Annihilation

Annihilation

A Global Military History of World War II

Thomas W. Zeiler
University of Colorado at Boulder

New York   Oxford
OXFORD UNIVERSITY PRESS
2011

Oxford University Press, Inc., publishes works that further Oxford University's
objective of excellence in research, scholarship, and education.

Oxford   New York
Auckland   Cape Town   Dar es Salaam   Hong Kong   Karachi
Kuala Lumpur   Madrid   Melbourne   Mexico City   Nairobi
New Delhi   Shanghai   Taipei   Toronto

With offices in
Argentina   Austria   Brazil   Chile   Czech Republic   France   Greece
Guatemala   Hungary   Italy   Japan   Poland   Portugal   Singapore
South Korea   Switzerland   Thailand   Turkey   Ukraine   Vietnam

Published by Oxford University Press, Inc.
198 Madison Avenue, New York, New York 10016
http://www.oup.com

Oxford is a registered trademark of Oxford University Press

ISBN 978-0-19-973473-3 (paper)

Printed in the United States of America
on acid-free paper

CONTENTS

Maps vii

Preface ix

Introduction 1

Part I **Origins and Outbreak, 1919–1939** 9

Chapter 1 Europe Unsettled 11

Chapter 2 Democracies in Crisis 27

Chapter 3 Militarism in Asia 37

Chapter 4 Phony and European War 53

Part II **Axis Advance, 1939–1942** 67

Chapter 5 German Expansion, North and West 69

Chapter 6 Blitzkrieg and Blitz 83

Chapter 7 America and the Atlantic 100

Chapter 8 Battles for the Mediterranean 117

Chapter 9 Attack on the Soviet Union 135

Chapter 10 Expansion of Imperial Japan 151

Part III **Turning Points, 1942–1943** 169

Chapter 11 Japan in Triumph and Stalemate 171

Chapter 12 Cataclysm on the Eastern Front 191

Chapter 13 Shifting Fortunes in the Mediterranean 204

Chapter 14 War of Words, the Sea, and the Air 224

Chapter 15 Allied Offensives in Asia and the Pacific 242

Part IV **Grinding Rollback, 1943–1944** 255

Chapter 16 Penetrating Japan's Defenses 257

Chapter 17 Costly Italy 274

Chapter 18 Soviet Rout 282

Chapter 19 Western European Front 294

Chapter 20 Island-Hopping in the Pacific 315

Part V   Annihilation, 1944–1945 327

Chapter 21 German Resistance in the West 329

Chapter 22 Red Army Sweep 346

Chapter 23 Shrinking the Japanese Empire 361

Chapter 24 Fall of the Third Reich 378

Chapter 25 The Inner Ring 386

Conclusion 407

References 419

Bibliography 435

Index 463

MAPS

Map 1.1   Europe in 1939 12
Map 3.1   Imperialism in Asia 38
Map 3.2   Pacific and Asia 41
Map 3.3   Japanese Expansion in China to 1938 48
Map 4.1   Invasion of Poland 59
Map 4.2   Hunt for Graf Spee 65
Map 5.1   Winter War 70
Map 5.2   Norway Campaign 75
Map 5.3   Invasion of Low Countries and France 81
Map 7.1   Battle of the Atlantic 109
Map 8.1   Mediterranean 118
Map 9.1   Barbarossa 139
Map 9.2   Moscow Attack and Counterattack 149
Map 10.1   Japanese Approach Pearl Harbor 161
Map 11.1   Japan in the Pacific and Asia 173
Map 11.2   New Guinea and Coral Sea 181
Map 12.1   Eastern Front, 1942 192
Map 13.1   North Africa 213
Map 14.1   Air War in Europe 234
Map 14.2   Convoys 240
Map 15.1   Southwest and Central Pacific Campaigns 250
Map 16.1   China-Burma-India theater 268
Map 17.1   Italy 275
Map 18.1   Kursk 284
Map 18.2   Soviet Offensives, 1943–44 289
Map 19.1   D-Day Landings 301
Map 19.2   Normandy Campaign 306
Map 19.3   Liberation of France 311
Map 20.1   The Pacific War 317
Map 20.2   Battle of the Philippine Sea 320
Map 21.1   Market-Garden and Scheldt Estuary 331
Map 21.2   Battle of the Bulge 338
Map 22.1   Third Reich defeated 348
Map 23.1   Battle of Leyte Gulf 364
Map 25.1   Okinawa 391
Map 25.2   Air War on Japan 398

PREFACE

In 1995, the 50th anniversary of World War II's end, I taught a course on that conflict to hundreds of undergraduates. Prompted by the commemorations that were so much in the news, or moved by the stories of their elder relatives who had taken part in this tremendous conflict, students in that course (as well as others at the time) claimed that they would have jumped at the opportunity to fight in the "Big One." Whether the topic was fascism, the a-bombs, D-Day in Normandy, or other issues, many had the same lament: by being born too late, they had missed out on the greatest moments in history—that of defeating evil in a "good war." To be sure, they soberly expressed this opinion, understanding the costs of fighting. They certainly registered such terrible events as the Holocaust. But gung-ho many of them were all the same. When I tried to show how horrifying the fighting was, I ran up against the popular notion that the war had been a good thing for the United States because it had launched the American Century of power and prosperity. So, I began looking into the war's toll and discovered that, in contrast to popular belief, even Americans killed on a mass scale. Over the past fifteen years, this has not been a very popular reminder for audiences; victors tend to write glowing histories of themselves and blame their enemies for atrocities. This book is an attempt to right the record for students, not by castigating any one nation but by stressing that the Second World War was a shared experience of annihilation. There was evil, and there was good, but history is much more complex than that, and reveals some uncomfortable truths about ourselves.

So many people helped me in what remains a daunting and massive undertaking over the past five years that I fear they might be overlooked. But let me try here to give my appreciation. Peter Coveney, formerly of Oxford University Press and now at Blackwell, asked me to consider this project. He was persuasive, and although there were times I cursed him and felt like backing out, he was always there with his encouragement. Brian Wheel then took over and guided this project to its conclusion. The manuscript was greatly improved by his keen judgments regarding everything—content, argument, writing, and images. Also at Oxford, and also indispensable, were Barbara Mathieu, who oversaw production, and Charles Cavaliere, who guided the book's launch. I spent the year 2004/5 in Tokyo on a Fulbright fellowship, which I deeply appreciate. Colleagues and students at the University of Tokyo's Center for Asian and Pacific Studies, and especially Yujin Yaguchi and Masako Notoji, were very encouraging. Also in Japan, I wish to thank Ambassador Takeo Iguchi, Akira Horie, and Haruo Iguchi as well as the University of Nagasaki, the Embassy of the United States, and Kyoto University for hosting me. On the Pacific War, it has always been a source of learning for me to participate in the University of Colorado's Teaching

ix

Asia Program under the innovative and welcoming Lynn Parisi and the National Center for Teaching Asia series of lectures for high school teachers coordinated by Meredith Melzer, who is just about the most energetic, enthusiastic, and dedicated person around. Sue McConaughy and Jean Fonden got me onto Iwo Jima and in contact with relatives of the soldiers as well as introducing me to Bill Bauer, a Doolittle flyer. Their passion for memorializing World War II remains infectious. Thanks also to these veterans (as well as those in the Colorado branch of the Eighth U.S. Army Air Force) for sharing their stories. I have always been lucky to have such good friends and colleagues who have corrected my manuscripts over the years. Thanks go to the expert eyes of Marc Gallicchio, Ron Story, Jeff Engel, Mark Stoler, and the several anonymous reviewers for Oxford University Press as well as Luca Micheletti in Rome. A conference in Poland introduced me to scholars who helped set the record straight on the European war. These included Andrzej Kaminski and his program on Recovering Forgotten History at the Institute of Civic Space and Public Policy, Lazarski School of Commerce and Law in Warsaw, and wonderful colleagues he invited: Wojciech Falkowski, Daria Nalecz, Krzysztof Lazarski, and Robert Kostro from Poland; John Merriman, Randy Roberts, Ted Weeks, and Sally McKee from the United States; and the American editors who attended—Ashley Dodge, Nancy Blaine, and my great editor Brian Wheel. Thanks also to Ken Osgood and the students, staff, faculty, and community of Florida Atlantic University for inviting me to speak on the war. Special thanks to Bill Miller, who saved me through guidance with military history and was always on call to search for more images. He is a true student of World War II and a committed historian. Nathan Matlock joined Bill in tracking down numerous images by giving me access to the photo holdings of the Center for the Study of War Experience at Regis University in Denver, Colorado. If his valuable help is any indication, his scholarly career will be a great success. I wish to thank the Center and Regis University for permission to use the photos as well as for inviting me to speak about my argument at a conference on the war held at the Center. At the University of Colorado at Boulder, my Dean, Todd Gleeson, and Associate Dean, Graham Oddie, have given support to the project since its inception. For technical magic in preparing the images, thanks to Jessica Wilson who also carries the burden in a program we direct so that I had more time to write and complain about this manuscript. Shelly Anderson also helped with the numerous copies and mailings. My relatives have always been there for me. My Mom and Dad, as usual, were always there with support and stories, and the latter gave me his typical close and critical reading that led to a minor overhaul of the book. My uncle Jess Strum was a source of World War II scholarship. Always ready to listen and joke with me in wonderment that anything could be new in history were my siblings and their spouses, Jeanie and Ralf, Diana and Howie, and Doug and Rachel and their simply wonderful kids: Ryan, Alex, Nina, Madeleine, Eli, and Aden. There is one family to whom I am indebted forever, and that is my very own. Jackson and Ella endured side trips to World War II sites including Guam, Normandy, and numerous American memorials and museums. These were not the worst burdens, but they must have wondered about my sanity. Above all, my wife Rocio is more than patient with me as I spent countless hours in my "dungeon" office. She has been a source of love and support for well over a quarter century since we met by chance on a bus in Paris. The French public transportation system will always hold an important place in my heart, but she is the true force behind my life.

Of course, another reason not to talk about war is that it's
unspeakable.

KURT VONNEGUT
A Man Without a Country

The military history of the Second World War offers a story of heroism and cooperation, calamity and loss, attrition and abundance, tactics and strategies, maneuver and operations, calculation and luck, politics and diplomacy, and production and
destruction. It also needs an injection of realism to counter the mythology that World
War II was a so-called good war. From 1937 to 1945, the world witnessed a succession
of savage military policies, innovations, and actions on the field, in the water, and in
the skies that resulted in butchery of over fifty million people. Whole armies, cities, and
nearly entire ethnic groups were exterminated; millions of others were decimated by
the carnage of war. The necessity of defeating great evil explains the violence, but we
must acknowledge that the Second World War brought us closer to Armageddon than
ever before.

STRATEGY OF ANNIHILATION
The conceptual architecture of this study is the linkage of military historian Russell
Weigley's "strategy of annihilation" framework to the idea of a "war of annihilation"
drawn from the work of Geoffrey Megargee. The latter applies the annihilation thesis
to one theater of war in arguing that the Eastern front saw criminal behavior alongside
conventional military action. Weigley employs the term "annihilation" in a strategic
sense. My meaning is close to Weigley's but applies the concept to every theater in
World War II; it is broader than Megargee's by including in the definition noncriminal
policies such as strategic bombing. In short, scholars use the term to emphasize the
focus on civilians and homefronts in the military campaigns.

The consummate war of annihilation, World War II had its strategic roots deep
in the previous century. American Civil War General William Sherman noted in 1864
during his devastating advance through the state of Georgia that "we are not only fighting hostile armies, but a hostile people, and must make old and young, rich and poor,
feel the hard hand of war, as well as the organized armies." This, in short, was a strategy

of annihilation, or what Mark Grimsley has referred to as a "hard war" policy to undercut "the enemy's will to resist" by "subjecting the civilian population to the pressures of war." It spoke to the ability of the United States to destroy the enemy's military capacity rather than erode it by attrition. Although American in origin, the strategy of annihilation was adopted by all sides in World War II—immediately by some (such as Germany and the Soviet Union on the Eastern front and Japan in China) and gradually by others (the United States and Japan in the Pacific and Anglo-American bombing forces in Europe). The complete defeat of the enemy through the waging of an unlimited war explains the strategies, operations, and tactics of both Axis and Allied forces.

The strategy of annihilation led to destruction of such scope and intensity that World War II must be seen as a unique conflict. The First World War witnessed immense carnage, but it evolved into a war of attrition in which militaries exhausted themselves but the homefronts remained largely outside the field of battle. Its successor evolved into a "total war" of expansive war aims, mobilization of resources by government and society, and the blurring of combatants to include civilians as well as the military. The overall purpose of victory whatever the cost and the utter destruction of the enemy in a form of warfare unlimited by economic, diplomatic, or (on the whole) moral constraints—in which civilians are military targets and not immune from warfare—defined the World War II strategy of annihilation. Germany, the Soviet Union, Great Britain, Japan, the United States, and Italy all engaged in this strategy, although to varying degrees, with unique intentions, and arrived at by diverse ways and at different times.

A marked difference existed between Axis war aims, strategy, and behavior and that of the Allies, so much so that although every theater experienced the horrors of annihilation, there is no moral equivalence between Nazi extermination policies and, say, Anglo-American strategic bombing. The Nazis sought to annihilate an entire people (the Jews and other "undesirables," as well as a nation, the USSR); the Japanese tried to eliminate China as an entity as did Italy in Ethiopia before the war. The United States, Great Britain, and their allies took aim on their enemies' ability to make war by attacking civilians. No doubt the Allies crossed moral thresholds—Dresden, Hiroshima, taking human war trophies on Pacific islands, shooting German and Italian prisoners, and a host of Soviet atrocities—but they did so to speed an end to the war. The Germans, Japanese, and Italians, on the other hand, sought to annihilate whole populations as the purpose of the war itself. But at least one of the Allied nations followed this example by the end of the conflict. Chris Bellamy wrote that the Soviet Union's approach to Germany was predicated on the notion of "absolute war." This reflected the "Trinity" of Prussian military theorist Carl von Clausewitz: political decisions, chance, and for my purposes, "primordial violence, hatred and enmity." Looked at another way, the Allies knew that their surrender meant their liquidation. Thus, they gradually adopted a strategy of annihilation to prevent the Axis powers from effecting theirs, which was in place from the very start of the war.

The strategy of annihilation preoccupied all sides, but it was not in play all the time. The reader should note that the strategy emerged throughout the war in the Allies' march to victory and that attrition warfare characterized many battles and campaigns. Annihilation as a driving force will not always appear in every issue of the war, although reminders will be constant. And because all sides eventually engaged in a hard war of violence against militaries and civilians alike, the strategy stands as the guiding theme of this textbook. In short, this study explores how the Axis military machines rose and fell and how their Allied counterparts fell and rose, and both wreaked havoc across the world.

TOTAL WAR

A vicious approach to war indicated the way the conflict was fought and how armed forces were maintained in the field. The objectives might have been the same as General Sherman's, but the process was immensely expanded in World War II. The global scope of this conflict—logistical, technological, and geographical—was a striking aspect (along with the enormity of the killing). Herculean efforts by all nations placed in battle the destructive power of new offensive and defensive weaponry—from ships and submarines to guns, tanks, and airplanes. Belligerents fueled their efforts by stockpiling a tremendous amount and wide array of resources acquired from by homegrown or conquered labor. They produced killing tools in large numbers and sent them into battle. Huge bureaucracies and expensive research centers developed weapons and organized other methods of fighting—from atomic bombs to intelligence decoding operations. Drawing on protective ship convoys, aircraft transport, and overland hauling by machine and animal, delivery systems were devised and personnel deployed around the world. As nations had learned from World War I, in Field Marshal Bernard Montgomery's words, "80 per cent of our problems were of a logistic nature."

Logistics played a unique role in this truly global conflict by influencing where and how fighting occurred across the globe. Adolf Hitler's pursuit of eastern European territory and Japanese penetration of China and Southeast Asia are two examples of logistical determination. The directions of the war and the venues of fighting derived from the material needs of the belligerents. Victory or defeat depended on supply, and success in this regard relied on the military acumen, luck, and performance of the armed forces. World War II required nations to pour vast sums of money, energy, and resources into the combat zones to effect the goal of destroying opposing armed forces and noncombatants alike.

This total war touched almost everyone in the world in mostly negative ways. German submariners, American seamen, British bombardiers, Japanese kamikazes, Finnish sharp-shooters, French resistance fighters, Chinese communists, Polish flyers, infantry from a host of nations and colonies in the British empire, convoys in the Arctic, aircraft carrier mechanics, Burmese and Indian scouts, and Russian artillerymen all sought to wipe out their enemy. The battles were horrendous affairs; Kasserine Pass, Kursk, Myitkyina, Alamein, Leyte Gulf, Narvik, Anzio, Guadalcanal, Stalingrad, Dresden, Dunkirk, Crete, Falaise, Hollandia, Okinawa, and Hurtgen Forest joined the rolls of death and destruction along with many more in the war of supply at sea, strategic bombing campaigns, blitzkrieg, tank battles, carrier and battleship fights, and amphibious landings. And, of course, there were such gruesome reminders of civilians at war as the Holocaust—the murder of over six million Jews—of which a third were children.

World War II was so devastating because it exposed people in every corner of the world to anguish and barbarism as a normal course of events. While 28 nations fought in the First World War, 61 participated in the Second. Some home fronts were removed from battle, as in America, but commonly the warzone and home were indistinguishable. While about 5 percent of civilians accounted for the deaths in the Great War of 1914–18, over two-thirds of the dead were civilians in the 1937–45 conflict. In Belgium, China, the Soviet Union, Norway, Poland, and Greece, more noncombatants died than did military personnel. That the war involved the most industrialized battle and technological sophistication ever seen greatly augmented civilian casualties. Bombing from the air proved devastating but so did premeditated, systematic murder by gas and modern weaponry. The strategy of annihilation extended the battlefields to cities, towns, villages, and farms, as leaders believed that victory could be achieved by exterminating populations by military force. As a result, as Hugh Strachan has written, total war "was far worse than prewar figurings; reality had outstripped imagination."

GOOD WAR?

Although there is recognition of the brutality, the impulse to glorify this war has enshrined it in the pantheon of great events and thereby cast the period from 1937 to 1945 in a nostalgic light. This is often the case on tours of military battlefields or lectures by relatives of those who fought in the war. People at the time knew how terrible the war was, and we have since acknowledged its horrors. Justice must also be done to the immense sacrifice of soldiers and civilians and the leadership of statesmen and military commanders. Nobody died in vain. Undeniably, the war was an essential fight against the aggression and genocide perpetuated by fascism and militarism. Revisionists of the war have argued that the global conflict was the unnecessary result of blundering diplomacy, especially on the part of the British. Perhaps or perhaps not; but for my purposes, they have engaged in a healthy questioning of ingrained almost worshipful approaches to the Allied cause. Others have begun to demythologize a conflict portrayed in a half century of retelling the war as a holy crusade—a paragon of justness in which even questioning the process and nature of the war or even the greatness of Allied leaders like Winston Churchill attracts scorn from a majority who venerate the winning effort.

This is particularly so among the participants who have selectively memorialized certain aspects of the war but forgotten its cardinal destructive characteristic. They constructed histories of the war from their own experiences and position after the conflict to serve political purposes. For the United States, the war was a moment of its launch to global preeminence. The victory clearly showed a well-meaning and determined nation mobilized to defeat evil and then establish a world order based on democracy, stability, prosperity, and justice. The notion of a good war emanates largely from American audiences who look on World War II as a just crusade won by a just nation.

Others are not immune from confusing heroism with reality and means with ends. For its part, the Soviet Union mythologized the deaths of tens of millions of people as the "Great Patriotic War." The Russians even downplayed their tremendous sacrifices in a strategy designed to deceive the West into believing Moscow was fully prepared to confront capitalism after the war. Britain went into steep decline but proudly upheld its leadership, stalwart suffering of its population, and democratic impulses during the war as evidence of backbone developed by decades of grand imperial rule. Japan never fully placed itself in the category of aggressor and has not entirely acknowledged its guilt for war crimes in China and elsewhere; nationalists hold that their nation shaped the destinies of others while confronting the white western imperialists. Meanwhile, mainstream Japanese view the good war as a means of converting from pernicious militarism to the economic miracle of the postwar years. In addition, numerous colonies understood the Second World War to be a catalyst to independence, although they were less enamored by the idea that this big power conflict was good because their imperial masters—many of whom were Allied nations—remained after the war. France, Germany, Italy, and China did not view the struggle as a good war, for they were losers in the conflict, although their populations welcomed the overthrow of dictatorships and occupiers.

This good war thesis is no straw man but a powerful idea based on myth, arrogance, and sanitizing of the record. For Americans in particular, it justifies the nation's postwar foreign and war policies by invoking the sad lessons of appeasement and the necessity of confronting aggression immediately wherever in the world it arose. In light of the postwar U.S. preponderance of power, the term does raise the issue of why and how the nation fought. Unfortunately, it emphasizes the notion of American exceptionalism in warfare, enshrining World War II in a pantheon of greatness that does an injustice to its soldiers who grinded it out on the fronts as well as the historical complexities of the conflict. While their objectives differed from the fascists, America or the USSR, in the end, were no different than other nations in fighting a vicious war and in exceeding the bounds of morality at times. Yet the quickening passing of the World War II generation and intervening postwar occurrences of questionable or ambiguous wars heightened efforts to memorialize the victors and place them on a pedestal of civic and familial pride. This good war—necessary, heroic, and even romantic when compared to the faceless nuclear age and brutal third world wars after 1945—had clear objectives and transformed life for hundreds of millions of people. But by placing World War II in a separate category from other conflicts, we tend to forget that tens of millions perished, needlessly and horribly. The good war argument presents an inaccurately antiseptic view of the Second World War. This was not a good war or even an honorable crusade, although honorable men and women fought it.

Readers and World War II hobbyists have simply missed the irony in the term "good war." They have misinterpreted such book titles as Michael Adams' *The Best War Ever,* Studs Terkel's *The Good War,* or several (including one for youth by Stephen Ambrose called *The Good Fight)* as sanctioning the conflict because it saved democracy, destroyed genocidal maniacs, and ended the Great Depression. Some long for this supposedly golden age of inspirational leaders who united people in a grand cause on behalf of future generations. Memorials to the passing of the World War II generation, however, as well as battlefield tours and video games, have glossed over and maybe even cheapened the real meaning of the Second World War. The objective was to kill—to eliminate the enemy threat physically, ideologically, and totally. Millions of soldiers and civilians perished, many of them in face-to-face encounters and more by technologically driven mass death. Millions simply killed others, for that was the purpose of war. Nobody escaped the wrath of a war of annihilation and certainly, soldiers saw no glamour in it. Nobody since should desire to fight in "the Big One," for World War II was a hell of massive death, crime, and destruction. It was far from a good war.

This is not to say that good and evil is indistinguishable, but only that all sides took part in the killing and therefore legitimized the cataclysm they perpetuated. The Allies triumphed over the horror of the Nazi regime, but the Soviets massacred millions, the Americans and British indiscriminately eviscerated entire cities by firebombing and two atomic bombs, and partisan supporters got revenge on their occupiers by murder. The winners also insisted on unconditional surrender of their enemies, which, because it abandoned compromise, meant that the war's end depended on the complete defeat of the Axis powers. In other words, the requirement of unconditional surrender encouraged the war of annihilation by using all the tools of total war at the Allies' disposal. The Fascists perpetrated terrible crimes beyond the normal standards of wartime behavior and military action. The Japanese brooked capitulation of enemies as unacceptable and punishable by death. Barbarity reigned on the part of all belligerents. This was a good war?

CONTENT AND ORGANIZATION

This is a fairly standard military history textbook that draws on the immense secondary source research of battles, campaigns, and personalities and the invaluable interpretations of historians. Recent historiography of the war has investigated strategic bombing, intelligence gathering, and resistance movements, and this book will integrate those aspects into the military history. As Gerhard Weinberg has demonstrated in his magisterial *A World at Arms,* viewing the war in terms of its global impact shows how places, states, people, ideas, and developments were linked by a worldwide military conflict. Yet the intention is not to explore war and society; home fronts are addressed only in their relationship to the conflict and not as topics in and of themselves. This is a military history with a purpose of analyzing strategic planning, war theaters and campaigns, operational coordination, and battlefield tactics and their effects on people.

My contribution is twofold. The first is the interpretive architecture. I argue that the Second World War was the most atrocious event in history because a strategy of annihilation—followed either continually or gradually by all belligerents—swept millions into a cataclysm of total destruction. The perspective of soldiers and civilians help show the tragedy behind the military campaigns in terms of real-life situations. Social history provides a supplement to the military campaigns. I hope the combined effect will be a direct challenge to the notion of a good war while validating the conflict as a war of annihilation.

The second contribution deals with organization. I take a two-tier approach to the war's story, both chronological and geographic. A chronological approach provides a full picture of the scope of the conflict and of the violence as it happened around the world. Typically, the Pacific theater has been examined separately after the European war reaches, say, the gates of Stalingrad in 1942. Instead, I place the theaters side by side, in parts delineated by time periods, to emphasize that events were happening simultaneously. This might help convey the Axis march to victory in the early part of the war, the precarious nature of the Allies' situation, and the overwhelming defeat of fascism and militarism at war's end in a holistic fashion. African, Asian, and particularly the Soviet/Eastern front theaters receive equal status to Western Europe. As well, lesser known aspects of the war, such as the sea battles in the North Atlantic, the China-Burma-India theater, the Allies' capture of New Guinea and the southern Philippines, the extended German retreat on the Eastern front, and campaigns in Scandinavia are included in more detail than usual. Militaries and politicians working in real time had to weigh events in various theaters and make their calculations accordingly. Policies and actions were made in conjunction with events as they occurred.

NOTE ON CITATIONS

To avoid distraction from the narrative, citations will appear in a section entitled References at the end of the book. They are organized alphabetically by Introduction and by each Part in which they reference material.

NOTE ON TERMS

Military terms are explained or implied in the text, but the following table will be helpful in reference to military units.

Table I.1 Military Organization: Nominal Infantry Units

Unit	Composition	Size (men)	Normally Commanded by
Squad		c.12	Sergeant
Platoon	Three squads + HQ	20–50	Lieutenant
Company	Three to five platoons	100–200	Captain
Battalion	Four to six companies +	600–1,100	Major or Lieutenant Colonel
Regiment or brigade	Two or more battalions + HQ	1,800–3,200	Colonel or Brigadier General (one star)
Division	Three or more regiments/ brigades + supporting arms.	10,000–20,000	Major General (two star)
Corps	Two or more divisions + specialist units	c.50,000	Major General or Lieutenant General (three star)
Army	Two or more corps + specialist units	c.100,000	Lieutenant General or General (four star)
Army group or front	Two or more armies	c.500,000	General (four star)

Source: Williamson Murray and Allan R. Millett, *A War To Be Won: Fighting the Second World War* (Cambridge: Belknap Press, 2000), 580.

This infantry table is broadly applicable across nations although it draws on U.S. terminology. Details about rank, composition, and unit size vary internationally.

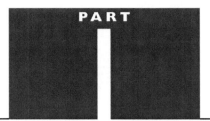

Origins and Outbreak

1919–1939

This time of madness in Europe.

JOYCE CAROL OATES
The Gravedigger's Daughter

"Periods of crisis have been common in history," concluded the noted political scientist E. H. Carr in his classic study of the breakdown of international order published just after Adolf Hitler launched the war in Europe in September 1939. Tensions resulting in war throughout the world and through the ages bore him out. But the crisis in international politics of the twenty years after the First World War until the Japanese invaded China in 1937 was different from others, for it led to more death and upheaval than the world had ever seen by powers wielding a strategy of annihilation.

A second global conflict of the twentieth century emerged just two decades after the dreadful World War I. The Treaty of Versailles of 1919, the peace settlement of that war, addressed difficult issues for victors and losers alike, but a settlement it was all the same. The treaty gave rise to an era of false optimism, unstable recovery, and above all, grounds for underlying recrimination and hatred. By the 1930s, the world spiraled down on a path of social, political, and economic turmoil. Demagogues took advantage of the unrest and disorder in much of the world while those fortunate to live in relative quiescence, namely, in the western democracies, still suffered from economic instability. The Second World War might not have been an inevitable consequence of the uneasy peace that preceded it—indeed, for awhile in the 1920s, the international community seemed benign—but aggressors soon exploited the terms and results of that peace.

CHAPTER I

Europe Unsettled

VERSAILLES TREATY

The international crisis emerged from the ashes of Verdun and Passchendaele—catastrophic battles of World War I—as political disagreement spurred momentum toward war. Whereas 27 countries appeared at the Paris Peace Conference in January 1919 at the close of hostilities, the Treaty of Versailles' provisions for defeated Germany were primarily derived from negotiations among Britain, France, the United States, and Italy. These "Big Four" imposed peace terms on Germany, ensured the dissolution of the Austro-Hungarian Empire, and froze out the infant communist government of the Soviet Union from diplomatic affairs. Although not unduly harsh in the long run, the peace dictated by the western democracies instigated resentment in Germany and elsewhere, even as the American leader, President Woodrow Wilson, counseled fairness. With his cherished League of Nations, he planned a world consultative body to elevate diplomacy over war as the primary tool in world affairs. The League came into being (though without America's membership), but it failed ultimately to reduce arms, spread prosperity, or bring about a permanent peace. And the treaty neither fully subjugated nor forgave Germany, thereby creating an uneasy peace in Europe.

Rather than create a lasting peace, the treaty reflected the grasping of nations for advantage. The Versailles settlement did not work from a blank slate; many ensuing territorial changes stemmed from boundary disputes created from revolutions, war, and diplomatic treaties stretching back decades if not centuries. Tensions were already prevalent, and the treaty added to or created more dangerously emotional nationalist sentiment. For instance, Belgium, Denmark, Italy, and Poland received pieces of territory from the disintegrated Austro-Hungarian Empire, but these claims involved the absorption of ethnic Germans and other minorities that stirred German nationalism.

In the case of Poland, the new country (carved up among big powers since 1772) won access rights to the city of Danzig on the Baltic Sea through a narrow strip called the *Polish Corridor*, a Nazi propaganda term used to deny Poland its historical rights to this land. This maritime access divided East Prussia from the rest of Germany where smoldering bitterness over the seizure of Pomerania was easily inflamed by nationalist rhetoric. Similarly, Italy ignored Wilson's cherished principle of national self-determination, in which people democratically expressed their preference for sovereignty and form of government, and held on to Trieste and Trent. As a result, Italy presided uneasily over thousands of Germans and Slavs and along with Greece and Yugoslavia, the Italians also eyed parts of Albania.

The Wilsonian dream of democratic choice could not overcome the fragmented map of central Europe in which the Austrian, Russian, and Turkish empires had disintegrated into new countries made up of a mix of minority nationalities. The new

Map 1.1 Europe in 1939. Credit: Ronald Story, *Concise Historical Atlas of World War II: The Geography of Conflict*, Map 6, p. 17.

Czechoslovakia, partitioned from the Hapsburg Empire, included a large bloc of unhappy Sudeten Germans ripe for agitation by those pursuing liberation from perceived foreign occupiers. Romania grew from Hungarian and Russian lands with restive minorities, whereas the German-speaking part of the Austro-Hungarian Empire became Austria, which was forbidden from linking to Germany itself. Still, Germany emerged from the peace settlement relatively stronger than the multiethnic, divided countries of southern and eastern Europe. Greece's armed conflict with Turkey persisted past the Paris conference. France and Britain, which assumed control of the Turkish "mandate" (a territory assigned by the League of Nations to a big power for administration), faced Arab and Jewish leaders who contested each other for Palestine. Britain, France, and Greece divided up Ottoman lands, although a rebellion led by Mustafa Kemal galvanized Turkish nationalists who routed Greece in 1921–1922 and prompted a painful population resettlement. In all, the flawed territorial settlement dictated by the Treaty of Versailles fueled anger toward minority groups and nationalistic hatreds that years later manifested themselves in a global war of annihilation.

THE GERMAN QUESTION

The Versailles Treaty also forced Germany to dispose of much of its merchant navy and deliver large amounts of coal to France, Italy, and Belgium for ten years. Its military limited to 100,000 soldiers, Germany was also stripped of submarines and military planes, lost most of its naval surface ships, and could not fortify or put troops in a demilitarized zone stretching fifty kilometers east of the Rhine River. The Allies began an armed occupation on the western bank of the Rhine for fifteen years. They also took away Germany's colonies and an eighth of its European territory (where one-tenth of its population resided), together with much of its iron, steel, and shipping capacity. This appeared to be a punitive peace, but even though Germany struggled economically after the war, so did other European nations. The problem was really more psychological and political: the Germans believed that they had merely laid down their arms in 1918 rather than surrendered. Yet they were forced to concede their guilt for creating the entire conflict. As a result, Versailles ominously planted seeds of German supernationalism to redress through violence if need be the supposedly unjust settlement of the Great War.

Germany's rivals in Europe undermined the long-term peace by forcing Wilson to compromise on his plan for a lasting peace. The American president's Fourteen Points included territorial changes under the doctrine of democratic self-determination and also called for freedom of the seas and trade, disarmament of militaries, and the League of Nations. Britain sought to protect its economic supremacy abroad by maintaining its large navy, weakening German military power, and holding on to its empire. London supported French demands for Berlin to pay out over several years a large bill of reparations for mending the Allied economies. Included was a German promise to pay for all damage to civilian property during the war at a rate of $5 billion per year until 1921 when new reparations requirements would be issued. Although Germany returned to a competitive economic position by mid-decade relative to France and Britain, the reparations amount was very burdensome. Not only that, but it was assessed after the

Treaty's signing, so Germany had no redress. At one point, the bill amounted to $33 billion (roughly $373 billion in 2007 dollars) to be paid out over thirty years. Yet there also existed a seemingly unsolvable paradox: a weak Germany could not fulfill its reparations obligation, but a solvent Germany appeared a threat to France. With the help of American bankers and international agreements under the Dawes and Young Plans, Germany lowered the tab. In 1932, Germany stopped paying reparations altogether, and Hitler refused further discussion on the matter. The peace settlement therefore hurt but did not crush Germany.

German viability was not a result that French strategists desired. In seeking a vengeful peace, Paris feared another invasion by Germany. World War I had devastated more French lives and property than those of any other nation. France thus depended on outside help to safeguard its borders. Yet allies, particularly the British, were unreliable, and alliances had not stopped the last war anyway. Furthermore, whereas France had counted on Russia to balance the German threat before the war, Paris had no arrangement with the new Soviet Union after it. In an incoherent policy of desperation, French policy makers tried to draw in allies for security and also sapped the budget to rearm. After the Fourteen Points authorized the return of its eastern territories of Alsace-Lorraine, France also focused on further punishing Germany. Not only did Paris impose a huge reparations bill but it demanded the coal-rich Saar Basin of Germany and the west bank of the Rhine River to serve as a buffer between the two countries and weaken its erstwhile enemy. The Americans and British opposed French machinations, which in any event further angered Germans. When Germany and the Union of Soviet Socialist Republics (USSR) signed the Rapallo agreement in 1922 to ease relations and secretly cooperate on military issues, West Europeans and the new states of East and Central Europe tried to yank Germany out of Russian hands under the Locarno Treaty of 1925 that set the western borders of Germany and opened discussion of its eastern borders. The hopeful signs at Locarno belied deep-seated security worries on the part of France.

France wanted Berlin to pay for postwar reconstruction. As inflation whittled away the value of the franc and with it the stability of the lower middle class, the country encountered political volatility. When the Great Depression hit in 1930, rightwing paramilitary groups demonstrated against the government while the Left went on strike. The Popular Front of socialists and communists under Premier Léon Blum gave labor more rights; partly nationalized the banking system, railroads, and munitions industries; and outlawed fascist paramilitary squads but also angered citizens with higher taxes and overspent on a costly rearmament program in 1937. An anticommunist movement was also quite strong at the time. Blum soon resigned, but the new government had trouble steadying the economy while faced with Italian, German, and Spanish militarists on its borders and insurgents in the colonies. The nation divided along class lines as the wealthy leaned toward fascism to solve the instability.

France was psychologically and economically sick as well as being inadequately armed for war. The French believed Germany was to blame, but the punitive peace soon helped provoke Berlin into a radical right turn that worsened France's predicament. Paris counted on the support of Great Britain to quell a renascent German military threat and banked on the United States to backstop Anglo-French security should there be a need. Neither the financially strapped and World War I damaged British nor the isolationist Americans offered firm and clear security guarantees to France. As Hitler rose to power, the western democracies chose appeasement—giving in to the demands of an aggressor as a way to calm tensions—over resolute defense.

The influential British delegate to the Versailles conference, John Maynard Keynes, warned of the consequences of a peace that prevented the German economic engine from revving up rather than idling. Germany was the industrial heart of Europe, and without its factories, recovery would be stymied and Germans victimized. Such nationalists such as Adolf Hitler harped on the humiliating terms of the treaty, calling it a dictated peace in which weak German democrats had sold out their country to nemesis France. Hitler's clever manipulation of the peace settlement by harboring grievances against the Allies and blaming the Jews for Germany's predicament and Europe's degradation exploited patriotic sentiment to such an extent that he was able to undo much of the treaty's restrictions on his march to power and ultimately war.

Hitler became chancellor of Germany in 1933 by capitalizing on resentments and a vision of greatness and hate. The National Socialist German Worker's Party (Nazi) perpetuated a fascist ideology in which Hitler—called the *Fuhrer* or *Leader*—set out to consolidate a dictatorship at home and expand abroad against supposed enemies. In the Nazi view of the world, races (rather than classes, as communists argued) competed for survival through acquisition of territory. Based on contrived models and legends drawn from ancient martial and pastoral Germany, Rome, and Sparta, Nazism elevated the Germanic people above "barbarian" races. They asserted the racial superiority of so-called *Aryans*—actually a term for prehistoric Indo-Europeans but one twisted by Nazi mythology to connote a racist occult of northern Germans and Austrians. As descendants of a sacred class of warriors who emerged from primeval forests, Aryans were to expel, enslave, or kill the residents of lands they coveted. This meant a war of annihilation—the destruction of inferior subhumans such as Jews, homosexuals, Slavs, Gypsies, and the infirm. Hitler eyed Eastern Europe as the key area to build and sustain his thousand year Third Reich under the creed of German expansion, termed *lebensraum* or living space for Aryans. His goals were to conquer and enslave the USSR to rid the world of communism and to expel (and eventually to exterminate) Jews and Slavs from Eastern Europe. France remained an implacable foe, but the Fuhrer expected Britain, as a largely Aryan nation with a powerful empire, to join him in the crusade against Soviet communism as the Third Reich became the center of a sweeping Romanesque system of conquered states, colonies, and sycophantic allies.

The forty-three-year-old Hitler was an eloquent Austrian who rose to fame in a failed coup against the German government in the early 1920s. At his trial, he denounced German democracy and Treaty of Versailles and then served out his prison term writing the doctrinal guide of the Nazi (an abbreviation of National) Party, entitled *Mein Kampf,* or "My Struggle." He expressed his agenda of conquest and extermination. Hitler planned to restore the *volk*—simple and pure peasants—to power through his dictatorship and then go to war. "The father of all things," war, he wrote, would purify Germany and save the world from the twin evils of Judaism and communism. He was not alone in this way of thinking. Many members of the elite Waffen-SS—the highly obedient army of the Nazi Party formed in 1940 under the command of SS (the Schutz-staffel or Protective Squadron, Hitler's bodyguard and private army) leader Heinrich Himmler—embraced Nazi doctrine because of their alarm over communist insurrections in Germany after World War I. They did not necessarily agree with his anti-Semitic views, but they were disposed to National Socialism's objectives of suppressing Soviet communism, restoring the economy, and pursuit of Germany expansion. War would forge a new elite to serve the German good.

Economic recovery in the mid-1920s put Nazi plans on hold, but Hitler's chance came soon enough with the renewal of the twenty years' crisis. Germany's stock abroad rose when it was admitted into the League of Nations and then assented to the Kellogg–Briand Pact in 1929, which outlawed war. That same year, U.S. bankers eased its reparations burden. In 1930, German rehabilitation continued as the former Allies vacated the industrial Rhineland. Yet the onset of the Great Depression—the deepest economic crisis in modern times—wracked Europe and the United States, prompting the withdrawal of credit and drying up capital and industrial production with it. The gloom chillingly reminded Germans of its recent past when rampant inflationary times of the early post-World War I period forced consumers to cart wheelbarrows of paper money to market. The Austrian banking establishment tumbled first in the great crash, followed by American, German, and British financial houses. Fascist state planning and economic nationalism seemed to provide an answer to the chaos and rising unemployment, and fascist syndicalism and regimentation were preferable to Soviet-style centralization. In addition, not only were workers hard hit, but the middle classes in all the industrial countries now suffered. The disenchanted and struggling lower middle classes in Germany implored their leaders for help. Demagogues gave them clear answers, casting blame on Marxists, Jews, and Western bankers. Hitler emerged from the shadows to champion the downtrodden and angry.

Hitler prepared the Nazi hierarchy to do an end run around German democracy and assume control. Promised authority over an expanded air force, Hermann Göring joined Hitler's ranks and lent military credibility. He had garnered the Pour le Merite medal for recording at least twenty kills by air during World War I. A secret police force, the Gestapo, became the core of the SS elite of black-shirted guards under Heinrich Himmler. The SS rounded up opponents and terrorized the population, enforcing Nazi doctrine. Only the presidency of Germany eluded Hitler. Yet because the Nazi leader had fared well in the runoff against the eighty-four-year-old Paul von Hindenburg, the aged Field Marshal's hastily built coalition of aristocrats, businessmen, and the military could not prevent the relentless Nazi quest for power. Minister of Propaganda Joseph Goebbels predicated Nazism on appeals to economic nationalism; paeans to past greatness of the Teutonic race; and race, ethnic, and class hatreds. Poor Hindenburg could merely counter with calls for order and democracy, though Hitler dared not confront the old hero just yet.

Electoral maneuvering by Nazi opponents backfired until Hindenburg accepted Hitler as Chancellor in January 1933. Soon afterward, the rule of law disappeared. In February, Hitler used the burning of the parliament building by a Dutch communist as a pretext to crack down on leftist opponents. Once Hindenburg died in 1934, the Fuhrer consolidated his leadership into one-man rule (Hitler's henchman were mostly ideologues or loyalists to him, themselves unqualified to manage state affairs). Hitler transformed German democracy into a dictatorship. He cleaned house that year, assassinating rival Ernst Rohm, head of the Sturm Abteilung, or SA, who wished to supplant the German Army generals with his men. The German Army was grateful to Hitler for his ruthlessness.

As important as ousting Rohm was the Fuhrer's support from the military hierarchy. Although many generals thought little of the Fuhrer as a military leader and few realized the true purpose of lebensraum and annihilation behind his grand military vision, many bought into his expansionist, supernationalist, and racist plans. Anti-Semitism was strong among German Army leaders, and racist propaganda immunized enlisted men to genocidal acts instigated by Nazi ideology. The command structure became so politicized that Hitler did not act on his own when he went to war but instead won the backing of his general staff. The German armed forces, called the Wehrmacht (renamed from the Reichswehr in 1935), willingly helped to forge his thousand-year Reich of glory, racial purity, and world domination through war and extermination.

The Nazis designed a martial nation. Dramatic mass meetings, oftentimes lit up at night, and a stress on physical fitness and a military spirit replaced the arts and culture of Germany. The nation was one and all. Unemployment of six million people, or around 30% of the working population in 1932 before Hitler assumed power, dropped precipitously by 1937 to around one million as the Nazis turned to public works to stimulate the economy and, under a second Four-Year Plan, to rearmament and war industries. By 1937, Germany enjoyed agricultural self-sufficiency. The output of raw materials rose, benefitting industrialists and arms makers. Modern expressways (the autobahns) whisked goods and people around Germany while the new Göring Iron Works compensated for the loss of Alsace-Lorraine by manufacturing low-end ores and synthetic materials at government expense. Industrial organization centered on monopolies that regularized production and distribution under state authority. Stability, growth, conformism, and centralization joined ruthless totalitarianism and terror, preparing Nazi Germany for Hitler's ultimate objectives to be obtained by force.

GERMAN MILITARY POWER

Conquest of vast spaces depended on the Wehrmacht's doctrine of mobile warfare, based on speed, surprise, exploitation of the enemy's weaknesses at a certain moment, and the judgment of officers in the field. Well before they possessed tanks, military leaders starting in the 1920s had investigated the integration of motorized infantry, artillery, engineers, and communications (signal) troops with armored units. In the vanguard as well as in a supporting role of these troops was the "panzer arm" that had developed a doctrine of armored warfare in collaboration with the Soviet Union during the interwar period. Actually, all major powers had explored armored doctrine, but although some effective use of tanks during the First World War had occurred, they held more promise than performance. The decision to motorize the German Army required supply services by train and truck, which necessitated high consumption of fuel, personnel, and spare parts if the Wehrmacht were to maintain its superiority in speed and cover great distances. Problems of incomplete motorization and inadequate organization plagued the Germans well into the war. Mobile warfare tactics actually did not revolutionize German doctrine; the Wehrmacht also drew on traditional infantry maneuvers including the use of horses.

The blitzkrieg (lightning war) tactic used in Poland was new. The infantry still predominated in the German Army, and the rearmament program mechanized only a small portion of the forces in an effort that nearly bankrupted the government. The British had pioneered the blitzkrieg concept. Top military analyst Sir Basil Henry Liddell Hart, as well as his underappreciated mentor Major-General Percy Hobart, envisioned mechanized armies penetrating deeply into enemy territory in a constant movement forward that would destabilize defenses and sow chaos. Based on Hart's theories, General Heinz Guderian and the Germans put the doctrine to early use. Three panzer divisions were established in 1935, although they were equipped only with light tanks at the time for use as infantry support. By September 1939, 3,200 armored vehicles were in service with just 300 new and well-armed medium tanks. The rapidly growing armored panzer arm intimidated German enemies. As one historian has put it, "the central fact stood out with stark clarity: Germany moved in six years from being one of the weakest land powers in Europe to being the strongest."

Wehrmacht expansion took place alongside reorganization. In 1938, Hitler dissolved the war ministry and established the Oberkommando der Wehrmacht (OKW), the Armed Forces High Command, with the Fuhrer as the supreme commander. All officers swore allegiance to Hitler's leadership, including the Waffen-SS whose membership rose to over 800,000 fanatical adherents by 1945 who were integrated into the Wehrmacht. The Fuhrer tightened his control over the Wehrmacht by discrediting and removing many of its key senior leaders. Hitler did not have unlimited resources at his disposal, however, as the birth rate and the procurement of arms could not keep pace with his territorial ambitions during the war of annihilation. Still, in 1939, the Wehrmacht boasted over 4.5 million men under arms and in training. The German Army was truly impressive considering it was not as well trained or equipped as the World War I force. The Army's size skyrocketed under great pressure, and reorganization by mid-1939 resulted in 103 divisions, split into active and reserves, with 3.74 million under arms once mobilization began.

On the other hand, the German Navy was a comparatively weak link for the Wehrmacht. It had the lowest priority for resources of the three branches, but the surface fleet in particular was really intended more as a diplomatic tool to pressure Britain rather than for effective wartime use. An agreement with Britain in 1935 forced Germany to limit the Navy, but such regulations also turned the focus toward submarine construction. Although the German Navy could not challenge the British warship fleet, Grand Admiral Erich Raeder embarked on an ambitious building program that commissioned two battle cruisers in 1939 and planned to expand the surface fleet by 1944 to attack the British merchant fleet. Two large battleships, *Bismarck* and *Tirpitz*, neared completion in 1939, but the Navy's battleships were overage, with batteries smaller than the World War II average of fifteen- to sixteen-inch guns. The closest the

Germans came to battleships were the *Scharnhorst* and *Gneisenau*, two battle cruisers with eleven-inch guns. In addition, the Navy possessed three "pocket" battleships (special, powerful cruisers), one heavy and six light cruisers, 21 destroyers, 12 fast torpedo boats, and 57 U-boats or submarines. The latter fleet was surprisingly small given the success of German submarines against Allied shipping in World War I, but U-boats were considered secondary to the German surface fleet.

Under the command of Admiral Karl Donitz, the German U-boat fleet aimed for a submarine war close to the British Isles rather than in the Atlantic and beyond. But not only did Donitz have a mere 26 ocean-going submarines in 1939 and an additional 35 more in the first year of war (he lost 28), but the new U-boats were small as a response to tonnage limits imposed by the 1930 London Naval Treaty. Their size cut down on the number of torpedoes they carried, and they were uncomfortable to boot. Although they were more maneuverable near shore, these Type VII subs were less effective in the mid-Atlantic. Still, because of their overall efficiency, the Type VII remained the foundation of the U-boat fleet, and 704 were eventually built. Nonetheless, Hitler's ignorance of naval affairs streamlined the Navy, undermined the U-boat campaign against Atlantic convoys from the very start, and made Germany vulnerable to innovative operational tactics by the British Royal Navy.

Hitler was more interested in his air force—the Luftwaffe—led by Hermann Göring. Hitler's chosen successor, a member of the Nazi inner circle, and Germany's economic czar, Göring evolved during the war into a grotesque megalomaniac. Before the war, however, he was not only the Luftwaffe's commander-in-chief but the Reich aviation minister who built the air force from the ruins of the Versailles Treaty limitations. Capitalizing on the general interest at the time in airpower and Hitler's demand that planes support ground troops, Göring began a rapid expansion of the Luftwaffe in an attempt to match the larger forces of Britain and France. With the Fuhrer also desirous of having the capability of bombing America, Göring also launched work in 1937 on a four-engine plane that could reach the United States.

From 1935 onward, the Germans met production goals for aircraft, building an average of 5,500 per year until 1938. Thereafter, the government stepped up the pressure even more, targeting 45,700 planes by 1942. This goal was never realized because resources were not available, but the buildup was prodigious nonetheless. By the time they declared war against Poland, the Germans had roughly 2,500 serviceable frontline aircraft and 1,500 transports and seaplanes. These aircraft were suited for decisive engagements and obtaining short-term air superiority. The fleet included one of the best fighter planes of the early war, the superb Me (Messerschmitt AG) 109, as well as the Ju87 dive-bomber tried out during the Spanish Civil War (1936–1939) and a long-range escort fighter, the Me110. The Germans also developed strategic bombing capabilities, although heavy bombers capable of flying great distances never went into full production. But the nearly 1,200 medium-range bombers, mainly the Do17 and the He111, reached Britain, France, and Central European capitals. Because of action over Spain, the Luftwaffe was better prepared than the Allies to hit targets on the ground. The Germans had high-tech navigation systems, blind-bombing devices, and a pathfinder force well before the Royal Air Force deployed similar technologies. Quality aircraft and advancements, and a decent number of planes and pilots, made the Luftwaffe a formidable force that kept the Allies on their heels in the first years of the war.

AUTHORITARIANISM FROM THE LEFT

Hitler intended to focus his military on the Soviet Union; but ironically, his cardinal enemy also had grievances stemming from World War I that it sought to remedy by military force and dictatorship during the twenty years' crisis. Western democracies seemingly feared communism emanating from the USSR more than right-wing authoritarianism. The Russians, however, posed less of a strategic threat to them than did fascism prior to the Second World War. Revolution in 1917 brought the communists to power and also ushered Russia out of World War I. As a price for immediate peace under the Treaty of Brest-Litovsk, the new state lost Ukraine as well as any claims to the provinces of Estonia, Latvia, Lithuania, and Finland. Russia lost a third of its population and almost all of its iron and coal production. The advent of Soviet communism inspired revolutions in Germany and Hungary, but the USSR assumed a largely defensive stance in international affairs, focusing on internal recovery and development while fending off external threats.

Soviet leaders, and especially Josef Stalin—who took dictatorial control of the state in the mid-1920s—believed that the capitalist countries were bent on destroying the young communist state. Mutual suspicion between the capitalist West and the so-called Reds festered from the time of the USSR's conception. French, Japanese, British, and American forces entered the country during its civil war from 1918 to 1921 to prevent supplies from falling into German hands and to rescue Czech soldiers stranded in Siberia, but the Soviets saw them as counterrevolutionaries against the fledgling Reds. These suspicions appeared valid. The West backed Polish aims to reestablish its Russian frontier of 1772 and absorb Ukraine, the old Czarist Belorussia (White Russia), Latvia, and Lithuania into a loose federation. Poland received a large tract of Belorussia and western Ukraine as well as hundreds of thousands of ethnic minorities whose mistreatment made the country largely ungovernable during the twenty years' crisis.

The USSR was ripe for strongman rule. Devastated by war, millions died of malnutrition and disease, and industry and agriculture functioned at pitiful levels. The distractions of the Western powers by other international issues and their own economies gave the Reds some breathing room, however, as former political commissar Stalin emerged to lead the economic recovery through the Communist Party. He consolidated his power by solidifying his hold over the Party, strengthening its hold on the state, and then crushing opposition. Stalinism—political consolidation, dictatorial rule, and crash industrialization—strengthened communism and the Soviet state at great cost. Peasants slaughtered their livestock rather than turn them over to the state in the early 1930s while millions died of famine as land lay unplanted. Industry adhered to vigorous five-year plans that quickened the pace of production, although targets were not met. A growing worker proletariat labored in the second five-year plan of modernization from 1932–37 to boost production of steel, electric power, cement, coal, and oil. Output reached that of Germany in all of these sectors by 1940, though the everyday hardships on workers multiplied as they were forced into factories, farms, and cities such as Moscow and Leningrad. The majority toiled in deprivation, though the new bureaucrats, skilled laborers, artists, and model athletes became the elite and intellectuals kept quiet or fled.

The country witnessed sheer terror under the Stalinist purges of the 1930s. Paranoid and pathological, fearful of rivals to his leadership, and seeking discipline from the masses and bureaucrats to meet the goals of his five-year plan, Stalin massacred his rivals after public trials from 1934–38. Like Hitler, Stalin engaged in a domestic version of the strategy of annihilation against his opponents. In June 1937, he turned on Red Army commanders, "liquidated" on grounds that they had conspired with Germany to undermine the Soviet state. Judges, vice-commissars, ambassadors, Communist Partymembers, generals, secret police chiefs, and prime ministers of the Soviet republics disappeared. By 1938, over a million Soviet citizens sat in jail, nearly nine million had been arrested and sent to camps, and 700,000 executed. By 1940, there were no pretenders to Stalin's throne, as even the purgers themselves were rounded up and shot. Safe from his foes, Stalin then used carrots to maintain his power and national security. Among his reforms, the Red Army witnessed the restoration of ranks from the Czarist era, a new officer corps, and the naming of marshals. Revolutionary ideology went into receivership, replaced by pragmatic measures to secure the homeland against presumed foreign predators. Boosting production and the birth rate, science and technical skills, and patriotism through the nationalistic arts prepared the Soviet Union for the inevitable attack from Nazi Germany, Fascist Italy, and anti-Soviet Eastern European countries that Stalin lumped with the capitalist West as those bent on overthrowing communism.

Stalin aimed to protect the country with the duplicity, realism, and brutality that typified his rule. In 1934, the USSR joined the League of Nations and crusaded for universal disarmament within the forum. Yet Stalin allowed the Nazis to build their air force secretly on Soviet soil in the hopes of appeasing Hitler and receiving training for Red Army officers in return. The dictator was no dupe, but he had a knack of ignoring

Stalin with military and political leaders (Zhukov is second from right).   Credit: Imperial War Museum.

Hitler's core message that Germany intended to subjugate the Soviet Union. This was due to his obsessive concern with capitalist enemies abroad and personal ones inside the country and incredulity that the USSR could be overrun. The USSR and Germany, in fact, exhibited a mutual interest in reversing the Versailles Treaty's territorial settlements and drawing new borders. Cynically playing the other side, Stalin also hoped to enlist the Western democracies against Nazism. In 1935, Stalin signed mutual aid pacts with France and Czechoslovakia and softened his anti-Western propaganda. He backed the Spanish government against the Franco military revolutionaries who Nazi Germany and Fascist Italy supported. This was not out of devotion to a cause but to draw Britain and France into a commitment to fight Hitler. The democracies refused aid to Spain, however, which along with their appeasement of Germany ultimately convinced Stalin of their intention to let the Germans destroy his state. As the twenty-years' crisis ended in war, Stalin determined to contest both fascist intimidation and capitalist flaccidity on his own, if need be, with his substantial military (analyzed in a later chapter) and a strategy of annihilating any invaders who dared to enter the Soviet Union.

FASCISM EMERGENT

Stalin readied to fight fascism, the most dynamic ideology of the times. Fascism had its first triumph in Italy, a nation that lost not only 650,000 people in World War I but also many of its territorial demands at the Paris Peace Conference. This failure, coupled with a slumping postwar economy, stimulated outrage from nationalists and workers, resulting in the temporary occupation of the city of Fiume on the Dalmatian coast in Yugoslavia. Chased out by Italian troops, the nationalist occupiers were inspired by Gabriele d'Annunzio, whose straight-arm salute, black-shirted garb, haranguing oratory and mass chants, and plans for Italian territorial expansion and corporatist economic organization influenced Benito Mussolini. This founder of Italian fascism came to power in 1922 and built a dictatorship that ruled the country for over two decades. Mussolini showed right-wing extremists throughout Europe that adventurism abroad and staunch anticommunism at home served nationalist purposes. Murderous campaigns against fascist opponents, the quashing of dissent and of democratic institutions, and inspirational rhetoric solidified the rule of Mussolini, also known as Il Duce.

Having established his fascist state, Il Duce set out to reclaim the glories of ancient Rome. He called the Mediterranean area Italy's "mare nostrum" or "our sea." Backed by a fascist militia of nearly 200,000 followers and an enlarged but ill-equipped army that pledged allegiance to him, Mussolini also rebuilt Italian seaports and created a large merchant fleet and navy that numerically eclipsed the French and British flotillas in the Mediterranean. As early as 1923, he sent settlers into Libya and meddled in border issues in Albania and Greece. At odds with the League of Nations, he later clashed with France and Britain over his invasions of Ethiopia and Albania, military adventurism in Spain, and demands for French withdrawal from Corsica, Tunisia, Nice, and Savoy in actions that drove him closer to Hitler. World War II in Europe did not begin in the Mediterranean, but its origins derived partly from conflicts caused by Il Duce. By May 1939, Mussolini had formally allied with Hitler's Germany under the so-called Pact of

Steel, eventually acquiescing to expunge all Italian Jews (only 70,000) from the Fascist party and heading toward war against former allies France and England.

Strategically vulnerable and economically weak, Italy faced an uphill battle in trying to achieve its grandiose vision of mare nostrum. Italy could be invaded from all sides, land and sea, and it was unprepared for such an eventuality. In addition, the war in Ethiopia and support for Spain's Franco had run the national account into a large deficit and by 1939 compelled the first rationing measures (on sugar and soap). Italy was an importer of coal and lagged well behind other European producers of steel. Its auto industry was good but small, while its aircraft manufacturing rested on knockoffs of foreign models. A major plague on the Italian war effort was the inability to coordinate the military, politicians, and industrialists under a regime of modern warfare. Rome had trouble mobilizing whatever inadequate resources for modern, industrial warfare, and tactical and strategic military cohesion was sorely lacking. In large part, Mussolini's reach exceeded his grasp; he could not conduct a war of annihilation unless allied with a stronger power.

The Italian Army's bad training and an opportunistic approach to war by its high command dimmed the prospects for permanent victory. Il Duce's general staff were at best a bunch of slackers who cared little about studying planning and more for internal political intrigue and patronage. Although Italy spent nearly 23% more than France did on defense (with less than half the national income of the French), Mussolini directed that money to the war in Ethiopia and Spain. Spending on empire and civil war from 1935–1940 amounted to 77 billion lire of the total 116 billion allocated. The diversion of funds meant that the Army never reached its target of 126 divisions.

Mussolini did not help matters, consumed as he was by the difficulties of his conquests and later insecurity in the face of Hitlerian economic and military superiority. He took over the post of minister of armed forces and in 1938 became a "first marshal of the empire." By 1940, King Victor Emmanuel III (also proclaimed King of Abyssinia) had named Il Duce the personal military commander of Italian forces. World War I hero Marshal Pietro Badoglio, the chief of the commando supreme of the armed forces, merely played the role of peacemaker between crown and public who trusted him despite his complete ineffectiveness at corralling Mussolini. And Il Duce needed reigning in. While his military advisors warned of Italy's total lack of preparedness for war, Mussolini sought to dispel notions that he played second fiddle to the Nazi concertmaster and that Italian diplomacy was adrift. No amount of bravado could substitute for the weaknesses of his military should he choose to follow his grand course of dominating mare nostrum.

A closer look at Mussolini's military might revealed it was based on bluff and defects. The Army numbered 1.6 million soldiers, 600,000 of these overseas. Included were more than 300,000 Blackshirts, the fascist militia. In 1927, Mussolini claimed there were 5 million soldiers under arms; nine years later, he took as a slogan "eight million bayonets." Inflated numbers belied the fact that this army, though more maneuverable due to a reorganization scheme begun in late 1938, was not nearly so large. Italy possessed three armored divisions, yet they were equipped only with light tanks and armor and manned machine-guns rather than cannon. Artillery was

Mussolini and Hitler.   Credit: Center for the Study of War Experience at Regis University, Denver, Colorado.

outmoded, modernization proceeded slowly, and Italy had weak supply and transport services.

The air force, Mussolini's pride, was not much better. Boasting that his air fleet was so large that the planes would blot out the sun, Il Duce pointed to the strategic bombing theories of native son Giulio Douhet whom the other big powers revered. He adored the image of airpower; Italian aircraft had set speed and altitude records and were adept at public displays such as flying in formation across the Atlantic. In actuality, Mussolini's target 8,500-plane fleet remained a dream, as the conflict in Spain drained away 700 aircraft. The air force became old-fashioned due to a lack of funding. Of the 1,753 front-line aircraft in the Italian force, only 900 were modernized with radios, night-flying technology, and aerial torpedoes. Fully 250 planes in the fleet were inferior to the British Hurricane and Spitfire, and no Italian fighters bested the British in speed. Later in the war, Italy had access to advanced German engines but still produced few respectable fighter planes. Command disjuncture made matters worse. Resting on the reputation of Douhet, the Italian Air Force, to its detriment, never collaborated with the Navy.

As independent-minded as the air force but better equipped, the Italian Navy of 6 battleships, 19 cruisers, 100 smaller vessels, and 113 submarines compared well to the British and French, with the added benefit of being located in the center of the Mediterranean. Its flaws lay in outlook, narrow vision, and resources. The Navy believed that the next war would center on battleship slugfests rather than airpower. In any case, Italian construction did not keep pace with France or Britain. The service was outmoded, lacking carriers, radar, and submarine detection devices as well as sufficient armor, although its ships were speedy. It was also starved for oil. Italy stockpiled petroleum, but during World War II, the country counted on imports from Romania.

Italy was simply unprepared for a major war. Strategic coordination among the services did not exist; both the army and navy planned for defensive battles against the Western democracies. Still, Mussolini planted his flag with Hitler, which exacerbated the gap between his grandiose rhetoric and military realities. Courted by democracies and fascists alike, Mussolini's ability to blow smoke kept his star high in the sky over Europe. Despite its deficiencies, the Italian armed forces could still bully small countries. Il Duce's performance on the large European stage was abysmal, but he was able to wreak destruction in his Mediterranean arena by bluster backed by force.

EUROPEAN AGGRESSORS

With Italy and Germany pointed toward dictatorship, other nations followed along the authoritarian path, some under the influence of the Fuhrer's ambitions. Antonio Salazar gradually seized outright power in Portugal in 1932, becoming a neutral in World War II but remaining dictator for 36 years. The disintegrated Austro-Hungarian Empire entered a troubled period after 1918, wracked by economic problems and the siren of pan-Germanism. Torn between Nazism and democracy, Austria went the way of fascism but not before Mussolini frustrated Hitler's early attempts to unite the nation with Germany. Pro-Nazi Austrians finally ended this uneasy situation by chipping away at Austrian independence until Hitler peacefully "invaded" the country in March 1938. A plebiscite resulted in the *Anschluss*—a union of Germany and Austria.

The other part of the former empire, Hungary, lost so much land to new Eastern European states after World War I that a nationalist movement sprung forth to reclaim the territory. Under the regent Miklos Horthy, these nationalists linked with Mussolini who supplied them with arms. After absorbing Austria, Hitler backed the revisionist campaign and cozied up to the Hungarian dictatorship. Fascists in the country took power, invoked anti-Semitic laws, and withdrew from the League of Nations in 1939 in anticipation of gaining land from Slovakia and Romania. Like all East-Central European states except Czechoslovakia, multinational Yugoslavia chose dictatorship over democracy and succumbed to the rivalries of its many nationalities. Fascists appealed for a bridge to Hitler, but peasants opposed them, preferring their freedom instead in the Serbian-dominated former kingdom. Dictatorship under King Alexander II prevailed until his assassination in 1934. Serbs dominated Slovenes and tried to suppress Croats who themselves looked to Italy and Hungary for support. As German power grew in the 1930s, the dictatorship turned to the Nazis. Engulfed by the world war, the Balkans took sides according to ethic groups. Yugoslavia split between the Axis and Allied causes.

Elsewhere, tension mounted as nationalists were attracted either to Nazi ideology, fascism, or simply Italo-German meddling. Poland's General Josef Pilsudski came to power in a coup in 1926 but remained wary of German influences and the Soviet nemesis on the eastern border. Romania adopted a form of Nazism so alarming to King Carol

II that he installed his own fascist dictatorship to prevent a Nazi coup. Yet Romania fell victim to Soviet, Hungarian, and German territorial intrigues, and in 1940, the King abdicated to Hitler's chosen henchmen. Royal dictatorship prevailed in Bulgaria, torn by Russian and Italian sympathizers, but not until King Boris supplanted a military coup with his dictatorship in 1935. Weighing monarchy or democracy after World War I, Greece remained politically unstable due to a series of military coups. Communists gained in the countryside and among workers; but the most fascist general of all, John Metaxas, took power in 1936 and initiated political persecution, censorship, and a program of public works. He performed an about-face when Italy invaded Albania in 1939 and the Greeks futilely decided to resist the Nazis.

In 1936, a vicious civil war erupted in Spain. This bloody conflict pitted republican government loyalists, socialists, anarchists, and revolutionaries (including ex-patriots from America and Europe as well as the Soviet Union) against conservative forces of General Francisco Franco supported by monarchists, the clergy, the army, aristocrats, and an emerging fascist party. Franco triumphed in 1939. Over half a million lives were lost, or the equivalent of total British deaths in both world wars, in a civil conflict that resembled a war of annihilation. Italy and Germany used the war as a testing ground for their air forces. Pablo Picasso's painting, *Guernica,* graphically displayed the horrors of the bombing of a small northern Spanish Basque town on market day. Along with the Soviets, the Italians and Germans learned the efficacy of coordinated ground and air attacks that paid dividends in Poland and the Eastern front during World War II and the potential for devastation and panic produced by dive-bombers. Franco, a traditional Catholic conservative rather than a fascist, remained neutral in the Second World War and played both sides of that global conflict depending on the course of the war. Hitler pleaded with him to join the Axis or at least to let German troops use his soil. Franco refused, and his stubbornness worked; he was one of the few dictators to survive the war because of his neutral stance.

The Spanish Civil War revealed telling insights into the political situation in Europe. Dictatorships were the dynamos of change, as authoritarians in Germany, Italy, the Soviet Union, and elsewhere vied to transform the World War I peace settlement to their advantage. The harped on perceived injustices but also on economic anxieties and ideological hatreds to ready their populations for righting the errors of the Versailles Treaty and redressing historical national hatreds. Hitler intensified the twenty-years' crisis, but others had objectives to be achieved by violence as well. It was left to the democracies to quell the dissent, provide for security and peace, and prevent the slide toward a war of annihilation caused by fascist and communist loathing.

CHAPTER 2

Democracies in Crisis

I see wars, horrible wars.
VIRGIL
Aeneid, VI, 86

BRITAIN AND IMPERIAL CONCERNS

The rise of fascist and military aggression in Europe and Asia during the 1930s challenged the Western democracies. Their inability to stop or appease the dictators was not a simple matter of succumbing to the iron will of the aggressors. Britain and France had suffered enormous losses in World War I, and both had pushed for peace terms from Germany that paid for recovery and the liquidation of debts. Both were preoccupied in the 1920s with domestic problems of labor disputes, farm sector woes, and the like while they warily eyed Germany and the USSR. The Great Depression taxed them mightily by shrinking trade and international revenues. Along with a general sentiment that precluded military buildup in the face of fascist demands, both countries also had limited military budgets. Neither could count on support from the United States, which engaged economically and culturally in Europe but shunned political and military involvement. In the face of fascist and militarist determination, the European democracies sputtered uncertainly. They perceived the fascist threat, but they also had few options available to halt it except by exacting promises of better behavior from the dictators.

Like so much of Europe, Britain had begun to recover from World War I by the late 1920s, but then the Depression set in and rendered peace in Europe all the more important. This island outpost depended on exports of goods and services mostly to imperial domains to buy food for domestic consumption and raw materials for factories. As British unemployment skyrocketed, a coalition government took the nation off the gold standard in 1932 to devalue the pound and drop the price of exports. Britain then reneged on its war debts to the United States. The economy stumbled along as global trade plummeted. By 1936, the economic picture had brightened, but fascist moves on the continent preoccupied the country. Britain resolved to avoid a repeat of

World War I by engaging in diplomacy to prevent another local conflict from blossoming into a large war and by disarming land forces while maintaining its Royal Navy. This passivity gave little solace to French strategists who looked to Britain and America for support against Germany. London's efforts to unify the democracies against Italy and Germany proved disastrous due to well-meaning and politically expedient antiwar thinking derived from the cemeteries of World War I. The problem lay with Mussolini and Hitler, who responded little to international pressure. Il Duce was an opportunist, but the Fuhrer had a plan to first nullify neighboring enemies before turning on the USSR and England. There was no place for British diplomatic niceties in the grand schemes of the future Axis powers, but neither did the democracies have alternatives to confront fascism short of war.

Britain also had worries within its own empire. In the crown jewel, India, the anticolonial nationalist Mohandas Gandhi had lobbied for independence since World War I. The British steadily gave in as civil disobedience erupted from 1930 onward. Gandhi believed that dominion status was in the offing. In 1935, Britain separated Burma and India, and then wrote a constitution that provided for full self-government in the Indian provinces. Independence was delayed, though, as the European dictators compelled Britain to rely on Indian troops and others from the Commonwealth to combat fascism. Japan also emerged as a considerable threat to British holdings in Asia.

In the *Middle East*—a wartime term for the lands of Persia and the former Ottoman Empire in Asia and Africa—oil focused Britain, as well as France, the United States, and Germany, on imperial domains. Converting a protectorate in Egypt to an independent monarchy beholden to them, the British retained the right to station troops in the country. An agreement in 1936 called for the eventual withdrawal of British soldiers except at the Suez Canal, the strategic waterway linking the Mediterranean Sea with the Indian Ocean that served as an economic lifeline for Britain to the Commonwealth. Egypt remained an ally. Iraq, which also possessed major oil fields, won independence from Britain in 1930. Turkey and Iran remained neutral during the war (the Reza Shah Pahlavi leaned toward the Nazis until he was deposed by British and Russian troops in 1941), and the United States bought off the friendship of Saudi Arabia. Britain had a trickier time with its Palestine mandate where Arab revolts and violence against British subjects had long influenced London's policy in the area. Arab nationalists had the ear of Hitler in demanding an end to Jewish immigration into Palestine, which raised the percentage of the Jewish population there to just under a third. The British restricted Jewish land purchases as well as the inflow of people, mindful of Nazi attempts to appeal to the Arab world. Arabs were not appeased, making Britain's position in the Middle East ever more tenuous.

The French were less willing to grant concessions for independence to their mandates. In 1936, Syria won a promise of independence from France; but on the brink of war a few years later, Paris withdrew its pledge. It did the same in Lebanon. The Arabs reacted in fury, but the French held on in the Levant. In North Africa, Moroccan nationalists joined with anti-French forces in Algeria and Tunisia to try to loosen France's colonial hold. Islamic nationalists in particular were open to the fascists who sought to deprive the resources of these areas to France and Britain. Italy already exercised power over Libya, integrating the territory into its state after nearly doubling the Italian population of farmers and builders there (some brought in to complete a coast road from Tunisia to the Egyptian frontier) during the mid-1930s. The Great Depression also hurt small Muslim farmers in French North Africa, especially in Morocco and Tunisia, where the colonized areas were smaller than in Algeria and were less likely to receive special trade benefits. Revolution was brewing, but an anticolonial reckoning awaited the catalyzing effects of the Second World War.

The Western imperial powers faced desires for independence from their colonial subjects the world over. The Japanese in particular aimed to exploit these nationalist dreams by signifying commonalities of race and ethnicity between them and Asian subjects. As early as 1926, communists rose against the Dutch in Java, portending further difficulties in Asia for the white Netherlands, France, and the United States. In 1933, America voted to grant the Philippines independence within ten years (extended until 1946 due to the war's interruption). Communist nationalists led by Ho Chi Minh made demands for freedom on the French in Indochina, although they ran up against resistance not just from France but from Japanese as well, which occupied the northern part of the colony in 1940. Ethiopia contended with Mussolini in Italian Somaliland, which Il Duce invaded in 1935 and conquered the year after. The future democratic allies wished to avoid aggressive means of holding on to their interests and the militarists took advantage.

ANGLO-FRENCH ARMIES

The British and French did not want war. Why did the two Western democracies acquiesce and engage in appeasement when they had substantial military forces that could confront the fascists? The answer arose from the imperial commitments of Britain, the weakened state of the French economy, and the horrific losses from World War I, which caused both nations to prefer to accommodate rather than confront an aggressive Germany.

For Britain, until early 1939, public opinion and politicians stipulated that the British Army's overseas duties included a policing role in the colonies but not fighting responsibilities on the European continent. This policy meant that 64 infantry battalions remained at home, but 47 battalions served in India, 18 in the Middle East and the Mediterranean, 8 in the Far East, and a single one in the West Indies. Britain possessed the only European army comprised solely of regular soldiers as conscription ended in 1920. Its total strength of 387,000 troops, about half of which derived from units in the Indian Army, made it equal to France's Army, but Britain lacked reserves. By the time of the Munich crisis in September 1938, Britain had available only two divisions for possible deployment to France if war erupted. When war did come a year later, the British Expeditionary Force marshaled just four divisions compared to France's 84 and Germany's 103 divisions. When the British reintroduced the draft in May 1939, there were still severe limitations. For instance, service lasted for just six months unless a state of war existed, and 40% of the 200,000 yearly conscripts (many of them women) served in antiaircraft units rather than combat units. The first draftees were not called until August, on the very eve of war.

The numbers game and geographical dispersion of troops represented a losing cause for Britain. Parliament authorized a rearmament program in February 1936, but financial limitations until September 1938 greatly restricted funds for the three services. Civilian demands on industrial output during the Depression compelled the government to quash significant military spending hikes. British free-market ideology and an erroneous belief that war would be won by the most stable, prosperous economy combined with restraints on borrowing from the United States to weaken the Army.

Troop levels, imperial overstretch, and money problems also had a bearing on Britain's feeble military response to fascism on the Continent. The Army was its own worst enemy, namely, in its inability to innovate under constraints and with new technology. Experiments with armored vehicles had occurred since the 1920s, but there was no coherent plan to integrate tanks into the rest of the British Army or coordinate armor with airpower as in Germany. A combined-arms doctrine was nonexistent. Although the Army was comprised of cavalry and infantry under a regimental system that encouraged a sense of belonging for each soldier, that same philosophy hindered organization, especially once casualties required replacements. Prime Minister Neville Chamberlain decided to protect the home country first, safeguard trade routes, defend the empire, and last to help out European allies. An Army spread out around the globe necessitated fighting at sea and in the air and avoidance of trench warfare that had cost so many lives in World War I. Britain left the massive French Army, therefore, to handle the land war. This did not appeal in the least to Paris nor did it make sense by 1939 when the Nazi threat woke up the British to the realization that if France fell, so might they. The Chamberlain cabinet finally authorized an expansion of 32 divisions very late in the game.

France's Army had different problems, for it shunned the lessons of the past. The French War College examined the battles of 1918 that had maximized firepower and limited casualties, and these "successes" became models. The French banked on the next war involving the same sort of tactics, but Germany did not oblige, and France was left unprepared. A falling birthrate had prompted legislation in 1935 to raise the period of military service to two years, but it took the mobilization of the reserves and the consequent economic dislocation that followed from removing these men from their regular jobs to bring the French Army up to full strength. This effort and the long period required to train the reservists bore on the diplomats who faced Mussolini and Hitler from 1936 to 1939. The French knew their forces were not ready for war.

Yet the Army numbered just under 5 million soldiers in 84 divisions in September 1939 and 2 million reserves in the French empire, a force that even Stalin held to be the most formidable in the world. British strategists banked on France to protect Britain with this army.

France possessed a defensive mind-set, however, that precluded strategy for a short war. By 1939, the Popular Front government had ordered 6,600 antitank guns and 3,200 mostly light tanks despite its commitment to domestic social programs. Yet serious shortages ensued, as factories and the Army could not coordinate the flood of orders.

Table 2.1 Peak Uniformed Manpower

	Army	Navy	Air Force	Total
Germany	6,900,000	700,000	1,000,000	7,800,000
Japan	5,500,000	1,700,000		7,200,000
United Kingdom	2,931,000	789,000	963,000	4,683,000
United States	5,851,000	3,744,000	2,282,000	11,877,000
USSR	6,000,000	?	?	12,400,000

Source: John Ellis, *World War II—A Statistical Survey* (New York: Facts on File, 1993), 227–28.

The disorganization might be overcome by the Maginot Line, a wall of defensive for-tresses guarding France from Germany that the French worked on since 1929 at great expense. This system of high-tech fortifications manned by 400,000 soldiers ran along the French border with Italy, Switzerland, Luxembourg, and southern Belgium. The Maginot Line was deemed unbreachable, although its northern side running along the rough terrain of the Belgian border was not completed to the Atlantic Ocean, a result of deliberate French strategy. French military doctrine called for a prolonged war against Germany as in World War I, with the hopes that a blockade would drain the Nazis over time. The desperate Germans then would either futilely assault the Maginot Line or invade France. If the latter, the large French Army would respond. This was defensive war. Some, like Chief of Staff General Maxime Weygand, tinkered with the mobile war concept by attaching tank units to the infantry; but politicians, the public, and the mil-itary in general were committed to a wait-and-see response. Neither the French nor the British were truly ready for confrontation and wholly lacking a mind-set to fight a war of annihilation.

Because the French and British hoped to avoid a repeat of the mass slaughter of the First World War, both thought about airpower as a means for victory even though they had not solved the problems of inaccuracy in bombing. In the end, the French were mired in prior experiences as leaders and believed wars would be won only on the ground and not in the air. An air force independent of the army and navy finally came into existence in 1933, with only 1,000 or so first-line aircraft dating from the 1920s. The French Air Ministry presented ambitious targets to boost delivery to 2,400 aircraft by June 1940, but stocks did not move much past 500 planes between 1935 and 1938. As a result, France had little to show in the air in 1939. The fighter it had developed proved obsolete when the Germans attacked in 1940, and its bomber force was in poor con-dition due to slow and old planes. France remained well behind Germany and Britain when it came to maintenance, experience, and operations. The country had no plans for offensive use of airpower, only support for ground troops. Thus, France's Air Force lacked modern aircraft and air doctrine heading into war.

This was not the case for Britain. The Royal Air Force (RAF) was the newest of Britain's three military services, but the Air Ministry spent more than the Admiralty or War Office by the late 1930s. The Air Ministry set out to build a bomber and fighter fleet in response to claims that London might suffer as many as 20,000 casualties in the first

Table 2.2 Peak Air Strength

Ellis	Europe Dec. 1944	Pacific Jul. 1945
Germany	5,041	
Japan	—	4,600
United Kingdom	8,395	
United States, Europe	19,892	
United States, Pacific	—	21,908
USSR	14,500	

Source: John Ellis, *World War II—A Statistical Survey* (New York: Facts on File, 1993), 231, 239.

The table does not include figures for the Royal Navy Fleet Air Arm deployed against Japan, nor U.S. naval aircraft deployed in the Atlantic on antisubmarine duty.

day of a German bombing raid. Memories of German raids in World War I, coupled with newsreels of air assaults in the Spanish Civil War, convinced the public that Britain must have a protective fleet of aircraft at the ready. By the Munich crisis of September 1938, the RAF had nearly doubled the number of aircraft stationed at home over four years to 1,102, and this expanded to over 250 more when Hitler invaded Poland the next year. The new Hurricanes and Spitfires improved the quality of the RAF's fighter fleet, although the bombers were older models. Added to the Fleet Air Arm and overseas aircraft, the number of planes in the arsenal hit nearly 2,000 by September 1939 and allowed the country to survive Germany's air assault the following year. During the 1920s, the independent RAF developed under the command of Chief Air Marshal Hugh Trenchard who lobbied for strategic bombing as an answer to the problems of aerial combat. Such targeting of enemy economic and population centers would win wars efficiently and without the massive loss of life. Proponents of this belief included his successors Cyril Newall and Charles Portal as well as the head of the RAF's bomber command, Arthur Harris. They also adhered to the ideas of air prophets Guilio Douhet and the American Billy Mitchell. Yet technological aids in navigation and targeting were needed to make bombing effective. The RAF joined research and development into a system of air defense, but airpower in Britain was defensive rather than offensive until the war was underway.

However enticing air power was, Britain still had the Royal Navy as its ace card. Although politicians held a tight leash on the naval budget, in the event of war, Britain would certainly resort to a naval blockade to choke Germany. The Royal Navy remained the preeminent surface fleet in the world, relying on an antisubmarine active detection system by sound waves that by 1943 they called by its American term, *sonar* (sound navigation ranging). They also used good-weather training to confront threats from submarines. But the Atlantic offered distinct spatial and weather problems, which hindered preparations to protect slow convoys in the mid-Atlantic against German U-boats. The British also still favored the battleship over the aircraft carrier, although this weakness revealed itself in the Pacific rather than European theater. The fleet was aging, with the newest of its 12 battleships built in 1927 and most having sailed in

World War I. Only one of Britain's six carriers was new, although many of the 68 cruisers and 201 destroyers were later models. From 1936 onward, the government decided to expand the fleet, but the vessels were in the process of being built when war arrived. Bereft of innovative thinking when it came to its 69 subs and 2,000 aircraft, the Royal Navy could handle the inept Italians in the Mediterranean but learned the hard way how to combat German U-boats. Meanwhile, the Home Fleet—a defensive force of all of Britain's battle cruisers, 5 battleships, 17 modern destroyers, 2 aircraft carriers, and a handful of light and heavy cruisers—was compelled to await Germany's initiative. Still, the fact that naval vessels were under construction showed that Britain had awakened to the German threat.

For its part, France had the world's fourth largest fleet, which was recently renovated. Although the new ships lacked cutting-edge technology like radar and sonar, they were manned by highly professional officers and seamen. The fleet was deemed worthy, for even though its five battleships were old, the French Navy had modern battle cruisers, cruisers, destroyers, and submarines. It even sported an aircraft carrier. This force could easily match Italy in the Mediterranean, confront Germany's pocket battleships intended for raiding convoys, and team up effectively with the Royal Navy.

Anglo-French naval power, as well as the defensively minded French Army and developing air forces, could confront the fascists, but politicians hoped to avoid war through diplomacy. In the midst of reorganizing its Army, France counted on its alliances with Eastern European states and cooperation with the British to hold off aggressors. A military agreement with Italy in 1935 to guarantee Italian troop support for France in the event of war with Germany fell victim to Mussolini's war in Ethiopia and the subsequent sanctions insisted on by Britain. Yet in 1936, the British Army consented only to sending two divisions to the Continent if war erupted, and these without air support. This lack of commitment exasperated the French who based their defensive posture against Germany on a long war aided by allies, particularly Britain. France gave little credence to its alliance with the Poles in the late 1930s, as military contacts were practically nonexistent. Anyway, Poland had little faith in French security pledges after the Locarno Pact had not guaranteed Germany's eastern borders, thereby depriving the Poles of a secure boundary. The Soviet Union remained off limits because of its

Table 2.3 Naval Strengths, Major Combatant Vessels

	Aircraft Carriers	Battleships	Cruisers	Destroyers	Escorts	Submarines	Total Built	Strength at War's Start	Loss
Germany		2		17		1,141	1,160	95	845
Japan	16	2	9	63		167	257	232	329
United Kingdom	14	5	32	240	413	167	871	289	288
United States	141	8	48	349	498	203	1,247	344	157
USSR		2		25		52	79	126	137

Source: John Ellis, *World War II—A Statistical Survey* (New York: Facts on File, 1993), 245, 261, 262, 266.

The chart is a composite that reflects net major warship production in relation to beginning fleet strength and overall wartime losses.

communist ideology. In addition, there was a tendency in French military circles to overestimate German military power, particularly the Luftwaffe. In contrast, the British generally underestimated Wehrmacht strength. After two decades of preparing for the defense of France, the French Army, Air Ministry, and Navy believed by 1939 that a war with Germany could be won as long as Britain helped out and Poland held out for a time. This seemed a reasonable supposition at the time.

With all the economic and political problems facing them, the Western democracies opted for diplomacy and appeasement of fascism over deterrence. Britain sought to reduce the number of its global enemies, shield itself from bombing, and protect its imports of resources by settling at the negotiating table. Meanwhile, France—having the Maginot Line, its alliances, and its big army—counted on Britain's diplomatic skills. Appeasement was the temporary answer to fascism—a solution of constraint, diplomacy, and hope that temporarily kept the peace but in no way deterred the relentless Hitler who was not open to reasonable persuasion.

AMERICA DELIBERATES

Britain and France might also count on salvation from the United States, a country that emerged from World War I in relatively good shape compared to its coalition partners. America returned to "normalcy" in the 1920s by focusing on business expansion and a foreign policy of isolationism that rejected the League of Nations, restricted immigration on a large scale for the first time in three centuries, and raised tariffs to protect its workers and industry. America did not withdraw from abroad, but it took a cautious hands-off approach to Europe in particular. The country demanded repayment of war debts owed by France and Britain, engaged in plans to reduce German reparations, and supported investments and sales the world over. Most alarming to its friends in Europe was the rejection by the U.S. Senate of a treaty to guarantee support for France should Germany attack. Britain followed the American lead by withdrawing a security promise to France. The Senate turned back the Versailles Treaty twice, thus also rejecting the League, but the failure of the security treaty most undermined the plans of France, which was then compelled to rely on alliances with small countries like Czechoslovakia, Belgium, and Poland. America would not send a rescue brigade to fight future aggressors.

That the Americans were not wholly absent from global affairs after World War I did not make the democracies any more secure. Washington sponsored a naval disarmament conference in 1921–22 that limited battleships according to a ratio of 5 British and U.S. vessels for every 3 Japanese, protected the territorial status quo in the Pacific, and safeguarded Chinese integrity. But these treaties, like its sponsorship of the Kellogg-Briand pact of 1928 to ban war, provided the illusion of security. The democracies disarmed their sizable militaries to great acclaim just as the militarists built their armies, navies, and air forces. Still, the Americans did not naively think that these pacts prevented war. Rather they were hopeful that the various agreements would increase the prospects for peace and avoid the bilateral security deal with France that would commit the nation to fight in Europe. Meanwhile, the United States also eyed cooperation with Japan, with whom relations had been fairly good in the 1920s.

Japan felt slighted by the Washington naval treaty because it was not given equality in the ratio of battleships commensurate with its self-perceived status as a great power. A follow-up conference in 1930 had less success in limiting the number of cruisers, submarines, and other auxiliary ships; and a League of Nations meeting two years later failed to halt increases in land armaments. American strategic calculations and goodwill were found wanting.

The American response to the dictators suffered from the same woes of its future allies: misplaced faith in disarmament, economic difficulty that curbed the willingness to arm, a lack of confidence in leaders and in cooperation abroad, and a misplaced faith that Hitler would halt his ambitions. The roaring Twenties honeymoon abruptly ceased during the Great Depression, which hurt the United States more than any other nation. One-third of the labor force was unemployed by the early 1930s, and gross production was cut in half. Into the breach came President Franklin D. Roosevelt and his interventionist New Deal program of recovery for the United States. Yet he also faced isolationists who protested attempts at a forceful response to Hitler, Mussolini, and Franco. A superb gauge of domestic political winds, Roosevelt trod carefully. There would be no united front of the democracies either led or joined by the United States. The League of Nations lacked credibility as the decade wore on, for the United States was not even a member. Roosevelt monitored the worldwide threat of the dictators and attended to building up American military power. But the democracies did not muster a common defense against the momentum of fascism and militarism. The twenty years' crisis was nearing a tipping point.

The way was open to the dynamic aggressors. After withdrawing from the League in 1933, Hitler denounced the Treaty of Versailles. He openly built his army and air force. Britain responded by the naval agreement of 1935 to limit the German navy and also looked to France and the USSR for a security treaty. Mussolini then invaded Ethiopia in October despite a trade embargo imposed by the League. The move lacked teeth, however, as oil was not included on list of sanctions, for neither the British nor the French stomached a confrontation with Il Duce in Africa. Soon Japan and Italy quit the League. Nazi reoccupation of the Rhineland, the section of western Germany previously demilitarized under the Versailles Treaty, followed in March 1936. No protests arose from the democracies even though a forceful response might have halted Hitler in his tracks. The year closed with the Spanish Civil War underway and Hitler and Mussolini signing the Rome-Berlin Axis agreement. The British and French wrung their hands; the Soviets and Americans remained aloof.

How had the international community reached this threshold? Certainly it is easy to blame the democracies for weakness, but calling them futile pacifists is unfair. They were pragmatically responding to the sentiments for peace among their populations and somewhat crippled by the unwillingness of the United States to provide military guarantees to European friends. In hindsight, Hitler would not stop his aggression until he had achieved his grand objectives for territory and racial purity, but his intentions became clear after the fact. The democracies could only decide and act in the present as they made history rather than learned from it. Still, they were simply not prepared to fight the type of war the Fuhrer envisioned—a brutal obliteration of all foes, military and civilian alike. Hitler's ambitions would reward Germany with dominance or he would drag the German people down with him in the abyss of total destruction implied by his strategy of annihilation. It is unlikely that the democracies could have done anything to stop him short of war; appeasing this violent megalomaniac and his allies would not suffice. Although they had determined to avoid it, the democracies now faced war—the most destructive in history—by mid-1937. Just as distressing as the failure of diplomacy was the fact that fighting broke out not in Europe but across the world, in Asia.

CHAPTER 3

Militarism in Asia

I have fought for good causes. Important causes. But I mourn every man I've killed...And not merely for the best reason, because killing is so terrible, but because there is no point to so many deaths.

SCOTT TUROW
Ordinary Heroes

JAPAN AND CHINA

Two authoritarian states in Asia also edged toward war. China became the victim of Japan as the Second World War began in China. This development was testimony to the fact that ideologies of aggression took root as much in Asia as they did in Europe, fueled by long-held Japanese perceptions of Western racism and paternalism as well as Tokyo's vision of empire. The experiences of Japan and China showed the global linkage of events, ideas, movements, and very clearly, the strategy of annihilation. Against the Chinese, the Imperial Japanese Army applied the concept in a most brutal fashion.

Japan emerged from the European age of imperialism as the first independent industrial modern nation in Asia. After Versailles, political and economic modernization liberalized society and sent business abroad looking for markets rather than solely counting on home consumption. Although disappointed by a peace settlement that denied Tokyo's claims to German colonies and a racial equality clause in the League charter, the government focused on reforms at home. The Great Depression rocked Japan, however, giving conservative army and navy officers sway over anguished citizens susceptible to the siren call of extremists. Antiliberal traditionalists in the military vilified western influences by embracing the premodern age of the feudal samurai. They elevated the emperor to divine status over political affairs, using him to further their militaristic ambitions while condoning assassinations of moderate reformers. Japanese democracy withered under the increasingly bold and dictatorial pressure of the Imperial Army and Navy. Thought police demanded expansion in the Pacific and Asia to remedy the economic downturn and grant Japan its rightful place among white imperial powers.

Japan mimicked Germany and Italy in claiming that it was a victim of circumstances and nature. The population had boomed during the late nineteenth and early twentieth centuries to sixty million by the 1930s, double the number recorded in 1850. This placed great pressure on the economy, and desperation magnified during the Depression. Trade markets abroad could provide one answer for self-sufficiency, but the military preferred territorial expansion. Japan had registered major military victories that had propelled it to big power status, namely by inflicting a series of defeats

Map 3.1 Imperialism in Asia.   Credit: Ronald Story, *Concise Historical Atlas of World War II: The Geography of Conflict,* Map 50, p. 105.

on Russia in 1904–1905, including the stunning destruction of the Russian Baltic Fleet. This was the first time a nation of color had bested a European power. In regard to fellow Asians, Tokyo had annexed Formosa (Taiwan) in 1895 after its triumph in the Sino-Japanese War and Korea fifteen years later and then turned on China. The Western powers and Japan had carved up this decrepit former empire. It was Russia's claims to ports and territory in China that had led to war with Japan in 1904 in the first place. In 1922, the big powers signed the Nine-Power Treaty to guarantee the independence of China. The Japanese military had other ideas. At the risk of war with the United States, which sponsored the Treaty, the Imperial Army designed to seize China and absorb parts of it into the Japanese homeland.

The Chinese empire had decayed under pressure from imperialism and internal strife. Revolution overthrew the Manchu dynasty in 1911, but world war hurt the nascent Republic of China. Warlords—largely independent regional military leaders—loosely coalesced under the banner of the Koumintang, or the Nationalist government under Chiang Kai-shek who was a former army officer trained in Japan. He returned to China during the 1911 revolution and then succeeded Sun Yat-Sen in the 1920s as head of the Nationalists. Vying for power with Chiang were communists and the Japanese. Guided but not significantly materially supported by the Soviets, the communists were feeble at this time. As a result, Chiang chased them to the far north of the country. His Nationalist state then set out to unify the country of nearly 500 million peasants, but the Great Depression, and the Japanese invasion of Manchuria, intervened.

In attacking this northeastern area of China in 1931, Japan sought resources and an economic base in which to exploit the rest of the Chinese mainland and Asia. Manchuria abutted Korea, which Japan already controlled. The Japanese rationalized that they had a rightful claim to the region because they had driven out the Russians in 1905. Japan proclaimed Manchuria as a state independent from China and installed a puppet ruler. The Chinese responded with a boycott of Japanese goods, and Japan countered with an attack on the port city of Shanghai. When the Western powers and League of Nations did little more than wag their fingers at Japan, China gave in, and Japan solidified its hold on Manchuria. The Tokyo generals made their next move by maneuvering into an undeclared war on China itself that began World War II. War came to Asia because of the economic pressures of the Great Depression. Resource poor (except for coal in Manchuria), Japan turned to expansionism to feed its population of 70 million in 1937. Control of Taiwan, Korea, and Manchuria did not provide enough sustenance from imports; China answered that need by providing new markets, cheap labor, and raw materials. Tokyo militarists sought a "Greater East Asia Co-Prosperity Sphere" in the region, an economic system to reduce dependence on outside nations for such key goods as oil and scrap metal.

For the most strident Imperial Army and Navy nationalists in the government, the pursuit of self-sufficiency through tight controls on imports was preferable to reliance on trade with America and the European colonies. The country enjoyed steeply rising industrial production at home and healthy trade and capital surpluses with its colony of Manchuria, but it also counted on credits and commerce from abroad to maintain decent living standards. When the Depression dried up the flow of money and trade, the militarists looked for expansionist options. In 1936, Japan still bought two-thirds of its oil from America and all of its rubber and tin from the European colonies in Southeast Asia. Expansionists reasoned that Japan had no other options but to move into China as well as build its own refineries and synthetic plants. With economic negotiations at a standstill with Chiang Kai-shek, who demanded that Japan relinquish Manchuria, war presented the best opportunity to achieve self-sufficiency through empire. Such ambitions seemed unavoidable due to Japan's general isolation in Asia and its turn to antidemocratic extremism. By 1937, Tokyo signed a military pact with Nazi Germany, but it offered no economic rewards short of riding on Hitler's coattails to defeat their shared enemy, the USSR. Through the efforts of the Kwantung Army in Manchuria, the military subdued the coastal areas of China and defended Manchuria by securing Inner Mongolia against the Soviet Union.

Since World War I, the militarists had prepared for conflict against China and the USSR on land and with the United States and Britain at sea. Boasting over 200,000 officers and men in 17 divisions by 1930, the Imperial Army required compulsory military training. It indoctrinated the troops with patriotic and martial values and the notion that every soldier owed his life to the Emperor. But the Emperor was only the theoretical head of the military; real power lay with the rival war and naval ministries. Who controlled the military, however, was unclear. The Manchurian Kwantung Army under General Hideki Tojo enjoyed semiautonomy as did the armies in Formosa and Korea. The radicalized Imperial Army officer corps was divided between a faction committed to expansion in China and defense against the USSR, and another bent on dictatorship by the Emperor at home. This latter group led the assassination movement in Japan during the early 1930s but was eventually disabled by the expansionist bloc.

Ardently opposed to communism, the Soviet Union, and Moscow's close relationship with Chiang, the expansionist faction under Prime Minister Fumimaro Konoe took power. He believed that domination over the warlords of northern China would split them from Chiang and thereby weaken the Nationalists. In the meantime, Japan would garner the economic benefits of occupation and also geographic depth in the area of Inner Mongolia to prepare for inevitable war against the Russians. In November 1936, a small army of Mongols sent by General Tojo confronted the warlord Fu Tso-yi, but it met defeat at Suiyuan. Tojo believed the Soviet Union had directed this Chinese performance, which gave the expansionists all the more reason to sign the Anti-Comintern Pact with Germany. This agreement pledged to combat international communism and the Soviet Union while Germany recognized Japan's control of Manchuria. The Japanese had gained a free hand in China, as neither the Americans nor Europeans issued more than a moral protest, focused as they were on Hitler's annexation of Austria at the time. Furthermore, the U.S. Congress warned Franklin Roosevelt not to intervene in hot spots abroad.

JAPANESE MILITARY STRENGTH

Japan's war in China profited from a dramatic rise in defense spending during the 1930s as the Imperial Army modernized from rifles to machine guns and from artillery pieces to tanks. Although a generation behind European models, these weapons proved cheap

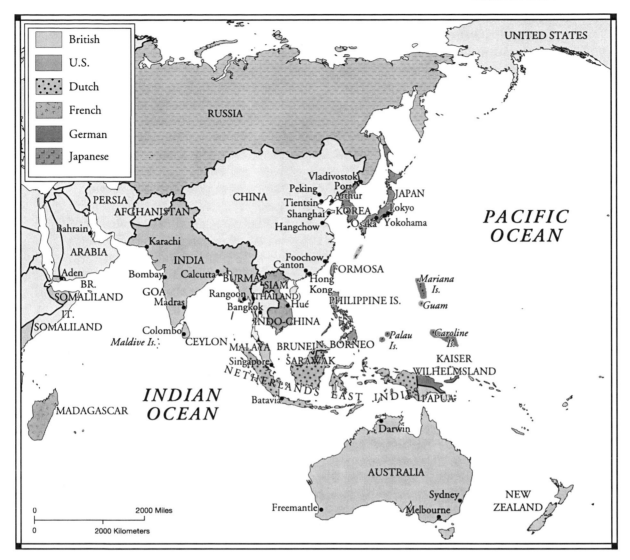

Map 3.2 Pacific and Asia. Credit: Ronald Story, *Concise Historical Atlas of World War II: The Geography of Conflict,* Map 34, p. 73.

to produce and easy to maintain. Japanese doctrine also stressed surprise, night fighting, and risk. This approach created formidable defense, although it was vulnerable on offense. The Army believed it had insuperable advantages. For starters, they believed the superior training and character of the Japanese fighting man compensated for inferior, lightweight weapons and an undersized army.

This "bushido" spirit, or way of the warrior, represented a special approach to fighting. The Imperial Army kept alive the notion that a soldier must die rather than face capture. Indeed, whereas one Western soldier died to every four captured in

World War II, the Japanese ratio of captured to killed was 1:40. The military demanded either total merciless victory over the enemy or death for Japanese troops. The samurai cult frowned on prisoners of war as cowards and thus oftentimes mistreated them. Furthermore, the bushido spirit drove Japanese soldiers to such fanatical lengths in the war years to come as the suicide missions of the kamikaze pilots; reckless banzai charges by the infantry; and their own *seppuku,* literally "stomach-cutting" or suicide by disembowelment to avoid disgrace. An arrogance and headiness permeated the bushido outlook that also led to a "victory disease." That is, this zealous attitude convinced the military it could ignore material deficiencies, shrewd warnings about overreaching capabilities, and information gleaned from intelligence and still proceed headlong into battle. This was "spirit" warfare—an ideology fueled by patriotism, emotion, religion, inbred confidence, and a long history of racial hierarchy with Japan perched at the top. It led directly to a strategy of annihilation derived from contempt for the enemy and eventually desperation. The approach made sense to Japanese strategists, for the nation could not husband the resources of the United States or the population and distances of China. Thus, the bushido spirit necessitated offense; sacrifice; and quick, decisive, and brutal engagements resulting in pitiless military campaigns of annihilation.

The High Command in Tokyo banked on an inspired fighting force to overcome deficient numbers and inadequate equipment. By 1937, the Imperial Army fielded just 17 divisions and only 31 when it went to war with the United States in 1941. The strength of the Kwantung Army rose from 5 to 13 divisions. At the outbreak of the war, these forces appeared enough to conquer China. In any event, during the first phase of war in China, the Imperial Army had adequate tanks, artillery, and services to support the advance of the infantry and ensure victory.

Meanwhile, the proud Imperial Japanese Navy prepared for war against its only nemesis in the Pacific: the United States. The Imperial Navy emerged from World War I ranked third in warships and tonnage to the American and British. Although the two Western powers limited Japan's capital ships (the most important, heavily armed vessels) to 60% of their own under the Five-Power Treaty of 1922, Japanese construction of carriers and heavy cruisers exceeded the ratio by the late 1930s. By the time of the attack on Pearl Harbor, over 311,000 officers and men sailed in a fleet of 391 commissioned vessels. This elite force was well trained and skilled, but its small size meant that replacements could only arrive at the expense of efficiency. This problem afflicted the Japanese as the Pacific War wore on. Added to these units were 3,500 "Sea Eagles," naval aviators who were also irreplaceable in sufficient numbers. Sorely lacking in its ability to add industrial and man power, Japan would face shortages in ships and aircraft after the first year of engagement with the Americans. Yet the Imperial Navy was formidable competition to the United States in terms of strength and technology; its two Yamato-class battleships launched in 1940 were unparalleled as the most powerful warships in history.

The Imperial Navy envisioned a strategy directed at the Americans. Japan assumed that it could not maintain a fleet equal to America's, so it planned to fight a "decisive" battle that also revealed the aggressive bushido spirit as well as faith in its qualitative superiority in arms. First, the Imperial Navy counted on advances in airpower, submarine, and torpedo technology to best the larger U.S. fleet. In this regard, the Yamato class of battleships exemplified the thinking that no U.S. vessel could hope to sink these immense warships, nor could the Americans build a comparably sized ship because they could not squeeze such a behemoth through the Panama Canal. Second, Japan fortified forward bases—Truk and Palau in the Carolines and Saipan and Tinian in the Marianas chain—which supported the fleet with submarines and reconnaissance planes. Tokyo aimed to erode U.S. superiority and defeat America's War Plan Orange strategy that sought to consolidate naval strength in California, link with forces in Guam and the Philippines, and fight the Japanese in a decisive battle in the Western Pacific. To counter Plan Orange, the Imperial Navy planned pitched battles way out in the Pacific. After chipping away at the U.S. fleet and reaching parity in force strength, the Imperial Navy would win the decisive battle as it moved from its bases in and near the Japanese Home Islands and attacked the overextended American fleet. While awaiting the key engagement, the Imperial Navy prepared by consolidating holdings in the Western Pacific and stockpiling resources, such as a two-year's supply of oil.

WAR COMES TO ASIA

On the night of July 7, 1937 junior officers in the Imperial Army of Japan provoked Japanese and Chinese troops into a skirmish at the twelfth-century Marco Polo Bridge outside of Peking. The "China Incident," as it is known in Japanese history, punctuated the lull in fighting between the Chinese and Japanese since the seizure of Manchuria six years before. The Nationalists had sought to redress the loss of Manchuria, but Japan instigated war. Confident of holding the Soviet Union at bay, Japan mobilized to conquer China as brutally as need be. The Germans actually tried to prevent this war by playing both sides. They helped train Chiang's army in the hopes of defending the lower Yangtze River area should Germany end up an enemy of Japan, but at the same time they allied with Tokyo. Hitler preferred for Japan to assault the European colonies. The League of Nations also attempted to intervene, yet its consideration of sanctions was futile without American involvement. For its part, the United States demanded that Japan honor its pledge to uphold Chinese sovereignty. All attempts at mediation failed. Sporadic fighting preceded major operations launched by the Imperial Army in an eight-year campaign for which the country was ill prepared but determined to win by sheer willpower if necessary.

Japan went on a war footing and in the process emasculated its struggling democracy. Converting to a quasi-wartime economy to boost military production and industrial efficiency, the government encouraged monopolies, banned foreign luxuries, and prevented exports deemed crucial to the military effort. Citizens faced rising state intervention in their lives. This led to civic mobilization by patriotic movements and governmental crackdowns on leftists, pacifists, and labor organizers. Discipline intensified over the next few years, school curriculums added the martial arts, and restaurants closed early to focus the nation on the war in China. Controls on prices and production tightened across the economy, and a vigorous black market emerged.

So mobilized, the Japanese moved quickly in China, at least at first, in battles of annihilation. They had a relatively easy time early in the war, as the Army drew on secure supply lines stretching into Manchuria. But the Nationalists countered with a strategy of attrition. China resisted attempts to subdue central and northern regions of the country. Chiang Kai-shek pledged to fight for every inch of territory and asked people to sacrifice, but only 33 German-trained divisions under the Nationalist banner enjoyed modern weaponry and communications. The Chinese Communist Eighth Route Army was more effective particularly because Mao Tse-tung had established a social system and government that reformed corrupt practices and lowered rents for peasants in north China. Mao built bases in the north and then in central China to undergird increasingly popular communist political regimes. The bulk of the Chinese forces were lightly armed, however, and unwilling to fight beyond their home regions. Morale sunk as the Japanese picked off each Chinese army one by one. The Nationalists registered only one victory against a Japanese brigade, at Pingsingkuan, in September 1937. To quell the ardor against its invasion, the Imperial Army resorted to military force and humiliation once mediation failed. After taking Peking and Tientsin in August, the Japanese moved west and south on the railroads, seizing China's northern provinces by October.

The Chinese response involved buying time. The Nationalists suffered from an inferior fighting capability, but their advantages lay in the numbers of people who could be mobilized and distance. China's population and geography were vast, and its human base of 480 million people (mostly peasants) seemed inexhaustible. When the Sino-Japanese conflict began, Chiang's Central Armies numbered 300,000 troops, among them an elite German-trained group of 80,000 soldiers. Units under warlords and other diverse loyalties built the Nationalist forces to about 1.5 million in 1937; but the best of the troops, including the elite group, were decimated during the war's first year. Western observers reported massacres of troops; in August, outside of Peking, an American officer came across the bodies of fifteen Chinese soldiers and two generals whose truck and cars had been ambushed by machine gun fire. He held out little hope for the Nationalist Army in direct confrontations with the Japanese and their strategy of annihilation. Sure enough, at Shanghai, Nanking, and the Japanese advance on Hankow in October 1938, the Nationalists lost about a million troops. A draft and additions from various regions replaced some of the dead, injured, and deserted; but attrition warfare in the face of Japan's slaughtering approach of military and civilians alike remained Chiang's only viable option and a weak one at that.

Rout after rout spurred the confidence of the Japanese in their ruthless onslaught. With the north subdued, they decided to open another front centered on Shanghai. The Imperial Army initiated the attack by a successful amphibious landing, although it was undertaken against an undefended site (American Marines would perfect amphibious landings at defended areas). The Nationalists had no answer.

Chiang vowed to make a stand there, aided by a German adviser, General Alexander von Falkenhausen. They made headway until the fighting erupted out of control in mid-August. The nearly four-month vicious battle for Shanghai destroyed an area of three square miles. The large international community watched as Chiang sent 50 divisions (700,000 soldiers) to fight the 300,000 Japanese infantry and marines. In an attempt to bomb Japanese air units on August 14, the Nationalists inadvertently hit the International Settlement and killed 2,000 people, most of them Chinese. Some saw it as a ploy to encourage foreign intervention in the Sino-Chinese war, and they may have been right. The intrigue, along with the savagery and criminal behavior, marked Shanghai at this time as a particularly terrifying place. It was an early exemplar of this war of annihilation. The Japanese reinforced their outnumbered forces with amphibious landings north and south of city and then unleashing a hellish campaign of extermination that expelled the Nationalists from Shanghai by November. The world watched in horror. Half the Chinese forces were routed, and an estimated 270,000 were killed and wounded. *Life* magazine's owner, the conservative pro-Chiang Henry Luce, ran a front-page, staged photo in the October 4, 1937 issue of his popular weekly picturing a lone crying baby sitting among the ruins of a bombed railroad yard. The propaganda was precious for Chiang and, ironically, the destruction he suffered might possibly have saved his forces by attracting American and other foreign support for his defense.

For the moment, however, he was on the run. Breaking out of Shanghai, the Imperial Army proceeded to chase the retreating Nationalists westward up the Yangtze River toward Nanking, Chiang's seat of government. Despite the presence of U.S. and British warships, and mediation by German emissaries, the battle raged on. The belligerents refused to compromise, as the Japanese bombarded Nanking from land and air and then loosed the usually disciplined Central China Expeditionary forces on the city on December 13. The Nationalists did not abandon the fight, which enraged the Imperial Army even more. What ensued has been termed genocide by some, although the term has been contested because Japan did not aim to exterminate the Chinese people. If genocide is construed more broadly to mean massive killings sponsored by government, than the events in Nanking (and elsewhere in China, where estimates range to approximately ten million Chinese war dead) certainly qualify the Japanese, at least, as engaged in indiscriminate slaughter bordering on ethnic cleansing. Annihilation of Chinese military personnel and civilians was the objective.

The Japanese issued a frenzy of killing, raping, mutilating, beheading, and torturing that rivaled any massacre of the World War II era. Mass executions of men of conscription age, prisoners, and soldiers out of uniform were common. The first rapes became public on December 16 and escalated thereafter. "One poor woman was raped seven times. Another had her five months infant deliberately smothered by the brute to stop its crying while he abused her," reported a U.S. official. The horror continued unabated, even descending to the depths of "recreational rape" because the Japanese grew bored by the monotony of mass murder. This prompted women to smear their faces to look like men or paste disease warning badges on their bodies to ward off rapists. The American observer saw 50 corpses in some ponds on December 22, "obviously civilians, hands bound behind backs, one with the top of his head completely cut off. Were they used for sabre practice?" The next day revealed a "ghastly sight" of a man burned black, his eyes and ears gauged out and his nose partly gone. The victim died, one of hundreds "to be tied together, then gasoline thrown over them and set afire." Soldiers competed for who could behead the most victims in a certain time period or thought up novel ways to kill such as burying people alive and then trampling them

Japanese soldiers taking bayonet practice on Chinese prisoners at Nanking.   Credit: Center for the Study of War Experience at Regis University, Denver, Colorado.

with horses, crushing them with tanks, or setting German shepherds on them. Screams rang out miles away in the countryside.

In the two months after Nanking fell, 200,000 Chinese died at the hands of the Japanese Army. Europeans fled or died in panic. At the American embassy, the U.S. flag still waved, but the bodies of servants lay scattered around the house. Even the U.S. Navy came under attack. The small river gunboat, *Panay,* took hits from Japanese aircraft, which killed two and wounded 50 sailors and passengers. The Japanese immediately apologized and paid an indemnity, not wishing to inflame American emotions. But they had no similar regard for the Chinese during the infamous "rape of Nanking," which also set a pattern of conquest by annihilation under the bushido spirit for the rest of World War II. The campaign in China would be no "good war."

The Japanese appeared unstoppable by the close of 1937. Chiang was forced out of desperation to move his capital up the Yangtze River to Chungking and turn to the USSR and Germany for help. None was forthcoming. Moscow proved unreliable and focused on European affairs, while Hitler embraced Japan as a means to undermine British and Russian interests in Asia and discourage intervention by the United States. The Imperial Army pursued Chiang into the Yangtze delta, took Shansi province, and overran most of northern and central Shantung province by January 1938. At that point, Tokyo decided to search for pliant, native puppet governors rather than recognize the Nationalists as the Chinese government. Collaborators proved unreliable and unpopular; even the more successful Wang Ching-wei regime in Nanking encountered substantial local resistance.

Japan was locked into a war mentality. Like Mussolini in Ethiopia and later in Albania, the Japanese picked on a helpless state. Prince Konoe further expanded the mission of empire and boosted the military. He announced in November 1937 his aim to claim Asia for Asians and end white colonialism under the Greater East Asia Co-Prosperity Sphere. In February 1938, Konoe pressured the Diet of Japan to pass a mobilization law allowing his cabinet to bypass parliament and rule uncontested. This gave supremacy to the military state. Rationing began while military spending rose to 75% of public funding. Imports flowed in from occupied China (as well as from Britain and the United States) to support the economy. The democracies had trouble reconciling their trade with Japan as that nation marched on China, but Britain had a commercial agreement with Japan and America was obligated to sell under contracts.

China fought on as the weak power facing the powerful and merciless Japanese annihilators. The willingness to sacrifice land and lives became apparent as Chiang refused to compromise either with the Japanese or with his potential military ally (but detested ideological rival), the communist Mao Tse-tung. As the Japanese advanced into the rest of Shantung province, Chiang won just a sole victory, at Taierhchwang, in April 1938. About 16,000 Japanese were killed (and Chinese casualties reached 15,000), but the victory merely checked the Imperial Army. Its Central China Expeditionary Army broke from the lower Yangtze River area and swept aside the Nationalists by mid-May. As a Japanese soldier attested, "the battles were always severe. There are many creeks in Central China. The dead Japanese and Chinese would just fall into them and get tangled up on the surface. Many hundreds at once. It was a gruesome thing. The corpses would block your way. If you pushed at them with a stick, they moved easily, the whole mass floating away." The fall of Suchow, Kaifeng, and Chengchow in June completed the encirclement, and capture of Hsuchow on the Yellow River six weeks later led to the loss of half of the Chinese Second Group Army of 600,000 soldiers.

Unable to slow down the invaders, retreating Chinese troops blew the dikes on the Yellow River, diverting it hundreds of miles but drowning tens of thousands of people in the flooded areas in the process. The catastrophe slowed Japanese operations for months but ultimately did not deter Second Army, which moved on the Wuhan province cities, took Hankow on the north bank of the Yangtze River on October 25, and completed the capture of other key cities (including Canton) by mid-November 1938. Officials in Hankow warned residents to ready for a wicked occupation, urging women especially not to come anywhere near the city. General Kenji Doihara's success gave the Japanese command of all the railroads leading out of China and a pivotal site on the Yangtze River. Chiang had to regroup, and some of his forces resorted to guerrilla warfare after the fall of Wuhan. Partisans scored some spectacular successes by killing traitors, bombing enemy units, and disrupting Japanese communications. Still, there was much credibility to Tokyo's claim that the campaign in China was virtually over at the end of 1938.

The steamrolling Japanese now began formulating principles for a settlement with China to end the war and give them occupation rights, but the intention of their military

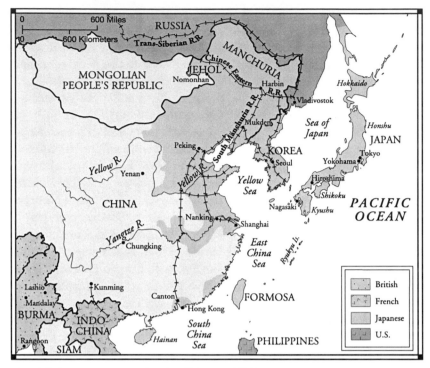

Map 3.3 Japanese expansion in China to 1938.   Credit: Ronald Story, *Concise Historical Atlas of World War II: The Geography of Conflict*, Map 36, p. 77.

doctrine of pacification was clear. This was the so-called three alls policy of "kill all, loot all, burn all." In province after province from 1938 to the end of the war, the Japanese engaged in campaigns of annihilation against the Chinese. Sino-Japanese battles were more numerous, fought with greater ferocity, and caused the Chinese more casualties than typically was the case in Western Europe or the Pacific theaters. For civilians, the outcome of the three alls approach was horrendous. In city after city, they brutalized the population into submission, encouraging corruption, narcotics, and plunder to float local economies. If the mistreatment of prisoners was not bad enough, the Japanese also engaged in practice surgery sessions on civilian captives. Vivisection was common, as patients—oftentimes farmers—were strapped to gurneys, drugged, and had their limbs and inner organs dissected before being killed. The near-genocidal campaign of annihilation created mass graves throughout North China in which "people reducing kilns" burned bodies of the victims. It was official Japanese policy to depopulate the countryside and pacify and punish those who lived.

The militarists in Tokyo had the establishment of their "New Order" in Asia in sight. This entailed ridding the region of European imperialism and Soviet-led communism and asserting Japan's leadership over the Greater East Asia Co-Prosperity Sphere. The Imperial Army moved south along the coast, taking Canton and then Hainan Island in the Gulf of Tonkin to strengthen their blockade of China and menace French Indochina to the west and the American Philippines to the east. In a declaration of victory in November 1938, Prince Konoe claimed the end of Western influence. Chiang denounced the plan, but his was a defiant yet feeble response at the time against the strategy of extinguishing Chinese resistance and white colonialism in Asia.

Chiang was remarkably confident that he could wait out the Japanese while he focused on containing the communists, his most hated threat to his rule. By 1939, Japan had completed most of its territorial gains. The aggressors seized Hainan Island in February and the Spratley Islands the next month, allowed them to cut off Chiang's supply lines from the south. They also conquered coastal areas in southern China in June and blockaded western outposts. Yet the Imperial Army now faced a tiring occupation and bogged down in its effort to advance north of Wuhan. China proved too vast to overrun and subdue. Meanwhile, events in Europe played into Chiang's favor. Just after the Wuhan area battles, the Munich Pact divided Czechoslovakia and thereby shifted German attention away from aiding Japan in China. To be sure, Chiang and Mao also had to go it alone, for the British and Americans balked at a military response on the Asian mainland. Attrition, appeals to the democracies, and civil war against the communists became staples that saw Chiang through the Sino-Japanese fighting in World War II.

Japan tried to address the problem of distance and Chinese attrition tactics through airpower. To extend their reach in southern and southwestern China and sever Nationalist links to the outside world, since 1937, the Japanese began the first effective strategic bombing campaign in history. The naval air service brought in its long-range aircraft, for the Imperial Army had just one 4-engine bomber available. It took until mid-1938 for fighter and bomber units to learn to fly in formation, and Chinese pilots took advantage by shooting down unescorted bombers in daylight raids over Nanking. When Chiang put 450 miles of territory between him and Japanese forces by moving to Chungking, bombing became even more of a challenge. Lack of planes further burdened the Japanese air campaign, as bomber formations stayed at low numbers of 50–90 aircraft until 1940. Imperial Army planes deployed to resupply troops as they marched up the Yangtze River in 1938, but their strategic bombing spread the Japanese thinly over China until the operation ceased in early December 1941. Flyers did inflict damage and nearly scored a major success when they just about wiped out Chiang's staff in a raid in August 1941. In addition, Operation 100 from May to October 1939 leveled several cities and damaged Chungking, which was nearly destroyed the next year during Operation 101. But the 1939 campaign largely failed to cut key supply lines from the Soviet Union to Sinkiang and from Kunming to Burma, or interrupt rail links to French-Indochina, or break Chinese morale. Tokyo reduced the number of aircraft to 150 in recognition of the general ineffectiveness of the bombing missions.

Chiang could hardly claim victory because fewer bombs fell on China than might have been the case, but the year 1939 proved difficult particularly due to the fusion of Asian with European and American events. The year before, the Americans sent Chiang a small loan that at least acknowledged Congress' understanding that the United States had to intervene in some way in the Chinese crisis. Madame Chiang,

Chiang Kai-shek, Madame Chiang, and Joseph Stilwell.
Credit: George Rodger from Magnum.

the Christian and English-speaking T.V. Soong, proved an effective propagandist for her husband's cause against Japan as did Henry Luce in *Time* and *Life* magazines. Born in China, Luce became an ardent supporter of the Nationalist cause through these popular publications and an influential advisor to the Republican Party. Due in part to their pressure, in July 1939, Congress ended the trade treaty with Japan, though it did not yet impose trade sanctions. For their part, the Soviets sent a steady flow of planes to Chiang, which he used to counter enemy air attacks. European diplomacy the next month provided an even more critical influence on the Sino-Japanese clash. The Nazis signed a nonaggression pact with the USSR, thereby dashing Japanese hopes that German force would distract the Red Army from Asia to Europe. The agreement stunned the Chinese, too, who counted on support from an antifascist coalition of America, Britain, and the Soviet Union. Yet Chiang could do without. Japan, on the other hand, faced a hostile archenemy in the USSR at least temporarily free of fear of an attack from Europe.

NOMONHON

As early as August 1938, Soviet and Japanese clashes had occurred where Manchuria, Korea, and the Maritime provinces met in the Changkufeng area. Two hills exchanged hands twice until the Soviets held them after a truce, but the Japanese vowed revenge. Along the wind-swept border of Outer Mongolia, a region of Soviet influence and Japanese Manchuria tensions erupted in May 1939, as both raided enemy positions from the air. Tokyo did not authorize reprisals by the Kwantung Army. This was a wise choice, for the USSR issued a large air offensive that employed over 200 aircraft in a single battle. By July, Kwantung Army troops and tanks and artillery crossed the Halha River into Mongolia twice, only to be halted by Soviet defenses. The threats alarmed Stalin, who feared a Japanese assault on the Trans-Siberian Railroad—the only way to transport troops to the Far East. He sent General Georgi Zhukov to organize the First Army Group along the border. A month of trench warfare and concealed buildup and movement of troops preceded a Soviet counterattack on August 20. After tricking the Japanese through open radio messages into thinking he was building up troops for a defense in the autumn or winter, Zhukov, a former czarist cavalry officer, blasted over the border with 35 infantry battalions, 20 cavalry squadrons, 500 tanks, and 500 aircraft.

Four hundred miles from the nearest railhead, Red Army firepower spilled past the frontier post of Kalkhin-Gol (Halha River), known as Nomonhon in Japanese. Zhukov believed his trump card was armor to be used immediately to crush the enemy. The Soviets overwhelmed inferior Japanese units and drove nearly 19 miles into Manchuria in ten days. Under Zhukov's brilliant leadership, tanks, artillery, soldiers, and aircraft were integrated into an offensive for the first time in military history. He revealed traits of bold initiative, innovation, and acceptance of heavy casualties that served the effort. By August 31, the Russians encircled and destroyed the Twenty-third Division of the Kwantung Army, causing casualties of 17,405 men. The diary of a fallen Japanese soldier read later by Zhukov recorded the misery of constant shelling as the "moans of soldiers and the explosions remind one of hell" amidst the confusion of constant and immense bombardment. Tokyo sent reinforcements in mid-September but had little desire for battling an enemy with superior armor, mechanized power, and artillery and air support.

Both sides signed a truce, and the Changkufeng and Nomonhon border disputes were resolved in June 1940; but the casualty toll on both sides totaled over 30,000. Still, the Imperial Army saw its reputation sullied. Military investigations urged preparations for better defenses and fortifications in the future. Zhukov reported to Stalin that although enemy troops had been well trained and dogged in combat, their generals lacked the initiative and thus confirmed stereotypes of the Japanese. Worse, except for aircraft, Imperial Army armaments were obsolete—the tanks old and the artillery less effective than Red Army models. Manchuria became a sideshow until the very end of the war, but the campaign there did indicate Japanese thinking. The Soviets, Japan's military leaders opined, relied too much on arms and materiel. To be sure, Japan needed adequate and better armor as well as more combat training, but leaders also reaffirmed their belief in the bushido warrior spirit over materialism. A superior mind and determination could supposedly overcome deficiencies in power. Still, Japan seemed to have both spirit and equipment. Western observers noted that by the end of 1939, Japan was "stronger in man-power, morale, experience of war, and reserves of munitions than ever before in its history." This view would be sorely tested in the coming years.

Diplomatic and strategic considerations—and losses—took the fight out of the Japanese in China. The Kwantung Army lusted for revenge, but Nomonhon cautioned the High Command in Tokyo about overextension beyond its capabilities, especially if it had to deal with the Red Army to the north and the committed Nationalists and smaller Communist forces farther south. An unhappy solution arrived on August 23, 1939, in the form of the Nazi-Soviet Pact just as Soviet troops drove past Nomonhon. With German power now added to Russian strength, Japan played a weak hand. Betrayed by the Nazis, Tokyo rescinded the Anti-Comintern Pact. Yet Hitler's attack on Poland a week later convinced Stalin that he needed an agreement with the Japanese so he could focus on the European war. The USSR and Japan reached a neutrality accord in mid-September that both honored until August 1945. By 1940, Stalin halted aid to China out of fear of insufficient resources for defenses in Europe. Until then, the USSR provided a good deal more military assistance to the Nationalists than did the United States. The Soviet cutoff did not help the Japanese, however, for they still could not complete their task in China.

The Kwantung Army wanted revenge on the USSR, but the Nomonhon debacle, Soviet-Japan neutrality treaty, and difficulties in China turned the militarists in Tokyo toward reorienting the focus from Manchuria in the north. No matter how grim and harsh on the Chinese population, the Japanese strategy of annihilation had not won a total victory. As their war in China ground on, Japan pondered British, Dutch, and French colonial holdings in Asia as a means of achieving their Greater East Asian Co-Prosperity Sphere. Rapprochement with the Soviets freed up the Imperial Navy to expand the empire at the expense of the Western powers. The Imperial Army came over to that view particularly because cinching victory in China seemed to be a ways off. Even the most adventurist Imperial Navy viewpoint (and the radicals soon held sway over policy decisions) had to admit, however, that a southern strategy might prompt war with the United States. But at least Tokyo could deal with that eventuality on its own terms, at a place and time of its own choosing.

CHAPTER 4

Phony and European War

There will never be a shortage of people to fight wars.

Ivan Doig
The Eleventh Man

WAR CLOUDS IN EUROPE

Four months after the outbreak of war in China, Adolf Hitler, his ministers of war and foreign affairs, and the commanders-in-chief of the army, navy, and air force gathered in Berlin. During this six-hour-long meeting in November 1937, the Fuhrer confirmed his unwavering desire to achieve living space for Germany by subjugating Europe. Like the Tokyo militarists, the Nazis knew their aggression might spark a large conflict, but both were risk takers who welcomed the opportunity to put their strategies of annihilation into effect and accomplish their ambitions. Although the Asian conflict preceded the European conflict of 1939 by two years, both merged into the monumental conflagration of World War II. Thus, a bridge in China and a room in Berlin immersed the world in a war of unpredictable ruin.

When the United States hardly lifted a finger to help the Chinese, Great Britain and France took note. Hitler had rearmed Germany and increasingly made demands on Austria and Czechoslovakia in 1937. Mussolini had conquered Ethiopia in 1936. Both regimes tested out their air forces in Spain and both gutted the diplomatic arena by withdrawing from the League of Nations. While Il Duce consolidated colonies of Italian East Africa—comprised of Eritrea, Italian Somaliland, and Ethiopia—Germany undertook the war-making initiative. The European democracies worried about America's isolation; if they could not count on U.S. military aid, then they stood alone against the menacing fascists. The Western Europeans believed that appeasement—giving into the demands of the dictators in the hopes they would be satisfied and not ask for more concessions—seemed the most reasonable course until the democracies were better armed. Appeasement meant acquiescing to Hitler's plans to absorb people of German descent into the Third Reich and acquiescing to Il Duce's grandiose plans for control of the Mediterranean basin. Hitler's vision was more expansive than simple ethnic solidarity, however, and Mussolini's quest for mare nostrum promised harsh suppression.

The Fuhrer put into motion his plans for a greater Germany by rebuilding his armed forces beginning in 1935 and then wielding them as a stick to join Austria into a union with Germany. Not only did Austria have a population of seven million ethnic Germans; it also possessed farmland, minerals, and large gold reserves. France and Italy had denied Austria its desire for annexation to Germany, or *Anschluss,* after World War I, and Mussolini enforced that policy by sending troops to the border of Austria in 1934 when Hitler made noises about union. Three years later, Italo-German rapprochement and Il Duce's preoccupations elsewhere gave the Nazis another chance. An ultimatum of either *Anschluss* or German invasion in February 1938 caused the resignation of the Austrian chancellor and the handover of power to the Nazis. Hitler followed up by sending troops across the border in March, sealing Austria's fate as a province of the Third Reich. The democracies acquiesced to the coup.

Appeasement helped Hitler's hands again with respect to democratic Czechoslovakia. Boasting twice the population of Austria, Czechoslovakia contained a plethora of minority nationalities, among them nearly four million ethnic Germans in the western region of the Sudentenland. The country enjoyed economic robustness because its stable industrial and farm sectors remained relatively healthy despite the Great Depression. The Czech Skoda Works produced excellent tanks and artillery. Local Nazis stirred up trouble with propaganda and street demonstrations, insisting on protection by their German brethren. Czechoslovakia looked to Britain and France for aid when the Fuhrer demanded the Sudetenland. Both demurred. Although they were greatly concerned about Hitler, they were not yet at full military strength, especially in airpower. Britain did not believe Czech independence worth fighting for, and France worried that a defense of the country would draw in the USSR and expand the conflict. In September 1938, the two democracies agreed to meet Hitler and Mussolini in Munich to find a solution to the crisis. French leader Edouard Deladier and British Prime Minister Neville Chamberlain handed Czechoslovakia to Hitler. The country was dismembered and compelled to give the Sudetenland to Germany (as well as its northeastern borderlands to Poland) in exchange for Hitler's dubious promise that he sought no new lands. Having lost its mountain fortifications, Czechoslovakia lay vulnerable to invasion. In March 1939, Hitler completed the coup by sending the German Army into Prague. Without firing a shot, Germany succeeded in its territorial ambitions to date. A week after the occupation of Czechoslovakia, Germany took Memel, a city of ethnic Germans claimed by Lithuania in 1923. The Versailles Treaty settlement in Eastern Europe had disintegrated.

Benito Mussolini now played a card in typical opportunistic fashion. His military might be deficient in many respects, but when victims and their protectors were at their most vulnerable, Italy pounced. The Kingdom of Albania's one million inhabitants faced an Italian invasion on Good Friday, April 7, 1939, just three weeks after the Nazi coup in Prague. The campaign was over quickly, and King Zog, his queen, and new baby son managed to escape to England. Victor Emmanuel III became King of Albania, and the Italians, who had coveted the country for two decades, added another element to their empire on the Mediterranean Sea. Albanian resistance sprung up immediately, as partisan groups of nationalists, liberals, intellectuals, and communists pestered Mussolini's occupation throughout World War II. The attack on Albania angered the British, in particular, because it breached the five-month-old Anglo-Italian pact safeguarding the Mediterranean area from conflict. As rumors swirled that Mussolini planned to invade the Greek island of Corfu, the British and French acted. Within a week of the Italian assault on Albania, both Western democracies followed up their public guarantees of defense to Poland with similar ones to Greece and Romania. Italy and Germany moved closer to a formal alliance while they consolidated gains in Europe. Il Duce was Hitler's second; but as a team, they were formidable.

By the Spring of 1939, the situation in Europe was tense and glum, but the democracies took heart. Britain and France finally turned away from appeasement, yet mutual recrimination and a lack of an alliance with the USSR plagued the security of the Western Allies. From the Baltic to the Mediterranean, the two nations pledged to defend victims of fascism. Britain also launched a peacetime draft. British observers optimistically analyzed their newfound toughness. Intelligence reports predicted that aircraft production would exceed German output by the Fall of 1939, that Nazi factories had reached their limits and could not sustain a long war, and that new radar installations promised to prevent German bombers from penetrating British defenses. Only the first assumption proved correct, but it was increasingly evident that if Hitler did go to war, he would have to conquer quickly before running out of steam. Thus, the British moved toward confrontation, believing aggression by Germany, Italy, and Japan would ultimately peter out.

The democracies miscalculated. The Germans in particular seemed up to the task of war. Hitler now possessed more territory and readied for an attack on Poland to bring him nearer to the despised Soviet Union. Appeasement had failed to stop the fascists, for even the clownish Il Duce taunted the democracies. The policy was useful diplomatically by sustaining the Anglo-French alliance, and militarily helpful because the Royal Air Force had not had sufficient strength until the end of 1939. But German power had much more strength, endurance, and skill backing it than the Western nations had bargained for.

TARGET POLAND

On the ground and in the air, the German military remained flexible and potent, though Hitler proved to be the dynamic strategist. He pushed his cautious generals, who feared a long war, to build up the military and engineer a lightning-strike tactic to stun and overwhelm German enemies. Historians have pondered what kind of war Hitler sought. He possibly envisioned a series of short campaigns that avoided attrition and high casualties and preserved German living standards while rearmament went forth. On the other hand, the Fuhrer told the Wehrmacht High Command to prepare for the long haul; synthetic oil and rubber programs hinted that Hitler anticipated a prolonged war. In any case, German rearmament provided a wide if not deep range of military tools to launch a series of brief wars.

Hitler stepped up his demands on Poland, a state of indefensible frontiers and many ethnic groups including Poles, Germans, Ukrainians, Jews, and Belorussians. Germans resented the very existence of the new nation (as did the Soviets, who had fought Poles aligned against the Bolsheviks in the Russian Civil War in 1920–1921), and enmity worsened because of the 800,000 ethnic Germans now living in Poland, of which roughly a quarter resided in the so-called (by the Nazis) Polish Corridor access route. They comprised 96% of the city of Danzig at the mouth of the Vistula River on the Baltic, which was administered by the Germans but under Polish customs and foreign policy regulations since 1933. Hitler turned to remedying this unhappy situation once and for all by exploiting the idea that the supposedly repressed ethnic Germans in Poland, or Volkdeutsch, were really part of the Third Reich.

Despite a lack of modern military equipment, Warsaw made clear it would fight Germany rather than yield sovereignty in the access route to Danzig. When Hitler took Czechoslovakia, British and French backbones stiffened, and both discussed security guarantees with Poland. Unfortunately, they dickered over the meaning of such alliances through the summer of 1939, giving Hitler added evidence that the Western democracies might protest but not interfere should he attack Poland. With a million men under arms, the Poles hoped to hold on long enough until Anglo-French troops reached them through Germany. Thus, they delayed their mobilization, not wishing to provoke Germany into a hasty attack. That plan proved to be illusionary; Britain's army was not in Europe, and France hid behind the Maginot Line. Poland's real hope lay with its mortal enemy, the Soviet Union.

Hitler then entered the diplomatic hall with great skill. By breaking off talks with Poland in April 1939, signing the Pact of Steel with Italy in May, and readying his military for war during the next three months, the Fuhrer courted the cynical Stalin. The Western democracies blundered by believing their security guarantees to Poland would deter either Germany or the USSR. This stance played into Hitler's hands. Although sworn to anticommunism, the Fuhrer sent Foreign Minister Joachim von Ribbentrop to Moscow in mid-August. The Soviet dictator eyed Poland, and now Hitler offered him a deal to obtain part of it. After the Munich debacle, Stalin feared that Britain and France would let the Germans and Russians fight it out over Poland. Stalin agreed to avoid war (the Soviets were currently engaged in their own war at Nomonhon against Japan), bought time and territory in the event Hitler did attack the USSR, and assured that conflict would come between Germany and the Western powers. None of the democracies could give Stalin such rewards, but the Third Reich could. The Nazi-Soviet Pact was a secret protocol that divided up Poland. The Soviets would scoop up the eastern provinces of the Polish state, populated mainly by Ukrainians and Belorussians, and deport Polish citizens and military personnel. The Germans would occupy the Lublin and Warsaw areas and western Poland. Stalin salivated at the prospects of seizing Estonia, Latvia, and Lithuania astride the Baltic Sea (Germany would get a share of the latter) and control of the Bessarabian province of Romania. Hitler had his hands free for war, and Stalin could expand the Soviet frontier westward once Germany acted. Ruthless realism, combined with paranoia, criminal behavior, and a nascent strategy of annihilation ready for the battlefield, guided both dictators.

War was imminent. Poland called up its reserves, the British put its fleet to sea, and French troops took up their stations on the Maginot Line. Hitler sent the Wehrmacht to the border of East Prussia and his new territory of Slovakia, placed the Luftwaffe on alert, and issued an ultimatum to Poland. Told to turn over Danzig to Germany, the Poles mobilized the next day. One day later, on August 31, German operatives disguised as Polish soldiers seized a radio station at Gleiwitz, Germany and broadcast an anti-German message in Poland to provoke the Poles into war. Up to the last minute and even past the German invasion date, the British sought a peaceful settlement. Some historians believe that Prime Minister Chamberlain wished for another Munich-type arrangement in which Germany would back off from war in return for carving up Poland. But appeasement was dead; the time for war had arrived.

At dawn on September 1, 1939, the German training battleship *Schleswig-Holstein,* a pre-World War I vessel armed with eleven-inch guns, was anchored in Danzig harbor on a supposed courtesy visit. The ship began World War II in Europe by bombarding Polish naval installations. Along the border, artillery shelled Polish defenses and communications while armored panzer units and infantry raced into Silesia behind Stuka dive bombers and Messerschmidt fighters that hit airfields, railway lines, and roads. Even German troops on the border were dumbstruck by the thundering artillery; after all the practice and years of tension in foreign affairs, the shooting was now real. Of no political or military significance, Wielun became the first town completely leveled by the Luftwaffe in the launching of the campaign of annihilation in the East. An Austrian infantryman remarked in surprise when villagers handed him flowers as the Wehrmacht marched into Poland, but the large majority of citizens were not friendly. Snipers killed soldiers and collaborators. In Berlin, stunned people gathered in Wilhelmplatz to hear the news of war. The Nazis understood their audacity meant general war; and sure enough, the French and British obliged by declaring war on September 3. In the United States, a frustrated Roosevelt announced that America would remain officially neutral, but its conscience lay with Poland. Europe joined Asia at war, but unlike Japan's quagmire in China, Poland's fate was sealed quickly.

The badly disadvantaged Polish military stood in the way of the Germans and Soviets. Germany possessed over 100 active and reserve Wehrmacht divisions and a cavalry brigade, including mobile troops under the command of the foremost tank warfare theorist, General Heinz Guderian. He had laid the foundation for Germany's panzer divisions of 300 tanks each. The Wehrmacht depended on horse transport, but it also added mechanized and motorized units, artillery, and other weaponry to the 1 million soldiers who attacked the roughly 600,000 mixed trained and reservist soldiers of the Polish Army. Just a third of the Polish Army was at full strength since Poland had earlier avoided general mobilization so as not to provoke Germany. Overwhelmed on the ground, the Poles sailed a naval force in the Baltic miniscule in comparison to the German Navy. In the air, the Luftwaffe enjoyed a 7-to-1 advantage in combat aircraft, all of which were more technically advanced than the mostly obsolete Polish planes. Outmoded also defined Polish armor, which amounted to 310 old tanks in the face of 1,500 panzers, although most of the Germans were armed only with machine guns or light cannon.

If the superiority in numbers was not enough, the Germans also readied their blitzkrieg technique of combined air power, tanks, and infiltration led by dynamic command through radio and rapidly laid lines of communications. Guderian had advocated the constant movement and speed of mobile tank warfare because an army had "to be able to move faster than has hitherto been done: to keep moving despite the enemy's defensive fire and thus to make it harder for him to build up fresh defensive positions: and finally to carry the attack deep into the enemy's defences." Movement, combined with proper armor plating and huge bursts of firepower, rendered the tank unbeatable. "Pity the artillery! It is already hundreds of years old. Pity the air force! Age is creeping up on it in the form of anti-aircraft," he confidently predicted. Actually, blitzkrieg tactics were not fully deployed in Poland. Coordination of the three services, a panzer army, and blanket Luftwaffe support of ground forces did not yet exist nor did the organization and bureaucracy. Poland became more of a proving ground for German armor at a tactical level rather than in a fully incorporated operation. Yet what they did have served the Germans well. The Poles planned to maneuver World War I style in a linear defense; and when these formations on the border broke down, they had nothing left. Speedy German envelopment tactics were so effective that they outpaced logistical supplies. The rout was certain and inevitable, especially because the Poles stood by themselves.

The Wehrmacht plan called for constant and quick movement forward, so fast that the Germans isolated the bulk of the Polish Army at the western edge of the country and penetrated over one hundred miles from Pomerania into Poland on the first day. Across one exposed border came German Army Group North with 530,000 men in two armies. Supported by First Air Fleet's 500 bombers, 180 Stuka dive bombers, 120 fighters, and an armored corps, General Feodor von Bock sent Fourth Army's General Gunther von Kluge into Poland from Germany and across the Polish Corridor. Kluge linked with Third Army, which included Guderian's XIX Panzer Corps, in East Prussia. Kluge cut the Polish Corridor by September 3, thereby destroying Poland's *Pomorze* Army while Third Army rammed through the Lodz and Cracow Armies. Third and Fourth Armies joined for the descent southward on Warsaw. Blasting up from the Slovakian frontier came the three armies of Army Group South, commanded by the consummate Prussian military officer, the elderly General Gerd von Rundstedt, who had come out of retirement at Hitler's request. Accompanied by the Fourth Air Fleet's 310 bombers, 160 Stukas, and 120 fighters, Rundstedt's Tenth Army headed northeast to Warsaw protected by Eighth Army on its left flanks and Fourteenth Army on the right.

The Poles did not lie down under the onslaught, which also included troops from neighboring countries entering Poland for the kill. They knew where the Wehrmacht would attack, but the German hurricane was just too much. Geography undermined the country's defenses; no natural impediments blocked Poland's frontiers, its flatlands aided the velocity of the blitzkrieg tactics, and its industrial areas were easily captured. Polish forces concentrated on the western frontier had no time to fall back and regroup. The Polish Air Force fought valiantly and contrary to legend, was not destroyed on the first day. It bravely rose to the skies and combated the Germans and

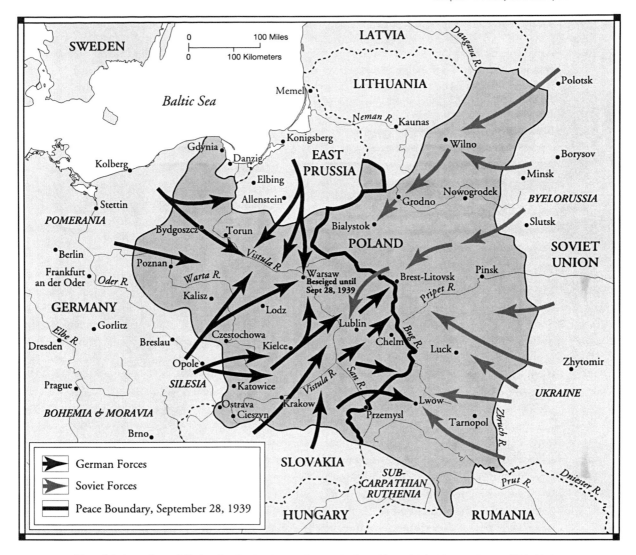

Map 4.1 Invasion of Poland.   Credit: Norman Davies, *No Simple Victory: World War II in Europe, 1939–1945*, p. 39.

then hopped to new airfields to preserve what was left of the fleet. The Luftwaffe swept aside the Polish flyers. In sum, the defenders fought hard but to no avail. Blitzkrieg sliced across the country; and by the third day, when Britain and France declared war, the Wehrmacht turned to wiping out the remaining Polish units as it closed on Warsaw.

Falling back to defend their capital, the Poznan Army under General Tadeusz Kutrzeba faced Guderian's panzers barreling down from the north and Tenth Army led by Lieutenant General Walther von Reichenau rising from the south. On September 7, the Polish government evacuated Warsaw and fled eastward to Lublin. Two days later, the Germans surrounded Warsaw and pounded Poznan Army as it attempted to break out to the south. On September 9, the only serious Polish counterattack occurred. In the battle of Kutno, Poznan Army destroyed a German division, buying time for the defense. The Germans withdrew around Piatek and fled in disarray the next day. This was just a reprieve for Poland. Reichenau sent reinforcements and saturated the Poles with air attacks over the next four days; just half of Kutrzeba's force remained after merciless artillery and Stuka pounding. His communications and command structures shattered, Polish Commander-in-Chief Edward Smigly-Rydz escaped to Romania, and 52,000 soldiers either surrendered on September 17 or crossed into neighboring countries. German Army Groups North and South began mopping up and linked together at Brest-Litovsk east of Warsaw.

SOVIET MILITARY OPPORTUNISM

The day that Poland's commander raised the white flag, the Soviets entered the war. Hitler had urged Stalin to attack along with the Germans, but the USSR delayed. That Stalin hesitated was perhaps part of his plan to let the capitalists destroy each other so that the Soviets would maximize their political gains. But his obligation to honor his pact with Hitler, made easier once he noted no Western rush to help Poland militarily, guided his decision to invade. On September 10, the Fuhrer asked again for a Soviet move, but Stalin waited another week before the Belorussian *front* (army group) poured across the Polish border from the north and the Ukrainian *front* moved from the south. Stalin explained that he aimed only to protect ethnic minorities; but in reality, he sought territory and resources. The Red Army met little resistance, as the Poles focused on fighting in the west and defending Warsaw. The Soviets rounded up prisoners as they advanced toward the German lines at Brest-Litovsk.

Professionalized and modernized during the mid-1930s, the Red Army had finally gone into action. Needed to cover the vast expanses of the USSR, it comprised two independent forces, one in the east and another in the west. Commanders innovatively stressed modern warfare, especially air and tank forces that benefited from cooperation with the Germans. In 1932, the USSR had built its first mechanized corps, three years before the German's established their panzer divisions. A parachute corps was cutting edge; later Soviet experiments in dropping troops from aircraft in April 1941 were the first of their kind. By the late 1930s, the military procured more of the national budget and resources (over one-quarter of the annual budget went to the army in 1939), and aircraft and tank production rose dramatically. Aircraft output doubled, and within two years, the Soviets had 28,800 armored fighting vehicles of all types—tanks, self-propelled artillery, and assault guns. The air force was an extension of the Red Army. It was the largest air force in Europe; by 1938, the USSR had 5,000 aircraft and produced about that many per year in support. The totals belied weaknesses, however. The Soviets had laid the foundation for a sizable industrial effort to support airplane production, but the Stalinist purges delayed modernization until 1941. As a result, on the eve of war, most Soviet aircraft were obsolete; bombers and biplane fighters encountered serious service problems.

The stalled transition to state-of-the-art air power revealed the Red Army's beleaguered leadership and organization. During the purges, Stalin killed or imprisoned about half of his 70,000 officers. The secret police murdered three of five marshals, 14 of 16 army commanders, 60 of 67 corps commanders, 136 of 199 division commanders, and all deputy defense commissars and commanders of military districts. Many of these officers were hacks, but the immensity of the removals erased any semblance of technical expertise and management. To be sure, the Nomonhon victory showed positive signs among the remaining officer corps, but they were terrified of Stalin. The Red Army became mindlessly obedient, even turning away from high-tech armored warfare and relying on traditional infantry movement. This left the military with numerous tanks, which were either old, unwieldy, or too light. The successful T-34 medium tank was not produced until 1940.

The Soviets banked on an offensive warfare doctrine in which invading troops would assist with the uprisings of the proletariat in each country or territory; but in Poland, Stalin was left with an inexperienced and scared command and a badly trained force. The Red Army might look impressive on paper, with five million soldiers by the time of the German invasion in 1941, but its performance raised eyebrows. Stalin's answer to a potential two-front war was the Nazi-Soviet Pact and the opportunity it provided to buy time to rebuild and gain territory as a buffer against a likely German invasion. Occupation of eastern Poland got him both. When the two Soviet armies entered the country, they quickened the collapse of the remaining organized Polish military resistance centered in Warsaw. The Red Army swept up about 200,000 Poles fleeing eastward away from the Germans. The number included 2,500 officers, many of whom were later murdered. In reality, Stalin lent little military significance to the campaign. Rather, the Soviets contributed to the disappearance of Poland once the Germans completed their triumph.

Warsaw held out until September 27. Under bombardment from the air and artillery, its citizens tried to conserve food and water and contain raging fires. Soldiers roamed aimlessly through the streets, and defense consisted of warning announcements and the playing of Poland's national anthem. A Luftwaffe general asked for the destruction of the city to effect the strategy of annihilation; Wehrmacht headquarters decided to eliminate only facilities required to maintain civilian life. Once those were gone, the city capitulated. The Modlin fortress surrendered the next day, ending any hopes for a formal armed Polish response by October 5. An underground resistance movement sprang up, eventually replete with a Home Army and civil administration.

Blitzkrieg tactics had succeeded, although the Germans had not escaped unscathed during the four-week campaign. Over 13,000 died or were missing in action, and the wounded numbered over 27,200. Because of the losses, the tough Polish resistance helped the Wehrmacht mature as a fighting force. The Poles, however, suffered badly. About 133,000 wounded and 70,000 officers and men were killed in addition to the 800,000 taken prisoner. Civilians also felt the wrath of the invaders, who had initiated their strategy of annihilation.

TOWARD THE HOLOCAUST

In their occupation of Poland, the Germans moved from institutional brutality to reprisal, and finally to atrocity. Nazi SS *Einsatzgruppen,* or paramilitary groups under the command of Security Police Chief Reinhard Heydrich, had the task of slaughtering undesirables. So began an extermination campaign called Operation Tannenberg aimed at wiping out Poland's top social and political classes as well as the millions of Jews living in the country. Not until Fall of 1941 did the Nazis consider the complete physical elimination of the Jews; before then, they looked for a "territorial" solution, such as shipping them out of Europe. Yet in Poland, the murdering of Jews and other Poles began immediately. The Nazis sought to Germanize the country and eliminate all vestiges of Polish national identity. Mass killings were the tool. It was clear that Wehrmacht officers did not mind the arrests and imprisonment of the enemy, although many soldiers blanched at such treatment of civilians. Prewar hatred of the Jews, stimulated by Nazi propaganda and widespread German abhorrence of the Poles, rendered vulnerable Poland's three million Jews (the largest Jewish population in Europe outside of the USSR) to the Germany Army. After the war, the Wehrmacht tried to absolve itself by blaming Hitler for the brutality, but from generals on down, the Army took part in genocide.

The SS did the dirty work, and the ensuing violence against person and property escalated as the Nazis moved across Poland. In Zloczew, the Wehrmacht disemboweled a ten-year-old girl in the street while another soldier crushed the skull of a baby. Three regiments of the 10th Infantry Division killed several elderly in Torzeniec after meeting fierce resistance from civilians. Jews became favorite targets of execution, but others, including Polish soldiers, were also massacred. In an infamous episode, the 15th Motorized Infantry Regiment ordered 300 Poles to strip off their tunics. The Germans then cut their suspenders so the captives could not run away and marched them down a road to be machine-gunned into a ditch. Operation Tannenberg lacked the systematic and technological perfection of the later killing machine of 1941, but the terror was immense. German troops became more radicalized in their actions, as murder of civilians was legitimized by the state as a defense against dangerous, barbaric Jews and partisans. This was the start of Nazi genocide and an instrumental part of Germany's strategy of annihilation. That wide-ranging scourge included razing hundreds of villages, hundreds of mass executions based on the collective responsibility for supposed crimes against the occupiers, organizing Jews into ghettos and killing them, and the liquidation of Polish culture by eliminating the intelligentsia.

Hitler and Stalin carved up their winnings, rearranging Eastern Europe according to their interests. Because Stalin coveted Lithuania, he offered to revise the Nazi-Soviet Pact. Lithuania would be given to the USSR. In return, Germany would control all Polish-speaking territory. The partition gave Germany 9.5 million Poles in a western zone. A central "General Government" area, which included the cities of Warsaw and Cracow, converted 12 million inhabitants into a labor force (unless they were murdered or imprisoned). In 1941, Hitler decided to Germanize the region and incorporate it into the Third Reich. The territorial arrangements also gave the Soviets an enlarged buffer zone in the west. Soviet control encompassed more territory than Germany but 10 million less people than the German zone. The population suffered nearly as much under the Russians as the Germans. The Red Army arrested authority figures such

The Siege of Warsaw.   Credit: Blitzkrieg (*Time-Life Books*, p. 43).

as Polish military officers, imposed taxes on churches, and generally tried to eradicate the nation's cultural, political, and economic identity. Deportations, jailings, and killing—the annihilation—halted once Germany attacked the Soviet Union, but the Poles became subject to the whims of their occupiers. Soviets and Nazis gloated about their decisive initial triumph in World War II.

PHONY WAR

German leaders had no plans should Britain and France actually fight for Poland, but they need not have worried. After Poland's demise, the democracies perpetuated a "phony war" of propaganda, feint-hearted probes into German lines, and basic inaction. France fully mobilized with 85 divisions facing Germany. With artillery, tanks, and aircraft added to Britain's force, the French vastly outnumbered the Wehrmacht. France could have attacked the Saar area, where nearly 80% of Germany's coal was produced, but Paris merely sent out patrols into Germany and withdrew them to safety behind the Maginot Line after Poland surrendered. The British bomber force of 800 planes could strike the vulnerable German western front. Indeed, the RAF launched ineffective and costly air attacks against German military targets as early as September 4. In mid-December, the Germans parried three such raids around the Wilhelmshaven naval base in the battle of Heligoland Bight. They downed several Wellington bombers previously thought to be impervious to German fighters. The Me109s and 110s shot them down and chased the rest back across the North

Sea. Chamberlain preferred to preserve the fleet and turned to dropping leaflets on Germany that urged peace. Like France, Britain believed itself lacking in armaments when compared to Germany, although that was not necessarily true and bred a defensive mentality. In any case, Chamberlain's diplomacy proved as unproductive as the Wellington raids.

No nation came to Poland's rescue. In reality, saving the country would have required upending Western military doctrine. Short of a guarantee of victory, the democracies decided to do nothing, hoping that an economic blockade would snuff out Hitler's ambitions or would generate a shouting match over the morality of Germany's actions. But they really had no viable military options; for the French had little offensive military capacity, and British bombers would have been useless. Words took the place of military action; the democracies adopted a stern exterior that transparently revealed their unwillingness to help Poland. Meanwhile, Polish leaders and troops fled through Romania for France to set up the first exile government of the war, military units were reestablished throughout Europe, and the underground focused on sabotaging the German war effort. Just as Czechoslovakia had been a "far away country" of little import to Britain, now nobody was willing to "die for Danzig" as the French slogan went. The dictators also took Anglo-French timidity as a signal to expand the war, although Mussolini delayed his plans for joining Hitler's aggression after intense Anglo-French efforts at appeasing him. He felt torn between his kinship with German fascism and his reluctance to fight the big Western powers.

The so-called phony war belied the fact that there were some clashes, especially on the high seas. Within hours of the British declaration of war on September 3, German submarines mistook the British liner *Athenia* for a Royal Navy auxiliary cruiser and sunk it off the coast of Scotland's west coast. Going down with the ship were 128 souls, including 28 Americans. The next month, 833 sailors lost their lives when another U-boat torpedoed the battleship *Royal Oak* at its anchorage in the British Home Fleet base at Scapa Flow in Scotland.

The British enjoyed a measure of revenge when they tracked the German pocket battleship *Admiral Graf Spee* all the way to South America, to the River Plate port of Montevideo, Uruguay. She and her supply ship had departed from Germany in late August before the outbreak of war. They scoured the Indian Ocean and South Atlantic for targets (an indication of the global reach of World War II), eventually sinking nine enemy transports. Attempting to score a last hit on a convoy before returning home for repairs, *Graf Spee* ran into a Royal Navy hunting party that lay in wait on the open seas at the approaches to the Rio de la Plata shipping lanes. On December 13, 1939, the Battle of River Plate lasted eighty minutes and resulted in damage to three British cruisers. The German vessel took sanctuary at Montevideo for repairs. On learning that reinforcements were on the way for Britain and that the Uruguayans had denied his request for an extension of time in port, Captain Hans Langsdorff scuttled *Graf Spee* and committed suicide. The British rejoiced, a sign that victories, however far away, were in much demand during the phony war period, especially for the harassed Allies.

Map 4.2 Hunt for Graf Spee.   Credit: Terry Hughes and John Costello, *The Battle of the Atlantic* p. 53.

Latin America would see no more campaigns in World War II, but the region became an important support area for the Allies. The Axis threat in the hemisphere, and particularly to the Panama Canal, ended after the Allied landings in North Africa in late 1942. Latin American losses of life and property were relatively light.

But a Brazilian Expeditionary Force saw heavy fighting in Italy, and over 250,000 Mexicans fought in the United States military (about 1,000 died). The region was more significant for its logistical contributions, as several nations served key roles in terms of resources, transit points for men and materiel, and bases. Brazil's northeast coast, which was the closest land to Africa, became an important departure point for trans-Atlantic supply and air shipments across the Atlantic. From the Caribbean to Brazil, a series of naval and air stations housed submarines and planes that prevented Germany from seizing assets in the South Atlantic and that replaced Allied losses caused by the European conflict. Venezuela and Mexico proved crucial in supplying oil to the United States, and Brazil granted America access to bases that became part of America's first response to the war, called "Hemispheric Defense." The attention placed Latin American nations in a position of economic ascendancy during and after the war that brought social changes to the region as well as international influence for Brazil, which received the first nonpermanent seat at the postwar United Nations institution.

The militarists and dictators had capitalized on their plans while the democracies searched for ways to stop the tide of aggression without going to war. They moved from appeasement to inaction. The standoff might have been phony in terms of extensive direct engagements, but Poland learned that war was real enough at the hands of the German strategy of annihilation and opportunistic Russian treatment. Despite the naval encounters of Fall 1939, the first bombings of Britain (in the Shetland Islands on November 13, 1939), and the first British fatality in France in December, the phony war with the Western democracies endured into April 1940. Even Adolf Hitler, who ordered his reluctant generals to prepare for war, an invasion of France by November 1939 was slowed by winter weather. Yet he readied to convert what might have been a small campaign of dividing up Poland into a Europe-wide struggle.

Axis Advance

1939–1942

CHAPTER 5

German Expansion, North and West

The potency of myth is that it allows us to make sense of
mayhem and violent death. It gives a justification to what is
often nothing more than gross human cruelty and stupidity.

CHRIS HEDGES
War Is a Force That Gives Us Meaning

WINTER WAR IN FINLAND

In Europe, the Soviets acted first to spread the war. Stalin sought a buffer zone on his
western border to protect against an attack from the Nazi military machine he had just
witnessed in Poland. Such territory hinged on dominating the Baltic states of Latvia,
Lithuania, and Estonia, which Stalin eventually occupied with the Red Army. Key
areas of Finland preoccupied the USSR. These included part of the Karelian Isthmus
just north of Leningrad, a naval base at Hango, islands in the Gulf of Finland, and an
Arctic area that threatened Russia's port of Murmansk. Independent since 1917, Finland
refused to trade these territories for others offered by Stalin. The Soviet dictator hoped
to exercise the option rapidly over Finland that he had gained under the Nazi-Soviet
Pact. He feared that by waiting, the Western powers might choose to protect the Baltic
States and Finland.

Rebuffed in its attempt to wrest Finnish territory close to Leningrad and military-
industrial sites, the USSR initiated the so-called Winter War in November 1939. The Red
Army bombed the capital of Helsinki and attacked across a 600-mile frontier, confident
of besting Finland's inadequately equipped army of a mere ten divisions and some special units. During the conflict, the Soviets employed 1.2 million men in 26 divisions
using motor transport and artillery and backed by 1,500 tanks and 3,000 aircraft. The
300,000 Finnish troops lacked sufficient guns, ammunition, tents, uniforms, and other
war materiel; and their air force and navy were tiny. But they made up for the deficiencies by clever training and determination. Soldiers learned how to negotiate on skis in
winter and on foot in summer through the thick wilderness that served as excellent
defensive terrain.

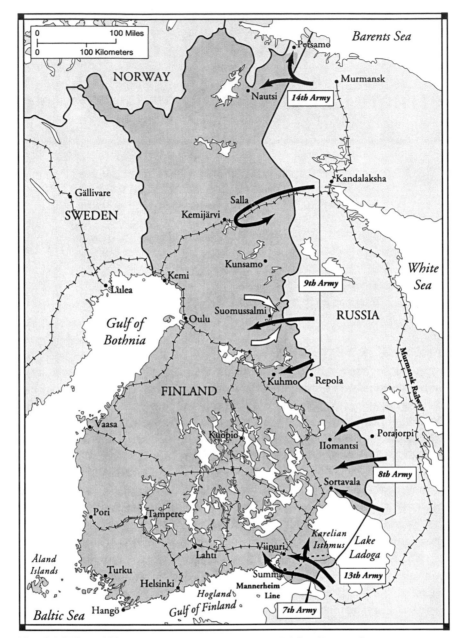

Map 5.1 Winter War.   Credit: Michael J. Lyons, *World War II: A Short History*, p. 81.

Taking advantage of the time gained from a month of prewar parley between diplomats, Marshal Baron Carl Gustaf Mannerheim prepared Finland's forces behind a defensive barrier of trenches and 44 concrete bunkers placed between fieldworks on the Karelian peninsula. This Mannerheim Line was outfitted with automatic weapons but no antitank guns or artillery to impede the Russians until outside help arrived from Swedish and Norwegian volunteers or even Franco-British forces. Commander Mannerheim had a reserve force of 100,000 Civic Guards who occupied the 700-mile frontier from Lake Ladoga to the Arctic with the same number of women's auxiliary in support.

The Soviets quickly encountered problems. Their thought they could intimidate the Finns with their sheer numbers. But as the chief of staff to Ninth Army commander General Vasili Chuikov reported, Soviet "units, saturated by technology (especially artillery and transport vehicles), are incapable of maneuver and combat in this theater" and could use only roads. They were "frightened by the forest and cannot ski." The Goliath Red Army was simply unprepared for war against the Finnish David in four hours of sunlight per day, −30°F temperatures, and screaming blizzards. The Russians wore dark uniforms, which made them easy targets against a background of snow, and antifrost protection for their equipment. Cockiness about victory exacerbated their ignorance and incompetence in fighting—a product of bad leadership. The toll of purges haunted the Red Army. The advantage went to the Finns. Underestimation of the enemy, Finnish fighting effectiveness, and inadequate preparation humiliated the overwhelming Soviet force. Without good leadership in the field and training in winter fighting, the ill-equipped Russians assailed the Mannerheim Line. The aggressors attacked en masse, neglectful of the waiting Finns huddled in their bunkers in snow-white outfits. Finnish reserves adjusted to the onslaught. They left towns lightly defended to provide the Soviets with few clear targets. The Red Army air force flew long-distance missions, losing 800 aircraft as a result. An amphibious penetration was also repulsed.

The USSR bogged down. The Finns panicked at first against the tanks, which they had never encountered and, in any case, lacked appropriate equipment to combat. But they soon improvised by throwing Molotov cocktails, first used in the Spanish Civil War but given their moniker in the Winter War. Ignited by a rag stuck in the top, these gasoline-filled bottles broke on contact, spattering the target with burning gasoline. The Finns also used their 20 mm Lathi antitank gun to good effect. With no coordination of tanks and infantry, the Soviets proved easier pickings once isolated after dark. The Mannerheim Line held, and on December 27, the Soviets ceased their assault on the Karelian peninsula. They did manage to advance from the north in large numbers. Amphibious troops overpowered the Arctic port of Petsamo as the Soviets poured in from Murmansk, cutting off Finland from the Arctic Ocean. On neither front could the Soviets close out the campaign, however.

The Finns required outside help to survive. Helsinki appealed to the League of Nations and hoped for supplies from Norway and Sweden. The League booted out the USSR, but Berlin and Moscow blocked trade in Scandinavia. Two battalions of volunteers and some weapons did enter Finland from neutral Sweden. In late December, the Finns counterattacked on the eastern front, skiing through the forests to outflank, cut off, and chop away at the unwieldy groups of Soviet troops stuck on the few roads in central Finland. Heavy equipment mired the troops in four feet of snow and Arctic temperatures. When tanks tried to break out across frozen lakes, they dropped through

Finnish troops with Russian corpses.   Credit: Center for the Study of War Experience at Regis University, Denver, Colorado: From the archives of the Finnish Defense Forces.

holes in the ice made by Finnish shelling. The Finns focused on destroying supplies and shelters to strand the Red Army. The tactic worked. Four Soviet divisions were destroyed between December 24 and January 5, with their heavy equipment absorbed by Mannerheim's army.

By February 1940, the defense waned, however. Finland could not endure alone against such a colossus. The Russians moved massive reinforcements to the front. The Finns took heart in an Anglo-French plan to send an expedition through Scandinavia into their country, but neither neutral Norway nor Sweden would let it transit through out of a fear of provoking intervention by Germany or Russia. The democracies mostly aimed to deny Swedish iron ore mines to the Germans rather than rescue Finland. They realized that geography and logistics made military intervention impossible. Help for the beleaguered Finns never materialized.

Soviet forces were soon stripped of ineffective officers and reorganized under Semyon Timoshenko and a reinforced Thirteenth Army. Timoshenko was a future Marshal of the USSR, defense commissar, and titular head of the armed forces who had survived the Stalinist purges. He rushed in from Poland where he commanded a Ukrainian army group. After studying the lessons of the confrontations with the Finns, he issued a new battle order that took into account severe winter conditions and the need for maneuverability. Timoshenko's plan adopted new combined-arms (infantry and tanks) tactics for assailing the Mannerheim Line and created ski brigades for reconnaissance patrols. Changes in the command structure decentralized the targeting of artillery. No longer reliant on haphazard barrages of fire that did not awe the Finns, the USSR adopted a doctrine of careful observation from the field and communications between infantry patrols and battery commanders. Timoshenko launched a devastating ten-week battle of attrition in Finland in January 1940. Hastily taught and retrained Red Army forces bombarded the Mannerheim Line, and combined infantry and tanks followed under air support. The Soviets broke through at Summa on February 11. Falling back to intermediate positions of field works and obstacles, the Finns awaited the next Soviet attack. They were overrun on February 25. At Viipuri a week later, the Finns faced Timoshenko from their rear position on the Karelian peninsula. Soviet tank and troops assaulted them behind the lines from the west over the sea ice. President Mannerheim advised his government a few days later to come to terms with Stalin.

Finland decided to cut its losses. Having suffered 25,000 killed and losing one-tenth of its territory, the nation made peace on March 12, 1940. Fighting ended the next day. Mannerheim turned over the entire Karelian isthmus in return for Petsamo in the far north. Stalin might have pursued total victory, but the Russians incurred 200,000 dead and lost mountains of equipment. This disastrous performance against an underdog compelled the Kremlin to recognize that a reorganization of the Red Army was in order. The USSR proceeded with reforms over the next year. The Germans disdainfully judged the Red Army incapable of defending its homeland; after all, the Russians could barely defeat miniscule Finnish forces. Perhaps the USSR might be easier pickings than Hitler had thought. In any event, the Soviets were strategically more vulnerable than before, as Leningrad, Murmansk, and the Murmansk railroad lay exposed to attack.

The Winter War was not a complete negative for Finland. The Finns retained some independence as well as enduring hostility toward the Soviets. They repaired their forces with a 16-division army outfitted with modern equipment. The initiative returned to Hitler, who the Finns joined in 1941 to eradicate the Red Army from their soil. This occurred even though the Germans had refused to let Italy send planes to Finland to honor the Nazi-Soviet Pact. Throwing their lot in with Germany was not palatable, for they knew from discussions with the Wehrmacht that Berlin simply wanted to use Finland as a pathway to the USSR. But this was a better option than being subsumed by the USSR, like the Baltic States. Finland made a deal with another devil by committing to a German invasion of the Soviet Union. The reason was to use Hitler to free itself from Stalin's grip.

SCANDINAVIAN CALCULATIONS

The Fuhrer had considerations with the north countries that might confound his plans to subjugate France and Britain before he turned eastward for lebensraum. He hoped to subdue the west before attacking in the east; but preparatory to overrunning the democracies, Hitler sought to secure his northern flank and to procure access for his navy and submarines to the North Atlantic. Above all, he needed to safeguard shipments of Swedish iron ore to Germany by controlling Scandinavia. The Germans depended on the iron ore for their economy and war machine. Extracted from the Gallivare fields in warm weather, this vital product went by rail to the Swedish port of Lulea before heading south by ship through the Baltic to Germany. With the Gulf of Bothnia frozen in winter, trains took the ore north to the Norwegian port of Narvik from which it was shipped southward along the coast. The Allies turned to the possibility of occupying the Gallivare fields themselves. This would tighten the British naval blockade, thereby repeating the World War I era squeeze on the German economy. Under the prodding of British First Lord of the Admiralty Winston Churchill, the Anglo-French Supreme War Council decided to lay mines along the Norwegian coast. The purpose was to flush out German vessels from Narvik into open water so that the Royal Navy could attack. The British also decided to land troops in neutral Norway, exhibiting an impulsiveness that led to a poorly planned and confusingly run campaign. This was neither Churchill's nor the Allies' finest hour.

The potential for havoc worried Hitler, especially after the Navy's commander-in-chief, Grand Admiral Erich Raeder, warned that the Royal Navy could prove troublesome by its willingness to violate Norwegian neutrality and attack German warships and iron-ore carriers. That fear came true in mid-February 1940 when the British intercepted *Graf Spee*'s former supply ship, *Altmark,* as it plied down the Norwegian coast on its way home with 300 British prisoners in its hold. The Royal Navy rescued the captives even thought it meant disregarding Norway's neutrality. Hitler was alarmed. The democracies could apparently tighten their blockade at will, prevent iron ore from reaching Germany, and upset his plans for the conquest of Europe. Anglo-French planners also realized these possibilities. They began gathering troops in Scotland for transit to Finland through Scandinavia. Merely transiting Norway and Sweden honored their neutral rights and also gave the British a presence in the region. But the Winter War ended, and the forces could not be justified. Hitler had no such concerns with legal pretenses. As always, he forced the issue. The Fuhrer listened to Admiral Raeder's counsel against defense in favor of seizing Norwegian coastal ports from which to attack British shipping in the north Atlantic and break out of the confines of the North Sea. In the larger picture, the Scandinavian campaign would make possible the strategy of annihilation in eastern Europe.

Raeder convinced Hitler to move on Scandinavia with Operation Weserubung. The plan for the campaigns in Denmark and Norway involved the type of stopgap, short-term thinking that typified German naval policies for the remainder of the war. Norway's long coastline was hard to guard. An invasion demanded the commitment of the entire Navy and then a taxing occupation to maintain security. Under pressure from Raeder, Hitler decided to gamble by surprising the Royal Navy with overwhelming force and seizing essential Norwegian ports and air bases. In February 1940, he named General Nikolaus von Falkenhorst to command the operation. The General spent an afternoon making his plans with the help of a travel-guide book.

To facilitate access to Norway, Germany attacked the democratic monarchy of Denmark. This small, flat, exposed, and thus essentially defenseless nation began modernizing its army as the Nazi threat loomed. Yet the Danes were caught on their heels because they neglected leaked information about an impending German invasion. Preparation would not have mattered in the long run, however. They possessed just 14,000 troops, over half of which had been drafted just two months before, and a

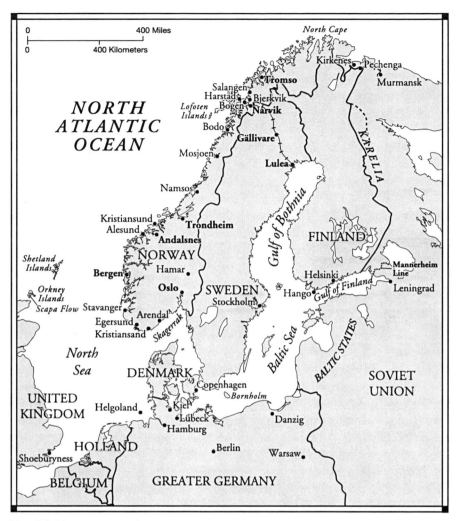

Map 5.2 Norway campaign.   Credit: Martin Gilbert, *The Second World War: A Complete History*, p. 41.

miniscule coastal navy and air force of mostly obsolete planes. Denmark posed little challenge to Germany. Hasty mobilization around Copenhagen and near the German border occurred a day before the April 9 attack, and the Danish Army fought for a few hours in North Schleswig. The Danish Navy never fired a shot, for it never went on alert. As a result, a German troopship sailed freely into Copenhagen. The Germans also launched the first parachute operation in history and then seized the land bridge of Masnedo and the Aalborg airport in the north. They took two hours to secure the capital city. A Danish coalition government negotiated an uneasy collaborative relationship with Germany into August 1943 when the Nazis officially took over the country. Perched at the entrance to the Baltic Sea and with air bases 200 miles farther north of Germany, Hitler now had his stepping stone to Norway.

The attack on Norway occurred the same day as Germany invaded Denmark. Rather than last two hours, this part of Operation Weserubung lasted two months. Worried about the assembling Allied forces in Scotland, Admiral Raeder ordered supply ships out of port on April 3 and sent to Norwegian waters. In the meantime, the British Royal Navy had mined the Norwegian coast unaware that Germany's entire navy was on its way. This was not the only oversight. Norway itself focused on the actions of the Western Allies rather than the fact that the Germans could invade regardless of Allied plans. Its conscripted peacetime army, when fully mobilized and joined by territorial units, consisted of 106,000 men lacking armor, antitank, and antiaircraft weapons. Yet they had to oversee an area of land and coastline of 125,000 square miles. An air force of 40 mostly old planes offered negligible support. The Norwegian Navy of 5,000 sailors on four new escort destroyers and a new minelayer, a few larger coastal vessels, and a scattering of smaller ships patrolled Europe's longest coastline. The democracies counted on Royal Navy superiority and discounted the possibility that the Germans could mount anything other than small counterattacks against British vessels. Bereft of decent military intelligence, the Western Allies underestimated Operation Weserubung.

Convinced of the foolhardiness of an operation against the Royal Navy, the British and the Norwegians were stunned when the German Navy achieved both strategic and tactical surprise. Britain believed that the oncoming German fleet sought to break out into the Atlantic; the troops were carried on warships, after all, and not on transport vessels. When the attack began, the Royal Navy found itself sailing for an interception point somewhere in the North Sea while the Norwegians faced a multipronged German offensive. The Norwegians fell back, barely responding except to mail out mobilization orders. British ships came upon German vessels by chance. Although victorious on occasion, they squandered their advantages due to mistaken assumptions and faulty intelligence.

Both sides won engagements. The destroyer *Glowworm* found herself facing the pocket battleship *Hipper* and four destroyers who were about to land troops at Trondheim. The British ship desperately rammed *Hipper* but went to the bottom soon afterward. A British submarine, *Truant,* caught the German cruiser *Karlsruhe* between Denmark and Sweden and crippled it so badly that the Germans themselves later sunk it. A Polish submarine torpedoed a transport, and dive bombers sank another German cruiser in Bergen Harbor. On April 10, the second day of battle, a torpedo from the British submarine *Spearfish* wrecked the stern, rudder, and propellers of the German pocket battleship *Lutzow,* taking the vessel out of action for a year. In actuality, Germany's margin for error was slim; captured sailors tipped off the British that Norway was their target. Yet they awaited the next German move and thus lost the initiative.

Falkenhorst ordered attacks on several key cities up and down the coast. On the first day (April 9), parachutists took Oslo's airport and subdued the city until troops from merchant ships and air transports took over. Within hours, the Germans poured ashore. They seized Kristiansand, dropped 2,500 men by air at Stavanger, and took Bergen and Trondheim by beaching 2,000 soldiers from ships with damage to only two light cruisers, *Karlsruhe* and *Koenigsberg.* Ten destroyers backed by the battle cruisers *Scharnhorst* and *Gneisenau* put another 2,000 troops ashore at Narvik although not without a high-speed gunnery duel between *Gneisenau* and the more heavily armed British battle cruiser *Renown*. The outgunned Norwegian Navy rolled over to German forces. Only the coastal fortresses provided some hope. Norwegian reservists fired torpedoes and shells from the Oscarsborg Fortress in the Oslo Fjord, sinking the new heavy cruiser *Blucher* that had led a convoy of troopships destined for the capital. Other vessels took hits, but the Fortress did not follow up with more, and the German convoy backed up and unloaded lower down the fjord. Overall, the German Navy enjoyed two good days of battle.

The phony war had come to an end. King Haakon VII and Norway's government escaped into the southern interior, refused a German surrender ultimatum, and denied recognition as head of state to the Norwegian fascist party leader, Vidkun Quisling. Instead the government organized a fighting retreat under the command of Major-General Otto Ruge, hoping to hold on until French and British aid arrived. The feeble response by the Western democracies failed to wrest Trondheim from German hands and adequately reinforce Ruge's southern flank over the next several weeks. About 30,000 Anglo-French forces put ashore at Andalsnes and Namsos south and north of Trondheim, respectively. The former linked up with the Norwegians to the south in the valleys surrounding Oslo. But despite British advances, around Oslo and Trondheim, the Luftwaffe strafed and overwhelmed the Allies and their support ships, and German ground forces pushed enemy troops back to sea. The Norwegians surrendered the south by May 3, and the government scurried northward to the Tromso area.

Slightly better news for the Allies came from Narvik, the major port in the far north of the Western Fjord. Mines laid by the British on April 8 did not deter the 2,000 German troops. Surprise was a key element. The Germans disembarked from ten destroyers the next day because a British group of five destroyers, commanded by Captain Bernard Warburton-Lee, arrived too late to stop them. U-boats failed to detect his flotilla when it finally showed up, however. The British destroyers penetrated the harbor on April 10 to sink two vessels and six merchant ships. The British commander himself was killed, his flagship grounded, and two destroyers were sent to the bottom and another damaged by the crossfire from a group of German destroyers that came to the rescue. The remaining British destroyers escaped under covering fire. That the Germans did not finish off the Royal Navy force proved a costly mistake. Three days later (April 13), the British battleship *Warspite* and nine destroyers sank the remaining German destroyers and a U-boat. Because German air cover did not reach this far north, a ground force of 24,000 French, British, Poles, and Norwegians counterattacked in and around Narvik. They slowly crept into and seized the town on May 28. The Germans retreated to the Swedish border by the time the German invasion of France had reached its climax. This compelled the democracies to abandon Norway, and the King's government left for Britain on June 7.

The campaign in Norway was over. As the Royal Navy returned home, the German 31,000 ton battler-cruiser *Scharnhorst* sank the aircraft carrier *Glorious* and her two destroyer escorts with a loss of 1,500 lives. That was roughly a third of the British casualties in the campaign. The Norwegians suffered 1,800 dead, the French and Polish together about 500, and Germans killed numbered 5,500. The material loss for Germany was significant. Half of the Raeder's destroyer fleet sank to the bottom. Even *Scharnhost* and its sister battle cruiser *Gneisenau* were put out of action until December 1940. Raeder had just a heavy cruiser, two light ones, and four destroyers remaining available for combat. Losses drastically reduced the forces available to support a cross-channel invasion of Britain in the coming months. The German Navy was crippled for the remainder of the war.

The Norwegian campaign both hurt and benefited the Third Reich. Hitler dreamed of Scandinavians as partner Aryans who could provide a strategic location for his military forces. Fearful of a nonexistent Allied attack, he garrisoned up to 500,000 troops there. This manpower might have been better used elsewhere once the world war expanded eastward and into Africa. Yet it was hard to argue with his logic at the time (and indeed, the British Army and Royal Marine Commandos raided the Norwegian coast several times over the next three years).As in Poland, the Wehrmacht overcame obstacles and setbacks and cinched the campaign in a matter of weeks. Germany also secured the Gallivare deposits and opened naval and submarine bases on the Norwegian coast. Their fortified submarine pens in Trondheim and Narvik complicated Allied efforts to control U-boat attacks on shipping over the next several years. In addition, German control of the airfields proved the worth of land-based airpower early on in the European war.

All the British had to cheer about was the sinking of German vessels. The Royal Navy reeled from the shock of encountering German airpower that could reach beyond its borders and across the sea. At home, the Norway campaign roiled politics and precipitated a change in leadership that ultimately benefited Britain. Winston Churchill showed his willingness to fight. In early April, Neville Chamberlain ridiculed Hitler as a has-been, convinced that the Allied blockade had dashed Nazi hopes for aggrandizement. But the Nazi war machine had been alive and well. In the midst of the Allied march on Narvik, Chamberlain fell from power. The appeaser was gone. In his place as prime minister stood Churchill, a forty-year veteran of military strategy and politics at the highest levels. Churchill believed in attrition warfare (and soon a strategy of annihilation), the skilled use of intelligence, and the British Empire. He was a blend of romantic and pragmatist who offered the people the promise of perseverance against fascism. To the public he was a fighter.

GERMANY TURNS WESTWARD

From Nanking to Warsaw and from Oslo to Montevideo, the ominous presence of the Tokyo militarists, Hitler, Mussolini, and Stalin cast a shadow over Europe and Asia. Hitler urged his reluctant generals to move to the next theaters in the west and north. The democracies were on guard. Churchill pushed the Egyptian government to put its country under martial law, sever relations with Italy and Germany, and maintain access to its resources for Britain. In Asia, Japan had devastated parts of China but found itself mired in a war of attrition and on the wrong side of a battle against the USSR, although it continued its war of annihilation against the Chinese. If a common denominator shaped events, it was that the dictators seized on the opportunity for war. For his part,

Hitler chose a wider war, finding western Europe ripe for conquer. He took aim there because he believed that defeating France and Britain were instrumental to his most cherished objective of destroying the Soviet Union. Military victory in the west was critical to instituting his ideological war of annihilation against allegedly subhuman people in the east.

Hitler had bigger fish to fry than those in the frigid nations in the northern reaches of Europe. Nearly thirty postponements of Operation Gelb since November 1939—the offensive on France—had given the Wehrmacht pause in its plan of attack. Generals Franz Halder and Walter von Brauchitsch, two weak-kneed leaders opposed to confrontation with Hitler, conceived of moving in a northern swing through the Low Countries. In an updated version of the First World War Schlieffen Plan, Army Group B under Generaloberst Fedor von Bock would take parts of France and Belgium and speed Britain's defeat. Chief of staff of Army Group A, General Erich von Manstein, counseled instead a bold southern thrust through the seemingly impenetrable Ardennes Forest in Luxembourg and across the Meuse River in an attempt to destroy the Allied armies. Backed by the Luftwaffe, Guderian's panzers would push through the heavily forested Ardennes and around the Maginot Line, slicing through the French at their weakest point. They would then drive to the English Channel as they encircled the French armies bent on protecting Belgium and Holland, meanwhile permitting commanders to take advantage of any opportunity that arose. The infantryman Manstein asked Guderian, a tank man, if the sickle cut could be done through the Ardennes. Guderian said yes, and Hitler was ecstatic.

The Allies took an opposite passive tack. Germany had absorbed real wartime experience already, whereas the democracies had only theory and training exercises to guide them. The British Expeditionary Force had built up its strength to about 400,000 soldiers by Spring 1940, but there was insufficient coordination with the French, Dutch, and Belgians. The latter two had capable militaries, but Belgium demanded strict neutrality and hence steadfastly refused to permit British and French forward deployment on their soil. That the Soviets could also not be counted on for Anglo-French appeasement policies convinced them that the democracies lacked the stomach to deter Germany. Britain planned a naval blockade to stymie Germany and feared Luftwaffe retaliation to a bombing campaign by the RAF while the French looked on the Maginot Line as their savior. The British worried about a French army plagued by bad intelligence and seemingly pointless defensive exercises. The French had long believed that Britain's small field army was inadequate to help defend France. Defeatism and faulty leadership threatened France's effort against the vengeful Germans. Prime Minister Paul Reynaud came to power by partnering with politicians who did not wish to fight. For France, the phony war persisted.

The innovative Allied commander-in-chief, Maurice Gustave Gamelin, also began to make some key planning mistakes. His command structure was faulty. He put General Alphonse Georges in control of the Northeast (France and the Low Countries) area's several armies, but Gamelin's interference sowed confusion. He took little notice of Nazi blitzkrieg tactics in Poland and erroneously believed that France could win by relying on the British blockade. Furthermore, Gamelin situated his headquarters close to Paris (to keep tabs on political developments) but far from the military front, thereby isolating himself with no radio communications. Operational plans posed further problems. Gamelin proposed to defend the Low Countries by extending his forces into Belgium to the Dyle River. This meant moving his Seventh Army away from the Ardennes and north to Breda in the Netherlands. Gamelin expected a plodding attack by Germany in the north. The French especially had learned little from Germany's smashing of Poland. Their tactics were outdated, and their armor scattered. France had neither changed nor adapted to new circumstances. Its leaders counted on outnumbering the Germans in men and materiel. The Wehrmacht, however, had created a new environment backed by a fanatical ruler bent on imposing a war of annihilation at all cost. The first step was to issue a swift smashing blow to France.

The weather that had so bedeviled Nazis was perfect on the night of May 9, 1940, when Hitler told his general staff, "Gentleman, you are about to witness the most famous victory in history." The next day, the Wehrmacht invaded neutral Luxembourg, Belgium, and Holland. Tiny Luxembourg was occupied that day with seven of its 87 defenders injured. The ruling family and the government fled to Britain. Those left behind faced conscription into the German army. King Leopold commanded Belgian forces of 600,000 men but with no navy or antiaircraft artillery, only ten tanks, and 250 mostly aged planes—half of which were reconnaissance aircraft. British and French troops entered the country on May 10 ready to defend Gamelin's Dyle Line between Antwerp and Namur. The German assault through the Ardennes that day threatened the Line.

The Wehrmacht was equally impressive against the Eben Emael fortress' steel and concrete emplacements between Liege and Maastricht that guarded the bridges over the Albert Canal. This was the world's biggest fortress. Perched on the steep incline of a river, it offered up to 1,200 men protection by thick walls, barbed wire, a moat, and two artillery batteries placed in immense domed cupolas. Tunnels transported men and materiel. When Leopold's army made its initial stand at Eben Emael, the Belgians had 750 soldiers in the fortress. Supposedly Hitler himself then ordered German gliders carrying 78 engineers in the Loch Assault Detachment to drop on to the fortress. Germany had developed glider technology since 1930, and under the guidance of World War I flyer General Kurt Student, Hitler could put his brainchild to the test. The results were sensational. Facing ten times their number of men the first day, the glider men blew up some of this modern fortification with hollow, shaped charges and flamethrowers. Belgian forces fought back, but the key bridges and the rest of the Eben Emael structures were captured the next day. If the fortress had held, the French might have fended off the blitzkrieg by fighting north from the Maginot Line. But before the Allies knew it, the Germans swept past the Canal and Liege aiming for the Dyle Line. The French and British raced up to confront them too late, on May 12. Worse, the Wehrmacht welcomed Anglo-French forces taking the bait because by rushing to defend Belgium, they weakened their positions around the Ardennes. The defense of France now had holes everywhere.

Meanwhile, the Dutch put into effect their "Fortress Holland" plan with largely the same results as the Belgian effort at Eben Emael. They counted on flooding the country

Map 5.3 Invasion of Low Countries and France. Credit: Ronald Story, *Concise Historical Atlas of World War II: The Geography of Conflict*, Map 8, p. 21.

then defending themselves behind three fortified lines. With 400,000 soldiers but not a tank and few armored cars and heavy guns, the Dutch Army inflicted some reversals on the invaders yet lost 4,800 men including 2,100 dead. Holland's home navy of a destroyer, a cruiser, and some smaller vessels fell victim to the Luftwaffe's 1,100 planes. German flyers sank the destroyer while the other ships were either scuttled or sent to England. They also destroyed 62 of the 132 serviceable aircraft in the Dutch army. On the ground, two German airborne divisions blasted through the Lake IJssel Line in the west and then hit strategic positions such as the critically strategic bridge on the Waal River at Moerdijk that exposed Holland's major cities.

This landing represented the main thrust for the Germans, although their 22nd Airlanding Division captured airfields around The Hague before being driven off to surrounding villages. German paratroopers resisted Dutch counterattacks until Holland surrendered and The Hague fell, although the Wehrmacht lost 80% of its air transport force in the operation. Back on the bridges and rivers that guarded Fortress Holland, the German 9th Armored Division reinforced the paratroopers and drove on Rotterdam. French troops melted away south while Dutch marines defended the bridges of Rotterdam before German paratroopers outmuscled them. Unbeknownst to Luftwaffe bombers, surrender discussions began on May 14. Messages aborting a raid on Rotterdam did not reach the pilots until they dropped 57 of their 100 bomb loads on the city. Rotterdam went up in flames—a victim of the strategy of annihilation that had no bounds—with upward of 980 civilians killed. This was considered an atrocity at the time. A further 78,000 were left homeless. Outraged by the killing of innocents, the British retaliated with the first strategic air offensive against Germany—the birth of their own strategy of annihilation—by hitting the Ruhr. But Holland had surrendered the previous evening just four days into the campaign.

Nazi Germany appeared invulnerable. As the Wehrmacht moved westward, the strategic and military flaws of the Western democracies became readily apparent. If France did not recover from its torpor and block Hitler's path, the Fuhrer would wipe out Germany's long-time foe. The Third Reich would then turn on Britain as the last obstacle to taking aim on his ultimate prize: lebensraum in the east.

CHAPTER 6

Blitzkrieg and Blitz

Peeking out, I saw direct hits on two holes at the far perimeter and the soldiers, already dead, flying toward me.

SCOTT TUROW
Ordinary Heroes

BLITZKRIEG IN FRANCE

The attack in the Low Countries was really a feint, a "matador's cloak" waved to trick the democracies into thinking that German Army Group B would lead the main thrust northward. All the while, Rundstedt's Army Group A, with 44 divisions and all of the fast panzer units, would conduct an end run around the Maginot Line in the Ardennes Forest. Gamelin banked on the old war plan, sending the French Seventh Army (his last mobile reserve) north to Breda just before the Germans attacked Holland. He left himself with virtually no reserves to contest Rundstedt. In addition, German Army Group C under General Wilhelm Ritter von Leeb, who had recently come out of retirement, waved the matador's cloak from Luxembourg south along the Maginot Line. He tied down 30 French divisions to prevent them from contesting Rundstedt's move through the Ardennes. The French possessed more tanks than the Germans, but these were spread out thinly, having not trained in the mass formations that the Wehrmacht had used effectively in Poland. Britain had ten divisions and a small air force in France, but the superb Spitfire fighter remained at home for defense, and the Royal Air Force lacked effective tactical bombers. For instance, the Fairey Battle bombers were single-engine light aircraft easily shot down. The French air force was inferior and poorly deployed.

On came the Luftwaffe, integrated smoothly into the blitzing offensive with fleets of medium bombers hitting behind enemy lines and the JU-87 Stuka dive-bombers supporting the tanks and infantry. To be sure, the Luftwaffe suffered large losses. On May 10, 83 aircraft went down in the biggest one-day loss for the Germans in all of 1940. But the confusion sown and psychological damage done—terror, intimidation, and the impression of domination—devastated the Belgians, Dutch, and French.

As Army Group B and defense of the Dyle Line distracted the Allies, Rundstedt's three panzer corps moved through the Ardennes with no resistance other than that of traffic jams on narrow dirt roads. Two companies of the infantry Belgian Chasseurs (Rifles) Ardennais resisted the 1st Panzer Division for a day, but neither French infantry nor 32 British Fairey Battle light bombers could stop the German advance. French Ninth and Second Armies took up positions on the western side of the Ardennes to await the Germans. On day three of the attack (May 12), the panzers emerged from the forest. They had penetrated the seemingly impassable and made it to the east bank of the Meuse River. Having outflanked the Maginot Line and reached Gamelin's Dyle Line, they confronted the main French defense. The bold Erwin Rommel, a devotee of mobile warfare, rested at Dinant in the north while Polish campaign veteran Heinz Guderian held the Sedan area in the south. They stood at the elbow or hinge of the Allied line at the Meuse. Guderian later confessed that success for Operation Gelb was far from certain between May 13 and 15.

General Gamelin desperately tried to shift reinforcements to help his two armies but still believed that the big assault would develop in the north. Guderian attacked across the Meuse at Sedan. He now occupied high ground in such a short time that he thought it a miracle. Supported by several hundred Stuka dive-bombers from the Eighth Flying Corps that screamed down on the terrified gunners and infantry of French Second Army, Messerschmidts eliminated any French aircraft daring to interfere. The 1st Panzer Division had created a pontoon bridgehead downstream on the Iges Peninsula and expanded it to three miles wide and four to six miles deep along the Meuse. The French 3rd Armored Division proved too slow to destroy the bridgehead and British bombers failed to concentrate in sufficient numbers to dislodge the Germans whose antiaircraft defenses were superb. Some French soldiers fled, others held their ground. But they were all outmaneuvered as the Germans moved at mechanized speed.

The future of France was in jeopardy. On May 13, the ruthless Guderian, backed by the Luftwaffe, hit the poorly trained and ineptly led French troops defending Sedan. The 2nd Panzer Division got only one of its eight assault boats across the river and was stalled until the 1st Panzer Division finally wore down the French. The 10th Panzer Division to the south experienced heavy losses, with nearly all its assault rafts sunk. The 1st Panzer Division's success fully decimated French defenses and landed engineers who built a bridge and continued the advance after hard fighting. When the elite Grossdeutschland army guard unit crossed by evening, the French either panicked and ran away or lacked the necessary artillery to destroy the bridges. Having sent French Second Army reeling, Guderian now unleashed Rommel on the Ninth Army. Rommel's 7th Panzer Division pushed four miles into French forces and crossed the Belgian Meuse in rubber rafts under heavy machine-gun fire that inflicted significant casualties on the Germans. But Rommel pressed his force onward by capitalizing on disorganization in the French ranks. By afternoon, he established a bridgehead defended with light machine guns. Bolstering his heroic reputation, he helped build additional bridges for tanks to move across that evening. The 5th Panzer Division meanwhile engaged the French in a diversion that took pressure off Rommel.

Guderian with Enigma machines during the assault on France.   Credit: Bundesarchiv, Koblenz, Germany, Bild_1011-769-0229-12A[1].

The Germans secured three bridgeheads across the Meuse. The French fought valiantly but were no match for Rommel's inspirational and resourceful leadership. For example, he cleverly ordered houses above one crossing point set ablaze to create a smoke screen. Rommel also assumed command of a battalion and traversed the Meuse in one of the first boats to join a contingent that had crossed earlier. Reinhardt's XLI Panzer Corps had a rougher time than did Rommel's 7th Panzer Division. They attacked at Montherme, well north of Sedan where the river flowed swiftly between defensible cliffs. The XLI Corps established a bridgehead but could not bring tanks across. Nonetheless, on May 14, it dawned on the French that they were in deep trouble. In High Command headquarters near Paris, silence greeted the news that the Germans had breached the Meuse. "The atmosphere was that of a family in which there has been a death," reported a general. "Our front has been broken at Sedan! There has been a collapse," proclaimed an officer who broke into tears. The French and British losses mounted as Guderian aimed the panzers westward toward the English Channel.

The French planned a counterattack. As the XIX Panzer Corps penetrated French lines on May 14, the British RAF finally attacked Sedan with light bombers after diverting airpower to Belgium. Because the Blenheim and Fairey Battle bombers were thin skinned, unwieldy, and slowed by their bomb loads, they were vulnerable to fast German fighters. The RAF experienced the highest rate of loss of the war, as 30 out of 71 bombers were shot down. So wasted were the British that bombing halted for a day. The French faced the same destruction on the ground. The next day, France's ground forces registered some initial success until enough German tanks arrived to destroy the light French ones. Divisions fell like dominoes. The 102nd Fortress Division that had held off Reinhardt gave way on May 15 so that nothing blocked his way into France. Troops led by General André Corap withdrew on foot in the face of the motorized Wehrmacht. The Germans had attacked in three large groups of tanks, whereas the French had so dispersed their armor that the infantry was left with little protection. On May 16, French tanks at Stonne fought well, but the effort was too late. General J. A. R. L. Flavigny had the 3rd Armored and 3rd Motorized Divisions in reserve, but he stayed on the defensive. If he had counterattacked, he might have breached Guderian's southeastern flank. Not doing so allowed the 19th Panzer Division to reinforce its flank before barreling on westward, leaving the French in its dust and heading unimpeded toward the Channel.

The French Second Army also fell back, opening the way to the Channel and to Paris. The Germans could take their pick of targets. All seven panzer divisions were across the Meuse in a fluid attack in which panzers had raced ahead, Stukas strafed the defenders, and refugees clogged the roads. Guderian was ordered to halt because his superiors, including Hitler, were so stunned by the disintegration of the enemy that they feared the panzers had exposed their flanks to French reserves. By audaciously motoring ahead of the infantry and artillery, Rommel captured 10,000 soldiers, 100 tanks, and 30 armored cars as he drove through a 50-mile wide gap in the French line. He mopped up the French army. By now France had abandoned the fight and on May 16, Prime Minister Paul Reynaud informed a visiting Winston Churchill that all was lost. He had no reserves, and Gamelin had no idea where the Germans were headed. The appalled Churchill returned to London.

Some did not give up. By advancing so rapidly, the Germans had outrun their supply lines and provided an opportunity for a counterattack against their southern flank. Colonel Charles de Gaulle, a rather undistinguished officer to this point, hastily assembled the 4th Armored Division. It hit the Germans at Laon on May 18–19, but within three days fell back to be pulverized. De Gaulle's mobile tank engagement with the Germans again at Abbeville between May 28 and 30 earned him a promotion to brigadier general. The effort showed that mobile armor might at least slow the Germans. Yet Gamelin still insisted on keeping the initiative in the hands of his deputy, General Alphonse Georges, who had collapsed from mental exhaustion. Actually, the Germans hardly took notice of de Gaulle. On May 19, Guderian's 2nd Panzer Division reached the English Channel, having traveled 200 miles in ten days. The next day, Reynaud fired Gamelin.

The 73-year old Maxime Weygand flew in from his command in Syria as a replacement. He proceeded with his Weygand Plan to assault the German "panzer corridor" stretching to the coast from two directions. A few days before, Rundstedt had ordered his panzers to pause because he worried that his forces were overstretched. But an outraged Guderian, as well as Georg-Hans Reinhardt and Rommel, maneuvered around the order using the permission granted for reconnaissance as an excuse to push onward. The Weygand Plan failed, trapping elite British and French forces against the sea. The British had success with a tank attack toward Arras to the south, but the French provided no support. Rommel's antitank battalion countered effectively, and the British Expeditionary Force retreated to Dunkirk on the English Channel for a last stand. General Ewald von Kleist, commanding three panzer corps that included Guderian's 19th Corps, chomped at the bit at the edge of the Dunkirk pocket.

DUNKIRK

With some logic, Hitler intervened by ordering the panzers to halt on May 24 for two days. He did so, some believe, because he still held out hope for a peace deal with Britain. In reality, the area of canals and ditches around Dunkirk was not good panzer territory. Why not let the infantry move in rather than armor? The British tank attack near Arras, followed by a small French V Corps action on May 22, had worried German headquarters that the Wehrmacht might face a more determined enemy than the campaign had thus far revealed. A dilemma of rapid armored warfare was also revealed: the need to maintain forward momentum exposed the flanks of tank columns to attack as the panzers swiftly advanced. Rundstedt wanted to rest his tanks for their move south. He told Hitler (who needed no convincing on this score) that a German attack might bog down around Dunkirk into a prolonged World War I style siege. The rapidity and totality of the Nazi's overwhelming victory in the west may have led the Fuhrer to stop and count his winnings. The campaign had perhaps gone too well, so maybe there was a chance that the Third Reich's luck had finally run out. In any event, Air Minister Hermann Göring told Hitler that the Luftwaffe would wipe out the escaping British Expeditionary Force as it tried to cross the Channel. Better to give the enemy a narrow window for flight and ensure that the British vacate Europe, and then crush the English lion later.

The halt order allowed for the organization of the evacuation of Allied troops under the protection of the French First Army and the Royal Air Force. Lord Gort, a World War I hero but a mediocre officer who now commanded the British Expeditionary Force, had made a monumental decision against orders on May 25. Instead of attacking to the south along the lines of the Weygand Plan, he ordered his troops to cover the positions of the retreating Belgian army to the north. This allowed for a shift in Allied forces to the south and delayed the Belgian collapse, both of which gave the Dunkirk evacuees precious additional time. Under Operation Dynamo, the British and French navies planned to take out 45,000 men on anything afloat. During the nine days of the evacuation beginning May 27, fishing boats, tugs, dinghies, and ferries shuttled across the Channel. The Germans relentlessly bombed the vessels and the beaches. Allied troops trudged to boats in the darkness, treaded water in the oil-drenched black sea awaiting rescue, or drowned if their craft was hit. On June 1, Weygand told Churchill that the evacuation had reached a crisis point, as

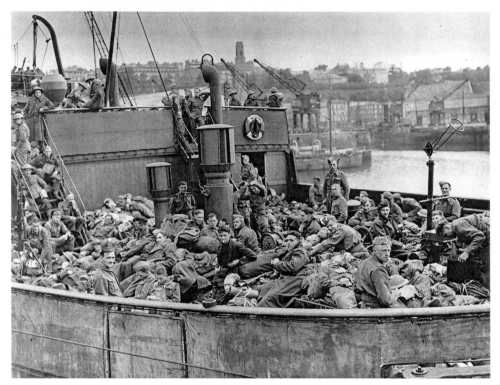

British troops evacuating from Dunkirk.   Credit: Imperial War Museum.

six ships full of troops were sunk from the air and by artillery fire despite the continual presence of five fighter squadrons. Weygand pledged to hold but worried that all might be lost.

The evacuation became, in Churchill's words, the "miracle of deliverance." Even though slowed by poor weather, the Luftwaffe obliterated the town of Dunkirk and blasted the RAF out of the sky. But smoke from the smoldering buildings and overcast skies provided enough cover to get the troops out. The British lost 177 planes and numerous rescue vessels. Tension erupted when the French wanted as many of their soldiers pulled out as the British and also hoped to hold the perimeter against the Germans. This latter demand led to the sacrifice of the 51st Highland Division, which tried to defend a front in northeastern France that the Germans overran by June 12. In trying to buy time, 8,000 British troops were captured. Despite Anglo-French squabbling, the evacuation ended successfully in the early hours of June 4 and the British Expeditionary Force was saved to fight another day. The public learned of the heroic escape but also realized that the Allies had been routed. About 160,000 British and 250,000 French remained trapped in the north, but 288,000 troops—including 193,000 from the British Expeditionary Force and 30,000 Polish troops—made it out. Virtually all of their artillery, vehicles, and stores were seized by the Germans. In the meantime, Belgium surrendered on May 28.

Despite the miracle, disaster and death were still the order of the day. During their campaign, the Nazis committed atrocities that forewarned of the strategy of annihilation. Surrounded in the town of Le Paradis in the Pas de Calais, 97 British soldiers were taken captive by the SS and machine-gunned before an open pit. The injured were bayoneted although a few men survived to tell their tale by shielding themselves under the bodies. A German major validated the survivors' story. Waffen-SS war correspondent Gunter d'Alquen noted unhelmeted corpses in British uniforms with head wounds, evidence that they had been executed at close range. At Wormhout the next day some 80 to 90 prisoners were also mowed down. Other incidents of mistreatment included manhunts of civilians by organized patrols as reprisals for the deaths of German officers. Rampaging soldiers burned down farms and houses and killed anyone suspected of shooting back at them during the Dunkirk operations. In the village of Vinkt, Belgium, on May 27, thirty-nine-year-old Maurice Martens was ordered with a family member to stand against a wall. Machine guns open fired and he recoiled. "Two bodies fell on to my back. They saved my life.... After the firing stopped, a German in front of us fired another two bullets into the pile on top of me, thinking they were still alive." Mertens later crawled away, but most others present were not so lucky. In 1949, the testimony of two survivors led to the execution of SS company commander Fritz Knoechlein as punishment for the atrocity.

The war in the west was firmly in German hands. For all intents, British ground force was eliminated from the Continent. Dutch and Belgian forces also disappeared. The Allies had lost 61 divisions and three-quarters of their equipment, leaving them with just 51 divisions, 200 tanks, and 175 fighter planes against 104 Wehrmacht divisions. On June 5, a day after the Dunkirk evacuation, the Germans wheeled southwards to root out the dug-in French along the Weygand Line running along the Somme and Aisne Rivers. Given a week to regroup and resupply, the panzers readied for the endgame. The Wehrmacht had a three-to-one advantage in divisions and mastery in mechanized and air warfare. Rundstedt directed Army Group A toward the Aisne and the Maginot Line, forcing the French back to the Marne as Guderian's tanks broke through at Chalons and raced south toward the Swiss border. Bock's Army Group B headed across the Somme west of Paris and reached the Seine River in three days. Leeb's Army Group C attacked the southern end of the Maginot Line before linking up with Rundstedt. Before the final offensive, French losses of men and materiel were already staggering; 24 of their 67 infantry divisions and half of their motorized divisions were destroyed. After vicious desperate fighting, including the German massacre of a captured black colonial infantry division near Lyon, the French evacuated the government south to Bordeaux. The Germans roared to Paris. As refugees streamed out of the city, Weygand counseled Reynaud to seek an armistice.

Franklin Roosevelt (FDR) claimed that Mussolini stuck in the knife on June 10 when Il Duce declared war to stake Italy's claim to southeastern France and Corsica, but blitzkrieg had already broken the French. Declared an open city to spare it from destruction, Paris then played host to Reynaud's resignation and the recall of the elderly World War I hero Marshal Philippe Pétain from Spain. Reynaud hoped Pétain would galvanize the army's war spirit, but the old man was a defeatist. He believed that France had gone bad and must surrender to purge itself of its sins. France and Britain, however, had pledged not to seek an armistice without the consent of the other. Arguments ensued, as did suggestions of the French government fleeing to North Africa or joining in a union with Britain. Reynaud appealed to the Americans for help, but FDR could not intervene due to isolationist sentiment in the United States. This, even as millions of Americans as well as British reacted tearfully to the fall of Paris—a beloved city now occupied by wide-eyed German soldier tourists who sat in cafes and took photos of the Eiffel Tower. France had nowhere to turn.

Petain replaced the discredited Reynaud on June 17. Three days later, after ten days of mobilization, the Italians attacked the border only to be beaten back and embarrassed by small French units. But France was finished. Petain ordered the fighting ended as the Germans reached the Swiss frontier behind the Maginot Line. He called for every city with a population of more than 20,000 to be declared open. Many continued to fight while refugees streamed south. De Gaulle left for England and some planes and ships took shelter in Britain and North Africa. On June 22, Petain agreed to a cease-fire and three days later signed a humiliating armistice at Compiegne in the same railway car in which Germany had surrendered to end the First World War. The armistice limited the French army to 100,000 men and compelled France to pay for a German occupation that stretched from the north down the Atlantic coast, including major industrial areas. Hitler left the southern part of France unoccupied and under the control of Petain's government headquartered in the resort town of Vichy. Pending the defeat of Britain, a treaty would settle authority over the entire country. French prisoners were held as hostages to assure the good behavior of the Vichy France government. Nazis paraded through the Arc de Triomphe, and the Fuhrer exalted over avenging his country's past debasement by France.

Hitler's excitement was merited, for Operation Gelb had been a rousing success. At the expense of over 163, 213 casualties (29,640 dead), the Third Reich bagged western Europe in just 35 days. France suffered 123,000 dead and 200,000 wounded, with 1.9 million taken prisoner or missing; and Britain lost tens of thousands of men and all of their tanks, trucks, and guns. In what many Frenchmen later claimed to be the beginning of their resurrection, Charles De Gaulle broadcast from London on June 18 to those interested in joining him as part of a Free France movement to reclaim the nation. But that happy day would not come soon.

France needed scapegoats to explain the surrender, considered the most shameful event in its history. So devastating was the loss that just a handful of French wrote about the defeat in the 30 years after the war. The archives largely remained closed, writers relied on memoirs for sources, and those historians who took up the topic were mostly foreigners. In the end, the consensus was that French troops fought bravely, but a general defeatism coupled with inept political and military leaders failed the troops. Although the Wehrmacht had faced resupply, transport, and organizational weaknesses, blitzkrieg had capitalized on Anglo-French problems to win a rousing triumph.

ASSAULT ON BRITAIN

Hitler assumed that Britain would become his next victim. This was reasonable owing to the disaster at Dunkirk, the magnitude of his victory in western Europe, and the willingness of many British leaders to negotiate a peace settlement. Churchill would have none of such talk, having earlier promised "nothing but blood, toil, tears, and sweat" to emerge victorious over the monster of fascism. As France fell, he urged terrified citizens to fight in the seas, air, beaches, fields, hills, and streets to defend their island—"we shall never surrender," he proclaimed. But the uncertainty of U.S. aid made his case seem unrealistic. Britain also faced a juggernaut of enemies. Though unreliable, Italy nonetheless added to German power. Also, Spain's Francisco Franco wanted to join the Axis powers. Because of Spanish infirmities after its civil war, the country might not be able to oust the British from fortified Gibraltar and close the Mediterranean, but its addition to the Axis could help harass Allied trade and transportation routes. North Africa and the Middle East lay open for conquest. Such neutrals as Turkey, Sweden, Yugoslavia, and Romania negotiated trade concessions with Germany that bought their chrome, iron ore, copper, and petroleum. The Atlantic coast yielded Germany bases for submarines to raid shipping. So stocked with power, the Fuhrer had his own answer to Churchill's rhetoric.

Convinced of their superiority and ability to destroy any European nation in their path, the Germans believed that Britain would roll over under the threat of attack. This would allow an attack on the Soviet Union, perhaps the biggest loser in the fall of France because Hitler could avoid the sort of ruinous two-front war that plagued Germany in World War I. So the Fuhrer pursued the prize of subduing Britain. In the likely event that diplomacy failed to convince the British to relent, he readied an invasion plan called Operation Sealion. The Wehrmacht viewed it as an occupation operation to be undertaken when Britain had surrendered; but in Hitler's eyes, his great war machine would follow in the path across the English Channel taken by Julius Caesar and William the Conqueror. Not much stood in his way. The British lacked heavy equipment (most of it left in France), and a pittance of materiel exited its factories or arrived from America. London even planned to use poison gas attacks as a last resort once the Germans landed on the beaches in England and Ireland. Other than that, Britain had the Royal Air Force and Navy in the English Channel, the amateurish Home Guard—known as "Dad's Army"—of hunt clubs with shotguns in the southeastern counties, the hastily reorganized but depleted British Expeditionary Force, and the prime minister's eloquence.

In their euphoria over Operation Gelb, the Wehrmacht did not carefully consider how best to take care of Britain. Given the strength of the Royal Navy and the difficulty of an amphibious landing, Operation Sealion hinged on a strategic bombing campaign by the Luftwaffe. To date, the Luftwaffe had engaged in ground support operations but not in an air war by itself. Thus, decisions remained on hold on whether to target people, cities, industrial plants, military installations, or some combination. The Luftwaffe also needed to recover its losses from the campaign in France where 30% of its bombers and twin-engine fighters, 40% of its transports, and 15% of its fighter pilots had gone down.

Britain's secret advantage was that intelligence had begun breaking ENIGMA, the German signals encryption machine. Cryptographers continually adapted throughout the war to the changing ENIGMA codes, which numbering in the millions of combinations for each letter of the alphabet, the Germans deemed unbreakable. But there were enough mathematical possibilities that operatives wormed their way into the entire system. At their disposal was ULTRA, the British code name for the signals intelligence used to unravel the ENIGMA cipher. ULTRA had been wielded rather ineffectively to track Luftwaffe operations during the Norway and French campaigns, but the British drew on the system to estimate Luftwaffe strength and losses. This gave them a good idea of how long Germany could sustain the battle of Britain. ULTRA derived from an Allied group effort. Polish cryptographers had been reading a large amount of cable traffic in the ENIGMA cipher since 1933 after they had painstakingly duplicated a German machine. They passed on some of their equipment to the French in 1938 and then took a few to Britain before Hitler invaded Poland. At Bletchley Park in Britain, mathematicians examined the machines and developed ULTRA. Despite precautions taken by Germany to safeguard its code, the British, and later the Americans, worked diligently to reveal the secrets. They had trouble with the ENIGMA ciphers of the German Army and Navy, but the Luftwaffe—more lax in protecting its secrets—offered entry into the other services' messages. The British deciphered new ENIGMA "keys" to intercept more traffic.

ULTRA offered a distinct edge, but it also created risks by its very existence. It was more reliable than interrogation and spying, but it required skilled staff to interpret the random mass of communications. Deciphering was one thing; understanding was another. During the battle of Britain, for instance, a scientist in the British Air Ministry figured out that German bombers were being directed in a certain direction to targets by radio beams. Thus, he uncovered a mystery behind a special ENIGMA key. Preserving the secret that ENIGMA had been revealed added to the burden. Thousands of cryptographers who revealed, translated, and sent decoded ENIGMA messages by the Axis powers never leaked the secret during the war or for that matter, neither did Polish and French loyalists. Historians place greater emphasis on the decisive aid given by ULTRA in winning key battles, campaigns, and the war itself. Much more than the Axis powers, the Allies relied on the acquisition of information, its analysis and interpretation, and its use to good effect in every aspect of the war, including judgments of Axis atomic capabilities. Cryptanalysis also cost less in terms of manpower and lives lost than resistance by partisans and others who comprised the other major noncombat force in the war.

It was difficult to believe that intelligence of any sort mattered at first, however, for confidence in Operation Sealion reigned through the Third Reich hierarchy. The Luftwaffe simply ignored the British radar system (in existence since 1938) on which air defenses rested. Despite a lack of systematic strategizing and miscalculations about the RAF's adaptability through radar, Air Marshal Göring authorized the campaign to commence in early July 1940 after having moved Luftwaffe units to Channel airfields in France, Belgium, and Holland. Battle-tested commanders led the assault. Field Marshals Albert Kesselring, a founder of the Luftwaffe who had commanded air fleets in Poland and France; Hugo Sperrle, a Spanish Civil War and French campaign veteran; and General Hans-Jurgen Stümpff, commander of air operations in Norway had 2,800 aircraft at their disposal. Because they would have to fly long distances, they could not draw on single-engine fighters for cover and thus had roughly two-thirds of the fleet available at any one time. Göring was ready despite the shortfall. The battle of Britain began.

England was handicapped by the Air Ministry's reluctance to consider close fighter combat. Not until 1938 did the head of Fighter Command, Air Chief Marshal Hugh Dowding, receive full attention from the RAF. A rather aloof man, "Stuffy" Dowding understood the complexities of coordinating the human and technological defensive network based on radio and radar. His was a daunting task. Not only had radar been first tested just five years before, but the Spitfire and Hurricane fighters capable of handling enemy planes became available in sufficient numbers only in 1939. Nonetheless, Dowding developed a system of fighter control that regardless of flaws, integrated planes and defense sectors together and overcame RAF losses of men incurred over the past year. He also knew how to guard resources, having refused Churchill's request to send more fighters into the hopeless battle for France.

Dowding's problem was not so much a lack of aircraft. Industry largely replaced losses starting in the summer under the energetic supervision of Canadian businessman Lord Beaverbrook, the Minister of Aircraft Production. The difficulty lay with a dearth of pilots. By September, just 60 squadrons (each with 10–24 planes) were available for Dowding's four Fighter Command Groups. This was less than half deemed necessary by the Air Ministry. They might have cut dashing figures in jackets and silk scarves, but the flyers were young and vulnerable. Compared to Luftwaffe crews who had served over Spain, Poland, and France, relatively inexperienced pilots took to the air for the Royal Air Force. The British also counted on some Americans and several Czech and Polish pilots (indeed, a Polish pilot shot down the most enemy planes during the air war) who made up about 20% of the RAF total during the battle. Dowding dispersed his forces judiciously. He placed Fighter Command 13 Group in the north of England and Scotland as a reserve and 10 Group in the southwest. He expected most of the attacks on Air Vice Marshal Keith Park's 11 Group, which guarded the southeastern part of Britain, and on 12 Group under Air Vice Marshal Trafford Leigh-Mallory in Anglia and the Midlands.

Along with the pilot shortage there were also arguments over tactics. Park and Leigh-Mallory approached the impending sky war in conflicting ways. Dowding's senior air staff officer and commander of a fighter group during the Dunkirk evacuation, Keith Park oftentimes flew his own Hurricane, one of the few top officers in the world who could pilot modern fighters. He adjusted rapidly to different Luftwaffe tactics. Morale in his Fighter Group 11 remained high under his approach, which Dowding favored, of having aircraft arrive separately to do battle. On the other hand, Trafford Leigh-Mallory, who would command the Allied Expeditionary Air Force during the Normandy landings in 1944, preferred a "Big Wing" tactic of massing a large formation of squadrons for the attack. The argument eventually went in his favor, so much so that he replaced Dowding when the Battle of Britain ended (and after Dowding was accused of permitting the bombing of Coventry to keep ULTRA under wraps) in December. Yet these turf wars were more important for the long term than in the immediate crisis. The key point was that the RAF, unlike the British Army, was still intact despite

Dunkirk. And the British benefited from a web of radar that warned them of approaching German planes.

The first stage of the battle took place over the English Channel during July and the first half of August 1940. The Luftwaffe attempted to eat away at Dowding's limited resources by attacking shipping and drawing out escorting British fighters. Light raids on the southeastern coast of Britain also occurred in the "Channel Battle," as the Germans called it. About 30,000 tons of shipping went to the bottom, but the attrition strategy failed. The Luftwaffe lost twice as many planes as the British in a haphazard operation. The Germans hit factories, then ports, then convoys rather than systematically attacking certain targets. All the while, they were harassed by Spitfire fighters. British aviators and radar operators gained some valuable experience during this phase. Meanwhile, snafus in Operation Sealion persisted to the point that Hitler agreed to delay the invasion until mid-September. The Channel Battle was only the preliminary stage of the bigger campaign to destroy the RAF with the Luftwaffe's "Eagle Attack."

On August 12, Adlertag or "Eagle Day," the Luftwaffe launched the first large-scale attack across the Channel against British aerodromes and the Ventnor radar station. The Ventnor facility was silenced. But the next day, bad weather cancelled the assault, although only half of the German units received the order. Thus, that afternoon 1,500 sorties bombed British targets. Two days later, the weather undermined coordination; but the Germans attacked not only from the Channel airfields but from Denmark and Norway as well. Luftwaffe aircraft darkened the skies over England over the next two weeks. Germany's experienced pilots well outnumbered British flyers. They shunned independent action and attacked in large numbers with the odds in their favor.

During this time, the Germans corrected the one-sided loss ratio they had suffered during the Channel Battle, but they encountered trouble all the same. First, they did not hit significant targets. Second, three Luftflotten groups attacked in concert, including Stumpff's from Norway. But the Bf109e single-seat fighter and the Me110 (a twin-engine two seater), the Stuka dive-bomber, and the old Heinkel and Dornier long-range bombers met RAF Fighter Command Group 12 and 13's tough and plentiful Hurricanes and agile Spitfires. The latter were slightly superior to the German Me110, and both aided the inexperienced British pilots by mounting eight machine guns on the wings to give a good spread of fire. Seventy-five enemy aircraft went down, doubling British losses. The Luftwaffe's inattention to intelligence led the Germans to believe that Dowding had just 200 front-line planes left in his Fighter Commands. In reality, he had triple that number. Furthermore, when the RAF lost fighters, the pilot could bail out over home territory and thus survive to fly another day. In contrast, German aircrews became prisoners in British jails. Dowding also responded to German tactics by changing his own. He intercepted the attackers farther out in the Channel to break up their formations before they reached land. The new approach ushered in the next stage of the air war for Britain—one that implied that the Germans sought a war of annihilation.

Göring continued bombing but focused on air combat in an effort to eliminate what he erroneously believed was the last of the British fighters. On August 24, small groups of morale-busting Luftwaffe bombers headed for raids on factories and homes, accompanied by large numbers of fighter escorts that aimed to destroy the remaining Spitfires and Hurricanes. The tactic worked initially, as Göring urged Kesselring and Sperrle to hit Britain with everything they had. Airfields on Biggin Hill, Hornchurch, North Weald, and West Malling at the end of the month and beginning of September strained under the efforts of Park's Fighter Group 11. Fighter Group 12 protected the bases while Park's flyers battled the Germans. Leigh-Mallory complained that the massing of defensive formations—the Big Wing—would work better than Park's dogfights. In any case, both the Luftwaffe and RAF endured heavy casualties during the German attempt to deliver the knockout blow in this aerial prizefight.

Sensing that the British stood on the edge of a precipice, the Luftwaffe shifted tactics again by bombing London on September 7. This date was as memorable for the British as December 7, 1941 became for Americans. The Germans usually flew up the Thames River to attack the airfields ringing London and the docks and suburbs where factories were located. They had not purposely bombed civilian targets, having learned after Rotterdam that the RAF would respond with retaliatory strikes on German cities. Lost on the night of August 25, a stray Luftwaffe pilot had dropped bombs on the center of London and ignited huge fires. British Bomber Command reacted by attacking Berlin with a tiny force of 50 bombers, embarrassing Göring who had boasted that Germans would be safe and outraging Hitler even though just two people were injured. This unfortunate exchange not only instigated the German "Blitz" on London, but the reprisals rationalized the strategic air campaigns of annihilation—by both the Axis and Allies—for the remainder of the war.

Perhaps Hitler thought that by destroying the British capital in the Blitz he could forego Operation Sealion and also defeat the remains of the RAF. The Germans understood that British factories could not produce enough replacement planes. Nighttime raids caught Fighter Command unprepared to defend the city, and the Luftwaffe used the erupting fires in the East End as guidance for their nighttime bombings. Göring traveled to Boulogne to watch his air fleet pass overhead on its way to London.

The destruction was immense. The first day and night of the Blitz killed 306 Londoners and injured 1,337. This was the last mass daylight raid, but an ensuing nighttime attack by 247 bombers ignited large fires. Within three weeks, about 7,000 British lay dead; by summer 1941, over 40,000 civilians were killed. In late December 1940, the Germans hit a two-mile area around St. Paul's Cathedral, engulfing it in flames that burned at 1,000 degrees Fahrenheit. Soon 1,500 separate fires in London raged, their glow visible from 30 miles away, and tens of thousands of homes and businesses burnt to the ground. Witnesses recalled feeling the compression, their eyeballs seemingly being sucked out and their clothes ripped off them by the explosions. A British Broadcasting Corporation employee saw two soldiers with their feet sticking out of a wall of the BBC building when it was hit in October and fire engulfed the area. One had his trousers blown off him, the other's arms dangled like a rag doll. He compared the scene to Dante's *Inferno.*

People adjusted to the disruption of sleep and work caused by the raids. Many escaped to nearby Epping Forest, to department store basements, or into hotels. By mid-September, half of Stepney had evacuated; and a few weeks later, one-quarter of Londoners had fled the capital. Those who remained, usually the lower classes of society, sought protection at home or in less-targeted areas of London. Some packed into bomb shelters every night in subway stations and tunnels where adequate toilets and water were lacking. Firefighters were not well organized, and blazes grew out of control. A plethora of aid agencies competing with local groups complicated the feeding and billeting of civilians. Homelessness was a problem for the poor until the end of September, when 25,000 people were accommodated in converted schools and derelict buildings.

This was certainly no good war, yet the Blitz generated pride and hope. Just hearing the antiaircraft guns perked up people. They rose to the challenge, as Churchill thought they would. The government evacuated 300,000 children, mothers, and other vulnerable elements of London's population in a process that had begun a year before the bombings. A total of 1.45 million people were moved to safer areas. The British withstood the Blitz, thereby disproving strategic air power theory that nations would sue for peace once their populations became targets. In actuality, the opposite was true. Despite being targets of a strategy of annihilation, the British withstood the atrocities of the bombings and morale actually strengthened. "Traumatic years they were," wrote a woman from Manchester, a city also badly damaged, "but they were happy ones. You could leave your door open when the sirens sounded and rush to the shelters to find everything intact when you returned." Echoed another, we "were petrified, of course. I was, many a time. But I wouldn't change for anything those years. There was good comradeship all around." Once people habituated to the nightly raids, and the chaos and panic in the streets subsided as the sirens went off, a grim determination set in that defeated Hitler's intentions of undermining British spirits. The victims soon sought revenge.

The Blitz aided the RAF by giving it a week's respite. On September 15, the five fighter squadrons of the Duxford (Big) Wing of Fighter Command Group 12 rose to meet 100 German bombers over southwest London. On this so-called Battle of Britain Day, the Germans stupidly junked their policy of trying to trick British radar with diversionary tactics. Out of frustration, impatience, and confidence that they could simply overwhelm the British, the Luftwaffe gave full notice to its enemy and came straight onward in the second major attack. Fighters escorted some 150 Dorniers and Heinkels, and the 175 Hurricanes and Spitfires of Park's Fighter Command 11 awaited them. As the Duxford Wing met the Germans east of London, Park hit them as well. Luftwaffe bombers scattered their payloads and turned back toward the coast. Over 60 German aircraft were shot down; the week's losses totaled 175 planes. What a difference a week made as the September 7 disaster in London was avenged by the RAF. The Luftwaffe could not win air supremacy. In the meantime, the British continued to bomb Berlin. Britain had given the Allies their first victory over Adolf Hitler.

The Germans were stunned. They had seemed on the verge of sewing up their campaign in the west with Hitler having ordered the cross-Channel invasion ready for September 14. But he postponed the operation for another ten days. On September 19, Wehrmacht High Command ordered a halt to the further deployment of transport

West End London tube station during battle of Britain.
Credit: Library of Congress, Call #: Lot 3476, Reproduction #LC-USZ62-42748.

ships. By early October, the Fuhrer called off Operation Sealion altogether, although he kept it as an option should circumstances improve. They never did. Germany was fast approaching an unofficial but critical deadline imposed by autumnal and winter nautical weather conditions that made an invasion ever more problematic. Hitler soon lost interest in the Channel crossing.

Britain had survived. Daylight raids continued into October until poor weather compelled Göring to switch to night bombings with fewer aircraft than before. He counted on Knickebein and X-Gerat navigational radio-beam devices to direct the bombers, but ULTRA intelligence and other information nullified their effectiveness. With defeat of Britain now impossible, German tactics evolved into terror bombing the population and seeking to destroy factories. The British responded by radar and communications-based integrated air defenses and also retaliated with their own campaign of targeting civilians. By the end of October 1940, Germany had lost nearly 1,300 planes and the British 788. If the RAF had been destroyed, Britain would most likely have sued for peace; yet the air force replaced many of its losses more successfully than the Luftwaffe. The British more than held their own in this battle of part attrition and part annihilation. The battle of Britain began as a war-clinching campaign for Nazism but ended as England's savior.

AMERICA BEYOND THE WAR ZONES

Tactical errors, negligence, and arrogance doomed the Luftwaffe air campaign, but the Germans might also catalyzed American sympathy for Britain. President Franklin Roosevelt had tried to push the American public and Congress into recognizing that Nazism was such a global menace that the nation must end its post-World War I policy of isolationism and aid fellow democracies at war. Britain's plight convinced Americans of the threat from the aggressors.

The United States hovered above the war clouds, though not for want of FDR's trying. In January 1939, he pushed through legislation in Congress that authorized defensive measures to fortify the Virgin Islands, Puerto Rico, and the Pacific entry to the Panama Canal. But Roosevelt fought a losing cause against pacifism and complacency. Such outrages as Japan's sinking of the American gunboat, the *Panay*, in December 1937 caused but a ripple of protest. In early 1938, the House of Representatives barely turned aside a resolution to require a national referendum if the president issued a declaration of war. The legislation would have prevented the country from ever fighting abroad unless attacked. FDR also asked Hitler and Mussolini in April 1939 not to attack certain nations. The dictators responded either by ignoring or denouncing such pretensions from a country that remained aloof from the League of Nations. Such was the isolationist mood that the Neutrality Acts, which placed restrictions on loans, travel, and arms shipments, remained in force. The attack on Poland prompted Congress to repeal the arms embargo but compelled Roosevelt to declare neutrality in the European war. France, Holland, and Britain placed orders for aircraft, although only a small number arrived before the first two nations succumbed to the Wehrmacht. Still, the orders jumpstarted the American production giant that had lain dormant during the Depression. Under the revamped Neutrality Act of 1937 and its "cash and carry" provision, an ally could procure U.S. military goods only in hard currency (not credit) with delivery by their own vessels. These provisions prevented America from being sucked into war. Public and official opinion alike believed that France and Britain could contain Hitler and Mussolini in Europe and that diplomacy could deny China to Japan. Ambassador to Britain Joseph Kennedy and other isolationists warned Roosevelt against intervention.

The rapidity of the Blitzkrieg in Poland and France, the ruthlessness of the Russian attack in Finland (the only nation that repaid its World War I debts to the United States), and most dramatically, photos of St. Paul's Cathedral shrouded in smoke awakened the Americans. They read of the sacrifices of Londoners who extinguished fires, saved victims, and buried their countrymen. Americans listened to the riveting broadcasts of Edward R. Murrow from London in the midst of the Blitz. The bombing of the British industrial city of Coventry on November 12–15, 1940, obliterated the city's famous cathedral and killed 380 people and injured 865 more. This further enraged the public. Churchill played on this sentiment to coax the United States into tangible support. Americans turned from passivity to an active pro-British stance. As the Imperial Japanese Army rampaged in China, the Roosevelt administration rethought its assumptions. When the Germans marched into France and then assailed Britain, the public and Congress began to change their attitudes as well.

On September 27, 1940, ten days after Hitler postponed the invasion of Britain, the Axis powers solidified their alliance by signing the Tripartite Pact in Berlin. In part aimed to forestall the entry of the United States into the war, the alliance pledged Germany, Italy, and Japan to aid each other should any of them come under attack by a nation not yet at war. The Americans were not intimidated. They increased aid to China and criticism of Japan. The Pact was also symbolic in that the Axis partners did not agree on a grand strategy. Instead they tried to recruit others to their ranks. They asked the USSR to join, but Stalin's terms turned out to be unacceptable to Hitler. That month, however, Hungary, Romania, and Slovakia acceded to the Tripartite alliance; and in March 1941, Bulgaria and Yugoslavia followed (although a coup in the latter prompted Belgrade to revoke the agreement two days afterward). Croatia was the final signatory in June. By that time, nine months had passed since the Berlin ceremony heralding the Tripartite Pact, a period in which the world war raged beyond Hitlerite Western and Northern Europe.

America and the Atlantic

Each side reduces the other to objects—eventually in the
form of corpses.

CHRIS HEDGES
War Is a Force That Gives Us Meaning

AMERICAN MOBILIZATION

America fell short of intervention, but it did edge toward mobilization. In May 1940,
FDR asked Congress to fund construction of 50,000 aircraft. As France surrendered
in June 1940, Congress introduced a tax bill to raise $1 billion a year and lifted the ceil-
ing on the national debt. The War Department studied resources to bolster defense
of the western hemisphere and Pacific possessions. In July, Congress appropriated
$37 billion—more than had been spent on World War I in its entirety—to build a
two-ocean navy and make more guns, tanks, and planes. In August, the administration federalized the National Guard and Congress approved the Selective Service
Act, also known as the draft. Many Republicans went along despite party opposition
to the Democrat in the White House. Roosevelt helped by reorganizing his cabinet,
bringing in Republicans Frank Knox as secretary of the navy and Henry Stimson as
secretary of war. He also declared his intentions to run for president for an unprecedented third term.

More immediate actions addressed the future projection of U.S. power and aid for
the Allies. As Hurricanes and Spitfires battled the Messerschmidts above England in
September, the United States and Britain negotiated their first major weapons deal. This
followed Winston Churchill's personal appeal to FDR that Britain could only hold out
against the Germans if America lent his nation 40 or 50 old destroyers to protect shipping until construction brought the Royal Navy up to speed. At first Roosevelt refused
due to his concern for isolationist sentiment and his lack of certainty about British
resolve to stay the course against Hitler. The heroics of the battle of Britain convinced
him of the latter. To quell the critics at home, FDR offered 50 mothballed destroyers in
return for 99-year leases on six bases in the British West Indies, one in Bermuda, and

Chapter 7: America and the Atlantic   101

another in Newfoundland. Churchill also pledged not to scuttle his fleet (like the French had after their surrender) should Operation Sealion succeed. By the end of 1940, only 9 destroyers had arrived in Britain, and haggling continued over the British territories, but America had become a partner in war. FDR did everything "short of war" to aid Britain. Public opinion turned toward more intervention. Roosevelt was reelected for a third term in November 1940, his smallest margin to date, yet the nation was nearly unanimous in deciding to rearm. By September, Congress appropriated $78 billion for war spending at a time when the country's gross national product was $101 billion. Along with the draft of two million men (1.2 million soldiers and 800,000 reserves) over the next year, the National Guard of 300,000 reserves based in the 48 states was also mobilized. By October, over 16 million men had registered under the Selective Training and Service Act. America had an ample supply of military manpower.

The country lacked the materiel to give to these soldiers, but officials and business soon harnessed the economy for rearmament. Organization was critical to prepared-ness. In mid-1940, the president reactivated the World War I National Defense Advisory Commission to bring producers in line with military needs. Dredging the economy out of the Depression, industrialists and corporate executives came to Washington, D.C., to reverse years of sluggish production, food surpluses, deflated prices, and the highest unemployment rate (15% in 1940) among the major nations. The colossal engine of pro-duction sparked to life with prodigious war plant construction. By the following year, steel mills climbed above the 82% capacity of 1940 and the manufacture of machine tools—the very basis of production—shot up. The average work week expanded beyond 38 hours, and productivity rose. Crop and food production skyrocketed. The American economy would soon mark the world war by its massive contributions to the fight against aggression and convert any doubters about U.S. capabilities to support a strat-egy of annihilation.

In 1940, Americans and their allies talked about the *future* rather than the reality of U.S. power, but sheer economic potential inspired them nonetheless. Roosevelt's pledge to build 50,000 aircraft amazed foreign observers. In the end, America manufactured six times that amount. Meanwhile, aircraft companies converted their factories into huge facilities where they could but also built entirely new plants funded by the gov-ernment-sponsored Defense Plant Corporation. Automakers retooled their assembly lines to make planes and tanks, although on the whole, they did not readily convert to airframe production except for Ford's huge Willow Run plant. This Michigan fac-tory eventually assembled B-24 bombers at the rate of one every 63 minutes. Detroit best converted to production of military vehicles, including armored units, and mainly produced subassemblies of airplanes. For instance, new Chrysler factories in Warren, Michigan, built tens of thousands of Sherman tanks.

The government-business partnership of new production facilities led to the notion that America was really democracy's arsenal. Modern shipyards in coastal cities from 1939 onward not only made war vessels but began the most prodigious construction in history of cargo carriers, tankers, and other merchant marine ships. Government armories, as well as several dozen state-owned but contractor-operated munitions plants, geared up to make rifles, cannon, shells, and ammunition. Many of the munitions

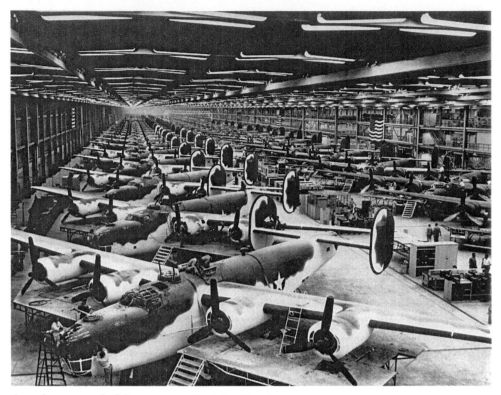

American arsenal of democracy.   Credit: San Diego Aerospace Museum.

depots stretched twenty-five square miles in size and were designed to store, process, and ship a massive torrent of explosive ordnance. Scientists and engineers injected their expertise in such critical areas as producing volumes of high-octane aviation fuel, the top-secret proximity fuse (radio devices that detonated projectiles near their targets), the programmable electronic computer, and atomic weapons. These developments were not for immediate use, but Churchill and others knew that they would be brought to bear in lethal ways against militarism and fascism once the U.S. economic machine went into full swing.

America's preparations included a growing military. In 1939, the regular army had 190,000 soldiers and Philippine scouts. After having analyzed the World War I experience to know that another war would require greater mobility and firepower, the U.S. Army trained for tactical combat rather than big operational maneuvers. It was also poorly trained and undermanned. As a result of budgetary constraints during the Depression, the standing Army lacked equipment and weapons as well as a sufficiently large professional officer corps. Historians have noted the irony that the United States was the most mechanized nation in the world but lacked adequate tanks and other high-tech weaponry. Japan and Germany enjoyed superiority or, at the very least, equality in arms capability with the United States. The money flowed by mid-1940, however, and strategic, operational, and tactical planning went forward. Eventually mobilizing 89 divisions

Table 7.1 Production

	Tanks and Self-propelled Guns	Artillery	Aircraft	Warships	Mortars	Artillery and Mortars	Merchant Ship Tonnage
Germany	46,857	159,144	189,307	1,141 (subs)	73,484	232,628	?
Japan	2,515	13,350	76,320	257	?	?	4,152,361
United Kingdom	27,896	124,877	131,750	871	102,950	227,827	6,378,899
United States	88,410	257,390	324,750	1,247	105,054	362,444	33,993,230
USSR	105,251	516,648	157,261	79	403,300	919,948	?

Source: John Ellis, *World War II—A Statistical Survey* (New York: Facts on File, 1993), 277–80.

(joined by six Marine divisions under the U.S. Navy), the United States Army matured into a potent force that learned through hard experience early in the war.

Drawing on American expertise in mechanization, Army Chief of Staff Douglas MacArthur had stressed during the 1930s mobility of men and artillery through the motorized combination of trucks, soldiers, and ammunition. He capitalized on the M2A1, 105-mm, towed howitzer. This weapon represented the strength of the American and British arsenal: guns capable of improvement and endurance that could be produced in great numbers. MacArthur's successor, Malin Craig, sponsored the Garand M-1 semiautomatic rifle in another nod to modernization. The howitzer and rifle proved to be America's most deadly ground weapons in the war; but the U.S. Army added mortars, flamethrowers, and antitank rocket launchers and guns that rivaled enemy equipment. Experimentation through 1940 with combined-arms exercises yielded a highly mobile ground force with mechanized infantry and an armored force that was speedy and skilled in surrounding the enemy (envelopment) but weak in coordinating tanks with infantry in battle. Further maneuvers highlighted the need for radio communications from the top levels to infantry platoons, the problem of gas consumption by tanks, and the ability for artillery to hit targets by using maps or observers rather than by direct sight.

The numbers mobilized were astonishing. The U.S. Army planned a "Victory Program" to put 6.7 million men under arms in 213 divisions—half of these armored or mechanized—and an army air force of 2.9 million personnel in 195 groups of more than 400 flying squadrons, half of these bombers. Incredibly, the military first determined how much manpower was required for production and then mobilized soldiers, sailors, and flyers based on the leftover. Other nations could not afford such a luxury. How to divvy up logistical support between European and Asian theaters and how to balance ground and air forces loomed as the U.S. Army's biggest challenges. The answers came from expert management and organization, which led to the addition of layers of bureaucracy. A new building, the Pentagon, broke ground in 1941 to house these agencies. Training camps and bases blossomed. These were issues of riches not constraints.

The father of the Army Air Corps, Major-General Henry "Hap" Arnold, who had been taught to fly by the Wright Brothers in 1911, initially commanded only 20,000 men on 17 bases and 2,470 mostly obsolete aircraft in 1938. Advocates of airpower clashed with those favoring ground and naval power. They endorsed General Billy Mitchell's crusade for making land and sea forces redundant to the airplane during the 1920s. Unlike the British, the Americans had no plans to bomb civilians in a strategy of annihilation, at least not at first. They focused on destroying economic hubs such as electricity grids, transportation networks, and vital industries and on experimenting with large-scale airborne operations. The Army's Air Corps school did instill the notion that large formations of heavily armed bombers could make their way to enemy targets without the need for long-range fighters. This tactic received priority over supporting ground forces, although the Air Corps, as part of the Army, had to pay lip service to protecting the infantry. In October 1940, Arnold became the deputy to the stern and highly respected Army Chief of Staff, George C. Marshall. One of Roosevelt's key wartime advisors, Marshall allowed Arnold to expand the Army Air Corps from a few thousand planes to 79,908 aircraft at its peak in July 1944. By war's end, nearly 1.9 million men and women, including 39,000 Women's Army Corps personnel or WACs, and several thousand Women Air Force Service Pilots called WASPs, served in the U.S. Army Air Force on almost 700 bases and fields in America alone.

The U.S. Navy also transformed into a formidable force. In September 1939, Chief of Naval Operations Admiral Harold Stark had 15 battleships, including one built back in 1912, 5 carriers, 18 heavy cruisers, 19 light cruisers, 61 submarines, and dozens of other craft such as destroyers and wooden submarine chasers. The U.S. Navy had its own air arm under the Bureau of Naval Aeronautics and just under 11,000 aviation personnel of which over a third were pilots. In 1940, naval strength centered in the Pacific Fleet based in the Hawaiian Islands. The Philippines headquartered a small Asiatic Fleet and an Atlantic Squadron patrolled the Atlantic with four old battleships, an aircraft carrier, four cruisers, and a destroyer squadron. This latter became the Patrol Force United States Fleet on November 1, 1940, and the Atlantic Fleet three months later. It fell under the command of Vice-Admiral Ernest King, a brilliant and rigid master of all things naval who would direct the Pacific campaign against Japan. Thanks to naval expansion bills beginning in 1938, Congress abandoned the Washington Treaty limitations and raced to construct a "Navy second to none" within ten years. The Navy Expansion Act of 1938, coupled with the Two Ocean Navy Act of 1940, appropriated funds to double naval tonnage. The laws added nine battleships to the three already planned as well as 11 carriers and 44 cruisers. They expanded the naval fleet air arm to 8,000 pilots and 15,000 new aircraft. By war's end, this force grew to 60,747 pilots and a total of over 437,000 personnel, including 86,000 Women Accepted for Voluntary Emergency Service (WAVES).

After discovering in the late 1920s that massed formations of planes were the most effective means of aircraft carrier tactics, the U.S. Navy brought in innovations such as crash barriers and arresting hooks that reduced the space for launching and landing. The changes allowed for more planes to be placed on board carriers. New air-cooled radial engine technology—with cylinders arranged around the crankshaft—made planes much more serviceable and robust in combat because they lacked vulnerable plumbing of water-cooled engines. Research and development led to a synergistic relationship between the Army Air Force and civilian manufacturers who designed cutting-edge bombers and fighters such as the B-17, B-24, B-29, and P-47. The intimate ties between companies and the military extended to the U.S. Navy. Debates raged about the viability of airpower at night or in bad weather, but the admirals readied their vessels with antiaircraft guns and radar. War gaming tested the aircraft carrier as well as amphibious warfare, resulting in important doctrines that would guide sea and land forces in the war.

A separate service within the U.S. Navy, the Marine Corps was the U.S. Navy's soldiers but also possessed its own aviation. Evolved during the interwar period to conduct amphibious landings in anticipation of warfare in the Pacific, by mid-1939, the Marines Corps had roughly 20,000 men in two brigades—one in Quantico, Virginia, and the other in San Diego—each supported by an aviation group. Plans focused on assaulting enemy naval bases, which could then be converted into ports for warships and landing strips for aircraft. This modern thinking proved timely because the Pacific soon drew the U.S. Navy's attention.

Despite the huge construction effort underway and the recognition of Japan as the U.S. Navy's top enemy, the American fleet (like other services) was simply not ready for war in 1940. Providing manpower, ammunition, fuel, ships, landing craft, planes, and developed bases beyond home shores was still in the works. Because Japan preoccupied the admirals, the U.S. Navy neglected planning for battle against German submarines and protecting merchants in the Atlantic. Despite FDR's Europe-First strategy, the Atlantic did not wean Admiral King from his concern with the Pacific. Thus, the Americans were more onlookers to war than participants. They did not lack for money and resources, but they trailed in combat-ready forces, mobilization, and experience. Their contribution to aiding friends already engaged in war remained to be seen, but at least the dormant Americans had arisen from their slumber. Although the expanding war did not include direct U.S. intervention, the potential could only give Berlin, Rome, and Tokyo pause.

WOLF PACKS IN THE ATLANTIC

The Axis pileup of successes decidedly concerned the United States. Roosevelt and Churchill agreed to a set of war aims incorporated into the Atlantic Charter in August 1940. Seven months later, after his reelection to a third term, FDR used this document as the basis of his commitment to the "Four Freedoms" of speech, worship, decent living standards, and protection from fear. Such rhetorical support of the Allies was crucial to the American role in the global war, but it was still more powerful when the United States gradually put its economic and military muscle behind the words.

The Roosevelt administration directed assistance to China, but its main effort focused on the so-called battle of the Atlantic. The Allies began this six-year campaign in 1939 to secure trade and supply routes between the western hemisphere and Europe from the German naval menace. In a reversal of Britain's successful World War I blockade, the Germans used surface raiders, mines, and U-boat submarines to sink and impede enormous amounts of Allied tonnage in a war of attrition covering thousands of miles. They lacked resources, but Hitler could disrupt the flow of goods across the Atlantic. Historians have argued that if the Germans had poured their meager naval assets into submarines rather than battleships, the battle of the Atlantic might have yielded substantial returns for the Nazis. In any case, although this campaign involved industrial output, technology, and intelligence as well as the cunning and perseverance of its participants, it tended not to grab attention unless a dramatic action occurred. It was an epic struggle that stretched well outside the Atlantic, even into the Indian Ocean, as U-boats sought out British supply arteries from Australia, Malaysia, and around Africa into the Suez Canal. The North Atlantic proved unforgiving in terms of the toll on men and materiel.

The German Navy was unprepared for such a campaign, having ignored Admiral Raeder's request in 1939 to build up the fleet and then having lost much of it in the invasion of Norway in 1940. The survival of surface raiders was questionable, as the British sinking of the *Graf Spee* had demonstrated. Actually, surface vessels and mines were responsible for around just a little more than 6% of Allied shipping sunk during the war. Aircraft put another 13% on the bottom. But the innovative use of submarines moving out of ports in Norway and France in the summer of 1940 showed that the German Navy's capacity to inflict heavy blows on trans-Atlantic commerce. U-boats accounted for about 70% of the wartime sinkings in the Atlantic. It took Raeder until the end of the French campaign before he realized the importance they could play.

The Germans could access the Atlantic from several French ports and avoid northern bottlenecks between Norway, Scotland, Iceland, and Greenland. They also broke through the gap between Greenland and Britain to harass Allied shipping. The brilliant commander of the submarine fleet, Vice-Admiral Karl Donitz, eventually had at his disposal 1,168 vessels, although his average deployment ran at 115 U-boats in 1943. He innovatively deployed them in groups—"wolf packs"—that converged on convoys of ships to impose of sea strategy of annihilation on merchant vessels. Another effective move was his willingness to launch night surface attacks rather than rely on submerged assaults in daytime. The U-boat arm of this Hitler loyalist notched some remarkable achievements against the enemy. The sinking of *Courageous* at sea by U-boat 29 in mid-September 1939 was a notable one, for it represented the first carrier in history ever lost and the first major Royal Navy vessel sunk in World War II. The torpedoing of the British battleship *Royal Oak* inside the Scottish base of Scapa Flow, in which 833 sailors died, followed the next month. There were also ignoble deeds that smacked of annihilation, such as the U-boat sinking of the passenger liner *Athenia* the day Germany invaded Poland. By late 1939, Donitz eyed the U.S. and British vessels plying the Atlantic, hoping to sink 750,000 tons a month and bring Britain to its knees.

During the first "happy time" for the German Navy, from 1939 to early 1941, the subs could have inflicted mortal damage on Britain. The British lacked the average-speed, lightly armed corvettes (adapted from whale hunters) used mainly to hunt submarines with depth charges. They had lost much of their fleet escort force in the Norwegian campaign as well as the help of the French Navy once France succumbed. During this time, the Germans sunk 250,000 tons of ships a month, twice the amount that the British could add to the merchant fleet. The Royal Navy focused more on defense by aircraft than the sea, but air escort for convoys remained scant. The British

German U-Boat pens on Atlantic.   Credit: Imperial War Museum.

tried catapulting Hurricanes off merchant ships (some of these were later converted to escort carriers with small decks), but the plane could not land at sea. In the meantime, Germany sent 638 British ships to the bottom in the last half of 1940. In the first half of 1941, more than 700 were lost.

The Germans estimated that defeat of Britain required a tripling of sinkings, but they lacked vessels to do the job. In August 1940, Donitz had a mere 27 U-boats available and just 22 by the following February. Roughly a third were on station at any one time while another third were under repair and the rest in transit. His surface fleet expanded significantly by Spring 1941, as did the size of the U-boats and their capability to reach farther out in the ocean. Manpower also rose even though the Army and Luftwaffe enjoyed the lion's share of draftees. Submariners sailed as volunteers rather than as conscripts, which meant that morale and skills remained high. No U-boater could last long if incompetent. Yet the strategic possibilities of scoring an important victory in the Atlantic had diminished by that time, regardless of Italian and German victories in the Mediterranean. Allied tactics also proved effective in routing ships away from danger through ULTRA signals intelligence using aircraft to chase U-boats away and calling on support groups of cruisers, battleships, and destroyers to escort merchant vessels in open water. This forced submarines to operate close to shore or submerged, and thus risk greater detection.

Donitz's skillful adjustment of his pioneering wolf-pack technique avoided shoreline traffic and sent subs out to sea where the pickings were more plentiful. Guided by shore-based radio communications, U-boat lines patrolled perpendicular to convoy routes that covered vast ocean spaces. Once found, the convoy's position was signaled to shore command, which directed submarines gathered in wolf packs to attack. Then, usually acting at night, the submarines separated and infiltrated through escort screens and the merchant vessels with devastating effects. Oil tankers burned for hours and even days, as their compartmentalization required to carry bulk liquids gave them durability, while ships plodding along with weighty iron ore often sank in a minute. Sailors slept on deck if their ship was carrying a heavy load since they would have just seconds to abandon ship if torpedoed. Those with dry goods or other such general cargo could sleep below decks, dressed and ready to flee. If the ship held fuel, sailors could undress and sleep with the door closed; they could not escape an exploding ship. All the while the subs either maneuvered on the surface amidst the convoy to avoid escorts and engage targets or dove to flee from depth charges dropped by frantically pursuing escorts. The next morning, the wolf packs gathered behind the convoy ready to mop up the stragglers.

Near the end of October 1940, the unprepared Royal Navy could not protect a slow convoy (SC-7) of 30 ships. As a result, subs sunk 21 vessels. Among those going in for the kill was U-99 captained by ace Otto Kretschmer, who sank six ships. A faster convoy of 49 vessels, called HX79, lost 12 ships. Over three days, a total of 38 British vessels went to the bottom while nary a U-boat was damaged. The Germans often exaggerated their kills, and the British replaced their losses to the point that by the end of 1941, they enjoyed a surplus in tonnage. Many merchants even traveled without escorts. But London could not ignore the fact that 352,407 tons were sunk in October, a high for the death and destruction wrought by Donitz's wolf packs.

The British had no answer other than to expand convoy protection westward into the Atlantic. The problem of an "air gap" south of Greenland persisted for much of the battle of the Atlantic, in which aircraft could not reach this remote area. The British turned to the convoy system—or groups of naval escorts for merchant ships—which they had used in World War I. Research quickly improved radar and sonar for submarine detection for these convoys. In March 1941, the British killed or captured four U-boat captains, two of them aces who had accounted for a large percentage of convoy sinkings. But geography favored the Germans. They occupied bases on the French coast, at Cherbourg, Brest, Lorient, and points farther south on the Atlantic seaboard, building huge and strong reinforced concrete hangar pens for subs with roofs over twenty feet thick that withstood Allied bombings. These ports actually placed them as far west into the ocean as Britain. Pens in the Norwegian Sea (Trondheim and Bergen) also let them intercept ships headed for Russia. For the Allies, antisubmarine air and naval bases in Iceland, established in April 1941,

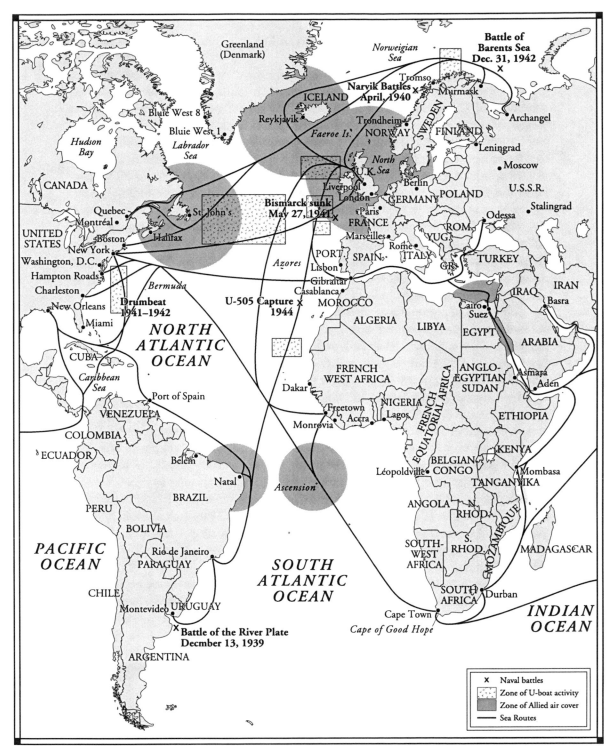

Map 7.1 Battle of the Atlantic. Credit: Douglas Brinkley and Michael E. Haskew, *The World War II Desk Reference*, p. 232.

stretched defensive cover to 35 degrees west of London; but the vulnerable gap still existed between this point and Canada.

Remedies appeared in May 1941. The Royal Canadian Navy based 13 destroyers, 4 sloops, and 21 frigates (about 1,400 tons) out of St. Johns, Newfoundland under the command of Commodore Leonard Murray. The only Canadian to head a wartime theater, Murray escorted merchants from the Grand Banks to Iceland. Air cover was still limited, but at least aircraft could reach 600 miles east and 400 miles south from Newfoundland while planes could fly 700 miles from bases in Northern Ireland. This still left a hole of 300 miles in which merchant sinkings were high. The advent of long-range B-24 Liberator bombers—a versatile plane that was faster and could fly greater distances than its cousin the B-17—finally closed the gap in May 1943. Other air holes that affected South Atlantic and African routes existed until then, including the "Black Pit" west of the Azores, so named by the Germans because they sunk so many ships there. Despite the new air blanket, the wolf packs did not let up. They sank 324,550 Allied tons in May 1941 and almost as much the next month. By July, Donitz had 65 submarines to roam the Atlantic and more were added thereafter.

The threat of conventional surface attack also persisted. In January 1941, the refitted battle cruisers *Scharnhorst* and *Gneisenau,* which had been damaged off Norway, broke out into the Atlantic. They sank over 115,000 tons in two months, altered the convoy routes, and then retired to the safety of Brest on the French coast where the RAF damaged *Gniesenau* in dry dock. Raeder then turned to a bold idea to impress Hitler with the German Navy's daring and skill. He readied for action his two heavy cruisers, *Prinz Eugen* and *Hipper,* as well as the mightiest battleship in his fleet, *Bismarck.* This 50,000 ton vessel not only reached speeds equal to any comparable ship in the British Navy, but its eight 15-inch guns in four turrets could engage any enemy. In search of convoys, Raeder sent *Bismarck* into the north Atlantic over the protest of his surface fleet commander who saw no good in a single battleship engaging an entire convoy. But Raeder wanted a victory. The formidable ship powered through Kattegat strait between Sweden and Denmark on May 20, 1941, and then Skaggerak channel between Norway and Denmark the next day en route to Bergen, Norway. On May 23, Swedish and British reconnaissance spotted *Bismarck* as she left Bergen. Churchill wanted the behemoth sunk.

The next morning, *Bismarck* encountered the lightly armored battle cruiser *Hood* and the new battleship *Prince of Wales.* Moving on a parallel course that benefited the German ship's long-range guns and restricted the British vessels' angle of fire, *Bismarck* sank *Hood* in the Denmark Straits on May 24, leaving just three survivors. *Prince of Wales* withdrew, but British cruisers tracked *Bismarck,* now leaking oil after being hit during the engagement by a 14-inch shell fired by *Prince of Wales.* The giant fled for the safety of Brest without help from *Prinz Eugen,* which had initially accompanied it out of port but disappeared westward. After *Bismarck* imprudently signaled its location by radio, a U.S. Navy-piloted Catalina patrol aircraft picked up the solitary battleship in mid-ocean on May 26. Flying off the carrier *Ark Royal,* a vessel from Britain's Gibraltar task force, a Swordfish torpedo aircraft disabled one of *Bismarck's* rudders. The battleship helplessly turned circles making it easy prey for two battleships and a cruiser to sink it the next day. Because of its size, only a relentless pounding sent the heavily clad *Bismarck* to the bottom, although some believed it had been scuttled. Its remains were discovered in 1989. Of the 2,222 crew members only 115 survived in a bloody ending.

Bismarck's demise further disillusioned Hitler with Raeder's surface fleet, and he turned to Admiral Donitz's plan of intercepting convoys with U-boats. Alarmed that the British Home Fleet and four British battleships were now free to roam the seas, the Fuhrer feared an invasion of Norway. To guard Swedish ore and prevent supplies from transiting across Scandinavia to Russia, Hitler ordered Bismarck's sister ship, *Tirpitz,* to Trondheim and planned to transfer the two battle cruisers, *Scharnhorst* and *Gneisenau,* and the heavy cruiser *Prinz Eugen* from Brest to Norway. These fateful decisions weakened the German Navy in the Atlantic. Salvation came for the British in 1941 because the Germans lacked enough U-boats at a critical juncture when they could have done the most damage. After winter 1940–41, the Royal Navy adjusted to new routes and better managed port congestion, and the Americans and Soviets boosted the Allied supply effort. The USSR deflected Germany's attention and resources from the Atlantic once Hitler attacked in mid-June; the United States helped with supplies, convoy escorts, and eventually, convoys. The German Navy not only shifted airpower eastward but moved U-boats into defensive positions off Norway and sailed into the Mediterranean by Fall 1941 to provide support against the British counteroffensive in North Africa. Donitz's fleet was still deadly but also thinner than before.

Intelligence took on greater importance. In March 1941, the British seized a German armed trawler north of Norway and found the enciphering tables for ENIGMA, the Wehrmacht's classified communications code. In May, the Royal Navy captured a weather ship and then U-110, a submarine that they stripped of all ENIGMA equipment including the keys that allowed deciphering of "officers only" messages. The Germans continued to deny that Enigma could be compromised. ULTRA revealed wolf pack positions and plans mainly because the micromanager Donitz sent and received hundreds of messages containing information. Intelligence against the submarines became the Allies' biggest coup of the war.

AMERICAN AID

Now convoys worked better because the British became more efficient in carrying goods with the aid of the United States. British officials had pleaded with Roosevelt for cash and goods after the battle of Britain, but FDR could not break the Neutrality Act and hand out loans to belligerents. He elasticized the Neutrality Act to its limits with the destroyers-for-bases agreement, and he searched for ways to get money into London's hands; but the British did not have much left to trade. Roosevelt looked for ways short of war to rescue the Allies. Churchill eloquently reminded him that Britain would fight "for future generations on both sides of the Atlantic" if the U.S. provided support. Removing the "silly, foolish old dollar sign," Roosevelt—once reelected and with wider latitude for intervention—announced in mid-December 1940 an idea to aid Britain without soldiers or illegal transfers of cash. Lend-Lease, as it was called when Congress passed the law in March 1941, rented out the American arsenal of democracy to friends abroad.

In the debate over intervention swirling around the Lend-Lease legislation, it became clear that Congress opted to help the Allies. The subsidies for Britain, the Free French, China, and the Soviet Union were enormous, eventually totaling upwards of $50 billion in food, military and industrial goods, oil, and services. Britain and the Chinese Empire received over half of this sum. The USSR got one-fifth—most prominently trucks and airplanes—via the initial main northern route to Murmansk and Archangel before southern access opened through Iran in 1942 and air delivery began from Alaska to Siberia. Chiang Kai-shek received a modest $2 billion because more goods could not reach him once Japan shut down supply routes into China from Burma. Although Washington attached strings to Lend-Lease to shape the postwar world, the assistance was critical. The Red Army relied on U.S. trucks in their war against Germany, food sustained the British and their colonial subjects, and soldiers around the world carried Lend-Lease arms. American production could not keep pace with demand.

Perhaps the biggest challenge for Lend-Lease was to deliver the tons of stuff to the Allies. Aircraft flew across the Atlantic or the Bering Strait while aid for the Asian theaters went through Indian ports. Arctic convoys escorted Lend-Lease ships at great peril north of Scandinavia. Yet the dearth of merchant shipping and the waiting wolf packs plagued the effort across the Atlantic until 1943. In the summer of 1941, Roosevelt's huge merchant shipbuilding program started to pay dividends as Henry Kaiser's and other (Bethlehem steel among them) shipyards launched the first "Liberty" vessels. Perfecting production by welding together whole sections of vessels rather than ponderously riveting panels, Kaiser churned out ships at such a rate that the U-boat campaign became less relevant to the Allied supply chain. His shipyards could make a Liberty ship in four and a half days. This was remarkable but no more so than the average time across all shipyards by 1942 of fifty days per ship or the fact that over 2,700 Liberty ships, and 5,777 total vessels (including troopships, improved Liberties called Victory ships, and tankers), were built during the war.

The alarm bells of October 1940 had rung in Washington, and the Americans responded with a massive production program that provided the foundation for the later American strategy of annihilation against fascists in Europe and militarists in Japan. In addition, by June 1941, they were involved in a sort of phony war with the Axis powers. After the passage of Lend-Lease, the War Department divided the continental United States itself into four Defense Commands and incorporated territories outside of the country—Alaska, Hawaii, the Philippines, and Caribbean holdings—into training and operational centers. The phony war involved no shooting, but it did usher in a period of military mobilization to assist the Allies. The United States prepared for hot war should developments in Europe, Africa, and Asia so demand.

In 1941, U-boats still lurked in the frigid Arctic seas and the Atlantic. Having first sailed from Scapa Flow in August with ships headed out from Iceland the next month, the Allied Arctic convoys were intended to aid the USSR. In the early stages of their invasion of the USSR, the Germans took little interest in these ships. As their luck ran out around Moscow, however, they realized the Eastern front campaign would be a long one. Thus, Donitz's submarine fleet moved north of Norway to pick off convoys. The British Admiralty decided to guard convoys traveling in both directions for adequate

U.S. Coastguardsman (*USS Menges*) in the Atlantic.   Credit:
Center for the Study of War Experience at Regis University, Denver, Colorado.

coverage. The protection also extended as far into the Arctic as possible as the merchant vessels made for Murmansk, Archangel, and Molotovsk. This widening of both the convoy system and U-boat warfare in these bitterly icy and stormy waters resulted in deadly encounters on both sides in 1942.

The wolf packs proved less decisive by mid-1941 due to ULTRA and the increasing American presence. The former saved many ships from calamity; in July 1941, the amount of tons sunk per month dropped to the levels of May 1940. Luftwaffe monitoring of convoys between Gibraltar and Britain in September and October 1941 gave Donitz more scores. After suspending trips along this route, the British sent convoy HG 76 from Gibraltar with 16 escorts guarding 32 merchantmen in mid-December. In command of the surface navy vessels was the skilled Johnny Walker. *Audacity*, Britain's first escort carrier (a merchant ship fitted with a small flight deck), sailed under a separate commander. The convoy engaged U-boats on the third day out of port. Over the next two days, the British lost a destroyer, sank a few subs, and chased off the rest.

Neglecting Walker's advice, *Audacity's* commander occasionally pulled his ship outside of the destroyer screen. On December 21, it went to the bottom. The Germans fled, minus four U-boats, having sunk only two merchant ships along with *Audacity* and a destroyer.

The Americans provided protection and a morale boost to the British and Soviets. In July 1941, after a sub tried to attack an American battleship off Iceland, a U.S. Marine brigade assumed control over Iceland. Within two weeks, FDR instructed the Navy to escort ships from any friendly country in the Western Atlantic. Admiral Raeder saw this as a declaration of war, but Hitler counseled caution, not wanting to add the Americans to his list of foes at the same time he was rolling through the Soviet Union. Raeder persisted; in September , he visited Hitler again, with Donitz, but the Fuhrer rebuffed him once more. Yet Berlin could not deny the rising tension on the high seas between the United States and Germany.

Once the German attack on the USSR was underway in the summer 1941, America took measures to send war materiel to Britain and the USSR. The Americans supplemented their merchant marine building once again by constructing more Liberty ships to expand shipments of Lend-Lease aid. The U.S. Navy took responsibility for Allied merchantmen and FDR also considered naval escorts from U.S. shores to Iceland despite America's official neutrality. The month before, Chief of Naval Operations Harold Stark organized the western hemisphere's defense against submarines. He created four Sea Frontiers—East, Gulf, Caribbean, and Panama (both sides of the Canal)—that not only guarded convoys as they left or entered the Atlantic coast but extended U.S. protection 200 miles out to sea. Churchill and Roosevelt authorized the U.S. Navy to escort fast convoys between the Grand Banks and Iceland while the Canadians took slow convoys into the Atlantic with American help. This situation posed dangers, not least of which was that the prewar Canadian navy consisted of just six destroyers and five minesweepers split between Atlantic and Pacific coastal duty. As the Royal Canadian Navy struggled with its ponderous charges, U.S. vessels had repeated clashes and near-misses with U-boats. The Canadians labored to expand their navy fivefold during the war and improve their performance, but not until the Germans withdrew their submarines in November to the Mediterranean theater. By this time, the Americans were deeply involved in the convoy system.

SUSPECT NEUTRAL

The neutrality of the United States was in question. Encounters with German submarines revealed a de facto war. At first FDR justified his agreement with Churchill to extend protection to convoys, arguing that America supported the Allies by aid and not soldiers. On September 1, 1941, Admiral Ernest King presented plans for convoy operations in the Atlantic, but Roosevelt hesitated to act. A week later, twelve U-boats hit a slow convoy nearing Iceland over a three-day period, and 15 merchant ships were lost. The British had run short of destroyers and the new Arctic routes taxed the Royal Navy to the breaking point. Roosevelt wanted to help out without angering Congress, and on September 4, , he found a way. Carrying mail and passengers to Ireland, the destroyer *Greer* came under fire from a U-boat. Two torpedoes missed. FDR seized on

Churchill, FDR, and staff meet on the Atlantic Charter.   Credit: U.S. Naval Institute.

the news to announce that the vessel had been deliberately attacked, this despite the fact that *Greer* had been trailing the submarine for three hours to identify its location to a British patrol plane that dropped depth charges. When *Greer* did the same, the desperate U-boat captain fired the torpedoes. In a nationwide radio broadcast six days later, the President boldly accused Germany of "piracy" in unleashing the underwater "rattlesnakes of the Atlantic" on innocent neutrals. In addition to warning German and Italian naval vessels not to enter U.S. waters, he cautioned that destroyers would shoot on sight any vessel that attacked a convoy. The U.S. Navy was free to protect merchant ships.

The German Navy begged Hitler to respond with a declaration of war. He refused, but an undeclared naval war between Germany and the United States now existed. As convoys sailed the Atlantic, Hitler ordered Raeder to avoid attacks on merchant-men at least until mid-October 1941 when the Russian campaign would be over. The German Navy tried to heed his wishes, but it could not avoid the American-protected convoys.

Britain needed more help, and FDR looked for options that would not provoke domestic outcries. Wary of a backlash from Republicans and isolationists in Congress, he needed to convince legislators to ease restrictions on travel, trade, and aid under the Neutrality Acts. That legislation prevented the arming of merchant vessels, for example, making them sitting ducks to submarines that surfaced to sink them with gunfire. Merchant vessels were dependent on destroyers to save them. Roosevelt proposed to arm the merchantmen, but he needed another pretext to win skeptics on Capitol Hill. Donitz obliged him. On October 17, as Congress considered Roosevelt's request, the destroyer *Kearny* was torpedoed while defending a British convoy. Capitol Hill took note. *Kearny* limped back to port with 11 dead sailors on board. Congress accepted the changes to the Neutrality Acts. Actually, the U.S. Senate overturned the entire law, but Roosevelt preferred eliminating only parts to quell isolationist criticism. He proclaimed that a shooting war had begun and that the Germans had fired first. Two weeks after the *Kearny* attack, a U-boat sent the destroyer *Reuben James* to the bottom off Iceland along with 115 men. It was the American Navy's first loss in the undeclared war in the Atlantic. FDR's caution about junking the Neutrality Acts appeared sound. In November, by narrow votes in both the Senate and the House, Congress permitted armed merchantmen to enter the war zone which exposed them to German brutality but aided the Allied war effort.

Congress and the American people remained beyond the fighting, but the Neutrality Act had been gutted. Only restrictions on travel and loans remained, and Lend-Lease circumvented the latter restraint. Convoys welcomed the protection of the U.S. Navy but FDR could go no further down the road of belligerent status even though diplomacy with the Axis powers had virtually ceased. He monitored events on the Eastern front for the next opportunity to aid the Allies. Maybe Hitler would declare war. Or maybe one of his Axis partners would bring the United States into the global conflict.

CHAPTER 8

Battles for the Mediterranean

We still entered scenes that...seemed to have come from the *Inferno:* the dead with their faces knotted in anguish, weeping soldiers immobilized by fear, vehicles ablaze with the occupants sometimes still screaming inside, soldiers without limbs within vast mud-streaked halos of their own blood, and others careening about, blinded by wounds or pain.

SCOTT TUROW
Ordinary Heroes

THE MEDITERRANEAN

When Italy declared war on June 10, 1940, Benito Mussolini finally had his chance to achieve a new Roman empire. Nobody really knew what he sought exactly: empire, a role as intermediary between the Allies and Axis powers, or peacemaker. He lacked the ability or stomach for campaigns of annihilation, but he had grand ambitions. Il Duce had jealously watched Hitler march across Europe, and now he wanted a share of the spoils. The Mediterranean afforded opportunities, but obstacles to expansion abounded. Vichy France retained control of most French overseas possessions in the Middle East and North Africa, and Britain would also defend its colonies. Even fellow authoritarian Spain coveted many of the same territories he sought, such as British Gibraltar and French North Africa. Il Duce took aim on British and French possessions with the one goal of bolstering his Ethiopian-Eritrean empire. To do so, Italy needed to absorb Tunisia, Libya, and Egypt as well as coastal areas of Algeria and Morocco to the west. In east Africa, he sought the Sudan and the Horn territories, including French and British Somaliland (added to Italian Somaliland). The next phase of the war involved campaigns in the Mediterranean Sea itself, East Africa, and the Western African desert and inadvertently opened a fourth theater in the Balkans.

Britain stood in the way of Mussolini's dream of *mare nostrum*—domination of the Mediterranean Sea basin. By joining 250,000 troops in Libya and 350,000 in the Horn with 92,000 from Italy proper, he could overrun Britain's 10,000 soldiers garrisoned in Sudan, British Somaliland, and Kenya. Responsible for the Middle East theater, British General Sir Archibald Wavell had already tied down his 63,000-man force with patrolling East Africa, Egypt, Iraq, and Palestine. Mussolini could also bring to bear 500 aircraft based in Africa and another 1,200 from Italy against 370 RAF planes.

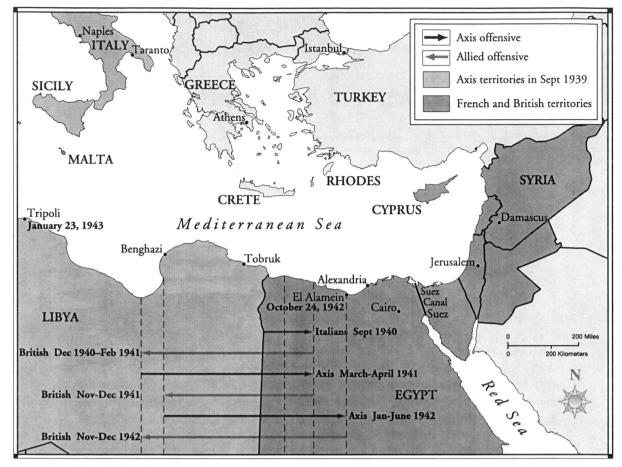

Map 8.1 Mediterranean.   Credit: Ronald Story, *Concise Historical Atlas of World War II: The Geography of Conflict*, Map 12, p. 29.

Yet there were decided weaknesses in the Italian armed forces. The army had expanded beyond its capabilities, the navy lacked leadership and a sound economic basis to sustain it at sea, and the air force needed more modern fighter aircraft to compete with the Allies' American-built Curtiss P40 and the British Hurricane. The invasion of the French Alps as France lay prostrate was a study in ineptitude. Il Duce had also failed to recall the Italian merchant marine and almost a million tons of shipping fell into Allied hands in 1940.

Furthermore, Italy's leadership did not evoke confidence. Much of the problem can be traced to Mussolini's superficial decision-making style in which he ranted at his commanders' failures but provided no fresh directions. The head of the armed forces, Marshal Pietro Badoglio, coordinated operations, but neither he nor the theater commanders possessed real power. All remained subordinate to Mussolini. The fascist revolution was also not deep seated; King Victor Emmanuel was autonomous, Roman politicians were strong, and the Mafia thrived tenaciously in the south. Mussolini's dictatorial rule more resembled Hideki Tojo's in Japan—subject to events—rather than institutionalized states with embedded ideologies that were guided by skilled strongmen such as the USSR and Germany. Thus, he relied on showing off, on theatrics. Mussolini preferred the "banner headline" to real progress. Thus, bored with details and partial to sensationalism, Il Duce followed a schizophrenic way of war.

Such an approach was unfortunate for Italy because Britain's hold on its territories in the Middle East and Africa was tenuous. The British maintained a military presence in Egypt by informal agreement and held Palestine and Iraq through League of Nations' mandates. Their top priority was to protect the strategic trade routes from Singapore and India to the Suez Canal by manning key naval bases in Alexandria, Cyprus, Malta, and Gibraltar. These allowed the Royal Navy to dominate the Mediterranean. Malta was in the middle of the Sea. Although it lacked extensive dockyard and repair facilities like Gibraltar and Alexandria, it accommodated major fleet units of carriers and battleships as well as tankers. Just five infantry battalions, some local reserves, and three old aircraft comprised the garrison in Malta. The British Admiralty considered a withdrawal from Cyprus and Malta to Gibraltar to evacuate the eastern reaches of the Mediterranean, but this would expose Egypt, the Suez Canal, Sudan, and the Horn colonies to Italian pressure. Churchill knew that the Mediterranean was the only place left to turn back the fascist tide. Besides, he had long believed that an invasion from the Mediterranean, which he termed "the soft underbelly of Fortress Europe," was the key to victory over the Axis powers.

The British position looked grim, however. Churchill anguished over the power vacuum left by France's defeat in the western Mediterranean. Fearing that the Axis could best the Royal Navy with the addition of the French fleet, the British seized France's squadron in Alexandria, Egypt, on July 3, 1940. They then issued an ultimatum to the French Mediterranean fleet anchored in the harbor of Mers el Kebir near Oran, Algeria, to surrender or face destruction. French Admiral Marcel Gensoul had sought to disarm the fleet and the British Admiralty accepted this option, but Churchill refused because the ships could fall into fascist hands. Confusion and intrigue prevailed until the British fired on the French, sinking a battleship, a cruiser, and several destroyers. Some 297 sailors on the battleship *Bretagne* were killed and 350 wounded. The British were sickened, the Americans uneasy, and the French apoplectic. The outraged Vichy government issued a retaliatory torpedo bomber raid on British Gibraltar, and Marshal Petain broke diplomatic relations with London. An uneasy accord ensued, but the threat of Vichy formally joining the Axis military effort existed thereafter. For now, Petain merely gave Germany some bases in the Middle East.

The Italians seized on this moment of Franco-British tension. They overran Sudanese border posts in July and the next month invaded British Somaliland after French Somaliland joined the Vichy regime. The British fled Somaliland, their first colony to fall to the Axis. This was the only territory that Italy seized from the Allies without German help. Fortunately for Britain, Rome rather than Berlin was the foe. Hitler had turned his attention to the USSR, although he welcomed the addition of African colonies for their resources. Africa was Italy's show, but the Italian record did not bode well for the future. Marshal Badoglio suggested an attack on Egypt, but the Italian Navy ignored the British ships exiting from Malta. In the battle of Calabria on July 9, the stronger and well-positioned Italian vessels fled after contact with the Royal Navy and the Australian Navy, which damaged the battleship *Cesare*. Italian aircraft inadvertently bombed their own forces. Most Italian generals no longer supported Mussolini's inchoate imperial reveries, including half-baked plans to partition Switzerland and take Yugoslavia and Greece. In August 1940, the worried Germans warned him that such adventurism distracted from their planning for the invasion of the Soviet Union. As a rule, however, the Axis powers did not listen to each other but vied over policy in an atmosphere of mistrust. Unlike the Allies, Germany and Italy had no common war aims or command structure. The delusional Mussolini forged ahead in Africa.

ITALY IN AFRICA

Il Duce ordered his commanders into battle. Although his forces vastly outnumbered British Commonwealth (Britain, Australia, South Africa, New Zealand, India, and colonial Africa) troops, tanks, and aircraft, the timid Duke of Aosta froze his soldiers in East Africa, near Sudan and Kenya. The excuse was that he lacked reinforcements and supplies, but this defensive strategy split his forces. They were preoccupied with preventing the British from mobilizing the Abyssinian "Patriots" to return the deposed Ethiopian emperor, Haile Selassie, to his throne. The Commander-in-Chief of Sudan, General William Platt, and Brigadier Sir William Slim launched campaigns in November to rid Ethiopia of the Italians. Platt focused on the frontier town of Gallabat while Slim, a twenty-year veteran of the British Indian Army, advanced into Ethiopia until the Italian air force drove him back. The fascists went on the defensive again, however, despite their numerical edge. British intelligence deciphered the secret codes of both the Italian Army and Air Force in East Africa, which allowed veteran Commander-in-Chief of the Middle East Wavell full knowledge of Italian battle plans.

Farther west, Army Chief of Staff and commander of Italian forces in Libya, Rodolfo Graziani, had directed General Mario Berti to send five badly equipped divisions of his Tenth Army across the Egyptian border in September 1940. Graziani did so with trepidation. He knew that Italy was not prepared for war. The military lacked motorized equipment and armor and counted on a small industrial base relative to the British for supplies. The undermanned Wavell had also bluffed by placing groups of troops along the Egyptian-Libyan border and sending quick raids against Graziani's positions. The tactics convinced Graziani that the British had substantial men under arms. He reluctantly decided to move. Berti's forces advanced into Egypt but not before they lost their way until the Air Force found them and resupplied them with water. They reached the town of Sidi Barrani when Berti—who had earned a reputation for fighting last-ditch battles during the Spanish Civil War—halted to await supplies. The Italian motorized forces simply stopped, bereft of leadership and materiel. The Italian Tenth Army faced two ragtag British mobile divisions under General Wavell, which stalled the Italian offensive until December.

The news turned worse for the Italians in the Western Desert. While Tenth Army awaited reinforcements in Egypt, Wavell took advantage of the new heavily armored Matilda tank, extra planes, and troops from India and Australia. He sent Lieutenant-

General Richard O'Connor in a surprise raid on December 9 on Sidi Barrani. Feinting a retreat that lured out the Italians, the counterattack aimed at coastal camps. The Italians only dented the Matildas while their light tanks were obliterated. British mobility exploited gaps in the Italian lines, and fortified camps were attacked from the rear, falling one by one. Only Italy's Cyrene Division got away, though without its supplies and equipment. This mere raid actually pushed the Italians out of Egypt in three days, giving the British Western Desert Force its first victory. Wavell took prisoner over 38,000 Italians, including four generals, while the British suffered just 624 casualties. Operations to remove Italy from Cyrenaica, the eastern province of Libya, escalated from this point.

O'Connor's 13th Brigade turned on the white-bearded General Annibale "Electric Whiskers" Bergonzoli's XXIII Italian Corps at Bardia, which Graziani and Mussolini pledged to hold. Underestimating Bergonzoli's strength and with a mere 31,000 troops at their disposal, the British struggled. Wavell sent the 4th Indian Division to Ethiopia and replaced it with the novice 6th Australian Division. This postponed O'Connor's successful attack on Bardia until January 1941. Aided by Royal Navy bombardment, he took 40,000 prisoners, dozens of tanks, and hundreds of guns and motor vehicles. The British pushed further into Cyrenaica and captured the key city of Tobruk on January 22, smashing through the sloppy defenses and claiming 25,000 more prisoners, guns, and tanks while losing just 400 troops. O'Connor now urged a run on Tripoli, where Graziani had fled. Wavell refused, worried that his forces were spread too thinly.

Instead, while the Australians pressed the Italians up the coast, O'Connor bypassed Tobruk and daringly cut 170 miles across the desert with the 7th Armored Division. This blocked the coastal road south of Beda Fomm and prevented a retreat by the Italian Tenth Army in February. Graziani had thought such a cross-desert maneuver impossible. The British endured sandstorms and freezing rain, but they made it, confident from intelligence that the Italians would be completely surprised. Hard fighting yielded another 25,000 Italian prisoners and destroyed both Tenth Army and the Italian Air Force. Amidst the battlefield of smoldering fires strewn with equipment, the Italians readied for the long march to British prison camps in Egypt. O'Connor now asked for permission to attack Tripoli; Wavell refused because he lacked comprehension of the speed of mechanized warfare. He assumed a defensive posture in the Western Desert. The 7th Armored Division returned to Egypt and the British rested at El Agheila. Wavell dispersed O'Connor's headquarters, leaving an armored brigade and an infantry division to keep the Italians at bay. The bulk of the troops embarked for the defense of Greece in February 1941.

They had not eliminated Italy from Libya, but the British had converted a numerical disadvantage into victories. In eight weeks of fighting, the Italians lost 130,000 soldiers; almost 1,000 guns; 500 tanks; and additional trucks, supplies, and ammunition. The British suffered 2,000 killed. Wavell might have ended the North African campaign by taking Tripoli and asserting control over all of Libya. That he did not allowed the Germans time to replace the futile Italians in early 1941. Yet for now the British were content. The 700,000 square mile Western Desert campaign gave them a rare success in this early stage of World War II. Mussolini ultimately suffered from his arrogance and poor command structure as well as from second-rate weapons. Low morale and timid leadership also played a role in defeat; Italian soldiers were not enthused about fighting the impressive British in Africa. Defeat in Libya caused all sorts of problems for Mussolini's rule and his ambitions. The Mediterranean could not be closed to British shipping. Italy itself could be attacked from the south, and Vichy's French colonies in north and West Africa might defect from the Axis cause. Due to these problems, the Germans soon decided to divert their energies from Europe to make a large commitment to holding North Africa.

In the meantime, Wavell's forces also moved in East Africa despite a lack of troops. The Duke of Aosta received permission to withdraw his forces to the Sudanese border but the British quickly decrypted this message and moved up their offensive by three weeks to mid-January 1941. General Platt drew on Indian troops to pursue the enemy. In the battle of the Lowlands, they captured the top officers and the soldiers of the Italian 41st Colonial Brigade. The commander in Eritrea, General Luigi Frusci, then ordered Aosta to make a stand with the Savoia Division southwest of the town of Keren. This was good ground for defense. Aosta held Keren until March 27, when Platt's 4th Indian Division overwhelmed him. The battle for Keren and for Asmara four days later initiated a series of critical losses for Italy in East Africa. Fascist setbacks from both engagements mounted to 3,000 dead while the British suffered 536 killed and over 3,200 injured. Allied troops headed toward the Red Sea port of Massawa, which surrendered on April 8, 1941 under pressure from Indian and Free French troops from French Somaliland. Six Italian destroyers then sailed northward, intent on raiding Port Sudan. Four were sunk and two scuttled before reaching their destination. Northern Eritrea was also in British hands.

The British objective now focused on Ethiopia. Up from Kenya came Lieutenant-General Alan Cunningham, younger brother of Admiral Sir Andrew Cunningham who was the Royal Navy Commander in Chief of the Mediterranean. Most of his 77,000 troops hailed from Africa. South African forces provided six air squadrons. In January 1941, the 1st South African Division and an East Africa brigade entered the southern province of Galla-Sidamo to find that Ethiopian Patriots had refused to rebel. This development forced a temporary retreat. In mid-February, Cunningham moved eastward into Italian Somaliland. At Kismayu, he precipitated an Italian withdrawal north of the Juba River; and within ten days, his troops pushed the enemy from Mogadishu. Capitalizing on a shorter supply line after the Royal Navy jumped from Aden to the port of Barbera on March 16, Cunningham then shot northward to Harar. It fell in ten days. He turned west and liberated the capital, Addis Ababa, on April 6, before dispersing his troops in all directions to make contact with his other forces. Some recaptured the frontier post of Moyale before heading northward through Galla-Sidamo while others turned north and joined Platt's forces in a pincer movement against Aosta's mountain redoubt at Amba Alagi. Covering 1,700 miles in eight weeks, Cunningham routed Italy's forces while he lost just 501 of his own along with eight planes.

The capture of Addis Ababa brought the demise of the Italian empire in Ethiopia and Emperor Hailie Selassie's return to the throne. The British and the native Patriots closed on the Italians at Amba Alagi. Aosta held out for 25 days as the Allies reduced his mountain lair peak by peak. He surrendered on May 16, 1941, although isolated units remained in Ethiopia until November. Meanwhile, Lieutenant-Colonel Orde Wingate escorted Selassie into Ethiopia. He fought his way in with the Gideon Force, an irregular group of 50 officers, 20 British noncommissioned officers, 800 soldiers from the Sudan Frontier Battalion, and 800 partly trained Ethiopian troops. They set up a base in the province of Gojjam, but then Wingate exceeded his orders by executing a guerilla campaign that used bluff and daring to bring the Emperor all the way to the capital. With Selassie installed as ruler in Addis Ababa, the mercurial Wingate wrote a summary of his actions that criticized the command above him, thereby earning his dismissal. He returned to action later, however, though this time in Asia.

The end of the East Africa campaign was good news for the Allies. For the first time, a country occupied by the Axis had been liberated. British cryptography had built confidence not only in ULTRA but in the ability of the military to put it to good effect. Troops were shifted to the Western Desert campaign to expel the Italians there. Il Duce's proudest achievement—the conquest of Ethiopia—was undone, and over 100,000 soldiers became prisoners of war. In a larger strategic sense, the removal of Italy from northeast Africa freed the western Indian Ocean from Axis control. Thus, once they entered the Pacific war, the Japanese could not intercept Allied shipping routes. As significant, Franklin Roosevelt could declare that the area was no longer a war zone once fighting concluded on the Red Sea and Gulf of Aden. On April 11, 1941, he overcame the technicalities of the Neutrality Act of 1939, which prohibited American vessels in combat areas, and announced that U.S. ships would supplement and replace overstretched British ships in the Suez area. American merchants could carry supplies through the Suez Canal directly to British forces in Egypt. That FDR was providing all aid short of war heartened the British.

GREEK TRAGEDY

Mussolini hatched another haphazard plan to dominate the Mediterranean by turning to the Balkans and specifically, Greece. He had no designs on Greece when he took Albania in April 1939. But Anglo-French promises to aid the Greeks in the event of an Axis invasion rankled him, as did old Greco-Italian animosities and his fear that Germany would expand its presence in southeastern Europe after having moved troops into Romania. Il Duce determined to preempt Hitler. After he charged Britain with violating Greek neutrality, Italy invaded with four columns from Albania on October 28, 1940. He did so from a weak position. Demobilization of the Italian army was underway, for the harvest at home required manpower. Italians also chafed at the prospects of a long war. Dwindling numbers in his own army and a gross underestimation of Greek military strength did not bode well. The Italians possessed more tanks, heavy guns, and airpower, but their tanks had light armor, and the Air Force had little training in bad weather. Greece had an advantage in artillery, machine guns, and troops once British reinforcements arrived. Four first-line divisions of the Greek Army faced six Italian divisions, though Greek units were larger. In addition, the Royal Air Force arrived with five squadrons, and the Soviets also sent aircraft. Because word of the invasion snuck in through intelligence, Greece mobilized beforehand. As in Africa, lack of preparation and enemy readiness hindered Italian operations.

The weather turned bad, thereby grounding the Italian air force and removing air support for the ground troops. The outcome was not surprising. Within two and half weeks, the Greeks halted the invaders. When General Visconti Prasca panicked, the defenders drove him back across the Albanian border. His replacement, General Ubaldo Soddu, preferred to write musical scores for movies rather than fight and thus took a defensive posture. The Greek commander-in-chief, General Alexandros Papagos, counterattacked against Santa Quaranta and Klissoura; and aided by British bombers based on Greek soil, he then advanced on the Albanian port of Valona. To make matters worse, Britain's Mediterranean Fleet under Admiral Andrew Cunningham made a habit of beating up on the Italian Navy. On November 11, 1940, he raided the Italian base of Taranto with 21 Swordfish biplanes flown off the aircraft carrier *Illustrious* that was stationed 180 miles away. Separated by an hour in time, two waves of planes followed behind flares that illuminated the Italian fleet and diverted antiaircraft guns. Thanks to timely photographic reconnaissance, the British avoided barrage balloons and netting over the battleships and swooped in by total surprise. The Swordfishes torpedoed Italy's three battleships—ruining one beyond repair—hit a cruiser, and damaged the dockyard. Cunningham lost just two planes. The effect of the Taranto mission was huge. It signaled that the battleship era had neared its end; the attack represented the first carrier-based operation against a fleet base in history, a development for which the Japanese took note before their attack on Pearl Harbor. The Italian fleet fled from Taranto to sanctuaries on the west coast, no longer able to threaten Allied convoys chugging through the Mediterranean. The raid was also another blow to Il Duce's rule.

The quest for *mare nostrum* in jeopardy, the fascist regime appeared more farcical by the day. Disaffection toward Mussolini's rule mounted. He could not dispel this sentiment merely by firing Marshal Badoglio; he needed to redeem his recklessness abroad. The double humiliation of Taranto and the Greek counteroffensive also alarmed Hitler. He had cheered on Rome's dreams of lebensraum in North Africa and Egypt as a benefit to Germany's campaign in the east, and he hoped that operations in Greece would mimic his own in Norway. Il Duce's abysmal inability to control the Balkans, however, jeopardized the Romanian oilfields and weakened Germany's southern flank just as Hitler poised to invade the Soviet Union. Recognizing that Mussolini's dictatorship kept Italy in the Axis alliance, the Fuhrer resolved to save his ally and Germany's own pursuit of lebensraum by assuming control of the Balkans theater.

As the Italians met Greek resistance and Graziani retreated in Cyrenaica, the Nazis began to build up a Luftwaffe presence in Bulgaria in November 1940 and sent troops to Romania in January 1941. They had carved up the latter earlier with the help of Hungary, the Soviet Union, and Bulgaria. Hitler now prepared for an assault on Greece, hoping to clear the Balkans of the British as well as the Russians. His mission to Romania included a panzer division, two fighter squadrons, and a motorized infantry division. ULTRA messages revealed his intentions of invading Greece to protect Romanian oil fields, but the real drama played out in Anglo-Greco diplomatic circles. Churchill worried that Athens would make a separate peace with Hitler and bow out of the war. He sent Foreign Secretary Anthony Eden to persuade Yugoslavia and Turkey to block the German invasion of Greece. By early March, Churchill thought he had a Greek pledge to withdraw to a new defensive position, the Aliakmon Line, in return for British reinforcements. But Prime Minister Papagos knew neither Yugoslavia nor Turkey wanted to fight the Nazis, and thus he did not pull back his troops from Thrace.

The initiative was Hitler's as the Balkan situation deteriorated. In February and March 1941, Italian counteroffensives failed on the Albanian border even though the fascists had more men. The Fuhrer had enough. He would overrun Yugoslavia with the Wehrmacht, mass troops inside Bulgaria, and head for the Greek frontier. Perhaps neutral Turkey might also be brought around by being offered a piece of Greek territory. Turkey leaned toward the Allies but served as a major German source of chrome, a critical war commodity used to harden steel. The Fuhrer hoped to master the Balkan situation by negotiation rather than force. On March 25, 1941, Nazi diplomats compelled Yugoslavia to join the Tripartite Pact and permit Germany transit rights, but Serbian air force officers staged a coup, renounced the alliance, and opened a dialogue with British diplomats. Having considered bypassing Yugoslavia, Hitler abandoned diplomacy and decided to smash that country along with Greece undergirded by a strategy of annihilation that Italy had been incapable of wielding in the Balkans and Africa.

Meanwhile, the British scored again against the Italian navy at Cape Matapan, off southern Greece, on March 28. ULTRA intercepts revealed that Italy planned to attack British troop convoys sailing from Egypt to Greece. Admiral Cunningham warned off the convoys and then raced from Alexandria with the British carrier *Formidable,* three battleships that had seen action at the World War I battle of Jutland in 1914, four cruisers, and nine destroyers to engage three Italian battle groups. Cunningham sank three cruisers and two destroyers in a risky night action aided by radar. As the historians Williamson Murray and Allan Millett have written, at this point, Mussolini's "parallel war" in the Mediterranean ended and Italy "was well on the way to becoming a German satellite."

The final straw for Germany was an agreement on strategy by the Greeks and British. Papagos agreed to pull back his troops to the Aliakmon Line. They joined the 6th and 7th Divisions of General Thomas Blamey's Australian I Corps and the New Zealand Division, with supporting tanks and artillery rushed in from the Middle East. Lieutenant-General Maitland Wilson, who had served in Egypt and Cyrenaica, commanded these forces. The Aliakmon Line required 35 divisions for its defense; the Allies had 23 on hand. The RAF provided seven squadrons boosted by two flown in from the Western Desert campaign. Another three and a half Greek divisions stood on the Mataxas Line around Salonika. Despite the agreement, the Allied forces did not match up well to the coming German onslaught.

The Wehrmacht went into action. Germany moved first on Yugoslavia. Outraged by the Serbian coup, Hitler ordered Belgrade razed under the aptly named Operation Punishment. The unmerciful destruction of the city by over 1,000 aircraft imported from as far away as southern France commenced on April 6, 1941. Bombing runs raised the dead to 17,000 people. The Germans also sent in Twelfth Army under Field Marshal

Siegmund List—victor in Poland and France—into southern Yugoslavia and Greece. Two days later, Germans, Italians, and Hungarians swept into Yugoslavia and overran an army of one million men shackled by obsolete equipment and ethnic rivalries, dissent, and mutiny. Croats and Serbs squared off as German infantry and mountain units took Zagreb. It took a mere six days and 151 German dead for Belgrade to fall to panzer units arriving from the north, east, and south. The Yugoslav government followed suit on April 17. Over 330,000 Yugoslavs were captured while a Croat government in Zagreb declared for Germany. Partisan bands cropped up in the mountains as the Wehrmacht quickly withdrew troops needed elsewhere. Regardless of these redeployments, the Germans kept the Balkan nationalists at bay and destroyed the formal Yugoslav Army in a strategy of annihilation that began with Belgrade's bombing and continued with vicious reprisals.

The quick victory permitted List's XL Corps to head from southern Yugoslavia around the Aliakmon Line into Greece while his XVIII Corps wiped aside the fortified Metaxas Line along the frontier with Bulgaria and took Salonika. A gap opened between Greek and British positions, and the Germans surged through. Split from British support, the Greek Army fell into a hopeless state. General Wilson could block an attack from Yugoslavia down the Bardar River Valley, but his left flank lay open. The Wehrmacht pushed the British from the Aliakmon Line before they could dig in. The Germans fought their way past Ptolemais to the south and chased the New Zealand units down the east side of Greece. Wilson withdrew to a new defensive line

German soldiers at the Acropolis in Athens.   Credit: Bundesarchiv, Koblenz, Germany, Bild_1011-165-0419-19A[1].

on April 10 on Mount Olympus. Lacking antiaircraft guns, he ordered British tanks to elevate their guns from hillside positions and shoot at the incoming German aircraft. He inflicted a blow on the Germans at the Olympus Pass four days later, but the Luftwaffe gained air supremacy. The Allies retreated again, across the plains to Thermopylae and Athens. Further resistance deemed pointless; Greek generals in Albania sued for peace.

The British decided to evacuate the same day, April 21, that the Greek Army surrendered to the Germans (and the Italians). Wilson's retreats had been orderly, timely, and punctuated with counterattacks guided by intelligence; he was the first field commander to receive access to ULTRA. Yet he was outnumbered ten to one in the air, his troops were exhausted, and he knew Greece had capitulated. He could do nothing else but depart. Cunningham scraped together 48 troopships as the New Zealand Division and Australian 6th division defended the Thermopylae Line to provide time for the withdrawal. This replay of Dunkirk began the night of April 24–25, 1941 from Athens and the beaches and lasted seven nights. Most troops ended up on the Greek island of Crete and others went to Alexandria. The proximity of both locations allowed the rescue ships to race back for soldiers. The few RAF planes also fled to Crete. Unimpeded by Allied air cover, the Luftwaffe sank two destroyers and four transports with heavy losses. Paratroopers took the Corinth Canal to protect the oil link between Italy and Romania and cut off the 4th New Zealand Brigade from the waiting vessels, but the troops were later picked up. The British evacuation continued to mop up harassed troops for months, but the main operation ended on the night of April 30 and May 1. Over 50,700 men made it out thanks to Royal Navy ships and flying boats. Still, some 7,000 Allied troops surrendered at Kalamata. The evacuees suffered an additional 5,000 casualties.

The Greek episode ended in another Allied loss to Germany and in great suffering for the population. Given responsibility by the Germans to feed the inhabitants, Italy tried to pressure the Bulgarians—who held Greece's most productive areas—to send 100,000 tons of grain. Bulgaria refused, although Yugoslavia, Romania, and Turkey provided foodstuffs. This was not enough, especially after the British sank a German ship carrying additional grain to Greece. As a result, during late 1941 and into much of the next year, a famine (one of the largest in Europe in terms of mortality of the twentieth century) killed over 50,000 people in Athens and Salonica alone until the Red Cross stepped in. A war of annihilation subdued the Greeks.

CRETE

Hitler had no interest in Crete, but Hermann Göring argued that seizing the island would eliminate the Royal Navy's dominance in the eastern Mediterranean. Some 35,000 British Commonwealth and Greek troops faced the Germans. This would be no ordinary landing. Germany could not count on the unreliable Italian Navy to guard surface transports across the Aegean Sea. The Wehrmacht opted instead for Operation Merkur, the first major independent airborne operation in history. They amassed 500 transport aircraft and 100 gliders—backed by 280 bombers, 150 dive bombers, 180 fighters, and 40 reconnaissance planes—for this daring mission.

Nearly 23,000 troops, including 10,000 paratroopers, 5,000 mountain soldiers, and 750 glider troops, were dropped from the air. The rest came by sea.

Crete's mountainous terrain made the Allied defense difficult as did the lack of heavy weapons, transport, and signals equipment, scarce aircraft cover, and coherent command and control. Lieutenant-General Bernard Freyberg, a highly decorated First World War veteran and notably relaxed commander of the New Zealand Division, led the Crete defense by spreading out his scanty resources. He had 28,000 weary troops and 14,000 ill-equipped Greeks. Nonetheless, morale was high, and the British troops were top notch. ULTRA gave Freyberg knowledge of Operation Merkur's objectives of seizing the airfields of Maleme, Haraklion, and Retimo after the Germans bombed, landed paratroopers, and reinforced the island of Milos. But it turned out that he could not use the information for fear of revealing ULTRA's existence. He also focused during the first day on a purported assault from the sea rather than the air. Freyberg's resistance was plagued by misjudgment and German perseverance.

For a day and a half, the British held on as vicious fighting swept the airfields. German paratroopers and gliders encountered thunderous antiaircraft batteries, and once on the ground, their radios did not work. Commonwealth forces repulsed the invaders at Milos by air and sea bombardments and bitterly contested the Heraklion and Retimo airstrips. Yet German airpower was overwhelming. After the 22nd New Zealand Battalion retreated from a hill overlooking the Maleme airfield, the Luftwaffe landed the 5th Mountain Division the next day. The Germans took the Maleme field on May 21, 1941 after muscling aside the one battalion watching over it. The Royal Navy did its job of denying reinforcements by chasing away the Italian escorts of captured Greek vessels that carried German soldiers, but Luftwaffe pressure intensified on the New Zealanders east of Canea. The Retimo airfield defenders soon surrendered. His position desperate, on May 26, Freyberg got permission to evacuate to Egypt. He ordered a retreat southward across Crete to Sphakia while arranging for warships to evacuate troops surrounding Heraklion. At Sphakia, after the Luftwaffe sunk three cruisers and six destroyers and damaged 17 other vessels, the evacuation was suspended on May 30. This left 5,000 Allied soldiers on the island, some of whom joined a resistance movement while the majority entered Axis prison camps.

The losses from the Crete campaign were staggering on all sides. The Allies suffered 1,742 killed and missing, 2,225 injured, and 11,370 taken prisoner. The Royal Navy lost 2,000 killed and 183 wounded. About 18,000 troops were rescued, but the harm done to the British Army and Navy was immense. German deaths numbered around 7,000 soldiers; the 7th Airborne Division lost more men than in the Greek and Yugoslav campaigns combined. This grim lesson persuaded the Nazis never again to undertake a major independent airborne operation against enemy-held territory. The Crete operation also did not attain the desired strategic possibilities, except by perpetuating the strategy of annihilation. For the residents, starvation constantly menaced. As well, the Germans shipped off about 200 Cretan Jews to their deaths at the hands of an Allied submarine attack. Those that survived were liquidated in Nazi concentration camps. The island proved to be a dead-end for Allied,

Axis, and civilian participants alike. Greece itself fell under a merciless occupation by Germany and Italy until 1944. People turned on their neighbors, the SS seized Jews for transport to death camps, and massacres were prevalent—a harsh reminder of the wages of war.

The loss of Crete undermined Britain's strategic position in the Balkans. The British could have harassed Romanian oil passing through the Aegean Sea and assailed that nation's oil fields. Also, Greece's resistance fighters might have been supplied from Crete. None of these scenarios were possible, as the Germans saved the day from the Italians and altered the balance of power in the region. With the Balkans under German control, Romania's oil was secure. The British had badly blundered by frittering away Wavell's Middle Eastern reserves to a losing cause. They had refused to engage in a futile rescue of Poland, but they tried to help Greece and failed abysmally. Churchill had gallantly fought for an ally, but the Greek campaign had weakened his military. Despite victories in East Africa, theaters in Libya and Egypt were exposed to German power. It was questionable whether the Royal Navy could protect the Middle East should the Fuhrer seek a campaign there. A pro-Nazi coup in Iraq further alarmed the British. They had opened the door to German penetration in the Western Desert and risked lifelines of supply in the Middle East. Most doubted that the Balkans merited the military debacle experienced by the Allies.

ROMMEL IN NORTH AFRICA

And now the Third Reich turned its attention to North Africa. The Germans were commanded by Erwin Rommel, whose humble background and heroic blitzkrieg across France had endeared him to Hitler. This former infantryman believed in armored warfare, and he aimed to put theories into practice in North Africa and the Middle East. His cunning and daring in the field soon earned him the nickname of the "Desert Fox." Rommel also greatly irritated his aristocratic superiors in the Wehrmacht. A desert campaign held no interest for them; they were in the process of planning the attack on the USSR. But Rommel's nominal superior was the Italian Comando Supremo Italo Gariboldi. Thus, the Desert Fox could act with impunity and cause consternation in Berlin. As Rommel pushed boldly into British lines, Wehrmacht staff officers feared he had gone off half-cocked in a dangerous foray. They sent to Rommel's headquarters in Libya Lieutenant-General Friedrich Paulus to urge caution in the desert. Rommel, however, was far from crazed, and far from cautious.

Contrary to British expectations, Rommel moved instantly. Wavell's forces that occupied Cyrenaica had been pulled away to Greece, leaving behind a feeble screening force under Lieutenant-General Philip Neame. The Middle East command predicted through ULTRA that Rommel would sit until May 1941 under orders from his superiors. On February 14, German troops disembarked in Tripoli Harbor, but Rommel saw no reason to hang around. After taking a reconnaissance flight over enemy territory, he ordered unloading to continue through the night. The next morning, Rommel assembled the troops and within a few days later, his tanks had moved 350 miles east. "The enemy can only run away from us," he wrote home. Placing the Italian Ariete Division under his German Afrika Corps and ignoring orders from his superiors (including

The Desert Fox.   Credit: Center for the Study of War Experience at Regis University, Denver, Colorado: U.S. National Archive photo. ARC Identifier 540148 / Local Identifier 242-EAPC-6(M713a).

Hitler), Rommel went on a rampage that made him the stuff of legend. Within a week of landing at Tripoli, he ordered reconnaissance eastward to Nofilia and then pushed farther down the coast to capture El Agheila on March 24, 1941 and Mersa Brega a week later. Comando Supremo Gariboldi berated him for disobeying orders from Rome to halt and conserve supplies. But Rommel would not let good opportunities go by, and he flatly refused to stop even if the full complement of forces had not yet arrived from Germany. He divided his forces into three prongs to dash into Cyrenaica. When his troops slowed, he dropped messages from his Storch airplane warning them that if they did not move at once, he would land and punish them.

The Luftwaffe flew from Sicily to neutralize the port of Benghazi, which Rommel seized in April 1941. To trick the British into thinking he had overwhelming numbers, the Desert Fox placed dummy tanks on Volkswagen frames. With the enemy on the run, he swept past Tobruk, captured Neame—and Lieutenant-General O'Connor to boot— and drove to Sollum. The Germans thereby retook all of the territory that O'Connor himself had conquered in the months before. The Luftwaffe now besieged the island of Malta from its North African airfields. As Rommel drove the British from Cyrenaica, he took aim on the Suez Canal itself. He reached the Egyptian border, although the British clung to Tobruk, which threatened his supply lines. The offensive not only shot Rommel to fame in Germany but it attracted the attention of King Farouk of Egypt, who secretly urged the Germans to rid him of British rule. Concerned about this possibility,

Churchill held back more troops in Egypt originally planned for dispatch to the Greek campaign.

In late April, 1941, German General Paulus arrived in Libya. While he agreed with Rommel that another attempt on British-held Tobruk should occur, Paulus doubted Egypt could be taken. He advised a defensive strategy and constraints by Berlin on Rommel. The siege of Tobruk lasted until the end of 1941. The Desert Fox assumed that the British wished to evacuate, so he hit Tobruk hard. But in a theater where supply lines stretched for hundreds of miles, Rommel faced a grave logistical weakness. His main supply depot was 900 miles away in Tripoli; the Allies used Alexandria and Cairo, a short distance from Tobruk. Rommel could shorten his supply chain by taking Tobruk, but without it, he had to build a bypass road (completed in three months) to advance into Egypt. Tobruk remained a nuisance, as the garrison held out under the resilient Australian 9th Division.

Churchill knew through ULTRA that Paulus counseled against the idea of bypassing Tobruk and shooting into Egypt. The Prime Minister saw an opportunity to reverse the British plight in North Africa by a counteroffensive against Rommel. He ordered two operations under theater commander Archibald Wavell. Operation Brevity began on May 15, 1941, and Battleaxe followed a month later. Both operations were premature, both badly planned and carried out, both worsened by terrible radio security, and both encountered Rommel's tactic of converting the 88 mm antiaircraft guns to an antitank weapon. It took the British a long time to adjust to this weapon. Drawing on the newly arrived 15th Panzer Division, the Desert Fox handled the Brevity operation quite easily. In three days, ending on June 17, he also beat back Battleaxe by defeating the attackers at Sollum, near the Halfaya Pass. His only regret was that the 5th Light and 15th Panzer Divisions had not sealed the British in a pocket to destroy their offensive capabilities. While Rommel lost just 25 tanks, the British left 220 tanks on the battlefield. The Desert Fox went up to the front to thank his troops, rejoicing in the rousing victory and the news that Churchill viewed the Sollum engagement as a crushing loss.

Wavell had failed miserably. A frustrated Churchill fired him for the defeat, but he was on the way out anyway after expressing doubts about the Battleaxe plan. His criticism had been justified. Defeats in Greece and Crete, plus the diversion of overthrowing the pro-Nazi regime in Iraq and blocking Vichy French forces from Syria, had depleted British power in the Middle East. Lieutenant-General Claude Auchinleck became the Commander-in-Chief Middle East Command two weeks later. "Auk" was a participant in the Norwegian campaign, organizer of the Home Guard before the battle of Britain, and had suppressed the Iraqi insurgency. Like Wavell, he decided on a slow buildup of strength against Rommel. Churchill reluctantly agreed.

Fighting in the Western Desert swung back and forth along the North African coast, dependent on which side had been reinforced with supplies. The desert was unforgiving; neither side counted on protection from its harsh conditions and vast distances. Logistics were the key. The Germans sustained forward bases with goods brought in through Tripoli while the British relied on Alexandria as their depot. Germany could not go too far eastward without stringing out its supply lines and exposing them to British air power from Egypt. The British paused before heading toward Benghazi or Tobruk because Rommel enjoyed good air coverage. In June 1941, the Germans had the edge even though Rommel's panzer force in Libya did not grow beyond three divisions until December 1942. The British were simply overextended, weak, and poorly equipped. Rommel was efficient, daring, and skilled—but also had to rely on secure supply lines. In the desert, a campaign of attrition rather than one of annihilation took place.

By the time Hitler initiated his war of annihilation against the Soviet Union in June 1941, logistics were clearly the challenge for Germany and Britain in the North African western desert. Auchinleck's appointment on July 1 came at a critical juncture in the fight against Rommel's panzers. He would not budge until ready and demanded a 50% reserve of tanks. Throughout the Summer and Fall of 1941 months, he constructed his forces for an offensive. Called Operation Crusader, this engagement with Rommel involved Alan Cunningham who was fresh from the liberation of Ethiopia. Except for holding Tobruk, Rommel dominated Libya, having nearly surrounded the British Eighth Army in June. His big weakness lay not in the sands but out at sea. German supply lines were vulnerable owing to the Italian Navy's inability to wrest the Mediterranean from British control and protect German convoys from British air and naval attacks from Malta.

With a restructured Eighth Army, also known as the Western Desert Force, Auchinleck unleashed Cunningham and Crusader on November 18, 1941. The goal was to extract the garrison at Tobruk and join other infantry and tanks in a sweep westward across eastern Libya. Cunningham called for an infantry advance along the coast in tandem with a tank thrust inland into Germany's newly named Panzer Group Africa, or Afrika Korps. Rommel had other ideas. He would capture Tobruk and rid this obstacle at long last from his path to Egypt. The British changed his plans, however. Cunningham's tanks advanced in such superior force—quadruple the number of the Afrika Korps—that the Desert Fox turned to defense. But Eighth Army's tanks dissipated in separate, unsupported attacks, and the British offensive stalled. Rommel then made his own stand on Sidi Rezegh, a ridge 20 miles southeast of Tobruk.

The bloody battle for Sidi Rezegh swung back and forth. The British captured the ridge, but when the 7th Armored Brigade tried to move beyond it, the Afrika Korps blocked its way. Rommel retook the ridge and almost destroyed the British unit in the process. Cunningham rushed in the 1st South African Division, and the battle turned more vicious. Joined by the Italian Ariete Armored Division, the Germans nearly wiped out a South African infantry brigade and its supply route on November 23. The battlefield presented a woeful picture. A soldier in the 6th Field Regiment of the New Zealand Artillery noted that "we were helpless, we could not fire, our own troops and trucks were all around the area and the German tanks advanced behind a shield of dust and Kiwi prisoners. Not a target for our guns. Each man sat or knelt at his post, many wished that we could at least fire, but it was just wicked to sit there and watch. Our Regiment was being cut up." The battle went down in German history as the Totensonntag or "Sunday of the Dead," the day when German Protestants prayed for the souls of the departed. It was the British who needed divine help, however. Convinced Crusader had failed, Cunningham asked Auchinleck for permission to withdraw. Auk refused and replaced him with his deputy chief of staff, Major-General Neil Ritchie on November 26, 1941. Meanwhile, Rommel charged for the Egyptian border to spell the German posts at Bardia and Halfaya Pass, which Crusader had isolated. Both positions guarded the coastal plains. Bardia, an anchor of the German defense, had withstood two British offensives. It now experienced a third.

When Rommel impulsively defended Halfaya Pass on November 26, the New Zealand Division captured Sidi Rezegh. Then British forces broke out of Tobruk. Alarmed, Rommel turned around and headed westward to Sidi Rezegh. Neither Allied infantry nor tanks could help the New Zealanders. On December 1, the Afrika Korps retook the ridge, overwhelmed South African and New Zealand troops, and closed off the route to besieged Tobruk. But the slugging match had depleted the Desert Fox's forces and supplies. Having lost half his tanks on the ridge, he pulled back on December 8 as Crusader ended. The battle for Sidi Rezegh caused high casualties on both sides. About 15% of British and Commonwealth troops—17,700 of the 118,000 who participated in Crusader—fell to the Germans. Some 20% of the Afrika Korps, or 24,500 men, were killed, injured, or missing. When the British captured the frontier posts of Bardia and Halfaya Pass in January, they netted 13,800 prisoners.

It appeared as if the British had won the day; but in the desert war, fortunes turned quickly. Rommel retreated back to El Agheila in Cyrenaica. German U-boats and a larger Luftwaffe presence in the central Mediterranean soon secured supply lines for the Afrika Korps. Hitler ordered the Second Air Force under Field Marshal Albert Kesselring to the Mediterranean from Russia. Energized by the extra fuel and tanks, Rommel dashed Auk's hopes of invading Tripolitania (western Libya). On January 21, 1942, he raided Mersa Brega. Panzers drove the British backward, all the way to Gazala. True to form, the Desert Fox ignored orders to halt and captured Benghazi before running out of steam. The British were in disarray. Their Cyrenaica airfields were lost again and their effectiveness against German convoys was somewhat neutralized. Auchinleck again decided on a slow buildup of forces before renewing the effort in the western desert. After all, the North African theater was larger than the Eastern Front but engaged far smaller forces. In the desert, both sides settled in to wait out the winter rains until Spring 1942.

The battle for the Mediterranean had seesawed back and forth. That the military engagements in the area were a distraction for Hitler was all too true, and the Middle East proved of negligible consequence to the overall war. For instance, the Royal Navy shifted supply routes from the Suez Canal to the South Africa's Cape of Good Hope. Although this imposed heavy penalties on a maritime fleet stretched to breaking by sinkings and increased wartime demands, the rerouting nullified Italy's ability to impede British shipping through the Mediterranean. Hitler thought of his friend Mussolini as an incompetent, but even the Fuhrer made mistakes with his unnecessary brutality in the Balkans. The region boiled in ethnic and class conflict, fueled by the ruthless German occupiers who hauled out food and raw materials with little regard for the human condition. Moreover, as Jews in Yugoslavia and Greece fled to the Italian zone to avoid being annihilated, the Germans increasingly criticized Italy's lack of anti-Semitism. Italy rejected Nazi racial policies and refused to persecute the Jews as the SS and Wehrmacht rounded up undesirables in the spring of 1941 and initiated their program of extermination the following fall. Thus, another fissure opened between the Axis powers, as Germany's Mediterranean campaign came to mimic the impending one in the east that Hitler had long relished.

CHAPTER 9

Attack on the Soviet Union

Five white bodies lay facedown in the white snow. A family of winter dead, the dead father still clutching his dead wife's hand, their dead children sprawled a short distance away.

DAVID BENIOFF
City of Thieves

LEBENSRAUM

Hitler was unwavering in his ambitions. In his book *Mein Kampf,* he had explained that lebensraum, or living space for the German population, depended on the subjugation of the USSR to provide oil, metals, food, and a labor base for the Third Reich. Comprised largely of Slavs, Jews, communists, and other "subhumans," the Soviet Union had no place in his worldview other than as slaves or enemies to be annihilated. The decision to invade the USSR proved to be the most momentous decision of World War II. It shaped the military calculations of the Axis and Allies thereafter. The Nazi-Soviet Pact was a marriage of convenience that provided mutual trade benefits—the Soviets sold the Germans raw materials and food and received finished goods in return. The Germans never fulfilled their export quotas, but Stalin was more than diligent. He sent more grain, cotton, and oil than called for in the agreement. He was either buying time for mobilization or oblivious to the gathering storm. Historical debate persists over the motivations behind his meekness, but it is clear that Stalin badly miscalculated. Hitler's Operation Barbarossa represented one of the great deceptions in history.

Named after Red Beard—the Holy Roman Emperor Frederick I who crusaded against the Muslims in the twelfth century—Barbarossa spawned the largest armed conflict on a single front in human history. The Soviets called this clash the Great Patriotic War. For nearly four years, two massive armies swept across vast areas in a front that ran over 1,700 miles long stretching from the Barents Sea in the north to the Black Sea in the south. Ten million troops engaged in battle. Roughly 80% of the entire Wehrmacht took part in the campaign, joined by Finns, Hungarians, Italians, and Romanians. Taken together, Barbarossa led to over half of the total deaths of World War II. From its very inception, the Eastern front (the German term) epitomized the strategy of annihilation and total war.

Barbarossa's objective was simple: rapidly destroy the Soviet military as close to the border as possible and then encircle the remaining enemy forces and subdue the entire country within eight to ten weeks. The USSR would merely cease to exist west of the Ural Mountains. Opposed to an extended war, Germany aimed to level such a massive blow on the Soviet military that the entire Stalinist structure would keel over in a matter of months. The Luftwaffe worried over supporting ground troops over vast distances, and the German Foreign Office opposed the whole idea of the invasion, but the Fuhrer believed that he could wipe out the world's largest state. His enthusiasm soon infected the usually sober thinking of the Wehrmacht. Historians argue about his intentions in World War II. It seems clear that he cared less about engaging the Western powers, prioritizing the obliteration of the USSR, communism, and the Jews instead. Crossing the English Channel could await the defeat of the Soviet Union., Barbarossa was Adolf Hitler's holy war.

The Soviets (and their future allies) engaged in misjudgments and self-deception when it came to Hitler's dream. Stalin was familiar with the Fuhrer's geopolitical views and ideology. As a result, he organized a defense on three fronts along the western border. Yet he also watched as the German war machine mobilized against him. The invasion of eastern Poland had actually weakened the USSR's forward defenses, which were in the process of being rebuilt on the new frontier. With such deficiencies in mind, Stalin refused to help the Yugoslavs against the German onslaught. When the Wehrmacht flooded into Poland in 1941, in preparation for Barbarossa, he called the action merely spring maneuvers. He downplayed the German threat and continued his long-standing appeasement of Hitler with more trade and other concessions to buy time for military preparedness. The Red Army also erred. Intelligence did not monitor Wehrmacht deployments despite Anglo-American advice gleaned from Polish information. The Red Army supposed that an attack would come from the southwest as Hitler tried to seize the resources of Ukraine and the oil-rich Caucasus. Thus, it diverted its strength there and away from what would be the main line of German attack. The Soviet General Staff, moreover, did not believe that the Wehrmacht could deploy in less than two weeks. So, the Russians would have plenty of time to respond. But the climate of fear Stalin had created paralyzed the military and intelligence services, causing this colossus to stumble badly in practice. The British also miscalculated, believing up to ten days before Barbarossa began that Berlin had no intention of attacking as long as its diplomatic negotiations with the USSR continued in Moscow.

For their part, the Germans scrutinized the plan at the highest levels. Operational planning began after the defeat of France and then map exercises took place in Fall 1940. In December, the Wehrmacht High Command argued with the Fuhrer over the invasion's direction. Hitler wanted the troops to thrust into the center. After breaking through enemy lines, the armies would split. Some forces would head for the industrialized Baltic north, and others would move on the resource-rich south and the Black Sea oil fields. His generals preferred a drive straight for Moscow. In either case, the Red Army west of the Dvina and Dneiper Rivers had to be crushed to allow Germany a permanent footing on the Volga River Line running from Archangel in the far north down to Astrakhan on the Caspian Sea. This would secure the critical resources of the Donets Basin as well as a base to seize Moscow, the USSR's political heart.

Logistical headaches abounded as the Germans brought in war materiel from all over Europe and calculated the complexities of supplying troops over hundreds of miles. Planners worried about weather, terrain, and condition of the roads, but they assumed that the Wehrmacht was so superior to the Red Army that any problems could be overcome. The High Command instructed troops to forage for food and fodder once they had penetrated deeply into the Soviet Union. This made abuse of the civilian populations, and a campaign of annihilation,more likely. Also, railroad repair troops did not receive much attention, though they were essential to the supply lines. Railroads were critical to limiting Soviet supplies and maintaining lifelines to Germany. Fuel was also important; but of the 103 Army divisions that began the war, only 16 were fully motorized. To a surprising degree, the Wehrmacht depended on horse-drawn transport. There was little need to obsess over logistics, Hitler surmised, if the Third Reich's victory was quick.

BARBAROSSA

After two postponements due to a late thaw and the diversion of German troops to the Balkans, Hitler sent over 3.6 million troops supported by 3,350 tanks and 2,770 aircraft across the Soviet border on June 22, 1941. These numbers far exceeded those in France, Poland, and North Africa; the aircraft alone represented 60% of the Luftwaffe's entire fleet. Six hours later, the German ambassador in Moscow delivered a declaration of war; but by that time, the largest force in European military history had raced ahead in Operation Barbarossa.

The three-pronged invasion on a broad front was led by the Field Marshal Walter von Brauchitsch. Army Group Center under Field Marshal Fedor von Bock, recipient of the Knight's Cross for his role in defeating Poland and participant in the blitzkrieg across Western Europe, led Fourth and Ninth Armies and 2nd and 3rd Panzer Groups from Warsaw toward Minsk and Smolensk. Commanding the most powerful of the three armies, Bock had designs on Moscow. General Wilhelm Ritter von Leeb's Army Group North came out of East Prussia, with the 4th Panzer Group and Sixteenth and Eighteenth Armies directed toward the Baltic and Leningrad. Leeb was a reluctant participant, having counseled against war with the USSR. Just as lukewarm toward Hitler but rewarded for service in Poland and the west, the highly respected General Gerd von Rundstedt headed from Czechoslovakia and Hungary for the Soviet grain center of Ukraine and then to Sevastopol on the Black Sea. His Army Group South included Eleventh and Seventeenth Armies, 1st Panzer Group, Third and Fourth Romanian Armies, and Hungarian forces. The three Army Groups—153 divisions in all—enjoyed support from three air fleets.

The Red Army faced the Germans with over 4 million troops, 2.9 million of which had been deployed in western defense in army groups, or *fronts,* with a half million in reserve. The troops were stationed north from the Pripet Marshes to the Baltic and south to the Black Sea. Stalin committed most of his military on this line to prevent the Germans from taking Ukraine and Moscow. Backing the ground troops were 7,500 old, slow aircraft, hindered by a confused command structure, and nearly 10,000 tanks. This represented 90% of the total number of planes and armor in the Soviet arsenal. Booming military production since 1939 yielded the USSR an enormous storehouse of guns, artillery pieces and mortars, tanks, and aircraft.

Stalin had weakened his forces, however, although it is debatable whether he could have stopped the blitzkrieg in any case. Because his purges had gutted its leadership ranks, the Red Army struggled to reinject initiative into noncommissioned and junior officers, coordinate units, and organize staffs. Despite the factory output, the Red Army had not been properly reequipped after the Winter War. It even lacked accurate maps of the USSR itself, which had been altered to thwart invaders. Stalin had also eliminated armored formations in 1939, requiring his military leaders to spend time rebuilding. Bureaucratic rivalry and command disorganization hampered intelligence analysis after German mobilization and Luftwaffe overflights had been detected in early 1941. Regarding tactics, the Red Army spread out its tanks superficially over an immense stretch of territory and packed the troops too close to the border. Soviet armies also focused in the south, vitiating an effective response in the country's center and north. More immediately, Stalin refused to acknowledge the imminent attack with a war alert until late June 21, just hours before the launching of Barbarossa. Full deployment might have slowed the Wehrmacht.

In hindsight, the Soviets bungled in the face of German power and skill. Some analysts argue that by pulling forces deeper into the Soviet Union, the Red Army could have marshaled a more concerted counterstrike. Others suggest that Russian forces should have been concentrated on the border to halt the Wehrmacht in its tracks. Still others believe that a more elastic mobile defensive posture, rather than opportunistic offensive jabs, might have worked. Marshal Georgi Zhukov later reflected that the main error arose from miscalculating the date of Germany's attack. In any case, Stalin settled on a grueling war of attrition. The problem was that the Germans roared through Soviet defensive lines, intent on effecting the strategy of annihilation by wiping out the Red Army in such quick order as to render attrition irrelevant.

When Barbarossa commenced on June 22, the Luftwaffe gained total control of the air after bombing the Soviet planes lined up in neat rows. Fliegerkorps IV destroyed 142 aircraft on the ground and 16 in the air in its first strikes. The USSR began its stand with 7,500 aircraft; by noon of the first day, it lost over 1,200 combat aircraft, another 1,800 the next day, and still 2,000 more by the sixth day of the invasion. Ordered to hold the western sector and counterattack by the acting Soviet Commander-in-Chief, Marshal Semyon Timoshenko, Red Army units were decimated before they even knew they were at war. The speed of the attack overwhelmed the chain of command paralyzed by stunned officers. The world's largest air force lay in tatters and exposed the devastation of the purges and the hollowness of Stalinist propaganda regarding Soviet power. In five days, the Germans arrived in Lithuania and Latvia. After a week, as the Goebbels propaganda machine blurted, "the Fuhrer's offensive has smashed the Red Army to splinters" and the USSR lay "like a limp virgin, in the mighty arms of the German Mars."

Army Group Center's two panzer groups undertook a double pincer movement 155 miles apart on parallel tracks that enveloped Bialystok. Ordered to stand his ground

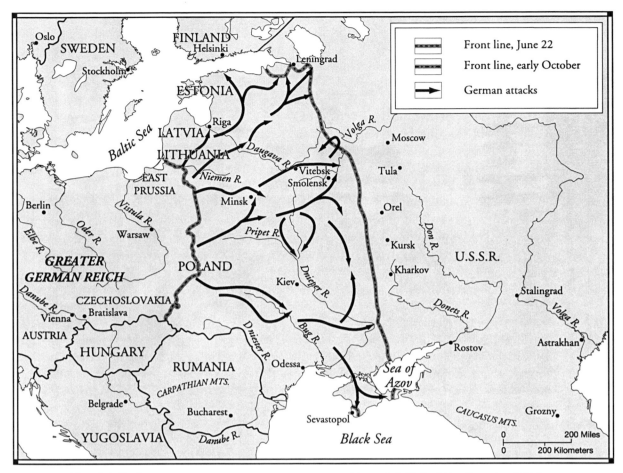

Map 9.1 Barbarossa.   Credit: Ronald Story, *Concise Historical Atlas of World War II: The Geography of Conflict,* Map 15, p. 35.

with his Western *front*, General D. G. Pavlov lost touch with his field commanders and superiors in Moscow as German commandos destroyed radio stations. The Luftwaffe took a mere 16 hours to separate the north and northwestern fronts. Hermann Hoth's 3rd and Heinz Guderian's 2nd Panzer Divisions pushed onward after discovering the chaos in the Soviet lines. They let the infantry close the Bialystok pocket while they sealed off Minsk on June 29. Russian soldiers fought on, unaware they were surrounded. Under orders to keep feeding in units despite the German encirclement, Pavlov mentally collapsed.

Disaster was at hand. The panzers moved 200 miles in a week, netting 328,000 prisoners, 3,300 tanks, and 1,800 artillery pieces. With infantry in tow, they reached the Smolensk gap—a 50-mile wide entryway to Moscow between the Dneiper and Dvina Rivers—a week later. The columns of armor seemed endless. Stalin recalled Pavlov to Moscow ,where the unfortunate General, his chief of staff, and artillery and intelligence chiefs were executed. Such brutal scapegoating disguised the fact that the dictator himself had nearly suffered a nervous breakdown over the shock of Barbarossa. Stalin despaired especially over the fall of Minsk and disappeared from view for a few weeks, as the fall of the USSR was imminent. He then emerged from hiding on July 3. Voicing martial rhetoric rather than the usual socialist utterances, Stalin called for a patriotic war of scorched earth policies and partisan warfare against the Nazis. The new commander of the Western front and a veteran of World War I, the civil war, and the Winter War, Marshal Timoshenko, put up determined resistance outside of the Smolensk gap with five armies.

They fought bravely, but with the help of the Fourth Air Fleet, Germany's Hoth thrust along the Dvina to occupy the north side of the gap. Guderian attacked across the Dneiper to the south. On July 16, Smolensk was in the Wehrmacht's hands. Timoshenko's troops dug in to prevent the two panzer groups from uniting, but he could not hold. The Germans closed the Smolensk gap on August 5. As Stuka dive-bombers leveled villages, the invaders captured another 310,000 men and an additional 38,000 south of the gap as well as 3,205 tanks and 3,000 guns. Soviet resolve was no match for the Germans who stood 220 miles from Moscow.

Meanwhile, the northern prong of the German fork stabbed into soft Soviet defenses. Capturing the old fortress of Shlisselburg at the conjunction of the Neva River and Lake Ladoga to the west of Leningrad, 4th Panzer Group under Erich Hoepner cut the city's land contact with Moscow. Leeb believed that by combining with Finnish forces moving around the lake toward Leningrad, Army Group North could seize this major urban area. But the Finns refused to advance farther south than the Svir River, the pre-1940 boundary 26 miles from Leningrad that divided Finland and the USSR, realizing the potential folly in arousing Soviet ire. Still, the city was isolated from the north. General Nikolaus von Falkenhorst, conquering commander of Norway, bogged down in bad weather before Murmansk, but the Germans stood at the gates of Leningrad in mid-August. The Russians began a Dunkirk-style evacuation, although the defenses held. If they had not, Stalin well understood that the Germans could outflank and envelop Moscow.

Hitler was convinced about victory. He stripped Leeb of the 4th Panzer Division staff and half of its tanks to assault Moscow and ordered the destruction of Leningrad. What the Germans did not destroy in Leningrad, the birthplace of Russian communism, starvation and disease would. The Soviets shipped out treasures from palaces and museums, and rations were reduced to a little more than a pound of bread a day for workers and half that for children. Food reserves neared exhaustion. Shipments entered sporadically but were inadequate to the task of feeding those stranded in the city. Still, residents manned antiaircraft positions on rooftops. There would be no surrender, either by the USSR or on Germany's part. Thus in September began the horrific 900-day siege of Leningrad, an event beyond the boundaries of humanity. The worst of the suffering occurred from November 1941 to January 1942, as 200,000 people died from hunger and diseases caused by malnutrition. Some subsisted on dogs, rats, and even wallpaper glue. Cannibalism occurred frequently. Citizens lived and died in a horrible war of annihilation.

Dead civilians in the streets of Leningrad.   Credit: Center for the Study of War Experience at Regis University, Denver, Colorado.

Barbarossa rapidly turned into a vicious campaign of survival for the Soviets and ruthless extermination on the part of the Germans. The USSR adopted scorched earth tactics as the only way left to boost morale and prevent the Germans from foraging. Chiang Kai-shek had acted similarly in 1938 when he flooded the Yellow River to slow the Japanese And tens of thousands of Chinese had perished as a result. Just as mercilessly, Moscow issued a stream of propaganda urging a fanatical defense of the homeland. "Teach them implacable hatred and rage against the enemy, ardently to crush the Fascist cur, to grind his face into the earth, to be prepared to fight to the last drop of their blood for every inch of Soviet soil," proclaimed one directive. Soldiers must stand up to tanks; desertion, retreat, and even panic were punishable by death. According to law, a corpse not identified or lost (to fire, rats, or explosion) was considered a deserter. The Red Army burned or removed everything in the German path—factories, towns, crops in fields. In battle after battle, soldiers fought with weapons and when those were gone, their bare hands. Whole divisions vanished, ground to dust by the Wehrmacht machine. German sharpshooters picked off the commissars of the Communist Party who ordered the Red Army soldiers to their deaths.

German soldiers were freed from any legal restraints on their behavior because the USSR was not a signatory to the Geneva conventions regarding humane treatment of noncombatants. But pure hatred and racism, rather than a neglect of legal niceties, drove the Nazi's furious attack. The Wehrmacht—and not just the SS—instigated a reign of murder. The military executed Red Army political commissars and civilians and committed other atrocities as it engaged the strategy of annihilation. General von Gunther von Kluge, a hero of the Polish campaign, ordered women prisoners in uniform to be shot. Despite a countermand from Berlin, soldiers performed the deed. Any civilian who aided the Red Army was executed under directives from the diligent Hitlerite Wilhelm Keitel, chief of the Armed Forces. Estimates show that Germany took 5.1 million Soviet prisoners into mid-1944, the point at which reliable figures on captives stops. Some 3.3 million died. (By then, the strategy of annihilation was used by both sides; 90–95% of German prisoners of war in the USSR did not survive). Many soldiers refused these commands, and some senior officers tried to moderate the policies. Others recognized the barbarity, but, in the words of one young German soldier, "[w]e were the victors. War excused our thefts, encouraged cruelty, and the need to survive didn't go around getting permission from conscience." In the end, efforts at leniency failed mainly because this was a pitiless campaign. The weak suffered at the hands of the oblivious, hungry, homesick, but focused German soldiers conditioned by Nazi racism and intent on carrying out orders from ideologues. The Nazi way of war lowered the threshold of acceptable behavior in terms of atrocities committed in the name of military victory.

Far to the south Rundstedt's forces also rolled toward Kiev, the capital of Ukraine. At the fore of Army Group South was the 1st Panzer Group under General Ewald von Kleist, a superb field commander in Poland, France, and Yugoslavia who did not embrace Nazism. Reaching the outer defensive ring of the city on July 11 and turning south along the Dneiper River, the Germans had gone 248 miles in just 18 days. The ecstatic generals abandoned their original plan of constraint shaped by logistical worries of limited means, and raced onward. But they bogged down after encountering the Soviet southwest *front*—four well-equipped armies under Lieutenant-General M. P. Kirponov. Kleist lacked the resources to encircle Kiev in early August, even though he pushed along the Dnieper. Exhausted troops rested and ate ravenously, mulling over such horrors as seeing their comrades' brains blown out by shells during their recent march to the Dnieper.

A cocky but frustrated Hitler now made the first of several critical decisions. Because aggression in the Rhineland, Czechoslovakia, Poland, Scandinavia, and France had worked, he was sure of his own infallibility as a military strategist. Contrary to the wishes of his generals, the Fuhrer halted Army Group Center's advance toward Moscow on July 29 and ordered a shift south toward Kiev. Guderian, and others urged Hitler to focus on Moscow, the economic and political solar plexus of the USSR. Its capture would have a huge psychological effect on Soviet citizens as well as the rest of the world. Besides, Army Group Center was poised to advance on Moscow. Changing now would waste time and point the Wehrmacht in the wrong direction. Hitler valued Ukraine's land and minerals and the Caucasus oilfields. He also worried about ending the war by winter, for the campaign had drained troops and materiel. There was only one winner in this argument. While Bock mopped up around Smolensk, the Fuhrer transferred 2nd Panzer Group to Rundstedt for an attack on Kiev, the birthplace of Russia.

On August 25, Guderian headed to Romny, 125 miles east of Kiev, to begin a pincer movement with Kleist's 1st Panzer Group. Once Guderian crossed the Desna River, which was the last natural obstacle before Kiev, Kleist's forces shot north from Kremenchug 160 miles downstream from Kiev. The two panzer groups met at Romny on September 16, thus closing the circle around Kiev and its 665,000 Russian soldiers. Kirponov's troops might have broken out because they were not in the way of the encircling panzers, but Stalin would not let them abandon the city. Luckily, the USSR gained some breathing room as the Germans moved their armies alongside and parallel to the *fronts* rather than directly into them. Hitler had his victory, and a vicious occupation commenced, but the German advance slowed.

In Ukraine, the SS and Wehrmacht demonstrated the horrors of Nazism by putting into practice the most evil elements of the strategy of annihilation. On September 29–30, 1941, at the Babi Yar a ravine outside of Kiev, 33,000 Jews were slaughtered. This was the largest single massacre during the entire Holocaust by the SS. Western European Jews had been deprived of civil liberties; but for the moment, they were safe from physical harm. Not so for Eastern European Jewry. The SS killing squads, or Einsatzgruppen, oftentimes worked in tandem with the Wehrmacht, local police, and Axis allies. They massacred nearly one million people during the first 6 months of Barbarossa, partly fulfilling preinvasion plans for mass killings. Particularly vulnerable were those in cities, such as the Jews of Kiev. Thousands of others died in ditches, fields, and pits throughout the rural areas of the Soviet Union that summer and fall. In anticipation of a pending victory and amid the realization that shipping several million Jews to "reservations" in Poland or elsewhere was impractical, Hitler first ordered what would be termed the "Final Solution." This was the murder of Europe's Jews under German control. From Barbarossa onward, the war of annihilation was in full swing.

The Germans lumped their enemies together. The slogan went "Where the partisan is, the Jew is, and where the Jew is, is the partisan"; and it gave the Wehrmacht and the SS license to kill. The Holocaust logically stemmed from this brutality. Although the Nazis conceived of answers to their Jewish problem and lebensraum through forced migration, plans were on the drawing board for death camps at this time to overcome the "inefficiency" of mass killings by roundups in villages. By summer's end, the SS had experimented with the poison gas Zyklon B and had carbon monoxide techniques, based on earlier euthanasia programs, under review. Discomfited by the Einsatzgruppen, both Leeb and Bock issued only mild protests, preferring to keep their distance from the atrocities yet not stop them. Most senior German commanders did the same. Field Marshals Walter von Reichenau and Rundstedt, as well as General Manstein, encouraged plunder and massacres of Jews and Slavs. The Wehrmacht followed orders.

As the first stages of the Final Solution got underway, the Wehrmacht made a mistake. Initially greeted as liberators by Ukrainians—victims of Stalin's collectivization of agriculture and foes of communism—the Germans so pillaged the region that they alienated these potential allies. Famine, looting, rape, and systematic killing prompted partisan warfare in which guerrillas harassed the Nazi murderers by sabotaging supply lines and railroads. In September 1941, Keitel ordered the death of 50–150 communists for every German life taken. Furthermore, over a million prisoners were transferred to Germany for labor and to prevent rebellion. Stalin appealed for people to defend the homeland regardless of their antipathy to communism. Propaganda cleverly spoke little of communism, focusing instead on patriotism and the trials of Mother Russia in its hour of need. Partisans responded by making life difficult for the occupiers. They killed collaborators, destroyed railways, and stirred resistance. The Germans retaliated ever more savagely in their campaign of annihilation, but Hitler had unnecessarily instigated an uprising.

SOVIET REBIRTH

After an aborted plan for a peace with Hitler through Bulgarian emissaries, Josef Stalin took control. A state committee on defense united all organs of government under him. Stalin named himself Supreme Commander in Chief and formed a military headquarters with seven members, called the Stavka, to reform the Red Army's structure and direct operations under his orders. He assumed ultimate authority over the USSR. A political functionary his entire career, Stalin was a novice on military affairs relative to, say, Winston Churchill. But this inexperience did not prevent his interference in Red Army affairs. In November 1941, he ordered a futile Soviet counteroffensive against the broadly deployed Germans. Within the first 6 months of the Great Patriotic War, most of the initial Red Army troops were killed or captured. Stalin worried not a bit about the human cost of his campaigns; indeed, the deaths of millions of military and citizens were his main weapon in a strategy of attrition adopted at this point to blunt the German onslaught. This approach, to be sure, could hardly be distinguished from one of annihilation in terms of the catastrophic loss of life.

With the fall of Kiev, the Soviets lost over 1.25 million troops, but Hitler's insistence on taking the city played to the Kremlin's favor by providing breathing room for six weeks. The Russians used the time to regroup and prepare new defensive positions around Moscow. They did not lack for manpower despite Red Army depletion. Stalin called up 5.3 million reserves at the end of June 1941, deploying 13 field armies in July and another 14 in August. Overall, the Red Army created 194 new divisions and 84 separate brigades during the summer. The Germans soon admitted that they had grossly underestimated Soviet strength. They grew worried as panzer units took heavier casualties, but trains with Russian prisoners seemingly never ceased moving westward to camps. And the more enemy soldiers, the longer the campaign lasted and the larger the logistical problems for the Germans. Resupply became harder and repairs of machinery more difficult. Fuel and ammunition ran short for Bock's panzers as well as for the Luftwaffe. Uncoordinated counterattacks by Timoshenko in early August did not change German plans, but they further drained men and resources and sapped momentum. Persuaded that logistics gave his generals nightmares, Hitler changed his mind in early September and agreed that Moscow should be the target. Having initiated Barbarossa in mid-June with 3.78 million men, the Germans had suffered 409,998 casualties three months later. Combat units required 200,000 more men, but there were no reserves. Less than half of the panzers were in working order. Hitler now planned to wield a giant pincer from Kiev in the south and Leningrad from the north. Brauchitsch restored the initiative to Army Group Center under Operation Typhoon, a two-sided assault on Moscow projected to end by the onset of the Soviet winter. It was time to finish off the communists.

In the final attempt of the year to destroy the Soviet Union, the Fuhrer launched Operation Typhoon on October 2. Bock had three armies and three panzer groups backed by a tactical air force and three air and antiaircraft artillery corps. He threw them at the Soviet West *front* of seven armies under Lieutenant-General Ivan Konev, a World War I and civil war hero, and at the Briansk *front* of three armies led by Major-General Andrey Eremenko. After the 4th Panzer Group separated the two army groups in a diversionary move, it joined the 3rd Panzer Group and Second Panzer Army coming from the north and south. Within the week, Bock enveloped nine Soviet armies and 663,000 soldiers in the Briansk-Vyazma pocket. The panzers left the infantry to take prisoners. Georgi Zhukov picked up the remaining free Russian troops and joined them with a reserve *front*. This hero of the Manchurian campaign against Japan always seemed to reappear at his country's most dire hour. As the Germans stood at the gates of Moscow and the Soviet Union on the brink of collapse, Stalin called "the Fireman" to service once again.

As the Nazi dictator detailed plans for the destruction of Moscow, the Germans tied up loose ends elsewhere. Rundstedt approached Rostov and entered the Crimea while Leeb pushed eastward to cut off supply routes across Lake Ladoga into Leningrad. The Soviets encountered weapons shortages. German Army Groups South and Center forced them to dismantle industrial complexes in the Donets Basin and around Moscow. Soviet ball bearing production almost came to a standstill, and precipitous drops in coal, iron, steel, and aluminum output ensued. Britain's first Arctic convoy had left its Scottish port in August for the USSR, but it did not carry enough supplies to matter. As looting and panic had erupted in the capital in mid-October 1941, U.S. and British military attaches in Moscow tacitly agreed with Hitler's propaganda. The war in the east was nearly over, and the war in Europe would likely soon end.

Weather and Zhukov gave the Soviets hope, however. Steady rain turned terrain and unpaved roads into impassable mud fields that stymied German progress into Moscow. Days stretched into weeks, further straining thin supply lines that stretched 700 miles to Prussia. Zhukov had orders to hold a north-south line centered on Mozhaisk, 62 miles west of Moscow. He lost his northern anchor, Kalinin, on October 14, but it took 4th Panzer Group five mud-laden days later than predicted to roll past Mozhaisk. The weather shut down action from Lake Ladoga in the north to the Sea of Azov in the south until early November. Revived by military and political organizations in unoccupied areas as well as the industrial capacity built in the 1930s or recently hauled out of the Moscow area behind the Urals and in Siberia, the Soviets responded. The three-week respite allowed for preparations. Nine reserve armies of 100,000 men each from Siberia and the Far East (the neutrality pact with Japan after the Soviet Nomonhon victory and Tokyo's southward gaze gave Stalin less insecurity in Asia) were brought up behind the Volga River and added to Zhukov's line. Most of these troops were too old, too young, or too unfit, but they were tough. In addition, logistics favored the USSR.

The Soviets had the advantage of a large rail network while the Germans had but one line. Stalin sent most of the government, Communist Party, and military leadership 500 miles eastward on the Volga to Kuibyshev. As a million Moscow residents evacuated in mid-October 1941, Lenin's coffin was hidden in a secret place and the Kremlin wired for demolition. With the Germans moving past Mozhaisk, Stalin called on Fortress Moscow to block the Nazi invaders.

By November 8, Hitler no longer spoke of blitzkrieg. Instead he pledged to take Moscow immediately then win the war outright in 1942 when the weather improved. The High Command urged the generals to surge ahead as far as possible before winter stopped them, but Berlin knew about the exhausted troops and the dearth of fuel for the panzers. The Wehrmacht had used up two-thirds of its tank strength and half of its manpower. There were no reserves at the depots. Hitler decided on a final attempt on Moscow, a show of will to nail down the Red Army coffin. The muddy quagmire was freezing, allowing the tanks to maneuver again. Bock thought it better to surround the city and envelop Zhukov's Western *front* rather than wait out the winter at the end of a railway line. After all, the Germans possessed most of Russia's coal and iron ore reserves and ruled over 35 million civilians. Bock argued for a final thrust for victory, and Hitler agreed. Operation Typhoon began anew on November 15, 1941, the Germans under time pressure fighting against the oncoming winter and dwindling supplies and the Russians banking on a numbing winter to rescue them.

A DECISIVE PHASE

On frozen ground, the Germans advanced so quickly that they ignored the dire supply situation. On the first day, a Soviet army across from German Ninth Army disintegrated; and in less than two weeks, the 3rd Panzer Group overran Klin on November 23 and broke open a wide hole in the Soviet defenses. The Germans rested on the Moscow-Volga Canal, 37 miles north of the capital. To the south, the 4th Panzer Group reached the suburbs, only twelve miles from the Kremlin. To the southeast, Second Panzer Army passed the town of Tula. Around Leningrad, Leeb had seized Tikhvin, cutting off the water supply to Lake Ladoga, and moved First Panzer Army toward Rostov-on-Don. Stalin desperately attacked Leeb, trying to divert Wehrmacht attention from Moscow. He declared martial law in the capital. Zhukov now revealed his most important traits: mule-headed stubbornness, courage, competence, and ruthlessness. The Fireman dominated the defense. Within weeks, he even persuaded Stalin to counterattack. Zhukov was one of the few leaders who could argue with the dictator and live to tell about it.

Tantalizingly close to marching into Red Square, the Germans faced their first serious trouble of World War II. New Soviet armies halted Guderian before Kashira and slowed the 3rd and 4th Panzer Groups to the south. Hitler learned that the Soviets had good planes and that the Luftwaffe no longer ruled the skies. Russian armored brigades not only appeared with British tanks, but the superior Russian T-34 finally exited assembly lines to replace obsolete tanks that the Germans had destroyed at the opening of Barbarossa. From his headquarters in East Prussia, Hitler intervened again. He fired Rundstedt after the general refused to cancel an order of retreat from Rostov. His replacement, long-time Hitler sycophant Walter von Reichenau, followed Rundstedt's lead, however. He pulled back Army Group Center. The snowy weather wreaked havoc on the Germans. Temperatures dropped as low as –29 degrees Fahrenheit. The cold jelled engine oil, fuel, and gun lubricants. Body parts froze, the weather congealing exposed skin and orifices. Men urinated on their numbed hands to warm them and cauterize the cracks in their fingers. On December 3, Leeb threatened to vacate Tikhvin if Bock failed to encircle Moscow.

Hitler had intended to bring most of the troops home before winter and send the remainder warm clothing stored in Poland once the rail lines were open. Snow and sabotage had closed them. Reopening the lines was imperative, especially when the spring thaw came and roads became impassable. But warmer weather was far off. Unprepared for a winter war, the panzers ground to a halt. Bock hoped to wait out the cold but instead, on December 5, he faced Zhukov's counteroffensive. Some Wehrmacht troops had seen the Kremlin through binoculars; most would never live to see Germany again. Because they had focused on pressing forward with mobile patrols, the Germans had not bothered to bolster their various fronts, and no reserves were on hand from other theaters. As a result, when the Red Army attack broke through and opened gaps in the German lines, the Wehrmacht itself faced encirclement. The whole Eastern front verged on collapse, an amazing reversal from just a week before. The Wehrmacht abandoned artillery and vehicles immobilized by the cold as it tried to fight the Soviets in front and behind. Blizzards shut roads and communications while troops fled westward, clogging the few exits. Discipline evaporated. Chief of the General Staff Franz Halder lamented that Germany faced its greatest crisis in two world wars. On December 15, the Soviet government returned to Moscow from Kuibyshev. Stalin expressed confidence that the tide had turned.

Hitler was frantic, dejected, and outraged. After the enemy ran through German positions north of Moscow and Tula, and Zhukov turned his armies westward, Bock requested sick leave on December 18. Hitler replaced him with Kluge and accepted Brauchitsch's resignation. The Fuhrer himself assumed the role of commander-in-chief of Barbarossa. He ordered all troops to stand their ground against the communists and forbid a retreat. Guderian refused such insanity, for his soldiers were freezing to death without shelter "in this abominable cold. It is frightful, unimaginable." Hitler dismissed him. Leeb and Hoepner, his remaining commanders, also lost their jobs. The change in leadership neither stopped the intense cold nor Russian pressure. While he knew Barbarossa had failed, Hitler had no intention of ending his crusade for lebensraum because he was convinced that salvation was around the corner and the Nazi military machine indefatigable. Just as Zhukov had counterattacked, the Japanese shocked the world by bombing the U.S. naval base at Pearl Harbor. The Fuhrer declared war on the United States, this in the midst of the biggest disaster facing Germany. But he could not disguise reality. By the month's end, the Wehrmacht's mystical reputation of invincibility lay in ruins along the 175 miles of retreat westward from Moscow.

Zhukov wanted to press onward with the attack. He believed that he could reach the jump-off point of Typhoon and then advance to Smolensk before the end of winter.

German soldiers in snow trench in the USSR.   Credit: Library of
Congress, Call #: Lot 6455, Reproduction # LC-USZ62-30749.

Stalin sought instead to encircle Army Group Center with a general offensive involving,
incredibly, nine entire army group. He scheduled this ambitious plan for a later in 1942
because the Moscow counteroffensive had petered out. The Russians also withered in
the freezing temperatures, although without the strategic consequences experienced by
the Third Reich.

In the meantime, the Russians and Germans assessed the results of Barbarossa's
first half year. By the end of January 1942, Germany suffered nearly 918,000 casualties, or almost 29% of the total soldiers involved. Hitler's dream of lebensraum and
his tactic of achieving it through the awesome power of blitzkrieg were in question.
He faced a two-front war as soon as the western allies, the United States included,
chose to attempt a reconquest of France. The Soviets, on the other hand, got back on
their feet despite the 3.35 million soldiers sent off to German prisoner camps. Those
were the lucky ones, for the Waffen-SS usually did not take captives at all. That Stalin

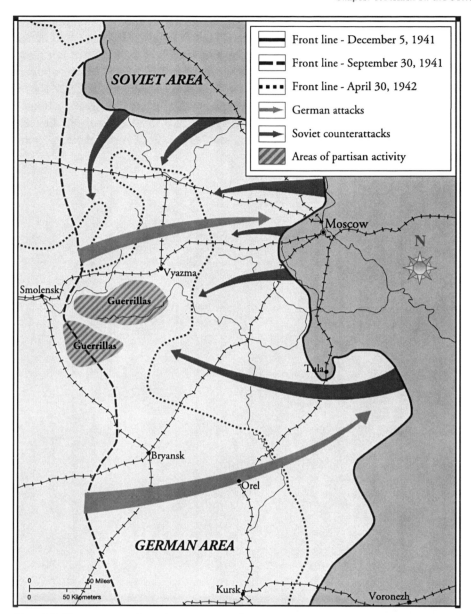

Map 9.2 Moscow attack and counterattack.   Credit: Ronald Story, *Concise Historical Atlas of World War II: The Geography of Conflict*, Map 16, p. 37.

and the Red Army defended Moscow alone without outside help boosted morale at home and Soviet prestige abroad. In part as a reward for its valor, the USSR became a signatory to the United Nations Declaration on January 1, 1942. Stalin's successful defense of Moscow assured that he would take a big role in world affairs during, and after, the war.

For the present, the fortunes of war shined down on the bleeding but breathing USSR. Hitler did not ponder his darker fate. He still believed that he could defeat the Allies; after all, he had nearly toppled Stalin, and would try again in warmer temperatures. In the end, Hitler misgauged the Soviet dictator, whose performance had oftentimes been self-defeating. The five to eight million dead citizens of the USSR attested to rule that had brought untold misery. Yet at great cost Stalin had defended the homeland. The Germans had erred by having no alternatives to a short campaign. The German invasion of the Soviet Union was monumental because it changed the very course of the Second World War.

CHAPTER 10

Expansion of Imperial Japan

Pearl Harbor and the Luftwaffe are signs enough to me they're
out to get us, and I don't like being got.

IVAN DOIG
The Eleventh Man

SINO-JAPANESE WAR

Across the Pacific, the Japanese watched Barbarossa with amazement and then dismay,
but they were most focused on American mobilization. U.S. naval expansion threatened
their grand imperial designs in Asia. The Imperial Navy had ordered the world's two biggest battleships, but it planned as late as July 1940 to convert to carriers and escort groups.
That would take eighteen months. The country faced other problems as well. Japan did
not have enough shipping tonnage to meet military and civilian needs. The war in China,
occupation of Manchuria, and the Army's mechanization program, moreover, had tripled the national budget and skewed expenditures. Industrial production did not met
projections, and the seven-year program of a synthetic oil law yielded no more than 8.3%
of targeted petroleum output through 1941. Tokyo still relied on high-octane aviation
fuel from America; and overall, bankruptcy loomed without favorable trade and financial
arrangements with the United States. The nation ran a balance of trade surplus within its
empire, but its account with the rest of the world was in deficit. Expansion into Southeast
Asia could solve these economic dilemmas. Only the U.S. Navy stood in the way.

Japan also remained mired in China, although the Chinese fought as much among
themselves as against their foreign enemy. In northern China, the Communists
endured the brunt of Japanese aggression as well as from Chiang Kai-Shek himself.
Mao Tse-tung's forces fought behind enemy lines but also struggled in a civil war
against the Nationalists. Between 1937 and 1940, the two sides had formed a United
Front that quintupled the size of Mao's Eighth Route Army in the north and expanded
his New Fourth Army in central China. Cooperation did not endure. By late 1939, the
Nationalists blockaded Communist-held cities. In the summer and fall of 1940, Mao

got revenge by victories in Anhwei and Kiangsu provinces; but Chiang struck back in January 1941 by destroying the New Fourth Army headquarters.

The Imperial Army capitalized on the infighting by pursuing its strategy of anni-hilation under the three alls policy to kill, loot, and burn everything in its path. It lay waste to large swaths of China. In Shanxi province from September to October 1940, Tokyo ordered the Army to kill all males ages 15 to 60 "having an enemy char-acter," destroy weapons and provisions, and burn down villages. The goal in 1940 and beyond was to create a no-man's land where ordinary life was impossible. In Xinglong county in eastern Hebei between 1942 and 1944, this policy caused the deaths of 15,400 civilians. Almost that many were sent to Manchuria for work, drop-ping the population by forty percent. One village witnessed 1,230 women, men, and children assembled in a courtyard and gunned down. The numbers lost to indis-criminate massacre ran upward of three-quarters of a million people in each of the border regions of JinJuLu Yu and JinchaJi. Campaigns in Spring 1940 in a county of Wuxiang province wiped out 10,688 lives. Subsequent "suppression and clean-up operations" resulted in a human cataclysm where infectious disease swept through the countryside. Just as horrifying in the annihilation policy was the starvation due to crop failures because of a dearth of farmers. Famine necessitated the cannibalism of corpses. In response, the Nationalists could mount no more than partisan attacks on the Imperial Army. Chiang fought a war of attrition to trade space for time in the hopes of rescue by the outside world.

The war in China yielded Japan territory and spoils but not victory. Over one mil-lion troops under the three separate commands of the Kwantung Army in Manchuria and the northern and central China headquarters fought in a quagmire. By 1941, man-power and materiel were eaten away in a land war in Asia against Nationalists and Communists alike. Japan intensified its campaigns and perpetrated atrocities against both, but the Imperial Japanese Army bogged down in northern China as Mao sabo-taged communications and transportation lines. And a shift in focus overshadowed the China war as European events changed the equation of military power in Asia.

The demise of western Europe under Hitler's advance also weakened colonial-ism in Asia. A day after France surrendered in June 1940, Tokyo demanded landing rights in northern Indochina, which the French were in no position to refuse. Japan compelled Britain to close the Burma Road between Lashio and Chungking—the key supply route to the Nationalists—in July 1940. In September, the Japanese occupied northern Indochina and joined Germany and Italy in the Tripartite Pact. Such actions worried the United States to the extent that it issued an embargo on steel exports to Japan on September 26. The restrictions had little effect on curbing the Tokyo milita-rists' desires for more colonial possessions given the European preoccupation with war. In December, British War Cabinet documents taken from a ship sunk in the Indian Ocean revealed that Britain had no plans to contest Japan in southeast Asia and would not send its fleet to Singapore if war broke out. Thus, Malaya was ripe for conquer. The Imperial Army began training for amphibious landings, including exercises on Hainan island that involved a 600-mile march to simulate an invasion down the Malay penin-sula. Jungle warfare training commenced in February 1941 on Formosa.

ACROSS THE PACIFIC

Whenever the Japanese made an expansionist move, the Americans responded with a countermeasure. This hardened Japan's stance ever more. Both sides believed that war was inevitable, making conflict a self-fulfilling prophecy. In 1940, the Imperial Navy of Japan reacted to U.S. naval expansion bills with boldness. It not only ordered a full mobilization by December 1941 but considered a suggestion to assault the U.S. Pacific Fleet in Hawaii. Roosevelt had kept the fleet in Hawaii after conducting exercises in May 1940. This made Pearl Harbor America's forward base, a signal to Japan that the United States was on guard in the Pacific.

The critical economic sphere drove Japanese militarism, however. In July 1940, Prime Minister Konoe named expansionist Hideki Tojo as his war minister and Yosuke Matsuoka the foreign minister. The latter loudly supported a Japanese empire to the south as an answer to U.S. trade restrictions and general dependence on American economic policies. Both elevated the military's power even higher in Tokyo government circles. The United States abrogated its commercial treaty with Japan in January 1940 and then passed legislation six months later to allow for the imposition of embargoes on goods deemed crucial to the Japanese war machine. Roosevelt banned 40 export items, including aircraft and machine tools. Furthermore, he insisted that the Imperial Army vacate China. Congressional sympathy for Chiang, Tokyo's threat to U.S. possessions in the Pacific, ethical opposition to aggression, and a vision of a friendly and important postwar China kept Chiang in the President's sights. FDR also had an affinity for China, as he traced the Roosevelt family's wealth to trade with the empire in the early 19th century.

With the Japanese unable to end the war, however, Washington found the emboldened Chiang as troublesome as the Imperial Army. The Japanese three alls policy punished China, but Tokyo abandoned hope of negotiating an armistice. It recognized a puppet regime under Wang Ching-wei, a former Nationalist leader, whose power rapidly collapsed. This allowed Chiang to resume the civil war against Mao by January 1941. The Roosevelt administration tried to refocus him on the Japanese threat because a civil war might allow the Imperial Army to remove troops from China and send them to Southeast Asia to fulfill the dream of the Co-Prosperity Sphere. But Roosevelt played a weak hand. The Nationalist leader was popular among American opinion makers. FDR endorsed a $100 million loan to Chiang to stave off the Wang government, but the Nationalist leader used it to destroy Mao's New Fourth Army along the Yangtze River and attack communist headquarters in Yenan. Meanwhile, he leveraged American concerns to win Lend-Lease aid in March 1941. From then onward, he had U.S. support to conduct a dual war—one against Japan and the other against the Communists.

The Americans were further sucked into the vortex of Chinese intrigue because they planned to build a Chinese-American air force. This would be used not only against the Japanese in China but also as a foundation for a strategic bombing campaign on Japan itself. The air force was the idea of Claire Chennault, a U.S. Army Air Force pilot who had served as a private military advisor to Chiang since 1936. In November 1940, Chennault and Chiang's brother-in-law, the political operative and financial whiz T. V. Soong, asked Treasury Secretary Henry Morgenthau to fund a 500-plane air force to be built and flown by Americans. Morgenthau approved; but without available planes, he advised the long-range bombing of Japanese cities instead. The War Department quashed both ideas. It opposed both a chain of command outside of the U.S. military and a strike that would provoke instantaneous war with Japan. FDR compromised by approving 100 fighters for use in China proper. They would be flown by U.S. pilots who had resigned their military commissions and signed up as volunteers as the core of Chennault's famed "Flying Tigers." As well, the pilots joined the Civil Air Transport during the war. Along with the aircraft came arms and a permanent U.S. Army mission to train the Nationalist army.

Faced with American resistance in an ever-stalemated war in China, the Tokyo militarists opted for aggressive expansion rather than negotiation to bring economic salvation. In August 1940, Matsuoka enunciated the Great East Asia Co-Prosperity Sphere to rid the region of European imperialism through Japanese military guidance. This area included Manchuria and northern China; European colonies in Indochina and Indonesia; and Borneo, New Zealand, Australia, India, Burma, and Thailand. The occupation of north Indochina in September 1940 was a first step toward controlling Southeast Asia and building the Co-Prosperity Sphere. The United States reacted with more export bans. Even FDR's wife urged the ultimate embargo of a cutoff of oil to Japan. The President refused such radical prescriptions because he did not wish to push Japan into a drive southward. But both sides stiffened ever more. The Konoe government bound extreme nationalist groups into the Nazi-style Imperial Rule Assistance Association. This gutted the political party system and cleared the way to total power for the militarists. Germany and Italy backed Japan's claims to a New Order in Asia while they created one in Europe. Matsuoka banked on the Axis alliance to scare off the Americans, but Konoe doubted a weakening of American resolve to stop Japanese expansion.

Japanese diplomats also implemented the Co-Prosperity Sphere by protecting their northern flank from Soviet attack. Matsuoka traveled to Europe in April 1941 to speak with Hitler and Stalin about a Russo-Japanese neutrality pact. The Fuhrer hinted at his designs on the Soviet Union (Barbarossa was two months away), which might upset Japan's plans. The Soviet leader welcomed the idea of an agreement obligating either country to observe strict neutrality toward each other for the next five years even if they were drawn into a larger war. The accord allowed Stalin to focus on the German threat and not worry about an Asian front. Japan could now head toward Southeast Asia without fear of a Soviet invasion in Manchuria. The neutrality agreement also undercut the Chinese effort against Japan by denying Chiang or Mao Soviet assistance. A shocked Roosevelt expanded aid to Chiang as a result, including a shipment of long-range bombers that Army Chief of Staff George Marshall warned could set all of Japan ablaze. Churchill rejoiced at the prospects for even more American intervention in Asia. Meanwhile, Matsuoka readied to convert the Co-Prosperity Sphere from theory to reality.

The neutrality pact gave the Japanese military a free hand to build an empire. As battles raged in the Mediterranean and the Atlantic in April and May 1941, a war in the Pacific did not seem outlandish. U.S. Secretary of State Cordell Hull insisted that Japan retreat from China and abandon its imperial dreams. Japan's Ambassador to the United States Kichisaburo Nomura wrongly told his superiors in Tokyo that the Americans were softening toward the occupation of Manchuria. American intelligence officers had broken Japan's diplomatic codes through the MAGIC intercepts. This allowed them to read the most secret cables, which informed Roosevelt of Nomura's misinformation campaign. Tokyo stood by its vision of the Co-Prosperity Sphere. The Japanese Army occupied the Saigon airport in southern Indochina and bought the colony's rice surplus at a discounted rate. Japan also bullied the Dutch for their oil fields in the East Indies. Field Marshal Pibul Songgram, the dictator of Thailand, aligned himself with Japan so that his country could regain disputed territories from the French along the borders of Cambodia and Laos. He did so in early 1941 with an army of 50,000 soldiers. For the rest of the war, Anglo-American secret services tried to win Thailand back to their side.

As the militarists in Asia became more overtly expansionist, the Americans became more reactive. They realized the probability of war with Japan was growing as Nomura stalled for time until the military prepared to seize the resources of Asia. Every Japanese military move forward meant a step backward in diplomatic relations. Events in Europe also sped the two nations faster toward war. Washington had less tolerance for aggression as Germany invaded the Balkans, contested the British in Africa, marched across the Soviet Union, and attacked merchant ships on the high seas. In mid-1941, the world stood on the brink of cataclysm as the Japanese hurried toward empire and a possible clash with the United States.

On June 25, 1941, Imperial Army and Navy officers met about the ramifications of Barbarossa and rising American belligerence. Germany appeared invincible, the European democracies' colonies were vulnerable, and the war in China was no closer to resolution. The Imperial Navy criticized the Army's quagmire in China, which could worsen as U.S. aid grew for Chiang Kai-shek. Both services decided it was time to grab the resources of Southeast Asia. A week later, government ministers at an imperial conference supported this idea, but they acknowledged that a southward advance might provoke war with the United States. Matsuoka counseled that Japan should help Germany and attack the USSR in the east, but he was overruled. The Imperial Navy formally declared its support for the move. A delay would allow the Americans to complete fleet construction and thus limit Japan's freedom to create the Co-Prosperity Sphere.

Such a course would bring sanctions from potential enemies, but Japan proceeded anyway. On July 25, 1941, the Imperial Army occupied all of French Indochina. The next day, the Americans froze Japanese assets and stopped trade between the two nations, and the British and Dutch followed suit. Roosevelt activated Western Hemisphere Defense Plan IV to ready his military for a conflict, although he still believed that hostilities could be halted short of war. But Japan had plans of its own. This entailed a neutralization of American power in the western Pacific by a bold strike at Pearl Harbor to cripple the U.S. Navy. To erect a defensible perimeter, Imperial forces would conquer the Philippines to guard the shipping lanes between the home islands and the invasion route to the Southeast Asian treasures of Malaysia and Indonesia. The only significant obstacle to these goals was the American Pacific Fleet in Hawaii.

The Japanese Navy Ministry worried over the superior strength of the United States as well as the logistical strain of shipping oil from the Dutch East Indies once America cut off its fuel exports, yet prospects for success looked good. The U.S. Navy had 347 warships, including seven aircraft carriers, and the Army Air Force had 150 four-engine bombers among its 1,200 combat aircraft. Most of these forces were pointed toward the Atlantic, convoying merchant vessels to Europe, or stationed in North America. Japan could bring 7,500 aircraft to bear on the enemy, including nearly 2,700 modern planes and 3,000 trained pilots per year. The Imperial Navy had fewer ships (about 230) than the Americans, but it was up to date and primed for battle. The Japanese, boasting 2.4 million trained troops and reserves of 3 million, outnumbered America's current 1.6 million men under arms. But according to the Japanese, the military also had an insuperable edge over all other nations, one that no other nation or race possessed— that of fighting spirit. On its side were the gods, surprise, and morality as well as men dedicated to the divine Emperor and trained to fight the soft Americans to the end. After all, Japan was supposedly weaker than China in 1894 and Russia in 1904 but had defeated both. The United States would be next.

The rivals slid toward conflict. The stoppage in August 1941 of oil sales to Japan, which counted on 60% of its petroleum demand from America, undermined diplomacy. This sudden and total economic slap accelerated Tokyo's preparations for war because the ban was lethal to Japanese well-being. Combined with the freeze on financial assets, the oil embargo placed the nation in a position of de facto bankruptcy. A negotiated settlement with the United States seemed out of the question. The American sanctions—for Japan, a declaration of war—hinted at the emerging U.S. strategy of annihilation that used economic as well as military weapons to crush its foe.

EYEING THE PHILIPPINES

Roosevelt vowed to take all precautions to protect American security in the Pacific. In July 1941, he asked General Douglas MacArthur to come out of retirement and command the new U.S. Army Forces in the Far East in the Philippines, where he resided as the chief military advisor to the commonwealth government. Most experts predicted that a Japanese war would begin in this American territory. These nearly 7,100 islands spread out east of Formosa and home to 17 million people had been tied United States since 1898. Filipinos attained commonwealth status in 1935 in preparation for independence shortly thereafter. A brilliant, West Pointer, MacArthur had served tours in the Philippines after World War I and then became chief of staff, the top post in the U.S. Army. MacArthur also had a huge ego, one capable of confronting the president of the United States and of playing to a cheering public fascinated by his personality and heroism. He disparaged FDR's plans to shore up the islands at this late date. The Philippine Army had ten reserve divisions, but they were just partially mobilized. A two-torpedo boat navy and 40 aircraft completed the small force. The General threw together a Philippine Division under the leadership of Major-General Jonathan Wainwright. This hastily built force comprised excellent Filipino and American troops. Along with a substantial garrison of coastal defense and associated forces and the small U.S. Asiatic Fleet, the Philippine Division nervously watched Japanese moves over the next months.

MacArthur.   Credit: Center for the Study of War Experience at
Regis University, Denver, Colorado: U.S. National Archives.

Left with just a year's worth of petroleum supplies, Japan decided to negotiate with
the United States about China and the occupation of Indochina while readying for
war. Some experts in America thought this was a positive sign, but the prevailing sentiment among diplomats was that Konoe would not be able to persuade the Imperial
Army and Navy to accept any agreement limiting expansion. Negotiations between
Foreign Minister Nomura and a resolutely pro-China Secretary of State Hull came to
naught. By October 1941, War Minister Tojo concluded that the Konoe diplomatic mission had exceeded its deadline. He demanded that the Army mobilize for war. Konoe
tendered his resignation. The son of a samurai who despised the decadence of the West
and America for its domination of Asia, Tojo replaced him. New negotiations in late
November between Hull and Nomura went through the motions. Japan raced headlong
into war.

As war clouds gathered, the two sides readied their militaries. Even before World
War I, the United States and Japan had eyed each other as potential enemies and they,
as well as other powers, had planned for a war in the Pacific. In the event of a Japanese
attack, the British and Dutch would fall back on the Malay Barrier, Malaya, and the
East Indies to await the arrival of the U.S. Pacific Fleet. America's Achilles heel was the
Philippines, just 200 miles from Japanese bases in Formosa but nearly 5,000 miles from
the protection of the Pacific Fleet in Hawaii. The islands were vulnerable to invasion by

Japan. Harbor defenses of Manila Bay were extensive, but little else in the vast Philippine archipelago was fortified. The original U.S. Navy War Plan Orange (the color representing Japan; rainbow war plans included a host of allies) called for a naval offensive from Pearl Harbor into the western Pacific to guard the Philippines and rescue the Malay Barrier.

FDR's decision to send in MacArthur did not change this inherently defensive approach. In the Allied strategy worked out largely by Roosevelt and Churchill, planners had decided that if the United States entered the war, the defeat of Germany would take priority over Japan. This involved landings somewhere in Western Europe as quickly as possible but only after a prudent buildup of forces could assure the liberation of France and ease the Soviet burden on the Eastern front. America might pull back to Alaska, Hawaii, and Panama as it fought its Europe First strategy, but with enough men and materiel, MacArthur believed he could deny the Philippines to Japan. He hoped to train the Filipinos with modern equipment and draw on the U.S. Army Air Force's new long-range bomber, the B-17 "Flying Fortress." Yet just a small number of weapons and planes arrived in the Philippines by December 1941, and scant evidence existed to show that bombing would have impressed the Japanese. In fact, as in the case of Germany, American strategy toward Japan rested on ground armies rather than air power alone.

The Japanese recognized the general drift of U.S. strategy to maintain a tenuous hold on the Philippines, so they decided to modify their original plan. They would act even more audaciously. When war broke out, they would snatch the Philippines and Guam from the Americans and capture Burma, Malaya, Thailand, Borneo, and the East Indies from the Europeans. The Imperial Navy also abandoned the idea of harassing the U.S. Navy as it moved across the Pacific to fight. A fervent advocate of airpower over the battleship, the commander of the Combined Fleet, Admiral Isoroku Yamamoto, argued against waiting on the American initiative. This hero of the Russo-Japanese War and participant in the historic victory in the battle of Tsushima Strait in 1905 (where he had lost two fingers) had lived in the United States, spoke fluent English, and saw the U.S. Navy as an effete social club incapable of engaging in bold planning or hard fighting. He also realistically understood that the United States was a powerhouse capable of crushing Japan. Yamamoto had no illusions. Japan could neither defeat the American colossus nor count on the U.S. Navy to seek out the Japanese for a decisive battle somewhere in the Pacific. The fleet might simply sit in Pearl Harbor until it grew large enough to overwhelm the Imperial Navy. Yamamoto preferred to set his own terms. Japan must consider taking the Philippines to prevent an American attack on the backside of the southward advance. To do so, the modern navy—replete with airpower—must knock out the U.S. fleet in Hawaii. A preemptive blow might just lead to Washington searching for a diplomatic solution to avert war altogether.

In late 1941, London sent the battleship *Prince of Wales* and battle cruiser *Repulse* to Singapore to beef up defenses there, but Japan did not need to fear European power in Asia. The British-Canadian brigade in Hong Kong was unimpressive, and the 90,000-man Commonwealth Army defending the Malay Barrier was comprised of second-rate Indian troops. The best soldiers had been sent to the Middle East and Africa,

Yamamoto.   Credit: Naval Historical Center.

leaving behind an amalgam of Commonwealth and indigenous forces. The 40,000-man Royal Netherlands East Indies Army was more of a colonial police constabulary than a fighting force, and the Dutch Navy was small and spread out over 2,000 miles. In the Philippines, MacArthur's training efforts had borne paltry results. The small U.S. Asiatic Fleet "that God forgot" under Admiral Thomas Hart consisted of a heavy cruiser, two light cruisers, 13 destroyers, 28 submarines, and auxiliaries. Prevent the Pacific Fleet from exiting Pearl Harbor, Yamamoto reasoned, and Japan's southward advance could be assured.

Through his charisma, expertise, and willpower, Yamamoto convinced Imperial General Headquarters to raid Pearl Harbor in conjunction with offensives in the Western Pacific and Southeast Asia. The Japanese Navy prevailed over the Imperial Army to expand the focus beyond MacArthur and the Philippines. To be sure, he counseled against going to war with the United States if it could be avoided and because of such sagacity, Admiral Yamamoto became a target of nationalist extremist assassins. Once Tokyo had decided to head south, however, he threw in his lot with the notion of fighting America. He would plan and direct a surprise strike under Operation Hawaii.

INFAMY AT PEARL HARBOR

As the Hull-Nomura diplomatic talks went nowhere, Yamamoto secretly sent out his striking force from Kure naval base between November 10 and 18, 1941. It assembled four days later in the Kuril Islands. Led by Vice-Admiral Chuichi Nagumo, who was not an air specialist but was noted for his daring, the force comprised a destroyer screen and eight vessels in support of two fleet and two light carriers, two other carriers converted from a battleship and a cruiser, two battleships, and two cruisers. A support group of eight tankers and supply ships followed behind. The group maintained strict radio silence to prevent detection from the U.S. Pacific Fleet. The Japanese skillfully deceived their foe. Rear-Admiral Husband Kimmel, the commander-in-chief of the U.S. Pacific Fleet, had no idea where the strike force had gone. From the Kuriles on November 26, Nagumo's flagship *Akagi* led the fleet across the Pacific, beneficiary of a winter storm that disguised its passage.

In the event of war with Japan, Kimmel had orders to attack the enemy in the Marshall Islands, 2,000 miles to the southwest. He saved his long-range aircraft for reconnaissance in that area, but it still was not enough to patrol over the vast seas. Meanwhile, the military focused on the Philippines, fearing sabotage and submarine but not aircraft at Pearl Harbor. The Navy ruled out bombings by torpedo-carrying planes because of the base's shallow waters. It also reinforced Wake Island defenses with a squadron of Marine Corps F4F Wildcat fighters from the carrier *Enterprise,* which put to sea to protect bombers headed for the Philippines. The carrier *Lexington* also left Pearl Harbor on December 5, to ferry Marine Corps dive bombers to Midway Island. Moving both aircraft carriers from their moorings at Pearl Harbor proved fortuitous. Yet the War Department deprived the base of anti-torpedo netting. Yamamoto had studied Britain's successful torpedo raid in the shallow waters of Taranto from the previous year. He prepared a similar attack with a new type of torpedo built for the Pearl Harbor operation.

Yamamoto also had the element of surprise on his side while the Americans neglected the signs and engaged in interservice rivalry that stymied the flow of information. Nagumo headed across the Pacific to a point 275 miles north of Pearl Harbor, far from reconnaissance planes and undetected by communications intelligence. Hawaii operators were unable to read the Japanese PURPLE diplomatic ciphers, the rough equivalent of Germany's ENIGMA system, because the decoding machine at Bletchley Park was under scrutiny. MAGIC did pick up the "East Winds" message sent by Japanese diplomats that signaled that relations with America had deteriorated to the point of war. The U.S. Navy knew about the message on December 4 or 5, but it failed to act. More available information, such as the fact that Japanese officials in Hawaii twice directed spies to pinpoint U.S. battleships in definable grids, was not reported to commanders at Pearl Harbor. Mistranslated MAGIC messages added to the general diplomatic misunderstandings, misperceptions, and stereotypes that rendered a defense difficult. On November 27, a final war warning went out to U.S. Army and Navy commanders, but there was no mention of Hawaii. Perhaps the Panama Canal would be the target. Despite the fact that the U.S. Navy had undertaken Hawaiian invasion exercises in the late 1930s, it was beyond imagination that the Imperial Navy would travel more than 90 degrees of longitude and almost 4,400 miles to reach the U.S. fleet.

Fearful of sabotage, both Kimmel and Hawaii's Army commander, Lieutenant-General Walter Short, went to high alert. Kimmel informed his superiors in Washington but they did not reply. As a result, antiaircraft guns lacked ammunition, and U.S. Army Air Force planes were grouped together on the ground (for better defense against

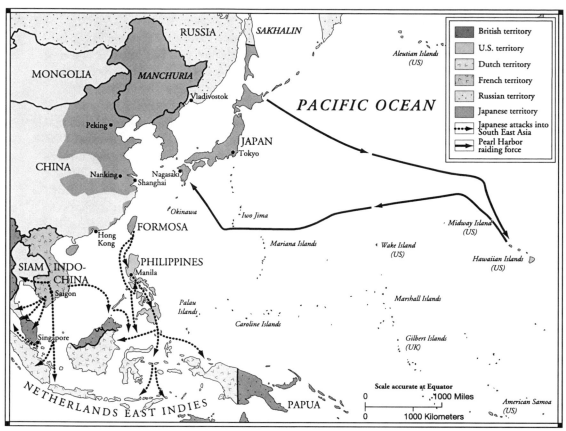

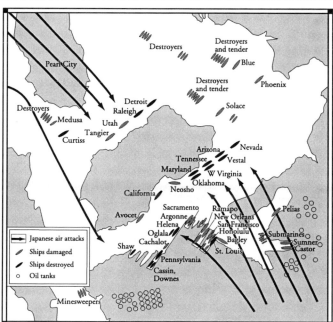

Map 10.1 Japanese approach Pearl Harbor. Credit: Ronald Story, *Concise Historical Atlas of World War II: The Geography of Conflict*, Map 38, p. 81.

saboteurs). Only one in four of the U.S. Navy's machine guns were manned (main batteries were never combat-ready in port) and, in the event of a call to battle stations, none had ready access to ammunition that remained secured in lockers. December 7 being a Sunday, a third of the ships' captains were ashore along with other officers.

Kimmel and Short faced six wartime investigations and one after the war into their supposed negligence at Pearl Harbor. Conspiracy theorists offered shaky evidence that either Roosevelt or Churchill knew about the impending attack. They argued that FDR needed the Pearl Harbor attack as a pretext to go to war. The reality was much more sobering. A myriad of information was either destroyed or disappeared amidst the hundreds of cables crossing the desks of intelligence and diplomatic officers. Included was the fact that the Americans knew Nomura in Washington had been ordered to burn his code books and present a declaration of war message to Hull in advance of the hour of attack. Recently unearthed documents showed that officials in the Roosevelt administration pondered the imminence of war and that the Imperial Navy's alert message had been decoded and intercepted three days before the attack. But in the end, Washington simply missed the warning signs. The British, meanwhile, noted Japanese fleet movements in the Gulf of Siam. They expected an attack on Malaya. Suffice to say that Kimmel and Short, like almost all Americans, were guilty of underestimating Japan's abilities. As a result, they took the fall for their negligent military bosses, Army-Navy squabbling that undermined readiness, and the failure of foresight by politicians. Amidst all the recrimination, critics should have noted the brilliance, efficiency, and intrepid effort of Yamamoto and his striking force.

Buoyed by the historic importance of his mission, Nagumo raised the flag that had flown in the battle of Tsushima Strait, where Japan had defeated the Russian fleet. As the sun rose on December 7, 1941, he ordered the air force Sea Eagles to Pearl Harbor. The first wave of 183 torpedo bombers, level bombers, dive-bombers, and fighters was followed by a second an hour later of 168 attack aircraft. Developed since 1918 and perfected by the Imperial Navy, Japanese midget submarines—dropped off by large I-type subs—were to enter the harbor and pick off any remaining ships not hit from the air. This mission ended in failure, as a patrolling U.S. destroyer sank a midget boat as it tried to enter Pearl Harbor. The aircraft performed beyond expectations, however.

A Japanese reconnaissance plane preceded Nagumo's first wave. The radar unit on Kahuku Point—its three operators in training—reported the presence of the scout plane. The duty officer thought little of the news, and he did not act again when operators informed him of the approaching swarm of Japanese attackers. After all, Pearl Harbor was expecting a delivery of B-17 bombers from the mainland. Unknown and unhindered, the Sea Eagles zeroed in on the rows of eight battleships and auxiliary craft (70 vessels in all). The clouds parted as the first wave reached Pearl Harbor. Directed by local music on the radio, grids provided by the consul in Hawaii, and by sight, torpedo and dive bombers blasted the ships and then Hickam air field for an hour or so. The second wave attacked after a fifteen-minute respite, after which high-level bombing pummeled the base. More dive-bombers appeared for a half hour before the second wave followed the first back to Nagumo's waiting carriers. Wheeler Field, Ewa Marine Corps Air Station, and Kanehoe Naval Air Station were also struck.

The destruction was spectacular and dreadful. A total of 2,403 U.S. servicemen and civilians perished and another 1,178 were wounded. Nagumo's forces sunk six of the big vessels lined up on Battleship Row (*Colorado* was in the United States for repairs) and damaged the two others. *Oklahoma* capsized while *West Virginia* and *California* sunk and *Nevada*, after making a run for the harbor's entrance, was beached. The explosion of *Arizona's* forward magazine entombed over one thousand crewmembers inside. Another three destroyers and three light cruisers, along with four other vessels, either rested on the bottom or were put out of action. Fortunately for the Americans, heavy cruisers were escorting two of the three fleet aircraft carriers to garrisons in the Pacific and another to the West Coast, thus sparing these ships. On the ground, 164 planes lay in ruins and some 128 damaged out of nearly 400 total aircraft. Japanese losses were comparatively light. Just 29 aircraft—only ten in the first wave—as well as six submarines went down.

Nagumo might have launched a third strike on repair and fuel installations to knock out Pearl Harbor for the foreseeable future, but he feared that two U.S. carrier task forces somewhere to the south might catch him. And he rightly argued later that

USS West Virginia.   Credit: Center for the Study of War Experience at Regis University, Denver, Colorado: U.S. National Archives.

the oil could be replaced quickly and dockyards rapidly rebuilt. The Americans did eventually return all but two battleships to service. Operation Hawaii had more short-term efficacy than long-term impact. An invasion of the islands might have brought more lasting effects but that was out of the question owing to the need for a secret Pacific crossing and a lack of Japanese capabilities. In terms of paralyzing the Pacific Fleet so that Japan could launch its move southwards in Asia, the Pearl Harbor attack was a dazzling success. The operation rivaled Barbarossa in shock value as one of the greatest military feats in history. On board Yamamoto's flagship, telegrams of congratulation flooded in. The Japanese Navy Ministry erupted in delight. "*We* planned this!" officers exclaimed as they swaggered up and down the hallways. Cheers resonated in stores and schools. "We really did it! Incredible! Wonderful!" remembered a middle schooler on hearing the news on the radio.

Yamamoto's endeavor sowed a whirlwind, of course. On hearing the news, Churchill slept soundly with the knowledge that American might would finally be brought to bear on the Allied side. When the U.S. strategy of annihilation went into effect, he noted contentedly, the Japanese "would be ground to powder." In vengeful fury, the Americans vowed to ruin the Japanese. Tokyo promised to give back the same. The United States and Japan exhibited an uncontrollable rage and hatred toward each other. Pearl Harbor ignited those feelings, and they never ceased until a war without mercy concluded nearly four years later. Roosevelt could not justify entering the war on the basis of defending European colonialism from Japanese encroachment, but the catastrophe of December 7 slammed the door on aloofness from the conflict. He requested a declaration of war, accusing Japan of an unprovoked attack on a "day that will live in infamy." Congress approved and Australia, New Zealand, and China joined America in war against Japan on December 9. After Germany and Italy backed Japan against America two days later (although this was not the last time that Tokyo failed to coordinate policies with its European allies), Congress declared war on all the Axis powers. Raging in Europe, Africa, and now the Pacific, this was truly a world war of annihilation.

PACIFIC WAR

The stunning attack at Pearl Harbor was not Japan's sole achievement in December 1941. Tokyo took aim on the central and western Pacific Ocean and Southeast Asia to secure the resources of the Co-Prosperity Sphere, isolate China, and build a wide defensive perimeter. The latter extended well into the Pacific—to the "unsinkable air-craft carriers" of the Mariana, Marshall, and Gilbert Island chains, as the military called them—from which to meet the impending U.S. offensive. Japan operated on a shoe-string of logistics. The Japanese Navy drew on just 49 oil tankers in 1941 compared to America's 425 and Britain's 389, with one-sixth of their tonnage. In the opening phase of the Pacific war, however, deficiencies in the economy of scale was overcome by planning, preparation, and synchronized operations. Combined with an offensive mentality and a tired, uncoordinated defense on the part of its enemies, these fighting elements gave Japan an edge over three imperial powers.

The campaigns varied in difficulty but were feasible. The unfortified American island of Guam in the Marianas, which succumbed on December 10, 1941 was easy prey. The Japanese also took New Britain Island and its strategic harbor of Rabaul, airfields on Bougainville and Buka in the northern Solomons, and Makin in the Gilbert chain. Within hours of the Pearl Harbor operation, the Japanese bombed the U.S. Marine garrison on Wake Island, about 2,000 miles west of Hawaii. On December 12, the Marine Corps repelled the invading force of Rear-Admiral Kajioka Sadamichi, sinking two destroyers and damaging a transport. Kimmel tried to reinforce the island, but he was fired five days later. His replacement did not send relief. After borrowing two of Nagumo's aircraft carriers that were returning from Pearl Harbor, Kajioka went in a second time. The U.S. Marines sank two more ships, a submarine, and 21 planes, but Japan occupied Wake for the remainder of the war. The Americans bypassed the island when they began their central Pacific campaign in 1943.

Meanwhile, despite his skills as a showman and manipulator, Douglas MacArthur could not simply will a defense of the Philippines. Because of Japanese power and American weakness, little could be done to save him. His 107 P-40 fighter planes and 35 B-17 bombers faced 500 aircraft of the Japanese 5th Air Group flying from Formosan bases. A day after Pearl Harbor, air raids destroyed Clark and Iba fields and hit the naval bases at Subic Bay and Cavite. The commander of the Far East Air Force, Major General Lewis Brereton, had parked the B-17s and P-40s on the tarmac in a similar fashion to the line-up at Hickam Field in Hawaii. Nearly all were destroyed.

Making a further mockery of MacArthur's preparations, Japanese Fourteenth Army under Lieutenant-General Masaharu Homma, who was familiar with Western military culture, landed on Luzon and marched on Manila in the Philippines. Two Filipino-American divisions did not stop him on the beaches or the roads. The Americans asked for support, but the British Eastern Fleet headed to the Dutch East Indies per a prewar agreement. Embracing the Europe-First strategy, FDR did nothing. MacArthur refused to enact a plan calling for a withdrawal to the Bataan Peninsula to await help and thereby squandered a month in which he might have built up the Bataan depots. As Homma approached Manila, MacArthur declared the capital a demilitarized open city to grant it immunity from attack and retreated to Corregidor, a fortified island two miles off Bataan. He awaited the oncoming Japanese siege, bereft of ammunition, food, and medicine. Due to his lofty stature, MacArthur was not court-martialed for his errors, but his blunders proved costly.

The Japanese also wanted to wipe out all vestiges of British rule in Asia. They targeted the tiny British colony of Hong Kong and its garrison of 12,000 men. Britain looked on Hong Kong with pride and thought its forces could hold the impregnable island against presumably mediocre enemy troops. This was no time for arrogance, however. Major-General Christopher Maltby could count on neither British nor Chinese reinforcements. Behind a three-mile long defensive line north of Kowloon, three battalions of Scottish and Indians troops tried to slow the Japanese. Another three battalions, including the first two Canadian units to see action in the war, manned Hong Kong Island along with a hodgepodge of local volunteers and artillery. Maltby had just a handful of old aircraft and a sea force of a destroyer, eight motor torpedo boats, and four gunboats. Sea Eagle bombers made quick work of the aircraft on the morning of December 8. The next day, Twenty-Third Army's 38th Division, under Lieutenant-General Sano Tadayoshi, reached the Kowloon line. Maltby evacuated from the mainland to Hong Kong, after which Sano bombarded his position until he finally put troops ashore on December 18. Royal Navy torpedo boats hit Japanese vessels trying to ferry across reinforcements, but Sano had air superiority and decimated Maltby's tiny fleet. Sano moved inland, splitting apart the British troops as his enraged troops pillaged the population of the city. It took a week before the Allied force gave up, exhausted and short of supplies. On Christmas evening, the governor of the colony surrendered even though a Canadian company of the Royal Rifles attacked Stanley Village that day. The invaders suffered 2,754 casualties and the garrison 4,400, or a third of its force. Some escaped, but most became prisoners of Japan, which held Hong Kong for the rest of the war.

The Japanese also bulldozed back the Commonwealth forces on the Malay peninsula. To guard their flanks in the Malayan campaign, they moved into southern Burma while the clever former commander of the Kwantung Army, Lieutenant-General Tomoyuki Yamashita, invaded northern Malaya and southern Thailand with Twenty-Fifth Army on the night of December 7. Perhaps his nation's best general, but banished from power twice due to political intrigues, Yamashita was supported by the able but cautious Vice Admiral Nobutake Kondo. His Southern Force controlled all air, naval, and amphibious operations in Malaya, the Philippines, and the East Indies. A modest advocate of naval airpower, Vice-Admiral Jizaburo Ozawa oversaw the landings with his Malayan Force. Recognizing his three divisions of 60,000 soldiers were outnumbered by the British, Yamashita supported them with superior naval and air power including 158 naval aircraft and 459 aircraft of the 3rd Air Division.

Shooting actually started before the Pearl Harbor attack when Sea Eagles downed a British flying boat to keep the attack force's whereabouts secret. Then Ozawa bombarded Kota Bharu in northern Malaya at 1:15 a.m., failing to coordinate with the Pearl Harbor attackers. It did not matter, as Yamashita's troops took control. They stormed ashore at Singora and Patani in supposedly neutral Thailand (although defense minister and future premier, Phibum Songkhram, was favorably disposed toward the Japanese) and over the next two days landed on the northern Malayan coast. The idea was to chip away at British strength and advance down the peninsula to Singapore. The British Commander-in-Chief Far East, Air Chief Marshal Robert Brooke-Popham, was an uninspired leader who oversaw a jumble of ineffective defensive arrangements of Singapore, Malaya, Burma, British Borneo, and Hong Kong. He called for more airpower to supplement his weak force of 158 outdated aircraft but did not press the matter. He also lacked tanks and above all, a workable plan of defense. Brooke-Popham sent troops everywhere to meet the Japanese, counting on inferior Indian soldiers to counter them. And he relied on the striking power of the Royal Navy's Task Force Z, which was sent to Singapore in October.

Japanese aircraft operated from the Singora and Patani airfields and strips in southern French Indochina to catch British planes on the ground at their forward bases and neutralize protection for Force Z. The task force was comprised of three destroyers and the battleships *Prince of Wales* and *Repulse,* which had been sent to Singapore in October. The aircraft carrier *Indomitable,* which usually accompanied Force Z, had run aground in the West Indies. Under the command of Admiral Tom Phillips, Force Z sortied from Singapore on December 8 to surprise Yamashita's convoys of troops. But the Japanese detected his movements. Without air cover from either land-based aircraft or from a carrier, the two battleships attempted to block the purported landings at Kuantan. Yet faulty intelligence not only revealed that the landings were not in process, but Phillips maintained radio silence and thereby denied himself air support. Meanwhile, after tracking *Prince of Wales* and *Repulse,* Rear-Admiral Matsunaga Sadaichi's First Air Force flew from Indochina on December 10 and attacked the battleships. *Repulse* rang the alarm bells but within an hour and a half had gone to the bottom. An hour later, *Prince of Wales* followed, taking 840 sailors including Phillips with it. They were the first capital ships sunk in battle in open sea by aircraft alone. A Japanese patrol plane dropped a wreath on their watery graves. The catastrophe did not approach the magnitude of Pearl Harbor, but the strategic situation was transformed. Japan now dominated the Western Pacific.

With the disappearance of Allied naval power, Malaya and Singapore lay exposed. Yamashita's 5th Division crossed the Malayan peninsula and routed Indian troops who had never seen a tank. The Imperial Guards Division occupied Bangkok as a prelude to descending down the west coast toward Singapore. The two forces linked up on December 24; and three weeks later, they seized the capital of Kuala Lumpur. The Koba and Takumi Detachments of the 18th Division flowed down the east coast. Untrained in jungle warfare, the invading troops were still veterans of the China campaign and thus able to adjust to circumstances. They used bicycles on the good roads in highly mobile maneuvers that leapfrogged them southward at great speed. The troops outflanked the British by jungle assaults or landings by sea in small boats. The Malayan population aided them out of pride as fellow Asians or to root out British colonialism.

The British withdrew the III Corps to Johore under the command of Lieutenant General Arthur Percival while elements of Australian and Indian divisions tried to halt the two-pronged offensive. Despite the vigorous defense of Johore led by Brooke-Popham's successor, Archibald Wavell (who arrived fresh from the Middle East), Commonwealth forces could not stem the tide. The Australians flooded surrounding mangrove swamps with oil and set them ablaze. Fearful of being burned to death, Japanese troops plunged forward with fixed bayonets. As machine-gunner Ochi Harumi remembered, "[n]o longer human at the hour of death, the Japanese darted after the enemy, goring anyone in their path with the bayonet. During the frenzied killing on the beach, the soldiers lost their spiritual balance." Resting troops then severed the wrist or fingers of fallen comrades, put them in a box to be disposed of later, and said a quick prayer. By January 31, 1942, British units had retreated to Singapore, the colony at the base of the Malayan peninsula. The base was fortified to fend off an attack from the sea—its guns turned toward the sea—but the Japanese approached from inland at the back side. The dire situation for the fortress symbolized a British empire teetering on the brink of extinction.

Simultaneous offensives also took the Japanese into the Netherlands East Indies, prized for their vast oil fields and other natural resources. The Imperial Command understood that an invasion had to be quick and multipronged to prevent a Dutch scorched-earth policy that might destroy these precious raw materials. On December 20, Lieutenant-General Hitoshi Imamura sent elements of Sixteenth Army from Mindanao in the Philippines to Dutch Borneo, Celebes, and the Moluccas. For the first time, Japanese paratroopers saw action, dropping on an airfield in north Celebes on January 11. Oil and airfields fell into Hitoshi's hands. More treasures were available once additional troops resisted raids on his holdings by Allied forces.

The Allies hastily reorganized at the Arcadia conference beginning on December 22, 1941, code name for the first Washington conference. Churchill and Roosevelt agreed to coordinate their military operations and discussed where to dispatch troops. General Archibald Wavell, fired from his Middle East duties, was appointed to head the ABDA (American-British-Dutch-Australian) combined command. Its first task was to defend Singapore and the Netherlands East Indies. Wavell put his headquarters at Lembang in Java. But coordination was too tricky, he had insufficient naval and air forces at his command and no strategic reserves, and member states fell to squabbling. ABDA was just an acronym with little capability of defending the Malay Barrier, itself a myth perpetuated by the so-called Singapore strategy of the Royal Navy. This involved the deployment of ships from European waters to the bastion of Singapore in the Far East. That strategy was little more than words, as the Japanese were in the process of demonstrating.

The Philippines were under siege; the U.S. Pacific fleet lay in tatters; and Indochina, Thailand, and all of the Malayan peninsula but the very tip was in Japanese hands. The Allies faced dark days ahead in Asia, but the sun was rising on the Empire of Japan. The Axis powers rejoiced. Across the world, the Germans had also made their mark. Although the North African desert war had reached a stalemate, they held a position that threatened British defense of Egypt. On the Eastern front, Barbarossa had ground to a halt; but it seemed just a matter of time—some months for winter to thaw—before the Third Reich renewed the attack. Whether the Allies could blunt Axis gains and save the fate of millions was a big question as the new year of 1942 dawned.

PART III

Turning Points

1942–1943

There were broken bodies and dead, sweet hearts. Still, it was better than the gas.

MARKUS ZUSAK
The Book Thief

At the end of 1941, Anglo-American officials forged their war aims at the Arcadia meeting. Twenty-four countries, including the Soviet Union and China, ultimately joined the United States and Great Britain in this United Nations Declaration. At the time, Germany occupied much of the USSR and North Africa, Italy roamed the Mediterranean, and Japan rolled through Asia. Despite the glum news, the Allies pledged to impose a strategy of annihilation that tolerated no compromise. Hitler, Mussolini, and Tojo were put on notice. The United Nations would cooperate to defeat—unconditionally and completely—the Axis enemies. This hard-line approach—a product of inter-Allied negotiations, vengeful public sentiment, and the pursuit of justice—assured a bloody fight to the finish that would brook no sympathy for military personnel and civilians alike. Thus, even as they scored victories in mid-1942, a shadow fell over the Axis. They held seemingly impregnable positions abroad, the Germans having recently made their biggest territorial acquisitions so far in the war Hundreds of millions around the world were subjugated to fascism and militarism. But grand thoughts of empire—a Third Reich stretched across the Eurasian landmass, a Co-Prosperity Sphere spanning Asia and the Pacific, a Mediterranean controlled from Rome—spoke to increasingly unrealistic ambitions over three years into World War II.

CHAPTER 11

Japan in Triumph and Stalemate

CONQUERING COLONIES

Regardless of the United Nations' intent, the facts on the ground in Asia belied the rhetoric. Japan's victories mounted in a stunning array that sent enemies reeling. These included the signatories of the UN Declaration as well as the ABDA Command. By mid-1942, Japan ruled the second biggest colonial empire in the world and had accomplished a cardinal goal of possessing the oil-rich Dutch East Indies.

Tokyo's foremost victim, Great Britain, pondered the fall of Singapore. Into this center of European imperialism and one of the biggest strategic harbors in the world, Arthur Percival, head of Malaya Command, withdrew the British garrison from the Straits of Johore on January 31, 1942. He had helped organize home defenses during the battle of Britain before transfer to Asia as a corps commander. Because of inexperience at this level, he misjudged the situation. Percival divided Malay, Australian, Indian, and British brigades among northern, southern, and western sectors of the island. They numbered about 70,000 troops plus 15,000 unarmed administrative personnel. But his troops were green, understrength, and demoralized from retreat. Determined to defend the entire 70 mile coastline, he spread out his forces thinly to repel the invasion from the sea. His air cover was inadequate while General Yamashita had plenty of planes and tanks to support his 35,000 Imperial Army troops. In addition, Singapore's fortress guns could be turned inland but lacked proper ammunition; they were stocked with armor-piercing shells designed to sink ships but too big to be effective against infantry and small transport boats. They might not be needed anyway, assumed Percival. He did not believe Yamashita could penetrate 200 miles down the peninsula through difficult jungle terrain.

Pressing Percival, the skilled Yamashita launched the attack on Singapore on the night of February 8–9, 1942. He landed battle-tested soldiers of the 5th and 18th Divisions on the northwest coast to envelop the British defense line and capture the city's reservoirs. The next night, the Imperial Guards Division came ashore west of the Causeway and overwhelmed the dogged defenders at great sacrifice. Within three days, Commonwealth forces were in a precarious situation, although the Japanese were also low on supplies. Percival ordered a perimeter defense and deserters fled while refugees flooded the city center in fits of drunkenness, looting, and mayhem. Morale and organization crumbled as the Japanese moved in without conscience. For example, Imperial Japanese soldiers entered the Alexandra Barracks Hospital on February 14 claiming that Indian snipers had fired on them from the building. They bayoneted several orderlies and patients—even one on the operating table—then marched the rest to a bungalow where they were systematically massacred the next day. On the afternoon of February 15, Percival heeded the advice of his commanders and surrendered. Over 62,000 troops were taken prisoner, though many Indian troops joined the Indian National Army formed in February by the Japanese and nationalist Giani Pritam Singh. The Japanese military police executed more than 30,000 Singapore Chinese on racial and political grounds as part of their strategy of annihilation.

Yamashita had nearly run out of supplies and thus considered withdrawing, but in the end, the resolute "Tiger of Malay" won the prize of Singapore at the expense of 1,714 dead and 3,378 wounded. On hilltops surrounding the city, cries of "Banzai!" erupted from incredulous Japanese troops. They were astounded over the rout of the British, many of whom lay submissively at their feet as prisoners. Incredibly, Japan took the entire Malayan peninsula in just 70 days, inflicting 38,000 casualties and taking over 130,000 prisoners. Some 50,000 Chinese lay dead in Malaya and Singapore by the end of the war. The triumph in Malaya was for the Japanese Army what Pearl Harbor was for the Imperial Navy: victory over a supposedly superior Western power. Churchill called the fall of Singapore "the greatest disaster in British military history," but the calamity was even worse than he admitted. The administrative and military bungling, compounded by desertions and the confused performance of the troops, was shameful. The Australians felt betrayed by the British whose propaganda blamed the disaster on poor Aussie discipline. In reality, Britain's "Singapore strategy" on which Australia based its entire defense was a masterpiece of illusion. It had called for dispatch of the Royal Navy from European waters to Singapore, but it relied on American help that was simply not forthcoming. Britain's empire was no more, and the Indian Ocean lay exposed. The best that can be said for the fall of Singapore from the Allied viewpoint was its minimal bearing on the larger war. Despite the psychological blow and the loss to Britain of Malayan resources, Singapore proved expendable for the Allies in a material sense.

More glory for Japan lay ahead. The ABDA Command had little answer for aggression in the Netherlands East Indies. Imperial Army forces seized airfields, oil centers, and other strategic resource and military points. By mid-February, Sixteenth Army paratroopers landed at the huge oil refinery at Palembang on southern Sumatra and then captured Dutch Timor. On February 19, 1942, bombers from the same carrier

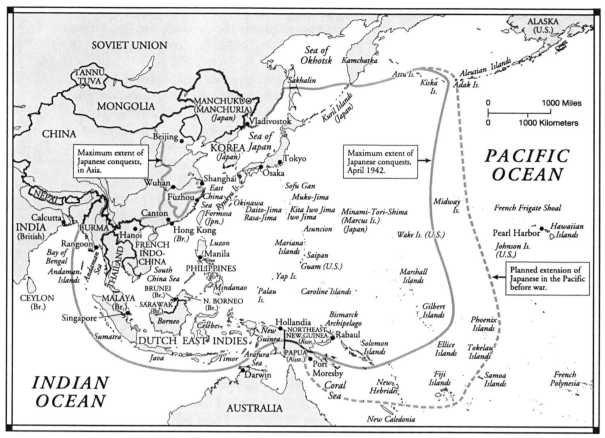

Map 11.1 Japan in the Pacific and Asia. Credit: Douglas Brinkley and Michael E. Haskew, *The World War II Desk Reference*, p. 80.

force that had been at Pearl Harbor attacked Darwin by surprise and destroyed the Australian port. Air raids knocked out Wavell's air power—the most crushing blow issued when 23 Zero fighters downed 40 Allied fighters. Although U.S. destroyers sank four transports and a patrol boat near Balikpapan, the Imperial Navy ruled the seas around the oil-rich Dutch East Indies. This became apparent during the battle of the Java Sea, fought on the afternoon and night of February 27, the first fleet encounter of the Pacific war.

The Japanese had isolated the island of Java—Wavell ABDA headquarters—and sent 41 transports to Surabaya under the command of Vice-Admiral Ibo Takahashi to finish off Allied forces. Vice-Admiral Takeo Takagi's four cruisers and 14 destroyers guarded the transports with superior firepower. They were armed with the large Long Lance torpedo—at 30 feet long with a diameter of two feet—which could travel up to 49 knots and deliver a half ton of explosives at a 12-mile range due to its use of oxygen instead of compressed air for combustion. The weapon gave the task force a decided advantage over the ABDA forces particularly when fired in numbers that saturated the waters around warships. Takagi's disciplined organization, superior to the ABDA jumble of cruisers and 9 destroyers under the command of Dutch Rear-Admiral Karel Doorman, also gave him a marked edge. In a confusing battle, the Japanese kept their heads.

The ABDA force suffered from bad to nonexistent communications, lack of coordination, and the fact that unlike Takagi (a participant in the Philippines invasion), Doorman had never engaged in a fleet action. His ships did not even have codebooks. Doorman banked on a night battle, so he left reconnaissance aircraft on shore and his ships without cover. Takagi hit the British cruiser *Exeter,* which withdrew; sank two Dutch cruisers and three destroyers; and killed Doorman himself. Only one Japanese destroyer was damaged, although the next night, the two remaining ABDA cruisers came on the rest of the invasion fleet anchored west of Batavia. They sank two vessels and damaged three others before the Imperial Navy arrived in relief and sent the Allied ships to the bottom. *Exeter* and two destroyers then fled Surabaya for Ceylon; but the next morning, March 1, Takagi's force caught them. Only four U.S. destroyers survived the calamity in the Java Sea by escaping early to Australia.

Temporarily delayed by the sea battle, the Japanese landed on Java on March 1 and marched on Bandung. Within a week, the Dutch governor surrendered along with 93,000 soldiers of the Royal Netherlands East Indies Army. Imperial Army forces sent from Singapore also invaded northern Sumatra that day and captured the entire island by the end of March. From there, they began landings on Dutch New Guinea. Sporadic resistance continued for months in Dutch Borneo and Celebes. The Japanese occupied Batvia, renamed this capital city Jakarta, and possessed the valuable natural resources of the Netherlands East Indies. Tokyo brought Sumatra under the Malayan military administration and handed over authority of Java to the Imperial Army. The Imperial Navy oversaw Celebes, Borneo, the Moluccas, and Dutch New Guinea. Guerrilla resistance appeared, especially on Timor. In general, however, the Japanese enjoyed the support of fellow Asians in the East Indies while they inflicted great suffering on the European colonialists who remained behind. Even before the battle, Wavell had dissolved the futile ABDA Command and pulled out to Burma to leave the Dutch holding the bag. Japan had the economic prize of its Greater Co-Prosperity Sphere—Dutch oil.

For many in the region, the Asian conflict was really a race war against white supremacy. The Japanese represented liberation from years of colonialism. As the Malayan campaign proceeded, Japan found support in its campaign in British Burma. Tokyo initially intended to deny the capital of Rangoon to the Americans and British as a supply depot, troop staging area, and air base for Claire Chennault's Flying Tigers. In December 1941, the Uno Force occupied the southernmost tip of Burma across from Thailand to interdict British air reinforcements to Malaya from India. A month later, two divisions of Lieutenant-General Ida Shojiro's Fifteenth Army moved up the Burmese coast backed by the 10th Air Brigade and the new Japanese-trained Burma Independence Army. This latter group of rebels opposed to 1,300 British forces were eventually absorbed into the Burma National Army, which Japan crafted in August 1943.

The British hoped to stop the fall of Rangoon, a port that so dominated communications and transportation that its loss would prompt the loss of Burma itself. Seventeenth Indian Army under Major-General John Smyth blew up the Sittang River bridge on February 23 as a delaying action. As a result of this controversial decision, he stranded two of his three brigades and almost all of his artillery and transports on the eastern bank of the river. The Commander-in-Chief Burma, Lieutenant-General Thomas Hutton, refused to retreat until too late, but Smyth's failure to build a solid defense made matters worse. Both he and Hutton were removed, the latter replaced by Harold Alexander who also failed to stem the enemy advance. British forces were just too strung out. Alexander even came close to capture at a roadblock, and only the decision of a local commander to withdraw toward Rangoon saved him. Outflanked on the ground and overpowered in the air, the British retreated. Japanese troops seized Rangoon on March 8, 1942.

Retreat was the order of the day for the Allies in Asia in Spring 1942. Chinese troops under U.S. Lieutenant-General Joseph Stilwell attempted to save the British. After the reinforced Fifteenth Japanese Army pushed back Wavell's run south on Toungoo, Stilwell's 38th Chinese Division rescued the 1st Burma Division defending the oil fields

Japanese troops in Burma. Credit: Center for the Study of War Experience at Regis University, Denver, Colorado: Mainichi Newspaper Company.

of Yenangyuang. It then vacated Burma for India. On March 19, Alexander created the Burma Corps under Lieutenant-General William Slim. Newly arrived from East Africa and Syria, Slim had commanded Indian troops since 1919. He now led the "Burcorps"— the remnants of 27,000 British and native forces of the Burma garrison—on a skillful fighting withdrawal from Rangoon into India. The retreat became the longest in the British Army's history. Wrenching total catastrophe from Japanese jaws, Slim's successful evacuation was the only light in the gloom of Britain's situation on the Asian subcontinent. And it was really a defeat all the same. Ida's divisions continued up to the border of China. On June 17, they reached their northernmost wartime point in Burma at Sumprabum, a town just over 1,200 miles from Kunming at one end of the Burma Road. Chinese Nationalist forces retreated into their homeland with 5,000 dead. Japanese forces also moved westward to Akyab on the Bay of Bengal, which fell on May 4. Now Commander-in-Chief India, Wavell launched a counteroffensive to recapture Burma. In December 1942, this also failed when the Imperial Army rebuffed the 14th Indian Division's assault on Akyab.

In four months, Japan had harassed Britain from its colony; and within a year, Tokyo sponsored the independence of Burma. Suffering over 13,463 casualties to Japan's 4,400 or so, Britain balked at another counteroffensive for a year. The supply route to China was cut. The British naval base at Ceylon remained safe even after air strikes sank the carrier *Hermes* and the cruisers *Dorsetshire* and *Cornwall*, and Britain could still reach India and replenish the Army for a renewed campaign against the Japanese. But as the Germans resumed their offensives in North Africa and Ukraine in mid-1942, it appeared that India might be invaded from both east and west. Loss of this imperial jewel would spell the ultimate disaster for the British. Tokyo encouraged Indian nationalism within a Japanese framework as British power in Asia reached its nadir, although the Indian Army remained largely loyal to its colonial mother. The Imperial Japanese Army certainly engaged in imperial overstretch as it tugged at the end of a long logistical line. For the moment, however, these difficulties did not mask Japan's sweeping triumph in Burma nor the brewing political rebellion against British rule in India.

AMERICA'S TURN

Japan did not spare the sword for the Americans, either. In the Philippines—the sole remaining Allied garrison in the northern hemisphere between Ceylon and Hawaii—Masaharu Homma's Kimura Detachment and the raw 65th Brigade readied to finish the job. Homma's forces smashed U.S.-Filipino defenses on the Bataan peninsula on January 9, but they stalled a month later when they could not breach the secondary defense line. Douglas MacArthur's troops and medical staff, including nurses, huddled in the Bataan garrison. Their stockpiles of food, fuel, medicine, and ammunition were petering out. U.S. Army Chief of Staff George Marshall hoped to save the Philippines, but the dwindling U.S. Asiatic Fleet was fighting for the Malay Barrier and thus there was no chance of convoying supplies and reinforcement into Manila Bay. On March 11, after lambasting Washington for not sending reinforcements, MacArthur departed the Philippines under FDR's orders and left his subordinate, Jonathan Wainwright, in charge. The president did not want General MacArthur, a potential political rival, to become a martyr. On arriving in Australia, MacArthur promised to return and rescue stranded U.S. forces. Debilitated in mind and body and with instructions not to surrender, many of these "battling bastards of Bataan" felt betrayed by his withdrawal.

MacArthur became a hero because of the heroism of his stranded troops. Wainwright's garrison hardly had enough supplies to last through March. The troops lived on 1,000 calories a day by the end of the month, less than a third of the nutritional requirement to prevent starvation. After reinforcing his spent Imperial Army troops, Homma renewed the attack on April 3. He fought a plodding, systematic siege. When Wainwright's counterattack failed, the ground commander, Major-General Edward King, capitulated six days later to avoid a massacre despite MacArthur's order to fight. The end came quickly and brutally. About 86,000 Filipinos and Americans, including 26,000 civilians, surrendered on April 9, 1942. A day later, they were forced to begin a 65-mile march to a railhead at San Fernando from which they would be sent by train to a prison camp. The frail physical conditions of the captives made such travel on the dust-choked and unshaded roads grueling. Moreover, because the Japanese thought there were only 25,000 prisoners at the end of Bataan, and not triple that number, logistics converted a grim situation into a nightmare.

The inexperience of the Japanese troops and their contempt for enemy warriors who chose surrender over noble death perpetrated the infamous two-week Bataan Death March. About 600 Americans and 7,000 Filipinos died along the way, felled by malnutrition, exhaustion, disease, or impatient captors. Many of the victims were clubbed to death, shot, or beheaded. So horrible was their treatment that Homma and his superior, Yamashita, were charged with war crimes and executed in 1946. Their trial sparked controversy because both shunned responsibility for the treatment meted out to their prisoners. They had been unaware of their subordinates' behavior. In any case, just like the Nazis in Ukraine, the Japanese made enemies among the Filipinos by their cruel war of annihilation on civilians. They also paid the price by provoking resistance. When news of the harsh episode leaked out, the Death March went down in history as one of the worst atrocities experienced by the United States in war. The treatment of prisoners in the Philippines—and most notably on Bataan—was a contributing factor to America's turn to vicious reprisals and their own strategy of annihilation later in the war against Japan.

As the captives fell in line for San Fernando, about 2,000 troops escaped to Corregidor two miles away to join the 9,000-member garrison. Corregidor and other harbor defenses denied the Japanese use of the superb Manila Bay harbor. The site of MacArthur's former headquarters, the rock of Corregidor possessed enough rations and strong fortifications to endure a six-month siege. A tunnel complex gave protection for hospitals and storerooms. Enemy aircraft bombed the island with little damage to these critical facilities. Moving artillery on to Bataan, however, Homma began a bombardment supplemented by air raids so intense that he changed the island's topography. The invaders blew away the shore road, for instance, and denuded the island of trees. The 4th Division then landed on Corregidor on May 5 and established a beachhead in which to bring in tanks and artillery. After pounding the garrison, the Japanese penetrated the tunnel system the next morning where 1,000 wounded hid.

March of death on Bataan.   Credit: Center for the Study of War Experience at Regis University, Denver, Colorado: U.S. National Archives.

General Wainwright capitulated. Remnants of his force scattered into the countryside to organize resistance movements with Filipino guerrillas, but most natives (including government officials) survived the occupation by varying degrees of collaboration. Japan took surrenders on the numerous islands over the next four weeks. These were essentially completed by June 9 on Cebu, Mindanao, the Visayans, Panay, Negros, Leyte, Samar, and Tacloban. More substantial resistance remained on the southern islands of Mindanao and Jolo. An exile government formed under President Manuel Quezon but the fears of opponents of U.S. expansionism at the turn of the century were realized. The Philippines had become America's Achilles' heel. All but collaborationists, anti-Americans, and the Marxist Hukbalahaps—the military arm of the Filipino Communist Party formed in 1942 to resist the Japanese—awaited the fulfillment of MacArthur's promise to return. Japan had routed the United States from its own territory.

Although large gaps existed at sea and on land, Japan's Asian-Pacific offensive was geographically vaster than the Third Reich's sweep across Europe and done faster. Its enemies were weaker than Germany's, but the distance covered and efficiency of force used compared impressively to the European theater. With just 11 divisions, two fleets, 700 army aircraft, and 1,500 naval planes, Japan invaded an area stretching over 7,000 miles from Pearl Harbor to southern Siam. The distance from the coast of France to Ukraine was less than half of that—roughly 3,300 miles—and from North Africa to northern Norway about 2,000 miles. Berlin was much closer to Moscow than Tokyo was to the port of Rabaul, its eastern outlying port some 3,500 miles from Japan. By mid-1942, Hitler had subjugated 206 million foreign people; Tojo controlled 371 million.

Yet like Germany, Japan faced the future with less certainty than six months before. At least the Germans readied to renew their assault on the Soviet Union. Neither the Imperial Navy nor Army knew what was next. They had no plan beyond their initial conquests, nor could they agree on one for the next phase of operations. Bureaucratic rivalry caused concern. The Imperial Army wanted to focus on China and the new conquests of Southeast Asia while the Imperial Navy sought to expand the defensive perimeter in the Pacific. Within the Imperial Navy itself, debate persisted over where to strike next or even whether offensive operations to shore up the perimeter were in the country's best interests. Japan was at the apex of its power in May 1942, but could it extend or defend its vast holdings? Perhaps, but strategists also knew that a U.S. response was in the wind.

INTO THE PACIFIC

While Japan pondered its options, the forlorn Allies responded by reorganization. The United States assumed nearly complete control of the Pacific war after the ABDA collapsed in February. Australia and New Zealand contributed large numbers of land forces—sometimes more than America—to the war against Japan, but the U.S. Navy and Army maintained their monopoly of command. Washington divided the Pacific into two main theaters. MacArthur ruled over the Southwest Pacific Area of Australia, New Guinea, the Solomons, the Philippines, Borneo, the Bismarck archipelago, and most of the Dutch East Indies. Japan held most of this territory. He fell under the authority of George Marshall. The U.S. Navy oversaw the rest of the vast Pacific Ocean Areas theater under Admiral Chester Nimitz, the commander of the U.S. Pacific Fleet. A former submariner admired by FDR, the genial but tough Nimitz was a superb strategist. He took orders from the irascible Ernest King, chief of naval operations and Commander in Chief of the United States Fleet. King, Marshall, and U.S. Army Air Force head Henry Arnold served on the newly created Joint Chiefs of Staff, a counterpart to the British Chiefs of Staff Committee. Because the Pacific theater evolved into the U.S. Navy's show, King ultimately called the shots.

At the behest of Roosevelt, these leaders considered ways to quiet the public clamor for a response to the Japanese whirlwind. They decided to bomb Japan itself by a raid launched from aircraft carriers because the Allies lacked land bases within range. Yet the flattops could not get too close to Japan or they risked discovery. Secrecy was a must in this publicity stunt meant to bolster morale at home. On April 1, 1942, the carrier *Hornet* left San Francisco loaded with sixteen twin-engine Army B-25 Mitchell bombers and volunteer pilots commanded by Colonel James Doolittle. They had trained on land for takeoff but never on a real carrier. Two weeks later *Hornet* rendezvoused with Task Force 16 under Vice-Admiral William "Bull" Halsey, the aggressive commander of the Pacific Fleet's carriers. After avoiding enemy patrols, Halsey sailed within 700 miles of Japan by dawn on April 18. Imperial Navy picket boats sighted the task force and forced him to alter course, but one alerted Tokyo. Detection compelled Doolittle to take off immediately rather than at night as planned. Each loaded with four 500-pound bombs, the B-25s attacked Kobe, Nagoya, Yakosuka naval yard, Yokohama, and Tokyo. Twelve hit the capital. One aborted to Vladivostok, and the rest crash-landed in China.

The Doolittle raid cheered Americans in the dark days of Spring 1942 while it alarmed Japanese officials. About 50 people were killed and 100 houses damaged mainly in Tokyo, but civilians seemed little impressed. Some even waved at the bombers because they mistook them for Japanese aircraft; the planes still had old identification emblems that included a red circle similar to the Rising Sun. Air-raid sirens did not sound until twenty minutes after the first bombs had dropped. The Imperial Army punished the Chinese who aided the downed crewmen, 71 of 80 of whom survived the raids, by launching an offensive in May on the Chekiang-Kiangsi area. Seeking revenge, the Imperial Army killed 250,000 peasants. They even resorted to biological warfare that infected peasants and Japanese troops themselves with cholera, typhoid, anthrax, and other diseases. The Japanese also caught eight members of the Doolittle crew. Three were eventually executed while another died in prison. Roosevelt condemned the punishment as inhumane. On both sides, the mentality of annihilation burgeoned.

Within Tokyo government and military circles, the Doolittle raid added fuel to arguments over whether to engage the U.S. Pacific fleet in a decisive battle. Some leaned toward attacking into the Indian Ocean in conjunction with Germany to complete the conquest of Southeast Asia. This course entailed risks because the Americans might launch operations on Japan's back door as the Imperial Navy focused on an invasion of Ceylon and other points in the Indian Ocean. In early April, surface ships and submarines attacked Ceylon and sank 36 British vessels, including 29 merchantmen in the Bay of Bengal. A force seized the Andaman Islands. This completed the Southeast Asian campaign. But Admiral Yamamoto could not get those Doolittle bombers out of his mind. They had penetrated Japan's defensive perimeter but from where? FDR coyly replied that they came from "Shangri-la." Yamamoto opted to extend the perimeter farther out into the central Pacific to meet the Americans, guessing that Shangri-La was either the island of Midway or a grouping of U.S. aircraft carriers. First, though, the Imperial Navy wanted to neutralize Australia, a potential base of offensive operations against Japanese military ports at Rabaul and Truk. The fleet sailed from Rabaul around New Guinea to capture Port Moresby on the south coast of the Australian territory of Papua. This would give Japan a means to cut Allied supply and transport lines to Australia, isolate the defenseless nation (whose main body of troops were in the Middle East), and secure New Guinea.

Japanese troops landed at Lae and Salamaua on New Guinea to the north of the Papua peninsula and followed with seaborne assaults in April. Two beleaguered Australian units blocked an overland march across the rugged Owen Stanley Mountain range to Port Moresby. Conditions were challenging, as both sides suffered from malaria and dysentery. The Japanese decided to get their prey by sea. Vice-Admiral Shigeyoshi Inoue steered his large invasion convoy around the peninsula under the watch of Rear-Admiral Aritomo Goto light carrier *Shoho,* four heavy cruisers, and one destroyer. A strike force of the fleet carriers *Shokaku* and *Zuikaku,* two heavy cruisers, and six destroyers under Vice-Admiral Takeo Takagi accompanied the group. Two

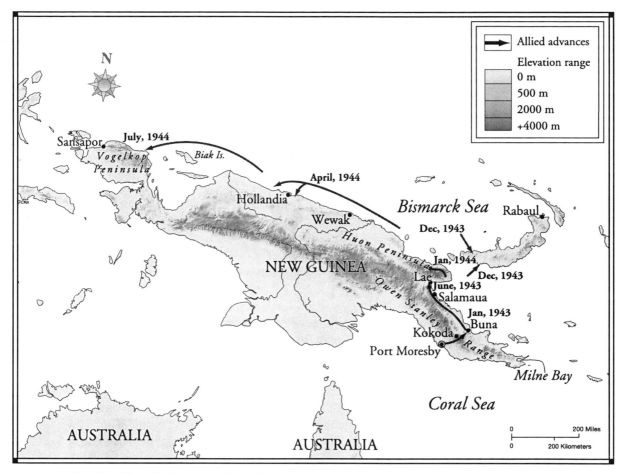

Map 11.2 New Guinea and Coral Sea.   Credit: Ronald Story, *Concise Historical Atlas of World War II: The Geography of Conflict*, Map 41, p. 87.

other convoys headed for neighboring Tulagi Island and the Louisiades to establish seaplane bases.

The stage was set for the battle of the Coral Sea. Tipped off by ULTRA intelligence intercepts, Nimitz added U.S. and Australian cruisers under British Rear-Admiral John Crace to two carrier task forces centered on the fleet carriers *Lexington* and *Yorktown*. On May 3, the Imperial Navy convoy took Tulagi without resistance; but aircraft from *Yorktown* beached a destroyer and sunk some smaller vessels the next day. Two days later, three Allied task forces under Rear-Admiral Jack Fletcher—whose recent decision to refuel his ships had left Wake Island unprotected—sailed toward Port Moresby. Inaccurate air reconnaissance led *Yorktown* to attack the convoys rather than the carriers, but Goto withdrew anyway. Planes from *Lexington* and *Yorktown* then sunk the carrier *Shoho*. Further confusion prevented attacks by both sides on the main fleets until they located each other the next day on May 8. The Japanese planes were superior in maneuverability and firepower. The Americans damaged *Shokaku* but did not find *Zuikaku*. *Lexington* took two torpedo and three bomb hits, though damage control parties restored it to even keel. Fumes from its generator ignited on subsequent hits, and the ensuing explosion caused wild fires that sunk the ship. Crews not killed in the bombing or drowned were also dreadfully burned by the high-octane gas. Takagi's aces also damaged *Yorktown*.

The slugging continued, but Vice-Admiral Takagi did not press home his advantage. This first-ever naval action between carriers in which opposing surface vessels never sighted each other ended up as a tally for the United States. The loss of *Yorktown* hurt, but it did not cripple Nimitz's fleet. Takagi failed to finish off the enemy. Furthermore, two of his large carriers (one of them hobbled) lost many of their 121 aircraft. The Japanese also did not capture Port Moresby by sea. They settled for holding the Solomons and the Tulagi base and beginning construction of an airfield on Guadalcanal, an island to the southeast. These changes, as well as Yamamoto's impatient refusal to replace the lost planes and so many skilled pilots, had a dramatic effect on his plans to do away with the Americans. The United States earned a strategic triumph.

MIDWAY

Neither side had time to learn lessons from the engagement because the Japanese made their move in the central Pacific less than three weeks after the fight in the Coral Sea. American pilots studied new tactics to confront the Zero such as the Thach Weave aerial maneuver, which lured enemy aircraft into a snare set by constantly crossing U.S. fighters. But these tactics were really still under development. Meanwhile, Yamamoto wished to divert attention from the central Pacific. He ordered an invasion of uninhabited Attu and Kiska islands in the Aleutians to the west of the Alaskan mainland. Led by Vice-Admiral Boshiro Hosogaya, the Fifth Fleet landed unopposed between June 5 and 7, 1942 to begin an occupation that lasted well into 1943. The Japanese endured the bitterly cold weather of the North Pacific before retreating to an equally brutal defense of the Kuril Islands. The Alaska campaigns remained largely hidden from view, run by secret intelligence forces. In any case, the Americans did not fall for the feint. Rear Admiral Robert Theobald withdrew his task force to Kodiak 400 miles to the south at the easternmost end of the Aleutian chain where it met the Alaskan mainland. The main American fleet headed for the base on Midway Island, 1,000 miles west of Hawaii in the central Pacific.

Believing that the bulk of Nimitz's fleet was preoccupied in the Aleutians, Yamamoto relished wiping out the remainder with his 145 warships at Midway, including six aircraft carriers and 11 battleships. This was the largest Japanese naval group in history, a "Combined Fleet" designed to destroy the inferior enemy in the decisive battle that Japan had sought for decades. It would then move down the Aleutian chain, take Hawaii, and then compel FDR to sue for peace. This bold and rather eccentric plan would determine the war in the Pacific. Yamamoto erred from the start, however. He left the engagement up to America's choice of exactly when and where to fight. The admiral also thought *Yorktown* had been sunk along with *Lexington* in the Coral Sea and that America's other two carriers, *Enterprise* and *Hornet,* were far from Midway.

He was wrong on all counts. In any event, he reacted too late in sending submarines to screen off the area from Pearl Harbor. With ULTRA up his sleeve, Nimitz knew of the plan to attack Midway. Until early May, he had surmised that they would focus on the southwest Pacific; but decrypts revealed buildups in the Marianas in preparation for a long-range operation. He was incredulous that Yamamoto might commit his entire Combined Fleet to the central Pacific. Tokyo eliminated the certainty of this news by changing intelligence codes on May 24. Still, Nimitz had Yamamoto's detailed orders of four days before. The Imperial Navy was on its way to Midway.

Nimitz readied an ambush by assembling two carrier groups at Pearl Harbor. One force centered on Fletcher's hastily repaired *Yorktown*. The other, commanded by cool decision maker Raymond Spruance, was built around the carriers *Enterprise* and *Yorktown*. The two groups also marshaled 233 aircraft escorted by eight cruisers and 15 destroyers as well as 19 submarines. Beyond the reach of Japanese search planes, they took stations northeast of Midway before the Japanese submarine screen was in place. Vice-Admiral Nagumo, hero at Pearl Harbor, sailed with an imposing Imperial strike force of four carriers, two battleships, and smaller escort ships. An invasion transport force convoyed by a light cruiser and 10 destroyers, and the main group of three battleships, trailed him. Yet his forces were vulnerable to the unseen American carriers who sowed confusion and concern among the Imperial Navy's admirals.

The battle involved several air strikes. Nagumo's planes attacked Midway at dawn on June 4 and damaged installations. Unaware of the lurking U.S. carriers, he decided on rearming his reserve planes on the upper deck to prepare for a response from the American ships and a second strike against Midway. His timing was atrocious. Spruance sent out his torpedo bombers once the strike force had been sighted. Along with Midway-based bombers, they struck just as Nagumo's bombers were returning from their runs. Almost all of the American torpedo planes were lost without scoring a hit. *Yorktown's* squadron lost 12 out of 13, *Enterprise* watched 11 of 14 go into the seas, and *Hornet* sacrificed all of its torpedo planes. But the slow U.S. aircraft had drawn down the Japanese fighters to sea-level—below swiftly incoming American dive-bombers at 19,000 feet—which prevented the Sea Eagles from engaging the dive-bombers until too late. The Americans had a clear field on the Japanese fleet and were unmolested by fighters. They obliterated three carriers and their aircraft being serviced. A fourth carrier, *Hiryu*, fled the scene but sank that afternoon. Before going to the bottom, her bombers damaged *Yorktown* and the destroyer *Hammann* to the extent that Fletcher switched ships and gave overall command to Spruance. Struck by torpedoes from a submarine on June 6, the smaller vessel sunk immediately and *Yorktown* finally went to the bottom the next day. Nonetheless, caught flat-footed by Dauntless dive-bombers, the Imperial Navy could not recover. Terrified sailors looked over the destruction, watching fires spread and the attackers disappear over the horizon. "Five minutes! Who would have dreamed that the tide of battle would shift completely in that brief interval of time," lamented an airman on *Akagi* as the bulk of the Imperial Navy's carrier fleet disappeared under the sea.

Believing he faced superior forces, Nagumo noted his fleet's utter confusion and ordered a withdrawal. Yamamoto reversed him, but the unflappable Spruance had already pulled back out of range. He did not know that the main Combined Fleet was steaming toward Midway, but his retreat made the action moot. Yamamoto then called off the Midway operation. Spruance mopped up, sinking one crippled Japanese cruiser and damaging another.

Midway was a big defeat for the Japanese who asked how such a golden opportunity to crush the U.S. Navy had turned sour. The answers centered on their own miscalculations, enemy brilliance, and a lot of luck. For the first time, the Americans defeated the Imperial Navy as the balance of power at sea shifted from battleships to carriers. True, *Yorktown* sank, but all four of Japan's big carriers lay on the bottom. In the meantime, Tokyo made a long-term decision. The Imperial Navy turned from battleship construction to aircraft carriers, yet there was no way to replace the carriers within a reasonable time. The Japanese also lost nearly 300 planes as well as vast numbers of experienced air crews and naval crewmen. Historians argue that the aircraft and aviator losses were even more important than the carriers. The Imperial Navy reconstituted the fleet in 1944, but could never replace veteran flyers. Tokyo also postponed offensives on New Caledonia, Fiji, Samoa, and New Guinea. The battle of Midway made the central Pacific safe from further Japanese offensives; the Imperial Navy lost the initiative and never regained it. Above all, the battle of Midway proved to the Tokyo regime that Washington's capitulation was out of the question. Yamamoto had long thought that confronting the United States would be risky, and now his worry was borne out. Japan had enjoyed six months of ranging through Asia and the Pacific before the Americans countered. Six months after Pearl Harbor, Midway made him a prophet.

GUADALCANAL

Although they had only marginal naval superiority and limited resources, the Americans hoped to use the victory at Midway as a springboard for offensives against Japan's defensive perimeter. Japan had other plans. MacArthur lobbied for a naval attack against the base at Rabaul, but Nimitz feared engagements in restricted waters. Cognizant of MacArthur's influence with the top brass and American public, Nimitz opted for a two-pronged convergence on Rabaul—from New Guinea and the Solomon Islands. Admiral King did not like the idea because the U.S. Navy was overstretched, but Roosevelt and Marshall endorsed operations in both sectors. The U.S. Navy and Nimitz, however, and not MacArthur would command the theater. As MacArthur advanced up the northeastern side of New Guinea to Rabaul, Nimitz would climb the Solomons to meet him. Australia was also a major concern. The Imperial Navy had a seaplane base on tiny Tulagi Island just twenty miles across a strait from the island of Guadalcanal. From there it could sever the U.S. link to Australia. Guadalcanal must be taken to shut down Japanese operations in the area. Smarting from Midway, Yamamoto schemed differently. He wanted to try again to draw the U.S. Pacific Fleet into a decisive battle. Midway had merely been a case of bad luck for his country and the inexperienced Americans had not yet beaten his superb fleet. He would seek them off of New Guinea or in the Solomons, whichever they preferred. When he realized that the United States had more in mind than a mere raid or reconnaissance on Guadalcanal, Yamamoto decided to defend the Japanese Empire's perimeter by a rapid response.

Around and on Guadalcanal, the Americans took the initiative for the first time in the Pacific war, excepting the sideshow Doolittle raid. A steamy British-owned island 90 miles long and 50 miles wide at the bottom of the Solomons, Guadalcanal epitomized the emerging war of annihilation in the Pacific. U.S. prospects hinged on the seizure of the airstrip near Lunga Point—called Henderson Field by the Americans—in the middle of Guadalcanal's north coast. Japan sought to wipe out the U.S. Navy and defend the airfield. The battle opened when the Americans raced to Guadalcanal on August 7, 1942. Robert Ghormley, Commander-in-Chief South Pacific Area, took charge of the operation with Midway's Frank Jack Fletcher in tactical command. The abrasive Rear-Admiral Richmond Kelly Turner, who was partly blamed for Pearl Harbor because of his infighting in naval circles, directed an amphibious force of 19,000 men of the 1st Marine Division under Major-General Alexander Vandegrift. It met little resistance, except on two islets, Gavutu and Tulagi. On the latter, 3,000 Marines were required to overwhelm 750 defenders. By this time, Tokyo had turned its attention from Papua New Guinea to defending Guadalcanal. What followed telescoped into the most destructive naval campaign since the mid-17th century and the first test of land strength between the two nations.

Not only did the 2,000-soldier garrison on Guadalcanal counterattack against badly organized U.S. defensive arrangements, but controlling the seas proved as important as the fight on the island. American forces failed to secure lines of communication and guard themselves from Japanese assault. They knew little about the topography and Japan's battle plans. On landing, the U.S. Marines penetrated only a few miles inland. To make matters worse, Vice-Admiral Gunichi Mikawa sailed from Rabaul with a powerful naval force backed by bombers to chase the Americans off the island. The first attack planes appeared from Rabaul on the afternoon of the invasion. Mikawa then sent his fleet down the "Slot," a big channel within the Solomon chain, and downed 21 aircraft from Fletcher's task force while losing 28 of his own. Coordinated numbers of Coast Watchers—mainly Europeans who had settled in the Pacific islands—tipped off the Americans about the incoming bombers, but the air cover allowed Mikawa to surprise an Allied screening force off Savo Island on August 9.

The battle of Savo Island tested U.S. plans. Debuting the formidable Long Lance torpedo, the Imperial Navy sank the Australian cruiser *Canberra* and three U.S. sister cruisers: *Astoria, Quincy,* and *Vincennes.* It also blew the bow off the cruiser *Chicago* with no losses other than to a cruiser hit by a submarine. The area appropriately became known as Iron Bottom Sound. With daylight approaching, and worried about U.S. aerial bombardment, Mikawa did not follow up with attacks on the transports exposed in Lunga Bay off Guadalcanal. He missed an opportunity to scuttle Nimitz's Guadalcanal campaign before the U.S. Marines had built their perimeter defense around the Henderson airstrip. But in a battle of equal forces, the Japanese humiliated the Americans by proving far superior in night fighting. The battle killed 1,534 U.S. sailors (more than died at Pearl Harbor) and injured 709. It also caused a chain of decisions that weakened the invasion. Vulnerable to air attack, Fletcher withdrew his carriers. Without air cover, Turner spent one more day on the beaches and then pulled out the transports with 1,400 troops still on board. This left the U.S. Marines on the island without essential supplies except for short rations and Japanese rice. They worried about capture until the Cactus Air Force—a mixed force of mostly Marine Corps aircraft flown into Henderson Field—ended their isolation on August 20. The Japanese took advantage by sending in Seventeenth Army to finish off the depleted U.S. Marines.

Yet Japan underestimated its needs. Because they did not land in concentrations of strength (a pattern throughout the campaign), Imperial forces let the Americans entrench themselves on Guadalcanal. Downplaying Marine Corps capabilities and limited by the availability of troops from other theaters, Lieutenant-General Hyakutake Haruyoshi injected his soldiers piecemeal into the battle. On August 18, part of the Ichiki Detachment under Manchurian veteran Colonel Kiyonao Ichiki assaulted Henderson Field in the battle of Tenaru River. The attack was premature. The Japanese lacked adequate numbers to overwhelm the perimeter defense of wire and machine guns. As a result, 900 men in the unit were wiped out while the U.S. Marines suffered just over 100 casualties. The Americans then added planes to the airstrip. Henderson Field played a crucial role for the United States, as the land-based aircraft tipped the balance of airpower to the American side and more than replaced naval aircraft.

The killing on Guadalcanal was terrible and constant, as U.S. Marines recorded in their diaries. In one case, men sleeping in foxholes "were caught unaware by the Japs who crossed the Lunga River. [Corporal] K. was stabbed by a Jap officer with his saber right thru his face. He then raised his sword and came down on the sleeping [Corporal]. The blow almost severed his leg. It hit him right on the knee bone"; but fortunately, the Corporal was built like a barrel, and survived. The dead were buried in Japanese blankets. On Guadalcanal, as elsewhere in the Pacific theater, the fighting in the so-called good war was of the most brutal nature. Rage on the part of the Americans precluded the taking of prisoners, although the Japanese preferred to die rather than give up. The dead lay and rotted where they fell on Guadalcanal. Cleanup was left to bulldozers treating the corpses as waste disposal rather than as human beings requiring burial.

Hyukatake countered with the so-called Tokyo Express, which was the Coast Watcher's nickname for convoys of destroyer transports under Rear-Admiral Raizo Tanaka who came from Rabaul down the Slot each night. Bomber cover flew unhindered five hours from Rabaul and the northern Solomons, even though the Coast Watchers monitored their clockwork missions. U.S. forces responded by attacking the reinforcements by day. But because General Hyukatake preferred to feed troops on to Guadalcanal rather than send a sizable counterinvasion force, the Americans not only held. They even expanded the perimeter with the help of Seabees (naval engineer and construction battalions), reinforcements from the 2nd Marine Division, and the Cactus Air Force. The Tokyo Express eventually brought in enough Japanese troops to even the numbers with the Americans on Guadalcanal by mid-October, but Hyakutake missed a chance to push enemy forces off the island.

Encounters in the surrounding seas revealed the seesaw nature of the campaign. In the cautiously fought battle of the Eastern Solomons on August 24, Yamamoto's force damaged the U.S. fleet carrier *Enterprise*, but it lost the light carrier *Ryujo* and suffered damage to a seaplane tender. Aircraft downings were substantial—20 on the American side and the Japanese triple that figure. But less than a week later, the fleet

Dead Japanese on Bloody Ridge, Guadalcanal.   Credit: Center for the Study of War Experience at Regis University, Denver, Colorado.

carrier *Saratoga* was sent home for three months of repairs after being torpedoed. On September 15, the smallest of the fleet carriers, *Wasp,* went to the bottom and the new battleship *North Carolina* was hit by Japanese submarines.

Meanwhile, the Japanese resolved to chase their foe, at long last, off Guadalcanal. The entire Ichiki Detachment and the Kawaguchi Brigade of 3,000 troops landed east of the U.S. Marine's beachhead and assailed U.S. lines on September 12, 1942. In a three-pronged attack south of Henderson Field, they pushed back a Raider battalion to within 1,000 yards of the airstrip. The Marine Corps countered with heavy machine guns, howitzer, and mortars in this battle of Bloody Ridge to mow down banzai charges of suicide attacks. The Americans lost 150 men and the Japanese ten times that many. The Kawaguchi brigade retreated in a two-week death march, the injured left trailside and survivors given handfuls of rice to stave off starvation. As thousands of troops from the Sendai Division landed west of Henderson Field in early October, battleships unleashed such an intense bombardment that they nearly wiped out the airstrip. By the time they tried again to take it, the Japanese outnumbered the Americans. On October 23, Japan's third offensive began, but the human banzai waves were poorly organized. Reinforced by 3,000 men of the 164th Regiment of the U.S. Army's Americal Division, U.S. Marines left over 2,000 dead enemy troops strung on their wires and lost 300 in return. The Americans then expanded their perimeter, no longer waiting on the defensive. The two sides were bent on annihilating the other.

The Imperial Navy would not relent in trying to put more troops ashore. Following up its gains in the battle of the Eastern Solomons, it initiated another night action in the battle of Cape Esperance. This time the Americans struck back. Using new surface radar, they surprised a force sent to shell the U.S. Marines. Rear-Admiral Norman Scott's task force sunk the heavy cruiser *Furutaka* and the destroyer *Fubuki,* damaged the heavy cruiser *Aoba,* and killed Rear-Admiral Goto. Aircraft sent down two more Japanese destroyers the next day, although enemy troops landed on the island. Three U.S. ships were damaged and *Boise* was sunk after it exposed itself by turning on its searchlights. Nonetheless, it was the Japanese who could not afford to lose such tonnage; their ship construction could not keep pace with their losses. The U.S. Navy chalked up its first nighttime victory and sailors on board and U.S. Marines on shore cheered the much-needed good news. A week afterward, on October 18, Nimitz heard complaints of lack of support by the Marine Corps, and he had evidence. Because the closest Allied deep-water port was 900 miles away in New Caledonia, supply ships waited for days to unload their goods on the island. Warships then put to sea for weeks at great risk to their crews. In one case, a destroyer vanished without a trace until discovered after the war; the cruiser *Juneau* exploded and sunk with almost all of her 700 men on board. As historian Ronald Spector has concluded, "[f]ear, horror, fatigue, anxiety: that was Guadalcanal for the navy as well as for the fliers, marines, and army troops."

Nimitz decided to act. He replaced Ghormley with Bull Halsey, and Admiral Thomas Kincaid took over from Fletcher. The next week, while the third banzai assault on the airstrip transpired, the unrelenting Halsey sent Kincaid after Mikawa's fleet. The carriers squared off in the battle of Santa Cruz Island, the biggest naval engagement between Midway and the battle of the Philippine Sea in June 1944. The Americans downed 100 planes and lost 74 of their own as well as the carrier *Hornet* that had carried the Doolittle raiders. *Enterprise* was also damaged again as were the heavy cruiser *Portland* and destroyers *Smith, Hughes,* and *Porter.* Japan had the heavy cruiser *Chikuma* and the carrier *Shokaku* forced from the battle. Despite the near ruinous loss of U.S. vessels—America had no operational carriers in the Pacific at this time—the battle was a draw. The pool of Japan's irreplaceable skilled pilots drained low. American flyers became more adept at combating the Zero fighter as their commanders shuttled squadrons in and out of Guadalcanal, now a base for U.S. aircraft.

Neither side conceded as the Guadalcanal campaign approached its climax. Their failures of the previous weeks should have convinced the Japanese to accept their losses and withdraw. But Guadalcanal had become the long-sought decisive battle for the Imperial Navy and Army. Hyakutake planned a last attempt at victory in mid-November 1942. He drew on reinforcements from the experienced 38th Division, a naval bombardment of Henderson Field, and the use of heavy artillery that had landed on the island. The Americans readied for these 13,000 enemy troops by transferring ships from other theaters despite the need for them in the impending invasion of North Africa. Both sides prepared for the final engagement. When Halsey demanded full support for the U.S. Marines, FDR personally authorized allocations of resources to Guadalcanal. Securing the island became his highest priority. Into Iron Bottom

Sound, Yamamoto sent the World War I battleships *Hiei* and *Kirishima,* screened by the light cruiser *Nagara,* and 14 destroyers. Later in the war, a torrent of U.S. construction would outmuscle the outdated battleships; but for the moment, Turner could not match this massive force. In desperation, he ordered his escort commander Admiral D. J. Callaghan to meet the Japanese with five cruisers and eight destroyers. The Imperial Navy had loaded up with bombardment shells rather than armor-piercing ordnance, so its response would be weakened.

The Americans waited in ambush as the huge enemy force appeared. Part of a three-day shootout, the key battle began on the night of November 12–13 and lasted just 24 minutes. The brevity belied the ferocity of the fighting. Nine ships were sunk—six American and three Japanese. In service less than a year, the cruiser *Juneau* went down with over 700 on board, including five brothers. In the confusion, both sides shot at each other and sometimes at friendlies. Callaghan died in the melee as did Norman Scott on his bridge. Due to the chaos at sea, Henderson Field was spared another massive bombardment, although cruisers shelled it that night. Still, the first phase of the grand battle gave the Americans a victory as Turner's force contested the Japanese flotilla. The next day, what remained of the Cactus Air Force hit the landing fleet. The aircraft sent a cruiser to the bottom and damaged three more before U.S. Marine aviators attacked the transports. Seven of the eleven were sunk, along with two cruisers. But the Imperial Navy would not quit. The Japanese sent their last battleship (*Kirishima*) in the area, four cruisers, and nine destroyers to bombard Henderson Field. Four U.S. destroyers and the new battleships *Washington* and *South Dakota* took on the task force. The latter was temporarily knocked out, but the *Washington* sunk *Kirishima* as well as a destroyer. Once *South Dakota* returned to the battle, the Japanese fled northward. The four remaining transports beached themselves, but U.S. aircraft decimated them the next morning. Ominously for the Imperial Navy, the arrival of the brand new vessels signaled a competition in ship production that Tokyo could not win.

There would be one last night engagement off Guadalcanal at Tassafaronga Point on November 30 because the Japanese would not abandon the island. Rear-Admiral Carleton Wright sent five cruisers and six destroyers of Task Force 67 against Admiral Tanaka's Tokyo Express force of two destroyers and six transport destroyers. Tanaka hoped to drop drums of supplies for troops on the island. He hit furiously at the Americans. Because Wright delayed his response, Tanaka damaged three cruisers and sank another, losing just the destroyer *Takanami.* The battle of Tassafaronga went to Japan; the U.S. Navy was lucky it did not lose its entire heavy cruiser group. Nonetheless, the Americans tightened their grip on the waters around the island. Although the Japanese continued to sail down the Slot and shell Henderson Field, sea battles slowed the Tokyo Express to a trickle in early 1943.

The clashes represented the peak of the struggle for Guadalcanal. The American 25th Infantry Division and the 2nd Marine Division replaced the 1st Marine Division in December 1942 and January 1943. The former leader of the Americal Division, Major-General Alexander Patch, activated the U.S. XIV Corps with over 50,000 men. In the face of such superiority, the Japanese moved north to form defensive lines on other islands. They consigned the dwindling number of troops on Guadalcanal to resupply by submarine rather than by the flotillas of the Tokyo Express. The 13,000 starving survivors including Hyakutake retreated to Cape Esperance by the end of January. Within a few weeks they executed the most successful evacuation since the British withdrew from the Dardanelles in 1915. Unbeknownst to the Americans, barges took the troops at night to waiting Imperial Navy destroyers.

The consequential campaign for Guadalcanal—seven naval engagements, numerous amphibious landings, several battles on land, and constant bombardment from air and sea—resulted in an American victory. The United States prevailed, even though, as at Midway, it had played a weaker hand. The losses were heavy. The U.S. Army and Marines suffered 6,111 casualties, among these 1,752 dead. The carnage was so substantial that the Navy refused to release its casualty figures for years afterward. Over 6,000 Japanese perished. The U.S. Navy saw two carriers, seven cruisers, and 15 other ships sunk; and Yamamoto lost two battleships, a light carrier, four cruisers, and 17 other warships, along with 1,200 naval aviators, 3,500 sailors, 14 transports, and over 500 planes. He decided to hold back his Combined Fleet for another decisive battle now that the balance of naval power had shifted decisively America's way.

Survivors remembered the horrendous fighting during the six-month campaign for Guadalcanal from early August 1942 to February 1943. The 1st Marine Division did not return to battle for an entire year afterward because it required such extensive rehabilitation. A Japanese veteran memorialized his time in the jungles of Guadalcanal with a poem: "Our rice is gone, eating roots and grass, along the ridges and cliffs, leaves hide the trail, we lose our way, stumble and get up, fall and get up, covered with mud from our falls, blood oozes from our wounds, no cloth to bind our cuts, flies swarm to the scabs, no strength to brush them away, fall down and cannot move, how many times I've thought of suicide."

Guadalcanal inflicted a grave blow on Japan. It was the first step to secure the Solomon chain for the United States and thereby prevented a flanking attack against Allied advances in New Guinea and Nimitz's eventual drive across the central Pacific. Supply lines to Australia remained intact. Above all, this long battle represented a true reversal of fortunes. The Imperial Navy's air arm and light naval forces never recovered from the contest. Midway stymied the Japanese, but the fleet was still stronger than America's. Guadalcanal was simply a campaign of attrition that Japan could ill afford. Naval engagements cost both sides 47 warships, or 16 percent of all major naval losses worldwide during 1942. But the Americans were rebuilding. The Japanese had entered the fray to halt a U.S. offensive, and they ended up on the defensive for the rest of the war. Derailing the Tokyo Express ultimately began a process that led to Japan's defeat.

The Americans had demonstrated their ability to beat superb air, land, and sea forces. U.S. forces respected but they did not fear the Japanese fighter. With materiel pouring into the Pacific theater, the demise of the Empire of Japan seemed more certain than six months before. The British and Soviets soon revealed German weaknesses in North Africa and the USSR, respectively; the Americans questioned Japanese invincibility on land and at sea. The battle of Tassafaronga sobered the U.S. Navy, but there would be more reckonings in a future that appeared brighter for the Allies after Guadalcanal.

CHAPTER 12

Cataclysm on the Eastern Front

> Still, we killed thousands of innocent people along with
> them.
>
> HILLARY JORDAN
> *Mudbound*

SOVIET INITIATIVE

Guadalcanal witnessed vicious fighting, but the Eastern front continued to defy imagination in terms of brutal conditions and carnage. The German offensive had ground to a halt, and in early 1942, the Russians took the initiative from the ill-prepared Wehrmacht. Stalin had no patience for defeatism but neither did the Fuhrer. Hitler prized Soviet resources and held to his dream of seizing the Caucasus oil fields in the south. Thus, under a renewed effort—Operation Blau—he aimed to occupy the Don River bend west of Stalingrad and then taking the city itself to cut off the oil flow to the Soviet Union. In the north and center of the USSR, the Wehrmacht would defend its positions. The key was progress southward to the Caucasus after which Germany could then turn back north and finish off the Soviet Union once and for all.

But this would be a battle to the end. Stalin acted first with a general offensive, putting nine army group *fronts* in action to free Leningrad from the German siege in the north, block further advances on Moscow in the center, and open up the Donets Basin and the Crimea in the south. Zhukov would encircle and liquidate German Army Group Center at Smolensk. Indeed, frozen terrain let his troops to reach Smolensk in early February 1942 against the fraying German front, but coordinated concentration of forces broke down over the long distances and the Soviet advance fizzled out. By this point, over 2.6 million Red Army soldiers had perished; for every German killed, the Soviets had lost twenty. As winter slid into the mud of spring, the Wehrmacht maintained its defensive hold, and the Red Army could not organize a massed thrust into German lines. German Field Marshal von Kluge sustained Army Group Center's 220-mile front by keeping open the Warsaw-Smolensk-Moscow road as well as railways running east to Vyazma, north to Rzhev, and south to Briansk. The spring thaw

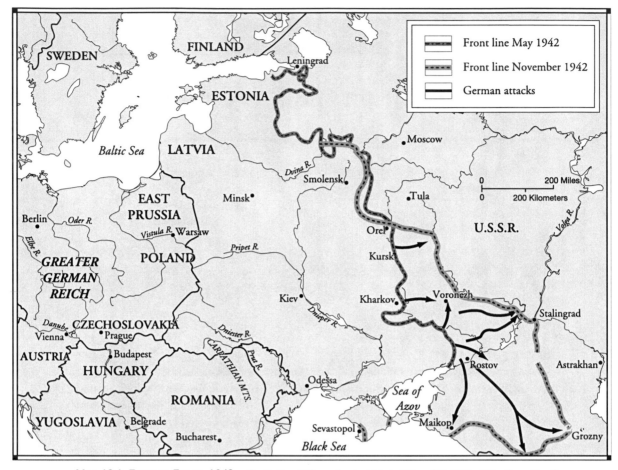

Map 12.1 Eastern Front, 1942.　Credit: Ronald Story, *Concise Historical Atlas of World War II: The Geography of Conflict*, Map 17, p. 39.

in March halted Soviet operations for weeks as both sides wallowed in the ooze. The Germans guessed correctly that the Red Army had not yet recovered from Barbarossa, but Hitler also knew that his forces were weakened to engage in a full-bore southern advance.

In the north, Soviet *fronts* had bulged the salients but had not broken through. This theater was not critical to Hitler, although he wanted it closed. The Volkhov army group pushed south of Leningrad, and the Northwest *front* protruded into enemy lines below Lake Ilmen, yet the Germans still besieged Leningrad. Leningrad Party head Andrew Zhdanov and the incompetent Kliment Voroshilov, commander of the Northwest army group, feared defeatism. They fixated on both rescuing the 2.5 million civilians in the city and on saving the Red Banner Fleet, the Soviet's northern navy on guard beyond the Arctic Circle. The hazardous lifeline across Lake Ladoga could not sustain the population who turned to scavenging and cannibalism to survive the winter war of annihilation. The dead were never fully counted, but nearly a million perished in Leningrad. Roughly 800,000 remained behind, and about that many were evacuated between January and July 1942. Finally, a narrow gap north of Lake Ilmen opened for Andrei Vlasov's Second Shock Army to advance 37 miles toward the city. A superb commander at Kiev and Moscow, Vlasov assumed the impossible assignment of relieving Leningrad without adequate support. When the spring thaw inevitably halted his advance, the Germans closed the gap, and Vlasov's army was pummeled after Stalin refused to let it withdraw. Irate, Hitler now demanded the total isolation of Leningrad.

Because his general offensive failed, Stalin ordered preemptive strikes over the wide Soviet front as the basis for an "active defense" against the impending German summer offensive of 1942. This was unwise; but like Hitler, Stalin did not listen to his generals. The ensuing Soviet "blows" placed masses of troops in vulnerable positions, allowing the Germans to regain their equilibrium and momentum of a year before. This became clear as the Wehrmacht ferociously met the Soviet advance. On May 12, 1942, General Timoshenko attempted to break out of the Izyum bulge with three armies and thrust toward Kharkov. They would cross the Donets River from a bridgehead at Izyum, 75 miles southwest of Kharkov, and encircle the Germans. Timoshenko misgauged enemy strength, however. German Seventeenth Army enjoyed substantial reserves. On May 17, the Russians sent two tank corps across the Donets. Sixth Army under the newly arrived Friedrich Paulus and Kleist's First Panzer army unsuspectingly converged from the north and south along the river. Forced to halt the tanks just 15 miles from Kharkov, Timoshenko could not prevent engulfment by the German spearheads. On May 28, he surrendered over 250,000 troops, 1,200 tanks, and more than 2,600 artillery pieces. Soviet reserves disappeared almost in their entirety. Kharkov was an unmitigated disaster and severely vitiated the Russians in the south. Hitler's Operation Blau was close to realization.

CRIMEAN STRUGGLE

To achieve the goal of securing the Caucasus oil fields, Paulus needed to clear the Soviets from his left flank around Stalingrad and from his right on the Black Sea. He began with the latter. In the Crimean, the Kerch peninsula traded hands, but the Germans eventually drove the Soviets into the sea. To the west on the Black Sea, three defense lines encircled the naval fortress of Sevastopol. By mid-November 1941, Lieutenant-General Erich von Manstein, commanding the seven divisions of Eleventh Army under Army Group South, had emptied the entire Crimean area except for Sevastopol of the Red Army. Lightly armed, plagued by badly trained Romanian troops, and befuddled by tricky terrain and rainy weather, Manstein delayed an assault on the fortress until December 17. In the meantime, Vice-Admiral F. S. Oktyabrsky took command of Sevastopol. He bolstered lines overseen by Major General I. Y. Petrov's Independent Marine Army. Okytyabrsky's attempts to disrupt the attack went awry when the Germans breached the first and second defense lines before the Soviets were even ready to repel them. In the ensuing slaughter, a German machine gunner moaned, "I can't just keep on killing!" as streams of bullets mowed down waves of Russians not more than fifty feet from his position.

Sevastopol, underground arms factory in the cliffs. Credit: Library of Congress, Call #LC-USW33-024231-C.

On the brink of blasting through the third line and capturing the fortress, Manstein suddenly found his entire Crimean position at risk. Soviet forces took a beachhead at Kerch on December 26 and landed troops at Feodosiya. Five days later, 40,000 Russians were ashore, and the Germans had to evacuate the Kerch Peninsula. Manstein broke off his siege of Sevastopol, for only a German division and Romanian troops guarded the 170-mile coast from Kerch to Yalta. He turned to recapturing of Feodosiya. In May 1942, good weather permitted deployment of infantry, a panzer division of 180 tanks, and two Romanian divisions against Major-General D. T. Kozlov's Crimea *front* of 21 infantry divisions and four brigades of 350 tanks. Landing under air cover by small vessels, Manstein—master of the blitzkrieg—drove back Kozlov in ten days. Stalin's refusal to allow a retreat let the Germans capture 170,000 prisoners as well as over 4,600 artillery pieces, 417 aircraft, and 500 tanks. The treeless marshes offered little shelter from German bombardment, which left bodies strewn on the ground. More than 176,000 Soviet soldiers died in just twelve days. The Kerch peninsula once again was empty of Soviet forces.

The remaining Soviet troops retreated to the limestone quarry of Adzhimuskai behind Kerch. They huddled in caves and tunnels chiseled from the stone; and when food supplies ran low, the 3,000 inhabitants turned to eating their horses or raiding German stores on the surface. The Wehrmacht planted explosives, sealed the exits, and released poison gas in the tunnels. The few who survived starved to death. Soviet mythology called the quarry another Leningrad, but in reality, the defenders had been forced to die there by political operatives who would not let them leave. And now

Kerch had fallen, putting in jeopardy Sevastopol itself. Petrov's 106,000 troops and over 80,000 naval personnel could hold the fortress as long as supplies reached it by sea. On June 2, however, Manstein brought 600 artillery pieces to bear on the shipping lanes. Yet the German advance stalled. Bombardment by artillery, including the gargantuan 31.5 inch railway gun "Gustav," could not dislodge the Soviets from their third and last defensive line. They placed machine guns and light artillery in hundreds of natural and man-made caves. The dead from both sides lay in ravines swelling and decomposing in the intense heat and emanating a sickly sweet smell. Hitler's June 23 deadline of taking Sevastopol passed, but the Germans did not concede. Persistence got them to the harbor on the city's north side. Manstein's forces surprised the Russians by an amphibious assault with LIV Army Corps across the harbor and the Soviet southern line gave way. Oktyabrusky evacuated a few hundred top officers and left the rest of the garrison to the Germans. Sevastopol and the Crimea were in Nazi hands by July 4, 1942, along with another 100,000 prisoners.

Hitler now had secured his right southern flank in preparation for taking the Caucasus oilfields. He promoted Manstein to field marshal but did not heed his advice to keep Eleventh Army in the south as a reserve for the impending summer offensive. The Fuhrer preferred instead to transfer that force to the left northern flank. This required a wasteful six-week train ride for Eleventh Army. The Wehrmacht prepared to move on Voronezh and the Don River bend by seizing Stalingrad before bombing around Baku to destroy 80% of the USSR's oil production. Taking the industrial center of Stalingrad would interrupt the flow of oil on the Volga River from Astrakhan to the north. Barbarossa's checkered ending was a memory; the losses around Moscow were blamed on winter weather rather than on Hitler's overstretch.

That the Fuhrer might be deluding himself never entered his mind. By mid-1942, both combatants were weak from the spring campaigns, but Red Army logistics had improved. Lend-Lease helped fill consumption gaps for an economy on the brink of collapse. The Russians also mobilized their own sparse resources from towns and the countryside often by the brute force of Stalin's diktats. Meanwhile, due to Hitler's meddling and attrition of German resources in the USSR, the Wehrmacht declined in capabilities despite the appointment of the brilliant architect Albert Speer to the position of minister for armaments and munitions. Although he rationalized German production, and output rose, Speer was no magician. German transport shortages, heavy consumption of ammunition and supplies, and failure to capture enough rolling stock to allow troops to live off the land hampered efforts to subdue the Red Army. The Third Reich also could not keep pace with Allied production. U.S. output alone dwarfed Germany's, and materiel poured into Stalin's depots as a result. This helped tip the logistical scale in the USSR's favor. Manpower also gave the Allies an edge. On the Eastern front in mid-1942, over 4.4 million Axis soldiers, including Romanians, Slovakians, Hungarians, Italians, and a Spanish division, faced 5.5 million Russians. But Hitler took the initiative again. His belief in Nazi invincibility was as strong as ever as he readied for the final phase of victory in his pursuit of lebensraum in the USSR.

GERMAN RENEWAL

Germany's position of strength on the Eastern front actually appeared unassailable. Hitler was in control of the army, German arms production was increasing (it would reach its peak in Summer 1944), and the Wehrmacht remained outside of Moscow while it battered Leningrad in the north. The battle of Kharkov had gone far toward destroying the Soviet presence in Ukraine. Sevastopol had fallen in a week. With another strategic victory, Hitler could tame the Russians in the south and possess enough raw materials and slave labor to wage a long-term global war. The war of annihilation on the Eastern front hinged on Operation Blau.

Hitler ordered Army Group South to be split. He reluctantly recalled Bock who he put in charge of Army Group B to oversee the sector on the left from Kursk to Izyum. List commanded Army Group A on the right between Izyum and Taganrog. Both aimed to destroy Soviet reserves (presumed to be few) and capture the Caucasus oil wells in three phases. The first targeted Stalingrad, and the second involved Army Group B holding the Don and Volga River areas. This would allow Army Group A to drive south to the Caucasus and complete the third phase. The plans were ill-advised. Axis forces on the Eastern front were outnumbered by a Soviet force of ten field armies and one tank army in the STAVKA reserve. American aid and domestic factory output gave the Russians new tank armies modeled on the German panzer divisions. Stalin' sent his substantial manpower and materiel to the wrong location, however. He stationed his reserves against Army Group Center and transferred three of the Briansk *front* army groups and its tank army to meet the supposed offensive against Moscow. This further weakened army groups in the south that had yet to recover from their whipping that spring. Even the discovery by the Red Army of the Blau plans from a downed plane did not turn the suspicious Soviets from their mistaken belief that the capital city was the target.

Army Group B struck south instead toward Voronezh and the Don River, thereby putting the Soviets on the defensive. Neither the Briansk nor Southwest *fronts* could stand in the way. Stalin ordered his first and only retreat on July 6, 1942, the day that Bock took Voronezh by blasting through two holes in Red Army lines. Paulus' Sixth Army reached the Don River and turned downriver toward the big bend situated forty miles from Stalingrad. Bock upgraded the Fourth Panzer division to an army under Hoth and sent it and Kleist's First Panzer Army south and east in a pincer movement toward Stalingrad. They captured fleeing soldiers at Millervo on July 13, although many Russians escaped. The Fuhrer grew impatient. Having moved his headquarters to the Ukraine to be closer to the action, he sacked Bock for supposedly misusing his armor. He replaced him with General Maximilan von Weichs, a successful corps commander in the Polish, Western, and Barbarossa campaigns. Hitler was unreasonable, for Operation Blau was a month ahead of schedule. Kleist and Hoth caught and destroyed the South *front* before it crossed the lower Don. In mid-July, the Germans encircled Rostov, although Russians escaped the Nazi net in droves. As two corps of Fourth Panzer Army neared the Chir River, Hitler shifted them to Sixth Army. The Fuhrer ordered Paulus, who had no experience as a field commander, to thrust toward the city and complete the first phase of Blau. Although the German generals still squabbled over resources, and their supply lines stretched ever thinner, the Wehrmacht plan to control the Don-Volga area and the Caucasus was moving along.

Hitler then complicated the effort by inserting into Operation Blau two new operations—Edelweiss and Heron. After Stalin activated the Stalingrad *front's* three reserve armies to block the Germans coming up from the Don bend, Paulus crossed the Chir on July 23 to confront this force that stood 87 miles west of Stalingrad. At this point, Hitler launched Operation Edelweiss, trying to accomplish all of his objectives without great concern for logistics. He ordered Army Group A to grab the Caucasus oil fields 745 miles away. Operation Heron called for Army Group B to capture Stalingrad and then shoot down the Volga to Astrakhan. Believing he had sufficient troops, the Fuhrer pulled Manstein and five infantry divisions and siege artillery from Sevastopol and sent them to help Army Group North finish off Leningrad. There was little resistance when Army Group A began its new mission, but constant movement depleted Sixth Army's fuel and ammunition. Hitler added a panzer and infantry corps to Army Group B's Heron assault, which prompted List to complain that Edelweiss was in jeopardy. Intelligence revealed that over three hundred Red Army divisions were still in formation, even though the Germans had wiped out over one hundred divisions already. The Wehrmacht generals were gloomy; they realized that they were outnumbered by at least 50 percent. Hitler would have none of their pessimism.

In late July 1942, his self-assurance seemed warranted, as the Red Army dissolved before Paulus. Tank armies disintegrated when crews abandoned their vehicles. The commander of the brief-lived North Caucasus army group—the inspirational hero of the Civil War Marshal Semyon Budyonny—could not stem the retreat. On July 28, Stalin acknowledged the mutinous situation and warned of harsh punishment for those who did not stand and fight. "Not a step back" he proclaimed in his famous Order 227. "This must be our chief slogan. It is necessary to defend to the last drop of blood every position, every meter of Soviet territory, to cling on to every shred of Soviet earth and to defend it to the utmost." Order 227 boosted morale, and Stalin made good on his threats. Roughly 13,500—but likely many more—supposed traitors to the motherland were shot around Stalingrad. Neither disciplinary pronouncements nor a willingness to engage in a counterwar of annihilation could stop the Germans, however. Sixth Army rolled onward. On August 7, Paulus destroyed another army and took 50,000 prisoners east of Kalach on the Don River. After replenishing his ammunition, he charged for the Volga River two weeks later. In two days, a panzer corps supported by dive-bombers broke through Soviet lines. The Germans rested just nine miles north of Stalingrad. Securing his flank by building a screening line between the Don and Volga, Paulus linked with Fourth Panzer Army on September 2, 1942. The end was near for Stalingrad. Even better news had come from the Caucasus. Despite a Soviet scorched-earth policy that ignited some oil wells, Operation Edelweiss was underway. First Panzer Army took the oilfields of Maikop on August 9 and then drove toward the Caspian Sea.

But the offensives had overreached German capabilities. The advance on the Caspian stalled out in late August, and Edelweiss lost momentum. Seventeenth German Army headed through the mountains for the Black Sea coast but slowed in early September due to snow. Army Group A now stood some 372 miles from Stalingrad. Hitler would not admit failure, blaming his generals as usual by claiming they were holdovers of an army based on class and technical proficiency rather than Nazi dedication, guts, and performance. After all, Barbarossa had aborted the year before. This time he would ensure that loyal instruments of the regime carried out his mission. The Fuhrer accused List of timidity and fired him from Army Group A, and he gave Halder notice as head of the Army General Staff. Hitler was not insane. He understood the challenges: winter was approaching and the Soviet reinforcements were on the way. Yet there was hope. Positions in the Caucasus and outside Stalingrad showed that the Third Reich and its multiethnic allies occupied solid fronts in the north and center of the USSR. The Caucasus campaign had won very little, and now bands of partisans (soon to number over 250,000) sabotaged the Wehrmacht. But it struck back with extermination policies that slaughtered millions of civilians. Reprisals by large-scale German Army, SS, and police unit sweeps intensified this war of annihilation even as the Red Army and partisans mounted their own effective responses to the Germans. And Hitler also still possessed two strong points at Voronezh and southeast of Stalingrad. Whether his recklessness would upend gains on the Don as it had outside of Moscow in December 1941 remained the question.

Developments surrounding Operation Heron did not bode well. In his drive to the Volga, Paulus had removed most of Army Group A's air support. Furthermore, the Russians tied down Sixth and Fourth Panzer Armies around Stalingrad by early September. Most notably, Stalin appointed Zhukov deputy supreme commander. For the moment, the dictator stressed the advice of his generals rather than their devotion to politics. The people soon got a clear sense that defending Stalingrad meant more than just a fight, for the city symbolized the very existence of the USSR. Monumental challenges influenced Stalin's transformation. The Soviet Union had lost half of its European territory, most of its iron and coal, and might relinquish 80% of its oil should Operation Edelweiss succeed. During the summer, hundreds of tanks and aircraft arrived on the battlefields from factories, but would incompetent commanders and intimidated troops fritter them away? The task for "the Fireman" Zhukov and his cocommander, the obscure but skilled Aleksandr Vasilevsky, was daunting: repeat the Moscow counterattack at Stalingrad.

STALINGRAD

The defense of Stalingrad did not go well for the USSR initially. Major-General Vasili Chuikov—defeated by the Finns in 1939–40 and banished to China before taking command of the defending Sixty-Second Army—could not block the German advance. Paulus outnumbered him by half in troops, tanks, and artillery pieces. Furthermore, the Luftwaffe bombed Stalingrad so mercilessly for twenty-four hours on September 3 that resistance nearly ceased. When the Wehrmacht entered the city nine days later, Hitler ordered them into annihilation mode to kill all males and ship the females to slave labor camps in Germany. With popular and world opinion in mind, a desperate Stalin vowed to hold his namesake city where he had served during the Russian Civil War in 1920. He rushed reinforcements to Chuikov—"General Stubbornness"—who fully agreed that holding the city was a do-or-die situation.

The Wehrmacht had no small task at hand. It was compelled to conquer a sizable city street by street. Stalingrad stretched along the bend on the Volga for miles, its western side of bluffs high on the river. As the battle raged into September 1942, the Russians ferried supplies across the Volga every night, and Soviet soldiers hid in the rubble created by the initial Luftwaffe bombing and subsequent bombardment. They contested the invaders in every building and on every block. Neither the Wehrmacht nor the Red Army desired this kind of street fighting, but this was a fight to the finish until one side exterminated the other. Stalingrad became the Eastern front's equivalent of the decisive battle sought by Japan in the Pacific. It also evolved into the Third Reich's version of World War I's most debilitating battle—the Verdun of the East. The Germans clawed their way through the city, and by September 30, they had two-thirds of Stalingrad in their possession. By that time, however, the Luftwaffe had suffered substantial losses, and its logistical system was sorely taxed.

As the street battles raged into November, and the Germans ground forward with massive aerial and artillery bombardments, Chuikov's fresh troops halted both Paulus and Hoth. After the Don *front* to the north and Stalingrad army group on the south counterattacked, Weichs rushed to the rescue after turning over the Don-Volga bend west of the Chir River to the Romanian and Italian armies. The Soviets pounced on the opportunity to maul these futile foes. A new Southwest *front* of four field armies and a tank army took up positions across from the Romanian Third Army and its weak neighbor, Eighth Italian Army. Stalingrad *front's* Fifty-First Army received an entire tank army to face the unimpressive Romanian Fourth Army. The assault could not begin, however, before the rains ended in mid-November 1942 and ice floes cleared from the Volga.

Stalingrad, therefore, endured but at great sacrifice. The Germans carved the city into four parts, so isolating each that the Soviets moved communications to the opposite side of the Volga. Less than two weeks later, Hoth reached the river itself in the southern suburbs. Deaths and injuries skyrocketed as Russians ferried across the Volga to fight—never to return—and the Germans poured in more soldiers from other fronts. Victory and defeat were measured in blocks and gullies, houses and stairwells. Hitler would not give up even when bad news poured in from North Africa, where Rommel's forces were in retreat. He was ever more determined to make an example of Stalingrad. Stalin also would not bow. He knew that the city's capture would give the Nazism a permanent hold in the south and threaten his oil supplies. Besides, he could expect no help from his allies. Churchill had visited in August to inform him that there would be no second front in Western Europe that year. The Soviets had to tough it out alone. Such circumstances permitted tactics of annihilation (although the Soviets focused purely on survival at this point) and devolved into a massacre. Hundreds of pitched battles took place in the rubble of factories and apartments, or what General Stubbornness coined the "Stalingrad Academy of Street Fighting." Fighting often occurred in the dark, hand to hand. Snipers on both sides preyed on those holed up in buildings who desperately sought water or other supplies. A Russian recalled picking off nine Germans his first day on duty and shooting women sent out by the enemy to stop Red Army fire. The Russians counted on reinforcements to arrive from across the river; the Germans relied

House-to-house fighting in Stalingrad.   Credit: Center for the Study of War Experience at Regis University, Denver, Colorado.

on superior firepower. When the 10,000 troops of the Soviet's elite 13th Guards Division went into action in the city center on September 14 and 15, many lacked ammunition. Close to 30% were killed; the division ended up with just 320 survivors. Chuikov's forces in total suffered 75% casualties. But the Red Army fought on for the homeland.

In August, journalist Vasily Grossman had accompanied the Red Army into the city to record the destruction. "Stalingrad is ashes" he wrote. He found the Palace of Culture "velvety from fire, and two snow-white nude statues stand out against this black background. There are children wandering about, there are many laughing faces. Many people are half insane." At sunset, Grossman felt a "feeling of calm. The city has died after much suffering and looks like the face of a dead man who was suffering from a lethal disease and finally has found eternal peace." His description came before the worst of Stalingrad's street fighting. In September, he walked along the Volga to observe the batteries camouflaged by vines and the military sitting on benches intended for strollers. "Wounded men in their bloodstained bandages are walking along the Volga, right by the water. Naked people are sitting over the pink-evening Volga, crushing lice in their underwear." On a cold morning he heard screams and weeping after the Luftwaffe killed seven women and children. "A girl in a bright yellow dress is screaming, 'Mama, Mama!' A man is wailing like a woman. His wife's arm has been torn off. She is speaking calmly, in a sleepy voice. A woman sick with typhoid fever has been hit in the stomach by a shell fragment. She hasn't died yet. Carts are moving, and blood is dripping from them."

By mid-November, the Russians were backed up to a strip along the Volga cliffs; yet respite lurked from secret Soviet counteroffensives. Red Army strength built to the north, and Zhukov launched the Uranus and Mars operations. The latter turned into a tremendous disaster, called Zhukov's Greatest Defeat. Mars attempted to obliterate German Ninth Army and destroy Army Group Center on the Rzhev salient but the Red Army faced relatively fresh troops under the skilled defensive commander in Ukraine, Walther Model, who countered eleven Soviet armies around the town of Belyi with six panzer divisions and two motorized infantry divisions. Mars resulted in 100,000 Russian dead and over 235,000 injured, or nearly three-quarters the number lost at Stalingrad and around the Don. It might have inhibited elements of Army Group Center from reinforcing the Stalingrad attack, but the operation turned into a horrific meat grinder.

SOVIET COUNTEROFFENSIVES

Operation Uranus had better prospects. With the Germans sucked into the vortex of Stalingrad, the Russians preyed on the Italians and Romanians by attacking their thinly protected flanks. Two field armies and a tank army of the Southwest *front* hit Third Romanian Army on November 19 with a 3,500-gun onslaught up and down the Don River. A day later, the Stalingrad army group assailed the other Romanian army. Both Romanian sides collapsed. Soviet tanks broke out and encircled them as well as Paulus' Sixth Army near Kalach on November 23. The Soviets now had two rings around Stalingrad, which made a German breakout next to impossible. When Paulus asked for permission to retreat with his twenty divisions and nearly 250,000 troops, Hitler told him to fight in the pocket until relief arrived. Luftwaffe chief Göring pledged to drop 300 tons of supplies a day to sustain Sixth Army while Hitler tapped Manstein to rescue Paulus with a new Army Group Don.

Not anticipating this response, Zhukov and Vasilevsky dallied while Manstein assembled Army Group Don 62 miles south of the pocket and came up behind the Russians. He ordered a break out, but the loyal Paulus awaited word from the Fuhrer. Hitler gave none. Also, because the Mediterranean theater had drained away air resources, the Luftwaffe's response was insufficient. As the Soviets closed in for the kill on the Stalingrad pocket, they captured airfields and forced the remaining Luftwaffe transports to pull back to Novocherkassk over 200 miles from the city. The rout was on. Zhukov launched Operation Little Saturn on December 16 to push Army Group Don away from Stalingrad. His Southwest *front* corralled the Italians and penetrated Manstein's northern flank while the Stalingrad army group turned southwest toward the lower Don. With Hoth's tanks held up at the Mishkova River 35 miles south of the trapped Sixth Army, Manstein fought for his life. On December 23, he told Hitler that he would have to withdraw a panzer division and urged Paulus again to break out of the pocket. If not, Sixth Army would wither away because bad weather and Soviet harassment had curbed Göring's air-dropped supplies. Depleted in transports and bombers, the Luftwaffe never fully recovered from the battle. The cold was also telling. An Italian soldier in the Don pocket recalled that exhausted troops fell to the ground, some turning into ice and others dying in a delirium caused by the bitter freeze. On December 28, with Hoth surrounded, Manstein allowed him to retreat.

Paulus was stranded in a pocket about 37 miles wide and 28 miles long. The snow and cold grew more intense by the day, the airlift sputtered, and supplies dwindled. Officers handed out ammunition cartridges one at a time. Soldiers wrote their last letters home. The Don army group, under Zhukov's trusted commander Lieutenant-General Konstantin Rokossovsky, cut the pocket in half by mid-January 1943, and seven armies tightened the noose on Sixth Army. Paulus asked for permission to surrender. He had lost his last airfield, thereby ending the resupply effort, and fought from two small areas. The Fuhrer refused his request, but with typical bluff, he promoted Paulus to field marshal a week later. In Stalingrad, the streets were scenes of horror where the wounded froze, the garrison starved, and discipline disappeared. The Soviets inched through the city. The Germans halted rations to the wounded and fought on desperately.

A day after his promotion, on January 31, 1943, Paulus gave up his pocket and became the first field marshal to surrender in German history. Hitler demanded the six divisions in the other pocket to fight to the last man. They did, with predictable results. Outside contact with the Tractor Works vanished, as German XI Corps fought until February 2. The Red Army used 911,000 artillery shells, 990,000 mortar shells, and 24 million rifle and machine gun rounds in January and early February alone. The Germans lost 200,000 troops, not including the 30,000 wounded taken out by air. Of one-quarter million soldiers, just 80,000 remained. Hitler called them cowards, which was gallingly unfair. They were certainly prisoners and in great jeopardy. Only 5,000 would ever see Germany again. Stalingrad was in Russian hands and defeat unwound the German offensive on the Eastern front.

As Rokossovsky sliced up the remainder of the pocket, Axis armies fell back elsewhere. The Leningrad and Volkhov army groups attacked in the north on January 12, 1943 and opened a six-mile wide corridor to Lake Ladoga. Leningrad barely survived the siege. In the south, First Panzer Army withdrew to the Don River and Seventeenth Army departed from the Maikop oil fields. The Voronezh *front* took twelve days to wipe out the Hungarian Army, pushed back Second German Army, and freed Voronezh. Kleist wanted to retreat to the Caucasus with Army Group A, but Hitler did not respond until the end of the month. By that time the South *front* (renamed from the Stalingrad *front*) stood just 31 miles from Rostov after blowing past Millerovo toward the Donets River. The Southwest army group withdrew to a bridgehead on the Taman peninsula as First Panzer Army retreated to Rostov-on-Don. After appointing Zhukov a marshal (Vassilevsky was elevated a month later) and awarding himself that rank as well, Stalin urged the troops to crush the enemy.

Hitler also vowed total war, but he was too late. Germany faced over six million troops in the USSR as well as a 24,000-unit disadvantage in armored vehicles and 7,000 in aircraft. The invaders might be more skilled in the field, but Zhukov and Vassilevsky had made improvements. And the sheer numbers marshaled by the Red Army were overwhelming. The Soviets hinted at impending offensives shaped increasingly by a counter-strategy of annihilation that did not yet embrace genocide of the German people but was nonetheless intended to dearly punish the Nazi regime. For now, the Russians continued to trade space for time. They lost fewer prisoners and set out to waste away the Wehrmacht. Their confidence also blossomed. German

Army Group Center appeared vulnerable, and Army Groups Don and A seemed unable to reach the Dneiper River. Stalin began Operation Leap on January 29, 1943, to trap them in the Donets basin. A group of tanks crossed the river east of Izyum and headed south to Mariupol on the Sea of Azov. At Stalingrad, Zhukov and Vasilevsky began the largest artillery barrage in history with 7,000 guns. They overran German headquarters and seized 100,000 prisoners, 500 planes, and a thousand pilots. They then sent the Voronezh *front* in two directions. One prong went southwest past Kharkov toward the Deniper, and the other headed northwest through Kursk toward Smolensk. His cleanup completed in the Stalingrad pocket, Rokossovsky joined this northern prong to the Central *front* on February 15 to destroy Army Group Center once and for all.

Amidst the cataclysm of Stalingrad, the Soviets took heart. They not only had unraveled the German gains of the summer but those of Barbarossa the year before. The battle of Stalingrad was a turning point on the Eastern front—a burial ground of the most important Wehrmacht offensive in the USSR. Bells in Moscow rang, the Volga River remained open, and the Germans reeled. The British press viewed the epic victory as the "salvation of European civilization" while the *New York Times* noted that in "the scale of its intensity, its destructiveness and its horror," Stalingrad was one of the most decisive battles in world military history. It was certainly a patriotic effort but certainly not indicative of a good war. Stalin was more subdued than his Western allies because the USSR had suffered around 2.5 million casualties. He lauded the great victory, but he knew the Nazis were far from finished. He ordered Stalingrad's civilians to stack up the frozen corpses and rebuild the factories. Bodies and body parts from this campaign of annihilation surfaced in the ground for several decades thereafter. One thing was certain: Hitler would no longer take the initiative against his archenemies, the Soviet communists.

CHAPTER 13

Shifting Fortunes in the Mediterranean

Nobody is actually ever prepared to die, are they—it's not human nature, the imagination can't handle obliteration.

IVAN DOIG
The Eleventh Man

PUNCHING IN NORTH AFRICA

Well before the wrenching Soviet victory at Stalingrad, the Germans encountered trouble in the western desert of North Africa in 1942. Rommel had exhausted his momentum, but Hitler was distracted elsewhere and unresponsive to demands for more resources. British Eighth Army welcomed General Claude Auchinleck's leadership, U.S. aid, and fresh troops. The Auk awaited Erwin Rommel's next move. He discovered through ULTRA that the daring Desert Fox planned a new attack for May. The news turned Auchinleck to defensive preparations. Unbeknownst to London, German intelligence intercepted over the first 6 months of 1942, reports to Washington of the U.S. military attaché in Cairo, Colonel Bonner Fellers. These discussed every aspect of Eighth Army's designs, strengths, positions, and supplies in the Middle East. Within hours, Axis high commands knew exactly what the British intended to do until the Allies detected the Fellers' affair and stopped the enemy's intelligence penetration. Yet the information allowed Rommel to roll onward. Mysstified by his genius, the British assumed he would hit the center of their defenses—the Gazala Line. They were wrong.

Anchored by the Free French fortress of Bir Hakeim at the southern end, the 35-mile long Gazala barrier was the last obstacle to Rommel's capture of Tobruk and hence his run to Egypt and the Suez Canal. Lieutenant-General Neil Ritchie, commander of Eighth Army, grouped his forces at strongpoints along this substantial but static Line. While Italian troops and armor undertook a diversionary frontal attack on the fortress, the Germans overran motorized units and then captured the 7th Armored Division's command post to try an end run south around Bir Hakeim. Bolstered by the new American M-3 medium tank (called the Grant by Britain), the Allies engaged the panzers in one of the fiercest slugfests of the Western Desert campaign. With his supply lines strung out, the Desert Fox halted his flanking maneuver on May 29 and withdrew to the "Cauldron," so named because of the heat generated when Ritchie counterpunched with his own armor. Yet he did so in an uncoordinated fashion that allowed Rommel to regroup, patch together supply lines, and renew his attack on Bir Hakeim with his 90th Light Division. The Afrika Corps wiped out over 100 Allied tanks, including the Grant, which proved sluggish and vulnerable due to its high silhouette, hull-mounted (rather than turret-mounted) main gun.

The Allies were in trouble. The 1st Free French Brigade Group under Major-General Marie Pierre Koenig—a veteran of campaigns in Norway, France, and Africa—absorbed Rommel's thrusts for ten days. The impressive showing prompted Charles de Gaulle to rename Koenig's forces the "Fighting French" and earned the French points with the Allies. But after roughly two-thirds of the 1st Brigade escaped the fortress, it surrendered on June 10, 1942. Encircling the defenses with a deep salient and pounding away with 88-mm guns adapted as an antitank weapon, Axis forces pushed back the British from the Gazala Line. Auchinleck ordered Ritchie to take up new positions, but by June 16, all British defenses had disappeared west of Tobruk. The city fell five days later. Rommel captured large amounts of supplies and two battalions of infantry. Having lost 90% of his tanks, Ritchie was fired and Auk's tenure in the theater was also in jeopardy.

With the North African campaign seemingly over and Britain's Mediterranean strategy in tatters, Hitler bestowed the rank of field marshal on Rommel. The Fuhrer decided to let him push on for Egypt rather than opt for an air assault on Malta, as Wehrmacht brass preferred. The Desert Fox crowed to his men that "[t]hrough your fighting spirit, the enemy has lost the nucleus of his standing army which was poised to spring back at us, and above all his powerful armored force." He urged them onward, for it was "time for the outright annihilation of the enemy. We must not rest easy, until the last elements of the British Eighth Army have been shattered." So dire was the crisis for Britain that Auk took personal command of Eighth Army as it retreated to the Egyptian port of Mersa Matruth. On Auchinleck's second day on the job, Rommel surrounded the X Corps after poor communications and coordination isolated the New Zealand Division. These troops broke out using bayonets and fled eastward to a new defensive line at the desert railway station of El Alamein. The Germans occupied Mersa Matruth on June 27 and took up the pursuit. Defeatist British commanders readied to retreat or evacuate if need be. Just 60 miles west of El Alamein, the Royal Navy's Mediterranean fleet departed from Alexandria. In Cairo, 152 miles beyond, panic set in. The Auk had failed both to halt Rommel and inspire the troops. His relations with Churchill soured as the Germans knocked at the door of the Suez Canal.

Rommel rumbled forward by attacking the British line on July 1, 1942 in the first battle of El Alamein. Aided by ULTRA and directed by a prewar founder of the mechanized army—Major-General Eric Dorman-Smith—the British formed into defensive boxes ringed with mines and wire around key points such as the railway depot. They could not counterattack, but neither could Rommel root them out. The operation succeeded because of the terrain. A flanking movement by the Afrika Korps was impossible due to the impasse of the Qattara Depression's vast salt marshes to the south. The Panzer Army could also not break through near Ruweisat Ridge, and the Desert Fox's offensive faltered due to geography, exhaustion, and Dorman-Smith's defense. The first battle of El Alamein checked German forward movement for the first time, the land equivalent of Midway's effect on the Japanese Navy at sea. The pendulum swung back to the British initiative. Reinforcements rushed in to both sides, and several pitched fights occurred during July. But neither side budged. Rommel understood the stakes. He had to eliminate Britain from North Africa before Anglo-American supplies arrived in Egypt to tip the logistical advantage. Churchill urged Auk to attack, but the commander merely sparred ineffectually into August 1942.

Auchinleck was done. Churchill arrived in Cairo with General Alan Brooke, the former commander of the II Corps at Dunkirk, organizer of the British Home Forces, and as Chairman of the Chiefs of Staff Committee, the key military advisor to the War Cabinet. He was one of the few officials who stood up to Churchill and managed through his intellect, clear communications skills, and professional demeanor to shape decisions. Churchill offered him command in the Middle East, but Brooke felt he could better serve as Chief of the Imperial General Staff in London. Among his protégés was Harold Alexander, who had recently led retreating forces out of Burma, and Bernard Montgomery. During the fall of France, the inspirational, adept, energetic, and self-centered "Monty"—the British version of America's MacArthur—had commanded the

Monty leads the charge in the desert.   Credit: Center for the Study of War Experience at Regis University, Denver, Colorado.

3rd Division of the British Expeditionary Force in 1940 with such skill and calm that Brooke remained forever awed. Brooke tapped Alexander to replace the Auk as commander of the theater and handed over British Eighth Army to Montgomery.

The confident Monty was just the cure. He rallied the troops, telling them they would stay on the Alam Halfa ridge alive or dead. The Germans tried demoralizing the Australians by dropping leaflets claiming that Americans were consorting with their wives while they ground it out in North Africa. Monty had a more powerful weapon than disinformation: ULTRA. Drawing on knowledge gleaned from German signals, he met Rommel's final attempt to break through the El Alamein line for the Nile River. At Alam Halfa during the first week of September 1942, British ground and air harmonization was stellar. Rommel attacked with paratroopers, rapid penetration across minefields, and a direct blow on Alam Halfa itself. A sandstorm covered the movement of the panzers who emerged with long-barreled 75 mm guns that terrified the British. Yet antitank guns silenced them. Knowing every move before hand, Monty refused to let his tanks be lured out into the open where the "Flak 88s" could destroy them. Tired and bereft of supplies, Rommel lost the initiative on September 5. Churchill sought an immediate offensive, but Montgomery focused on training his army for a new one, called Lightfoot, to begin at the end of October. This would give the Desert Fox a dose of his own medicine. By that time, Monty enjoyed a nearly four-to-one advantage in troop and aircraft strength, three-to-one advantage in tanks, and a secure supply base for sustained operations. The British outlook in North Africa brightened by Fall 1942.

EL ALAMEIN

The British had thwarted Rommel at El Alamein and now determined to push him back westward to Tunisia with Operation Lightfoot. Churchill prodded Monty to do so quickly because the Allies planned to land in North Africa in the first week of November. Monty would not be rushed. Rommel was at a distinct disadvantage both logistically and tactically by this time. He lacked sufficient fuel and transports, and Commonwealth forces had him outmanned and outgunned. The British numbered 195,000 troops to German-Italian Panzer Army's (renamed on October 25) total of 104,000 men. The Allies roughly doubled his number of tanks, antitank guns, and artillery and matched his aircraft. Resupply was possible for Monty thanks to the Royal Navy's dominance of the Mediterranean while the British base at Malta intercepted Rommel's logistical train to Libya. The Desert Fox faced major constraints.

The second battle of El Alamein was a study in contrasts. Operation Lightfoot aimed for a traditional battle of attrition with superior firepower. The terrain favored the British. Because the Qattara Depression forty miles to the south prevented flanking movements so cherished by Rommel, the battle required the careful preparation of a set engagement rather than surprise and mobility. The methodical Monty was perfect for such circumstances. He would not fritter away the British empire in Africa, the only place in the world it still thrived. Eighth Army readied a large force including artillery and 1,000 tanks, among them the new American M-4 Shermans with medium-velocity guns adaptable as antitank weapons or against armor and infantry. Monty then turned to training the troops, an effort that delayed Lightfoot by six weeks but instilled confidence. This time around, he intended to hit the enemy's most vulnerable place once he determined where that was. Rommel planned to meet the British with a static defense because they had him outmuscled. He would trap his enemy by employing 249,849 antitank mines and several small but deep minefields called "the Devil's gardens." His armor would form into six groups poised to fill the breach in his defensive line. Including antipersonnel explosives, engineers laid a total of 445,358 mines. Weak Italian troops were bracketed on each side by reliable Wehrmacht units. The defense had two weaknesses. First, British intelligence detected the minefields. Second, the defenders were initially without their leader. Rommel returned to Germany on September 23 sickened by exhaustion. Hitler and his ministers greeted him with wildly optimistic assessments regarding the possibility of reaching Cairo. A month later, Montgomery attacked.

On the night of October 23–24, 1942, Operation Lightfoot began with a rolling, World War I style, 882-gun barrage eight miles inland. This would soften up German lines for the infantry to clear a path for the armor. "No fury of sound had ever assailed our ears like that before, it cuffed, shattered and distorted the senses, and loosened the bowels alarmingly," noted a British bombardier. The Allies also feinted to the south to draw Rommel's forces from the offensive. The depth of the line saturated with minefields bogged down Commonwealth forces and delayed the British tanks. X Corp's armor got through some of the Devil's gardens, but it could only reach and not secure a planned infantry bridgehead in a line running southeast from Kidney Ridge. The 9th

British Universal Carrier passing burning Panzer III at El Alamein.
Credit: Center for the Study of War Experience at Regis University, Denver, Colorado.

Australian Division took Point 29 in their northern sector along the coastal road and developed a salient while 1st Armored Division attacked two key points on either side of the strategic Kidney Ridge. Australians, New Zealanders, South Africans, Indians, and Greeks as well as the British and French attacked Rommel's line in three days of roaring noise, fear, and death.

Rommel rushed back from his convalescence to replace General Georg Stumme who died of a heart attack when the battle began. He countered fiercely, but air and artillery bombardment issued a withering attack on his tanks and infantry. The Australians moved the salient outward toward the sea on October 30. To meet them, Rommel shifted his best troops from contesting the second attack by Allied infantry two nights later. This exposed Italian forces, which were ground up in the offensive. Montgomery's plan had gone well, albeit slowly and at great sacrifice. His tank losses quadruped Rommel's yet, the Axis could not afford even this ratio. Monty stuck to the plan of attrition, slugging away at the Axis defense. He was wise to do so. The New Zealand Division broke through and hit the German line north of Kidney Ridge and south of Rommel's elite troops. British armor poured through the gaps and Rommel's tanks were now outnumbered 20 to 1. Despite losses in the minefields, the British had 600 tanks whereas the Germans were down to 30. His troops facing disaster, the Desert Fox informed Hitler that he would withdraw to Tunisia. ULTRA operatives gave the message to Monty the next day, November 3. The Fuhrer refused to let Rommel retreat. Just as Paulus would defend the Stalingrad pocket a few weeks later, so must Germans stand in the desert. Rommel obeyed, but the British 51st Highland Division overran his lines. By the morning, the British rolled into Tell El Aqqaqir; and by midday, German defenses toppled. Hitler finally let Rommel retreat, although the bitter Desert Fox had not waited for word from Berlin to flee across Libya. He crossed the same stretches on which he triumphed earlier after taking Tobruk. El Alamein cost the Allies 13,560 casualties and half of their tank force, but the Germans left behind 30,000 men—mostly Italians—as prisoners.

Rommel conducted a brilliant retreat. He fought at several places along his 1,800 mile route to Tunisia, but he gave way at each, pounded by Eighth Army and the Allied Desert Air Force. Monty dogged the panzer army all the way with supplies from the Royal Navy, which leapfrogged materiel down the coast. The British tried to get ahead of Rommel to cut him off. They established an air base in front of him but to little avail, and British tanks could only cut away at the tail of his column. He traveled faster along the coast road than Monty could move in the desert. Montgomery's caution earned him criticism because Rommel's forces escaped into Tunisia after departing from Tripoli on January 23, 1943. The panzers hid behind the old Mareth Line in southern Tunisia, a French fortification. Rommel's own skills, plus heavy rain and exhausted pursuers, played a role in his evasion. Nonetheless the results were clear. The Desert Fox was a marked man. Tobruk came into British hands on November 13, Benghazi a week later, El Agheila in mid-December, and then Sirte on Christmas Day.

The last major battle of a desert campaign fought mostly by British and Commonwealth troops was a ringing victory. The Allies occupied Libya for the remainder of the war. ULTRA, as well as Polish intelligence, had again contributed to the outcome of a key battle. Monty had acted according to code-breakers' revelations about German-Italian Panzer Army. Furthermore, the British military was reborn after years of bungling and failures in Western Europe, the Balkans, and North Africa. The defeat paid political dividends as well. It sowed discord among the Axis powers by making the Germans more contemptuous of their Italian allies. And the Western Desert campaign was over. El Alamein turned back the two and one-half year Axis threat to Egypt and the critical lifeline of the Suez Canal. Blitzkrieg over the long empty expanses of the desert had not worked as effectively as in densely populated Europe where confusion through constant movement gave Germany an advantage. Rommel proved a brilliant tactical wonder, but he could not overcome logistical weaknesses. Because the German General Staff never endorsed the strategic plan to take the Suez Canal and link with Axis forces in the Soviet Union, the desert offensives always strained supply lines. The campaign actually rendered the Axis position on the African continent vulnerable to the inexorable buildup of Allied forces in the Mediterranean theater. Rommel's campaign aided the Allies in another critical way as well. The French finally agreed to cooperate in the new theater of North Africa.

OPERATION TORCH

Although of secondary importance to Hitler, the desert war disappointed him. Rommel's expulsion from Libya jeopardized the German presence in North Africa, and the crisis on the Eastern front raised the question of a retreat. Prospects worsened as Anglo-American forces began the Operation Torch landings in French Morocco and Algeria to drive the Axis powers from the African continent and open a second front in Europe. This giant pincer from the west began just as the panzers fled from El Alamein in the east. Allied plans had existed since the fall of France to occupy the French colonies of Algeria and Tunisia. Arguments erupted between Britain, which pushed for the landings in North Africa, and the reluctant Americans who preferred to focus on an invasion of France. A raid on the French port of Dieppe in August 1942 tested German defenses and served as a means to resolve the France versus North Africa debate.

Over 6,000 Allied troops—most of them Canadian—attacked Dieppe on August 19, and at a disadvantage. They lacked adequate air support, as leaders neglected a major preliminary aerial bombardment to soften up the defenders. In addition, 237 warships and landing craft divided into thirteen groups could not maneuver in the constrained space of the English Channel. In any event, the vessels did not provide sufficient cover for the landings. Once recovered from the surprise, the Wehrmacht counterattacked. The furious Luftwaffe response wiped out several landing craft. Faulty intelligence and communications created ineptitude on the ground when units landed at the wrong places or others arrived late. Only 15 of the 27 Allied tanks crossed the seawall, and those that climbed it met roadblocks. The Allies acknowledged the fiasco by early afternoon. Left behind were 3,367 Canadian dead, wounded, or prisoners and 275 British casualties. Over 550 Royal Navy servicemen were lost when the Germans eliminated a destroyer and 33 landing craft. German casualties numbered just 591 men. Only 48 of 945 Luftwaffe planes were shot down, but the RAF suffered 106 losses. Impatient as always, Churchill had pushed too far at Dieppe, and now the lessons were clear. The need for major bombardment prior to landings and the perils of direct amphibious assault on a port were evident. An open beach would better serve future invasions. And opening a second front in France at the moment was out of the question; the British won the debate.

The argument over the second front came with the baggage of politics. Anglo-American talks grew bitter and remained so over the location of the invasion. FDR still pursued the Europe-First strategy but because Americans were chomping at the bit for revenge for Pearl Harbor, he demanded an invasion of Europe to keep them focused on Hitler. Stalin also sought evidence of his Western Allies' willingness to ease pressure on the Eastern front by attacking Germany from the west. FDR's Chief of staff George Marshall favored France as the entry point, but Churchill preferred North Africa as the only viable option to a Channel crossing after the disastrous Dieppe engagement. Roosevelt agreed to attack in the Mediterranean even at risk of diverting resources from the primary theater in western Europe and protecting British imperial interests in Africa and the Middle East. German submarines, airpower, and a potential counter-attack simply made an invasion of France untenable at the time. As long as Operation Torch did not delay the eventual Channel crossing, the Americans were on board. The resistance of the autonomous Vichy French government and the rout of British forces in Libya after the battle of Gazala in June 1942 held up the project in North Africa. But by November, plans were in place. Ironically, considering British lobbying for Operation Torch, it was largely an American show.

Command was critical. The Combined Chiefs of Staff from the United States and Britain oversaw the Torch operation. They adopted a global advisory role by exercising jurisdiction over strategy and allocation of resources worldwide. The Combined Chiefs supervised the Mediterranean, European, and Atlantic theaters (leaving the Indian Ocean and Middle East to the British Chiefs and the Pacific to the U.S. Joint Chiefs of Staff) and the commander of the Allied Expeditionary Force, Lieutenant-General Dwight D. "Ike" Eisenhower. Eisenhower had enjoyed a meteoric rise through Army ranks. Marshall had tapped him to reorganize the War Plans Division until he took over command of the European Theater of Operations. Despite having no combat experi-ence, Eisenhower took command of the North African campaign because of his unique ability to facilitate inter-Allied cooperation and soothe big military egos. His talents would be tested. Operation Torch aimed to attack German-Italian Panzer Army from the rear, clear Tunisia of Axis forces, and seize control of North Africa from the Atlantic to the Red Sea.

Ike scored two diplomatic successes prior to the invasion. One coordinated com-mands at Allied Force Headquarters. Unlike Rommel and the rigid Jurgen von Arnim—German panzer commanders who differed sharply over strategy in a divided command in the North African theater—the Allies were a model of unity under Ike, his American major-generals, and British leaders. Eisenhower's deputy was the youthful and flam-boyant Mark Clark. James Doolittle led the Western Air Command, which supported landings at Casablanca and Oran under George Patton and Lloyd Fredenhall. Charles Ryder led the Eastern Force to Algiers. The rest of the commanders were British includ-ing Lieutenant-General Kenneth Anderson, Admiral Andrew Cunningham, and Air

Marshal William Welsh who oversaw the Eastern Air Command. By and large, they all got along thanks to Ike's mediation.

Bringing the French into the fold was Eisenhower's other goal. That Franco-Allied relations had been tense for two years is an understatement. The Royal Navy had scuttled the French fleet with great loss of life two years before at Mers el Kebir. The invasion of French Syria and Lebanon had then irritated France's leaders, including the dynamic Brigadier General Charles de Gaulle. In May 1942, French troops clashed with British forces when the latter captured Madagascar to guard the approaches to India. The French lost in every confrontation, but their Navy remained recalcitrant. Eisenhower feared they might rise up against Operation Torch.

To allay his concern, he clandestinely sent Mark Clark and diplomat Robert Murphy to seek a pledge from the commander of Vichy France's armed forces, Admiral Francois Darlan, that the French would not resist the Allied invasion. Darlan, who happened to be in Algiers visiting his son, assured them of a cease-fire, which allowed Anglo-American troops to land without fear of French resistance. This was bad news for the Axis powers. When Darlan tried to rescind the deal, the Americans arrested him. Vichy severed relations with the United States, but Hitler had had enough. On November 11, 1942, Nazi forces occupied all of France because the Fuhrer no longer trusted Vichy to prosecute the war and worried that the Riviera coast would be used for Allied landings. The Germans also took Tunisian airfields while the Italians occupied Corsica. The occupation of Vichy freed the cynical Darlan from his obligations to Pétain's government, and Eisenhower appointed him the high commissioner for French North Africa. This ignited a firestorm of criticism in Britain and America, but Ike made the deal with the devil because only Darlan could persuade loyal French forces—which doubled the 65,000 on the Allied side—not to fight. The decision earned de Gaulle's enmity for decades afterward. The French fleet was another matter. Pro-Allied French Navy officers scuttled the vessels in Toulon just weeks after the Torch landings in late November, although this also served Darlan's purpose of keeping them out of Axis hands.

Taking Tunisia was the first aim of Operation Torch. Some 650 warships, transports, and landing craft escorted the central and eastern forces from Britain. Patton's Western Task Force sailed directly across the Atlantic to Casablanca because the Americans worried that either the Luftwaffe might catch him in the Mediterranean should he land with the British, or Spain could attack from behind. A Franco-Polish network across North Africa gave intelligence on ports and airfields as well as the location of Vichy military units and installations. The military planning worked, although the diplomatic maneuvering did not totally appease the French. The invaders came ashore in the early morning of November 8, and Algiers fell that day. Fredenhall captured Oran two days later, even though the French blocked landings (the cease-fire had not yet gone into effect) in the harbor and U.S. paratroopers missed their marks by twenty miles. General Auguste Nogues, the resident-general so duplicitous that he was nicknamed General "No-yes," put up resistance around Casablanca. Pétain vowed a fight, but his troops were torn between adherence to the Vichy government and loyalty to Darlan. The Americans carried their flag ashore in the hopes the French would not fire on them but the mostly colonial troops ignored Old Glory. About 1,400 U.S. and

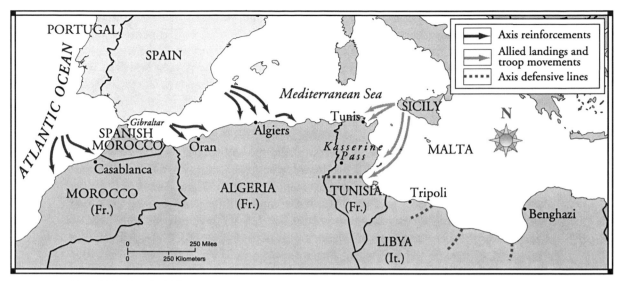

Map 13.1 North Africa.   Credit: Ronald Story, *Concise Historical Atlas of World War II: The Geography of Conflict*, Map 14, p. 33.

700 French troops died during the Casablanca engagement. General Nogues surrendered on November 11 on orders from Algiers, and he joined the Allied cause shortly thereafter as the French cease-fire went into effect. A month later, Darlan's life ended at the hands of an anti-fascist French student seeking to restore the monarchy.

NORTH AFRICAN CAMPAIGN
Because the Allies did not land further east than Algiers, Germans raced troops from Sicily to Tunisia to block a further advance. Luftwaffe bombings and the opposition of these 7,000 troops slowed down the invaders by the end of the month. By December, Field Marshal Albert Kesselring had named the ruthless Arnim to command Fifth Panzer Army in Tunisia. He instructed this former chief of the XXXIX Panzer Corps on the Eastern front to stop the Allies from capturing Tunis and reaching the central coastline. Arnim did as he was told. He halted the Allies 13 miles short of the capital and then widened a narrow bridgehead to link to Rommel in southern Tunisia. The 10th Panzer Division, Arnim's main striking force, attacked Kenneth Anderson's First British Army around Tebourba to good effect. The onset of rain and lack of air support bogged down the Allied force. The German defense at Longstop Hill from December 22 to 25, 1942, compelled Anderson to wait for reinforcements. In torrential rain, British Coldstream Guards took this critical rise—actually two crests split by a ravine—the first day, but the Americans relinquished it the next. On Christmas Day, the British recaptured Longstop Hill, but the Germans once again rebounded and seized the upper part later that morning. With infantry waterlogged on "Christmas Mountain," Ike halted the advance on Tunis. He counseled caution in Tunisia until reinforcements arrived. Longstop Hill remained in German hands until late April 1943, although both British and American skeletons in battle dress remained on top for months afterward.

Stifled at the northern end of the Tunisian coast, the Allies hoped for progress at the drier mountainous southern end where the Americans poured in. The panzers proved troublesome here, too. In mid-January 1943, the U.S. 1st Armored Division prepared for an assault toward the coast. Arnim beat Fredenhall to the punch, however. Fifth Panzer Army surprised poorly equipped French divisions by maneuvering tanks in the Eastern Dorsale Mountains and seizing the passes by month's end. From there, Arnim launched another offensive that won him Sid Bou Zid and Sbeitla farther west while Rommel pushed unopposed into Gafsa to the south. This forced the Allies to retreat to the Western Dorsales Mountains. They completed the withdrawal by February 19, but not before Fredenhall lost two tank, two infantry, and two artillery battalions. The situation got even dicier when Rommel sent his main German-Italian Panzer Army against the U.S. positions at Kasserine Pass. Because the Western Dorsales protected the Allied flank in Tunisia, holding the passes was critical. But U.S. II Corps reserves were inexperienced, and the Germans knew it. Worse, a misinterpretation of ULTRA information convinced Anderson and Fredenhall that Rommel would strike farther north. Thus Anderson moved up his main reserves and left American and French African troops to guard Kasserine Pass. This green force faced Rommel's battle-tested desert veterans. The Axis gained an added advantage when Arnim sent part of the 10th Panzer Division to join Rommel. Actually, they hoped to buy time. The Germans had planned to abandon North Africa but not without inflicting damage and diverting Allied troops away from a second front on the European continent.

Rommel performed his role, and sent the Americans reeling. German tank and air power were awesome. The light U.S. Stuart tanks could not dent the panzers (nor could these vehicles withstand Rommel's shells) and the Shermans performed badly. The 26th Infantry Regiment under Colonel Robert Stark blocked the Germans at Kasserine Pass on February 14; but by the fifth day, the panzers shifted their attack northwest. Rommel broke through the Pass with an Italian armored division and infantry bound for Tebessa. Arnim headed for Thala. In complete disarray, Fredenhall sent out confusing messages. His saving grace emerged on the German side when the mutual animosity between Arnim and Rommel spilled over into strategic planning. Rommel chafed at orders from the Italian Comando Supremo to move northward toward the Allied reserves at Le Kef rather than continue west to Tebessa. He correctly called the order shortsighted because it bogged him down in poor tank terrain amidst rain storms that persisted throughout the battle. Rommel broke off the offensive on February 22, 1943.

The Allies lost the battle of Kasserine Pass but with no long-lasting ill effects on their North African campaign. American losses climbed well over 6,000 men compared to about 1,000 German casualties. Mourning their dead and counting up the massive damage of materiel, the Americans were catalyzed to change. They reoccupied the Pass on February 24. Afterward, a furious Eisenhower replaced Fredenhall with the impetuous and hard-charging but competent Patton. The chief intelligence officer also got a pink slip. The battle served as a wake-up call. Regardless of their dubious reputation as fighters in British eyes, the Americans reformed into a potent military machine. Ike also learned about the personalities of his commanders and about organization, and took steps to change his command structure. In January 1943, he had met with the

Combined Chiefs of Staff, Churchill, and Roosevelt in a suburb of Casablanca to discuss strategy. Among other topics, these leaders formed the Eighteenth Army Group under Harold Alexander and a unified Mediterranean air command led by Air Chief Marshal Arthur Tedder. The Allies were now ready to eradicate the Axis menace from Africa.

Alexander's charge was to complete the North African campaign by the end of April 1943 so that the Allies could then cross the Mediterranean and invade Italy in August. Meeting the deadline meant a reorganization of the North African campaign. Despite Ike's best efforts, the theater suffered from chaos of command among Anglo-Franco-American officers, a lack of a plan, and the loss of initiative to the Axis. Alexander created national sectors of command, and he armed French units. The Wehrmacht regrouped, too. Rommel became Commander-in-Chief Army Group Afrika to coordinate strategy, and Arnim headed for a new offensive in the north to capitalize on the confusion sown at Kasserine Pass. By April 1, the Allies rebuffed him. Rommel found himself across from his old nemesis, Bernard Montgomery, in southern Tunisia.

To relieve the Americans at Kasserine Pass, in early March, Monty sent two divisions of British Eighth Army from Libya to attack Rommel's Mareth Line in southern Tunisia. The Desert Fox tried to outflank the British from the Matmata Hills while the German-Italian Army under General Giovanni Messe began a diversionary attack from the Mareth Line. ULTRA revealed details of the operation. Although outmuscled, Monty placed reinforcements in key areas and constructed antitank gun and infantry defenses in front of the town of Medenine. Keeping his armor in reserve, he lost not a tank as he drove away the Axis attackers. The victory on March 6 at Medenine represented a signal loss for the Axis. Rommel and Kesselring accused Messe of betraying them; but fortunately for the Allies, the Germans never launched an inquiry that might have exposed the existence of ULTRA. The Axis powers also lost their most able commander in the theater. The worn out Rommel left Africa three days later, never to return to the scene of his greatest triumphs.

His departure preceded the exit of the Axis from North Africa. Better equipped than Messe's Italian Army and with a superiority in tanks, Eighth Army attacked the Mareth Line. Backed by the Western Desert Air Force—a composite group (renamed later the First Tactical Air Force) comprised of British, American, South African, Australian, and other flyers—Monty finally rooted out Messe. The Italian withdrew further north to Wadi Akarit. Patton's II Corps charged up on Messe's flank and rear while Monty moved directly at him. Arnim warned that without reinforcements, Army Group Africa would fall. An Allied naval and air blockade from Malta denied him all but a trickle of help, however. He was forced to rely on vulnerable airlifts. Although the Germans blocked Patton's way to the coast, Monty broke through at Wadi Akarit and Messe backed into a shrinking pocket around Tunis. Patton's departure from the theater to plan the invasion of Sicily amply demonstrated that the Allies had things sewn up in North Africa. U.S. First Army cleared the hilly area north of Tunis, and the 2nd II Corps under the command of Patton's deputy, Lieutenant-General Omar Bradley, grabbed the northern flank by attacking Bizerta. These movements opened the way for the final offensive of the campaign. On April 22, Allied forces assaulted

Messe from all directions. Monty bogged down at Enfidaville and remained on the defensive. Yet in a grand gesture, Eighth Army offered two of its finest divisions to the Americans. Pummeled by a tremendous artillery and air barrage—the most intense ever in Africa—Arnim's line collapsed on the Medjez-Tunis road. In a day, Bizerta, Pont du Fahs, and Tunis itself fell, and two panzer armies fragmented into isolated groups. The Luftwaffe fled for Sicily, its transports harassed across the Mediterranean by the RAF and Royal Navy. The last of the panzers surrendered on May 13, 1943, as the Allies took 238,000 prisoners.

The North African campaign was over, its significance overshadowed by impending events on the European continent. The Allies had suffered 76,000 casualties. Critics concluded that the effort was not worth such losses, particularly because the campaign diverted forces from an invasion of France as the main way of defeating Hitler. Yet the theater provided valuable lessons regarding coordination and gave American troops their first taste of fighting. In any case, a cross-Channel invasion was operationally and logistically out of the question in 1943. Torch had been the best alternative to the second front in Europe.

What Churchill called "Tunisgrad" and others called the "Verdun of the Mediterranean" helped the Allies enormously. The defeat eliminated almost all of the Third Reich's reserves in the Mediterranean. Like Stalingrad, Operation Torch pierced the myth of German omnipotence. The capture of Tunis convinced important neighbors to turn away from the Axis. The French, for instance, leaned increasingly to the Allied side and the ever opportunist Francisco Franco in Spain also saw the writing on the wall. Earlier, he had turned over downed Allied aircraft to Germany, supported Axis sabotage operations in Gibraltar, placed his media at the disposal of Nazi propagandists, and offered to fight on the German side—the Blue Division of volunteers were sent to the Eastern front. Franco now refused to permit the Germans to cross his country and attack Gibraltar, whereas he let the Allies sail safely through the Straits. Significantly, Il Duce no longer lay claim to the Mediterranean, and Hitler's Third Reich existed only in Fortress Europe.

The Torch landings proved good practice for those who led the later invasions of Europe. Among them was Patton, who rivaled MacArthur and Monty in ego. MacArthur sported a pipe and Montgomery a beret as distinctive identifiers; the brusque Patton wore two ivory-handled pistols. He had served in World War I on General John Pershing's staff, commanded the largest U.S. tank force to go into action during that war and a new armored division after it, and then led a tank brigade during the war. In North Africa, Patton honed his skills as an offensive and inspirational combat officer. On the voyage across to Africa for the Torch landings, Patton exhorted his officers with the simple directive: "Always attack. Never surrender." They followed this "steamroller strategy" of annihilation into Italy and beyond. The campaign was also a sorting out for the Allies. To be sure, the British took a dim view of their American cousins after Kasserine Pass. The narrow-minded Monty never veered from this view, but Alexander came to a different position over time. Eisenhower worked to smooth over the differences. Although not directly involved in the campaign, he showed the fruits of inter-Allied cooperation in North Africa that were so pivotal during the invasion of France.

SICILY

Regardless of the aerial pounding Germany endured, fascism could be felled only on the ground, and that mean an invasion of the Third Reich. The Allies now had a foothold from which to advance into the continent. Churchill and FDR had compromised at the Casablanca conference. The former sought an invasion in Italy or the Balkans to open a second front, but Roosevelt still held out for France. They settled on Sicily out of an obligation to help Stalin while they prepared a cross-Channel attack. Both were aware that the USSR bore the brunt of the ground fighting. Besides, Italy appeared ripe for defeat.

That country teetered on the brink of ruin. Benito Mussolini's reign had little support, the fascists had lost their stomach for war, and his empire lay in tatters. He provoked little fear abroad; even Vichy France largely ignored him. To his great annoyance, he was clearly Hitler's subordinate as the Nazis had called the shots ever since the campaign in Greece. The Fuhrer compelled Italy to send troops to the Soviet Union (Mussolini preferred that the Third Reich make peace with the USSR as well as the Balkans). Italy committed 235,000 troops, nearly 1,000 heavy guns, 25,000 horses, 17,000 vehicles, and five dozen aircraft to the German cause in Russia; but it now wanted out of the Soviet Union. This was especially so after 30,000 soldiers had died and nearly double that number sat in captivity in the USSR by 1943. To quell the home front, Il Duce wanted his troops returned from the Eastern front to fight in Sicily, the entry point of the Allies into Europe. Instead, Hitler sent German troops to the island. This unhappy situation for Mussolini had a redeeming feature. In the Nazis, the Allies faced a troublesome foe that might sustain Italian fascism a bit longer.

Under the Sicilian invasion plan—Operation Husky—Eisenhower looked to Alexander and the newly formed Fifteenth Army Group. Its elements included Eighth Army and Patton's I Armored Corps, renamed Seventh Army, of eight divisions of infantry and armor along with airborne, commando, and Ranger units. In support were the Allied Naval Commander Andrew Cunningham and Arthur Tedder, the Allied Air Commander in the Mediterranean. Tedder reported to Ike while Cunningham took orders from the Allied Headquarters in Algiers. This jumbled command system, as well as Alexander's willingness to adhere to Monty's suggestions, hinted at problems to come. On July 10, 1943, the second largest landings (after Normandy) of the war took place after weeks of confused planning and Anglo-American bickering.

A deception operation called "Mincemeat" tricked the defenders into thinking that Sicily was a cover target for an invasion of the Balkans or Sardinia. The body of a dead, supposed Royal Marines attaché officer was dumped off Spain the previous April with papers revealing that Sicily was a feint. Fearful of landings in the Balkans, Hitler swallowed the ruse and sent troops there instead of Sicily and even Rommel rushed to Greece to meet the Allies. Despite this advantage of surprise, Husky did not start well. Even though bombing neutralized Sicilian airfields, strong winds and inadequate planning forced many of the gliders carrying the first large Allied airborne missions to ditch in the sea. What Germans were present to contest the landings were a demoralized lot, yet they offered stiff resistance. The Luftwaffe was beaten up and drained of veteran pilots. But the Axis had 350,000 troops on the island under Italian Alfred Guzzoni. While many were local coastal reserves who disliked the Germans, there were six mobile divisions, including the rebuilt Herman Göring unit and the new 15th Panzer Grenadiers, both under General Hans Hube's XIV Panzer Corps. These forces could not block all the landings, so they hoped to withdraw inland and seal the beaches from there.

Despite the obstacles of weather and heavy seas, the bulk of the 180,000 troops of the Husky invading force, backed by 2,590 ships, got ashore. Following the airborne assault, Monty's X and XIV Corps met sporadic resistance on the east beaches between Pozzallo and Syracuse. The latter fell into his hands the day of the landings. Arriving on the southwest coast between Cape Scaramia and Licata, the three American divisions had difficulties due to the adverse weather conditions and stronger opposition than on Sicily's east side. By the end of the day, however, the divisions made land. By the next day, July 11, U.S. Naval gunfire repelled a German armored counterattack around Gela. The Allies had landed in Fortress Europe.

That otherwise striking fact belied faulty strategy and bad Anglo-American blood that undermined harmony. British Eighth Army was to advance on two fronts up the right side of the island. The XIII Corps would go toward Catania and the XXX Corps to Leonforte and Enna. Both would mass around Mount Etna before Monty marched into Messina to end the campaign. Unimpressed by the American showing in Tunisia, Alexander directed Patton to guard Eighth Army's left flank in a subordinate role. This order prevented Bradley's U.S. II Corps from cutting the island in two and trapping the 15th Panzer Grenadiers. It also angered the hotheaded Patton. Worse, it did not work out as planned. Monty stalled on the plain of Catania for two weeks until August 5, blocked by Guzzoni who fought for the all-important Messina. Hube's formation dug in. An infuriated Patton regrouped under the Provisional Corps and aimed for Palermo. When Alexander demanded that he continue to protect Monty, Patton protested in person. The appeal worked. His force advanced on Palermo, took prisoners along the route, and captured the city a week later. Patton's temper would get the best of him when he slapped two U.S. soldiers who were convalescing in an infirmary but who he mistakenly believed were shirking their duties in the field. His reaction nearly got him dismissed from the U.S. Army.

At this point, the Allies received some good news. On July 25, 1943, Il Duce fell from power, fired by the King, the Italian Army, and some fascist chiefs. Surrender seemed inevitable after antifascist partisans and leftists had inspired huge strikes in Milan and Turin in March. King Victor Emmanuel III rallied to save the country, and a coup dissolved the Fascist Party in favor of restoring the constitutional monarchy. Mussolini was arrested. After Italy declared an armistice, however, Hitler freed him in September 1943 and named him the leader of a puppet regime designed to legitimize the German occupation of the country. The meddlesome Hitler had long refused to allow his troops to withdraw from Sicily but once Mussolini's regime ended and Italian soldiers abandoned the fight, the Germans began to pull back to the northeast corner of the island.

Hube remained on another defensive line in rough country that hindered the Allies' tanks and then fought a fierce five-day battle at Troina against the U.S. Big Red One Division while fending off Monty's forces around Adrano. As the line cracked,

Patton.   Credit: Center for the Study of War Experience at Regis
University, Denver, Colorado.

German Commander-in-Chief South-West Kesselring began a virtuoso evacuation on
the night of August 11–12. About 40,000 German and 62,000 Italian troops, most of
their supplies, and 10,000 vehicles escaped across the Strait of Messina to the Italian
mainland three miles away. Antiaircraft guns lined the Strait as troops were ferried
night and day. Alexander failed to capitalize on ULTRA that told him ten days before
the withdrawal exactly what would happen. Amphibious actions in which the British
advanced northeastward around Mount Etna and the Americans hopped along the
north coast came up short against the fleeing Axis powers. Operation Husky turned
out to be only a partial victory because the Germans escaped in force. Although Patton
famously won the race over Montgomery to Messina on August 16, by the next morning, the Germans had departed. The Allies registered 16,500 casualties, but the Axis
suffered 164,000 losses, most of them Italian prisoners. Nearly 32,000 Germans were
trapped, injured, or killed.

The sole remaining question was the disposition of Sicily. Alexander became the
governor of the island under the Allied Military Government of Occupied Territories.
This established a civilian government that recruited locals to the administration, among
whom were Mafia members whom Mussolini had suppressed. Their U.S. brethren ran
the port of New York efficiently and had contacted Sicilian families at the beginning of
Operation Husky for help in gathering information. Now in government positions, the
Mafia revived the lucrative black market and re-entrenched themselves in the Italian
economy.

ADVANCE INTO ITALY

With the central Mediterranean safe for shipping, the route from the Middle East to Asia thereby shortened, and Mussolini out of power, the Allies decided to invade the Italian mainland. Winston Churchill looked on Italy as the "soft underbelly" of Europe, and his chief advisor, Alan Brooke, advocated this idea. They believed an assault in southern Italy would aid the USSR by drawing German forces from the Eastern front, threaten the Axis in the Balkans, and bring the oil fields of Romania within striking distance of airfields around Foggia. The other option was to ship all the troops to England where they would lay idle for a year or so until a cross-Channel attack began. Instead, the British might score a much-needed victory. Renewing the American demand for a landing in western Europe, Franklin Roosevelt insisted on southern France as the next landing point but relented when Churchill promised a hard date of May 1, 1944, for the commencement of Overlord, the invasion of Normandy. The Americans reasoned that an invasion into southern Italy would provide air bases from which to bomb Germany.

Anglo-American planning again undermined the invasion. In fact, there had really been no planning beyond the capture of Sicily. Brooke envisaged the Allies running up the boot of Italy and reaching a point north of Florence from which they could strike at southern Germany. The Americans doubted this strategy would work and their skepticism prevented a coherent plan of attack. No clear aim existed at the operational level except for a surprise assault by amphibious landings. Tactics were improvised, strategy haphazardly planned, and politics muddled the decision-making process. Furthermore, the Allies were unsure whether the turnover of the Italian government met their terms of unconditional surrender. As the Allies dallied by discussion of this issue, the Wehrmacht moved sixteen divisions into Italy. The gentlemanly Alexander could not control his field commanders—the imperious Montgomery and the brash Mark Clark of the Anglo-American Fifth Army. As in Sicily, the Allies blundered by disorganization and misjudgment of their foe. Because the new Italian government under Marshal Badoglio was unwilling to surrender to the Allies or face the anger of the Germans, it delayed an active defense for weeks. During this time the Wehrmacht took up key positions in north and central Italy.

The Allied landings began on September 3, 1943 at Reggio di Calabria across the Strait of Messina. Bombardment by sea and air preceded a pincer advance by three Canadian brigades that were part of Eighth Army. The Germans had already conceded Calabria. Monty sought to clear the toe of Italy before heading up the west side of the boot along with the rest of the Allies who had come ashore at Salerno. His troops moved northward as expected. They took Taranto to seal of the heel and then moved northward beyond Foggia. Although slowed by bridges blown up by the retreating Germans, Eighth Army moved easily when contrasted with Clark's pincer movement. The amphibious assault by Fifth Army on September 9 in the Gulf of Salerno south of Naples did not go smoothly. Part of the reason was that Ike had announced the Italian armistice the day before, which led Allied leaders and troops to believe that their landing would be unopposed the next morning. They were sadly mistaken.

The invasion force lacked sufficient landing craft and the element of surprise but the landings at Salerno went ahead anyway, covered by the 627 ships of Force H and extra air cover from two fleet carriers and five escort carriers. The latter joined the operation when demands in the Pacific stripped the Mediterranean fleets. Because Salerno sat at the outer range of aircraft based in Sicily, these warships were imperative. Naples had been the intended target, but the land-based planes could not reach that far. The four divisions of Fifth Army's VI Corps commanded by Ernest Dawley and X Corps of Eighth Army under Richard McCreery led the invasion. A smart and inspiring leader, McCreery had served as Alexander's chief of staff in the Western Desert. His X Corps, comprised of two infantry and one armored division, came ashore around Salerno. U.S. Rangers and British commandos took the left, and two British divisions were on the right. Dawley hit the beaches to the south in Salerno Bay to protect McCreery's flank. One of the American units bogged down before the only panzer division in the area at the time. Kesselring recovered from his initial shock and ordered Hube to hold in the Gulf of Salerno. He also did away with his Italian allies because on September 8, Italy exited the war. The Italians fell into disarray and overestimated the Allied commitment to liberate the peninsula. The British and Americans figured Germany would shift attention elsewhere from Italy but the Germans rounded up their former allies, disarmed them, and either shipped them off to prison camps or shot them for betrayal. Tens of thousands of Italian soldiers melted into the countryside as partisans or joined the Allied cause. The war in Italy dragged on for twenty more months.

At Salerno, meanwhile, the defenders toughened. Green U.S. units and German resistance made the landing hard while part of the British 46th Division marched into a group of panzer grenadiers after wrongly guessing that the Germans had vacated when the Italians surrendered. The British seized the airfield at Montecorvino, but Tenth Army commander General Heinrich von Vietinghoff rushed in the LXXVI Panzer Corps from Calabria and a Panzergrenadier division from Rome. Their intense fire decommissioned the airfield, thereby limiting Allied air cover. Harassment continued even when the Allies tried to build airstrips elsewhere. By the end of the first day, both Dawley's and McCreery's landing forces were on the beaches; but a seven-mile gap stood between them. On September 11, the Germans damaged two cruisers with radio-controlled bombs then hit the battleship *Warspite*. The Allies could not break out of their beachhead for a week as enemy reinforcements poured in. They took Salerno and Vietri, but neither were usable as ports. The Wehrmacht soon capitulated on nearby Capri, but Vietinghoff began a counteroffensive that nearly drove the Allies back into the sea.

It was clear that while the Germans had rapidly coordinated their attacks, Clark, an able staff officer but a vain—and in this case inept—commander, had not built up his beachhead in time to oppose them. Neither the British nor the Americans had reserves to meet Vietinghoff's attack, and plans were hastily drawn up to evacuate the beaches. The situation grew desperate. Two battalions of the U.S. 82nd Airborne Division dropped on to the beaches as reinforcements and two British ships bombarded the German position. One knocked out a German Tiger tank while a cruiser fired 1,500 shells in ten minutes in a massive display of firepower. McCreery received a supplement of 1,500 troops from Tripoli, and Tedder sent his entire Mediterranean air force. The Germans finally had no answer. In northern Italy, Rommel refused to send more troops to Vietinghoff on the basis that Germany did not intend to make a stand below Rome. The Wehrmacht feared an amphibious attack above its defenses. Outgunned, the Germans on September 16 withdrew north of Naples and the city erupted in rebellion. This provoked the Nazis into a four-day massacre of hundreds—Hitler invoked his strategy of annihilation to Italy as well as other theaters—that ended when the Allies reached Naples on October 1, 1943. Meanwhile, the Americans linked with British Eighth Army coming up from Reggio di Calabria. The beachhead had been saved.

Optimistic about prospects below Rome, "Smiling Albert" Kesselring convinced Hitler that a defensive effort was worthwhile. The Germans decided to resist the Allies in Italy. The latter's sloppiness revealed weaknesses, while rivers and mountains provided superb defensive havens. The Wehrmacht built a series of imposing barriers—the Gustav, Winter, and Gothic Lines—that crossed Italy from the Mediterranean to the Adriatic. Behind these lines, they made their defensive campaign into the perfect image of attrition warfare. It involved a series of vicious battles fought in rain and snow. Allied leaders did not give Alexander enough resources to fight these battles but merely demanded victory. Furthermore, strategy did not account for geography. King Victor Emmanuel warned that the worst way to conquer the country was to advance south to north. The Allies did not listen. After all, Rome was just 80 miles away from the Gustav Line. Morale was also low. Learning that Italy played supporting actor to the starring roles of the Eastern and Western European theaters, Allied troops were oftentimes deflated by the campaign.

In the Fall of 1943, the Allies crawled up the Italian mainland through mud. No extra supplies, equipment, and vessels were available because the Pacific theater and the buildup for Normandy exhausted surplus shipping. The Foggia airfields were operable, but they sapped aircraft to the Balkans. Strained resources dashed hopes of a strong amphibious assault up the coast. In any case, the Apennine Mountains inland on the Mediterranean side prohibited flanking movement. By the end of the year, Anglo-American forces inched their way forward, but the troops were worn out. The Wehrmacht defended the Gustav Line while their enemies ground themselves to exhaustion. In late November, 1943, Eighth Army crossed the Sangro River and went up the Adriatic coast, but it could not make the critical town of Pescara. The Canadians took Ortona near Christmas but went no farther. To the west, U.S. Fifth Army crossed the Volturno River in October, and Rome lay just 100 miles north. Yet mountains ran to the sea in front of them, and the Gustav Line capitalized on this terrain. In bitter cold, the two sides battled ferociously in the mountains, carrying supplies by mule or manpower. Anglo-American forces broke through the Winter Line by taking Monte Camino, Monte Maggiore, and other villages. They reached the Gustav Line in mid-January 1944. Yet the German defenses blocked the way to Rome. Italy had proven to be the opposite of a soft underbelly.

Faced with a quagmire in Italy, politicians resorted to planning for future military success, making operational and strategic adjustments along the way. How the battles worked out on land, sea, and in the air were another matter. As the Japanese discovered in the Southwest Pacific, the Germans found out in North Africa, and Anglo-American troops realized in Italy, the Allied advances were brutal and unpredictable affairs. The year 1943 had seen the Allies and Axis switch places. The Allies took the initiative and charged on the offensive. The Axis powers were nowhere near to conceding, however. As a result, World War II entered a particularly atrocious stage of violence.

CHAPTER 14

War of Words, the Seas, and the Air

We never saw the faces of our enemies. When I thought of them at all, I pictured blank white ovals framed by blond crew cuts—never bangs or curls or pigtails, though I knew our bombs fell on plenty of women and kids too.

HILLARY JORDAN
Mudbound

THE BIG THREE

Despite the setbacks in Italy, diplomatic cooperation spurred Allied victories as much as military prowess, even though tensions had long infused negotiations over many issues. Of particular focus was the USSR. The democracies answered Josef Stalin's calls for help in this period with their economies and air and sea power. They sent more than 10,000 tanks to the USSR in 1942–1943, although they were too light for Soviet needs. Stalin preferred the more than 14,000 aircraft (mostly fighters) shipped by the Americans and the 4,000 British Hurricanes and Spitfires. Added to Russian production, the aid was important. Shipments of over 385,000 trucks as well as clothing, food, and signal equipment permitted Soviet factories to focus on the manufacture of guns and tanks. To be sure, much of the war materiel did not reach the Eastern front in large quantities until 1943, but they contributed to the USSR's war effort in 1942 all the same.

The issue of the second front was a thorn in Allied relations. Roosevelt knew that something had to be done but the alternatives were stark. Either Germany might defeat the USSR on the second try or demand parts of Eastern Europe as a buffer zone. Churchill opposed such appeasement; but like FDR, he worried that the Soviets might make a separate peace as they had done in World War I. A mutual security treaty was thus under consideration. Stalin's territorial demands—which ran counter to the spirit of openness and democratic self-determination ingrained in the recent United Nations Declaration—made it unlikely. As the Eastern front turned bad for the USSR in Spring 1942, the western allies refused to concede postwar boundaries. The resulting treaty did not mention borders and innocuously pledged the Allies to mutual aid and no separate treaties. Soviet diplomats urged a second front in 1942, but the invasion of North Africa the next year evolved as the preference. Discussions with Stalin remained stormy. He accused the Anglo-Americans of treachery.

It was a mark of their confidence in victory, however, that Churchill and FDR, and then Stalin, discussed the war and postwar plans at a succession of conferences in 1943. They first convened in Casablanca in January; and by the end of the year, they had met in Quebec, Cairo, and Teheran. The latter was Stalin's first summit with the other two leaders. Arguments erupted at each gathering, but the intention was the same: to wield a strategy of annihilation in their initiatives against the Axis powers. Diplomacy clearly reflected the Allies' counter-offensive mindset.

At Casablanca in mid-January 1943, Churchill and Roosevelt decided that the Axis powers must unconditionally surrender. That the communiqué of the meeting did not mention this stark demand was due to Churchill's hopes that Italy could be coaxed into quitting the war without an invasion rather than being pummelled. But FDR insisted on a complete defeat of all the Axis powers as the American public required. Regardless of their differences, the two agreed that unconditional surrender would best erase fascism and militarism and allow for the pacification and democratization of Germany, Japan, and Italy. No German demagogue would arise again to blame domestic politicians for defeat. The Allies would dictate terms to the Nazi regime. This would also show Stalin that the West would not stab him in the back and negotiate with the Germans. The goal was clear: total victory. Roosevelt assured that this did "not mean the destruction of the population of Germany, Italy, or Japan, but it does mean the destruction of the philosophies in those countries which are based on conquest and the subjugation of other people." That was more propaganda to coax a surrender. The means to the war's end really depended on the strategy of annihilation that would besiege citizens as well as soldiers.

That the war had devolved into a one of annihilation particularly on the Eastern front implied that massive destruction would actually persist because of the unconditional surrender decision. A month before the Casablanca meeting, the United Nations had issued a statement that promised justice for war crimes committed by the enemy. By October 1943, foreign ministers issued a declaration on Nazi atrocities that called for trials and punishment for war criminals. Much information about the Holocaust and other Nazi atrocities had reached the West by this time. For their part, the Germans—the Nazis as well as the Wehrmacht—determined after Casablanca to fight to the bitter end in part because they knew they had committed horrendous crimes. Their war of annihilation on the Jews and other undesirables instigated a campaign of annihilation against the Third Reich. This linked the Holocaust to the military side of the conflict in a horrible onslaught of inhumane violence.

Although officials left Casablanca embittered by the discord caused by such issues as unconditional surrender and the second front, FDR and Churchill exited with a strategic plan to defeat the Axis. This included a Casablanca Directive that called for the systematic destruction of the German economy and military, and the undermining of civilian morale by British aerial bombing at night and an American campaign by day. Alterations to this Combined Bomber Offensive followed at the Quebec meeting. The Allies pledged not to target civilians, even though they acknowledged that innocent populations could not be avoided. They stressed destruction of aircraft and factories to attain complete air supremacy before the invasion of western Europe. But the bombers' first priority targets were U-boat shipyards and submarine pens on the Atlantic because Anglo-American leaders gave the war at sea their fullest attention.

The conferences at Quebec, Cairo, and Teheran addressed these same European issues, and they also dwelled on the war in Asia and the Pacific. At the first Quebec meeting in August 1943, the Allies decided to isolate the major Japanese base at Rabaul. They also created a new theater—the Southeast Asia Command (SEAC)—which encompassed Burma, Malaya, Sumatra, and secret missions in Thailand and Indochina. Lord Louis Mountbatten, whose diplomatic dash exceeded his talents (he had masterminded the disaster at Dieppe), led SEAC. The command attempted to draw Japanese attention away from the Pacific and to increase supplies from India into China. At Cairo in late 1943, Mountbatten and Chiang Kai-shek pressed for amphibious operations in the Bay of Bengal to coincide with Chinese action in Burma. Roosevelt agreed. The subsequent Cairo Declaration coordinated future offensives against Japan. That enemy would lose all of its territories taken since 1895, including Formosa (Taiwan) and Korea.

Primed for action in war, the Allies also prepared for the peace. In Teheran at the same time as the Cairo conference in late 1943, the so-called Big Three of Roosevelt, Churchill, and Stalin decided to launch the Normandy landings by late Spring 1944. That Churchill tried to postpone the invasion gave this issue top billing; it encompassed three of the meeting's four days. FDR and Stalin stood firm, oftentimes taunting Churchill who realized that the weakened Britain was no match for the massive USSR and United States. Roosevelt also received the first nod from the Soviets that they would fight against Japan once the war ended with Germany.

However controversial the diplomatic wrangling was at these four conferences in 1943, their tenor was one of unremitting dedication to the total defeat of their enemies. The Allies took the initiative, backed by growing logistical power. Production of armaments, shipments of military aid, and induction of large numbers of personnel into their armed forces gave the Big Three a critical (and increasing) edge over the Axis powers. The latter failed to cooperate sufficiently—they had an alliance on paper but it lacked as a diplomatic tool to aid their war effort—and they lagged in logistical competition. The Allies had the luxury of deciding when and how to attack in the various theaters around the globe with masses of troops equipped with high-quality weapons and supported by long, safer, and more reliable supply lines.

AIR OFFENSIVES

The years 1942 and 1943 witnessed the coming of age of total war. The British escalated strategic air offensives into a major—and controversial—weapon in the Allied arsenal. Ruin wrought by the combined bomber campaign in Europe and later in Asia, and Germany's response in kind, was tremendous. Although the Third Reich had a larger air force than the RAF when war broke out, the Luftwaffe had no doctrine of strategic bombing. Neither side wanted to provoke the other; so it was not until France's demise in May 1940 that the British, desperate for any sort of victory, embarked on nighttime bombing raids. Bombers such as Whitleys, Wellingtons, and Hampdens had trouble hitting unseen targets at night, however, even though darkness provided them with protective cover. The Germans retaliated by night raids of their own during the battle of Britain that also missed their mark. Focused on specific targets such as factories, railroads, airfields, and bases, both nations' reconnaissance revealed that lighted urban areas were the best targets. Precision bombing was often not very precise; it was also difficult to hit small objectives. London's compulsion to counterattack against the unstoppable Nazis overrode the ethical issues of bombing civilian populations. By the end of 1941, after a year of experimentation, Britain adopted area bombing. Planes flew in a stream—essentially, one behind the other rather than formation—and saturated an area with a mix of explosives and incendiaries. The Germans initiated area bombing over Guernica, Warsaw, Rotterdam, and London; but the British perfected it. This was also safer for the bombers themselves, and it compelled the Luftwaffe to defend its home rather than carry out its own offensive missions.

The air war drew on science and technology. Germany improved its radar network and better orchestrated night-fighter aircraft response. As in Britain, German scientists worked with air crews to detect incoming bombers and direct their own toward targets. Bombers navigated by radio beams, which the British countered by warping the signal so pilots veered off course. In 1943, British bombers began dropping pieces of tinfoil that reflected their image back to German radar operators. This filled their instruments with "snow" that obscured the radar images and prevented bombers from distinguishing the real from the fake. Decoy planes also flew over the German coast to distract radar operators. Both sides made adjustments in this scientific war, but the British turned out to be more determined in mastering the technical aspects of the effort. The combatants also developed new bombers to carry more and heavier payloads and to travel farther distances. The British had the best night heavy bomber on any side—the Avro Lancaster—which became operational in March 1942, flew up to 1,660 miles, and dropped the most tonnage of all bombers in the war. It joined two other four-engine bombers, the Short Stirling and the Handley Page Halifax. The Germans did not progress as well. The Heinkel suffered engine complications, and the bigger Dornier Do217 and Ju188 were nothing more than sophisticated versions of older models. Still, Berlin produced the war's first bomber jet in 1944.

The Americans had already made the first modern, all-metal, four-engine bomber—the Boeing B-17—nicknamed the Flying Fortress because its World War II version was outfitted with six manned positions in twin-gunned powered turrets. The B-17 ranged to 1,850 miles and flew at lofty altitudes of a 35,000 feet ceiling. This was high enough for daylight missions that reduced risk from antiaircraft batteries, although it was not immune to the 88-mm gun that could reach to 48,000 feet. Yet not until mid-1942 was the Flying Fortress armed with enough power in the turrets and to a tail gunner for protection. The B-24 Liberator, a newer designed four-engine long-range bomber, first saw service with the RAF on antisubmarine patrols in the Atlantic. Over 18,300 were produced during the war, more than any other U.S. combat aircraft. Japan had its twin-engine "Betty," an Allied name for the Mitsubishi G4M, which was vulnerable to attack because protection for crews and fuel tanks (typical in the Allies' four-engine planes) was sacrificed to its long range of 3,765 miles. Yet Americans also paid a heavy price in terms of lost lives and planes due to their initially stubborn view that fighter escorts for bombers were unnecessary. The B-17, on the other hand, could not fly as far; but it was more durable, carried a greater bomb load, and could absorb great damage before returning to base. Although roughly half as many Liberators than B-17s were produced, the B-24s were deployed more widely, especially in the Pacific. The Flying Fortress dropped roughly one-third of the nearly 2 million tons of bombs by both the RAF and United States on the German war machine during the war.

By 1942, British military advisors justified area bombing at operational and tactical levels, but they also argued for strategic and psychological rationales as well. The bombers might change the correlations of power away from German and Soviet ground armies to the air and give Anglo-American forces means of winning the war from above and at sea. In 1942, the War Cabinet endorsed this approach and also advocated bombing as a means of breaking the enemies' will. The new Commander-in-Chief of British Bomber Command, Arthur Harris, enthusiastically embarked on a plan to carry out this theory. "Bomber" Harris had joined the new Royal Air Force in World War I. By 1939, he led a bomber group before serving on the Air Staff and leading the first RAF delegation to the United States. He observed incendiaries during the Blitz destroy much of London and thus decided that burning, rather than high explosives, would be most effective against Germany. On his appointment to Bomber Command in February 1942, he set out to prove the point by firebombing raids on Lubeck and Rostock. Initially he had only 300 planes at his disposal, fewer than existed in 1940. The problem was that his superiors saw no good reason to justify an increase in bombers. Harris set out to give them one.

His campaign created a new epoch of annihilation in which the battlefield was potentially infinite. Harris ordered his entire second line of operational training units into massive attacks on cities. He scoured for pilots. Engineers developed guidance systems, timed waves of bombers for maximum effect, and tinkered with the ratios of high-explosive bombs and incendiaries. The new Lancaster and Halifax heavy bombers could drop enormous payloads to ignite self-perpetuating firestorms that would suck the oxygen out of the air and consume all forms of life. The goal of this air strategy of annihilation was to prove the efficacy of strategic bombing and to show the Germans that they could not survive against Anglo-American might. The raids began on Cologne on May 30. Some 1,050 planes dropped 1,455 tons of bombs, which caused fires to burn across 600 acres of the city for two days. Reconnaissance photographs showed 20,000 homes destroyed or damaged and 1,500 commercial properties leveled. Remarkably, the historic cathedral was spared. Five dozen factories closed, and communications and rail links were interrupted for two weeks. About 500 died or were hurt and a half million left homeless. Harris was disappointed by the results, especially after 44 planes did not return. Two nights later, Essen was hit by 956 aircraft that dropped their payloads on targets illuminated by flares. On June 25, it was Bremen's turn. Harris sent 1,006 bombers of which 49 were lost. The Luftwaffe had neither the strength nor the capability (lacking fleets of four-engine heavy bombers) to issue big reprisals.

Although the destruction in Essen and Bremen did not live up to expectations, Bomber Command's learning curve shot upward. Cologne had been bombed before, but the big raid demonstrated that huge bombings were more effective than small ones. Harris calculated that he needed 6,000 heavy bombers working round the clock. This was an unrealistic figure that was never attained. Manufacturers could not produce that many aircraft, and factories focused on other needs besides planes. Also erroneous was his belief that civilian morale would crumble under the crushing weight of such assaults. Like their British victims, bombed Germans instead became more patriotic and determined to survive. Harris would not let up, however. He returned to the industrial areas of the Ruhr, Saar, and Rhineland time and time again. Bomber Command ordered repeated poundings of the same targets and then threw in an attack on Berlin for good measure just to show the Nazis it could be done. The introduction of electronic navigational and bombing aids augmented the offensive, which opened with a damaging blow in the Ruhr in March 1942 and continuing through the next several months. The strategic air offensive shared such traits of the sea campaign as the large rate of casualties. Counting civilians, however, it far surpassed the battle of the Atlantic in number of people injured, killed, and missing.

The Americans firmly established the policy of merciless hammering when they joined the air war by August 1942. Due to training and doctrine, they first focused on daylight bombing to allow for precision hits on targets rather than British-style area bombing that strayed from factories to residences. Such was the thinking of Lieutenant-General Ira Eaker who led the first U.S. bomber raid in Europe on Rouen, France on August 17. He became head of the Eighth USAAF based in England. Eaker trained B-17 and B-24 crews, although his efforts were held up until squadrons were replenished in Spring 1943 after the North African campaign. First, though, the Allies argued over tactics. Harris claimed that daylight precision bombing was unfeasible, but Eaker countered that the Norden bombsight provided the means to hit targets dead on from 30,000 feet. A complex ballistic computer that calculated the trajectory of a bomb, the bombsight never dropped ordnance as accurately as alleged by its inventors. Yet flyers swore by it. Unescorted heavy bombers could not combat the Luftwaffe over German air space, countered Harris. Eaker responded that for protection, B-17s and B-24s possessed more machine guns of heavier caliber than those carried by the Lancaster, as well a more armor. This meant the payloads had to be lighter, claimed the British, and required more planes. So be it, responded Eaker. He would send masses of heavily armed bombers stacked in "boxes" against German fighters. Hitting a few essential targets rather than bombing indiscriminately would cause the collapse of the Third Reich's economy and the Nazi regime with it. "We won't do more talking until we have done more fighting," Eaker concluded. This turned out to be a good idea.

At the Casablanca conference in January 1943, the Allies discussed Eaker's idea for a Combined Bomber Offensive along the lines of the massive Cologne attack. The British would attack at night and the Americans by day. A directive required that the bombers focus first on destroying the Luftwaffe and airplane factories to establish air superiority over western Europe in preparation for the invasion of France. The RAF's Charles (Peter) Portal, an advocate of area bombing and advisor to Churchill, coordinated the Combined Bomber Offensive called Operation Pointblank. It began with attacks on Italian cities to unseat Mussolini and also pinpointed German submarine

First big raid by USAAF on Focke Wulf plant, Marienburg, Germany.
Credit: National Archives.

bases in St. Nazaire, Lorient, Brest, and La Pallice, France, in the winter of 1942–43. Raids followed on the Ruhr, Hamburg, Regensburg-Schweinfurt, and then Berlin in the second half of 1943 in an effort to bomb nonstop around the clock.

Operation Pointblank ushered in an era of sheer devastation. The Allies had no significant effect on U-boat operations due to the formidable strength of German shelters, but bombing cities was their real focus. The USAAF encountered similar problems as the RAF did earlier. In April 1943, half of the force was lost or damaged over the Folke Wulf aircraft factory near Bremen. In the Ruhr, 442 British planes struck Essen on the night of March 5–6 that launched the four-month campaign in this industrial heartland. Electronic navigation systems and the short distance from Britain helped the bombers, although decoys and smog wreaked havoc on accuracy. The Germans moved their factories to rural areas; but by the last raid—on Gelsenkirchen on the night of July 9–10—the Luftwaffe downed a rising number of bombers through improved electronic aids. An intense defense by fighters bagged 87 U.S. bombers over Hamburg, Hanover, Kassel, Kiel, and Warnemunde. Bomber Harris overestimated the damage done in the Ruhr offensive, which he halted due to the growing losses. Some 1,000 Allied planes went down with 7,000 of their crews (although many aircrews survived to become prisoners of war) in the battle of the Ruhr. At least the campaign diverted a higher number of Luftwaffe aircraft and 88-mm guns, which were deadly against tanks as well as planes from Italy and Russia.

Missions over Germany spoke to the horrors of war. In a raid over Vegesack in March, for instance, the Eighth USAAF's 93rd Bomb Group experienced German fighter defenses. After nearly two hours in hostile airspace, the B-24 *Shoot Luke* suffered severe damage from cannon shells and small caliber rounds. Seven of the ten men were wounded. Tail-gunner Paul Slankard was hurled halfway out of the aircraft with such force that doctors later dug out coins embedded in his hip from his trousers. His left leg nearly severed and the bleeding profuse, he received first aid from the bombardier who also struggled with his own head wounds. Crew members finally staunched the seepage from Slankard's wounds by exposing the pulped mass to the freezing air blasting in from a hole in the fuselage opened by enemy shells. The tail gunner suffered greatly because hypodermic needles containing pain-killers were also frozen despite an attempt by the bombardier to thaw them out by mouth. Slankard survived, one of the few flyers hit by a 20-mm shell who did not need amputation or did not endure a permanent major disability.

HAMBURG AND THE AIR WAR

By making adjustments to confuse radar defenses by using the "Window" device to drop large quantities of aluminum strips, the British targeted the port of Hamburg in July and August 1943. Germany's second biggest city was an industrial and shipping center. It had been bombed over 130 times already and thus had developed extensive civil defense shelters, warning systems, and firefighting organizations. Harris focused on Hamburg's wooden town center once again. Conditions were perfect for destruction; visibility was clear, and the weather hot and dry. In raids coded Gemorrah, over 3,000 RAF planes unleashed area bombing raids, alternating explosives with incendiaries. Delayed-action bombs also rained down on the city to hinder the firefighters who were stuck on the north side responding to the first bombs. The British bombed the night of July 24–25, and the Americans hit each of the next two days, although they lost an entire squadron to German fighters. The RAF (and Canadian Air Force) returned before midnight on July 27–28.

The bomber crews saw the results, but most had few regrets in the midst of war. Flying through heavy flak, probing searchlights, and night fighters, a British lieutenant readied for "a week of hell for the German port." He returned three days after his first run to view 16,000 feet below "a city still blazing" under drifting smoke. The RAF flyer returned to Hamburg just after the war in 1945 to see complete desolation, "acre upon acre of lifeless ruins, and I was more than glad that no one could point the finger and say where my bombs had fallen. It was one thing to bomb in the heat of battle and another to see one's contribution against the background of a defeated enemy." There was obvious discomfort with this "morale bombing" or "terror bombing" as it became known. The intentional targeting of civilians by all sides has elicited controversy over the supposed good war thesis ever since. From the view of those on the ground as well as from the air, the effect was dramatic evidence of the strategy of annihilation.

The first man-made firestorm of the war swept an area of Hamburg 8.5 square miles in size. Huge lumber yards fueled the inferno. Temperatures hit 1,000 degrees Fahrenheit. "The air was actually filled with fire," recalled a warden, and then "a storm

Hamburg bombing.   Credit: Center for the Study of War Experience at Regis University, Denver, Colorado.

started, a shrill howling in the street. It grew into a hurricane" that sounded, recalled another resident, like "the devil laughing." One had two choices: either leave a shelter and risk the firestorm or stay behind in cellars filling with smoke and rising in heat. In Hamburg—the "pan of a gigantic oven"—victims burned alive as they were sucked into a windstorm of fire that blew at upward of 300 miles per hour. Others suffocated in shelters deprived of oxygen or were baked by the raging street fires above them. Thousands were never found—turned to ashes and blown away by the wind. Firefighters could do little but rush to various spots as over 44,600 civilians and 800 servicemen died. With half the city reduced to rubble, nearly two-thirds of the survivors were evacuated. Mercy killings went on for days. Fires persisted for two days, and then the RAF returned to bomb the unaffected parts of the city. On the last night, August 4, the weather turned so cloudy that only the Lancasters made it through to drop another 1,400 bombs on the ruins. Hamburg had become a city of the dead. It also was a warning to Germany to expect similar devastation anywhere in the country.

In 1940, Germany had leveled 100 acres of Coventry; the Allies destroyed 6,000 acres and 300,000 homes in Hamburg. Along with the dead, 580 industrial establishments went up in flames or were damaged. The U-boat yards emerged relatively unscathed, however. About 75% of the city's electrical system, over half of its waterworks, and 90% of its gas network were destroyed. Industrial output dropped 40% for big factories and 80% for the smaller firms. Still, production returned to 80% of normal within five months. The Germans also turned to the effective "wild boar" night fighter tactics developed by Major Hajo Herrmann in which aircraft roamed at will rather than being tied to static lines of an air defense system susceptible to interruption by metal foil, or chaff. After reading about the carnage, Germans were fearful when they heard bombers overhead. Albert Speer, the armaments production chief, warned Hitler that six more raids like Hamburg and Germany's weapons factories would lie idle. The Fuhrer was unimpressed. He had little interest in defensive strategies despite the fact that the air war mocked his claims that the Third Reich was safe. He urged more production of fighters to defend German skies. Like the British before them, Germans also made do. Some reacted in anger, some were depressed. Soldiers returning from the front could not find peace. The RAF knocked out the rocket station at Peenemunde at this time. And to be sure, Harris and Eaker persisted in their destructive missions that took its increasing toll on enemy pilots, production, and people. But Bomber Command only emulated the destruction of Hamburg—such targets as Wurzburg, Kassel, Darmstadt, and Weser suffered from firestorms, though with fewer dead than Hamburg.

The American Eighth Air Force now took its turn in the Combined Bomber Offensive with attacks on five ball-bearing factories in Schweinfurt and a Messerschmidt aircraft plant in nearby Regensburg on August 17 and October 14. Harris viewed such attacks as a diversion, but the Quebec conferees had urged raids on factories to throttle the Luftwaffe. Eaker believed in precision bombing of industry; taking out factories might cause a chain reaction of disruption throughout all German war industries. Regensburg-Schweinfurt tested the notion. The first raid involved 376 bombers; 60 were lost and four were damaged beyond repair. The October mission included 291 planes of which another 60 were shot down by fighters and flak and 142 were damaged. In one day alone—"Black Thursday"—the USAAF lost over 10% of its planes and 17% of its crews. The Americans counted 43 wounded and 5 dead on returning aircraft and 594 missing in Germany (most of whom were taken prisoner). It was safer to fight one's way ashore in the Pacific as a Marine than to be a pilot in the European bombing campaign.

In between the failed Regensburg-Schweinfurt raids there were battles over Bremen and Vegesack and hits on factories in Anklam and Marienburg deep in Germany. Luftwaffe fighters blasted the lead formation as it entered and exited the country; not one of the 100th Bombardment Group's eight aircraft returned to base, and nearly a quarter of the bombers in the first wave went down. The results were familiar to the Germans. During the Battle of Britain, the Luftwaffe had had no answer for home-based defense because its fighters could not reach across the Channel. The Allies now discovered similar troubles over Germany. If continued, such losses would have gutted the Eighth USAAF. The days of the unescorted bomber were over. Bomber Command suspended runs deep into Germany until February 1944 when P-51 Mustangs, fitted with extra fuel "drop tanks" hung under their bellies or wings, provided long-range protection after shorter ranged Spitfire and Thunderbolt escorted bombers across western Europe. Meanwhile, the Germans dispersed some of their factories from towns and rebuilt the remainder (using slave labor and foreign conscripts as well as nationals) so rapidly that double shifts restored output to normal levels. Yet they also became more worried about the strategic air campaign, as cities like Kassel went up in smoke in October 1943 when the weather turned better.

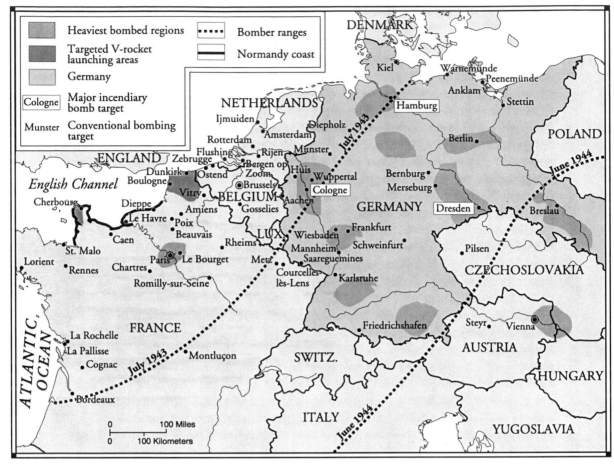

Map 14.1 Air war in Europe.   Credit: Ronald Story, *Concise Historical Atlas of World War II: The Geography of Conflict*, Map 22, p. 49.

Harris turned to Berlin. If he could level the Nazi capital, Hitler might surrender. This was violating the Quebec conference directive that forbid attacks on civilians. Harris had no such qualms, and the Combined Chiefs of Staffs put up no argument. He wrote Churchill that Berlin could be wrecked in its entirety. "It will cost us between 400–500 aircraft. It will cost Germany the war." American air force leaders argued that the chances of a concentrated attack terrorizing into submission a people conditioned by war were remote. Harris persisted from August 23 to September 4, 1943; the RAF hit Berlin in three attacks. The results were less evident on the ground, but in the air, 126 bombers out of 1,647 fell from the skies. He suspended the operation until the winter nights grew longer. Harris sought to enlist the Americans, but they had no taste for such raids after the Regensburg-Schweinfurt debacle. In any case, they had begun reassigning some aircraft to the newly created Fifteenth USAAF operating out of Italy. Bomber Harris was on his own. Undeterred, he hit Berlin again in mid-November and lost just nine of 444 bombers because of a diversionary raid against Mannheim-Ludwigshafen. The RAF mounted three more missions during the month with similar results of few casualties, but cloud cover prevented crews from actually seeing their targets. Between November 1943 and March 1944, bombing missions of at least 1,000 planes each hit the capital twenty-four times. Survivors noted the buildings reduced to heaps of rubble as firemen and prisoners of war pumped air into the ruins in the hopes of rescuing those trapped in collapsed cellars. Despite the destruction and a modicum of effective, Luftwaffe defense factories kept churning out war materiel.

How well the British were doing was thus unclear. Four more runs over Berlin in December raised the bomber loss rate again to nearly 5%. Harris would not give up even though raids in January, February, and March 1944 yielded ever worsening rates of planes shot down. Over 9% were lost on the night of March 24–25, the last mission before the Allies suspended the Combined Bomber in preparation for the Normandy landings. Overall, British Bomber Command lost 492 planes in the Berlin campaign. Although the city suffered great damage, it continued to function. In the final analysis, the RAF lost the battle of Berlin. The capital escaped destruction, Germans did not rise up against Hitler, and the campaign petered out.

The Combined Bomber Offensive remains controversial. Some accused the British of inhumane behavior because of the area-bombing tactic as opposed to the American precision attacks that targeted factories rather than civilians. It is hard to disagree. Tens of thousands of innocents perished including 150,000 French and Italian civilians and 100,000 foreign workers in Germany. Cities were wiped from the map. The campaign of aerial annihilation could not be rationalized by just or good war theory in which all means to defeat the evils of fascism absolved the Allies of sin. Area bombing ranked with genocide as a war crime. Deliberate bombing of civilians not engaged in the war effort, many of whom were children or elderly, represented the lowest form of ethical standards. The context, however, was total war. This adhered to the logic that any and all weapons could be used on any and all elements of the enemy, whether they were factories, soldiers, or civilians. After all, the ground campaigns inflicted more suffering. Total deaths from bombing amounted to about 1,000,000 people, less than the Germans caused in the siege of Leningrad. Besides, the Luftwaffe killed over 60,000 British civilians in reprisal raids as well as the Battle of Britain. Over 100,000 USAAF and RAF crewmembers also died. The campaign absorbed about 20% of the Allied military budgets. Harris wrote in his memoirs that bombing civilians was wicked, but all wars led to the mistreatment of noncombatants. Might not the effort have gone to more use elsewhere—on more or better weapons or to aid the partisans and resistance fighters against Nazism? Perhaps, but the bombing proved crucial to the Allied victory as well as assuring the Soviets that, barring a landing in western Europe, their allies were doing all they could to help defeat Nazi Germany.

Criticism of the Combined Bomber Offensive begs attention. Hamburg and Berlin lay in ruins, production slowed, and the Third Reich was forced to divert resources to defend cities that could have otherwise been used on the Eastern or Western fronts. For instance, in 1943, they had 2,132 batteries pointed toward the skies manned by 10,000 antiaircraft guns that might have been used as antitank weapons. Yet due to Hitler's offensive mindset, Germany avenged the strategic bombing campaign by developing complex and expensive rockets rather than a focus on restructuring the fighter defense system. In a public relations move designed to destroy English towns, the Luftwaffe produced the V-2 ballistic rocket and had under development the V-1 cruise missile by the end of 1943. Both efforts drained away precious resources. The Combined Bomber Offensive, therefore, reduced Germany's capacity to wage war.

In sum, losses on the battlefield rather than at home spelled doom for the Nazis, but the air war burdened the regime. Harris and his American partners promised more than they could deliver. Germany did not drop to its knees. In fact, the population survived and even triumphed over the bombers. Morale fell, but the will to resist heightened as in Britain. Aircraft production actually rose from 10,898 planes in 1943 to 25,285 in 1944, and tank output also shot up. But without Allied bombing, production would have been higher. Furthermore, disruptions of petroleum and aviation gas supplies by plant and transportation bombing reduced the amount of training given to replacement pilots. Improved targeting and damage assessment through air intelligence further inflicted damage on Germany. Thus, the Luftwaffe was increasingly at the mercy of more experienced Allied pilots. Late in the war, attacks on oil and communications facilities proved devastating; but the Third Reich stood on the edge of oblivion by that point anyway. Still, even in late 1943, the British had more viable options of destroying the German war economy other than indiscriminate killing from the air.

U-BOAT HUNTERS

At sea, the role of aggressor and victim was reversed from the airwar. A theater ripe for German submarine plunder was the U.S. eastern seaboard and the Caribbean. These areas were so thinly protected by the American Navy that German U-boat captains referred to Operation Drumbeat in the Western hemisphere as the second "happy time" of hunting. In February and March 1942, almost a million tons and 168 ships went down. Journalists pressed Roosevelt about the location of the U.S. Navy after the first attack by U-123 sunk a tanker, *Malay,* off Cape Hatteras, North Carolina. Their questions mounted as attacks multiplied. In April, a convoy system doubled aircraft patrols from Maine to Florida and thereby dramatically reduced the losses, but U-boats withdrew to the unprotected Gulf of Mexico and Caribbean. In May and June 1942 alone, subs sank over a million tons of shipping, or half of their total for the entire year 1941. The campaign netted them 3 million tons in the first half of 1942 alone. That year, the Allies lost more tanker tonnage than had vanished under the waves in the 27 months of war prior to 1942. Admiral Karl Donitz approached his objective of a decisive victory; but , his U-boats were just not plentiful enough to sustain these numbers. There were two reasons. By Fall 1942, U.S. industry pumped out such staggering amounts of goods and ships to carry them that the subs could not keep up. Second, the Americans corrected their blundering policies that allowed for more sinkings than necessary.

The United States relied on routine patrols by surface vessels and aircraft, protected shipping lanes on predictable schedules, and varied routing of coastal ships to defend convoys. There were no coastal convoys at first because the U.S. Navy believed weakly escorted ones were worse than none at all. Early in the war, the British had erred with these techniques. As a result, lone U-boats snuck close to shore to avoid patrols. To make matters worse, Washington did not enforce a blackout, thereby silhouetting convoys against the shoreline at night. The Americans stuck with the small convoy strategies learned from helping out the Canadians during the previous year despite British advice to adopt protective missions on a larger scale. As a consequence, not a German submarine was sunk until April 1942.

Changes were imminent. Air patrols expanded as the Navy widened and stretched the convoy system. Bombing and patrolling ahead in coordination with the convoy itself hindered the easily detectable wolf packs. Escorts also improved, but it was the broadened coverage of the system that worked best. In short, Donitz's submarines had no more easy victims. Worse, they faced counterattacks; the Allies compelled them to take rapid evasion measures after taking a shot or two from naval escorts. Tonnage sunk diminished through the year as subs sailed in a shrinking and more dangerous operating area. By July 1942, the tremendous output of the U.S. economy and the end of independent sailings by convoys cut U-boat kills by a third. Even though the Germans added a fourth wheel to the ENIGMA machine the previous February to prevent decryption of U-boat instructions for the rest of the year, prospects for convoys looked better by summer. The new strategy worked, especially when complemented by good leadership, experience, camouflaged planes, and better intelligence gleaned from radar operating on an automated 360-degree sweep. The improvements pointed the battle of the Atlantic toward a climax in early 1943.

For an unknown reason, Donitz focused more attention during the first half of 1942 on Arctic convoys than on those plying the North Atlantic. Only a quarter of Lend-Lease traveled this route. Half came through Siberia from the northern Pacific and a quarter went through the Persian Gulf and Iran. But the Arctic convoys served both as propaganda gestures to the USSR and as a decent source of supply. Most of them from Iceland and Scotland headed for ice-free Murmansk or seasonally ice-bound Archangel and Molotovsk on the White Sea, escorted by the Royal Navy and U.S. and Soviet ships. Limited air patrols helped out, along with British and Russian submarines that watched over the entrances of Norwegian fjords for U-boats and German surface raiders. Also available was the British Home Fleet. After the battleship *Tirpitz* (the sister ship of *Bismarck*) sailed out of Trondheim and attacked an Arctic convoy in March 1942, the Royal Navy sent the Home Fleet to sink the vessel. Communications errors and the inexperience of the British sailors allowed *Tirpitz* to escape, however.

The Germans took a greater interest in the convoys in March 1942 when they realized another massive offensive even more drawn out than Barbarossa was necessary to defeat the USSR. They built up their air and sea strength in northern Norway to prevent supplies from reaching the Russians. Convoy PQ-13 was their first victim. Attacked once it sailed on March 20, the convoy lost five ships. ULTRA picked up the trap, and escorts sent a destroyer to the bottom while damaging two others.

At the end of May, 108 waves of German aircraft assailed 25 vessels of the PQ-16 convoy and sunk seven merchant vessels, two escorting cruisers, and several other vessels. The carnage brought pressure on Churchill to end the Arctic convoys, but he would not annoy Stalin by doing so. On June 27, convoy PQ-17 left Iceland for the Soviet Union protected by a strong close escort, a powerful support group, and an even more potent covering force in the area. There were 47 warships in all. They moved alongside of the merchants particularly once the Admiralty got word through ULTRA that the Germans lay in wait. Ready to greet the escorts at the Altenfjord were *Tirpitz*, the cruisers *Hipper* and *Admiral Scheer*, the pocket battleship *Lutzow*, and several destroyers. An intimidated Admiral Dudley Pound ordered the convoy dispersed and the escort returned to base. As the ships broke ranks, U-boats and the Luftwaffe attacked. Only 11 of the 37 vessels in the convoy reached port; 3,850 trucks and vehicles, 430 tanks, and 2,500 aircraft went down with 153 sailors. The catastrophe prompted Churchill to suspend the Arctic convoys despite Stalin's protests. The perilous Arctic route soon went dormant, as the impending invasion of North Africa in November 1942 demanded the escorts.

In the Atlantic, the Allies had perfected their convoy system over eighteen months, but there were still dangerous gaps in coverage. Canadian escorts remained easy prey for U-boats because they still lacked modern equipment and enough destroyers. In addition, in early 1943, ULTRA intercepts picked up ominous trends. In January, Donitz took over the German Navy from Erich Raeder who Hitler blamed for a failed attack on a Murmansk convoy the month before. At long last Donitz possessed enough submarines and the freedom to direct them where he wanted. At his disposal were upward of 435 vessels of which 100 were operational each month of winter 1943. He embarked on the U-boat campaign's equivalent of the Japanese decisive battle. More subs, bad weather, and success at blocking the ULTRA decryption process by changing German codes during the first three weeks of March permitted the wolf packs to sow disaster on the seas. They pounced on half of the North Atlantic convoys and sunk nearly a quarter of the total Allied shipping.

The Allies were alarmed, but Churchill and FDR settled on a solution. Seeking to secure the logistical train across the Atlantic in preparation for the invasion of France, they prioritized the protection of convoys. As Donitz's subs rampaged below the seas, recommendations of a Washington Convoy Conference requested more aircraft, destroyers, and escort carrier groups to fill the Atlantic air gap. The Americans compromised by lending a few escort carriers from the Pacific campaign to the Atlantic cause while Canada and Britain assumed the burden over the convoy legs. This plan, as well as the reinstatement of ULTRA and better weather, gave the Allies an edge by April 1943. With one carrier added to each convoy group, more B-24s in service, and squadrons of antisubmarine flying boats available, the hunters harassed the wolf packs. As the battle of the Atlantic reached its climax, the Allies settled on a strategy of attrition. They were unable to reroute the convoys away from the submarines, but they traded a few vessels for a U-boat when it showed itself. The acquisition of a base in the Portuguese colony of the Azores sealed the air gap by late May. This success and the buildup of Allied convoy forces compelled Donitz to withdraw his decimated fleet at

U.S. Coastguard in convoy watch depth-charge explosion on U-boat.   Credit: National Archives.

the end of the month to safer locations. He soon acknowledged defeat, having lost 100 submarines in the first 5 months of 1943.

Although the battle of the Atlantic lacked the drama of some other theaters, it played a decisive part of the Allied victory in the war. ULTRA was critical, but ultimately convoys boosted by airpower kept the U-boats at bay. An average of 450,000 tons of Allied shipping went to the bottom from January to May 1943, but the 200,000 tons lost during the final seven months of the year were a marked improvement. In the last two years of World War II, roughly 50,000 tons a month were sunk. This was not enough to dent the huge output of ships and supplies generated by the American economy. Meanwhile, the Third Reich turned to drafting younger submariners and less experienced commanders as the bloodletting under the seas caused a manpower shortage. The cost of the U-boat campaign was great. The death rate in the Atlantic was among the highest in any theater of the war. A shocking 17% of British merchant seamen in convoys perished, which made the service more dangerous than joining the British Army, RAF, or Royal Navy. Over the span of the war, Germany lost 784 U-boats out of its total of 1,170 and 26,000 crew. The Allies saw 15 million tons of merchant shipping and 2,828 vessels, 175 warships, 40,000 sailors, and 30,000 merchant seamen go to the bottom. The deaths of so many civilians brought the battle of the Atlantic into the realm of the war of annihilation. German effectiveness was

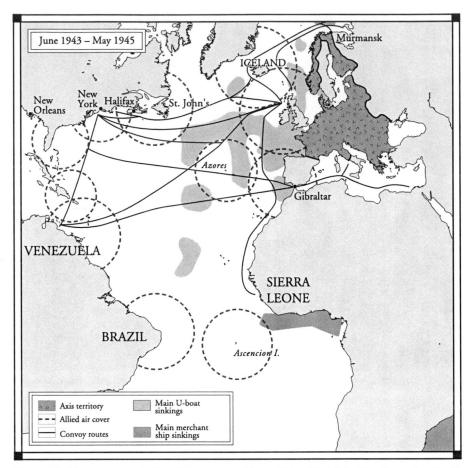

Map 14.2 Convoys.   Credit: Ronald Story, *Concise Historical Atlas of World War II: The Geography of Conflict,* Map 11B, bottom map, p. 27.

partly to blame, but some losses were due to Britain's neglect of antisubmarine warfare doctrine before 1939.

In any case, Donitz slowed the pace of Allied victory, but he eventually succumbed. The battle cruiser *Scharnhorst* went down on December 26, 1943 when it fled from an Arctic convoy. Only 36 of its almost 2,000 crewmembers were rescued by British sailors who soberly commemorated its bloody ending. The sister ship of the behemoth *Bismarck,* the new battleship *Tirpitz,* sank in late 1944 in the Norwegian harbor of Tromso after enduring a two-year campaign of bombings and midget submarine attacks. The German High Command had not paid enough attention to technological issues of intelligence and U-boat design until too late, and they failed to recognize the Allies' improvements in both areas. Donitz also made errors such as maintaining a small staff even as the battle of the Atlantic expanded. He might also have attacked American commerce in the Caribbean and western Atlantic with a much larger force when the United States first entered the war. The U-boats terrorized the Atlantic; but in the end, the sacrifice hurt the Third Reich more than the Allies.In Berlin, Rome, and Tokyo, the dictators and militarists persevered with their visions of expansion; but the Allies developed new strategies, tactics, and doctrines to combat them. In some theaters, such as North Africa, the Atlantic, the USSR, and the Pacific, the aggressors witnessed their first major losses or retreated from territory previously taken during their impressive early triumphs in the war. This trend would persist in some places. The dictators in the Axis capitals soon knew, however, that the intensifying Allied campaigns of annihilation—orchestrated by tough diplomacy and prosecuted on the ground, from the air, and in the seas—were spoiling their dreams of hegemony.

CHAPTER 15

Allied Offensives in Asia and the Pacific

> But war is a god...and its worship demands human
> sacrifice.
>
> CHRIS HEDGES
> *War Is a Force That Gives Us Meaning*

CHINA-BURMA-INDIA THEATER

Allied conferences focused attention on the war in Europe, but they also resolved the three-pronged strategy for defeating Japan. British Commonwealth forces would move eastward from India through Burma to Malaya and Hong Kong. Australia and America would head north and west in the southwest Pacific from the Solomon Islands and New Guinea into the Philippines and the Dutch East Indies. The third point of advance involved the U.S. Navy's westward movement across the central Pacific to the Philippines and Formosa. All three campaigns would converge on the Japanese home islands to annihilate the enemy. Plotting strategy proved much easier than putting it into action, however. Diplomacy oftentimes trumped military operations and tactics.

The China-Burma-India theater was an example. The Southeast Asia Command under Lord Mountbatten and his deputy Joseph Stilwell promised better integration of the Allied effort in the China-Burma-India theater but SEAC was no more effective in coordinating the military. The principals disagreed on strategy and goals. Chiang Kai-shek remained independent, although Stilwell served as a liaison between the China and Burma theaters. Chiang still obsessed over containing the power of the Chinese communists as he did over the Japanese. Furthermore, the British sought to regain control of their empire by clamping a lid on Indian nationalism that was promoted by collaboration with Japan. Preoccupied with reconquering Burma, Stilwell labored against British imperialist designs while he chided Chiang for not improving the Nationalist army. "Vinegar Joe" angered Britain and Chiang, who both complained to Roosevelt about Stilwell's abrasiveness. FDR listened because he had engaged Churchill in sensitive discussions about the postwar disposition of the British colonies. They settled on establishing international trusteeships run by the United Nations to prepare territories for independence. The president did not wish to provoke the prime minister over the "sore spot" of India and also hoped that the popular Chiang would serve as a leader over postwar Asia. Contrary to Stilwell's approach, Roosevelt determined to coddle Chiang to retain him as a stable ally and contributor to the peace.

Regardless of the political tensions, Commonwealth forces were simply not ready to retake Burma. General William Slim's Fourteenth Army conducted small probing offensives. In December 1942, the British tried to win back Akyab on the Bay of Bengal through an offensive in the rugged terrain of the Arakan. This failed, and so did another attempt in March 1943. The British remained where they were the previous October. Slim considered amphibious landings, but shipping resources were scarce. Demands in other theaters, and the fact that India was a very costly destination because of its location halfway around the world, crimped logistics. Although Britain's Fourteenth Army added Ghurka Rifles of Nepal, British Army infantry, and untested battalions from East and West Africa, Japanese Fifteenth Army led by Lieutenant-General Renya Mataguchi had doubled its size. Thus, Slim banked on a modest conventional overland campaign. Even this would have to wait until 1944 for more support, however.

The British turned to northern Burma by employing the services of the energetic and idiosyncratic Brigadier Orde Wingate. Operating behind Japanese lines in the first half of 1943, his band of Chindits attempted to disrupt communications between Mandalay and Myitkyina. A "Long-Range Penetration" group, the Chindits (a Burmese name derived from winged stone lions guarding Buddhist temples) began Operation Longcloth to sever railway links. In February 1943, one group cut the railway south of Wuntho then marched 250 miles across the country to rendezvous with the other unit to interrupt the railroad near Nanken. Both crossed the Irrawaddy River and attacked the Mandalay-Lashio railway, but the Japanese halted them in an area not conducive to guerrilla warfare. In March, the Chindits retreated back across the Irrawaddy. Wingate ordered them to disperse and make their way back to Burma, a thousand miles away. Of the 3,000 troops, nearly a third never returned. Still, Operation Longcloth was regaled at home and Churchill took Wingate to the Quebec conference where he convinced the U.S. Joint Chiefs of Staff that "deep penetration" was a workable tactic. The Americans granted resources to create another group of Chindits into a special force as well as an air commando group and a new Long-Range Penetration unit of 3,000 troops called Galahad. All would be deployed in 1944, with Galahad under Stilwell's control. The Imperial Japanese Army snubbed the whole effort. In March 1943, Tokyo established Burma Area Army under Lieutenant-General Kawabe Masakazu and five months later proclaimed the independence of Burma under Japanese tutelage.

Japanese political and military pressure presented challenges in Burma, even though the mountain tribes, which comprised 7 million of the country's 17 million people, largely backed the British. The Nagas, Kachins, and Karens had fought Japan since 1942, and they despised collaborators. The Kachins in particular were fierce warriors. All of these groups as well as Chans and Shins received weapons, funding, and equipment from Anglo-American special operations units. Nonetheless, guerrilla tactics designed to open the supply routes into China and liberate Burma from the Japanese made uneven progress in 1943. British incompetence and Japanese determination and

Chindits inspect damage to a Burmese village.   Credit: Center for
the Study of War Experience at Regis University, Denver, Colorado.

skill slowed the Allied effort to improve Chinese troops and open the Ledo extension
of the Burma Road—the key supply route from India into China.

In China, Claire Chennault and U.S. Army Air Force chief Hap Arnold made
airpower the prime focus for the Allied leaders who wanted a sign of progress. The
Fourteenth Air Force went into operation in mid-March 1943. P-40 fighters struck at
shipping and installations on the Red River in Indochina. In May and June, Japan countered with raids into western Hupei. Chiang and his U.S. supporters lauded the performance of Chinese troops, though, and this propaganda earned him more money
and air support. In August 1943, the Tenth U.S. Air Force opened for business in New
Delhi, and the first air battles over China since 1941 began above Hangchow, Heng-
yang, and Ch'ang-sa. Heavy bombers hit Burma in early October and raided Formosa
on November 25. This last operation persuaded the Japanese to begin their offensive in
central and southern China in 1944 to neutralize U.S. bombing missions. The air power
lobby in Washington insisted on sending hundreds of planes to China to fend them
off, but the State Department and Stilwell warned that assistance would disappear into
the rat hole of Chiang's corrupt regime. The air lobby prevailed because FDR remained
wedded to the idea of a strong Nationalist government during and after the war. He also
endorsed the Cairo Declaration to liberate Asia from Japanese rule. Chiang offered an
alternative to the Co-Prosperity Sphere that Tokyo had solidified at a meeting between
its members just weeks before the Cairo conference. The Americans might not count on
Chiang to defeat Japan, but Sino-American diplomacy determined that his Nationalists
remained favored elements of the Allied military cause in Asia.

NEW GUINEA
At the Casablanca conference in January 1943, the Allied Combined Chiefs of Staff were
instructed to allocate 30% of their resources to the war against Japan. The British balked

at such a precise formula, but they nevertheless encouraged the Americans to maintain their momentum gained at Guadalcanal. The three U.S. Pacific commanders, Douglas MacArthur, Chester Nimitz, and Bull Halsey, knew that they lacked the resources to conquer Rabaul in 1943. The Army Air Force also did not have enough long-range bombers to begin a major strategic air campaign against Japan. The U.S. Joint Chiefs instructed Halsey simply to move up the Solomon Islands in tandem with MacArthur's advance on New Guinea and converge on Rabaul. Behind these instructions was a kernel of an idea. While the Americans targeted the Philippines, they would also open a new theater in the vast central Pacific. This echoed the old Plan Orange that called for Japan's defeat by the shortest route possible. Drawing on the strength of Nimitz's naval and amphibious forces, island-hopping from the Gilberts through the Marshalls, Carolines, and Marianas was the most direct way. At the Quebec conference in August 1943, U.S. officials presented this plan to their allies. The British agreed to coordinate Mountbatten's SEAC campaign in Burma with the Americans' westward movement up and across the central Pacific toward Tokyo.

In the southwest Pacific area, the defense of Guadalcanal in Fall 1942 had weakened the Imperial Army's offensive on New Guinea. Japan designed this campaign to sever the Allied lifeline to Australia and expand its Pacific defense perimeter. Major-General Tomitaro Horii landed his South Seas Detachment on Papua's north coast on July 12, 1942, and pointed it down the Kokoda Trail. This malarial-infested, 1,000-mile impassable jungle track crossed the lofty Owen Stanley Mountains at Port Moresby. MacArthur was taken by surprise. Although reinforced by an Australian battalion, the Papuan Infantry Regiment could not defend Kokoda. By mid-August, Horii had a beachhead at Isurava down the coast where reinforcements flowed in. MacArthur sent two extra Australian battalions up the precipitous trail to Isurava, but they were overloaded by equipment and badly supplied by erratic air drops. The Japanese blocked them and drove them off the Kokoda Trail by flanking and ambush maneuvers. Soaked by constant rain, exhausted, wounded, and disease ridden, the Australians retreated to Ioribaiwa just north of Port Moresby.

In addition to worries on the Kokoda Trail, MacArthur turned to a landing at Milne Bay at the southern tip of Papua. He beat back the initial invasion of 2,000 enemy troops on August 30 by sending the 18th Australian Brigade to boost the Allied garrison. Engineers built airstrips from which two Aussie squadrons bombed the brave but sick and starving Japanese troops. Only 1,200 invaders were evacuated; the Australians killed 123 and wounded nearly 200 men. MacArthur claimed this as the first Allied ground victory against Japan but the Imperial Army resumed its march down the Kokoda Trail. Despite reinforcements, the Australians made a last defensive stand at Imita Ridge near Port Moresby. Private Jack Manol recalled the crisis. "Christ, there's no-one between us and Moresby, and if the Japs get through us and get to Moresby there, Australia's gone!" Journalists reported the gruesome picture of motley crews and rotting corpses. Pieces of trees marked graves with either ideographs or English messages that directed burial crews to hurriedly-disposed of bodies. A Japanese soldier described the endless toil in the endless rain. "Our guns rusted. Iron just rotted away. Wounds wouldn't heal." This was hell. "In New Guinea, we didn't know what was killing us. Who killed that one? Was it death from insanity? A suicide? A mercy killing? Maybe he couldn't endure the pain of living." Encountering two brothers, he noticed one had gone insane. As one laughed hysterically the other slapped him to make him stop calling out his name. "Finally, the elder brother shot him dead. I didn't even raise my voice. The brother and I dug a grave for him." New Guinea's soldiers did not find themselves in a good war.

MacArthur protested Australia's poor performance to Prime Minister John Curtin, and he replaced the commander with fellow Aussie Thomas Blamey. General Blamey had overseen the evacuation of Crete before returning home to lead the Allied Land Force under MacArthur. Blamey managed to hold off the Japanese thanks to dogged air attacks from American George Kenney's Fifth Army Air Force. Dwindling supplies and manpower compelled Horii to withdraw north to the beachhead. The New Guinea campaign suffered from the last Japanese effort on Guadalcanal; troops were drained from the former and sent to the latter. The Imperial Army did not provide Horii with reinforcements and food. In a horrifying development, the strapped Japanese resorted to cannibalism by eating Australian prisoners and their own dead. On New Guinea, the survival of captives and the injured was rarely an option.

MacArthur finally began the Allied offensive by trying to rout the enemy from its 11-mile perimeter beachhead in northern Papua. He sent two regiments of the U.S. 32nd Division to join the Australian 7th Division. In mid-November 1942, they hit

Australian troops at Gona.   Credit: CSWE, Center for the Study of War Experience at Regis University, Denver, Colorado.

the Kokoda Trail. The Australians moved on the northwestern end of the perimeter at Gona while the Americans drove toward the village of Buna to the southeast and on airstrips at Cape Endaiadare. The Australians were weakened, however, and MacArthur underestimated Imperial Army strength on the perimeter. As a result, the Australian 25th Brigade suffered over 200 casualties in three days and had to be relieved. Gona finally fell on December 8 after two extra battalions slogged through swamps to join the fight. But Australian casualties climbed to 750 men. The green and badly equipped U.S. 32nd Division also misjudged the number of Japanese on the southeastern end of the line. As casualties mounted, an angry MacArthur sent Lieutenant-General Robert Eichelberger to take command of the Advanced New Guinea Corps, which included the 32nd Division. MacArthur demanded that he capture Buna or die trying. Eichelberger relieved the senior commanders and sent demoralized soldiers stricken with malaria to Australia. Then he brought in supplies to feed the remaining starving troops and added more men and armor. A fresh battalion took Buna on December 14, although the Japanese held out on the perimeter until early January 1943.

The losses were staggering on both sides. The 32nd Division had a casualty rate of nearly 90%, as 9,688 troops out of 10,825 were sickened, killed, or wounded. It was so depleted that it stayed off the battlefield for most of 1943. Australian dead numbered 2,165, and a total of 930 Americans were killed. Of the roughly 20,000 Japanese in New Guinea, about 12,000 soldiers died in battle or of starvation and tropical disease, especially malaria. The only savior for the Allies was that the Japanese were in worse shape as evidenced by their using the dead for cover as well as sustenance. Americans learned the lesson of inadequate logistics the hard way; they would never again repeat the mistake of inadequate preparation for battle.

The Japanese tried one more time to get at Port Moresby. MacArthur attacked garrisons at Lae and Salamaua up the coast. Hatazo Adachi Eighteenth Army reinforced these positions in January before sending 2,500 troops into the Bululo valley to eradicate the Australian's Kanga Force and seize the airstrip at Wau. Fighting turned intense. The Australians prevailed after a brigade landed on the airstrip and drove back the defenders to Mubo through rotting jungles by February's end. With Guadalcanal, lost the Tokyo command doubled the effort to hold New Guinea. But MacArthur targeted Lae and Salamaua as a prelude to capturing the entire Huon Peninsula and isolating the huge base at Rabaul.

The Japanese built up to block MacArthur. Adachi attempted to land Eighteenth Army on the coast in early March 1943. Included were the 7,000 men of the 51st Division who had set out from Rabaul in late February in transports guarded by eight destroyers. ULTRA decoders detected them, however, and Kenney's Fifth USAAF awaited. On March 2, the Americans sank a transport and damaged two others in the opening of the battle of the Bismarck Sea. The next day Kenney attacked in waves by strafing or "skip" bombing, this latter a technique invented by the British in which light bombers flew just above the sea surface and released bombs that bounced horizontally into a ship's waterline. The first wave registered 28 hits with 500-pound bombs. Subsequent bombing runs, along with torpedoes from high-speed, 78-feet long PT (Patrol Torpedo) boats, sunk two damaged destroyers. Four destroyers escaped, but only 950 Japanese reached Lae, and others were rescued at sea. The dead of the 51st Division totaled 3,660 or over half of the unit. Adachi left two remaining regiments of the 51st Division on the Huon Peninsula while he moved his headquarters to Lae and continued the buildup. By April, he controlled the 20th Division at Wewak, the 41st Division at Madang, and the remnants of the 51st Division.

Tokyo wanted a victory. Imperial Headquarters created Fourth Air Army, and Admiral Yamamoto launched a series of surprise air-raids against Guadalcanal, New Guinea, Port Moresby, and Tulagi. By stripping planes from carriers and using land-based aircraft, he issued the largest attacks since Pearl Harbor. Vice Admiral Mineichi Koga, commander of the Third Fleet at Truk, transferred Sea Eagle flying aces from two carriers and combined them with land-based pilots on Rabaul and the northern Solomons island of Bougainville. This force of 340 planes of all types darkened the skies over New Guinea south to Milne Bay. Pilots claimed they inflicted massive blows on Allied ships and aircraft. They did not, but Yamamoto welcomed the news for its propaganda value particularly because only 40 planes were lost. In the end, however, Japan lost something next to irreplaceable. Admiral Yamamoto decided to reward the victorious pilots with a visit But the Americans discovered his plans through intercepted radio messages. On April 18, P-38 aircraft ambushed his plane near Buin, in the jungles of Bougainville. The Empire's grand strategist—the architect of Pearl Harbor and Japanese naval airpower—was gone.

By that time MacArthur had reorganized Allied forces into two groups. Americans in Lieutenant-General Walter Krueger's Sixth Army comprised most of the Alamo Force. This removed U.S. troops from Blamey's control and placed them completely under MacArthur. The Australians folded into New Guinea Force. With the restructuring finished, MacArthur launched Operation Cartwheel on June 29, 1943. The New Guinea campaign was part of Cartwheel's overall mission to seal off Rabaul and neutralize its considerable sea and airpower. The first step required nullifying Fourth Japanese Air Army at Wewak, which was beyond the range of Kenney's air force. ULTRA revealed a concentrated Japanese presence and Kenney responded by secretly constructing an airstrip 60 miles west of Lae. Although the enemy eventually discovered it, he launched 200 planes against Fourth Air Army on August 17. Lacking radar and telephones, the Japanese defenders were stunned when U.S. bombers appeared over Hansa Bay in a two-day raid that wiped out all but 38 aircraft and three of the four airstrips.

Without air cover, the Japanese fell to the mercy of MacArthur's ground troops. U.S. and Australian divisions marched on the Huon Peninsula and American paratroopers secured airstrips on which reinforcements were dropped. A feint toward Salamaua to draw Adachi's reinforcements from Lae preceded an amphibious landing by the 9th Australian Division east of the town and an overland assault by the 7th Australian Division from the north. By September 16, the Allies occupied the critical southern part of Huon Peninsula, and Adachi fled north over the mountains to Sio with 7,800 troops. In October, Finschhafen—at the tip of the peninsula—fell into Australian hands. The Japanese gamely defended the area around Settelberg peak until early December 1943. It took four months of vicious fighting to clear Adachi from the peninsula. Determined Australian troops pursued him, although he escaped the Allies' clutches once again despite a U.S. attempt to cut him off at Saidor on January 2, 1944. The chase up the coast of New Guinea continued.

SOUTHWEST PACIFIC

Tokyo planners had a good idea of the magnitude of the problems they faced because Cartwheel involved thirteen sometimes separate, other times simultaneous, operations under MacArthur on New Guinea and Halsey in the Southwest Pacific theater. Bull Halsey first aimed at the New Georgia chain in the central Solomons group to secure forward air bases from which he could bomb Rabaul. He lacked veteran amphibious units. Both the U.S. 1st and 2nd Marine Regiments had been shipped off, and the Guadalcanal units were regrouping. Cobbling together three divisions under U.S. Army XIV Corps, miscellaneous Marine units including Raider and defense battalions, and two New Zealand brigades, Halsey moved in New Georgia.

This opening campaign went well at first. With eastern New Guinea secured, the Americans landed on New Georgia Island on June 21, 1943, two days later on Woodlark Island, and a week afterward on Kriiwana. Halsey then sent a Raider battalion to the main island at Segi Point while U.S. Marines and the 43rd Army Division landed on Rendova, Vangunu, and western New Georgia over the next two weeks. The invasions prompted the Japanese to reinforce their troops. Tipped off by ULTRA, Task Force 18 of three cruisers and ten destroyers (including the New Zealand cruiser *Leander*) met a convoy of Japanese destroyer transports off Kolombangara Island. The U.S. Navy inflicted losses, but it could not stop the replenishment of garrisons on New Georgia. In the battle of Kula Gulf on the night of July 5–6, the Americans sank a destroyer but lost a cruiser. The enemy successfully landed troops and supplies. A week later, Halsey tried to surprise a Tokyo Express transport. History repeated itself. Despite using radar to track the ships, the U.S. Navy was still no match for Japan's in night battles. America's Guadalcanal nemesis Admiral Raizo Tanaka lost his flagship in the battle of Kolombangara, but his task force took a U.S. destroyer with it and crippled three cruisers. As at Kula Gulf, Imperial troops went ashore and bolstered Major-General Noboru Sasaki's garrison to a total of 14,500 men.

Sasaki focused on defending the airstrip at Munda point. He sent most of his new troops to infiltrate into the area at night in ways that spooked the green American troops. They were so unnerved that Major-General Oscar Griswold, commander of XIV Corps, reported that the 43rd Division was near useless. He replaced some units and brought in the Army's 37th Division. He then hit the Japanese on July 25. The fighting raged for a week until Sasaki withdrew inland on New Georgia Island to await reinforcements. This time more men did not arrive because in the battle of Vella Gulf on the night of August 6–7, U.S. destroyers sunk three transports. Sasaki evacuated 12,500 troops to Kolombangara Island. Munda became a U.S. Marine aviation base to support the next step up the New Georgia chain. Halsey decided to bypass the large garrison on Kolombangara and proceed beyond to the more lightly defended Vella Lavella. This tactic set a pattern for the U.S. Navy by mimicking MacArthur's New Guinea maneuvers and leapfrogging around Japanese strongpoints. On August 15, 1943, he secretly

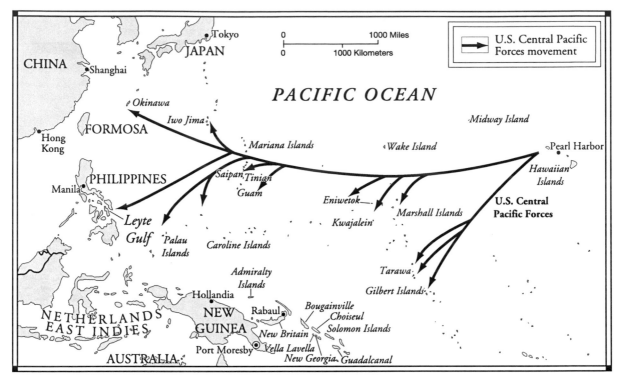

Map 15.1 Southwest and Central Pacific campaigns.   Credit: Ronald Story, *Concise Historical Atlas of World War II: The Geography of Conflict*, Map 42, p. 89.

landed 4,600 troops in just twelve hours. A month later, the 3rd New Zealand Division countered the 600 defenders who had rushed on to Vella Lavella. The Japanese issued 108 air raids, but they could not dislodge the Allies.

The Imperial command made the enemy pay as Sasaki retreated up the chain. He pulled out the garrison from Kolombangara to Rabaul on September 15 and looked to do the same at Vella Lavella. On the night of October 6–7, 1943, the two navies engaged in the battle of Vella Lavella. Both lost a destroyer, and the Americans had two damaged. They also failed to sink the transports that withdrew the enemy troops. But it was a loss for Japan all the same. Vella Lavella was in Allied hands. Bombing raids on Rabaul began from airstrips won in the New Georgia campaign. The effort cost the Americans 1,094 lives and 3,873 wounded in addition to thousands of noncombat casualties due to stress and disease. The Japanese suffered over double that number of deaths. Sasaki had fought and withdrawn brilliantly. He was so effective that the Americans had been compelled to bring in elements of four divisions when they planned for only one to go into action. Still he could not prevent Operation Cartwheel's advance up the Solomons.

The last bastion before Rabaul was the largest of the Solomon Islands—the 125-mile long Australian mandate of Bougainville at the northern end of the chain. Lieutenant-General Hyakutake Haruyoshi who had defended Guadalcanal placed his Seventeenth Army on Bougainville's southern tip and on surrounding islands. Once the

Phosphorous bombing on Rabaul.   Credit: Center for the Study of War Experience at Regis University, Denver, Colorado.

3rd New Zealand Division took the nearby Treasury Islands, on November 1, Halsey landed 14,000 men of the 3rd Marine Division and Army 37th Division at Bougainville's Empress Augusta Bay. Meeting minor resistance, the Marines established a beach-head, developed a perimeter, and quickly went to work on an airstrip. The battle of Empress Augusta Bay took place out at sea and above the invaders rather than on land the next day. Rear Admiral Aaron Stanton Merrill's Task Force 39 sank a cruiser and destroyer in Vice-Admiral Omori Sentaro's Eighth Fleet while Fifth Army Air Force hit Bougainville's airfields and defended the beachhead.

Yet Halsey was fixated on developments farther away at Rabaul. Vice-Admiral Takeo Kurita, who had participated in attacks on Malaya, Thailand, and the Dutch East Indies before commanding a force at Midway, assembled a fleet of over 500 aircraft to strike the Americans in the Solomons. Like Koga's sweep over New Guinea in April, Kurita sought a massive victory with his force launched from Rabaul. The prospect gave Halsey nightmares. Thus, on November 2, 1943, he ordered a preemptive raid by two carrier task forces—one under Rear-Admiral Forrest Sherman (whose son was on board a carrier) and the other commanded by Rear-Admiral Alfred Montgomery. The carrier strikes involved two big new carriers, *Bunker Hill* and *Essex,* and two new light carriers, *Princeton* and *Independence,* in addition to the stalwart *Saratoga.* The fast carriers continued to swell U.S. forces at an average rate of one every seven weeks through the rest of the war. As he sailed within range of Rabaul, Halsey expected to lose both carriers, but the risks were mitigated by the assurance of replacements. In addition, he hoped to wreak havoc on Kurita's fleet.

The gamble went better than predicted. Land-based planes prevented the carriers from being lost, and overhead the Americans shot down about 200 enemy planes and pilots. The effect on the Imperial Navy was substantial. An intimidated Kurita withdrew the entire task force to the Combined Fleet harbor at Truk, nearly 800 miles west in the Caroline Islands. He also lost command of the Combined Fleet. By late February 1944, all aircraft were removed from Rabaul and the Japanese never returned. From Bougainville and recently seized Cape Gloucester, U.S. planes leveled Rabaul and left the garrison of 90,000 troops to wither for the rest of the war.

Having neutralized Rabaul, the Americans landed the Army on Bougainville to annihilate the defenders. Griswold's forces marched inland and began a series of brutal battles. Hyakutake countered the Allied probes with troops that numbered 40,000 within five months. In the week-long battle of Piva Forks on November 24, 1943, the U.S. Marines let loose the most intense artillery bombardment so far in the Pacific war. It was so concentrated that American soldiers died from burst blood vessels due to the concussions of explosives. Using flame-throwers against the dug-in defenders, they inched forward on Bougainville. By mid-December, the first plane landed on a new airstrip. U.S. and Australian forces spent the remainder of the war pushing Hyakutake ever southward as both sides fought disease, scorching temperatures, rot, insects, and skin ulcers as well as enemy fire. When the battles on Bougainville ceased, 1,243 Australians and Americans lay dead and some 18,500 to 21,000 Japanese had perished from combat and sickness.

The Solomons and New Guinea campaigns disappeared in importance as the central Pacific offensive got underway on Tarawa in November 1943. But both proved instrumental in clearing out the Japanese from the Southwest theater and making Allied advances elsewhere possible. Japan could not afford the drain of men and materiel; the Empire was weakened by its defense of a perimeter over 3,300 miles from the military command center in Tokyo. The islands had arcane and forgettable names, but the Australian, American, and Japanese veterans who toiled in the inhumane conditions remembered them well.

Allied politicians and military brass decided that the war against Japan would be won in the central Pacific, where U.S. air and sea superiority as well as the ability to project a supply train thousands of miles beyond Hawaii could be brought to bear. The Southwest Pacific campaign and even MacArthur's toil on New Guinea were consigned to a status above the China-Burma-India theater in importance to defeating Japan, but secondary nonetheless. Even the invasion of France had to wait because Admiral Nimitz employed so many landing craft in the central Pacific that they were in short supply. With Navy personnel growing in numbers and the Marines becoming a permanent fighting force in the military from 1943 onward, Nimitz became the dynamic figure in the drive on Tokyo. By 1943's end, the Americans enjoyed growing advantages over Japan in carriers of all sizes, in naval aircrews and planes, and in battleships, cruisers, and destroyers. In terms of carriers alone, the U.S. Navy commissioned nine large *Essex*-class vessels each carrying 90 aircraft and nine *Independence*-class carriers with 30 aircraft aboard. These gave Nimitz 11 carriers—plus eight escort carriers with 28 aircraft each, five new fast battleships and seven prewar ones, numerous cruisers and destroyers, and amphibious and transport vessels—for the invasion of the Gilbert Islands. American production was fast overwhelming the Imperial Navy but so were the sinkings of Japanese transports and merchantmen. Carrier raids on Manus in August, the Gilberts in mid-September, and on Wake in early October were preludes to the central Pacific campaign.

Where and when victory over Japan would occur seemed the key questions by late 1943. Even as the Axis had scored victories in mid-1942, a shadow fell over their war effort even though they held seemingly impregnable positions abroad. The Germans had recently made their biggest territorial acquisitions of the war thus far. Hundreds of millions of people around the world remained subjugated to fascism and militarism. But Allied strategies and Axis overstretch had sapped the fortunes of war from Germany, Italy, and Japan. Grand thoughts of empire—a Third Reich across the Eurasian landmass, a Co-Prosperity Sphere spanning East Asia and the Pacific Ocean, the Mediterranean basin controlled from Rome—spoke to increasingly unrealistic ambitions. Over three years into the Second World War, the Allies began to turn the tables on their enemies in military engagements that changed the course of the conflict.

Grinding Rollback

1943–1944

Constant corpses, the accumulations of death on every
fought-over island, decay and flies always ahead of the burial
squads.

IVAN DOIG
The Eleventh Man

Operational pieces of the puzzle to defeat the Axis powers in Asia and Europe
came together in 1943. The North African campaign merged with the invasions of Sicily and the Italian mainland in a thrust upward from the Mediterranean
toward Germany. From the West, British and American leaders planned an assault
on the Atlantic side of Hitler's Fortress Europe. The USSR pressured the Germans
on the Eastern Front, the other large piece in the increasingly interrelated jigsaw of
the European theaters. Like Nazi Germany, Japan also faced a three-dimensional
Allied offensive: on the Asian mainland, from New Guinea in the southwest Pacific
area, and by the newest and most complex assault of all in the central Pacific. The
puzzle of Allied victory linked theaters within continents and regions and across
the globe. But the Germans, Japanese, and their minions vowed to convert the
appearance of defeat into resurgence. They tried to separate the puzzle pieces by
precipitating the greatest bloodshed possible. The time for annihilation had already
arrived, but their own people would increasingly fall victim as well to the strategy
that injected ever more brutal policies into the war.

CHAPTER 16

Penetrating Japan's Defenses

TARAWA

The onset of the drive across the central Pacific in November 1943 began in the Gilbert Islands, just 1,600 miles from Hawaii. The goal of Chester Nimitz was to hop westward from island to island—through the Gilbert, Marshall, and Mariana chains—to link with MacArthur in the Philippines and to bring Japan within range of bombers from the Marianas. Strategy resulted in part on the B-29 Superfortress coming off production lines beginning in the summer of 1943. Nimitz's boss, Ernest King, gave the Central Pacific operations primacy in terms of men and materiel. The invasion of the flat coral atolls of the Gilberts under Operation Galvanic would be easier than moving in the more distant Marshalls and yield high dividends. The islands could be converted into airstrips and also had lagoons with good anchorages for ships. Coral reefs ringing them provided good protection. The problem was that Tokyo treasured the Gilberts for these same reasons. Viewing the islands as "unsinkable carriers," the Japanese would defend them at great cost. U.S. admirals worried not about the Imperial Navy—the Fourth Japanese Fleet had just one naval air flotilla, 3 light cruisers, and 28,000 troops far to the west in the Marshalls—but they fretted about the amphibious landings required to take the islands. Tarawa atoll, the first of the Gilberts targeted for invasion, would test this landing technique.

Predicting trouble, Nimitz assembled a huge attack force. He was right to do so. The U.S. Fifth Fleet (previously Halsey's Third Fleet) was commanded by the cool Raymond Spruance, winner of the battle of Midway. At his disposal were nearly a dozen new aircraft carriers with 50 to 100 planes on each as well as battleships, cruisers, and smaller craft. The carriers had done well during the raids on Rabaul a few weeks earlier. Firepower was not at issue; the concern was the waiting Japanese. On the main island of Betio and two islets, Tarawa atoll housed over 4,500 soldiers under the able Rear Admiral Keiji Shibasaki. He had every right to boast that Tarawa could not be taken by a million men in a hundred years after the first day of battle. To be sure, the Combined Fleet would not come to his rescue because it was focused on defending the Marshalls. But Shibasaki had first-rate naval infantry and base defense forces that were reinforced in 1942 after an attack by a U.S. Marine commando-type unit called Carlson's Raiders. Some on board the approaching fleet predicted that the Japanese would abandon the atoll as they had done on Kiska in the Aleutian Islands three months before. Shibasaki had no such plan for Tarawa.

On Betio—an island just two and a half miles long—the defenders prepared to fight to the bitter end. Shibasaki constructed an intricate network of pillboxes, bunkers, and dugouts of palm logs and steel sunk in sand and concrete. The barriers withstood intense but brief bombardment from Spruance's ships and planes. U.S. Navy guns bombarded on a flat trajectory and thereby failed to dig out the Japanese positions. Because Spruance preferred fast, aggressive movement and not a World War I type bombardment, the U.S. Navy shelled the island for hours rather than days. It was the largest preliminary bombardment of the Pacific war to date, but the garrison survived. Shibasaki imported eight-inch guns from Singapore to defend the fortifications, which he covered with interlocking zones of fire. The cannons faced out to sea and left the lagoon vulnerable. Wrapped in thousand-stitch cloths around their waists, his forces readied to die for the Emperor. By November 13, the Americans had eliminated Japanese airpower but crack gunners and the pillboxes allowed Shibasaki to exploit difficult landing conditions. While the smaller Makin and Apamama islets were less heavily defended than Betio, all were surrounded by sharp-edged and shallow coral reefs that impeded landing craft carrying troops to shore. Two rings of coral encircled Betio. Wherever there were breaks, the Japanese had placed mines and wire, although Shibasaki had yet to complete his full defenses in this regard.

The green 27th Infantry Division comprised of New York National Guardsmen stationed in Hawaii headed for Makin, leaving the much more challenging Betio for the 17,000 men of the 2nd Marine Division. The latter had arrived from New Zealand a week before under the command of Major-General Holland Smith. They had engaged in combat but never an amphibious assault. The lack of experience required to send troops over a reef 1,000 yards from the Betio seawall into the lagoon made Operation Galvanic a challenging mission. Problems developed from the outset. Once the shelling ceased, Shibasaki moved guns to the north to hit landing craft floating offshore like sitting ducks. The 2nd Marine Division came ashore on November 20 with a company of amphibious tractors, the Landing Vehicle Tracked (LVT) that were nicknamed amtracs. This was their first use in an assault operation since their adaptation from rescue vehicles employed in Florida swamps. They transported troops across coral, mud, or swamps and gave covering fire. The amtracs did their job for the lead assault, but the operation soon ran short of them; the South Pacific theater stole the bulk. Landing craft carrying reinforcements filled the gap, but they ran aground on the inner reef in range of Japanese guns. Just getting to shore became an act of courage. Japanese Petty Officer Tadao Onuki recalled the massacre: "I in my tank kept shooting until the gun

Wading ashore on Makin. Credit: Center for the Study of War Experience at Regis University, Denver, Colorado: U.S.National Archives.

barrel became red hot" as the Americans pushed forward "in large numbers, one after another, floating the shallows, stepping over their friends' bodies."

A disaster was in the making. Five of the 14 new Sherman tanks flooded and stalled in the lagoon. The tractors were hit by mortars and artillery, and those that made it to the beaches could not climb the seawall. Troops waded ashore but as slow-moving ducks for Shibasaki's gunners. Correspondent Robert Sherrod went over the side when an amtrac bogged down. As machine gunners raked them with concentrated fire, he realized how "painfully slow" his unit advanced. The men had 700 yards to go. "I was scared, as I had never been scared before. But my head was clear. I was extremely alert, as though my brain were dictating that I live these last minutes for all they were worth." The defenders capitalized on the delays in the shallows by moving to Betio (which was essentially a big beach) and taking deadly aim. Meanwhile, the U.S. Navy stopped its supporting bombardment, fearful of hitting its own forces. The Marine Corps wanted to set up artillery on a nearby island, but the U.S. Navy did not want to hinder the invasion by such a distraction.

Pinned down on the beaches, the Americans hunkered down that night while some tanks and artillery got ashore. The next morning, the Marine Corps owned enough of a beachhead to call in airpower to hit the fortifications. Yet 350 reinforcements were lost in the waters. The U.S. Marines finally carved out a position on the south end of Betio by that afternoon. They built a defensive perimeter on the western shore where backup units poured in on the third day. The Americans divided and separated the defenders of Betio, and the Japanese countered with vicious banzai charges once they were forced into the island's eastern end. Sherrod described how a "Jap flared up like a piece of celluloid" after running from a pillbox where a U.S. Marine shot an intense stream of fire from a flamethrower. "He was dead instantly but the bullets in his cartridge belt exploded for a full sixty seconds after he had been charred almost to nothingness." By November 23, U.S. forces drew on an emerging strategy of military annihilation to secure the island. They ruthlessly cleared out the pillboxes and trenches. In the waters and on the island, 1,009 Americans lay dead and 2,101 wounded. The 2nd Marine Division had lost 263 men killed in six months on Guadalcanal; in three days on Tarawa, the death rate was ten times as much. Of the 4,500 Imperial troops and Korean laborers on the island, less than 100 of the latter were taken prisoner. Only 17 combat veterans surrendered, an emerging trend in this ever vicious Pacific war.

If the seizure of Betio was not grueling enough, the 27th Infantry Division of National Guardsmen on Makin did not coast to victory either. A regimental combat team of 6,500 soldiers landed on the islet, but it took three days to subdue about 400 Japanese. They suffered just 200 casualties, yet Holland Smith was disgusted by the battalions' inability to overrun the island quickly. The Army performed so badly that it endangered the mission offshore. For instance, an enemy submarine scored a direct hit on the bomb magazine of the escort carrier *Liscome Bay* waiting in support. The ensuing explosions blasted steel, oil, and human debris on to other ships over 5,000 yards away and the inferno killed 642 men. Only 272 survived, and these were badly injured with burns, concussions, and broken limbs. Watching in horror, sailors on *Coral Sea* and *Corregidor* realized the vulnerability of their 123 escort carriers, the lightly armed "little giants" commissioned during the war to provide support for sea-based assaults and cover from air attacks and submarines. In this case, all eyes narrowed on the National Guard. The New Yorkers never overcame their reputation for incompetence.

Tarawa provided an education on amphibious warfare. Preliminary bombardment—a critical element of amphibious warfare against an island's fortified positions—had not destroyed the pillboxes. Thus, the U.S. Navy looked into massive strikes in later campaigns. Furthermore, the premature lifting of the bombing itself was blamed on inadequate communications. In the future, a headquarters ship dedicated to oversee the operation from ship to shore would run the show. Amtracs, reconnaissance, and firepower would all be enhanced. The U.S. Navy conducted an investigation into the operation and found that the Marine Corps had paid a price for incompetence offshore. Tarawa was also a public relations mess. The high casualty rate shocked Americans back home. When the Marines exhibited photographs and film of the battle, citizens recoiled in horror. Even Nimitz turned sick at the stench of corpses awash in the steamy lagoon when he visited Betio. American dead were found bunched together before the pillboxes or hung up on the wires on the coral reefs, and Japanese bodies were charred inside the fortifications. Tarawa also conditioned planners to proceed with more caution and taught the troops to face the awful truth that the island-hopping drive would be a terrifying and bloody affair.

In fact, the conditioning of hatred that undergirded the strategy of annihilation intensified after Tarawa. The cultural, religious, and racial voids between the two enemies was so gaping that violence in the Pacific theater escalated to a furious level rivaled only by the carnage on the Soviet-German front. By the end of 1943, U.S. Army psychologists found that nearly half of newly activated infantrymen agreed that they wanted to kill Japanese soldiers. No more than nine percent felt the same about Germans. The Nazis had to be defeated; the Japanese must be wiped out. American soldiers had regrets and oftentimes shrunk in horror in the face of the killing. But the Pacific conflict devolved from Tarawa onward into a war of mutual extermination—a savage bloodletting based on racial denigration, fear, and a harsh environment—which drove soldiers on both sides to determine to destroy the enemy, without mercy.

INTO THE MARSHALLS

Tarawa's legacy prevailed into the Marshall Islands in January 1944. The 36 atolls in two island chains spread 125 miles apart had been mandated to Japan after World War I. Thus, the Marshalls comprised the official outer ring of defense for the Empire. From them, the Japanese menaced supply and communications lines and access to the Carolines and Marianas. Tokyo strategists had actually written off the Marshalls when they decided to bolster defenses closer to the home islands but the tactic of exacting a blood price on each step across the central Pacific was intended to erode American willpower. The world's largest atoll, Kwajalein, was the first place to make the enemy pay. It housed a large garrison under Vice Admiral Masashi Kobayashi and had under construction a 5,000-foot airstrip ideal for heavy bombers. With the harrowing Tarawa experience in mind, American forces prepared for a series of tough battles.

Admiral Mark Mitscher commanded the fast carrier Task Force 58, a powerful group of twelve carriers, six new fast battleships, a dozen cruisers, and more destroyers under the overall authority of the U.S. Fifth Fleet. Its carrier-based bombers erased Japanese air power in the islands as nearly 300 ships and landing craft made their way to the atolls. U.S. Marine and Army amphibious contingents numbered among the 85,000 combat, garrison, and construction personnel. Having practiced in Hawaii, naval gunners and pilots were linked by radio to ground and aerial spotters to improve their operational performance. This was a lesson learned from Tarawa. The second battalion of the 106th Infantry Regiment, with the assistance of the V Amphibious Corps Reconnaissance Company, went ashore on Majuro atoll. The island represented the first territory of Japan to be occupied by American troops during the war.

What followed was a tough but smooth (relative to Tarawa) invasion called Operation Flintlock into the heart of the Marshalls—landings on Kwajalein and neighboring Roi-Namur. The Japanese had moved troops to the outer atolls in anticipation of the attack, but intelligence informed Rear Admiral Forrest Sherman that the interior lagoons lay open. Thus, he neutralized the outer islands by three days of air bombings and sent five battalions of artillery to support the landings. Both efforts reflected alterations prompted by the Tarawa fiasco. U.S. Navy underwater demolition teams, the Frogmen, joined U.S. Army amphibious engineers to blow holes in the reefs. Kobayashi's defenses on Roi-Namur and Kwajalein were incomplete and the garrisons were equal to those on Tarawa but had to cover three times the area. The airfields on all three islands were put out of commission. The 4th Marine Division came ashore on Roi and Namur on January 31 transported in 240 amtracs and towing the new two-and-a-half ton amphibious trucks—the famous DUKW (nicknamed "Duck")—and the division's howitzers. Regardless of the massive power of the invading force, the defenders, the surf, and the reefs caused delays. Imperial troops rushed forward with bayonets or fought from trenches with small arms. Many committed suicide on Roi. On neighboring Namur, fighting was just as chaotic. Bombardment destroyed the communications center and killed the air commander of the Marshalls. Waiting in shell holes or in the thick undergrowth, the Japanese climbed up the sides of tanks with grenades before being blown off by raking machine-gun fire. Hand-to-hand combat like this was common. But within a day and a half, Roi and Namur, at the entrance of Kwajalein Lagoon, were in American hands.

The new tactics employed by the Americans, who proved fast studies of the Tarawa debacle, cost half the casualties they incurred on Betio. Meanwhile, almost all of the 10,000 Japanese defenders perished. On Kwajalein Island, the U.S. Army's 7th Infantry benefited from close-in naval bombardment and aerial assault from Task Force 58. Facing little opposition on the beaches, U.S. troops reached the airfield by the first night. Fanatical charges by the Japanese ensued, or an enemy soldier would squeeze a grenade from within a spider hole and kill himself. After four days, the island fell. Diverging from the norm, 49 Japanese refused suicide and surrendered. The Americans also found 125 Korean laborers. A week's worth of fighting and fewer than 400 dead—less than

Flamethrowers on Kwajalein.   Credit: Center for the Study of War Experience at Regis University, Denver, Colorado: U.S. National Archives.

2,000 casualties—gave Kwajalein to Nimitz. Out of 8,675 defenders, all but 800 died in the battle. Japanese on the outer atolls eluded capture until war's end. The Fifth Fleet so convincingly performed its amphibious and naval air assaults that Nimitz and King pushed the timetable forward by six weeks to take the last and most western Marshall atoll: Eniwetok.

On February 17, 1944, five U.S. Army and Marine battalions of 8,000 men landed on Eniwetok atoll's islands of Engebi, Parry, and Eniwetok. The Japanese waited with nearly 4,000 members of the elite First Amphibious Brigade, which arrived in January. The defenders inflicted losses when naval bombardment proved too hasty and inaccurate. They hid in networks of spider traps—oil drums set in the ground and camouflaged—which proved to be a deadly tactic. Sniping occurred through the night, and small packs of men raided from foxholes and trenches compelled the Americans to take three days to mop up on the atoll. They exposed the enemy by drawing on the first nighttime illumination of a battlefield from star shells fired from ships. The Americans had underestimated the numbers, but the skilled execution of the invasion, which cost them about a thousand casualties, showed that Tarawa's lessons had been heeded. Meanwhile, the elimination of the entire Japanese garrison of 3,400 revealed Tokyo's intention of sacrificing men for time.

The Japanese pulled back to the Marianas islands. They had no hope of reinforcing Wake Island to the north. It remained in their hands but played no role when the Americans swept past it. The completion of the operation proved of immense strategic value. Eniwetok served as an ideal naval and air staging area. American aircraft came within range of the Caroline Island chain and the key Marianas outposts of Guam, Saipan, and Tinian. The Japanese did not cut and run, however. Rather, they made adjustments in the Marianas in anticipation of the coming assault.

At the end of April 1944, Mitscher's Task Force 58 thundered toward the Combined Fleet base at Truk in the Carolines to prevent any retaliation. The Joint Chiefs pondered whether to invade the base and settled on leveling it from the air instead. This first radar-guided night bomber attack on shipping did not damage the Imperial Navy because Admiral Koga's fleet had vacated the base to safety a thousand miles to the west behind the Marianas. But 265 precious aircraft were destroyed and 50 ships and 140,000 tons of shipping went to the bottom. Truk itself took a major beating; its harbor was choked with cargo, sunken vessels, and bodies. The carrier *Intrepid* was hit by a torpedo bomber and four U.S. planes were lost, but by the second day of action, not one Japanese pilot took off. This was not the first or the last time that the Americans assailed this major port, but it was the most damaging of the thirty raids. For the first time in history, carrier aircraft had shut down a big base. The Joint Chiefs decided to bypass it and release troops designated for an invasion to the Marianas and Palau campaign. Truk, and Japanese garrisons in the Marshalls, were no longer factors in the Pacific War.

MACARTHUR IN THE SOUTHWEST PACIFIC

The chain's speedy capture advanced the central Pacific timetable by 20 weeks to June 1944 for an invasion of the Marianas, which were 1,500 miles closer to Japan. This worried

Douglas MacArthur, who feared that his Southwest Pacific theater would be forgotten as Nimitz charged toward Japan. The U.S. Joint Chiefs and the Allied Combined Chiefs rejected his plan to advance up the coast of New Guinea into the Philippines and then beyond to China using land-based airpower. They preferred the cheaper and more direct route to Japan of relying on the U.S. Navy to head through the central Pacific to the Philippines. Still, MacArthur recoiled at the idea that the U.S. Navy would beat him to the Philippines and thus prevent him from fulfilling his pledge to liberate the islands. He decided to bump up his schedule, too, in 1944. First he had to rid the theater of the specter of Rabaul's air and sea power just as Nimitz had done to Truk.

He took aim on Los Negros and Manus, the two principal islands of the Admiralty group that lay 200 miles northeast of New Guinea. Japan had taken them in 1942 and built air bases and a superb anchorage at Seeadler Harbor on Los Negros. Air commander George Kenney had not detected enemy activity, however. On February 29, 1944, Lieutenant-General Walter Krueger's Sixth Army, which had landed on New Britain, invaded the islands. The First Cavalry Division backed by the 73rd Wing of the Australian Air Force came ashore on Los Negros and then moved to Manus. ULTRA intercepts detected over 3,200 troops in a garrison that included two infantry battalions and naval detachments. The defenders came to life with a fury, killing 326 U.S. soldiers and injured nearly 1,200. But Colonel Yoshio Ezaki placed insufficient artillery and machine-guns at Hyane Harbor at the opposite end of Los Negros from Seeadler Harbor. Waves of U.S. amphibians swept over them and built a perimeter around the Los Negros airfield, to which the Americans held on to tenaciously. At one point, they fended off an infiltration attempt when Japanese troops silently swam around their rear. Los Negros was secured by early March 1944 and Manus held out for another two weeks until tanks and Australian aircraft pounded the defenders from their pillboxes. By May, the two islands were subdued with only 75 prisoners out of nearly 3,400 Japanese taken. Rabaul's encirclement was complete. Coupled with the end of the vicious fighting on Bougainville by late March, the Solomons-New Britain campaign was over.

With the Admiralties secured two months ahead of schedule, MacArthur capitalized on the momentum by preparing to advance up New Guinea. The Japanese realigned their defensive configuration accordingly. Troops traded their lives for time while Tokyo military planners drew a new perimeter running from the Kurils through the Marianas and Carolines to western New Guinea. From this line, Japan planned to lure out the Americans beyond their capabilities and then engage them in the long-sought decisive battle. In March 1944, General Adachi ceded overall control of the theater to Lieutenant-General Korechika Anami and waited for MacArthur up the coast of New Guinea. Anami transferred parts of Second Area Army in Manchuria to the New Guinea campaign. Facing this challenge, MacArthur struck.

As Australian and American forces pushed up the coast of New Guinea after fighting at Madang and Saidor, they had a surprise in store. Adachi's 40,000 troops stood between Hollandia and American-Australian forces farther down the coast, but MacArthur's gambling genius took hold. Ordering a diversionary air and naval attack on Wewak, he had his warships and 80,000 troops bypass Eighteenth Japanese Army and jump northward. In short, he hurdled his forces 580 miles up the coast to Hollandia. They leapt around enemy concentrations to the administrative center of Dutch New Guinea that had been converted into a major air and naval base. ULTRA greatly facilitated the leap-frogging maneuver because it exposed the exact whereabouts of Adachi's forces. MacArthur's leadership skills had paid dividends and the dearth of airpower prevented Japan from contesting the landings. Adachi placed his remaining 350 planes around Hollandia in the belief that U.S. bombers could not reach them but Kenney put 300-gallon wing tanks on his P-38 fighters and thereby extended their range by 300 miles. On March 31, they found Adachi's aircraft lined up. Kenney's assault left a mere 25 planes. Over the previous week, more than 3,000 Japanese were killed and another 600 were taken prisoner. Others fled into the jungles to die of disease, starvation, or enemy fire.

To complete this lightning strike, Robert Eichelberger moved ashore at Hollandia and Aitape. He took the airfields in three days against just 500 combat troops because most of the 11,000 defenders were construction crews and engineers. The General secured the entire area on June 6. A month later, Eighteenth Army retaliated at Aitape; but ULTRA and other intelligence gave Eichelberger enough warning to buttress the perimeter defense. U.S. XI Corps defended its position along the Driniumor River. Although the Japanese overran parts of the perimeter by August 25, they were done. Adachi lost 9,000 of the 20,000 men who had counterattacked. The Allies had their share of casualties during the two-month period of Hollandia's capture from April into June 1944. Yet over the next year, the Japanese Eighteenth Army shrunk to just 13,500 survivors who were harassed by Australian aircraft and ground forces in their diminishing pocket around Wewak. The Aussies mopped up on New Guinea as well as Bougainville and New Britain.

Meanwhile, MacArthur went after Anami's Second Area Army in western New Guinea in preparation for the invasion of the southern Philippines. The Americans searched for airstrips for heavy bombers and found one on the island of Biak in the Schouten Islands just north of Dutch New Guinea. On May 27, 1944, the U.S. 41st National Guard Division, which had seized Aitape a few weeks before, landed on Biak. Some 11,400 troops under the wily Colonel Naoyuki Kozume defended the air base. Tokyo added 1,200 reinforcements, although two destroyers were lost in the process. Americans walked into an ambush that ended with a tank rescue. The defenders continued to fight from the ridges on the island. MacArthur claimed the island secure on June 14 when Japan transferred troops into the Philippines, but in reality, the Americans still struggled against the garrison. Eichelberger and 6th Army Division were sent to relieve Major General Horace Fuller (at the latter's request) to finish the job; yet in the Ibdi Pocket, the Japanese held out in the interior's caves until July 28. An amphibious landing at Wardo Bay in mid-August finished them off. Biak was largely a wasted effort, however. It was taken to support Nimitz in the Marianas and Palaus, but it turned out to have no bearing on those operations. Some 2,000 men were wounded and 400 killed. All but 500 of the remaining 4,800 Imperial troops perished. Just as bad was a mysterious fever and scrub typhus that claimed over 7,000 nonbattle casualties. The grim New Guinea campaign revealed an impressive reduction among

Anglo-American soldiers in the incidence of disease and sickness occurred relative to the First World War. People the world over suffered health crises ranging from venereal disease to typhus. In general, American and British medicine made strides in disease prevention in Asia while the Japanese neglected this aspect of military life. Most telling was Tokyo's inattention to tropical maladies such as malaria. The Imperial Army did not even recognize the dangers of scrub typhus spread by the larvae of mites, which they labeled Wewak fever (from the New Guinea campaign) and confused with malaria. Troops were also not routinely given tetanus shots, which made them vulnerable to infection once wounded. Contrasted to this cavalier attitude, the Allies marshaled significant resources for medical research, prevention, and suppression of epidemics through insecticides and inoculation. They also exercised vigilance over hygiene and even sponsored weekly inspections of prostitutes. Malaria epidemics ceased after Spring 1943, and outbreaks were controlled. MacArthur welcomed the appointment of a public health officer to facilitate antimalarial spraying and the shipment of drugs and supplies because three-quarters of the American Army's disease deaths during the war occurred in the Southwest Pacific theater. Until the end of 1943, some 5,000 U.S. soldiers a month fell ill from malaria. But in jungle and island fighting, the Americans held a distinct advantage over the Japanese when it came to the treatment of casualties, organization, availability of staffs and hospitals, and overall, to surviving in the harsh tropical environment.

The stage was now set for a move into the Philippines. In addition to cutting off Adachi's Eighteenth Army in New Guinea, the U.S. also captured tiny Wakde Island and Sarmi on Dutch New Guinea. Both cost hundreds of casualties before troops cleared the Japanese from caves, pillboxes, bunkers, and spider holes. They also seized the island of Noemfoor after Kenney obliterated the Imperial Army garrison with 8,000 tons of bombs, although parachutists suffered a 10% casualty rate as they hit the coral-covered airfields. By the end of July 1944, the U.S. 6th Army Division undertook its last landings of the New Guinea campaign at Sansapor on the Vogelkop Peninsula. Bypassing a communications center on the island of Halmahera, General MacArthur then subdued Morotai to the north of New Guinea in September. He was just 300 miles from the Philippines.

The two-year New Guinea coastal battle was over. Until January 1944, the Allies had advanced 300 miles in twenty months and lost 24,000 mostly Australian casualties. From Hollandia in April 1944 until the Vogelkop invasion three months later, MacArthur covered 1,300 miles and suffered 9,500 mostly U.S. casualties. Japan buried 11,000 soldiers. Some 30,000 Imperial troops remained isolated on New Guinea while another 96,000 men were stranded on New Britain. Even MacArthur's harshest critics admitted that the campaign in New Guinea was one of the war's most innovative and economical in terms of casualties. His brilliant yet largely unheralded campaign got him his wish of returning to the Philippines. Gazing northward from the shores of Morotai, MacArthur remembered the disasters on Corrigedor and Bataan two and a half years before. "They are waiting for me there," he murmured.

Prime Minister Tojo and military officers blamed each other for the mishaps that had removed Rabaul and Truk as viable bases, brought MacArthur to the doorstep of the Philippines, and allowed the U.S. Navy to approach 1,300 miles closer to Japan. A reshuffling at the Ministry of War placed Tojo firmly in control in Spring 1944 yet even he realized that Yamamoto's prediction of defeat was coming true. Given the likelihood that assassination by militant Army officers awaited any leader who sued for peace, Tojo put diplomatic negotiations out of his mind. He sought instead a decisive victory—in the central Pacific, India, or China—to force the Allies to the peace table. The China-Burma-India theater provided the best prospects. MacArthur was not a great concern because the Philippines were less important than the resources of the East Indies. But the increasingly harmful Allied blockade intercepted the supply routes from the Asian mainland, and particularly China and Southeast Asia, to the home islands. This logistical crisis greatly troubled Tojo.

The U.S. Navy's tourniquet of submarine warfare tied around Tokyo in 1942 inexorably tightened in the years afterward. Crews adopted tactics to hunt in groups, attack merchants and military transports, and then retreat more effectively than before. American weaponry got better. They modified the Mark XIV torpedo, and the new (copied from a German design) electric Mark XVIII no longer had a faulty exploder and left no wake to boot. By January 1944, the U.S. possessed double the quantity of subs than in 1941, and the number rose by 50% more at the end of the year. ULTRA guided them to enemy shipping lanes. Unable to escape, over 600 Japanese ships went down in 1944. About 2.7 million precious tons of cargo—out of a total of 3.8 million tons coming from Southeast Asia and New Guinea—sunk before reaching the home islands. Japan could not afford such losses. Its merchant fleet was small to begin with, and got tinier still when cargo ships were converted to military use. Shipyards could not replace the losses. The Imperial Navy also neglected antisubmarine operations. Added to these woes were U.S. air attacks. Aircraft joined submarines in a double-edged American campaign of destruction. By mid-1944, Japan had lost so many tankers that the Combined Fleet moved into the Dutch East Indies to be closer to its fuel supply. Less than 200,000 tons of oil reached the home islands in 1944. The Allies squeezed the Empire of Japan from the seas and the air as well as on land.

CHINA-BURMA-INDIA CLASHES

In the China-India-Burma theater, the Allies also threatened Japan. To recapture Burma and free China, they retained their multipronged offensive plan. Under William Slim, British Fourteenth Army's XV Corps led by Philip Christison advanced southward in the Arakan to take Akyab. A central front targeted by Geoffrey Scoones' IV Corps pushed in Assam for Tiddim and Tamu. The irascible Vinegar Joe Stilwell moved in the north with Chinese and U.S. troops to secure the Ledo Road and also attack along the north-central border. They sought to open the land routes to China and then clear the Japanese out of Burma. Unlike the Pacific theaters, the campaigns in the China-Burma-India sector were not often in the spotlight. Yet the Allies proved to be inventive and adaptable in trying circumstances. The Japanese Twenty-eighth Army under Sakurai Shozo in the Arakan and Thirty-third Army under Masaki Honda in north Burma readied for the multidirectional counteroffensive. Masakuzu Kawabe Burma Area Army of eight ground divisions and a 100-aircraft division planned Operation

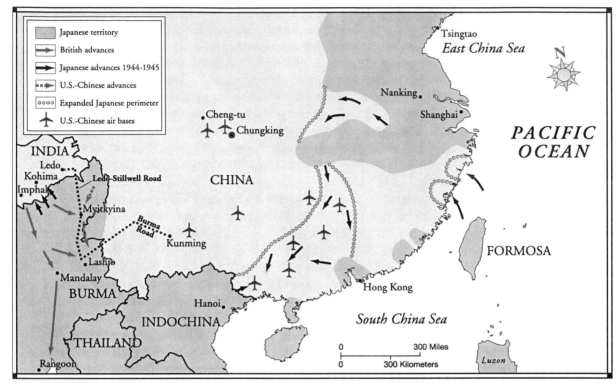

Map 16.1 China-Burma-India theater.   Credit: Ronald Story, *Concise Historical Atlas of World War II: The Geography of Conflict*, Map 46, p. 97.

Ha-Go to encircle and destroy two of Christison's divisions. This would not only under-mine British efforts to send reinforcements to Scoones in the central campaign, but Ha-Go would also distract attention away from a second operation, Operation U-Go. More familiarly known as the Imphal offensive, U-Go was led by Fifteenth Army under a bushido warrior, Renya Mutaguchi, a former chief of staff to Yamashita and an able commander in Malaya. He aimed to invade India across the Chindwin River and stem Slim's advance to block the center of the British front. The Japanese had big challenges ahead; they were confident they could defend Burma.

Stilwell had already entered northern Burma. He moved south along the Hukawng Valley with two weak Chinese formations that met stiff resistance. He also tried to trap Lieutenant General Honda's 18th Division with the unorthodox forces of Orde Wingate's Chindits, Kachin Rangers, and Galahad commandos under Brigadier General Frank Merrill. These "Merrill's Marauders" were created in the image of the Wingate's British force and included Sioux Indians and Japanese-Americans who served as intelligence and reconnaissance operatives. Stilwell trained the Marauders with the Chindits and teamed them with First Chinese Army and Kachin units to try to outflank Honda. While the Chindits dropped behind Japanese lines, the Marauders maneuvered around the ends of the front. The effort initially failed. In early March, the

Japanese escaped an ambush at Walawbun and then another in the Inkangahtawng jungle north of Kamaing. During the latter, they forced two Marauder battalions into the hills and nearly destroyed them. A vicious seesaw battle ensued. Honda's 18th Division outflanked the Chinese as they retreated and then Stilwell sent the Marauders on a debilitating jungle march to Nhpum Ga, directly in Honda's path. After taking the airstrip and water hole, the Japanese abandoned the village after a month-long slugging match. This grueling victory gave Stilwell the entire Hukawng Valley by the end of March 1944.

Stilwell pressured Chiang Kai-shek to send reinforcements. Having lost 700 men to combat, disease, and exhaustion, the Marauders joined new Chinese units and five brigades of 9,000 Chindits to pursue the 18th Division. This they did without Wingate who died in a plane crash in India on March 24. They focused on capturing the key airfield at Myitkyina in northern Burma where the Hukawng Valley met the Irrawaddy River. Merrill suffered his second heart attack, however, and the Marauders remained under the command of his deputy. Nonetheless, Stillwell ordered them to climb the muddy infested trails over the Kuman Mountains. The terrain and humidity were bad, and both added to the threat of malaria and dysentery that plagued all the armies in Burma. The Marauders emerged three weeks later and overran a surprised detachment of Japanese at Myitkyina airstrip on May 17.

The siege of the communications hub of Myitkyina itself was another matter. The Chindits could not continue to intercept resupply routes from their isolated positions without the town changing hands. Even though Chinese troops fought well, monsoons, exhaustion, and a tough but undersupplied Japanese defense required two and a half months of combat before the town fell. Major-General Mizukami Genzu held out for 79 days until August 3, 1944, against impossible odds after reinforcing the town with the few troops available. He remained to the last until he committed suicide while 790 troops in the garrison died and 1,180 were wounded. The few survivors fled across the Irrawaddy River rather than surrender. Such behavior illustrated the "inhuman fanaticism" of the enemy, remembered a British officer. When a Japanese foot patrol encountered three Grant tanks moving across a paddy, for example, they attacked it in open formation with fixed bayonets rather than dive back into the jungle. The sole remaining soldier did not surrender but leaped in front of a tank, which crushed him.

Myitkyina's fall allowed the completion of the Ledo Road in January 1945 that connected India to China through northern Burma, but the costs of victory rose for the Allies. Highway crews began paving the route (this was America's contribution to the Burma campaign) while gas pipelines sprung up alongside it. The airfield served transport planes that flew over the "Hump" with a shorter less precarious route into China than the previous Burma Road. From May to July 1944, deliveries to Chiang's forces doubled.

But acrimony swept over the Allied forces. Vinegar Joe demanded that hospitalized Marauders return to the battlefield, which was only fair, he insisted, because he had demanded that the British keep the exhausted Chindits in the field and that Chiang step up his efforts. Stilwell bestowed hardly an accolade on Merrill's Marauders. Debilitated

Ledo-Burma Road "21 Curves" near Annan, China.
Credit: National Archives.

to the point of reaching nonoperational status, the Marauders disbanded after the Myitkyina campaign. They suffered 272 killed and nearly 2,000 to injury and disease. The Chinese suffered 972 dead and over 3,100 injured.

Disaster also loomed on the Indo-Burmese border in March as the Japan Burma Area Army began the Imphal offensive to recapture Rangoon. By attacking from Burma into India, Mutaguchi's Fifteenth Army aimed to destroy William Slim's supply bases at Imphal and thus interrupt the British counteroffensive. Tokyo also hoped that success might also provoke a rebellion against British rule by the Japanese-sponsored Indian National Army of Subhas Chandra Bose. This was a pipe dream. Japan's harsh treatment of former European colonial subjects through slave labor, imprisonment, and execution made support for the offensive unlikely. Still, the Japanese enjoyed considerable military success. Prior to the offensive, Kawabe's Burma Area Army of 100,000 troops attacked into the Arakan to force Slim to commit his reserves and to block Christison's XV Corps that had already made it from India to Maungdaw. The British sought the

Akyab airfields, which were critical to recapturing Rangoon, and pledged that this time around the Japanese would not cut them off from supplies. Slim gave up the initiative to the Japanese. He was convinced that he could defeat them with superior air forces, weapons, and logistical networks.

The first step to retaking Rangoon depended on creating an administrative and supply base near Sinzweya. This was literally a box about 1,100 square yards to support Christison's offensive. The Japanese knew its importance. The 55th Division under Hanaya Tadashi moved on "Admin Box" in early February and achieved total surprise. Tadashi swarmed the 7th Indian Division and surrounded the area. Repeating the hospital massacre in Singapore of 1942, the Japanese shot several hand-cuffed British and Indian medical officers. Allied troops fought back using tanks, which Hanaya lacked, as well as air-dropped supplies, airpower, and artillery. These tactics defeated the Japanese and afterward, Indian Army units encircled the 55th Division and hunted down the escapees in the jungles. The British suffered over 3,500 casualties at Admin Box, and the Japanese suffered 3,100 killed and another 2,200 wounded. Slim took Maungdaw ridge and nearly broke through to Akyab, though the Japanese Imphal offensive forced him to divert his troops.

The British had more troops and firepower, including aircraft, so Mutaguchi gambled on speed and surprise for the Imphal operation. Slim expected the attack but he mistimed it as well as its strength. Mutaguchi's 100,000 veteran Japanese Fifteenth Army troops crossed the frontier into the Manipur plain. Part of this force drew British Fourteenth Army reserves away from the main thrust as Mutaguchi struck with his 33rd Division from the south on March 7. He forced Slim's 17th Division into retreat at Tiddim. The Japanese sought to control the Manipur plain by occupying Imphal at its southern end and Kohima to the north, and made significant progress toward this objective when the Yamamoto Force destroyed the British 10th Division at Tamu. A week later, the Japanese attacked into the center of British defenses and stormed across the Chindwin River into the Chin Hills. They ran into trouble, however, from the British 5th and 7th Divisions, which were airlifted to Imphal once the Arakan campaign halted. Mutaguchi was a mere 30 miles from Imphal by late March 1944. Slim had expected an attack on Kohima, so he placed just one division in Imphal. He had no idea that the Japanese 31st Division could bring in more than a regiment over the mountainous terrain. Kotuku Sato deployed his entire division, which annihilated the 50th Indian Parachute Brigade at Sangshak and then reached Kohima on April 3. The Allied supply route to Slim's main base at Dimapur to the northwest was now in jeopardy.

While Slim ordered the small Kohima garrison under Colonel Hugh Richards to hold fast, Mutaguchi readied to sever the Dimapur-Imphal artery. Sato attacked against a defensive box reinforced by artillery and a brigade of the 5th Indian Division. His 58th Regiment cut the road and surrounded the box and Kohima as well. Air-dropped supplies sustained Richards for awhile; but because he occupied such a small area, the materiel often missed its mark. Despite strafing by the RAF, the Japanese chiseled away at pockets of the garrison. By April 18, only Garrison Hill in Kohima remained in British hands. The outlook was bleak; Richards contested areas no bigger than a tennis court. But at long last the air attacks turned the tide and the XXXIII Corps rushed in from India to drive back Sato by the end of May. Against orders, he withdrew because his losses had climbed to over 6,000 men. British and Indian casualties approached 4,000, including three brigade commanders killed. The sacrifice was enormous in this remote area of the good war. The epitaph to the British Second Division that defended Kohima appropriately read "When You Go Home, Tell Them Of Us And Say, For Their Tomorrow, We Gave Our Today." The victory undercut the Imphal offensive and allowed Slim a golden opportunity for a reprisal.

Slim needed the break because Mutaguchi's 15th Division had made it to Kangpokpi, cut the Kohima-Imphal road, and stood just six miles from the British IV Corps outside of Imphal. But the Japanese had run out of steam. They were tired and bereft of necessary firepower, and also had no defense against enemy tanks. Slim received reinforcements from the air; over the next four months, the Third Tactical Air Force transported one million gallons of gas, 14 million pounds of rations, and 12,000 troops into the area. The logistical edge won the day. Supplies and men from Admin Box bolstered Commonwealth troops for a counteroffensive. With the garrison numbering 100,000 men, the 5th and 23rd Divisions broke the Japanese hold. Because he could not keep pace, Mutaguchi gambled again. He shot toward Imphal to take British supply dumps. When two divisions blocked his way, Mutaguchi tried another desperate ploy by exceeding orders and attacking Dimapur without success. Mutaguchi had predicated the Imphal offensive on living off British supplies, yet these were now denied to him. Burma Area Army chief Kawabe had always disliked the idea, however, and as a result, the Japanese fell into a holding pattern that played to British logistical strengths. Slim stabilized the front and steadily squeezed Mutaguchi's forces. Sato's retreat from Kohima, the arrival of the monsoon season, and disease and exhaustion added to the collapse of the Imphal offensive. By June 22, 1944, the battle for the Chin ridges resulted in an Allied triumph. The Dimapur-Imphal road reopened. A month later, Kawabe and Mutaguchi called off the Imphal operation and the latter retreated across the Chindwin, pursued by Slim's relentless forces.

The Imphal campaign was one of the deadliest operations of World War II. Fully 53,000 of the 85,000 Japanese troops became casualties, including 30,000 dead. The British suffered 17,000 casualties. Over 17,000 mules and pack ponies died. Not one heavy weapon made it off the battlefields. Imphal became a battle of attrition likened to some of the massacres of World War I. As historians Williamson Murray and Allan Millett have concluded, the battle for Imphal rivaled even the Eastern front of World War II for its "mindless savagery." The Imphal debacle represented the most telling defeat for the Imperial Army in the war and for that matter, in the entire history of the nation. Even though the battles of Imphal and Kohima occurred in India, they decisively weakened Japan's hold on Burma because the Army was bereft of mobile forces. The Burma Area Army lost all offensive capabilities and shifted to the defensive. There was no hope of conquering India. Slim now aimed to chase the Japanese from Burma and Thailand. His Fourteenth Army had suffered greatly, but it had learned to fight in the jungles and no longer feared the enemy. The British enjoyed a stable logistical supply train while medical care and evacuation support boosted discipline and morale. When Slim crossed into Burma in December 1944, both of his Japanese counterparts,

Kawabe and Mutaguchi, were sacked along with all but one of the Fifteenth Army staff. The skies over Japan's future in South and Southeast Asia had darkened due to the failure of the Imphal offensive.

Only in China could the Japanese enjoy a measure of success. They drove back a Chinese offensive intended to join the Myitkyina operations in June 1944. In April, the Imperial Army also began its own broad attack—the first in China since 1941—to show that U.S. airpower alone could not prevail on the mainland. Capturing railroad lines, transport and communications hubs, and airbases to secure an alternative supply route to the sea lanes prowled by enemy submarines, this Ichi-Go offensive swept across central and south China. Captured Allied air bases denied Claire Chennault the means of harassing shipping and troops in China and Formosa. Chinese Nationalist forces utterly collapsed amidst confusion and corruption during the height of the offensive from April to December 1944. The Japanese advanced on Chiang's capital of Chungking, and it appeared as if China might be ushered out of the war entirely.

Stilwell's insistence that Chiang be corralled and resources focused on a ground campaign seemed reasonable. He even convinced George Marshall to send a message with FDR's signature that demanded Chiang maintain an offensive with American-equipped forces in Yunnan called the Y-Force. But the Nationalist leader worked behind the scenes to get Vinegar Joe off his back. Sino-American politics as usual blocked attempts to reform the obstinate Chiang, who called the bluff of the United States once again. He knew the Americans banked on his leadership in Asia after the war, and he remained a darling of many U.S. politicians during it. Although a growing number of congressional members became disillusioned with the Nationalist chief, it was Stilwell who eventually departed the theater. America would not abandon its popular ally in China no matter how corrupt.

Although revealing of American and Chinese weaknesses, even Ichi-Go did not boost Japanese fortunes, yet the loss did not really matter to the larger war. As Chiang's troops fell back, the Chinese Communists proved more effective in combating the enemy. Chiang and Mao tied down about one million Japanese troops, in addition to Slim's successes that secured larger areas of Burma. But the United States turned away from the China-Burma-India theater. Chinese allies could not be counted on to chase Imperial troops from their land. It was possible that the north China coast might become a suitable landing area for U.S. troops if the country became a staging area for an invasion of Japan itself. By mid-1944, however, events in the central and south Pacific had elevated MacArthur and Nimitz to prominence. Stilwell, Chiang, and Slim were shunted aside in military significance, although they had engaged in a war of annihilation that rivaled the Eastern European front In the end, however, they fought in a theater on the periphery of the Second World War. The central focus in Asia was in the Pacific where the increasingly vicious fighting reflected the strategy of annihilation on all sides.

CHAPTER 17

Costly Italy

Mankind is falling into a long dark tunnel. It's the new Middle
Ages.... That's the bit that breaks my heart. I thought fascism
was the plague. But war is.

SCOTT TUROW
Ordinary Heroes

CARNAGE ON THE PENINSULA

Historians have labeled the Pacific theater as a killing zone and the Eastern front a killing field—both appropriate descriptions for a war of annihilation—but the terms are just as accurate when applied to Italy. Having slowed and bled the Allied advance up the mainland to Rome, the Germans stood behind the Gustav Line of defenses in central Italy. The position was situated in mountainous and river terrain ideal for hindering offensives as they had done for the past five months. Because its eastern end was anchored in the nearly impassable mountains and the western side ran into the sea, the Gustav Line could only be worn down by constant pressure. Allied commander Harold Alexander determined to go through it, but he did not relish attrition warfare. He had gotten to this point through poor planning and organization that had plagued the Italian campaign from the start. The Allies designed an attack, but prior errors had allowed the Germans the luxury of choosing where they wished to make a stand, and thus made the fighting all the more contested and brutal.

To get at the defenders, the Americans sought to cross the Rapido River and go through Cassino; the British corps of Fifth Army aimed for the Gustav Line at its sea terminus; and a plan for an amphibious landing behind the Line at the tiny port of Anzio was taken out of mothballs. Yet because Italy was a secondary theater, the invasions of Normandy and southern France took precedence when it came to equipping amphibious maneuvers. Even though the British had just a half-dozen Landing Ship Tanks (LST) available, they still considered further stripping Italy of amphibians by sending some to the Indian Ocean for an assault in the Bay of Bengal. Churchill approved the improvised and depleted Anzio operation—called Shingle—to begin on January 22, 1944. On the U.S. side, Mark Clark's Fifth Army prepared as best it could despite the

274

Map 17.1 Italy.   Credit: Ronald Story, *Concise Historical Atlas of World War II: The Geography of Conflict,* Map 23, p. 51.

lack of mental and material equipment necessary for a battle of attrition and harsh terrain that favored the enemy defense. Clark was obstinate, self-assured, and willing to sacrifice his men with few qualms—sort of like Stalin at Stalingrad. The Soviet dictator had had no choice but to throw troops and civilians into bloodshed. Clark had options to avoid a meat grinder, yet the assault on Cassino became a time for killing. "On few battlefields," claims one historian, "would soldiers endure harsher conditions or witness worse carnage."

The four battles for Monte Cassino from January to May 1944 involved fights for the town of Cassino and the steep and craggy Monastery Hill with its ancient abbey crowning the top. Sandwiched within the first and second battles was the fight for Anzio. The first battle commenced on the night of January 11–12. The French Expeditionary Corps—an amalgamation of Free French regulars, conscripts, and volunteers from the colonial empire—crashed through the first line of Wehrmacht barricades and headed for Atina before being stopped. On January 17, Clark ordered the British X Corps against the Gustav Line. It made progress but eventually bogged down. The British 46th Division then failed to cross the Garigliano River with only enough boats to hold a brigade. It was the turn of the depleted U.S. 36th Infantry Division to attempt to traverse the Rapido. The river was at its height, and the exhausted troops could not make it across. Neither the infantry nor engineers had coordinated their plans. An infuriated Clark demanded that they try again, but they failed once more. Over 1,000 men from the 36th Division died or were missing, and 600 were hurt in the first battle of Monte Cassino. The Allies turned to a new assault by landing troops at the port of Anzio just 30 miles south of Rome and targeting Cassino again.

There were high hopes for the U.S. VI Corps of Fifth Army under Major-General John Lucas. Achieving complete surprise on January 22, he sent in the 1st British Infantry Division and a British Commando Brigade north of Anzio. Supported by tanks and Ranger battalions, the U.S. 3rd Infantry Division landed in or south of the port. In all, a force of 36,000 Allied troops came ashore unopposed on the beaches. The Allies enjoyed control of the seas because of a flotilla of 378 ships, and the sizable Mediterranean Allied Tactical Air Force provided good air cover. In contrast, weak German naval forces relied on human torpedoes guided by one or two men sitting astride the tube and or in explosive boats who bailed out before impact. The defenders also hoped for harassing fire from the Luftwaffe, although this was not very effective during daytime. But even though the invaders met only four drunken German officers on shore and little enemy naval resistance, Lucas decided to dig in rather than move off the beaches into the mountains. Amphibious warfare doctrine called for hunkering down and the unimaginative Lucas adhered to his training. Such docility gave the Werhmacht time to mount a counterattack against Operation Shingle. Lucas counted on a buildup of materiel and men to consolidate his perimeter, but bad weather and Luftwaffe nighttime bombing (the Allies dominated the skies during the day) slowed the flow from ship to shore. The bomber raids, Lucas noted, were huge, and he worried about losing Anzio harbor and incurring more casualties.

Tarawa and Anzio shared a common characteristic: the invaders were not prepared for their enemy's skilled and determined defense. The difference was that at Anzio, the defenders did not contest the landings on the beaches but aimed to contain them in their perimeter. Theater commander Smiling Albert Kesselring quickly mustered six divisions into Fourteenth German Army under General Eberhard von Mackensen and sent it down from Rome to surround Lucas' forces. The Germans soon numbered 120,000 men. The Allies tried to break out in late January, but Mackensen ambushed two battalions of Rangers coming from Cisterna and inflicted 3,000 casualties on the U.S. 3rd Division. Aided by U.S. tanks, the British did a bit better in building a bulge toward Osteriaccia, but 2,100 were killed or injured in the effort. Cowed and worried by the response, Lucas withdrew to the defensive. The Germans wiped out the Osteriaccia salient, and Kesselring moved reinforcements around Aprilia to launch a counteroffensive. Thanks to ULTRA's pinpointing of tank movements around the Anzio line, the Allies had a chance. When Mackensen attacked on February 16, he was hit from the air and by concentrated artillery. The Allied perimeter held, and after suffering 5,389 casualties in four days, the Wehrmacht halted its assault. Two days later, Lucas was relieved of command, turning over VI Corps to his deputy, Major-General Lucian Truscott, veteran of the North African campaign. True to his dogged nature, Truscott resisted two more attacks but the Allies were stalled at Anzio.

Kesselring gave up on driving the Anzio beachhead into the sea, although he kept the Allies bottled up. Hitler wanted the invading force erased. He was unrealistic, yet the Germans enjoyed some success. A reinforced U.S. 6th Corps did not link up with the II Corps of Fifth Army until May 25, nearly three months later. In the meantime, Alexander had two static fronts to deal with, and his superiors chided him for siphoning off shipping from other theaters to the Italian front. In mid-February 1944, U.S. Secretary of War Henry Stimson hastily convened a press conference to quiet public outrage about the Anzio events. Alexander announced from Fifteenth Army Group headquarters that there was no basis for pessimism because the Germans had lost the battle. He had little reason to be so sanguine because on the beachhead, the view was much different. That Alexander asked reporters not to liken Anzio to Dunkirk spoke volumes about the dire situation.

The battle for Anzio cost the Allies 7,000 dead and over 36,000 injured or missing in action, while Germany lost 40,000 troops, including 5,000 killed. Shingle's objectives had never been confirmed. Alexander had expected Lucas to drive off the beaches into the Alban hills, cut German communication lines south of Rome, and help Fifth Army climb over the Gustav line. But a defensive mindset had evolved. Clark himself had to change his plans and try to save the Anzio perimeter. Designed to relieve Fifth Army, Anzio resulted in the opposite. When combined with the defeat at the first battle of Cassino, which caused 16,000 casualties in Fifth Army in exchange for just 7 miles of territory, Anzio was one of the Allies' biggest foul-ups of the so-called good war that led to the annihilation of an unexcusable number of men. Having endorsed the operation, Churchill now ridiculed it. Instead of a wildcat being hurled on shore, he complained, the Anzio mission had become a beached whale. The defense of Anzio was now embedded in three more battles for Cassino.

Alexander turned to the British command for help. Bernard Montgomery had departed for England to plan Operation Overlord—the invasion of France—in December 1943 and left General Oliver Leese in charge of Eighth Army. A skilled commander of XXX Corps during the Mediterranean theater campaigns, Leese tapped Bernard Freyberg's tough New Zealand Division to effect a breakthrough. A cunning commander who earned the respect of his troops for the failed but spirited defense on Crete in 1941, Freyberg first took aim on the Hitler Line, part of the Winter Line complex of defenses that included the Gustav Line.

Freyberg began the second battle of Cassino on February 15 by sending the New Zealanders against the town's railway station while the 4th Indian Division hit the sixth-century Benedictine Abbey at the top of Monte Cassino. The 4th Division's commander decided to destroy the monastery that overlooked the town. He believed that the Germans were using it as a fortress. Clark warned that its ruins could be used effectively as defensive positions, but Freyberg proceeded anyway with a tremendous artillery and aerial bombardment that destroyed the abbey. Not one enemy soldier was killed in the assault, although civilians who had taken refuge in the supposed sanctuary perished. Germany had promised the Vatican that the monastery would be avoided, and Berlin kept its word until the abbey was leveled. Then as Clark predicted, the Wehrmacht took advantage of the high ground by setting up observation posts in the rubble. Freyberg added to his woes by not coordinating the bombardment with ground operations. Fifth Army remained in place for an entire day and allowed the Germans to recover from the bombings. The four-day second Cassino battle ended like the first: an Allied embarrassment and a German success.

After bad weather delays, a month later the Allies began the third battle of Cassino on March 15, 1944. Once again massive bombardment preceded the assault by the New Zealand Division on the town and the 4th Indian Division attack on the mountain—this time below the abbey. The Germans still occupied their superb defensive position, however, and uncoordinated and unsupported ground movement beset the brave Allied troops once again. The huge bombing actually undermined their progress because it gave the defenders even more spots to hide. Despite air superiority, the Allies failed to interdict enemy lines of communications or root out German troops from the Gustav Line. The campaign in Italy was stalled.

The fourth and final battle of Cassino represented the last chance for the Allies to end the stalemate because resources would soon be shifted to the Normandy operation. Alexander finally had an operational goal: to destroy the German army south of Rome by smashing the Gustav Line and moving up the Liri Valley. A two-month breathing spell occurred between the third and fourth assaults on Cassino, the latter embedded in the overall Allied spring offensive to capture Rome called Operation Diadem. Alexander linked U.S. Fifth Army and British Eighth Army into a unified army group and then massed forces around Cassino and inside the Anzio perimeter. Troops from eight nations backed by 2,000 artillery pieces that unloosed a barrage of firepower began their attack on May 11. Meanwhile, the French Expeditionary Corps of Moroccans, Senegalese, Algerians, and metropolitan Frenchmen moved from the Garigliano River into the Aurunci mountains to blast the southern part of the Gustav Line. This was an unenviable assignment, but Clark—who had little respect for the French—sent them into the inhospitable terrain anyway. Remarkably, General Alphonse Juin's forces, spearheaded by the elite Mountain troops, successfully attacked the German rear and opened the way for the U.S. II Corps. Eighth Army's Indian and British troops then took the town of Cassino and moved into the Liri Valley. Leese sent Canadian troops in

New Zealanders assault Monte Cassino.   Credit: Center for the Study of War Experience at Regis University, Denver, Colorado.

XIII Corps spiraling up the Valley, and the British pushed into the Gustav Line farther north. Taking Monte Cassino would complete the breakthrough.

Leese ordered II Polish Corps to capture Monastery Hill. Members of this force had been released from Stalin's prison camps and joined the Allies. They met stiff resistance at Monte Cassino. Their first try resulted in the annihilation of two battalions. Every soldier was either killed or wounded. The next night the Poles took two parts of the hill, but the Germans remained on top. The violence was horrific. An American engineer came across three dead infantrymen. "They were killed by a shell concussion, skin on their face was burnt and rolled back, no eyelids or hair." Nearby a German helmet had "half a head still in it." By May 17, the Gustav Line was in trouble. German paratroopers withdrew from the abbey's ruins, though not before recording 3,500 Polish casualties. Not until 1969 did the Americans admit that the monastery at Monte Cassino had not been part of the Wehrmacht's defense plan. Its destruction remained controversial because of the loss of lives, so much so that the British suppressed an investigation of the bombardment for thirty years. The Allies, and especially the Poles, paid dearly for the bungling.

TO ROME

Still, the Gustav Line was no more, and Operation Diadem could point toward capturing Rome and ending the German occupation of Italy. Kesselring's reinforcements arrived too late to plug the breach. He hustled his troops back to the Hitler Line in the Liri Valley and then tried to bolster the Caesar Line in the Alban Hills. The Hitler defenses lasted five days until the British and Canadians overran it on May 23 and the Wehrmacht pulled out under harassment from fighter-bombers. Alexander then ordered the breakout on the Anzio beachhead by Eighth Army and its advance on Rome. The other half of Diadem required Clark's Fifth Army to attack the German rear around Valmontone west of the Alban Hills and just south of Rome and to round up Tenth German Army. The bold Truscott was ready to roll. On May 23, he exited Anzio with the U.S. VI Corps and closed in on ten enemy divisions near Valmontone.

With the conquest of Rome on his mind, the ambitious Clark butted in. This was still the Italian campaign, after all, where egos and organizational ineptitude got in the way of sound military practices. He focused on the glorious achievement of beating the British to the Eternal City. Instead of encircling Tenth Army as ordered, Clark had Truscott pivot and make a beeline for Rome. The Germans managed to hold him off in the Alban Hills for a week, stopping Truscott's momentum and separating him from Eighth Army. Enemy troops then escaped northward out of reach of the pincers and took up new positions on the Gothic Line that ran from Rimini on the Adriatic to Pisa. Alexander failed to pursue them three days after Rome's fall on June 4, 1944. By that time, attention as well as the logistical train had turned to the beaches of France. Clark's moment in the sun had lasted a few days. His capture of Rome, with its scant military value, became back-page news to the headlines of Operation Overlord.

Operation Diadem's goal of destroying the German army in Italy was in doubt. The Wehrmacht remained a potent force. Some historians believe that allowing Germany's retreat to the Gothic Line was the worst failure of the entire war for the Allies. The invaders advanced 200 miles up the Italian mainland and broke the Gustav Line, but the campaign left a bad taste in everyone's mouth. It prompted ill will among Anglo-American leaders who squabbled over responsibility for the destruction, the incompetence of command, and the missed opportunities. Although they forced Italy out of the war, the Allies lost 300,000 casualties including Poles, French, and Canadians sacrificed in the effort. The ruins of Monte Cassino caused much bad blood as did Alexander's poor leadership, Freyberg's mistakes, and Clark's showboating. U.S. Army Chief of Staff George Marshall called the Italian offensive an "expensive sideshow." He was correct in terms of the human costs and the deleterious effects the campaign had on inter-Allied relations.

Whether pushing back the Wehrmacht in Italy helped speed the end of Nazi terror is also debatable. Because of Allied pressure, the Germans oppressed the Italian population in a campaign of annihilation. They forced their puppet, Benito Mussolini, to round up Jews and partisans suspected of terrorist bombings against the SS. This was not the first time Italian Jews had been terrorized by the Germans. For example, over 1,200 Roman Jews were deported to Auschwitz in October 1943. In another case of the war of annihilation in March 1944, "Smiling Albert" Kesselring approved of an SS reprisal against 320 Italians murdered in the Ardeatine caves outside of Rome for killing 32 German policemen. This was but one instance of the Germans massacring civilians in Italy. In this theater, the idea of a good war actually resonates because the Allies had a moral justification for confronting Nazi evil waged on the population. Northern Italy continued to suffer from Hitler's tyranny, Il Duce's legacy, and Allied errors.

Long the stepchild of the European war, the Italian campaign became an orphan once the landings in western France took place. Even a secondary invasion along the Riviera in southern France took priority over Italy. Divisions were drained away from the Gothic Line to aid these French operations. The addition of six Italian battle groups in October 1944 had little effect, for the Italian government gave them few arms. Still, Alexander persevered. British Eighth Army began an offensive to trap Tenth Army in the Po River Valley. He had wanted to move on the Adriatic and Trieste then advance through the Alps to Vienna, but the loss of six divisions to the Normandy campaign cancelled those plans. The British believed that an assault on Vienna would have worked. This was nonsense because Germany would not have laid down in the highly defensible Alps. In any case, Alexander's remaining divisions failed in the Po valley. The east–west flow of the rivers impeded them. Reorganization took so long that autumn rains turned the terrain to mud. Eighth Army penetrated the Gothic Line north of Florence on September 3 and broke out to Romagna two weeks later before stalling. Once again, Leese plodded along, and Tenth Army took advantage by a swift counterattack. To make matters worse, Clark directed the U.S. 88th Infantry Division toward Bologna on September 10 in a futile try to outflank the city. Viewing Italy as a tertiary theater, the Combined Chiefs of Staff now ordered Alexander and Clark to keep an eye on the Wehrmacht in the Po Valley. This modest task occupied the Allies until April 1945. By that time the war in Europe was nearly over, and the Italian campaign was relegated to the history books.

Italy simply did not matter anymore because by the time the Allies began the process of tying down the Germans in the Po Valley, they believed the war was winding down in Europe. The Italian experience might have been negative, but in other theaters, the Axis powers were on the run. Besides, the Allies did not bank on the campaign in Italy to roll back the Third Reich on the ground. That would largely be the responsibility of the Soviet Union on the Eastern front beginning in early 1943, with the eventual assistance of the western nations the following year.

CHAPTER 18

Soviet Rout

> Your mother says to you: kill the German! Your children beg
> of you: kill the German! Your country groans and whispers:
> kill the German! Don't miss him! Don't let him escape! Kill!
>
> ILYA EHRENBURG IN CATHERINE MERRIDALE
> *Night of Stone: Death and Memory in*
> *Twentieth Century Russia*

ROUT ON THE EASTERN FRONT

As their allies discussed operations around the world, the Soviets moved from their monumental victory at Stalingrad to a multifront offensive against German forces in early 1943. Despite massive losses of men, their momentum appeared unstoppable, and their ability to answer Germany's strategy of annihilation with one of their own once they drove out the Nazis from the USSR and pushed westward through Poland and the Third Reich appeared a reality. In the north, at the expense of about 250,000 casualties, the Russians pried open a corridor to besieged Leningrad in January. The passageway was a most tenuous link. Enemy artillery remained 500 yards away, and only 76 trains slipped through the corridor. Yet the USSR built up forces to smash the blockade. In the center, the Wehrmacht retreated from Rzhev. Fighting was most ferocious in the south where the German position was no more advanced than it was a year before. The Soviets enjoyed a four-to-one manpower edge; Lend-Lease aid and their own factories were pouring weapons and supplies into various fronts, and Anglo-American bombing of the Third Reich diverted an increasing number of Luftwaffe forces from the Eastern front. By 1943, the USSR had accelerated the output of aircraft of all types—bombers, fighters, ground attack—and their pilots became more skilled. Included were hundreds of women who flew over 30,000 combat and support missions during the war.

Within weeks, however, the Wehrmacht had recovered. Clever leadership, skillful maneuvering, and a spoiling campaign offset their logistical inferiority. And Hitler brooked no defeatism. Unlike his generals, who hoped for a stalemate at best, he would not back out of the USSR without a fight. In his mind, the Fuhrer saw distinct possibilities for renewing the glory days of 1941. Thus, the German effort continued in the face of the Soviet advance. South-West *front* commander Nikolai Vatutin, a master of encirclement, failed to trap Army Group Don in the Donets Basin in mid-February 1943 but his forces and the Voronezh army group spanned the river north and west of Stavyansk by that time. Pressuring Army Group South, the Voronezh *front* took Kursk on February 8, Kharkov a week later, and by February 18 neared the Dnieper River. Hitler ordered three SS panzer divisions to hold Kharkov. Knowing this meant suicide, they refused and broke out to the south 115 miles before joining up with Hermann Hoth's Fourth Panzer Army. Under Hoth they turned around and reached Kharkov on March 9 as the terrain thawed.

Hitler decided to attach Second Army to Army Group Center and refashion Army Group South by removing Army Group B from its command. In charge of a 280-mile front between Belgorod and the Sea of Azov, Erich Manstein took over Army Group South. Because the 180-mile section from Belgorod to the north of Taganrog was weakly defended by the Russians, he set a trap. Manstein drew on panzer divisions, 100,000 troops flown from the Crimea, and the services of Hoth who was a skilled tactician of mobile warfare. When the Russians attempted to clear out the Orel and Briansk areas, Army Group Center held. To the south, the Soviet offensives marched beyond the reach of air support and right into Manstein's arms. The XL Panzer Corps surrounded A.F. Popov's army group on February 20 and although Popov pulled out some units, he lost a large amount of men and materiel. With First Panzer Army guarding his flank, Hoth then turned toward Kharkov to secure the Donets basin. He moved Fourth Panzer Army north of the Mius River to Dnepropetrovsk and Kharkov. The SS Totenkopf panzer division captured forces south of the Samara River while Hoth drove northeast. Blitzkrieg had returned. Mobile Wehrmacht forces swept up toward Kharkov, catching the Soviets by surprise. Hoth ordered the panzers around (and not into) the city but II SS Panzer Corps commander Paul Hausser disobeyed to make amends for the earlier retreat. Three days of house-to-house fighting ensued until Kharkov fell to the Germans on March 15, 1943. Thirty miles away, Hausser avoided a court martial by taking Belgorod in just four hours. The Red Army had been badly prepared, and paid a steep price, whereas the Luftwaffe performed brilliantly. This was the last time in the war German aircraft dominated Soviet skies, although the Luftwaffe lost 653 bombers and fighters. As the mud reached flood levels, Manstein ended the counteroffensive on a high note.

KURSK

Encouraged, Hitler went ahead with plans to eliminate the Soviet hold on the Kursk salient—or bulge, by using Kharkov as a staging area for the southern side of the pincer. His generals cautioned against another summer offensive because an Allied invasion of either France or the Mediterranean area seemed viable before the year was out. The Combined Bomber Offensive had also undermined the war effort. Some German strategists recommended a defensive posture on the Eastern front. Neither Hitler nor his sycophantic senior officers wished to sit, however, to await an attack by overwhelming Red Army forces. Manstein suggested letting the Soviets launch an offensive against Army Group South before responding, but the Fuhrer refused to lose more ground. When Manstein opted for encirclement of the Kursk salient, Hitler agreed. A quick and decisive victory at Kursk might give Stalin pause about further offensives that summer and might also allow Germany to seize the initiative on one part of the Eastern front and win a significant tactical victory. Yet weeks of debate allowed the Russians time to build up their defenses. To the north, Konstantin Rokossovsky, who had terminated the Stalingrad pocket, shifted his staff and an army by train to the Kursk area. He joined

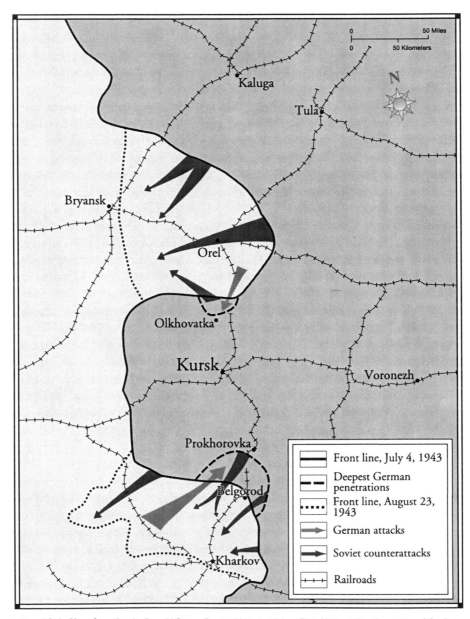

Map 18.1 Kursk.   Credit: Ronald Story, *Concise Historical Atlas of World War II: The Geography of Conflict,* Map 19, p. 43.

other forces into a Central *front* that targeted Smolensk. The thaw slowed him down, however, and on March 1, the Wehrmacht further complicated matters. Recognizing that attaining Moscow was no longer possible, Hitler withdrew Army Group Center from the huge Rzhev salient (about the size of East Prussia) west to a line from Velizh to Kirov. This freed up enough troops and armor to block Rokossovsky's advance. Now both German and Soviet forces lay exposed in bulges that both sought to exploit.

Three bulges—two German ones sandwiching a Soviet salient—catalyzed Stalin to act. Army Group Center sat on a front south of Kirov that extended eastward into a salient north of Orel. Central and Voronezh army groups occupied a bulge south of Orel around the railway center of Kursk. Farther south, Army Group South held a line from Belgorod to Kharkov. The Russians were squeezed. But Soviet military leaders saw an opportunity to strike the Orel salient with Operation Kutuzov and batter the Belgorod-Kharkov line with Operation Rumyantsev. Both would wedge open the German lines so that the Red Army could begin its first summer offensive. Access to good intelligence on enemy plans fueled their optimism. Also, young but combat-tested commanders, such as Rokossovsky and Vatutin, had emerged during the previous slugging matches on the Eastern Front to lead the effort. For Operation Kutuzov, they had 1.3 million soldiers, 3,400 tanks and assault guns, and 2,100 aircraft. The T-34 tank dominated their arsenal; its 250-mile range allowed it to avoid having to stop to refuel. Rokossovsky had three armies on the northern side of the Kursk *front* and Georgi Zhukov told him to hold the line or risk returning to the Gulag jails where he had resided in 1940. Vatutin commanded the Voronezh *front* of four armies with a fifth available if needed. Ivan Konev's Steppe *front* of five armies stayed in reserve. Zhukov decided to let the Germans make the first move, and then he would overwhelm them with fourteen armies in five army groups arranged in six belts—each with three to five trenches and wire—ringing the bulge and backed by another *front* of six Stavka reserve armies. He also had a million mines to bolster field fortifications. This was the most massive battlefield arrangement of forces and fortifications ever seen—dwarfing those of World War I.

On his side, a jittery but opportunistic Adolf Hitler planned Operation Citadel. Army Group Center's shortened front gave Ninth Army under Walther Model a chance to move south of Orel and encircle the Soviet's Kursk bulge. Fourth Panzer Army and Army Detachment Kempf would close from the south. Citadel involved 700,000 troops, 2,300 tanks, thousands of assault guns, and 1,800 aircraft. The Germans were outnumbered, so Hitler delayed the operation until Fourth Panzer Army had three new SS divisions. These were the first units to possess the 45-ton Panther, a superbly mobile but sufficiently armed (75-mm gun) tank, and the huge, heavily armored, and slow Tiger tanks. The Panther was Germany's answer to the Russian T-34, although not produced in such volume as the Soviet tank. Hitler hoped to intimidate the USSR with a big blitzkrieg assault not only to secure victory but to free some of the more than 3 million troops from the Eastern front for transit to the expected invasion of Europe in the west. Both sides sought their aims through a strategy of annihilation—to obliterate their opponent. Hitler obliged Stalin's willingness to await a German move. He lacked his usual bravado when he confessed to Guderian that just thinking of Operation Citadel made him sick to his stomach. Yet true to form, the Fuhrer determined to strike the first blow and undercut enemy preparations. In defiance of his generals, he also refused to trade terrain for Red Army soldiers. On July 5, 1943, Hitler gave the go-ahead for the beginning of the largest single battle in world history.

The Wehrmacht attacked, and by the second day, Model's three panzer corps nearly made the village of Okhavatka, a third of the way to Kursk, but Ninth Army came up short of Rokossovsky's third line of defense bolstered with reserves, Second Tank Army, and a tank corps. A slugfest ensued. German generals had dreaded such a development, and Model knew he had no chance. By July 9, he told Gunther von Kluge, the commander of Army Group Center, that Kursk was out of reach. Three days later, Kluge had to shore up Ninth Army's rear by taking two panzer divisions and artillery and rocket launchers from Model. From the south, the strong pincer movement under Hoth targeted Oboyan, halfway to Kursk. He attacked west of the Donets River with two panzer corps and the Kempf detachment. This surprised Vatutin, who had deployed east of the river. Although outnumbered, Hoth gained 12 miles in two days but then ran into the second line of defense. Vatutin recovered, but the II SS Panzer Corps crossed the last trench line on July 12 and ended up only 22 miles southeast of Oboyan when it met the Fifth Soviet Guards Tank Army. The elite Grossdeutschland Panzer Grenadiers lost 230 of its 300 tanks. Drawing on the Steppe army group, Vatutin launched a counterattack in this battle of Kursk that became the largest tank engagement in history until the Persian Gulf War of 1991, and the biggest in terms of tank losses until the battle for the Golan Heights in the Arab-Israeli War of 1973.

Over 1,200 tanks—three-quarters of them Soviet—sparred relentlessly during the day. The panzers did much damage, but the Red Army had numbers in its favor, and German tanks proved vulnerable. The Panther broke down and burned easily, and even the huge Tiger's defensive armament could not withstand the pounding of artillery. The T-34 was a well-equipped tank that maneuvered effectively in the mud. The Russians also adopted a deadly technique of having infantrymen climb on the Tigers and drop grenades into the hatches or blast flamethrowers into the vents. In addition, Soviet artillery unleashed an unceasing bombardment. At the end of the day, 400 Soviet tanks were out of action while Manstein lost 320. But the Russians were on their home turf; they could repair some of the tanks in shops on their own territory.

The ferocity of the engagement was inconceivable. "Every valley is bursting with artillery and infantry," reported a Red Army officer. "The nights are just an endless roar. Our aviation is working near the limit of the first defense lines. There's a mass of tanks." The Soviets had urgency on their side: they faced the collapse of their homeland. Thus, they unleashed a torrent of fire into the air. But the Wehrmacht reciprocated. A Russian air attack had preceded the tank duel, which left the ground littered with twisted machines and charred remains of soldiers. The rain came down in the unusually cool summer days, but veterans remembered "the inferno of burning metal, burning fuel and rubber, burning air." Those in antitank battalions felt lucky because their losses were light relative to infantry who died from gunfire, tanks, or planes. There were innumerable ways to die at Kursk. Tanks ironed over trenches where infantrymen crouched, and crushed the soldiers. In another case, a wounded officer—his hand torn

Soviets advancing at Kursk.   Credit: Center for the Study of War Experience at Regis University, Denver, Colorado.

off—aimed a battery against an oncoming German tank until it halted. Then he shot himself, not wishing to live as a cripple for the rest of his life. As Panthers and Tigers advanced on a village, the Luftwaffe killed or injured every Soviet soldier in a battery except for one. A commander of a nearby gun instructed the few remaining soldiers to open fire on the German machine gunners "at point–blank range with armour-piercing shells. That was a terrible sight," wrote a Russian war journalist.

The Kursk battle was another turning point on the Eastern front and in the world war as a whole for that matter. An equilibrium had characterized the Soviet–German war in the first half of 1943 yet now the scales tipped in Stalin's favor. As the tanks pounded away, the Allies broke out of the beachheads on Sicily and prompted Hitler to lose interest in the Kursk melee. On July 13, he decided to remove the elite II SS Panzer Corps, which he thought better than 20 Italian divisions, and ship them to Italy to meet the Anglo-American landing. In Sicily, the USSR, and the Atlantic, Germany was simply overstretched and had hard decisions to make. To Manstein's dismay, the Fuhrer called off Operation Citadel and removed more troops from the theater, and within ten days, the Germans had retreated to their two bulges while the Soviets initiated a counteroffensive on the Orel protrusion and the Karkhov salient. The Russians lost over 900,000 casualties and 6,000 tanks, but they had stopped a Wehrmacht summer offensive for the first time in three years. Germans died by the tens of thousands. The Third Reich lost valuable pilots and tank crews and the panzers never fully recovered because factories could not replace tanks in sufficient numbers to reach their previous strength. Kursk went down in history as the grave-yard of the German panzer armies, but it was also a cemetery of Hitler's dreams for lebensraum in the East.

PUNCHING WESTWARD

Deep down, Hitler understood the Eastern front was lost. His Kursk offensive had not budged the Soviets and the USSR now enjoyed a windfall of men and materiel. By Summer 1943, the Red Army outnumbered the Wehrmacht by over 2.7 million, its tanks more than tripled the panzers, and Stalin enjoyed a 13,000 antitank gun edge. Lend-Lease aid had provided much-needed logistical support and allowed Moscow to focus on producing weapons. By war's end, Lend-Lease shipments of 11,800 locomotives and railroad cars, 409,000 cargo trucks, and 47,000 jeeps (roughly half of the number in each category had reached the Red Army by the time of Citadel) proved a boon. In the last analysis, the particularly brutal brand of Soviet tactics proved decisive. The Russians could afford tactical mistakes and callous disregard for human life, but the Wehrmacht had no such margin of error. And now, with large reserve armies near the fronts, the Red Army prepared its own offensives.

The Germans could only react to the Soviet initiative. Given command of the Second Panzers as well as Ninth Army, Model restored order to the Orel bulge. Model's talents lay in defense, and he matched the Soviets until July 25, when Hitler warned Army Group Center that 24 divisions would be sent to Italy after Mussolini's fall from power. This prompted Model to abandon Orel. He orchestrated a phased two-week retreat to the north side of the salient on August 1. Zhukov decided to look elsewhere for vulnerabilities, choosing Kharkov, the northern anchor of the German line in Ukraine. On August 3, 1943, fourteen armies with 1.5 million troops began Operation Rumyantsev. Trying to wrest himself from Zhukov's, shadow, Konev sent the four armies of his Steppe *front* against Kharkov. A few days of hard fighting preceded the breakthrough in the German lines and the recapture of Belgorod by Vatutin. When Manstein pleaded for permission to withdraw because he lacked reserves to plug the gaps, Hitler refused him. He dispatched the Grossdeutschland Panzer Grenadiers and the 7th Panzer Division from Army Group Center to help out and delayed the departure for Italy of the Das Reich and Totenkopf SS Panzer Divisions. But the Red Army widened the hole around Kharkov and poured an entire army group through it. Counterattacks failed; Hitler told the Kempf Detachment to hold the city anyway. This was simply beyond the unit's capacity. On August 22, 1943, Vatutin liberated Kharkov.

Bursting with confidence, Josef Stalin mocked Nazi assumptions that the USSR could not accomplish a summer offensive. Indeed, things looked glum for Germany. Once Model and Manstein had retreated from Orel and Kharkov, Stalin prohibited encirclements, instead demanding frontal "cleaving blows" to destroy the enemy. These wore down, but did not defeat, the Germans. The Wehrmacht was vulnerable everywhere, however. Hitler refused more retreats in the face of constant pressure on one flank or area to another. Such shifting tactics prevented the Germans from getting a firm footing and counterattacking in a concerted way. By the end of August 1943, eight Soviet army groups opened nineteen parallel thrusts along a line 662 miles long from Nevel to Taganrog against Army Groups Center and South. The going was tough against Army Group North and Center because the Germans fought behind well-prepared lines, and Soviet breakthroughs oftentimes turned into death traps as German troops and bombers struck back at Red Army flanks. Russians remember advancing and then retreating amidst the "putrid odor of decay—the eternal concomitant to death" of decomposing bodies.

Yet the USSR inexorably moved forward. The Central *front* progressed toward Kiev by mid-September while Manstein faced problems on his left flank as First Panzer Army and Sixth Army lost ground on the open steppe. So powerful was the advance west of Kursk and Kharkov by XXIII Tank Corps and I Guards Mechanized Corps that on September 8, Hitler permitted a withdrawal behind the Dnieper River. The retreat was too late. Army Group South's weakened state demoralized the troops and prevented an organized defensive posture. The troops could cross the Dnieper at just five bridges, and the Red Army raced to cut them off at all of them between October and

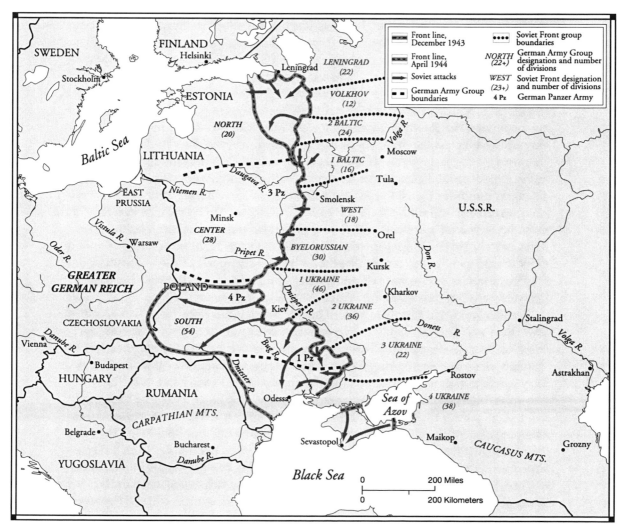

Map 18.2 Soviet offensives, 1943–44. Credit: Ronald Story, *Concise Historical Atlas of World War II: The Geography of Conflict*, Map 20, p. 45.

early December 1943. The First Ukrainian *front* beat Army Group South to Kiev, and the Second Ukrainian army group held Cherkassy, Kremenchug, and Dnepropetrovsk. Petrified German troops swam the river or were crushed by the tanks that ran through their ranks. Still, the northern Dnieper front was calm into November.

By December, Army Group Center had lost the entire southern half of the Dnieper salient as well as Smolensk. Both Army Group A and Seventeenth Army were isolated far to the south. When Stalin attended his first summit at Teheran, he had the Eastern front in hand, as he and his military advisors just had to decide where to attack next. Hitler, meanwhile, stewed on the implications of the impending invasion of France. The Fuhrer determined to contest the Soviets once again, but the Allied landings in Normandy immediately threatened key industrial centers. The distances required to fight on both sides were daunting. It was 375 miles from Normandy to Germany and 700 miles from Kiev to Berlin. The Third Reich could afford to divert resources from Soviet battlefields and lose some territory gained during Barbarossa, the Fuhrer reasoned, to buy time to focus on the Western Allies. But the Red Army was not about to allow the Germans the luxury of a slow and fitful retreat.

In the center, north, and south of the USSR, the Germans faced a colossal power. In the south, Manstein solidified his right flank and then temporarily blocked a Soviet breakout from the Bukrin bridgehead toward Kiev. The Red Army liberated the city but only after an assault from the swamps drowned many soldiers in their tanks. On January 27, 1944, Leningrad was liberated. Over one million inhabitants had perished in the siege of annihilation. Hitler refused to let Eighteenth Army retreat to a 117-mile defensive line from the Narva River to Lake Pskov, allowing the Russians to wreak havoc on Army Group North. At the end of the month, Model took charge. True to form, he pulled off a brilliant withdrawal to the line until spring mud halted operations, but the Soviets had returned to Estonia at a cost to Eighteenth Army of 31,000 of its 58,000 men. In the center, three army groups attempted to push westward, but they made just minor headway from January into March 1944. The now indefensible Dnieper River line loomed as the Wehrmacht's biggest problem.

Stalin's forces had already recovered half of the lands the Third Reich had occupied since June 1941 and the dictator determined to eradicate the Wehrmacht completely from his homeland's pre-1939 borders. Moscow decided to focus the main effort in Ukraine where four army groups enjoyed overwhelming superiority in men and arms. They would also keep the road open in the north to East Prussia and in the center to Poland and Germany to prepare for a march into the Third Reich itself. The Wehrmacht still had 26 panzer divisions with 2,300 tanks, 2.5 million soldiers and 700,000 from allied nations, and 3,000 aircraft, and so the Germans could put up a fight. They also remained convinced of their infallibility. But the numbers did not lie. The USSR possessed 6.4 million Red Army troops, 5,800 tanks, and 13,400 planes. Manstein continued to delude himself that the Wehrmacht could launch spearheads at will into Ukraine. The profound penetration of Nazi race-based hatred of communism—backed by severe punishment in case of disobedience—explained why Manstein kept his troops trained on their enemy, however futile the gesture.

The four Ukrainian army groups were plagued with problems, but their advance continued. Freezing and thawing limited movement, even though the Red Army had the famous two and a half ton all-wheel drive trucks—the American "deuce-and-a-half" vehicles—by this time. Yet man-made problems of disorganization and timing, as well as German acumen, stalled the southern offensive. Despite Zhukov's skills, his oversight of the First Ukrainian *front* did not result in coordination with the Second Ukrainian army group under Konev. The former attacked on December 24, but Konev's *front* could not get started until two weeks later. After the Third and Fourth Ukrainian army groups tried to launch their offensives on January 10, 1944, both halted the next day to reorganize over the next three weeks. Manstein's counterattacks failed nonetheless. On January 24, Konev finally broke through at Korsun-Shevchenkovskii and linked with Vatutin early the next month, trapping the Germans in the Cherkassy pocket on the Dnieper River. Zhukov won Stalin's approval to return to the policy of encirclement and the nihilistic, arrogant Hitler seemed amenable because he refused to let Manstein withdraw and reconstitute on the Bug River. In the Cherkassy pocket between Soviet bridgeheads, six German divisions were encircled by Konev and Vatutin. Some 30,000 soldiers broke out on February 17, some were captured and others escaped by swimming the icy Tikich River where many of them drowned. The pocket's main features were aptly named. "Hell's Gate" opened on to the "Valley of Death." In spite of the breakout, German officers lamented the insane orders to halt and hold the pocket in the first place. In the words of one, the operation "was unimaginable and simply irreplaceable, considering the men and materiel we lost by stubbornly sustaining positions and so-called 'strongholds' since Stalingrad." The Wehrmacht simply did not have the strength to counterpunch the Red Army.

By the end of February 1944, the four *fronts* readied to advance despite the inclement winter weather. The Soviets began a massive assault that caused the Germans to back away. Part of the Fourth Ukrainian army group drove on the Crimea where the Germans still held Sevastopol after withdrawing across the straits from the Taman Peninsula. First and Second Ukrainian *fronts* began their spring offensive on March 5 with parallel thrusts led by three tank armies each. They sent the reconstituted Sixth Army reeling backward to avoid being cut off between the Dniester and Bug Rivers. T-34 tanks proved matchless in frozen or muddy terrain. Their wide tracks and center of gravity in the middle provided excellent mobility compared to the Panthers and Tigers. Momentum was sustained by the mobile U.S.-made trucks that whisked supplies to the T-34 spearheads. By March 1944, the Wehrmacht lacked reserves to stop the Soviets; Manstein cobbled together defensive lines nonetheless. Zhukov countered with a constant flow of reinforcements. Sixtieth and First Guards Armies broke through at Staro Constantinov and sealed off the German LIX Corps. Three armies hit the invaders north of Uman and took the city. When Konev tried to join Zhukov and encircle the left wing of Army Group South, Manstein withdrew southward to the Bug River. He left much of his equipment in the mud. Zhukov hit with another spearhead between Tornopol and Proskurov on March 21. This drove 200 tanks through the German lines and separated First and Fourth Panzer Armies. Hitler wanted Manstein to hold the "fortress" of Tornopol, but Konev and Zhukov were on the brink of wiping out First Panzer Army.

On March 25, Manstein broke out after confronting Hitler. Two SS panzer divisions—the Hohenstaufen and Frundsberg—and two army divisions were rushed in from the western front. Manstein retreated aided by a blizzard that shielded his movements. First Panzer Army attacked to the rear while watching over its shoulder for the Soviets. Zhukov did not act fast enough to prevent the Germans from crossing the Seret River, and by April 10, the two SS divisions had come to the rescue. First Panzer Army was safe. Outraged by the constant retreats, Hitler replaced Manstein with Nazi tough-guy Model and Kleist gave way to Ferdinand Schorner, a ruthless commander of mountain troops in the Balkans, Crete, and Norway. He then renamed Army Group South and A as Army Group North and South Ukraine, respectively. Yet the reorganization could not disguise the fact that the Germans were in deep trouble. The troops knew it. Oftentimes they moved at night because to escape or advance during the daytime against Soviet tanks was suicide, and killing from sniper bullets was merciless. A Wehrmacht officer remembered the agonizing pleas of injured infantrymen out in the open fields as his unit waited for orders to move. He could not help without being blown to "pieces across a veritable shooting gallery." Russian tanks with infantry riding on them moved toward the calls for help and condemned the Germans to observe while their friends were annihilated. It was a "terrible ordeal."

By mid-April 1944, the new commanders confronted a Soviet line that reached from the Pripet marshes to the Carpathian foothills, and from the lower Dniester to the Crimea. The Red Army waited to attack in the Crimea until April 7, but Schorner did not put much value in the area. Hitler did, however, because he feared that the USSR would convert the Crimea into an air base to bomb Romanian oil fields, even though the Americans had already targeted the wells in March from Italy. The Fuhrer demanded a firm defense by the Wehrmacht and by the seven Romanian divisions that the heretofore pro-Nazi dictator Ion Antonescu wanted withdrawn to save his regime from revolution. After the Red Army overran Romanian and German bridgeheads, Schorner removed the defense lines to Sevastopol. Hitler told him to hold out for six weeks or so until the Allied landings in France had been rebuffed. That invasion did not come until June 1944, but the stand at Sevastopol lasted until May 12. A disastrous evacuation followed. Attacked by Soviet torpedo boats and submarines, 27 ships and barges went to the bottom and some 8,000 soldiers drowned. About 130,000 German and Romanian troops escaped to safety, but 78,000 were killed or taken prisoner. Within months, Soviet submarines had control of the western Black Sea, USSR's southern flank was clear of enemy troops, and the Red Army readied for an invasion of Romania and the Balkans. Romanians were so angry over the rout at Sevastopol that they rose up against the Hitlerite Antonescu a few months later.

The withdrawal did not change Hitler's thinking on the eve of Overlord, the Allied invasion of France. The Soviets had advanced westward to within miles of the post-1939 Polish border, but they were still 560 miles from Berlin in May 1944. By that time, the Fuhrer's attention turned to the Atlantic front. Having sent ten panzer divisions to the west for refitting to await the Normandy invasion and only two to the USSR, he predicted that Moscow would continue to target Ukraine in an effort to control the Balkans. The Wehrmacht accordingly reconstituted its forces in the region. Besides, the Red Army still suffered from operational problems with tanks against Army Groups Center and North. Thus, the Germans believed that Stalin would look southward for territorial and political gains and leave the Third Reich's fate to his Anglo-American allies. This freed Hitler to confront the Normandy invasion but it was clear that Germany faced crises on both sides.

By June 1944, calculations for defeating the Third Reich and the Empire of Japan had turned into actual equations on the fields and seas of battle. In bloody battle after battle, the Soviet Red Army had inched its way westward and sent the Germans reeling. The killing time in Italy had resulted in a last stand for the Nazis north of Rome. In Asia and the Pacific, Japan's imperial domains were contracting everywhere except eastern China. Turning points had been reached and the Allies were the beneficiaries. The war across the globe now centered on the pace of rolling back the Axis powers.

CHAPTER 19

Western European Front

We make war on Hitler. As we must. But millions get in the
way and die for the Fuhrer.

SCOTT TUROW
Ordinary Heroes

THE ATLANTIC WALL

The Allies exalted over the victories around the world, but at long last their western
front in Europe was near a reality. Since the Casablanca talks of 1943, planning proceeded for Operation Overlord—the liberation of northwestern Europe. The landings
across the English Channel were called Operation Neptune, which fell under the larger
Overlord umbrella. Overlord was a tremendously complex affair that tested Allied leadership, organization, resolve, and execution. Much of the operation involved a "war of
the accountants" to ensure the logistical side of the assault went as smoothly as the
combat itself. Bureaucratic obstacles, political constraints, competition from other theaters, and training problems risked undermining the entire mission. For example, just
one-twelfth of the tank-landing vessels were ready by late April 1944 because priorities
elsewhere sapped the rest away. Contrary to the mythology about Overlord, merely the
possession of superior resources did not guarantee success for the Allies. Nevertheless,
during the first part of 1944, 1.3 million U.S. troops and a huge amount of landing craft,
tanks, trucks, weapons, and other materiel poured into southern England in preparation for the opening of the western front.

By February 1944, Eisenhower brought his genius for mediation to bear as the
head of Overlord's unified command at Supreme Headquarters Allied Expeditionary
Force (SHAEF) in England. His skilled chief of staff, Walter Bedell Smith, ran SHAEF's
diplomatic and civil affairs while amiable Arthur Tedder organized the air units as
deputy SHAEF commander. Three other British leaders showed Ike's mastery of personnel matters. Monty oversaw the land forces. Trafford Leigh-Mallory, advocate of
the Big Wing tactic during the battle of Britain, ran the air campaign. And Bertram
Ramsay, the heroic commander at Dunkirk and a veteran of the Sicilian campaign,

Bradley, Eisenhower, and Major General Ira Wyche in Normandy.   Credit: Center for the Study of War Experience at Regis University, Denver, Colorado: U.S. National Archives.

directed forces at sea. Their command was not seamless. Even Eisenhower's American subordinates—the biting Bedell Smith, the dour former infantryman Omar Bradley, and the flamboyant Patton—could be ornery. But Ike worked hard to smooth over the differences.

The biggest decision centered on the landing spot for the invasion across the English Channel. The invasion of Sicily had put more men ashore than required by Overlord, but beefing up the beachhead to support about 40 divisions moving inland through France was the question. Normandy's Pas de Calais of Boulogne, Calais, and Dunkirk offered the shortest crossing to the Low Countries and France, but the Germans could reach these easily. The beaches had to be within range of aircraft cover (one of the lessons from the disastrous Dieppe episode) yet far enough away from Germany to make a rapid response and reinforcement difficult. There also had to be a major port for logistical support. Planners chose the Baie de la Seine between Le Havre and Cherbourg, the latter in Brittany. Both were big ports that bookended a series of beaches bounded by rocky headlands. These beaches were not totally safe for landing, but the Allies decided to bring along their own artificial harbors called Mulberries to compel the Wehrmacht to defend in multiple places. Good road networks ran behind the beaches to allow for lateral movement to link the various landing sites into a consolidated beachhead. Going ashore down the coast might also trick Hitler into thinking a larger invasion was coming at the Pas de Calais and thus freeze some of his forces.

Scheduling and secrecy were crucial to Operation Neptune's success. Because the operation required such enormous resources, a concurrent invasion of southern France was delayed until August 1944 and the date for Normandy was moved from May 1 to early June. In addition, the size, the complexity of the operations, and intimidating German defenses necessitated a dawn landing to ensure bombing support in daylight hours. The landing craft had to unload at low tide whereas paratroopers required a full moon. The calendar showed a convergence of those conditions between June 5 and 7 but bad weather pushed Neptune to June 6. Also, surprise was critical. The Germans could mass forces against the invaders if they knew the time and place of the landings. Strict security guidelines were imposed. Only authorized personnel traveled within a coastal belt in southern England. Couriers did not leave or enter the country. Diplomatic communications were limited to the Americans, British, Soviets, and the Polish exile government in London.

The Germans anticipated an invasion, but deception kept them guessing between the real landings and the diversionary ones. A unit of SHAEF orchestrated a series of feints and ploys to fool the Wehrmacht into thinking that the Normandy landing was phony. Developed after years of practice with visual and audio tricks, this was the most intricate Allied ruse of the war. Patton's notional U.S. First Army Group stationed in Kent and Essex served as a phantom force headed for the beaches south of Boulogne. Erwin Rommel would tend to think that nobody but the great Patton, who stationed dummy landing craft around his bases, could lead the invasion. As a result of using Patton as a decoy, German Fifteenth Army stayed out of Normandy for a time. Successful bombings of transportation lines that hindered enemy movement and prior German decisions not to react to the Normandy invasion were other reasons that the Wehrmacht did not react quickly to the invasion. The Wehrmacht kept its forces on the right bank of the Seine, expecting the Allies to fight there, and thus did not bolster its thin Normandy defenses until too late. The Germans continued to fall for Patton's fake operation and they experienced troop transfer delays even when Overlord was well underway.

The Germans faced strategic dilemmas as well. Neither Gerd von Rundstedt, the Commander-in-Chief West, nor Rommel who transferred from Italy to energize the defense of the Atlantic Wall with Army Group B had full control over land, naval, and air forces from Brittany to the Zuider Zee. The two also argued over ways to counter the landings. They disputed whether the Atlantic Wall of coastal fortifications that stretched for 1,670 miles from Denmark to Spain could hold back the Allies. These defenses of gun batteries, bunkers, observations towers, and radar stations had blocked the Dieppe raid. But could they stop a massive invasion at an unknown location? And could they do so while the Allies enjoyed air supremacy?

The conventional Rundstedt thought not, yet the daring Rommel saw no other option but to meet Overlord on the beaches. Rundstedt believed that the Atlantic Wall would be overrun, and therefore opted for holding a mobile force in reserve to counterattack with a maximum force in a decisive battle once the Allies were ashore. Waiting was not in the repertoire of either the Desert Fox or Hitler, however. In North Africa, Rommel had experienced Allied air power's destructive capacity on troop movements.

Therefore, he doubted that substantial forces would be able to maneuver freely against the invaders. Like the Fuhrer, Rommel preferred to prevent the landings at the Atlantic Wall itself. The decisive battle must occur as the Allies tried to make it to shore—"the longest day" he argued—or all was lost. But Hitler decided the debate in neither general's favor because he thought the invasion would come at the Pas de Calais. Thus, he held back the reserves contrary to Rommel's advice but did release them when Rundstedt needed them. As a result, Hitler crippled Germany's readiness and response to Overlord. Some historians believe that the high command had already determined that Normandy was a lost battle anyway, and that the Wehrmacht should make its stand behind the Seine.

In any case, Rommel focused on bolstering the Atlantic Wall. To hinder the landing craft in the shallows, he dug in a collection of beach obstacles. These included wooden poles embedded in the sand, steel beams welded to form by Xs and rigged with mines, and Element C or "Belgian Gates"—steel structures used as antitank barriers. He built thousands of bunkers and put "Rommel asparagus" or poles in fields to spear gliders. Log barriers and concrete emplacements would further impede the Allies. German Fifteenth Army in northern France and Seventh Army in Normandy received an infusion of troops by the end of May, and Rommel interlocked them into a network of concentrated firepower. The Germans counted 58 divisions: 25 on coastal defenses, 16 infantry and parachute, ten armored and mechanized, and seven in reserve. The force represented the best of the Wehrmacht's operational abilities of small-unit initiative, combined arms, mobility, and defensive technology. Yet there were weaknesses. Half of the divisions were training or coast units with little mobility. The German Third Air Fleet in France had only 319 aircraft available (although the numbers soon tripled to over a thousand) because the Soviet and Italian campaigns had decimated the Luftwaffe. To boot, the weak German Navy was another limitation. It had just four destroyers in Atlantic ports as well as 30 E-boats (small, fast torpedo craft that took their toll on invading troops during an Allied preinvasion rehearsal and later menaced the beachheads) and 39 submarines in the vicinity after the battle of the Atlantic. No matter the potent aspects of the Atlantic Wall; Rommel and Rundstedt also lacked intelligence as to where the landings would occur. The Germans were at a major disadvantage.

OVERLORD

As Rommel made adjustments, the Allies claimed control of the skies. British Bomber Command and the Eighth USAAF went on more than 200,000 missions over France from April to early June 1944. Some 11,000 aircraft bombed railways and roads, airfields, installations, industrial plants, and coastal defenses including radar posts. While almost 2,000 planes were shot down, the two-month torrent of 195,000 tons of bombs disrupted communications and supply routes as the Wehrmacht tried to rush reinforcements up to the coast. The attacks destroyed rail yards, depots, and bridges over the Seine River, and they caused great loss of civilian lives. But Free-French leader Charles de Gaulle tolerated the bombings for the greater good. By June 6, France's rail traffic had dropped to 30% of normal capacity. This compelled search for alternative means of transporting troops and supplies to the Atlantic Wall. The Anglo-American Combined Bomber Offensive on Germany and France transformed the western front.

Citizen resistance movements also hindered the Germans. Partisan bands operated in every country occupied by the Axis, although no unified movement existed. As the Nazi's brutal war of annihilation on Jews, Communists, and others escalated, even the authoritarian right realized that the Third Reich had no constructive intentions. Unlike previous conquerors, Hitler did not project himself as a universal leader for Europeans but rather aimed for the Nazi master race to destroy or, at best, enslave undesirables. Bent on survival, patriotic groups arose to confront fascist oppressors and their sympathizers. This was the case in Vichy France and much larger resistance movements in Yugoslavia and Poland. Outraged people of all political, religious, and national backgrounds joined to liberate their territory from Hitler's tyrannical hold. Some spied on the occupiers (and in the Nazi capital of Berlin itself). Others helped refugees, downed Allied aircrew, and operatives escape; and still others engaged in sabotage. Some went on strike, slowed down their work pace, hid and helped Jews, or made symbolic gestures of defiance. For instance, Norwegian clergy refused to abet the imposition of Nazi ideology in schools. Others refused to cheer German military parades or told jokes about the Fuhrer. Slave laborers took part in the resistance by making shoddy goods. In Palestine, the Jewish group Haganah stole guns from pro-Nazi Arab Palestinians (as well as from the British). Britain, Australia, and the U.S. Office of Strategic Services (OSS) focused on sabotage and intelligence in Burma, China, Thailand, Indochina, and Malaya. Although civilian resistance did not defeat the enemy, these movements bothered occupying forces and gave hope to those living under the Axis thumb.

In France, the resistance and secret forces, which in large proportion were organized by the communist party, were substantial. By the time of Overlord, the personnel of the British Special Operations Executive (SOE) or secret service peaked at 13,000 men and women. SOE ran six separate sections and an independent French unit designed to strengthen clandestine operations. They centered on bands of young Frenchmen called *Maquis*, a Corsican term for the local brushwood. A month before Overlord, Anglo-American secret services armed 100,000 Frenchmen who took orders from General Marie Pierre Koenig. Having restored the reputation of the French military during the battle of Bir Hakeim, Koenig now wore three hats. He was a delegate to SHAEF, a commander over the French Forces in Britain, and a leader of the French Forces of the Interior (FFI). This latter agency succeeded the Comité National de la Résistance that de Gaulle had established in 1943 to coordinate various resistance groups. The FFI became the provisional government of France after the Normandy operation. Roughly 35,000 Maquis were armed, although just a quarter had enough ammunition to last a day.

The French underground proved a worthy source of intelligence and a hindrance to Nazi rule. To be sure, it depended on Anglo-American aid and was itself penetrated by double agents. But partisans opened escape routes to Switzerland and Spain for downed pilots and prisoners. Maquis roamed the countryside, blew up factories, power stations, oil refineries, railroads, and highways and harassed Germans. Hitler did not take kindly to the Resistance, killing, torturing, or sending to camps over 90,000 members. Maquis were massacred by the thousands, and civilians also paid a horrible price in the Nazi response by annihilation. For instance, as Waffen SS units moved into Normandy after Overlord invasion, they discovered railway sabotage and partisan snipers. They retaliated against the town of Oradour-sur-Glane in central France. On June 10, 1944, the SS assembled the men in barns and murdered them by machine-gun and then herded the women and children into the church, which they burned down. The same fate awaited operatives and civilians in Norway, Poland, Czechoslovakia, and elsewhere. The Czech town of Lidice had been wiped off the map two years to the day before Oradour-sur-Glane after the assassination of top SS leader Rienhard Heydrich by SOE agents. Eisenhower weighted the French Resistance as the equivalent of six army divisions, but like partisans all over the world, it suffered for its role.

The Allies also sent in several crack teams of agents into France during and after the invasion to interrupt communications and transport. Eighteen 3-man uniformed "Cooney" teams of the French Special Air Service parachuted into Brittany on the night of July 7–8, 1944 to cut rail links to Normandy. Their effort prevented the German 3rd Parachute Division from exiting Brittany by train. In addition, 93 groups of "Jedburgh" teams comprised of uniformed Americans, French, and British coordinated the local resistance with Allied plans, supplied arms, and engaged in acts of demolition. It was dangerous work; 21 Jedburgh members died for their efforts. And 50 two-men "Sussex" teams recruited from French forces in North Africa and trained by the British dropped into France to report on Wehrmacht movements as the Normandy landings approached. They also parachuted behind enemy lines as the Allies moved across France. Unlike Jedburghs and Cooneys, Sussex teams did not wear uniforms.

While the Resistance continued its work, Operation Neptune commenced after midnight on June 6, 1944. The Allied task was enormous: to secure the beaches and push inland to take possession of western France between the Seine and Loire Rivers as well as lower Normandy, all of Brittany, and parts of Maine and Anjou. This coastal base would provide ports from which to reinforce land forces, airfields to support the ground troops, space to maneuver with mechanized warfare, and logistical and command installations. Neptune was the operation, therefore, on which pivoted Overlord and the entire second front in Europe.

Once Ike saw reports of improved weather after he had delayed Neptune a day due to high winds and driving rains, the assault on the Atlantic Wall went forth. Air transports dropped 23,400 paratroopers behind the landing beaches. The British 6th Airborne Division landed on the left flank on high ground east of the River Orne. Reflecting the Division's symbol of the winged horse, the paratroopers seized the soon-to-be-named Pegasus Bridge on the coast road over the Orne. The U.S. 82nd and 101st Airborne Divisions also faced a major challenge. Their mission targeted the right flank between St. Mere Eglise and Carentan at the base of the Cotentin Peninsula, but they struggled to control bridgeheads on the Merderet River. Soldiers also dropped on to beach exits and incurred heavy losses when many drowned in the swamps of the Douve River. U.S. outfits moved on St. Mere Eglise, which became the first French town to be liberated from Nazism. The preinvasion air drops confused the Germans and prevented concerted flanking maneuvers. Rundstedt complained about his small reserve forces, while Rommel had not yet completed his defenses. He also decried his lack of manpower.

The parachutists preceded the five beach assaults launched at 6:30 a.m. from an armada of 7,000 vessels, including landing craft, minesweepers, cargo vessels, small coastal craft, and warships. A total of 1,213 warships escorted them, bombarded the Atlantic Wall, and towed the two artificial harbors, the Mulberries. Destroyer screens and RAF coastal patrols held U-boats in check at both ends of the English Channel. Nearly four-fifths of the warships were British and Canadian, the rest were American, Dutch, French, Greek, Norwegian, and Polish. Altogether, 195,701 naval personnel took part in Overlord. The 11,590 aircraft of the Allied Expeditionary Air Forces (American, British, French, Canadian, Pole, and Czech) patrolled the skies, bombed gun emplacements facing the sea, and even created a ghost invasion force to trick enemy radar. Modified landing craft provided close-in gunfire support. Specialized tanks were equipped with flails to explode mines and also gain traction in the sand with carpet rolls. Mustered in England were 2.86 million troops, but 3,000 led the initial attack, followed by many more.

Some 75,215 British and Canadian troops and 57,500 American soldiers came ashore on D-Day (the D signified day) from the landing craft. Early plans written by Eisenhower's chief of staff Frederick Morgan had called for a three division-wide invasion, but Ike and Monty added two more. Because of the location of the troop buildup in southern England, the American landing beaches in Normandy were the farthest west on the Atlantic side of the invasion. Closest to Cherbourg, they were therefore charged with seizing the port. Canadian and British forces would move up the coast and inland by targeting the key cities of Caen and Bayeux. Patton's trickery had fooled the Germans into believing that the attack would come at the Pas de Calais, which appeared eerily calm. Thus, as the storm of men hit the coast farther south, Rommel drove back to Germany to celebrate his wife's birthday, convinced that there would be no imminent Allied attack. Because Hitler's aides did not awaken the Fuhrer when the invasion began, Rundstedt could not obtain the necessary mobile reserves. While Berlin slept, the Allies surged forward.

At the western end of the operation, 23,250 troops of the U.S. 4th Division made land on Utah beach south of Les Dunes de Varreville. It landed half a mile from its objective in a less heavily defended sector and was thus spared major casualties. Progress was much different down the shore to the east on Omaha beach between the Vire River and Port en Bessin. The U.S. 29th Division (a National Guard unit) joined the 1st (Big Red One) Division in the assault. Bradley's decision for a short naval bombardment as well as his neglect of special armored mine-clearing vehicles undermined the attack. Bombers also missed targets and the U.S. Navy dropped the 34 amphibious tanks of the 1st Division too far out at sea. Only five of 34 made it to the beach, the rest sank, dragging men in life belts behind them to their graves. At the water's edge, men died instantly or pitifully called for medics as they sank in the tide. Omaha witnessed the closest call for the Allies, as the veteran German 352nd Division nearly pushed the Americans into the sea. The beach itself was also not conducive to movement. A jungle of concrete and steel obstacles, it rose steeply to a shingle above which

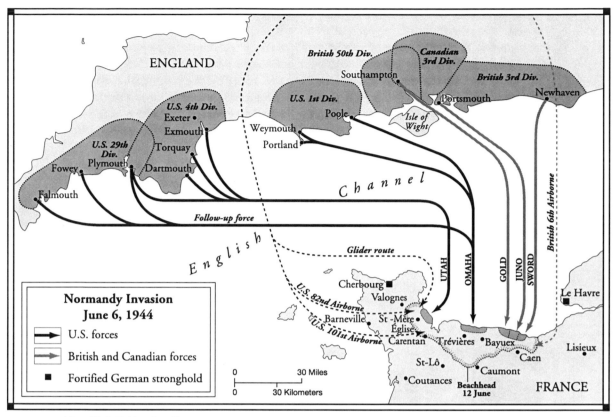

Map 19.1 D-Day landings.   Credit: C. L. Sulzberger, *The American Heritage Picture History of World War II*, p. 486.

the Wehrmacht enjoyed a sweeping view of the beach. Just to the west jutted Pointe du Hoc, which held a strongly fortified artillery battery. After bombarding this protrusion, the Americans sent a Ranger battalion to scale the cliffs and silence the big guns. They climbed 100-foot ropes that had been propelled to the top by rockets but took heavy losses in the process. And they found that the gun had not been emplaced, although troops occupying the position put up resistance. Like their comrades below them in the surf, the Rangers suffered from the American plan of attacking head-on in a direct thrust remarkable for its sheer hubris.

The guns above Omaha beach hammered the Americans in the surf. Amphibious tanks descended landing craft ramps into rough seas that battered their flotation gear until they sank. A radioman in 29th Division's Dog Green sector yelled for help as his heavy set pulled him under. One soldier described stepping into four feet of water. "I look behind, and the men are already off the boat and scattered for protection against the bullets that are singing around us but for the most part hitting the water. It was a hell of a feeling. We had about 500 yards of water to cross, we couldn't run cause the water was too deep, we couldn't crouch, we couldn't do anything except just what we did. Wade on into shore." Others struggled up to the shingle and huddled under makeshift shelters in the sand. Rifles clogged. Many found themselves in the wrong sectors without officers or communications. All the while German fire pinned them down. A second wave of troops came ashore at 7:00 a.m by slogging through the bloody water where corpses nudged against each other and shambled to land. The third and fourth waves followed but stopped short on the jammed beach. Men lay dazed and injured, crying in desperation. So terrible was the rate of death that the German commander of the fortifications actually reported the failure of the U.S. landing and Omar Bradley considered shutting down the beach entirely and sending reinforcements to Utah.

Historians debate the consequences of the decisions that led to such carnage. The Army did not take full advantage of naval bombardment and planners might have underestimated Wehrmacht intelligence and military capabilities and misread Rommel's conceptualization of defense. Still they also took actions to preserve the element of surprise. Overlord was costly as an infantry assault in daylight against prepared defenders but a night landing was out of the question, and the assumption of whether such an operation would have been more successful is dubious. SHAEF was responsible for sending hundreds of men to their untimely deaths, but Ike and his staff had carefully calculated the possibilities and made a judgment call in a bad situation.

D-Day. Credit: Center for the Study of War Experience at Regis University, Denver, Colorado: U.S. National Archives.

The Americans persevered on bloody Omaha, and the Allied invasion proceeded. The casualties on Omaha rose to about 2,500 or twice the number of Americans who perished on Tarawa. Most were in the Big Red One; several companies withered under a hail of machine-gun fire unleashed from the moment the Higgins boats dropped their ramps to the point they clung to life at the base of the bluffs. Yet acting on their own, small squads scampered across and up the shingle and penetrated the bluffs. The Wehrmacht lacked troops to stop them. Allied reinforcements came in, and the tide of battle turned. That evening of June 6, about 34,250 troops had a foothold, and by the next day, one of the 1.5 million ton Mulberries—hollow, concrete floating piers built in England and towed across the Channel—was installed at St. Laurent off Omaha beach, although an Atlantic gale destroyed it two weeks later.

The battle went smoother in the British sector farther eastward. Troops fixed in place another Mulberry at Arromanches as the British 50th Division waded on to French soil on Gold beach. Obstacles abounded, and several tanks with flotation devices sunk but the Division enjoyed good fire support offshore, and 24,970 troops rested at D-Day's end. Next door on Juno beach, 21,400 assault troops of the 3rd Canadian Division came ashore relatively unscathed between the Provence and St. Aubin-Sur-Mer. On Sword beach at the eastern extreme of the operation, the British 3rd Division got 28,845 troops ashore by nightfall. Overlord planners had expected Sword to be the most hotly contested. Indeed, most of the 200 casualties suffered on D-Day by the 2nd East York Regiment occurred in the first few minutes, yet although bloody, the fight was brief.

Outside of a German bunker.   Credit: Center for the Study of War Experience at Regis University, Denver, Colorado: U.S. National Archives.

German resistance did not disappear. About 155,000 Allied soldiers were put ashore, joined by 23,000 paratroopers and glider-borne infantry at the expense of 9,000 casualties. SHAEF judged these losses light considering the size and complexity of an invasion by eight divisions and three armored brigades. But when the British set out for their D-Day objective of the communications hub of Caen five miles off their beach, the 21st Panzer Division repulsed the advance. Other Waffen SS units were active. The 12th SS Panzer Division shot hundreds of Canadian prisoners near Juno beach, and the 2nd SS Panzer Division (responsible for the Oradour-sur-Glane massacre and a similar atrocity in the city of Tulle) cracked down on the French Resistance. Preinvasion developments ultimately hurt the Wehrmacht, though. With the railway and road travel disrupted by partisans and bombing, reinforcements arrived at the front in two weeks rather than two days. Fifteenth Army still fixated on the Pas de Calais; the high command continued to believe that the main attack had not yet occurred. In addition, ULTRA and the French underground showed the location of Panzer Group West's headquarters, which Tedder eliminated on June 10. Rommel's longest day had come to pass. Within a week, a forty-mile span of Allied roads and defensive works linked all five landing beaches to permit reinforcements of men and materiel to pour in. Neptune had resulted in an Allied victory. Hitler's foes stood on his Atlantic Wall and readied their own strategy of annihilation in western Europe.

PENETRATING NORMANDY

Piercing the Atlantic Wall was another matter. Traffic jams on the beachhead jeopardized SHAEF's timetable for progress inland. Ike wanted Normandy cleared within 17 days of D-Day so the Allies could arrive at the mouth of the Seine River by July 10 and then cut off Brittany and drive eastward. But the lodgment—a foothold expanded to a base of operations—was too small. The beachhead was one-fifth the required size, and few airfields existed to support the advance. Rundstedt decided on a counteroffensive to contain the invaders in the lodgment on the coast and then bolster the defense. Normandy's hedgerows, heaths, stone fences, and farms gave him excellent defensive terrain. Bradley noted that "the hedgerows formed a natural line of defense more formidable than any even Rommel could have contrived." Centuries of subdividing pastures yielded ramparts of earthen walls crowned with thorny brambles and trees, their roots reinforcing the walls, and deep drainage ditches backed the hedgerows. The situation was even more exasperating than the Americans had encountered in Tunisia though many made comparisons to the treacherous jungles of Guadalcanal. Tanks climbing the walls exposed their thinly armored undersides to German fire while troops crawling through the hedges could not get through fast enough without getting shot. The hedgerows added to the strains on the soldiers. Many fell victim to psychiatric disorders as the grind of battle followed the exhilaration of the Neptune landings. Furthermore, although crimped by railway disruptions, the Wehrmacht turned to barge transports on the Seine that had largely escaped Allied bombing. The Germans bogged down the Americans and turned to the danger posed by a potential Anglo-Canadian breakout at Caen.

To open up the lodgment in Normandy, the Allies needed to take Caen. The Americans occupied the bottom of the Cotentin Peninsula and reached the Atlantic by June 18. Cherbourg fell nine days later. Troops enjoyed the large stocks of wine left by the departing commander, but the port never fully functioned as a depot according to preinvasion plans because the Germans had destroyed it. The defenders focused, however, on the eastern flank of the lodgment and a British breakout around Caen, which stood at the edge of easier terrain for armored advances. They also considered the Americans a lesser foe than Anglo-Canadian forces. To be sure, when Bradley turned eastward to help the Caen effort, Rommel and Rundstedt pleaded with Hitler to release reserves from the Pas de Calais. Outraged by the request and miffed when Rundstedt counseled peace, the Fuhrer replaced him on July 2 with the Gunther Kluge who had just healed from a car crash on the Eastern front. Kluge warned the Desert Fox against defeatism. Rommel expressed pessimism, however, because the Wehrmacht had lost its last fresh armored units and the surge of Allied troops continued on the beaches. Within a month, Rommel's opinion no longer mattered. He returned home to recuperate from injuries sustained when a plane strafed his car, and afterward he got caught up in the July 20 attempt on Hitler's life. He committed suicide rather than face Nazi torture and execution.

The Wehrmacht blocked the way to the plains southward from Caen that stretched for eighteen miles to Falaise. Allied newsmen broadcast their impatience over the stalled beachhead and restricted lodgment. Caen had to be taken. As an option, Monty considered bombing and also mobile warfare in the flatlands. On July 7, Bomber Command obliterated Caen and Anglo-Canadian forces under Miles Dempsey of British Second Army then entered the city. The Germans vacated to a line on the south side of the Orne River. As Montgomery eyed them, he urged Bradley to move through bocage from the Cotentin Peninsula. To wield his tanks, Bradley searched for higher and drier ground around St.-Lo. Monty launched Operation Cobra to clear the hedgerows and allow the Americans turn toward Caen while Dempsey requested permission to advance on Falaise. To answer to the reporters, Monty decided on a two-punch offensive with Cobra and Dempsey's Operation Goodwood to break out into the plains. On July 18, after aircraft dropped 15,000 one thousand- and 500-pound bombs and followed an hour later with 76,000 twenty-pound fragmentation explosives, Goodwood began. The Germans crawled away and Dempsey quickly moved three miles south across the Orne until Kluge put up resistance and a thunderstorm halted the offensive. The mind-blowing air attacks had not knocked out all of the artillery or 88s, however, and some of the best Wehrmacht units constructed four lines in depth with the help of reinforcements that evening. Having lost 4,000 men and 500 tanks (over a third available on Normandy), Monty got cold feet and cancelled Operation Goodwood two days later. The breakout from Caen aborted again, and the press criticized his timidity.

The effort went better for U.S. forces. In command of U.S. Twelfth Army Group, Bradley made slow but steady headway in western Normandy. He advanced to the St.-Lo salient by July 21 with the aid of combined arms tactics and novel inventions. One was the Rhino device of steel beams welded to the front of Sherman tanks that cut

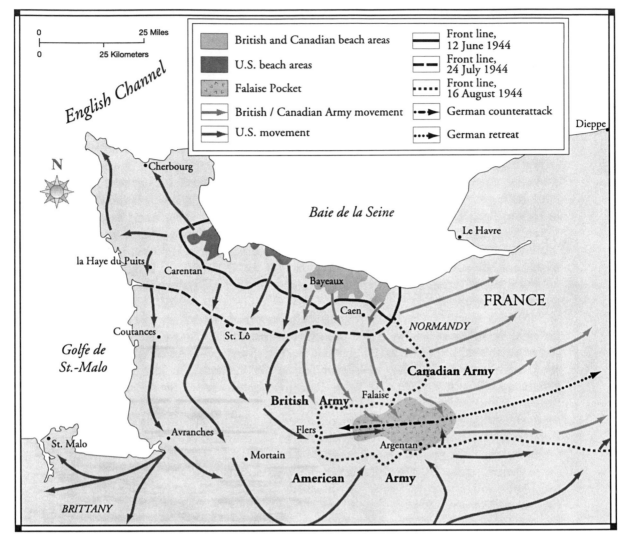

Map 19.2 Normandy campaign.   Credit: Ronald Story, *Concise Historical Atlas of World War II: The Geography of Conflict*, Map 25, p. 55.

through the hedges. The sacrifice was huge, however, as the Americans suffered 11,000 casualties. The losses, the weather, and errant bombing runs in which pilots dropped their charges short on friendly forces compelled Bradley to delay Operation Cobra and the advance toward the town of Coutances near the coast. But the storms finally broke, and bombers smashed the German lines. Panzer commanders lamented the growing number of grenadier, engineer, and tank crew deaths as the Americans raced through the gap in the defense toward Coutances and Avranches beyond. They seized the latter on July 30, to gaze on the famous Mont St. Michel. Blocking a counterattack, Bradley captured the key bridge at Pontaubault that linked Normandy to Brittany to the west, the Loire River valley to the south, and the Seine and Paris-Orleans salient eastward.

The Germans pulled back from the coast but accidentally ran into oncoming Allied forces and sustained large losses. The Americans had splintered the German line that ran from the west coast of Normandy to the Channel.

By the end of July 1944, the Wehrmacht's situation had deteriorated to the point that Ike could advance his plans to penetrate France. The Norman coast rested in Allied hands, and the Allies had broken into the interior. Eisenhower readied for the campaign by reshuffling commands in the field. Bradley turned over U.S. First Army to his deputy Courtney Hodges, a former chief of infantry school, and joined it to U.S. Third Army. The impetuous George Patton, the new Third Army commander, differed greatly from the cautious Hodges. He was raring to go after having spent two months playacting in London and Dover. Patton occupied the westernmost end of the Allied line by August 1 and headed into Brittany. He had orders to bypass the German line and arc northward to envelop Kluge's forces but urged Bradley to ignore Brittany and push the Germans eastward out of France entirely. Yet Ike's plan called for seizing the Brittany seaports. A corps indeed took Brittany but required two weeks of hard fighting to capture St. Malo and a month (and three divisions) for Brest. A quarantine of St. Nazaire and Lorient was also required an effort for the rest of the war even though Brittany became a sideshow. Patton's other corps wheeled left toward the Seine and the Orleans-Paris gap in the Wehrmacht defenses. Then trouble hit.

After Patton reached Le Mans in a week, the Germans struck back. On the left side of the Allied line, Henry Crerar's First Canadian Army, the only field army to fight under Canadian command and staff, aimed for Falaise accompanied by Dempsey's Second Army. But Hitler decided to drive westward through Mortain to Avranches in a tank offensive. The Mortain counteroffensive was designed to sever First and Third Armies from each other, destroy the left flank of the advancing U.S. spearhead, reestablish a narrow front to hinder Allied mobility, and then push the British and Canadians backwards. Kluge had his reservations about the idea due to Patton's considerable strength as well as terrain that favored the Americans. Nonetheless, he assembled four battered panzer divisions with just 145 tanks and 32 self-propelled guns for the attack on August 7. For three days, the Mortain battle raged. Aided by ULTRA, Bradley finally diverted reserves to boost the lines, and at St. Barthelmy north of Mortain, the 1st Battalion, 117th Infantry Regiment, held the 1st SS and 2nd Panzer Divisions. The Germans retook Mortain but then headed for cover as RAF and U.S. planes pummeled them over the next four days. Surveying the destruction, an enthralled Patton shouted to his driver, "Could anything be more magnificent?" The Wehrmacht withdrew out of a fear of being cut off. Over half of its tanks were destroyed. The Mortain counteroffensive ground to a halt by August 12, 1944. With Hitler's permission, German forces fled toward the closing escape hatch to the east around Falaise.

Kluge had retreat on his mind. Crerar massed Canadian armor and after carpet bombings from the air, he launched the ominous Operation Totalize toward Falaise, which quickly ran out of steam. A Polish and a Canadian division tried to jumpstart the offensive, but both were untested in combat and lacked coordination. By August 10, the effort had bogged down. Now Bradley determined to ensnare the Germans by maintaining Crerar's pressure on Falaise to the south and ordering Patton to move a corps due north from Le Mans to Alencon and Argentan to within 14 miles of Canadian First Army. This created the "Falaise pocket" to encircle and pinch off fragments of 21 German divisions. Monty had his eyes on Paris, but he permitted Dempsey and Hodges to herd the Wehrmacht into the trap and slam shut its jaws. On August 12, Patton grasped the import of the situation; the Allies could simply cinch the noose on the Falaise pocket. His rapid mobile forces drove to the outskirts of Argentan where the Allies mustered their largest armored force of the war on the Western Front. In the Falaise cauldron sat 100,000 troops facing two Allied armies. Patton asked Bradley to send the XV Corps north to Falaise and encircle the Germans but in a controversial move, Bradley refused out of the fear that the Americans would crash into the timid Canadians and a stampede of 19 enemy divisions desperate to escape. Bradley preferred to build a solid shoulder at Argentan, although Patton thought he simply lacked nerves. Although the Germans could not break out, Bradley's delaying decision allowed them to evacuate supplies and administrative units eastward through the Argentan-Falaise gap. On August 14, Crerar attacked again, and two days later had Falaise, yet as Bradley procrastinated, half of the German forces fled the pocket eastward in from rain and mist from August 13–20 despite incessant artillery and air bombardment.

The remainder of Wehrmacht forces prepared to defend the smaller and elongated pocket once Monty had sealed shut the Argentan-Falaise trap door after 50,000 Germans had escaped. Left behind sat 50,000 potential prisoners, and another 5,000 to

German dead in Falaise pocket. Credit: Center for the Study of War Experience at Regis University, Denver, Colorado: U.S. National Archives.

10,000 men lay dead alongside thousands of horses. The Germans left nearly all of their equipment, although Albert Speer's production miracles would replace much of it. The carnage was enormous. Flying over the battlefield, an RAF pilot smelled the stench of decaying bodies in his cockpit. "We thought that we were prepared for the dreadful scenes, which Eisenhower later said could only be described by Dante." These were the by-products of a strategy of annihilation.

The Normandy campaign spelled disaster for Germany. Walther Model took over Army Group B from Kluge. who committed suicide on August 18 after Hitler discovered that he had contacted the Allies for a cease-fire. The energetic Model had pulled off a stunning counterattack that halted the momentum of the Soviets on the East Prussian border and now the Fuhrer counted on him to save the Western Front. But Model could not deny the facts. The Atlantic Wall had crumbled along with hopes of defending the western border. For the remainder of the war, Hitler abandoned grand strategic concepts for a fierce but static defensive approach. He looked to new weapons such as rockets and stiff, inspired resistance—instead of mobile defense—to save the Third Reich. But gaps appeared in defensive lines, fronts vanished, and the collapse of Hitler's regime came nearer.

Ike had his Normandy lodgment in ten days less than he had expected, although he had also missed an opportunity because he could have destroyed the Wehrmacht in the west by sealing the Argentan-Falaise gap. Patton had seen the light, however. Taking cues from Patton, Eisenhower revised his plan to stop at the Seine, and instead aimed for the German border with a broad front. Monty and Brooke lobbied for a single drive—led by the British—along the northern flank into Germany. Yet, wary of the infighting within the SHAEF combined command, Ike rejected the idea. Besides, Patton was temperamentally better suited than Montgomery (or Bradley) to undertake an aggressive multipronged assault on the border.

LIBERATION

In the meantime, far to the south, the Allies targeted the French Riviera for a landing. First code-named Anvil, then called Operation Dragoon, this effort was conceived as a feint to divert German attention away from Overlord. Churchill opposed it because it drew forces from a thrust into Austria from Italy, and still sought to push the Wehrmacht into the Alps and out of northern Italy. The Americans disagreed. They viewed Italy as a brutal sideshow and besides, Ike did not think of the Riviera operation as a mere ploy because the Allies lacked a port in Normandy. Marseilles and other southern French harbors could serve as handy entry points for supplies and the backlog of American troops still in the United States. After much argument, Dragoon went forth.

Bombardment from five battleships, 21 cruisers, and 100 destroyers of the Western Naval Task Force, which included Free French warships, preceded the landings. Seven British and two U.S. carriers and some of the 2,000 aircraft of the Twelfth Tactical Air Force on Sardinia and Corsica added to the attack force. Substantial intelligence gathering and sabotage by special operations forces and the French resistance also cleared the way. The Task Force disgorging the assault troops included 887 warships and 1,370 landing craft. Lieutenant-General Alexander Patch, who had led ground forces

Daylight parachutists preceding Operation Anvil (similar to night drops before Overlord).   Credit: Imperial War Museum.

on Guadalcanal, sent ashore U.S. Seventh Army on August 15, 1944. Lucian Truscott, leader of the breakout at Anzio in February, landed three divisions of VI Corps in the initial assault between Cannes and Hyeres. Guarding his left were French commandos and the U.S. First Special Service Force. On his right at Le Muy parachuted the First Airborne Task Force, an ad hoc assemblage of Anglo-American units. Part of the French Expeditionary Force of seven divisions under General Jean-Marie de Lattre de Tassigny's Armée B followed. He had escaped the Vichy regime, served in Italy with Free French forces, and liberated Elba two months before. De Lattre had 256,000 troops including men from the Armée d'Afrique.

Patch directed a pursuit inland of the retreating Germans who had 10 divisions under Army Group G led by Johannes Blaskowitz. He had been removed from the Polish occupation force in 1940, after he protested Nazi Einsatzgruppen atrocities, to this minor theater. Blaskowitz had just three divisions on the coast while the Luftwaffe was only a tenth the strength of the Allies. Making matters worse, Hitler transferred some divisions to Normandy. The dearth of men prevented resistance on the southern beaches, and when ULTRA revealed that the Wehrmacht had no plans to attack from Italy, Truscott moved for Avignon and Sisteron to the northwest while de Lattre struck toward strongly fortified Toulon and Marseilles. The French forces overran both

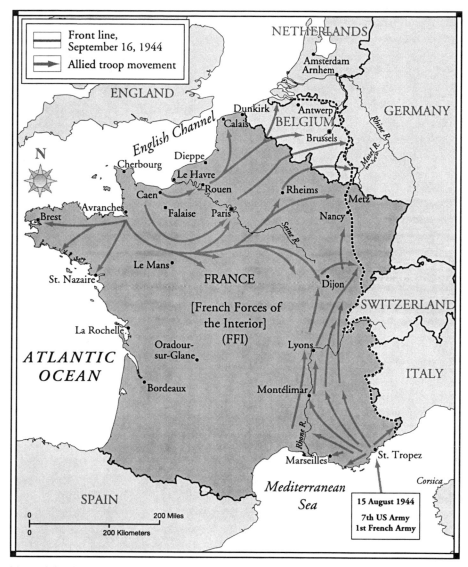

Map 19.3 Liberation of France.   Credit: Ronald Story, *Concise Historical Atlas of World War II: The Geography of Conflict*, Map 27, p. 59.

cities by August 28. Franco-American forces continued northward through France into September past Valence and Grenoble to link with Patton's army coming eastward. The Germans reeled from southern and central France.

Whether Dragoon had an impact on the Western front is debatable. The southern ports appeared important to the safe entry of supplies. Hitler seemed to neglect the region, but the Wehrmacht nonetheless sacrificed tens of thousands of soldiers and large amounts of irreplaceable materiel to defend the strongholds of Toulon and

Marseilles. It seemingly did so for no other reason other than to delay the retreat to Germany. Southwest France remained isolated; German garrisons held out until the French Forces of the Interior rounded them up as the war in Europe neared its end. Even the ports proved unnecessary, as supply depots moved further east in France. Churchill might have been correct all along in his desire to focus on Italy with these forces, yet Dragoon's success gave the Allies a long unbroken front running from the Channel to Switzerland, and undamaged Marseilles served as a useful port until Antwerp in Belgium was repaired in December 1944.

The campaign across Normandy proceeded so rapidly that Dragoon was relegated to a backwater. As Bradley closed the Falaise pocket, Patton divided his Third Army corps between Dreux, Chartres, and Orleans. Bradley halted him on the roads again by seeking territory rather than prisoners, but Patton liberated all three cities by August 18, 1944. He reached Mantes-Gassicourt just 37 miles downstream from Paris. One division crossed the Seine on August 19, the first Allied troops to bridge that river. German Falaise escapees formed pockets of resistance to avoid being cut off around Evreux and Rouen. American forces took a week to reach Louviers and Elbeuf and then tried to block off about 60 miles of the Seine to enemy troops seeking to cross to the far side by ferrying their equipment under constant air attack. British and Canadian armies also encountered resistance. Through the end of August, 240,000 German evacuees amazingly made it across the Seine even though all of the bridges were blown. Pursuit by U.S. Third Army continued as the Wehrmacht dispersed toward Belgium, Luxembourg, and Germany. Meanwhile, Lieutenant-General J. Lawton Collins and his VII Corps (Hodges' First Army) traversed the Seine at Melun and Fontainbleau, raced to the Yonne River and through Troyes, and arrived at the Meuse River at the end of the Ardennes Forest. The Wehrmacht had impressively crossed the Meuse four years before, but now moved in reverse. Patton reached a front that stood 186 miles beyond the Seine.

In the meantime, Paris awaited liberation. As the Allies neared it, railway workers and police went on strike, and when they heard of the Riviera landings, postal workers joined the work stoppages. Communists called for action, but Gaullists counseled calm, unsure if Eisenhower would support an uprising. The Allies had tried to keep de Gaulle out of France for as long as possible because they knew he would bypass their chain of command and complicate political affairs. Feeding the several million inhabitants was also a concern. But there was the issue of Warsaw. That city was in the midst of rebellion, and Hitler wanted it razed. Paris required a similar fate, he demanded. Should Ike save the capital from the strategy of annihilation? Eisenhower remained silent but events moved beyond his control. After fighting broke out. Hitler ordered General Dietrich von Choltitz, who had leveled Rotterdam and Sevastopol, to squash the uprising with his 20,000 occupying troops. City fathers persuaded Choltitz to behave honorably, however. When Eisenhower still balked, the BBC announced the city's liberation, and so shamed by the media, he permitted the 2nd French Armored Division under General Philippe Leclerc to enter Paris. Tanks reached the mayor's office on the evening of August 24. The next day, de Gaulle led his troops under the Arc de Triomphe and to Notre Dame in one of the most poignant moments of the war.

Resistance liberators.   Credit: Center for the Study of War Experience at Regis University, Denver, Colorado.

Choltitz surrendered, and the free city erupted in celebration. Paris had finally arisen from the depths of June 1940.

The City of Light's liberation and Patton's spectacular progress were not the only gains made by August's end. Generals Dempsey, Crerar, and Hodges led a multinational offensive that pushed the Wehrmacht out of Normandy, and Dempsey's Second Army took Amiens and pointed toward Brussels in early September 1944. In the first 10 days of September, the Americans got to Mons, Belgium and reached Antwerp before the Germans destroyed its important dock facilities. Canadian forces advanced up the Channel coast and isolated key ports, including Dieppe where so many of their countrymen had died in 1942. This touched off another outburst of festivities. Hodges's First Army captured Laon and shot toward eastern Belgium and Luxembourg. Hitler again turned to Rundstedt to assume the Western command, but the Field Marshal was no magician. German defenses were evaporating. Coming up from the south, Dragoon forces took Lyons, Besancon, and Dijon while Truscott made contact with Third Army. Patton had swept around Paris to take Verdun and Nancy, and just 45 miles from the German border, he headed for Metz. Dragoon fizzled, however, as the VI Corps failed to trap the enemy before they reached the Vosges Mountains at the Franco-German frontier. The Wehrmacht still possessed substantial numbers of troops and materiel in the area.

By mid-1944, Allied successes piled up on all the major fronts. In Europe, the Allies occupied Italy, the Soviets hammered the Wehrmacht westward, and the Nazi empire started to unravel in the Balkans to the south. Hitler faced a continent-wide pincer when the headline-grabbing Allied invasion of France opened the long-awaited second front. The Allies began to choke the German war machine and notably, this effort against fascism in France occurred concurrently with those on the other side of the world in the Pacific against Japan. The fact that the United States could launch these two massive campaigns on a global scale and with trained personnel, planes, ships, and equipment that had not existed three years before attested to the low odds of survival for the Axis power.

CHAPTER 20

Island-Hopping in the Pacific

The Pacific conflict was a strange piece-meal war, fought from island to island, mapping itself out more like a medieval storming of castles, if the castles had been of coral and moated by hundreds of miles of hostile water and defended by men committed to die for their emperor rather than surrender.

IVAN DOIG
The Eleventh Man

DECISIONS IN THE MARIANAS

As the Allies were preparing their invasion of Normandy, the Americans decided to crush Imperial Japan by a thrust through the central Pacific. After capturing the Gilberts and Eniwetok in the Marshalls, Nimitz needed to pivot northward toward Tokyo, but the best place to do so seemed, to his dismay, to be the Mariana Islands rather than the Philippines. The experience in Tarawa had so shaken him that he asked Chief of Naval Operations Ernest King whether taking the Marianas was necessary. With the isolation of Truk, the Japanese Combined Fleet had to fight in the Western Pacific far from support bases. Nimitz and MacArthur lobbied for the Philippines as the locus of the final move on Japan but King dashed their hopes by retaining the two-prong strategy of the Southwest and Central Pacific campaigns. Nimitz would facilitate a strategic bombing campaign by seizing the Marianas, he ordered, and MacArthur would retain the Seventh Fleet and pursue the Philippines. Under Nimitz's command, the U.S. Navy would implement a two-team command structure for the central Pacific force built around the fast carriers, alternating leadership between Raymond Spruance and Bull Halsey. When Spruance was in command, the force was called the Fifth Fleet, while Halsey and the Third Fleet planned the next set of operations. Command then switched, with the main fleet becoming the Third Fleet. This arrangement provided constant, well-prepared, and lethal pressure against Japan. Spruance and the Fifth Fleet would lead the charge in the Marianas, and Halsey would give support with the Third Fleet and prepare to assume control over the next operation. The American attack organization was set.

Because Eisenhower did not need amtracs in Normandy and skyrocketing ship output bolstered the fleets, Spruance began the assault in the Marianas with a huge force of 535 warships carrying 166,000 men. The effort required support from the base of operations at Pearl Harbor, 3,300 miles away. Smooth logistics were never easy. For instance, on May 21, 1944, hasty loading of fuel and ammunition on cargo ships berthed together at Pearl Harbor led to a massive explosion that killed 163 people and injured nearly 400 others. Six landing ships and the cargo vanished. The campaign for the Marianas was a grind, but the Americans also had growing confidence in their technological and industrial capacity to root the enemy from these islands. Earthmovers and other heavy equipment and daily items like insecticides accompanied the invading force. Lights used to illuminate stretches of coastlines to defeat darkness were tools in the arsenal. The Pacific environment could not be tamed, but it could be more amenable to the projection of U.S. power.

The three Mariana islands of Saipan, Tinian, and Guam were 1,500 miles closer to the Japanese home islands than the Marshalls, which put Japan within range of the new U.S. bomber, the B-29. Expressly built for strategic bombing campaigns, Superfortresses epitomized the emerging American strategy of annihilation to attack and destroy both military and civilian targets. Once the B-29 went into operation over Tokyo, the Japanese understood that their war was essentially over. Thus, because the Marianas lay at the edge of the Empire's inner sanctum, Japan prepared to contest the United States at sea, on land, and in the air. Americans could also not expect many friendly natives, for Saipan had long been home to Okinawan farmers loyal to Japan. Nimitz could also not hope for flat atolls as in the Gilberts and Marshalls. The Marianas possessed a deadly geography of hills, jungles, swamps, and caves surrounded by coral reefs. The conflict around and on Saipan—the first of the islands targeted and the administrative center of the Marianas chain—became the decisive battle that the Japanese had so long desired.

As the Americans hopped into the Marianas, the Japanese Navy lurked nearby awaiting an opportunity to strike. Spruance took no chances. Fifth Fleet focused on Saipan and Tinian while Marc Mitscher's Task Force 58 sailed into the Palaus to the southwest and to the Bonin group of islands to the north. Both forces aimed to isolate the garrison on Saipan and stop reinforcements to the islands. After the Americans secured the approaches to the Marianas, the 2nd and 4th Marines Division—part of Holland Smith's Northern Troops and Expeditionary Landing Force of over 250,000 men—landed on Saipan on June 14, 1944 to begin Operation Forager. So named for his hot-tempered impatience with troops, "Howlin' Mad" Smith commanded V Amphibious Corps and the Saipan operation. Roy Geiger headed for Tinian and Guam in command of the III Amphibious Corps which included the 3rd Marine Division, 1st Marine Brigade, and the green 77th Army Infantry Division in reserve. In tow were amphibious tractor battalions, substantial artillery and tanks, and engineering and logistical units. The Marines landed unscathed after negotiating the reefs that had been demolished by Frogmen. Ship-to-shore movement was superb; amtracs carried 8,000 U.S. Marines to the beaches in less than 30 minutes. But the men lay exposed to artillery and mortar fire. As if Tarawa had never happened, Richmond Turner's preliminary naval bombardment was insufficient because the fleet moved far out to sea to avoid mines. At least the U.S. Navy did not need to worry about air attacks because Mitscher was in the process of decimating the Japanese First Air Fleet.

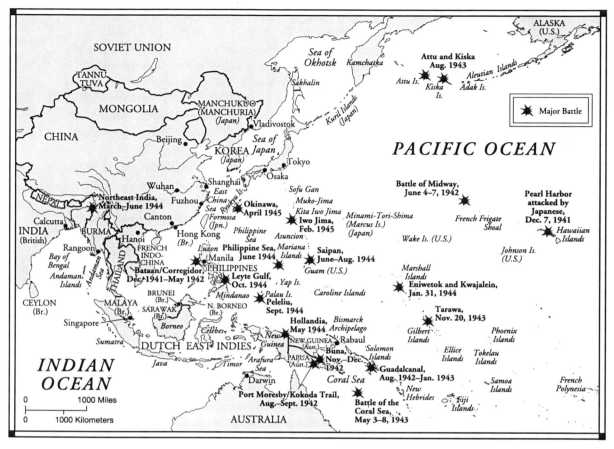

Map 20.1 The Pacific War.   Credit: Douglas Brinkley and Michael E. Haskew, *The World War II Desk Reference*, p. 276.

The defense of the island fell to the 32,000 troops of Lieutenant-General Yoshitsugu Saito's Thirty-First Army. It included the regular garrison, a regiment of 48 tanks, and 6,000 sailors from the original Pearl Harbor attack force, although reinforcements had been slow in arriving due to U.S. air and submarine strikes on transports. The garrison was also responsible for 20,000 civilians. Saito sought to keep control of the island's airstrips for use by carrier- and land-based aircraft, and thus made the most of his positions. The 14-mile long Saipan provided excellent defensive terrain. There was high ground for artillery and observation posts which overlooked the western landing beaches as well as caves, cliffs, and hills in which to hide and ambush the Americans. The lack of U.S. Naval bombardment gave Saito an opening and he responded with a two-day slaughter that caused over 4,000 casualties even though he misjudged the location of the landings. Without naval and air support, he could not expect to pin the U.S. Marines to the beaches. In any case, the Japanese had generally given up a defense at the water's edge on islands large enough to defend in depth, in terrain that enabled a war of attrition. As enemy troops, artillery, and flamethrowers poured on to the island

and the aerial attack intensified, Saito withdrew to the island's interior. The 2nd Marine Division headed north into the hills above the airfields while the 4th Division gave chase in lightly armored amtracs. Saito stopped them in their tracks, destroying 164 of the vehicles. The Japanese then fought a vicious holding action that extended the estimated three-day capture of Saipan to three weeks. This delay spurred bad blood between the U.S. Army brass, which preferred a methodical invasion, and the Marine Corps, which sought quick movement ashore and inland. As a result of the squabbling, Holland Smith of the U. S. Marines, who disliked the 27th Division after its poor performance in the Gilberts, relieved its commander Ralph Smith.

After the U.S. Marines took the Aslito airfield on June 18, the Americans hit Saito's defense line and found the defenders dug in amidst treacherous ravines and cliffs around Mount Tapotchau. The 27th Infantry Division attacked the sturdiest part of the line along a spine running through hills and woods but failed to break through. Howlin' Mad Smith reacted in outrage. The fighting was so ferocious that the site became known as Purple Heart Ridge, but other place names were just as symbolic of the brutality, such as Death Valley and Hell's Pocket. The U.S. Navy bombarded the Japanese positions in the valleys, which allowed the land forces to advance again. Despite his sickness, Saito had other ideas than giving up. On the night of July 6–7, he read and distributed his farewell address, and to stir his troops into a final courageous effort, he told them that they had no choice but death. "I will advance with those who remain to deliver still another blow to the American Devils, and leave my bones on Saipan as a bulwark of the Pacific." With no option but to confront the enemy strategy of annihilation, Saito ordered the biggest banzai charge of the war and then fell on his sword. The 3,000 screaming attackers hurtled forward with swords, rocks, and knives on poles. This amounted to mass suicide, but two U.S. Army infantry battalions and three Marine Corps artillery units were slaughtered in the process of being overrun. The desperate attack also represented the last large-scale organized resistance on the island. Skirmishes against small groups persisted until Smith declared Saipan secured on July 9.

Those that did not make the charge killed themselves to honor the Emperor. Even the naval commander shot himself and the head of the army committed hari kari. About 39,000 Japanese were killed whereas two-thirds of the civilians killed themselves, and just 736 prisoners were taken including 438 of Korean workers. The defenders caused 16,612 U.S. casualties, among these 3,225 dead. Egged on by government propaganda that the Americans were going to rape and kill, hundreds of civilians chose suicide over surrender. Many were forced to do so by Japanese troops who turned to lobbing grenades into the midst of entire families who resisted. Along with soldiers they jumped to their death from Marpi Point despite the pleas of Japanese-speaking U.S. soldiers, and they turned the waters red. Marpi Point was so densely filled with bodies that boats could not avoid running over them. Saipan became notorious for the shocking, deadly, and maniacal behavior of the Japanese defenders as a foreboding of more to come in the Pacific.

SHOWDOWN IN THE PHILIPPINE SEA

The ferocity of the Saipan battle led Spruance to delay the landings on neighboring Tinian and Guam. The next action occurred at sea. As they patrolled the Marianas and beyond, the big U.S. Fifth Fleet and Task Force 58 attracted attention. Tokyo sent the First Mobile Fleet—the best units of the Combined Fleet based at Tawitawi between Mindanao and Borneo—to defend the islands under the able command of naval air power advocate Vice-Admiral Jizaburo Ozawa. He had devastated the Royal Navy's Z Force off the Malayan coast in December 1941. The Japanese Navy's fleet commander-in-chief, Admiral Soemu Toyoda, ordered Ozawa to effect Plan A-Go to stop the enemy invasion of the Marianas. The aggressive Toyoda adopted the idea of assailing and destroying the U.S. fleet as it approached the island chain with the 1000-land-based aircraft of the First Air Fleet and submarines, then carriers and battleships would go in for the kill. Toyoda had initially planned for the Mobile Fleet to attack the warships supporting MacArthur, yet in response to Task Force 58's presence in the Palaus, he turned toward the Marianas. His carrier air fleet lacked experienced pilots because veterans had gone to Guam to fly the land-based aircraft, many of which now lay wrecked. Nonetheless, Ozawa's flagship, *Taiho,* was a formidable vessel; it was Japan's largest carrier and the first to have an armored flight deck. Although the sailors had not mastered its complicated machinery, the *Taiho* sailed after Toyoda carried out exercises under the Emperor's observation. Bad luck undercut the premise of a decisive victory over the Americans, however. A plane carrying the Japanese Navy's Chief of Staff had crashed in the Philippines with the details of A-Go on board. These gave Spruance information on the whereabouts of Ozawa's two oncoming groups of warships, and submarines and Coast Watchers reported them exiting from Tawitawi and passing through the Philippines toward the Marianas. Setting June 13 for the commencement of hostilities, Toyoda proclaimed that Japan's future rested on this crucial battle.

Regardless of Toyoda's rousing cry, Spruance held key cards as he readied to meet the First Mobile Fleet in the Philippine Sea. Marc Mitscher kept back two carrier task forces until the other two groups returned from the Bonins, and Spruance postponed the Guam invasion. He ordered Turner to withdraw his amphibious force from its support role of the forces ashore on Saipan, which stranded the U.S. Marines who feared a repeat of Guadalcanal. But at least this time around, they had three days of supplies and ammunition. Spruance had removed the vessels to put them out of reach of the Japanese strike force, refusing to be lured into a trap and determining to engage at a time and place of his own choosing. Also, preliminary feelers hurt the Japanese. One skirmish sunk 17 of 25 submarines, and this fleet never recovered. Without it, Toyoda's hope to wrest the initiative from the Americans was dashed. An attack by U.S. aircraft on airfields on Saipan, Tinian, and Guam also created havoc in the elite torpedo and bomber squadrons of the Japanese First Air Fleet. The Americans, therefore, immediately undermined A-Go's assumption that the U.S. fleet was susceptible to subs or land-based bombers shuttling from Marianas bases. Furthermore, the Fifth Fleet enjoyed numerical superiority by roughly doubling enemy carrier aircraft. Although Spruance had fewer heavy cruisers, he had two more battleships, 11 more light cruisers, and 41 more destroyers than the Japanese. Finally, Ozawa neglected communications security; unbeknownst to him, U.S. technicians listened into his squadron commander guiding pilots to the battle.

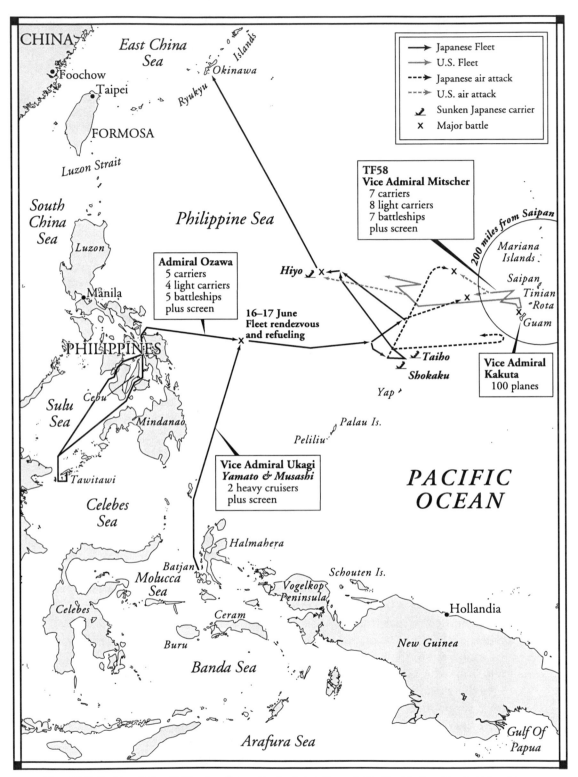

Map 20.2 Battle of the Philippine Sea. Credit: Craig L. Symonds, *The Naval Institute Historical Atlas of the U.S. Navy*, p. 171.

The Japanese predicted victory. Mobile Fleet's air scouts saw Task Force 58 first, and this allowed Ozawa to keep his fleet beyond the reach of Spruance while his planes flew with the trade winds into the Fifth Fleet to refuel on land if need be. Yet by directing the land-based aircraft toward the Americans, he broke radio silence, and his luck ran out afterward. Radar picked up the first of four attack waves of aircraft sent at 8:30 on the morning of June 19 about 150 miles from the Fifth Fleet. Spruance had nearly all fighter strength available; and having wiped out the land-based aircraft on Guam, he needed only to focus on Ozawa's carrier waves in the battle of the Philippine Sea. Mitscher counseled patience from his air group commanders. When radar picked up 69 incoming Sea Eagle fighters, he ordered dive-bombers and torpedo bombers off the decks and away to the east to safety and sent his more experienced pilots against the outnumbered and greener flyers of the Mobile Fleet in a defensive air fight. Hellcats roared at the lighter Japanese Zeros that were downed by one good burst of fire. The Japanese only hit the battleship *South Dakota* and shot just one plane out of the sky while Ozawa's first wave initially lost 42 aircraft.

Misfortune then plagued the next waves of attackers in what became known as the Great Marianas Turkey Shoot. American fighters and antiaircraft barrage devastated the enemy. The second Japanese attack wave approached with 128 Sea Eagles, but Hellcats met them 60 miles from the Fifth Fleet and shot down over half. The third wave searched in vain for Task Force 58, which turned out to be the best news of a bad day for Ozawa because this was the only large group of planes to survive. The fourth group of 82 Zeros got near the U.S. fleet but was almost completely eliminated. Dogfights over Guam cost Ozawa another 50 planes. At the same time, submarines sunk his flagship as well as the Pearl Harbor attack veteran *Shokaku*. Spruance lost just 29 planes but

Imperial Navy carrier maneuvers in the battle of the Philippine Sea. Credit: U.S. Naval Institute.

Japanese numbers were the reverse. Of the entire raid, nearly 300 Zeroes plunged into the sea. Ozawa retained just 11 Zeroes and 100 aircraft in total on his decks. The Turkey Shoot reduced the Imperial Navy's carrier strength to next to nothing.

To the annoyance of his admirals, Spruance called off the pursuit because he believed that his luck had run out and that Ozawa would ambush him. Ozawa thought he had gravely damaged enemy carrier power and planned to return to battle once he had rearmed and refueled. He erred considerably. Mitscher was sent to chase the retreating Mobile Fleet, and the next afternoon, June 20, scouts sighted Ozawa's ships for the first time. Spruance ordered 216 planes to attack even though day was quickly waning and the fleeing enemy remained at the extreme end of his range. Only a dangerous night landing would get them back safely; if fuel ran out, the pilots might ditch in the seas and hope for rescue. As the sun set the fighters and dive-bombers and torpedo bombers arrived above the Mobile Fleet. They sunk the carrier *Hiyo* and damaged two others and destroyed 65 planes, leaving Ozawa with a mere 35 aircraft. On the return, almost all of the U.S. aircrews were saved as destroyers risked detection by submarines by racing toward the planes. As a last resort, Spruance ordered the carriers to turn on their lights even though the Imperial Navy might see them. In the end, just 20 U.S. pilots were lost. This put a damper on the victory, although over 80 men either ended up in the water to be rescued or crash-landed on the carriers.

Among others, Mitscher believed that Spruance should have continued to chase the First Mobile Fleet and destroy it. Spruance and his supporters responded that his first job was to protect the Marine Corps stuck on land. He did so. And one could hardly complain about the devastation wrought on the Imperial Navy. The battle of the Philippine Sea was the largest carrier engagement of World War II. It nullified the Japanese carrier fleet, which returned home with decks and holds bare of aircraft. The Imperial Navy was not finished, but the late Yamamoto's air fleet had vanished.

TINIAN AND GUAM

The conquest of the Marianas now continued as the Americans moved on Tinian, just three miles from Saipan. Stationed on this ten-mile long island were 8,350 troops who had endured a 43-day sea and air blitz including from U.S. artillery on Saipan. On July 24, 1944, Major-General Harry Schmidt of the V Amphibious Corps sent the 2nd and 4th Marine Divisions ashore in a surprise landing on the more challenging northern shore rather than at the island's center. It took twelve days to overwhelm the Japanese defenders. The attack was rapid and methodical, although three months were required to root out pockets of resistance. Banzai charges were common. There were 2,000 U.S. casualties, though a relatively low 328 were killed. The Marine Corps fought skillfully, so much so that Holland Smith called the capture of Tinian the best amphibious operation of the Pacific war. It was also vitally important because Tinian became a base for the Superfortress bombers, two of which appeared over Hiroshima and Nagasaki in August 1945 after having taken off from the island.

The largest island in the Marianas was Guam, which had been under American control from 1898 until the U.S. Marines surrendered their small garrison on

December 10, 1941, to spare the lives of U.S. nationals. The island promised more challenges than Saipan because it was 34 miles long and equally as rugged. Guam was important because it had the only good supply of water in the Marianas, an excellent harbor, and it would serve as a jump-off point for the invasion of the Philippines. The difficulties in subduing Saipan and the duel in the Philippine Sea delayed the invasion of Guam until July 21. At that time, Roy Geiger sent in III Amphibious Corps of 55,000 men who had been plowing circles in the seas awaiting the destruction of the First Mobile Fleet.

By the time that the 3rd Marine Division and 1st Provisional Marine Brigade did land with the 77th Infantry Division in reserve, 19,000 veteran Japanese troops had built beach defenses. These pestered the invaders, but underwater demolition teams cleared the mines and debris. The U.S. Navy then began the most intensive and extensive air and sea bombardment of the Pacific war—a thirteen-day barrage from close-in positions. Unlike Holland Smith, Geiger—a veteran of Guadalcanal and Bougainville—worked well with his Army counterpart Andrew Bruce. Their cooperation proved lethal. Their attack unhinged the defenders and allowed the Americans to move across the island. U.S. forces killed 10,646 men while they lost a tenth of that number. Many Japanese committed suicide by exploding grenades against their bodies, jumping from cliffs, or cutting their throats, and even the commanding general sent the Emperor news of the defeat and then committed suicide. Imperial forces fought sporadically but fiercely, however. They prolonged the island's capture with banzai charges and instigated several friendly-fire mishaps. It took three weeks for Guam to be fully secured. U.S. casualty figures mounted to 7,800, with roughly 2,000 dead, by the end of the battle. Many Guamanians suffered as well, although 20,000 Chamorro civilians were freed from prisons. Mopping up continued throughout the war and afterward as well; incredibly, the last defender came out of hiding in 1972. In general, the population welcomed back U.S. control as the old Marine Corps barracks hosted a moving flag-raising ceremony. Nimitz arrived to declare Apra Harbor his new headquarters for the duration of the war.

The Marianas campaign paid big dividends for the United States. The Japanese fleet was routed and its airpower gutted even as the Imperial Navy turned to desperate acts in an attempt to stem the American advance across the Pacific. Guam became a base for American bombers, submarines, and services but most significant, land-based bombers could now penetrate into the home islands from the Marianas. Saipan was just 1,200 miles from Tokyo and the same distance to the Philippines. Even as the invasion was occurring, a strategic air offensive began. Fifty Superfortresses from the China-based Twentieth USAAF blasted steel mills on Kyushu on June 15, 1944. Most of the 50 sorties flown from China targeted the mainland and Southeast Asia with little strategic effect. On the other hand, the airfields in the Marianas were critical. Over 29,000 sorties during the next year dropped 157,000 tons of explosives and incendiaries (and two atomic bombs) that killed 260,000 people and left over 9 million homeless. The capture of Tinian represented the coming of age of the American strategy of annihilation in Asia.

Two other results stemmed from the capture of the Marianas. First, the Tojo government fell from power. The Prime Minister had incurred criticism for shortages that plagued Japan, and when he had named himself Army Chief of Staff in February 1944, his critics protested even more. The fall of Saipan was the last straw, however. Although a remote island, it was still part of the old Empire and the loss was psychologically unsettling. Senior statesmen, navy leaders, and some of the Emperor's court demanded his resignation in this hour of national crisis. In July 1944, he succumbed to the pressure and withdrew into obscurity, giving way to another hard-line belligerent, Lieutenant-General Kuniaki Koiso. This Army officer, a former chief of staff of the Kwantung Army in Manchuria and later the governor-general of Korea was Tojo's equal in staying the course. But as the reality of Japan's predicament came closer to home in the form of American bombers overhead, Koiso also lost his job by April 1945.

The other major consequence of the Marianas campaign affected American thinking. As news arose of banzai charges, beheadings, mass suicides, and civilian murder, military planners determined that Japan would stop fighting only after being invaded and subdued. This war without mercy—shaped by racism, fear, and hatred on both sides—spiraled into a conflict of annihilation. The enemy drew on such ruses as using civilians as decoys which compelled the U.S. Marines to bayonet all bodies they came across to be safe. Their motto became "if it didn't stink, stick it." Japanese defenders pledged to fight to the last man, woman, and child, and innocent civilians had shown a willingness to die. This prompted hand-wringing and disbelief but also anger and vengeance on the part of American soldiers. Flying hero Charles Lindbergh captured the sentiment. Writing from Australia as he reflected on the behavior in the field, he lamented that the GIs "treat the Jap with less respect than they would give to an animal, and these acts are condoned by almost everyone. We claim to be fighting for civilization, but the more I see of this war in the Pacific the less right I think we have to claim to be civilized." Convinced that the enemy was inhuman, Washington prepared to exterminate these supposed beasts by a war of annihilation.

PELELIU

With the Marianas secure by the end of July 1944 and the Philippines awaiting liberation, Japan's focus on defense centered on Peleliu and Angaur in the Palau Islands. This group of islands sat 800 miles west of the Philippines at the edge of the Caroline chain. Attention to the seven-square-mile coral island of Peleliu arose because the Palaus guarded MacArthur's flank as he moved up into the Philippines. In preparation for the invasion, the U.S. Navy shifted personnel and commands. Nimitz sent Spruance and his commanders off to the north and put Bull Halsey in charge of the Third Fleet. Mitscher remained at the helm of Task Force 58, which was transformed into Task Force 38. The Third Fleet took aim on Peleliu after MacArthur complained that he lacked enough carriers to protect operations in the Philippines. The cooperative Nimitz wished to prove his worth to General MacArthur by seizing the Palaus. What the U.S. Navy most wanted were the airfields on Peleliu, Angaur, and Ulithi atoll to support carrier-based aircraft. On Angaur, the 81st Army Division blasted away the garrison of 1,500 in just four days, but Peleliu was a different matter. On September 15, the 1st Marine Division went in but this so-called Old Breed of veterans found themselves at the wrong end of enemy artillery. The small island with Umurbrogol Mountain as its highest point had been so hammered by a three-day naval bombardment that Major-General William Rupertus predicted Peleliu's capture in four days. He grossly underestimated the timing and task at hand.

Colonel Nakegawa Kunio, commander of the 10,600 man garrison, switched tactics from previous island defenses. Rather than trying to push the invaders off the beaches and into the sea, he prepared his main defenses inland where he dug out impassable defenses that took advantage of the Umurbrogol's rugged terrain. His forces attacked from these points and caused major casualties. The airstrip fell into U.S. hands after eight days, but Nakegawa was only beginning to fight. He retreated to a network of interconnecting caves and bunkers inside the Umurbrogol Mountain—soon renamed Bloody Nose Ridge—which American assaults did not reduce until November. Nakegawa was also creative in this pocket. He blocked cave entrances with concrete or oil drums, put steel doors on some, and cut escape hatches at the back. Some tunnels had various levels, and a few had electric lights and ventilation systems. The 10,000 defenders had to be dug out—cave by cave—U.S. Marines did not completely eradicate them until November 27, seventy-three days after the invasion began. Albeit tiny, the entire island was not free of Japanese until February 1945. By then the Old Breed had been reduced by casualties. Combat in rough terrain and temperatures that soared above 115 degrees made Peleliu a living hell. The shelling drove men crazy, the stink of rotting flesh nauseated them, and in the muggy air, stench from puffy-faced corpses was unavoidable. Blowflies and land crabs feasted at night. The campaign so brutalized the troops that senseless cruelty ensued. During lulls in the fighting, U.S. soldiers pried gold teeth out of the mouths of living Japanese, while other times they pitched pebbles into the open skulls of the dead. In general, the troops were simply shocked and fatigued. On sailing away, one U.S. Marine recalled that even at a distance, Peleliu was ugly. This island fight hardly exemplified a good war.

Eventually, two regiments from the 81st Infantry Division had to come over from Angaur to secure Peleliu by October 15, 1944. By that time, the one-month battle had become one of the bloodiest confrontations of the war for the United States, wasting away the 1st Marine Division. While most of the Japanese perished—only 400 of the 13,600 defenders were taken prisoner—the Americans suffered over 6,500 casualties, including 1,252 killed. The Marine Corps also noted the change in tactics from banzai charges to tenacious defense, a new approach that typified the remaining battles of the Pacific war and worsened the killing in the ground war of annihilation.

Peleliu was not worth the effort. The operation finally succeeded, but only Ulithi in the Palaus proved important to the seizure of the Philippines and the central Pacific campaign because its deep harbor became an assembly area for the invasions of Iwo Jima and Okinawa. Peleliu was irrelevant to the capture and protection of the Philippines. The attack did wipe out the veteran 14th Division, one of Japan's finest, and also sealed off a marine base at Koror as well as 250,000 troops elsewhere in the Carolines. In addition, a patrol bomber from Peleliu sited the torpedoed *Indianapolis* on July 17, 1945, which led to the rescue of 316 sailors, although 1,196 were lost to the attacking Japanese, exposure, and sharks in the worst sea disaster in U.S. naval history. But these positives did not figure into the larger strategic operations of the war. As the

Americans moved up through the Pacific, they left Peleliu orphaned outside the sphere of conflict as a bloody reminder of the wages of war. Perhaps Peleliu's highest value derived from the warning of what lay ahead for the Americans. Indeed, as skirmishing persisted on Peleliu, the Joint Chiefs finally come to a decision about the direction of the Pacific war.

Both Nimitz and MacArthur focused on the Philippines. They believed that Leyte, in the heart of the central Philippines, could not be attacked until they secured surrounding islands. But U.S. Navy chief Ernest King hoped to bypass the Philippines entirely in favor of bombing Formosa or the home islands. MacArthur reacted in fury, arguing that the United States owed the Filipinos their liberation. In the midst of his fourth presidential campaign, Franklin Roosevelt weighed in. He heard out MacArthur and Nimitz in July 1944 after traveling to Hawaii to discuss strategy and take photographs with the famous general. Invading the Philippines was good politics. Yet events, and not the election, changed King's mind. In late July, Admiral Toyoda had activated a plan to defend the Philippines by forming two large naval task forces for Operation Sho Go. This was the final attempt at a decisive sea battle with the United States. Two months later, Halsey's Third Fleet roamed the Western Pacific and destroyed 500 enemy aircraft bound for the Philippines. U.S. Task Force 38 assailed Yap, the Palaus, Formosa, and Mindanao, finding the southern Philippines lightly defended. Halsey urged MacArthur not to focus on Mindanao but attack Leyte. Nimitz recommended targeting the island of Luzon itself where the capital of Manila was located rather than moving up through the islands from the south, and MacArthur agreed. He quickly jumped up the timetable for an invasion from December to October 20, 1944. King's Formosa option simply lacked the manpower for an invasion, claimed even his own staff, and Nimitz counseled that that the island could be subdued from the air. The central Pacific offensive would assume responsibility for Formosa before moving north toward Japan. King relented. MacArthur and Nimitz were instructed to invade Luzon on December 20 as the United States poised for huge gains as the Summer of 1944 turned into fall.

Since June 1944, the Allies in all theaters of the war had thrown back the Axis powers, and this reality was no more clear than in the case of Japan. The Empire was in retreat everywhere but China. Tokyo politicians and military commanders were under pressure to produce positive results, but their days of victories had passed. The United States advanced on the home islands and in the process systematically destroyed Japan's airpower and sea power. On land, fanatical resistance could not disguise the fact that the Americans were hopping ever closer toward the Philippines and Japan itself. In the Pacific, the Japanese hoped for a miracle to reverse their fortunes. In Europe, their German Axis partner had one in mind.

PART

V

Annihilation

1944–1945

I don't remember what battle that was, it was somewhere in
Belgium—Bastogne maybe, or Tillet. There was just fighting,
on and on, the crack of rifles and the ack ack ack of machine
guns, bazookas firing, shells and mines exploding, men
screaming and groaning and dying. And every day knowing
you could be next, it could be your blood spattered all over
your buddies.

HILLARY JORDAN
MudboundI

The Allies' surge toward their enemies' homelands by late summer 1944 did not
compel the Axis powers to surrender. On the contrary, as the USSR approached
from the east and Allied forces stood on his western doorstep, Hitler resolved to
defend the Third Reich to the bitter end. Japan, too, did not abandon the fight
even as the U.S. sea-air juggernaut guided by the strategy of annihilation came ever
closer to home. Because the Axis was losing, it became more senselessly brutal.
Germany and Japan fought tenaciously. In return, the Allies showed no mercy. As
the jaws of defeat closed inexorably on them, the fascists and militarists wantonly
calculated to exact the last bit of blood from their enemies in the hopes of miraculously saving themselves. The war of annihilation was very much in evidence.

CHAPTER 21

German Resistance in the West

THE WEST WALL

After their second meeting at Quebec in mid-September 1944, the Allied Chiefs of Staff transferred European resources to the Pacific. The units were solely naval forces and thus had no big impact on the campaign against Germany, but because no ground or air forces were moved, the decision reflected caution about the situation in western Europe. Eisenhower moved SHAEF offices to Paris in anticipation of an invasion of Germany proper yet logistical problems turned out to be a larger problem than expected. The Allies paid the price for their destruction of the French railway system since no trains ran at all. By the second week of September, their bloated and impeded supply chain became a crisis that shut down offensive operations. In the face of the Allied sweep across France, Germany resorted to a last-ditch defense in northwest Europe. Rundstedt reestablished a defensive line from Switzerland to the English Channel. The Wehrmacht held the north bank of Antwerp's Scheldt Estuary and thereby denied the vital port to the Allies.

By September 1944, six armies stood within reach of Germany: Crerar's First Canadian, Dempsey's British Second, three American (Hodges' First, Patton's Third, and Patch's Seventh), and de Lattre's French First Army in the south. All had outrun their supplies, which necessitated an alteration of the original plan of advancing on a broad front; but each general hoped his army would lead the charge to Berlin. Dempsey or one of the Americans was the candidate. Because he often condescended to the Americans, Crerar was not considered for the honor of invading Germany. Instead, he got the task of clearing the Channel ports. In any case, Dempsey moved forward to Brussels and Antwerp, backed on the right by First Army although the waterways of Belgium bogged him down. U.S. armies entered Luxembourg, neared the Ardennes Forest (where the

Germans had boldly broken out into France in 1940), and abutted the fortifications of the so-called German West Wall that guarded the Rhine River. Third Army went as far as supplies would take it, ending up in Metz and the Meuse River just miles from the German border. An alarmed Hitler urged Rundstedt to defend the West Wall.

When Monty's Twenty-First Army Group comprised of Dempsey's and Crerar's forces arrived at the gates of Antwerp on September 4, the Germans had no time to destroy the port's docks and lock system, yet these could only be accessed from the Scheldt River estuary. The Wehrmacht occupied the estuary's islands of Walcheren and South Beveland, and alternative ports such as Amsterdam and Rotterdam also remained in German hands. Monty had a plan, however, and one totally out of character. Normally, he ploddingly built up strength before attacking and occupied territory rather than opting for a swift advance. But given supply priority, he audaciously offered Operation Market-Garden to vault the lower Rhine River (a wide, fast-flowing obstacle to military campaigns throughout history), turn right, and advance on the Third Reich's industrial heartland in the Ruhr valley. Allied troops would capture bridges leading to Arnhem in the Netherlands so that Twenty-First Army Group could cross the Rhine River and sweep into the north German plain. Market-Garden would also take Rotterdam and Amsterdam and nullify the need to contest the Germans in the Scheldt estuary. It was a daring idea.

The prospects looked good. Fifteenth Army under Gustav-Adolph von Zangen was isolated on the west bank of the Scheldt and Monty could exploit his 70-mile separation from the West Wall by sending Second Army up the estuary. The 300-mile West Wall fortifications, also known as the Siegfried Line, faced the French Maginot Line. Begun in 1936, the West Wall from Basel to Cleves consisted of natural barriers linked to concrete antitank defenses that acted as a deterrent that could delay but not halt the invaders. In 1944, divisions of Volksgrenadiers—replacement troops comprised of the remnants of units that fought in Normandy and on the Eastern front—defended the West Wall. German Fifteenth Army was stuck in the Scheldt estuary unable to reach them, or so the Allies thought. ULTRA revealed Hitler's intention to fight in the Scheldt estuary, but the Allies ignored the information out of confidence that victory was imminent after Normandy. A mere 18-mile advance would have trapped the Wehrmacht, but the British stopped at Antwerp on the grounds that they were out of fuel. This was not true. The decision was inexplicable unless Monty orchestrated it to justify Operation Market-Garden and get credit for issuing the ultimate blow to Germany in the northwest Europe campaign.

The halt allowed the Germans to escape for the second time in 1944 and save themselves once again from destruction in the west. Crerar's First Canadian Army lacked the strength to cut off the withdrawal of German Fifteenth Army's 80,000 troops being ferried from Breskens to Flushing, which was on the way to the Beveland isthmus just north of Antwerp. Two Canadian armored divisions aimed for Fifteenth Army but missed at Breskens; and on September 20, a Polish infantry brigade also fell short. RAF bombers failed to slow the evacuation because Bomber Command had directed the planes to support operations on the Channel ports. Wehrmacht resistance stiffened along the front as the Allies approached the German border at the Rhine. The 85-day

Map 21.1 Market-Garden and Scheldt Estuary. Credit: Ronald Story,
Concise Historical Atlas of World War II: The Geography of Conflict, Map 28A, top, p. 61.

campaign to surround Zangen and grab the Scheldt estuary bogged down from the
start. Crerar gave II Corps responsibility for clearing the banks of the Scheldt by landing on Walcheren and then moving through South Beveland, but after their successful
evacuation, the Germans deployed across this area and into Holland just north of the
British. They had a lock hold on the Scheldt estuary and reserves to defend southern
Holland. Crerar soon returned to England for medical reasons and turned over command of II Corps to fellow Canadian Guy Simonds. This veteran of campaigns in Italy
and Normandy settled in for a prolonged assault on the estuary but he also was hampered by the supply problem caused by the diversion of men and materiel to Monty's
bold strike into Holland under Operation Market-Garden.

Montgomery had projected Market-Garden to win the war earlier than planned by
a drive into Germany spearheaded by the British. With a bridgehead across the lower
Rhine in the Dutch town of Arnhem, the Allies could outflank the West Wall and shoot
directly to Berlin through the Ruhr valley. Eisenhower gave Monty fuel, additional units
pulled from other parts of the theater, and several divisions of paratroopers under First

Allied Airborne Army. The undistinguished army aviator Lewis Brererton, who had recently led the U.S. Far East Army Air Forces in the Philippines before moving on to Libya, led First Allied Airborne Army. It would drop behind German lines to establish a corridor extending roughly from Eindhoven to the Rhine at Arnhem by capturing eight bridges and securing 40 miles of highway connecting the cities. Brererton had no experience with airborne or ground operations despite his new post.

The operation had air (Market) and ground (Garden) components. Market was under the tactical command of Brererton's deputy Frederick Browning, a pioneer of airborne forces during the campaigns in North Africa, Sicily, and Normandy. He had never taken part in combat but decided to land the troops in gliders. Browning warned Monty that by trying to capture the farthest water obstacle—the Rhine River crossing at Arnhem—there was the danger of "going a bridge too far." Yet he also ignored reports of substantial enemy armor surrounding Arnhem. Browning did not add antitank mines and weapons to the supplies of 1st Airborne Division but merely went ahead with the airborne attack. Garden involved a rapid advance across the bridges by the XXX Corps of Dempsey's Second Army under Brian Horrocks. A popular corps commander who had long served under Monty until suffering severe wounds in an air raid in August 1944, Horrocks would have to speed to Arnhem from the Meuse-Escaut Canal 59 miles away in just three days. The Dutch government helped by calling a railway strike to paralyze shipments of German supplies (that prompted vicious Nazi reprisals). Omar Bradley thought the plan too risky because it would cripple the joint offensive against the Rhine. Ike stayed the course, however, seeing the Market-Garden gamble as having a fair chance of success.

The risky operation began on September 17, 1944, as airborne units flew from England. The 16,500 paratroopers and 3,500 glider troops targeted the bridges: 101st U.S. Airborne Division between Eindhoven and Veghel, the 82nd U.S. Airborne Division around Grave and Groesbeek, and the 1st British Airborne Division near Arnhem. British paratroopers were less experienced than the Americans, yet they were responsible for the most dangerous assignment of dropping on Arnhem at the extreme end of the operation. The 1st Airborne's divisional commander, Roy Urquhart, had no history with airborne landings, and making matters worse, radios at the bridgehead failed and kept him beyond the guidance of his superiors. Fear of flak steered air transport away from Arnhem. Released with supplies six miles away, the British trudged four hours on foot to reach the bridges. The mission's armored jeeps were lost and reinforcements were available only once a day. The rest of the 1st Airborne Division came in on the second day, and the Polish Independent Parachute Brigade under World War I veteran Stanislaw Sosabowski took two days to arrive. The Germans captured the operational orders carried by an unauthorized U.S. officer killed in a glider crash. The most serious problem of all was the Wehrmacht's presence.

Having let the German army escape from the Falaise pocket came back to haunt the Allies. Resting and refitting after their flight from Normandy, elements of the battle-hardened 9th and 10th SS Panzer Divisions trained in the area. Allied intelligence knew they were there, but the information was ignored. Such carelessness persisted when the Dutch underground reported that German armor had grouped around Arnhem. But neither Monty nor the airborne commanders took note out of the belief that they had more than enough forces and a good plan to achieve their aims. Commander of Army Group B, the wily Walther Model, moved his headquarters near Arnhem. In addition, paratrooper General Kurt Student, who had led the attack on Holland in 1940, arrived to direct the defensive efforts along the Albert Canal. After practicing how to stop an airborne landing, the two panzer divisions reacted with a swift, aggressive, and well-executed defense in the best tradition of German tactical brilliance.

Things soured quickly for the Allies at Arnhem as resistance blocked their way. The Germans destroyed the targeted railway bridge, and a battalion of the 1st Airborne Division led by John Frost took an end of the road bridge but not in sufficient strength for the main body to move across. Bad weather delayed the arrival of the reinforcing Polish Parachute Brigade. The Germans isolated Frost, cut off Urquhart in the town, and prevented a rescue by stopping enemy troops from crossing the Lower Rhine after being dropped nearby at Driel. Arnhem's bridge was indeed too far from Allied reach.

Down the airborne corridor, Horrocks' XXX Corps joined the 101st Airborne Division near Eindhoven as it tried to open the sixty-mile passage to Arnhem. Horrocks fell 33 hours farther behind schedule when compelled to build a Bailey bridge, a modular steel roadway held together by pins in place of one ruined by the Wehrmacht. Dempsey urged on his troops, but the slowly creeping British VII and XII Corps exposed the 101st Airborne Division's flanks along the Eindhoven-Nijmegen road. The defenders subjected the unit to vicious attacks and severed the road soon known as "Hell's Highway." The British backtracked repeatedly to retake positions lost. Horrock's delay also undermined the 82nd Airborne Division's position on the Groesbeek Ridge. Those troops guarded against counterattacks and captured bridges leading to Nijmegen, but weather prevented reinforcements for the paratroopers. On September 20, Horrocks' men finally crossed the Waal River in assault boats to seize both Nijmegen bridges but took a full day more to advance toward Arnhem. They halted for tea as the 82nd Airborne Division paratroopers watched in rage. By the time Horrocks started moving, the British were driven off the bridge in Arnhem and German artillery went across it to block his advance to Ressen. The corridor was so narrow and straight that the Germans could hit it with artillery from both sides; tanks moving in single file were easily stopped by one well-placed gun. The march was diverted to Driel, though a large-scale crossing there was impossible anyway.

Operation Market-Garden failed. The British withdrew their remaining paratroopers to the river and evacuated the night of September 25. Over 2,100 of the 1st Airborne Division troops escaped along with 160 Poles and 75 of the 250 men who crossed at Driel, but more than 6,000 troops—half of them wounded—became prisoners of the Third Reich. Overall, 1st Airborne Division suffered 8,000 casualties. The two U.S. airborne divisions suffered 3,532 losses over the next two months. Horrocks' 1,500 casualties stood in marked contrast to these large sacrifices, which was testimony to his slowness. The British scapegoated the Polish Airborne Brigade commander Sosabowski even though he had issued a warning that the operation would be tougher than Monty, Dempsey, and Browning thought.

The German defenders had prevented a bridgehead across the Lower Rhine, and the West Wall held. Their discipline, speed, and decentralized decision-making structure reaped dividends against the command incompetence of the Allies. The best that could be said about Market-Garden is that it gave the Allies a salient from which they launched the final battle for Germany in February 1945. The debacle also allowed Eisenhower to reassert his command and regain the spotlight from Monty. Yet the operation exhausted Allied supplies, wasted personnel, and halted Patton's drive on Metz by diverting fuel-supply planes to Arnhem. It also exposed Monty's vanity. To his credit, it was no accident that the Germans based two elite SS panzer divisions to guard the north German plain and Ruhr where Market-Garden posed the greater risk to Germany rather than in front of Patton whose thrust labored through wooded, hilly country toward the Rhine. This area was a less immediate threat to the Reich's existence. The failure showed that the Allies were not strong enough to defeat Nazism in 1944.

The disaster around Arnhem also took valuable supplies and troops from the Scheldt estuary to the southwest. If given its proper attention, this operation might have inflicted a killing blow on Germany. At this point, Operation Dragoon in southern France saved the day by supplying nearly 40% of the Allied advance war effort through Marseilles. By October 1944, the 2nd Canadian Division under Simond advanced toward the South Beveland isthmus from Antwerp. Monty also tried to root out Fifteenth Army from the Breskens pocket, which the Wehrmacht called the Scheldt Fortress South. Allied power reduced the pocket over the next few weeks, but logistics caught up to Montgomery and his forces ran out of steam. Under intense criticism, he ordered Simonds to focus the entire First Canadian Army on clearing both sides of the Scheldt. Simonds directed the 2nd Canadian Division to the eastern bank as well as the South Beveland isthmus, which two brigades from the British 52nd Division overran by the end of October.

This advance showed how much effort lay ahead in excavating the Germans from the estuary. To take Welcheren Island required crossing an exposed 1,200 yard straight causeway in the Sloe Channel. The Canadians failed three times to traverse it, but two brigades of the 52nd Division finally crossed. The Breskens pocket closed, at long last, and the town itself was taken on October 21. Knocke and the Zeebrugge fell in early November and a British Royal Marine Commando brigade backed by armor struck at Walcheren. A group assaulted Flushing while another landed on a dyke on the western tip at Westkapelle with the aid of 27 amtracs. The operations succeeded, although the latter was harrowing. Bad weather cancelled a preliminary bombardment against the impressive defenses of pillboxes, concealed flamethrowers, and mines surrounding three heavy naval coastal batteries. Rocket-firing aircraft and the armed landing craft could not dent the wall. Because all but seven of the landing craft were sunk and damaged, the Allies incurred 300 casualties. Still, aircraft drew the attention of the German batteries; and as a result, the commandos made it to shore. They seized the batteries and minesweepers began to clear the Scheldt River. An artillery bombardment preceded an assault by the commandos at Flushing. The 155th Brigade of the British 52nd Division fought the Germans in the streets before Flushing was secured, and the unit then crossed the flooded dykes to reach Walcheren's capital of Middleburg where the Germans capitulated on November 5. Mopping up on the island lasted for three days.

The Allies could finally use Antwerp's docks, and Hitler's logistical nightmare had come true. The port was critical to supplying the Allies as they turned toward Germany. Hitler knew its import. The capture of Antwerp and the Scheldt estuary prompted him to attack the convoys with midget submarines and speedy E-boats armed with two torpedoes. He also aimed more V-weapons (flying bombs) on London and Antwerp; the latter endured almost as many V-1 guided rocket and V-2 ballistic missile attacks as England, and in half the time. As the supplies poured in and the Allies closed on the Rhine, the Fuhrer decided on a bold initiative to recapture Antwerp and thereby safe-guard the West Wall.

HITLER'S COUNTEROFFENSIVE

Up to this point in December 1944, Allied miscalculations aided Hitler's efforts. Allied infantry losses were heavy, and reserves grew scarce. The British suffered particularly in this regard, and as a result, Monty resorted to breaking up units for replacements elsewhere. A Canadian conscription crisis in November temporarily halted the flow of troops overseas. And having decided on an 89-division army, even the Americans lacked sufficient manpower. Soldiers remained in battle, and reinforcements did not replace them but joined them on the lines. The Allies also underestimated Wehrmacht troop strength and its ability to reorganize. In the field, there were also problems. Rain flooded the plains of southern Holland where the Germans rested after being pushed from the Scheldt area, and the weather made rapid advance impossible by October. Eisenhower divided the American drive toward Germany. In support of Monty, Hodges' First Army took Aachen on October 21 but only after breaking a two-week enemy effort to prevent encirclement. He then stalled in the Hurtgen Forest, where the Germans could halt an intrusion from the north by releasing water from the dams surrounding the forest. The Americans might have attacked from the southeast, but Hodges was ordered to protect the flanks of the VII Corps from the north. The Germans valued the Hurtgen Forest because losing it would jeopardize their position in front of the Rhine. Thus, they packed the area with mines, machine-gun nests, barbed wire, and pillboxes that mimicked Japanese defenses in the Pacific. The Americans faced prohibitive tacti-cal disadvantages. They were restricted to logging trails that accessed the gorges while the Wehrmacht held the roads for easy transport. The battle for Hurtgen Forest prom-ised to be fierce, for the stakes were high and the enemy was well placed.

The Americans quickly realized the challenges as they moved just a mile within five days of the battle's opening salvos on October 6. Ten days more yielded the 9th Infantry Division just another mile. They lost 5,000 casualties in the process, and still the Germans held the dams. Both sides ambushed the other. They took "an atavistic, savage pleasure whenever they caught the enemy off guard," recalled one soldier, with such tricks as tying grenades to telephone lines to kill engineers or shelling food carts destined for hungry infantrymen. Round after round of mortar attacks moved lines back and forth amidst the blackened trees in this "death fac-tory." Noted a U.S. air commander, the battle was "our Paschendale," a reference to the slaughter of British troops in World War I. In November, the new U.S. Ninth Army under W. H. Simpson pushed to the Roer River but could not cross it. Hodges insisted on taking the Forest rather than the dams. Heavy fighting cost the 28th Infantry Division over 6,000 casualties as the Americans were driven out of the key town of Schmidt before they seized the Hurtgen Forest in December. The cost was great. They lost most of four divisions or 25,000 men. Some 2,500 black infantrymen were also thrown into the breach, and men with just eight weeks of training then joined them. The fighting was so harrowing that some thought of escape. As a warning, the Army shot deserter Private Eddie Slovik in January 1945, the only American executed for that crime during the war. At first glance, the battle of the Hurtgen Forest did not seem critical to the general drive eastward but as things turned out, the troubles encountered there vitiated the middle of the Allied lines. Hodges' struggle in the Hurtgen death factory proved more significant than Monty's setback with Operation Market-Garden.

To the south, Patton met more trouble. In September, he assailed Metz but took many casualties as shortages of manpower and materiel plagued his effort. Third Army climbed on to Fort Driant, a fortress guarding Metz, only to be bombarded by the occupiers who called on their own artillery to hit the exposed Americans. On October 12–13, Patton withdrew from Driant and pondered ways to take the city. To encircle Metz, he ordered an attack on the Maginot Line by XII Corps, and when its commander asked for a delay because of rain, Patton refused. Heavy artillery bombardment broke through the clouds, and armor ground up the German lines. A pincer of two Allied infantry divisions swung from the north to meet the 5th Armored Division moving up from the south around Metz by November 19. The weather slowed the Americans enough to allow the garrison to escape. Even though he took Metz three days later, Patton had studied the history of sieges in France's Lorraine province. He knew that his effort was sheer folly.

The German's held the West Wall, and the Allied advance petered out. Jacob Devers' new Sixth Army Group, comprised of Dragoon forces, liberated Strasbourg; but it could not break through in the north and could not cross the Rhine because of an enemy bridgehead at Colmar. U.S. Seventh Army Patch simply moved up to the West Wall and stopped. Bad weather bogged down Patton. Bradley attempted a resupply, but winter clothes were lacking. Combat casualties in November doubled those of October and were ten thousand above the July numbers when the fighting had been most ferocious. Equipment losses were equally taxing. Washington readied to ship the heavily armored M-26 Pershing tank armed with its 90-mm gun, but senior commanders stuck with the M-4 Shermans that proved vulnerable. That Bradley lacked a precise objective for his forces, which he sent in multidirectional attacks against the West Wall, signaled another real weakness, and Hitler seized on the opportunity presented by meandering Allied movements.

The Fuhrer planned to split the Allied armies and recapture Antwerp. Against the wishes of his generals, he ruled out a counteroffensive against the USSR because its advance from the east could be stopped only by bringing full force to bear. Besides, the Soviets had halted in Poland and turned south toward the Balkans and away, at least temporarily, from Germany. With less respect for the Western Allies than the USSR's capacity to wage war, Hitler calculated that a big blow might demoralize the Americans or prompt a surrender by the British. This was the usual self-deception and hubris; but after the reprisals he took against the generals who tried to kill him on July 20, no commander would contest him. Hitler considered a strike against untested American troops in the Ardennes forest to begin his drive on Antwerp to batter the Allied armies into abandoning the fight. He looked to replay May 1940 when Germany had scored its startling successes in the west. Rundstedt and Model demurred; Hitler raged and got his way.

By the end of September 1944, the Wehrmacht began preparations that SHAEF ignored. Surely, opined Allied headquarters, the Germans could not start another major offensive. For starters, they lacked fuel to drive even halfway to Antwerp, and strategic bombing had destroyed their oil depots. Patton knew better because he recognized that Hitler was a gambler. ULTRA showed that Berlin had withdrawn SS and panzer divisions off the lines for refitting, ordered the Luftwaffe to patrol the Rhine bridges behind the Ardennes, and sent in trains to dump loads of men and materiel. By December 16, the Germans tripled the Allies in soldiers, doubled them in tanks, and had more artillery, and they only suffered a disadvantage in airpower. Hitler remedied that by attacking in bad weather to neutralize the USAAF and RAF. Success depended on mobility and a quick breakthrough. Hitler created Sixth SS Panzer Army under Josef "Sepp" Dietrich who had transformed the Fuhrer's bodyguard into a Waffen SS unit called the 1st Liebstandarte Adolf Hitler, which participated in most campaigns of the war. In the Ardennes, the fanatical Dietrich enjoyed the help of an excellent staff and the aid of Fifth Panzer Army under the skilled Hasso-Eccard von Manteuffel. He had fought in North Africa and the USSR and now would hit St. Vith in the center of the Ardennes. German Seventh Army, led by the competent Erich Brandenberger would go farther south. The Wehrmacht possessed 30 divisions in total and 1,000 aircraft flown by the II Fighter Corps. But Hitler cleverly disguised his intentions. He gave the plan the defensive name "Watch on the Rhine," secretly assembled his forces, and even kept Rundstedt—the Western front commander—in the dark.

Allied responsibility for the Ardennes rested with First Army. Hodges mustered adequate forces in the north around Aachen and the Roer River dams, but in the Ardennes, they were weak. He concentrated on resting his worn out troops after the Hurtgen Forest battle and training new ones. There were five divisions there, but only the 99th possessed sufficient strength. To the south of Monschau, two infantry divisions of VII Corps rested after Hurtgen Forest. The 106th Infantry occupied the Schnee Eifel on a 20-mile front but was green, and the 9th Armored Division stood in reserve. Third Army was farther south around Luxembourg City. The Ardennes was clearly vulnerable. A lack of aerial reconnaissance due to clouds, German radio silence, and Allied misjudgments made Hitler's audacious operation a complete shock.

Preceded by paratrooper drops intended to capture the Meuse bridges and speed the way to Antwerp, the Germans struck with artillery on December 16. Airborne operations included a commando group under Colonel Otto Skorzeny who had rescued Mussolini from prison as well as English-speaking Germans in American garb. They

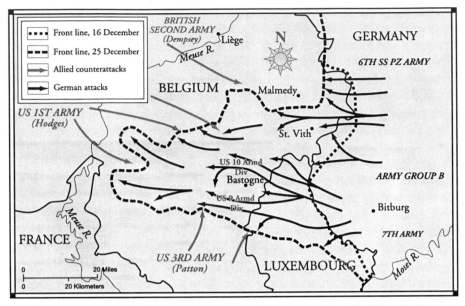

Map 21.2 Battle of the Bulge   Credit: Ronald Story, *Concise Historical Atlas of World War II: The Geography of Conflict*, Map 28B, bottom, p. 61.

sowed confusion. An SS battle group sped past the town of Malmedy, taking 149 prisoners and killing 86 of them before being subdued. This massacre—driven by a strategy of annihilation—was the largest but just one of many such incidents that earned its perpetrators indictments on war crimes. Meanwhile, Dietrich launched the main thrust in the north Ardennes around Monschau at 5:30 a.m. guided by searchlights. Artillery knocked out telephone lines, so Bradley was slow to hear the news. When asked if he expected a counterattack, Bradley responded in the affirmative but confessed that "I'll be damned if I wanted one this big."

Eisenhower responded quicker than his commanders. He sent the 10th Armored Division north against the German left flank, and to reinforce Hodges' beleaguered infantry, the 7th Armored Division from Ninth Army went south against the enemy right flank. They barely held on in the face of fierce attacks. When three divisions arrived to support the 99th Division, Dietrich could not get past the Americans around the Elsenborn ridge east of Malmedy. To the south, U.S. troops held back Brandenberger. The Allies occupied both shoulders of the emerging bulge in their lines, but trouble arose in the center against Manteuffel's panzers. The depleted 28th and inexperienced 106th Divisions collapsed as the Germans roared toward St. Vith and Bastogne to capture 8,000 men in two regiments. A third regiment held out desperately around St. Vith until December 21 before succumbing. This greatest military disaster ever inflicted on the United States ended at the hands of the inexperienced Eighteenth Volksgrenadier (People's) Division, a unit thrown together from replacements and army and air force personnel rather than from SS fanatics or elite commando forces.

At the road hub of Bastogne, the 101st Airborne and part of the 10th Armored Division encircled the town with a defensive ring. Yet Dietrich surrounded them

Bastogne resupplied by air.   Credit: Center for the Study of War Experience at Regis University,
Denver, Colorado: U.S. National Archives.

in turn. The 28th Infantry Division delayed the advance by blowing up bridges and manning artillery batteries until the last moment, yet by December 22, the Germans created a horseshoe—a bulge—that penetrated westward into the center of the line. The Allies pinched at both ends. Bastogne was the key defensive point in this battle of the Bulge. Bradley now realized that Hitler had grander goals than guarding the Roer dams; the Fuhrer sought a stalemate on the entire Western front. Patton saw a chance at Bastogne, however, believing that Dietrich had "stuck his head in the meat-grinder... And this time I've got hold of the handle." Eisenhower also understood the gravity of the situation. He cancelled all operations and gave Montgomery command in the north after the Germans cut Bradley's communication lines. Ike ordered Patton to rescue the besieged 101st Airborne Division that fought desperately inside the ring at Bastogne. As his ammunition supplies dwindled, Anthony McAuliffe, commander of the 101st Airborne, learned that Patton was racing north through the snow. When the Germans demanded he surrender, McAuliffe refused by famously replying "Nuts!" His stubbornness paid off. The skies cleared. Not only did Allied planes bomb the attackers, but he received more ammunition by air on Christmas Day. Patton's tanks broke through. The Germans attacked twice more to wipe out resistance in the bulge, but Patton held his ground. He then directed the counterattack from his open jeep in the bitter cold.

The center of the front now emerged as the critical area. Monty took command of Bradley's two northern armies and sent his reserve XXX Corps between Liege and Louvain. This gave Hodges the freedom to counterattack but not before part of his VII Corps was committed to blocking Manteuffel's 2nd Panzer Division at Foy-Notre Dame just 3 miles from the Meuse on December 24. Hitler switched attention from Dietrich's Sixth Panzer Army at Bastogne to the more dynamic Manteuffel. The Allied goal was to stop the panzers and reduce the bulge. It was soon clear that the Germans could not even make the Meuse much less Antwerp.

Rundstedt realized the operation was at risk but Hitler would not let him withdraw. A weather front allowed the Ninth U.S. Army Air Force to begin the first of 1,300 sorties on several targets. A blizzard of 2,000 planes and McAuliffe's resistance at Bastogne restricted 2nd Panzer Division. With town fuel dumps unavailable, the Germans stopped. On Christmas day, U.S. ground troops and planes smashed into the panzers, and just two miles from the Meuse, Manteuffel retreated under the barrage. Dietrich could not dislodge the Americans from Elsenborn ridge. Although his troops nearly broke out west of Malmedy, they were eventually beaten back. One final German air attack took place on New Year's Day, destroying 156 planes but costing the Luftwaffe over 300 of its own. It never recovered from this catastrophe, and neither did Manteuffel. His thrust to Foy-Notre Dame stretched the bulge to its limit of 40 miles wide and 60 miles deep yet Bastogne obstructed his way, and he stalled. Patton advised bagging the Germans, but the cautious Bradley, Hodges, and Montgomery wanted to reduce the bulge, and they prevailed. Hodges attacked southward, and Patton's six divisions pushed northward from Houffalize. The salient slowly disappeared. The pincers did not close until January 16 due to deep snow, and the delay allowed the winterized enemy to escape, but Dietrich and Manteuffel suffered 100,000 casualties—a fifth of their troops—and lost nearly all of their tanks, guns, and planes. The Allies experienced the same number of casualties and lost many weapons, yet the Wehrmacht could not replace its losses. Hitler had expended his last reserves of men and materiel on his audacious but rash counteroffensive.

The Allies had the West Wall in sight once again but at a price. Their command decisions had been found wanting. Hitler had compelled Ike to consider worst-case contingencies; at one point, SHAEF called for all available soldiers in America as well as 100,000 U.S. Marines (and Eisenhower disliked the Marine Corps) to be sent to Europe. Allied commanders had begged the Soviets to begin their offensive in the east to relieve the pressure in the west. And Hodges and Bradley had let the Wehrmacht escape. A rapid response had saved the situation, but the errors were numerous. The battle of the Bulge resulted from several failures, including the inability to coordinate forces to breach the Rhine in 1944, the ineptitude of leaders, and logistical problems. Germany had responded with a punishing counterattack that fell short only because resources had run dry. The strategic bombing campaign undercut factory output and the weapons program, and there were no manpower reserves left anyway to use the diminishing materiel. The Japanese ambassador in Berlin opined that Germany's mistaken attack in the West in 1918 had lost World War I. Had the same now occurred in 1944? With little strength left yet determined to pursue victory, Hitler could only await the invasion of the Third Reich itself. He ordered the dwindling number of people at home to mobilize for fanatical resistance under a Nazi militia, the Volkssturm. But he could also not forget his eastern flank. As the Ardennes fell silent, the Russians continued to advance.

CLOSING FROM THE WEST

The Allies raced for Germany. Hitler still denigrated the Western Allies' abilities and thus ordered another offensive on January 1, 1945 to recapture Strasbourg. Ike might have let the Germans advance to fritter away time to allow his forces and the USSR to close on Berlin, but de Gaulle refused to surrender another French city. Thus, Sixth Army Group blocked the way on the Moder River, and the German offensive petered out by the end of the month. As it did so, Anglo-American forces cleaned out the Colmar pocket west of the upper Rhine where the Wehrmacht still had troop concentrations. That Twelfth Army Group could stop an offensive and begin one of its own should have given Hitler pause about dreams of a breakthrough. The Allies began to wrap up the campaign on the West Wall. Three days after Stalin began a huge offensive, Eisenhower repopulated the line that had been depleted during the Battle of the Bulge. The Combined Chiefs approved a final western offensive for which main responsibility went to Montgomery's Twenty-First Army Group. Comprised of the First Canadian, Second British, and U.S. Ninth Armies, Monty's force would cross the Rhine north of the Ruhr and head for Berlin. The three remaining American armies and a French army would clear the Rhineland and thrust south of the Ruhr without draining men and supplies from Monty's effort. British Bomber Command and U.S. Eighth Army Air Force would also hit railways in eastern Germany to aid the USSR and honor a commitment to Stalin made at the Yalta conference in February 1945.

This bombing campaign called Thunderclap turned out to be another tragedy resulting from the strategy of annihilation. Arthur Harris and General Carl "Tooey" Spaatz of the USAAF had launched daylight raids on Berlin and Magdeburg on February 3 with cover, incidentally, from black Tuskegee Airmen in P-51 fighters. Missions over Chemnitz and Magdeburg followed twice more the next week. The goal was to add to the chaos on the ground from refugees fleeing the Soviets and give Stalin evidence of his allies' good will. Bomber Harris took aim on the historic city of Dresden, the capital of Saxony on the Elbe River. Famous for its architecture and fine china, the city had endured bombings before, and now Harris saw an opportunity to upend its defenses once and for all. On the night of February 13, 1944, he launched one of the most controversial raids in the strategic bombing campaign—a mission that tested morality even in the total-war clime of the Second World War.

The RAF sent 796 Lancaster bombers and nine de Havilland Mosquito bombers in two waves, three hours apart. The effects were horrific. Air defenses shot down just six Lancasters whereas some 478 tons of high explosives and 1,182 tons of incendiaries leveled the city and touched off a firestorm. After the Americans followed the next day with 311 B-17s aimed at railroad marshaling yards, about 35,000 residents and refugees lay dead. The ensuing debate over Dresden's utility to the war laid bare the morality of the strategic bombing campaign. An American infantryman taken prisoner at the battle

Dresden from above.   Credit: Center for the Study of War
Experience at Regis University, Denver, Colorado.

of the Bulge, future author Kurt Vonnegut, was underground when the bombs hit. He immortalized the tragedy in his novel *Slaughterhouse-Five* by satirizing the notion that human life is meaningless in the face of inevitable war. Allied reporters expressed little remorse for the two-day bombing, however. Joseph Goebbels propagandized about the depravity of his enemies in attacking a target supposedly bereft of military significance. Even Churchill had qualms about Thunderclap, which he had previously endorsed. And some of the aircrew were bothered long after the war by the notion of bombing women, children, and the elderly in a campaign of annihilation.

Research has revealed that Dresden was far from an innocent bystander when it came to war making. The city possessed 127 factories that made consumer products convertible into war industries (for instance, camera lenses to bombsights) and communications and other service facilities alongside its cultural sites. Still, the city came under attack because of the timing. The war in Europe did not seem to be slowing, memories of the Bulge were sharp, and there were fears that Allied winter offensives might stall. The Americans were also a week from the horrific invasion of Iwo Jima and had already experienced high casualties in the Pacific. The context for Dresden, therefore, was a raging world war guided by a strategy of annihilation. Bomber Harris remained true to his nickname. He was unrepentant, and implied that he would ruin the entire Third Reich if given the chance. Dresden became a symbol of the immorality of mass terror bombing, although the death toll from firestorms in Hamburg and Tokyo was higher.

As the bombing peaked in Dresden, the Allies maneuvered to the Rhine in two operations. To build a bridgehead over the river, First Canadian Army and the British XXX Corps launched Operation Veritable on February 8, 1945. After clearing out the Roermond triangle east of Nijmegen, they commenced the largest artillery barrage so far in northwest Europe. The carnage allowed four divisions to smash through German lines and then breach the old Siegfried Line the next day. By February 13, troops reached the Rhine at Emmerich. Bad weather and obstinate defense stymied them, however. In the Reichswald Forest, a sudden thaw followed by heavy rain bogged down Crerar's units that faced five lines of defense made more intractable when the Germans flooded the area. This compelled Crerar to attack on a narrow front in a ferocious battle that lasted for nearly a month. The casualties rose from Veritable despite intense RAF bombing.

Relief arrived when Simpson's Ninth Army drove from the south to link with Veritable. This Operation Grenade was delayed until February 23 after the Germans flooded the Ruhr River in front of the approaching army. Simpson finally arrived at the Rhine on March 2 to join the Canadians at Geldern. Distracted by Operation Veritable, the Germans lost 70,000 men. Monty suffered 15,000 casualties in Veritable but half that number in Grenade. Rundstedt and Model asked for permission to withdraw, but Hitler refused. The major breakthrough across the Rhine occurred in Grenade's waning days. Hodges captured the Ludendorff railway bridge at Remagen on March 7 when the Germans failed to destroy it. This stroke of luck let 8,000 troops and heavy weapons across the Rhine bridgehead during the next day. Outraged by the incompetence of his army, Hitler replaced Rundstedt with Albert Kesselring and shot five officers he held responsible. He even launched V-2 rockets at the bridge in their only tactical use of the war. Kesselring ordered Model to counterattack at the bridgehead. The bridge at Remagen collapsed on March 17, but pontoons had already been installed, and five Allied divisions were across by this time.

Once Montgomery and Bradley stood on the Rhine at the Dutch border near Koblenz, their armies poured across the Rhine into Germany, yet politics proved more insuperable. The rift between them gaped beyond repair. After the battle of the Bulge, Monty claimed credit for repelling the Germans, and Bradley and Patton were deeply insulted. As a result, the defeat of the Third Reich became a matter of beating the British (and Russians) to Berlin. The Americans scored the first win as the first to traverse the Rhine. Allied troops worked to clear the Saar and Palatinate and then Patton seized a bridgehead at the confluence of the Rhine and Main Rivers near Mainz and Oppenheim on March 22 and drove northeast through the Saar into central Germany. Third Army made 75 miles in just days. Meanwhile, Devers took Patch's Seventh Army and de Lattre's First French Army south from the Palatinate toward Austria. The Germans no longer fought west of the Rhine. They had inflicted 10,000 casualties, but this was a fraction of their 60,000 dead and 250,000 prisoners.

At Remagen, Bradley expanded the bridgehead and advanced south of the Ruhr. Always sensitive to combined command, Ike had Hodges join Montgomery to cross the Rhine at Wesel to the north on March 24. A three-day thumping from Anglo-American aircraft on the roads and rails in the area preceded this pincer that encircled three army groups. Smiling Albert Kesselring was no longer such an optimist because his 55 weak divisions could not stand up to Eisenhower's 85. The Allies also operated at strength and enjoyed dominating air support. U.S. First Army headed for Marburg, but then Ike sent it north to link with Ninth Army now under Monty's command but soon to switch to Bradley. With the rest of Monty's forces guarding U.S. flanks—to the British general's disdain and the Americans' delight—Army Group B was trapped. At Lippstadt, Hodges and Simpson linked on April 1 to create a Ruhr pocket. The desperate and increasingly depraved Hitler declared it a fortress and forbid his forces to break out. As at Stalingrad, they would fight to the end. Model was an expert at defense, but faced with such overwhelming odds he stood not a chance. Army Group B and Fifth Panzer Army disappeared and the Ruhr industrial heartland fell to the Western Allies. Model killed himself on April 17, 1945 as 317,000 of his troops entered prison camps. This was the largest surrender of the war by the Third Reich.

With victory within reach, Ike stepped into the politics of military decision making by altering Allied plans on March 31. He had placed Monty in a supporting role to the Americans, who were poised to advance from Erfurt to Liepzig and Dresden. Chief of the Imperial General Staff Alan Brooke campaigned diligently to turn the ground war over to Montgomery for a drive north of the Ruhr to Berlin. This Ike would not do. He worried about bypassing the southern area from the Rhine to Czechoslovakia because of a fantastic concern that the Nazis planned a last stand to prolong the war from a "National Redoubt" around Hitler's Bavarian mountain retreat at Berchtesgaden. The British also protested SHAEF's attempt to link with the Red Army along the Erfurt-Leipzig-Dresden line. This was the area where the Nazis were most likely to move their government. Churchill viewed Eisenhower's request for a meeting on the issues as an unwarranted military intrusion into political affairs. And contrary to western diplomatic policies, the Americans appeared to be leaving Berlin to the USSR.

At the heart of SHAEF's plan was the reality that Berlin was no longer so strategically important to ending the war. This the British accepted, although they got assurances from Ike and the U.S. Joint Chiefs that agreements for Allied sharing of interests in Berlin would be upheld. Yet Canadian and British troops played a decided second fiddle in the last campaign in Europe. The Canadians (and Poles) liberated Holland while the British shot for the North Sea port of Bremerhaven and then Hamburg and Lubeck farther east before moving into Denmark. The demise of Nazi Germany now centered on the Americans and the Soviets, but Stalin took issue with Ike's shift in plans. In fact, he was stunned by Eisenhower's message requesting consultation on the endgame in Berlin but hid his alarm behind a bland reply. The note indicated that the Americans could press deep into the Soviet zone of influence in Germany. After all, Dresden was further east even than Berlin, which was the original U.S. target. The Soviets could not abide this change. Stalin urged Zhukov and Konev to redirect their forces for a massive attack on Berlin to end the war quickly, and three days later, he accused Roosevelt and

Churchill of seeking a secret deal with Hitler. In exchange for conditional surrender to the Americans and British, the Germans would ease their defense of the Western front while stiffening against the USSR. A 125-mile wide largely undefended gap beyond the Ruhr pocket seemed to validate Stalin's suspicions. This was especially so due to Hitler's refusal to let Model break out.

In Ike's favor, the opportunity presented by this vacuum to be filled by U.S. forces trumped high politics. Simpson, Hodges, and Patton roared forward on a broad front, meeting intermittent resistance even in defensible places like the Harz Mountains, Thuringian Forest, and towns and cities. There was no cohesiveness to the Wehrmacht, although isolated pockets fought effectively. The Americans suffered as many casualties in this drive as they had during the first month of the Normandy operations. In the meantime, Anglo-Canadian troops eyed the Baltic and Scandinavia to root out the Wehrmacht. By early April 1945, prisoners flooded westward to meet Allied forces, but until Hitler gave up, his troops would fight on. Lack of usable railroads slowed the Allied armies as they zeroed in on Dresden. On April 7, they reached the intersection of the Weser and Werra Rivers, which was the halfway point from the Rhine to the Elbe. Three days later Patton arrived in Erfurt and two days after that Simpson had the Elbe between Wittenberg and Tangermunde in his sights. Three American armies occupied territory deep within the Soviet zone. On April 12, Bradley ordered Hodges to halt before Dresden. There, just west of the Elbe River, American forces awaited the Soviet Red Army.

By mid-April 1945, the Allied pincers had all but squeezed the Axis powers to death. Nazi enemies roamed inside Germany, tearing up the Third Reich and leaving the remnants for later as they stormed toward Hitler and Berlin. Resistance in northern Italy was over. Across the Pacific, American forces stood on the doorstep of the Japanese homeland. The United Nations conference had already convened in San Francisco in March. The gathering of delegates from fifty nations ushered in the postwar world even before the great military conflict had ended. They prayed that the war of annihilation might soon be over.

CHAPTER 22

Red Army Sweep

The arithmetic was brutal but brutal arithmetic always
worked in Russia's favor.

DAVID BENIOFF
City of Thieves

EASTERN FRONT CALCULATIONS

Two weeks after Anglo-American-Polish-Canadian troops went ashore in Normandy,
the Red Army began Operation Bagration in mid-June 1944. Intended to coincide with
Overlord, this huge campaign involved drives into the Balkans to the south, the Baltic
and Prussia in the north, and Warsaw and Berlin in the center. Fighting over the past
two years on the Eastern front had largely taken place in Ukraine. The north had been
relatively quiescent. Stalin changed this pattern in Summer 1944 as the Russians moved
in all directions and in all areas. With Germany having committed its last reserves to
the West Wall, Bagration was guaranteed a rapid advance but Stalin had more than victory over Nazism in mind. He gazed beyond military matters to the politics of the postwar period. Like his allies, Stalin knew that the war had reconfigured the global power
structure. He enjoyed a distinct advantage over them, however, because the Red Army
occupied large swaths of territory to ensure Soviet domination over Eastern Europe.
As he fought a war of annihilation against the Third Reich, Stalin would also spread
communism, promote Soviet influence, protect his nation from future invasions, and
bolster his own rule.

The USSR first looked northward. After sporadic negotiations ended by early
1944, Stalin sought the surrender of difficult Finland for the second time in the war.
Because the Russians had double the number of troops and five times more artillery and mortars than the Finns, the chances of repeating the humiliation of 1939–
1940 were slim. A massive assault north of Leningrad on June 9 by Twenty-First
and Twenty-Third Soviet Armies drove back the Finns beyond Viipuri and another
attack rocked Karelia. General Mannerheim turned to Hitler for emergency assistance in return for a pledge not to sign a separate peace, and as a result of German

aid, the front stabilized in early August along the lines of the 1940 border. But the losses were just too great. On September 19, Mannerheim signed an armistice with Moscow and thereby reneged on his promise to Berlin. In exchange for the separate peace, the USSR restored the 1940 frontier, traded the Porkkala for the Hanko base, and imposed large reparations. The punishing deal saved Finland from the fate of its neighbors: postwar Soviet occupation. In the neighboring Baltics on the other hand, the Soviets had occupied Estonia since January 1944 and Lithuania since April. Latvia remained contested until the end of the war because of a German presence on the Courland peninsula. All of these states had seen their Jewish populations devastated. Under Soviet rule, the three also witnessed communist terror. Collectivization of agriculture made Baltic farmers slaves to Moscow's dictates, and in a way continued the war of annihilation.

Meanwhile the Red Army targeted German Army Group Center under Operation Bagration. Stalin deceived the Germans into thinking that he was focused in the south and north by using false signals, dummy positions, and camouflaged troops. Falling for the trickery, Hitler pulled panzer divisions from Army Group Center and distributed eight each to Army Groups North Ukraine and South Ukraine. With a lack of reconnaissance aircraft, the Wehrmacht defended the wrong places on the Eastern front, just as it had in Normandy. The first objective was Belorussia where Army Group Center was enclosed around Minsk. Georgi Zhukov returned to Moscow in May 1944 to plan the operation. It involved no less than 2.4 million men, 5,200 tanks, and 5,300 aircraft involved in six *fronts* and nine separate thrusts toward Minsk; Bagration was double the size of the two Kursk operations combined. Hitler calculated that the Russians could not mount an offensive against the German center in the summer. Zhukov set out to prove him wrong.

The colossal Soviet offensive commenced on June 22, 1944 against Field Marshal Ernst Busch's Army Group Center. A Nazi enthusiast with limited talents, Busch would follow Hitler's orders forbidding a retreat but such blind obedience put at risk his 700,000 troops. Nonetheless, he adhered to the Fuhrer's will. He did not protest when Hitler stripped him of nine-tenths of his tanks, half of his tank destroyers, a third of his heavy artillery, and a quarter of his self-propelled guns in May and sent them to Army Group North Ukraine. Busch adapted by taking a leaf from the Fuhrer's book of inspirational warfare and designating the towns of Vitebsk, Orsha, Mogilev, and Bobruisk as fortresses to be defended to the death.

Launched three years to the day after Barbarossa, Operation Bagration has been termed "the destruction of Army Group Center." After committing his reserves over a four-day period, Busch could not stop any of the nine thrusts that isolated his four fortress towns. With five divisions left in Vitebsk, Third Panzer Army wandered the countryside and Fourth and Ninth Armies struggled in the marshes along the Beresina River. Fourth Army's Kurt von Tippelskirch tried to retreat, but Busch reversed the order and tried to plug the holes in his shattered defensive lines. It was a futile gesture. Hitler then replaced him with Model. As commander of both Army Group Center and North Ukraine, the Field Marshal could order shifts in reserves where needed from north to south, and vice versa. The first phase of the Soviet attack ended on July 5 with

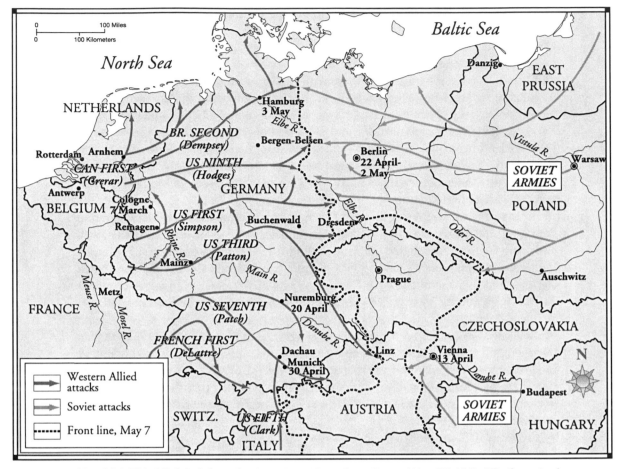

Map 22.1 Third Reich defeated.   Credit: Ronald Story, *Concise Historical Atlas of World War II: The Geography of Conflict*, Map 29, p. 63.

the Russians east of Minsk. They inflicted 130,000 casualties on the 165,000 troops of Fourth Army. Tippelskirch escaped a trap at Mogilev, but the Red Army at Minsk enveloped his forces. Third Panzer and Ninth Armies essentially ceased to exist, and Army Group Center lost control in just twelve days as 25 divisions disappeared. Russian deaths totaled many tens of thousands, but the state absorbed the losses. Hitler and the Wehrmacht High Command helplessly watched the Red storm of Operation Bagration roll over their comparatively dwarfed forces.

The result was a terrifying example of the strategy of annihilation in action. "Corpses, hundreds and thousands of them, pave the road, lie in ditches, under the pines, in the green barley," wrote a journalist after the battle for Bobruisk. "In some places, vehicles have to drive over the corpses, so densely they lie upon the ground." Burials could not keep pace with the killings. People went insane with revenge and misery. A common story related the vengeance meted out on two soldiers by a partisan whose daughters they had brutalized. After the father killed the Germans with a stake, he propped up their bodies on a tree stump and beat their skulls to splinters. Barbarossa had been a brutal campaign replete with the systematic killings of civilians by the Einsatzgruppen. Now the Soviets returned some of the slaughter in kind.

Bagration began its second phase once the Soviets took Minsk in July and continued westward. The Wehrmacht banked on the overstretched Red Army to halt and regroup, but the offensive did not cease as Soviet factory output and the persistent infusion of U.S. trucks kept the fronts moving forward. First Belorussian army group turned toward Warsaw while Second and Third Belorussian *fronts* pointed in the direction of East Prussia and Lithuania. By July 8, Vilnius was surrounded, and spearheads nearly cut the links between German Army Groups Center and North. Konstantin Rokossovky crossed the post-1939 border into Poland and rounded up prisoners. Stalin ordered 50,000 of them shipped to Moscow and paraded in Red Square, desirous that his people remember the enemy. To the south, Ivan Konev went after Army Group North Ukraine. After meeting resistance, he broke through with First Guards Tank Army and separated First and Fourth Panzer Armies. By July 18, the Russians trapped the XIII Corps east of Lvov and fresh troops poured through the gap between the two panzer armies. High Command chief Heinz Guderian ordered the troops to stand against Konev's steamroller in southern Poland. They listened for the ominous "Urrah!" as the Russians approached for the kill.

Germany's plight was suicidal as the Red Army penetrated Poland. While Fourth Panzer Army had its flanks exposed, Soviet Fourth Tank Army crossed the San River between Jarsolaw and Przemysl on July 25. That night Second Tank Army swarmed Siedlce just 50 miles east of Warsaw. First Ukrainian *front* moved into Lvov, pushed out First Panzer Army, and advanced on the Vistula River. Citizens exalted. "We waited for it like for God!" said one about the imminent Russian arrival. Yet bitterness followed. About 220 miles away, Warsaw witnessed a brutal purge of the Polish underground after partisans had risen up and demanded aid. But Stalin halted the drive at the end of July as Second Tank Army stood just seven miles from Warsaw. Did he wish for the Germans to crush the Polish uprising and eliminate potential competitors to Soviet rule after the war? Western observers believed so. Political factors weighed heavily in Stalin's calculus yet it was also evident that the USSR had reached the end of its logistical tether. The Red Army was low on fuel and ammunition, and the battle for Minsk had tired the troops. The Wehrmacht destroyed the III Soviet Tank Corps northeast of the Polish capital and battered the VIII Guards Tank Corps and Soviet Second Tank Army turned south of Warsaw away from the rebels in the city. The Soviets tried establishing a beachhead on the western bank of the Vistula but were pushed away. The Polish Home Army fought the Germans alone, and Stalin even refused to give his Allies access to air bases to land supplies until mid-September when Eighth USAAF flew a few missions. This callous decision indicated his desire to infuse the battlefield with realpolitik.

This was the second Warsaw uprising in the campaigns of annihilation in Poland. The first had occurred in April 1943 when Jews trapped in their ghetto desperately decided to fight as a symbol of resistance to Nazism rather than succumb without resistance. Nobody came to their aid. They prepared to die with dignity rather than in a gas chamber. That stance claimed 14,000 lives. The remaining 7,000 Jews left for the

Germans burning Warsaw.   Credit: Center for the Study of War Experience at Regis University, Denver, Colorado: Deutsches Bundesarchiv (German Federal Archive), Bild 146-1996-057-10A.

Treblinka and Majdanek death camps. The Germans had 400 dead and 1,000 hurt as they diverted resources in personnel and transport away from the Wehrmacht to perpetuate crimes against the Jews.

The second city-wide Warsaw uprising lasted 63 days. Genocide was not the issue this time around, however. The rebels hoped that their defiance against Germany and the USSR would attract help from the Allies, yet the 37,600 people who fought mostly for the Polish Home Army lacked arms. Just 14% had rifles, machine guns, or handguns. The 21,300 troops sent by Heinrich Himmler flattened the Warsaw uprising block by bloody block in a campaign that rivaled the most atrocious treatment anywhere during the war. Citizens fighting door-to-door with Allied grenades and homemade Molotov Cocktails attempted to counter German airpower. By the time that the Soviets allowed American aircraft on Russian-held airfields on September 9, the Germans had nearly subsumed the city. The commander of the Polish Home Army, Tadeusz Komorowski, decided to surrender on October 1. In an unprecedented act, the capital was totally evacuated and then Warsaw disappeared under the rubble as the Germans leveled 83% of the city. About 15,000 insurgents died as well as 250,000 civilians. The Wehrmacht lost 17,000 dead and missing and 9,000 injured (though Himmler downplayed the casualties). Many of the survivors were executed or sent to concentration camps under the Third Reich's race-based strategy of annihilation. Stalin now had few rivals to his rule. The Home Army was gutted, and after the Germans left, the Poles accepted the reality of Soviet power.

The Soviets turned to defense even though Army Group Center no longer posed a threat. By mid-August 1944, First Belorussian and Ukrainian *fronts* had bridgeheads on the Vistula. The Red Army decided to regroup and resupply. Operation Bagration had wiped out 30 German divisions and caused a half million casualties in its 200 mile advance west. The Soviets lost over 243,000 dead and more than 811,000 wounded. It needed rest. The respite allowed Model to ease backward to the Prussian border and the Vistula.

Bad news also greeted the Third Reich in the north. In Bagration's second phase, all three Baltic *fronts* under Aleksander Vasilevsky struck the 400,000 troops of Army Group North on July 18. The generals warned Hitler that they could not hold the 400-mile salient from the Narva River to a point west of Leningrad. He did not listen. He sent in panzer commander Ferdinand Schorner who was a specialist in pulling victory from the jaws of defeat. When the First Baltic front broke through west of Riga, Schorner counterattacked and stabilized the line, maintaining contact with Army Group Center through a narrow corridor along the Baltic coast west of Riga. He lacked the numbers to hold for long, however. Vasilevsky took a month to reinforce his army groups and then he joined them with the Leningrad *front* under Leonid Govorov, an artilleryman who had defended Moscow and helped free Leningrad. With double the number of troops, triple the armor, and a 6-to-1 advantage in aircraft, Govorov assailed the German position on September 14. Even the fanatical Schorner realized his helplessness but Hitler did not let him withdraw for four days. Vasilevsky hoped to prevent Schorner from evacuating through the corridor. He sent the First Baltic *front* under the veteran Ivan Bagramyan due west toward Memel on the Lithuanian coast. By October 13, the Germans departed Estonia and eastern Latvia, and Schorner fled to the Courland peninsula. With open seas to the west and the Bay of Riga protecting his rear and eastern flank, he planned to open another corridor to resupply Army Group North.

Army Group Center impinged on his plans. Three Soviet armies hit Model to the south and powered across the East Prussian border as the first enemy troops to enter the German homeland. As the shock spread across the Third Reich, Hitler ordered Schorner to send several divisions to Army Group Center and push back the communist invaders. This left Army Group North weakened. By November 1944, the gap widened between his forces and Memel. Schorner could not cross it without abandoning Courland itself but Hitler would not permit that course. By January 1945, the Fuhrer rejected counsel of his military staff who wanted the 300,000 troops evacuated to reinforce defenses farther west along the Vistula-Oder line. Later in the month, however, the Soviet offensive bore down on Berlin itself. This compelled Hitler to remove the divisions off the isolated Courland peninsula. He transferred Schorner to the main defensive front.

SOVIET SATELLITES

With the Baltic area and northern campaign in hand, the Soviets turned their attention to military and political affairs in southeastern Europe. Hitler hoped that territorial greed would fracture the Allies by bringing the British (who sought to protect their interests in Greece) into conflict with the USSR. Instead, Churchill and Stalin carved up the Balkans and surrounding areas in a "percentages" agreement of October 1944. In the deal, Britain got influence in Greece. Stalin would dominate Romania, Bulgaria, and Yugoslavia. Still, Hitler could hope. Churchill had long obsessed about the rise of communism in Greece where partisans had resisted the Germans since late 1942. These groups were split by those who backed the return of King George II and the communists who fought Nazism independent of Soviet guidance. Accommodation for a unified resistance movement proved impossible. As the Germans evacuated in October 1944, Churchill permitted a government that included leftist groups backed by the USSR in an uneasy coalition with the conservative, pro-British forces of Prime Minister Andreas Papandreou. By December, armed struggle replaced negotiations over the incorporation of guerrilla fighters into a national army. British Foreign Secretary Anthony Eden flew to Athens to broker a cease-fire between rival factions and the fighting stopped in January 1945 as Papandreou gave way to a regency. Greece devolved into civil war as its participation in the world war ended. The chaos did not disrupt the grand alliance, although Anglo-Soviet posturing over Greece fed into the Cold War rivalry.

The Fuhrer looked to direct confrontation elsewhere in southeastern Europe, and Romania gave him grounds for optimism. On the Romanian border massed 1.31 million troops of Second and Third Ukrainian front. These were the first Russian troops to occupy capitalist lands. The Wehrmacht marshaled over 900,000 German and Romanian soldiers, but it possessed a mere 170 tanks to the USSR's 1,874 tanks and assault guns. Romania's two armies at Stalingrad had lost over 155,000 casualties, or one quarter of the nation's military personnel. The dictator Antonescu had backed Hitler with 50 divisions, but he wisely kept half of the army in Romania to guard the border against the USSR. Antonescu had no following anymore. The people were disillusioned, even though the military had fended off a Soviet invasion in May 1944. To hold the Vistula Line, Guderian pulled five panzer and six infantry divisions from Army Group South Ukraine to rebuild Army Group Center. This left the Wehrmacht in Romania with only a panzer, panzer grenadier, and an armored division. Antonescu pleaded with Hitler not to retreat behind the Carpathians but instead hold a line on the Dnestr River. However hopeless the situation, the Fuhrer agreed to resist with Sixth Army flanked by Fourth and Third Romanian Armies. All of these armies had been wiped out at Stalingrad but were now reconstituted.

The USSR attacked Romania on August 20, 1944. Despite fanatical resistance, Sixth Army buckled as the Romanians fled or capitulated. The next day, Third Romanian Army was trapped along the Black Sea and it surrendered. The Dnestr Line collapsed along with the Antonescu government in Bucharest, and King Michael took power in a coup on August 23. He announced that Romania would join the Allied cause. The entire frontier was opened to the Red Army while the Romanian military either disarmed or rebelled against the 26 German divisions of 612,000 men. Hitler's attempt to save them by attacking the capital failed. The Soviets trapped remnants of Sixth Army on the west side of the Siret River and destroyed it for the second time. The march on Bucharest cost the Germans 5,000 men and 53,000 prisoners, including nine generals, while the Romanians suffered 5,000 killed. Germany lost 300,000 men in total in Romania. After the rout of Sixth Army, the Soviets swept through the Carpathians and Transylvanian Alps into Hungary. An armistice with Moscow signed on September 12 required Romania to join the Allies with no less than 12 infantry divisions. Romania had surrendered to Nazism in 1940. Five years later it generated the fourth largest number of Allied troops behind the United States, Britain, and the USSR. The country also lost nearly 160,000 men in the final assaults on Germany.

Bulgaria was next on the Soviet liberation list. Aligned against the western powers but not having declared war on the USSR, Bulgaria represented Hitler's best bet to divide the Allies. Leftist partisan activity boosted resistance units to about 11,000 men under a Fatherland Front, and Allied bombings and Soviet political pressure in Spring 1944 turned most Bulgarians against the Nazis. But Stalin took no chances. A pro-Western government searched for ways to escape the war. The coup in Romania, however, doomed his efforts before the Red Army showed up. The Soviets then turned up the heat. They declared war on Bulgaria on September 5 and sent the Third Ukrainian army group into the country three days later. The new prime minister, Konstantin Muraviev, sued for peace the next day. He turned over power to the communists under the Fatherland Front. First, Second, and Fourth Bulgarian Armies of 339,000 troops joined the Third Ukrainian *front* as it pushed into the Balkans and eventually Hungary and Austria. Over 32,000 troops were killed. In December 1944, Red Army veteran Ivan Kinov assumed the position of commander-in-chief of the Bulgarian armed forces after three months of purges removed 800 officers suspected of harboring anticommunist tendencies. The satellite Bulgaria soon orbited the USSR.

The Soviet way now opened into Hungary. This country also wished to leave the war. Army Group South Ukraine (renamed Army Group South in late September) stabilized in Hungary after the Soviet Fourth Ukrainian *front* had inched its way over the Carpathian Mountains into Slovakia. Prohibitive losses for Hungary's Second Army at Stalingrad and Voronezh—estimates placed casualties at 190,000 men—had led to peace feelers. Hitler exerted great effort to prevent a Hungarian surrender. In March 1944, he installed a pro-Nazi government in Budapest that sent most of Hungary's 400,000 Jews to Auschwitz. Knowing that Hungary wanted to call it quits, the Germans occupied the country that month, reorganized its defenses, and resisted the Red Army from April to October. Yet with the Russians just 140 miles from Budapest, the government tried again for an armistice that Berlin quashed. By late September, the Soviets passed the Carpathians and broke out of the Hungarian Plain. A coup escalated army defections even though the Germans cracked down on discipline. To combat the Allied advance in Bulgaria, Army Group E under Maximilian von Weichs mobilized 600,000 service troops from Trieste to Crete and withdrew forces from Greece and southern Yugoslavia. Both actions guarded his right flank from Fourth Ukrainian *front*. On the left he faced Second and Third Ukrainian army groups under Rodion Malinovsky and Fedor Tolbukhin, respectively. Fighting erupted between the Hungarians and Romanians. When Russians joined the fight, the Hungarians panicked and lost Arad on September 21. The drama now centered on the capital of Budapest.

Ranked by both Hitler and Stalin as approaching Stalingrad in prestige, Budapest was a major prize. The Fuhrer ordered the city into fortress mode, but Stalin determined to encircle and seize it. On October 15, the regent, Admiral Miklos Horthy, announced an armistice with the USSR, but the SS removed him and installed a puppet leader. Such action caused Hungarian officers and troops to desert the Germans, but the Wehrmacht had advantages that permitted them to stay and fight. Against Tolbukhin they oversaw Buda on the Danube River's west bank from the Galerthey Heights and Palace Hill. On the east bank facing Malinovsky, Pest had fortified factories and government buildings from which the Germans could mount a viable defense.

The Germans fought heroically. At the end of October, they encircled three Soviet corps that had advanced too far and fast, yet the Red Army shoved them back toward Budapest. In the city waited the German 13th Division and three SS divisions, which held off the Red Army for nearly two months before being surrounded on December 26. Army Group South commander Johannes Freissner, a veteran in the Balkans, divided his armor and infantry into two groups. The armor defended Budapest's northern approaches, and the infantry protected the south. Neither stopped Malinovsky. While Tolbukhin stalled, Malinovsky moved into the eastern suburbs, his artillery blasting away at Buda. Beginning on January 12, 1945, the Budapest Group Corps pushed through the city. German troops contested every block, street, and building but six days later, Malinovsky had Pest. The Wehrmacht suffered 35,000 dead and lost 62,000 prisoners. The end was not so imminent, however. Tolbukhin continued to parry German panzers as Malinovsky assailed Buda from Pest. A counterattack against Tolbukhin brought the IV Panzer Corps within 15 miles of the city center on January 24 but Hitler wanted Budapest defended not rescued. This was not to be. The Werhmacht abandoned the Gelerthey Heights on February 13 and another 30,000 prisoners fell to Malinovsky. The garrison held for three more days before a breakout caused its destruction by March 1945. In actuality, Hitler's last offensive occurred not at the battle of the Bulge but in Budapest, but the results were the same. There would be no more liberation on the Eastern front. Stalin had his Hungarian satellite at the cost of over 240,000 casualties. He now turned toward Berlin.

Stalin readied for the kill. In November 1944, he had assumed control of the military by placing the Supreme Commander-in-Chief and the General Staff in charge of strategic planning. He assigned Rokossovsky to Second Belorussian *front* and gave Zhukov the honor of taking Berlin as the commander of First Belorussian army group. Stalin left Zhukov as deputy commander-in-chief to negotiate with the Western Allies—namely Eisenhower—as a nominal peer. As Soviets forces mopped up in Budapest in February 1945, Vasilevsky took over Third Belorussian *front*. Soviet forces planned a 45-day drive to the capital of the Third Reich—15 days to the Oder River from the Vistula and a month to the Elbe. Some 2.2 million troops of First Belorussian and First Ukrainian *fronts* mobilized against Army Group A's 400,000 soldiers. Second and Third Belorussian Army groups' 1.6 million troops aimed for East Prussia and the Baltic coast.

How times had changed. In 1941, Germany had swept into the USSR but three years later, the Russians adopted a version of tank blitzkrieg by attacking from the Baltic to the Mediterranean Seas. No army matched the Soviets who bested the Germans 11-to-1 in troops, 7-to-1 in tanks, and 20-to-1 in artillery and planes. With overwhelming numbers, communist doctrine at hand, revenge on their minds, and a well-tested strategy of annihilation, the Red Army was omnipotent. From Estonia through Poland to Yugoslavia (which partisan leader Josef Broz Tito ran without Soviet interference), the Germans faced a tidal wave. Army Group Center disintegrated as the Red Army advanced through the Baltic States. Army Group South Ukraine was largely destroyed as the Russians moved 500 miles into Romania, Bulgaria, and Hungary. Had Stalin not sought political aims in southeastern Europe he might have defeated Nazism at the end of 1944, but there was plenty of time after he consolidated his territorial and political gains. In early 1945, the Red Army finally took aim on the Third Reich to open the final chapter on Hitler's Germany.

REVENGE AND COLLAPSE

The Allies compressed the Third Reich from two directions, but Hitler encountered the most debilitating losses on the Eastern front to date. In Italy, Anglo-American forces pinned down an army group and prevented it from being transferred to the West Wall. On the Western front, the Allies readied to advance across Germany. Stalin beat them to the Nazi homeland. The USSR began the entire war's biggest single offensive on January 12, 1945, led by multiple armies over three days. Zhukov's First Belorussian *front* in Prussia and Konev's First Ukrainian army group south of him above the Carpathian Mountains centered on the bridgeheads at the Vistula River. They massed just less than 4 million troops that outnumbered by 11-to-1 Schorner's Army Group A. Second Belorussian *front* under Rokossovky and Third Belorussian *front* waited in reserve. The Soviets had seven times more tanks and a 20-to-1 edge in aircraft and artillery than the Germans thanks to a reliable logistical train. The Wehrmacht was starved for fuel and supplies. The master escape artist Schorner tried to pull off another miracle with the help of SS chief Himmler, who activated Army Group Vistula on January 23, but in less than two weeks, the Belorussian army groups were on the Oder River just 35 miles east of Berlin and on the Czech border. Clear, dry, and frosty weather sped along the spearheads. Mobile forces "moved around the clock, giving the enemy no time to stop, rest, or fortify," remembered a Red Army soldier.

Just as Guderian had predicted, the Red Army charged toward Germany. Hitler could not fortify the Eastern front in any depth even though a surprising January thaw delayed the Russians a week. Guderian warned Hitler about the offensive, but the Fuhrer erupted in rage. He argued that the panicked Wehrmacht overestimated enemy strength but as the USSR steadily built up the panzer divisions in the east, the Germans were spread out too thinly and unevenly. Seven remained in Budapest, two were isolated in the Courland pensinsula, and only five guarded central Poland. German Ninth Army collapsed under bombardment while counterattacks died under withering aerial assaults. Still, the Soviet drive also became somewhat haphazard. Moscow ordered the Second Belorussian *front* to move north and cut off East Prussia from the rest of Germany. It did so on January 24 when it reached the Baltic. This exposed Zhukov's northern flank, however. The danger did not halt the Red Army, which took Warsaw, Lodz, and Cracow. General Chuikov, the hero of Stalingrad, encircled Posnan and 60,000 enemy troops. Second Guards Tank Army got to the Oder River fortress of Kostrin across the Polish border in Germany.

The offensive was a vicious affair that clearly reflected the strategy of annihilation as a seemingly boundless orgy of rape, murder, and pillaging ensued. By no means were all soldiers bent on revenge; some Russians took pity on German captives and especially the young. But others meted out years of pent up rage on the civilian population, stirred by calls to redeem the motherland. Abusing their victims merited hardly a thought, they posited, when compared to the misery the Germans had perpetrated on loved ones. To the Russians, Nazi crimes justified reciprocity in the form of torture, mutilation, and sadism. The Red Army had come upon the Majdanek death camp the previous summer and Treblinka afterward. The hellish conditions angered soldiers even more when they saw evidence of SS attempts to disguise the camps by burning the crematoriums and tidying up the living quarters. The Nazis had seemingly reduced genocide to a matter of housekeeping. Further insight into Soviet behavior arose when a group of women from Konigsberg were gang-raped and asked to be put out of their misery. "Russian soldiers do not shoot women," an officer replied. "Only German soldiers do that." Perversity, cruelty, and barbarism went hand in hand. Old men were shot by looters and girls cringed in horror and fear. A German woman brought her bruised teenage daughter to army headquarters to encounter her attacker—"pink-cheeked, fat-faced, sleepy"—under unenthusiastic interrogation by his commandant. A mother was raped in a barn as her relatives pleaded for a break to let her nurse her hungry baby. The Soviet soldiers relented in a so-called happy ending since she avoided death. In another case, a patrol raped two sisters. When the mother complained, a Red Army commander compelled the perpetrators to take the honorable road (and avoid execution) and marry the daughters.

Cover-up of such psychopathy was not usual. The scourge of rape erupted in Hungary where officers locked up females and assaulted them during orgies of food and wine. They even broke into a mental hospital to rape and kill women ages sixteen to sixty. Romanians also experienced Soviet bestiality. In East Prussia—the entry point to the Third Reich—the victims received the full dose of three years of Russian hatred as gangs of troops descended into the depths of animal conduct. Women, mothers, and children faced grunting soldiers with their pants down. Observers noted that "women who are bleeding or losing consciousness get shoved to one side, and our men shoot the ones who try to save their children." Grinning officers directed the horror to ensure that every soldier took part. German, Japanese, American, British, and other armies also brutalized women. In contrast to the heroic good war image of the U.S. soldier, some were executed for rapes in Britain and France, although none got death sentences for violence against Germans. The youngest recorded victim was three years old. Still, that behavior could be explained as an individual choice driven by pathological sex criminality or hatred. In the case of the Soviet Red Army, raping served as an official tool of the strategy of annihilation. That torture had become policy was further revealed by other monstrosities—some so grisly as to defy belief—such as the crucifixion of a school room of children. Verification is difficult (and episodes like this oftentimes apocrophal), and both sides had axes to grind. But even considering the tendency to politicize atrocities, the treatment of civilians on the Eastern front was simply inhuman and the scale of violence unimaginable.

In the midst of winter, tens of thousands of people fled the merciless Soviet armies. While American tanks displayed such logos as Donald Duck, Red Army vehicles called

Lager Nordhausen Gestapo death camp.   Credit: Center for the Study of War Experience at Regis University, Denver, Colorado: U.S. National Archives.

for a reign of terror on Germany. The Soviets cared little about how the postwar period would be influenced by such behavior. They thought instead of the past. As a soldier explained after finding two dead children in an East Prussian house, "the Germans deserve the atrocities that they unleashed. It's certainly cruel to have killed those children, but the cold-bloodedness of the Germans at Majdanek was a thousand times worse." Another vengeful combatant added that the defenders "are going to remember this march by our army over German territory for a long, long time."

PLANNING THE END

As Germany cowered from the Soviet onslaught, Stalin decided to slow the offensive and consult with his allies in Yalta on the Crimean peninsula of the Black Sea. From February 4 to 11, 1945, Churchill, FDR, and Stalin met for the last time as the Big Three. Along with 700 military and diplomatic advisors, they discussed all aspects of the war and postwar plans that influenced events around the globe. At Yalta, Stalin secretly told Roosevelt that the USSR would break its neutrality accord with Japan and enter the war in Asia three months after Germany's defeat. The disposition of Germany was also a key topic. The Allies decided to combine military operations and then divide the Third Reich into occupation zones, yet the specter of Soviet omnipotence hung over the talks. The contours of the Cold War emerged from Yalta. Stalin held up agreement on voting rights in the United Nations Organization to be established in San Francisco a few months later, insisting that all 15 Soviet republics get a seat in the General Assembly. Also he sought veto power in the governing Security Council, on which the USSR held one of the five permanent seats. He got his way on the veto issue but not on the republics. Stalin was satisfied, however, because he injected a demand that his puppet government represent Poland in the United Nations. The seat remained vacant at San Francisco due to American resistance.

The Soviet dictator did not back down from his policy on Poland. He insisted that a Polish government derive from the Communist Party, provisionally headquartered in Lublin and bossed by Moscow. Once the Red Army liberated Lublin in July 1944, the party agreed to turn over more than half of prewar eastern Poland to the USSR and expel 4.5 million residents. The Soviets arrested sixteen underground leaders including the commander of the Home Army and officials of the exiled government. They were tried in Moscow, and most never returned. To compensate Poland, its border with Germany was shifted westward from the Oder to the Neisse Rivers. The Neisse line was contested by Western diplomats, but the Red Army was the unchallenged occupying force and Roosevelt and Churchill could merely appeal to Stalin's sense of fairness to align the borders. Although the Soviet leader did not exude much sympathy, he gave lip service to Yalta's Declaration on Liberated Europe to placate his future adversaries. Based on the principles of self-determination, the Yalta Declaration required free elections in liberated nations. Stalin essentially ignored these lofty aims. He set up undemocratic pro-Soviet governments in Romania in March and in Poland a few months later. The coalition against Hitler began to fracture.

An aging Roosevelt hoped to hold his Soviet ally to his word, but he also understood that goodwill was not Stalin's forte. He continued to voice support for the USSR as an ally that had won the ground war against Nazism and that could help to defeat Japan. Such a stance built hopes that the postwar world would abandon power politics and that the budding superpowers would avoid conflict. FDR counted on the United Nations to resolve the tensions. He boosted the organization as a means to wean his country from isolationism and commit to an interventionist foreign policy that could deal with Stalin. Privately, President Roosevelt and Churchill held no illusions about cooperation with the USSR after the war. The prime minister had already recognized the reality of power politics by his percentages deal over the Balkans in 1944, and Roosevelt also understood the realities of Russian power. The Red Army occupied Eastern Europe and had reached Berlin's doorstep. Thus, FDR put great stock in the Declaration of Liberated Europe to moderate Stalin's imperial behavior. It was his only option in light of Allied military needs and Soviet strength.

As the Yalta conference concluded with varnished images of Allied cooperation, Stalin returned to the battlefield. He decided against a rapid advance through Germany and therefore, during February and March 1945, the Eastern front saw a series of random fights. Danzig fell and parts of Pomerania were occupied. While the Wehrmacht wilted, Rokossovsky and Vasilevsky slowly moved into East Prussia. The former received help from Zhukov who sent up two tank armies and a field army. Konev's First Ukrainian *front* crossed the Oder and progressed halfway to the Neisse to seize the industrial center of Upper Silesia. To the north, the Second and Third Baltic *fronts* kept Army Group Courland cooped up but they could not break defensive positions that had been weakened by ammunition and food shortages even after pounding Schorner in January, February, and March. The Nazis still believed they fought for the last bastion of European culture. To the south, the battle for Budapest ended in mid-February 1945 but the Red Army remained in a defensive stance in southeastern Europe. Stalin decided there was no need for a concerted rush to Berlin.

Hitler took advantage of the slack by ordering a showy attack. This was his first offensive on the Eastern front since Citadel in July 1943. He ordered remnants of Sixth SS Panzer Army from the Ardennes to Hungary for a defense of his Austrian birthplace. Disrupted railways and bad weather delayed its arrival until the end of February when the Wehrmacht attacked the Second and Third Ukrainian army groups as Guderian protested the futility of the campaign. On March 16, the Russians hit the strung-out offensive called by the delusional name of Operation Awakening of Spring. By early April, Hitler ordered General Lothar Rendulic, commander-in-chief Army Group South, to save Vienna or let it succumb like Budapest. The operation was really just a spoiling campaign at best. It wasted forces that would have been better concentrated in East Prussia and Silesia. Rendulic fought for five days and then withdrew north into the mountains on April 13. That same day the Red Army took Vienna. The Third Reich was reduced to a strip of land 50 to 100 miles wide running from the Baltic to Yugoslavia and Italy.

Stalin's attention turned abruptly back to Germany when the Western Allies broke across the Rhine and encircled the Ruhr Valley at the end of March. The prize was Berlin, and capturing this core symbol of fascism meant the death of Hitler, Nazism, and the Third Reich. Berlin also was the key to claims of occupation rights, territorial gains, and governance over the postwar order of central Europe. Stalin wanted the city. On March 31, he propelled the First and Second Belorussian *fronts* on a determined march past Berlin to blunt Western penetration. Zhukov took aim on Wehrmacht positions while Rokossovsky and Konev pushed to the Elbe River on his flanks. Army Group Vistula met these assaults. Army Group Center stood ready on the Neisse and Czech border yet Stalin's panic prompted a Russian quickstep directly to Berlin. The defenders had enough left to slow the attack during the first 3 days of April. Rokossovsky and Konev were forced to divert away from the Elbe and toward Berlin. The Soviet offensive on the capital began in earnest on April 16. The Western powers advanced east and north after Anglo-American air commanders ended the strategic bombing campaign.

A meeting of the two great fronts in the European war was imminent. Allied armor raced on the autobahns as the German collapse accelerated. Italy came into Allied hands. On April 19, Second British Army got to Hamburg almost at the mouth of the Elbe while U.S. First Army captured Leipzig. Patton, Patch, and de Lattre turned south across the Danube to attack the supposed National Redoubt. Patton ended up in Austria and Czechoslovakia by early May, and he wished to continue into Prague. If he had done so, it is possible the Czechs would not have fallen into the Soviet Cold War orbit. Reconnaissance teams moved across the Elbe to Torgau where First Army joined Konev's forces on April 25. The first Soviet-American contact had been made in the

Young German soldiers captured.   Credit: Center for the Study of War Experience at Regis University, Denver, Colorado.

village of Stehla ten miles to the southeast a few hours earlier as both sides embraced and toasted each other for having cut the Third Reich in two.

Axis and Allies had run the gamut of emotions up to 1945. Euphoric victory, grim determination to defend their gains, and sparks of defiant counterattacks amidst terrible losses described the Axis experience during the war. They had numerous allies in those early days but fewer as defeats mounted. On the other hand, the Allies witnessed depressing and stunning defeats at first, resolute rollback of their enemy, and triumphant liberation by 1944. More and more nations joined the Allied cause, including those in the Middle East and Latin America (even Nazi-sympathizer Argentina declared war on the Axis in late March 1945). The military initiative changed hands. What had been a flood of blitzkrieg on the part of the Axis turned into resistance and eventually a porous defense. Rather than orchestrating pincer movements, Germany and Japan became their unwilling targets. And instead of wielding the strategy of annihilation, the Axis powers now felt its effects in a most brutal fashion.

CHAPTER 23

Shrinking the Japanese Empire

> In the end there would be a seaful of dead sailors from both
> sides.
>
> Ivan Doig
The Eleventh Man

RETURNING TO THE PHILIPPINES

The war in the Pacific had certainly turned against the Empire of Japan, and as in Europe, it also turned increasingly vicious as the defenders desperately tried to block the invaders. It was like trying to plug the holes in the proverbial dyke; the Japanese could not stop the flood of American men and arms. The Philippines was a good case in point. The United States worked to liberate the islands as guerrilla groups of communists, partisans, and civilians disrupted communications, provided intelligence, and boosted morale. Three weeks after Ernest King agreed to invade the Philippines rather than target Formosa, the Southwest Pacific and Central Pacific campaigns converged on the island of Leyte. Despite their meager intelligence services, the Japanese predicted a landing and thus determined to contest the assault. Japan's tenuous supply, transport, and communication lines from Southeast Asia and the East Indies depended on holding the Philippines.

In September 1944, U.S. aircraft pummeled airfields in central Luzon and destroyed about 400 planes to give the Americans air superiority in the Philippines. Douglas MacArthur gathered a huge fleet of over 700 ships that carried hundreds of planes and 160,000 troops to Leyte. At dawn on October 20, warships bombarded for four hours, after which three islands in Leyte Gulf were taken by the 6th Ranger Battalion, and four divisions of Walter Krueger's Sixth Army secured the beachhead near the island's capital of Tacloban. By nightfall, the troops took the neighboring airstrip—Japan's biggest on Leyte—for use by Kenney's air forces. In only one sector did the some of the 60,000 defenders mount enough resistance to turn away the landing craft. Accompanied by the exiled Philippine President Sergio Osmena, MacArthur waded ashore the next day (for the first of many times) in a photo made famous by requisitioned cameramen as he memorably pronounced "I have returned" after nearly three years since his 1942 departure from Corregidor. The next day, the Americans had Tacloban, and MacArthur and Osmena presided over the restoration of civilian rule to the country. A large island with a population of over 900,000 people, Leyte required time to secure. U.S. forces proceeded to enlarge their foothold by landing more troops and equipment in the Pacific war's largest amphibious operation to date. They moved south through swamps and north over mountains to capture airfields and fanatically determined Japanese soldiers.

The key battle for the Philippines actually occurred off the coast. The Imperial Navy and Army sought to chase off the invaders by luring away carrier protection and then bombarding the beachhead. Despite irreplaceable losses of carriers and planes since Midway, the Japanese still had reserves for such a desperation ploy. Thus followed the biggest naval encounter in history involving 282 U.S., Australian, and Japanese vessels; 200,000 men; and 100,000 square miles. Drawing on every type of vessel, weapon, and tactic in naval warfare, the massive battle of Leyte Gulf began four days after the U.S. landing on Leyte itself. Admiral Soemu Toyoda went for broke with Operation Sho Ichi Go or Victory Plan 1 in what seemed to be an impossible gamble. His forces lacked land-based aircraft cover and he had little intelligence on the location and size of the enemy fleets, while Chester Nimitz and Bull Halsey were informed of Sho Ichi Go. Toyoda operated under the illusion that the air battles over Formosa had devastated the Americans but quite the contrary was true. Japan had not only lost hundreds of planes but shipping and base facilities as well. Nonetheless, Toyoda was defiant in the face of such overwhelming odds. Should his forces make the same sacrifices as the recent mass suicides at Marpi Point on Saipan, he was certain that victory was possible.

Sho Ichi Go had two parts. First, the Mobile Force of Jizaburo Ozawa would serve as a decoy. Ozawa's four-ship Carrier Force would sail in circles east of Luzon to pull away to the north Marc Mitscher's sixteen-carrier Task Force 38. Second, a seaborne pincer movement led by two strike forces would hit the Americans on land and at sea. The First Striking Force under Takeo Kurita would approach Leyte from the south. Part of this group—Force A—would head into the San Bernardino Strait. Force A contained the two biggest battleships on earth. The 73,000 thousand ton *Musashi* and *Yamato* possessed 18.1-inch guns (the largest naval artillery ever put to sea) and armor with main turret face plates over two feet thick. Force C, the other part of Kurita's First Striking Force, sailed under Shojo Nishimura and would penetrate Leyte Gulf through Surigao Strait. Meanwhile, the other element of the pincer, Kiyohide Shima's Second Striking Force, would follow Nishimura's path from Japan to Leyte as an escort and then would attack the amphibious assault ships under Thomas Kinkaid's Seventh Fleet. Converging from different directions, the four groups would doom the beachhead. The complex Shi Ichi Go began on October 23, 1944 with the first of six naval encounters.

Toyoda encountered problems from the outset but because he demanded radio silence and changed codes. U.S. monitors did not detect his forces at first. Still, U.S. submarines caught Kurita's Force A in the South China Sea and sank two cruisers including his flagship *Atago*, and crippled a third. The next day, October 24, Mitscher sent out Task Groups 38.2 and 38.3 after he detected Kurita crossing the Sibuyan Sea toward the San Bernardino Strait. They disabled the enormous *Musashi* and struck the other battleships. A return torpedo and air attack finished off the superbattleship and 1,039 of her crew. Force A then reversed course and thereby threw off the Imperial Navy's schedule for arriving in Leyte Gulf, even though Kurita turned back toward the Strait later that night. Halsey assumed that Kurita was through and thus directed the bulk of Task Force 38 and the fast battleships and cruisers of Task Force 34 under Guadalcanal veteran Willis Lee to chase after the decoy Ozawa. Despite the setbacks of the first two rounds, Toyoda appeared to have set his trap.

In the third encounter of the battle of Leyte Gulf, Japanese Carrier Force aircraft sunk the light carrier *Princeton* and damaged the cruiser *Birmingham* at the cost of two-thirds of its planes. Yet the Americans scored, too, as flying ace David McCambell's Hellcat set a record by taking out nine enemy planes in a day. Unaware that Kurita had changed his mind and was again heading for San Bernardino Strait into Leyte Gulf, Halsey still pursued Ozawa. After entering the narrow Surigao Strait on the night of October 24, Nishimura's Force C was discovered by Jesse Oldendorf who was stationed across the Strait a shore bombardment force of five battleships that had been sunk or damaged at Pearl Harbor. Thirty-nine pesky PT boats harassed Nishimura for 25 miles and darting destroyers launched torpedoes. Oldendorf then pulled out his big radar-controlled guns. The battleships and cruisers lined up broadside across the head of the oncoming column of enemy ships, "crossing the T" in a classic textbook naval maneuver. The Americans sailed back and forth across the mouth of Surigao Strait and devastated Force C. Within fifteen minutes, Nishimura died, and two battleships, all of his cruisers, and three of four destroyers went down with him in this battle of Surigao Strait. Trailing behind, Shima encountered the sole fleeing destroyer of Force C, which prompted him to withdraw Second Striking Force. He later lost two ships to pursuing U.S. planes. The fourth round of the battle of Leyte Gulf went to the Americans.

Prospects looked up for the Japanese, though, even if Kurita's arm of the pincer was all that remained. The next morning Force A appeared off Samar Island and stunned one of the Seventh Fleet's tiny escort carrier groups under Clifton Sprague. Kurita was also surprised but because he feared that a much American stronger force was in the vicinity, he ordered an immediate attack on Sprague's "Taffy 3" group. This was an error. In the first daylight surface naval action since the Java Sea in February 1942, U.S. aircraft destroyed two Imperial cruisers and a destroyer damaged another. Sprague threw aircraft at Kurita to deceive the Vice-Admiral that they came from Halsey's approaching fleet. Yet Kurita possessed four battleships and several cruisers and destroyers to Sprague's six escort carriers and handful of destroyers and destroyer escorts, and the Americans had nothing larger than a five-inch gun on board to ping away at the huge battleships. Fighter planes dropped small fragmentation bombs but desperately outgunned, Sprague fled southward and lost two escort carriers in the process. One fell victim to a kamikaze. These suicidal attacks were named in honor of the so-called divine wind that had miraculously destroyed two invading Mongol fleets in the 13th century. The brainchild of Takijiro Onishi of the First Air Fleet, who knew Japan was heavily outnumbered in men and planes, the first kamikazes took off on their one-way

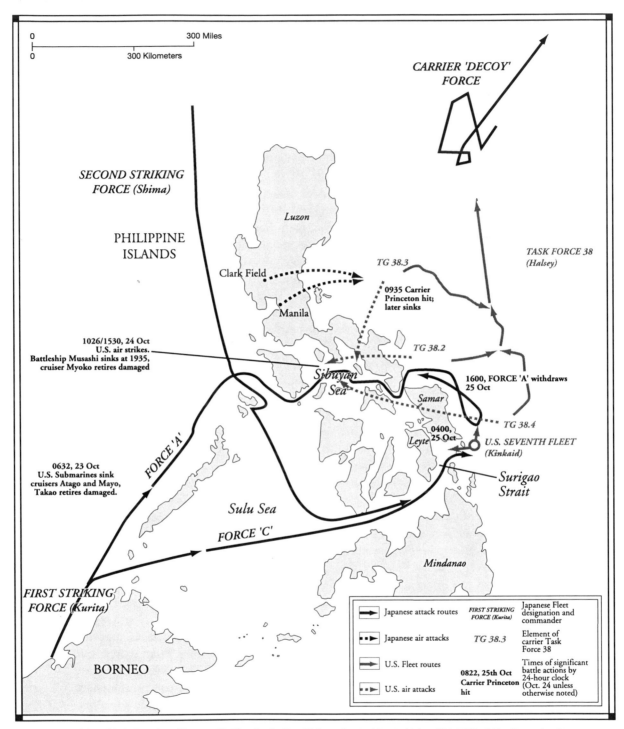

Map 23.1 Battle of Leyte Gulf. Credit: Ronald Story, *Concise Historical Atlas of World War II: The Geography of Conflict*, Map 43, p. 91.

Kamikaze attack on the USS St. Lo.   Credit: Center for the Study of War Experience at Regis University, Denver, Colorado: U.S. National Archive.

missions from Luzon. Essentially airborne banzai attackers, the kamikazes targeted troop transports but then zeroed in on the American escort fleet. In the battle of Leyte Gulf, they did little damage except for sinking the carrier *St. Lo* and damaging several of the other Taffy escort carriers but they were terrifying all the same and indicated that the Japanese would try to annihilate their enemy to the very end.

They unleashed a campaign of terror. A sailor recounted the air full of scrap and bullets as kamikazes screamed into his ship. When a dive bomber crashed, part of a motor embedded in the body of a fellow crew member while the rest were wounded. Gasoline sprayed everywhere. The deck near his position "was covered with blood, guts, brains, tongues, scalps, hearts, arms etc. from" the pilot. Horrified seamen were convinced that the enemy lacked all reason; the kamikaze combined the medieval creed of the samurai with modern technology. Such thinking shaped extremely negative American perceptions of the Japanese in terms of the mounting brutality of the Pacific war. The tragic use of kamikaze attacks (pilot recruits were increasingly college students or farmers initially bent on honoring their families and the Emperor) further escalated this war without mercy. Soon the kamikazes organized into divisions of the Thunder God Corps. The Americans believed they had no other option but to obliterate Japan through a total war of annihilation.

Back at sea, Clifton Sprague yelled for help to save his tiny fleet from the Japanese. Hearing the cries, Kinkaid launched air attacks, and the outgunned Taffy 2 under Felix Stump came charging up from the south. The U.S. escort carrier *Gambier Bay* was sunk along with destroyers and a destroyer escort, *Hoel, Johnston,* and *Samuel B. Roberts* as the Americans conducted their own suicide charges against ships thirty times their size. Ironically, Kurita had too much firepower; because his refrigerator-sized armor-piercing shells were designed for battleships, many of them went right through the lightly built carriers. Yet after two hours, the Americans looked doomed. Kinkaid frantically radioed for relief. Oldendorf was engaged, Stump still charged onward, and Lee's Task Force 34 sailed after Ozawa with Halsey diverted to the north. Help was far away. In the sixth round of the battle, Mitscher had taken out a destroyer and would sink four carriers in the Battle of Cape Engaño. But Halsey did not wish to break off his chase, although he soon learned of the surprising battle between the Goliath Kurita and the David Sprague. Kinkaid's pleas for aid reached all the way to Pearl Harbor, and in response, Nimitz sent an unintentionally insulting but crystal clear message over the airwaves by asking "Where is Task Force 34?" A communications ensign added the jarring "the world wonders" as padding to disguise the real message. Whereas naval historians chuckled over this wording mishap, Bull Halsey was not amused at the time. So chastised, he turned the task force and Lee's fast battleship support group away from the decoy and to the south. Kinkaid rushed in from the Surigao Strait yet Sprague's rescuers were still three hours away. Kurita's Force A pushed both of his carriers as well as Stump's recently arrived group into Letye Gulf for the kill.

Then a miracle happened. At 9:30 a.m., Kurita suddenly quit the battle and departed. Short of fuel and worried that Halsey and Lee lurked nearby, he decided to retire through San Bernardino Strait. In his defense, Force A had been ordered both to attack the Seventh Fleet in Leyte Gulf and pursue Halsey's carriers from the rear, two tasks that were irreconcilable. In addition, Kurita knew that Force C had been destroyed and Ozawa's situation was unknown. So, prudence dictated that he withdraw. The Americans could not believe their eyes as they watched Kurita go, for Sprague had expected to be dog-paddling by this time. Aircraft harried the retreating Force A and sunk a light cruiser in the Sulu Sea. Still, the events blackened Halsey's name. He had failed to cut off Kurita's exit and erase the Combined Fleet when he fell for Ozawa's ploy. Such criticism was unfair, however. Halsey had done more to boost morale after the dark days of Pearl Harbor than any other figure. Hospitalization for a skin rash during the battle of Midway had excluded him from the major engagements thus far. Thus he was primed to destroy the carriers of the Mobile Fleet, and so had eagerly gone after Ozawa. Above all, he emerged victorious.

The three-day clash at Leyte Gulf ended with major implications. Although Toyoda's fleet was not completely destroyed, it was useless for any further large operations. The U.S. Navy lost 6 light warships, 200 planes, and 3,000 dead; but Japan watched four carriers, 3 battleships, 12 destroyers, over 300 planes, and 10,000 flyers and sailors go down. A total of 300,000 tons of Imperial Navy vessels rested on the bottom. This was also the last old-style engagement between battleships, and the first and last time a battleship sunk a U.S. aircraft carrier. In short, the Imperial Navy was no longer a viable attack force and essentially assumed the status of a coast guard. The battle also safeguarded U.S. operations in the Philippines without fear of Japanese naval interference.

Turning to the islands, MacArthur viewed the capture of Leyte as necessary to host aircraft bases for the assault on his main objective of Luzon but the Japanese had a different idea. Because they thought that the battle of Leyte Gulf had resulted in a victory, they hoped to trap MacArthur on Leyte.

The new commander of Imperial forces in the Philippines, the "Tiger of Malay," General Tomoyuki Yamashita, commanded the 432,000 troops of a reinforced Thirty-Fifth Army. When Tojo fell from power in July 1944, the conqueror of Singapore flew from the Manchurian backwater where he had been exiled to assume leadership of the islands' defense in early October. Yamashita understood that losing the Philippines meant the unraveling of the entire logistical network that supported the Co-Prosperity Sphere in Asia. Thus, like Macarthur, he elevated Leyte to a top priority. Zipping 50,000 fresh troops in fast transports past U.S. air coverage, Yamashita bolstered the garrison of the 16th Division of Thirty-Fifth Army under Sosaku Suzuki. The troops assembled defensive positions on a line running along the central interior mountain spine. Yamashita decided to fight as long as possible. He ordered rounds of aerial assaults from Japan and Formosa, commando raids on airfields, and garrisoned 70,000 troops on Leyte alongside Fourth Air Army and First Air Fleet.

The reinforcements and attacks compelled MacArthur to drag out the campaign on Leyte longer than he wished. He underestimated the size of the garrison and his own troop levels of 200,000 men, and also wrongly assumed that the Fifth Air Force would have airfields to replace the carrier-based support. Bad weather slowed their construction. And Yamashita escalated air attacks, decimating the U.S. planes in a way not seen since MacArthur's days on New Guinea. By early November 1944, only two American airstrips were operable, and a monsoon and typhoon further limited progress. Expecting no air support, Krueger's two corps of 202,500 troops slugged it out against 16th Division in Leyte's mountains. MacArthur detected enemy reinforcements entering through the port of Ormoc on the western side of the island and so urged Krueger to close off access. Sixth Army labored for a month with artillery and tank support to cross the mountains into the Ormoc valley. Krueger pondered an amphibious envelopment like MacArthur had pulled off in New Guinea, but his superior told him to move forward on land. A quick pace was important because the Luzon landings needed to go forth, but MacArthur delayed the invasion of Mindoro by ten days to provide landing craft to Sixth Army. Krueger used them to put troops ashore near Ormoc Bay. A Japanese counteroffensive including the use of crack parachute troops followed against U.S. airfields, and Yamashita also tied down Sixth Army's rear areas and the Fifth Air Force for a week in early December. But Krueger's artillery blasted away one division, and after the 77th Infantry Division landed three miles from Ormoc, it linked up with X Corps coming down the valley. Both outflanked Yamashita's forces and shut the tap on his reinforcements.

The Imperial Army lacked the resources to hold. Within a week, Suzuki's defense lines began to collapse and the Americans split his forces in two. Ormoc Town saw U.S. troops inch through and fight with flamethrowers, grenades, and bayonets until they cleared out the enemy by December 21. Stragglers remained on the island until May 1945. True to form, the Japanese defenders fought to the bitter end. Over 70,000 died and less than 1,000 members of Suzuki's 16th Division surrendered. Yamashita still had over 250,000 troops in the Philippines, but they were now on the defensive. American dead numbered 3,504, and 12,080 were wounded. At the same time that the Germans succumbed in the Ardennes, MacArthur relayed the good news that Leyte was his. Like the battle of the Bulge, the invasion of Leyte had been prolonged but it was blessed by superb interservice cooperation. At the time, the battle of the Bulge and the invasion of Iwo Jima drew much more attention than the campaign in Leyte Gulf, yet this latter was at least as significant because of its devastating impact on the Imperial Navy. Had Toyoda won, he could have disrupted plans to take Luzon, and such a setback might have even affected FDR's reelection bid a few weeks later. Japan had banked on a miracle; Leyte Gulf indeed was the decisive naval battle that Tokyo had long sought. The Imperial High Command in Tokyo learned that miracles did not always happen, however.

The Americans now looked across San Bernardino Strait to the prize of Luzon and the Filipino capital of Manila. After setting up airstrips on the island of Mindoro, MacArthur readied for an invasion through Lingayen Gulf. Japan had followed this path in its successful campaign in 1941, and he would try to use in three years later. In Manila, he would restore a pro-American government to office and then the U.S. Army would mop up the Philippine islands south of Leyte. The invasion of Leyte represented the last conventional pitched battle with the Japanese. From Luzon onward, Imperial forces responded to attacks in ways ranging from suicide to vicious island defense.

BATTERING AND SQUEEZING

The American advance across the Pacific seemed unstoppable. Amphibious, naval, and ground forces had pushed the Japanese out of the central and southwest Pacific, killed tens of thousands of men, and nullified the Imperial Navy. Japan also felt the ill effects of the blockade of the home islands, the term for the archipelago of Kyushu, Shikoku, Hokkaido, and Honshu (Tokyo was situated on the latter). Protected by radar, U.S. submarines from the Marianas carried more electric torpedoes that were hard to detect because they left no wake. Japan lost 300,000 tons of shipping in October alone, and in 1944, a total of 3 million tons went to the bottom due to the aptly named Operation Starvation. In 1945, nearly 5 million tons were lost to subs, along with 2 million tons from mines and air strikes. Merchants plied the Sea of Japan at great peril. From mid-1944 onward, American submarines sunk 1,300 ships along with a battleship, eight carriers, and eleven cruisers, leaving Japan with half the merchant tonnage with which it began the war. The United States lost just 52 vessels out of 288, but 128 of the 200 Japanese subs went down. This is not to trivialize the grave risks involved for the American predators, for even the new, sturdy, and powerful fleet boats could be rammed or sunk by explosives. Such was the case for *Flier*. In August 1944, it hit a mine in the Sulu Sea and quickly disappeared with all but 14 of its 86 crew. Most victims drowned or suffocated from chlorine gas in the batteries. Sunburnt, dehydrated, and cold, eight survivors paddled twelve miles to a remote island behind enemy lines and eventually evacuated to safety. They were the lucky ones in the harrowing combat under and on the seas.

The jaws of defeat also fastened on Japan through the search for more efficient ways to win the war than simply conventional, hand-to-hand combat. For instance, the Americans relied on the flamethrower to subdue the Japanese (as well as enemies in other theaters), but humidity sometimes caused malfunctions. They resorted to a "blowtorch and corkscrew" technique in which rifle teams covered the flamethrowers that torched enemy firing apertures, and then engineers or infantry destroyed the fortified position with satchel charges, or primed canvas briefcases with twenty-pound demolition blocks. This was dangerous work because of the Imperial Army's interlocking network of defenses that cut down anyone who approached. As a result, by early 1945, the Americans contemplated using chemical agents rather than blowtorch and corkscrew as a safer method of attack.

The United States unveiled another weapon that it had used for over two years in Europe. A strategic air offensive brought the war home to Japan itself in an ever more devastating way once the USAAF adopted its strategy of annihilation. The Twentieth Bomber Command had inflicted little strategic damage since June 1944 when B-29s from China bombed in Asia in missions that offered little more than giving crews some experience in combat. When Twenty-first Bomber Command flew its first sorties over the home islands from the Marianas, that situation changed. They aimed to destroy aircraft production facilities. Eighty unescorted Superfortresses targeted the Nakajima factory in Tokyo. Brigadier-General Haywood Hansell defended precision bombing; and for the next two months, he ordered daylight attacks on aircraft plants. These resulted in lowering Japanese output, but bad weather, the jet stream, mechanical problems, and fighter defense hindered the effort. Such troubles did not help Hansell's argument to skeptics in Washington, including Army Air Force General Hap Arnold, that precision bombing worked.

Arnold advocated a new approach of firebombing entire areas rather than pinpointing targets. This called for a more expansive policy, and as in the bombings in Germany, civilians would be attacked. Flying at night at a low altitude, B-29s carried heavy loads of incendiary bombs that ignited large swaths of Japan's paper and wood cities. Indiscriminate bombing appalled Hansell, but Arnold ordered the tactic tried on Nagoya. Superfortresses hit the city on January 3, 1945, but the results were inconclusive. Arnold still believed that area bombing would inflict maximum damage and soon replaced Hansell with Curtis LeMay, the chief of Twentieth Bomber Command in India and China. The Army's youngest two-star general and an innovative tactician, LeMay continued precision bombing runs but mixed them with incendiary raids. He preferred to fly the latter during the day at safe altitudes. When they yielded encouraging results, he and Arnold decided to increase firebombing missions. Neither had moral qualms about intensifying the air war of annihilation. LeMay reflected that soldiers cared not how their enemy died but how they themselves might perish. So "to worry about the *morality* of what we were doing-Nuts. A soldier has to fight. We fought. If we accomplished the job in any given battle without exterminating too many of our own folks, we considered that we'd had a pretty good day." Great carnage awaited Japan in the coming months.

Once the Twentieth Air Force opted for low-altitude incendiary raids along with high-level precision bombing, destruction in the home islands spiraled upward. On

February 25, 1945, 150 Superfortresses firebombed Tokyo and the devastation convinced Arnold to alter tactics again to maximize the bomb loads and burn Tokyo to the ground with incendiaries. Experimentation proved that the most effective way to level the Japanese capital was to leave the buildings standing (instead of knocking them down with high explosives) and drop small bombs filled with napalm. The napalm would splatter on the walls, find its way into crevices, and burn furnishings and equipment inside, and then drafts created by thousands of small fires would rapidly reproduce to create a huge conflagration. LeMay turned to low-flying nighttime raids to minimize harassment from Japanese fighters (which were most effective in daytime), avoid strong winds and cloud cover, and cut fuel and engine strain. This allowed more air time with heavier bomb loads.

The upshot was the most cataclysmic mission of the war, once again over Tokyo, and further slaughter in other cities. On the night of March 9–10, 1945, 279 Superfortresses dropped 1,665 tons of incendiaries from heights of between 5,000 and 9,000 feet. The B-29s crisscrossed the capital at will as enemy fire or equipment failure downed just 14 of the American planes in two hours. As the densely populated city was bombed, winds fanned flames into a firestorm. A girl explained that people panicked as the fire came nearer. "Running, screaming. We're all going to die!" The wind and flames whipped more wildly. "We were in Hell. All the houses were burning, debris raining down on us. It was horrible. Sparks flew everywhere. Electric wires sparked and toppled." The girl's mother ran through the fire with her baby brother on her back. The mother emerged but the baby disappeared, leaving burn marks where his legs had touched her body. A quarter of Tokyo—16 square miles—lay in ruins, and some 85,000 people died and 41,000 were hurt. These amounted to more initial casualties than from the atomic bombings five months later. In this single most destructive bombing raid in history, the Americans hit twenty key industrial targets. LeMay kept up the pace over the next ten days. Incendiaries burnt sections of Nagoya, Kobe, and Osaka, and two more missions swept over the Tokyo-Kawasaki area before Bomber Command turned its attention to Okinawa. By that time, LeMay had run out of firebombs, although he returned shortly to resume the air war.

Like the bombing of Germany, the strategic bombing campaign in the Pacific prompted a concern in the U.S. command and political structure that the apocalyptic missions were killing thousands of civilians. Le May supported bombing as a means of speeding up Japan's surrender and rendering an amphibious invasion unnecessary. Like the European air theorists, he believed that bombing undermined morale. That it did not (Japan did not surrender until the atomic bombs were dropped) begs the question. The campaign curbed production and avenged the hardships endured by American soldiers in the Pacific. This was a brutal war without mercy with few limits to its savagery. Noted an officer in the Fifth Air Force, "the entire population of Japan is a proper Military Target . . . there are no civilians in Japan." From the military's standpoint, bombers worked in tandem with submarines in a grand strategy of annihilation to choke the Japanese war economy. B-29s also flew 1,528 sorties to sow 13,102 mines that closed harbors. Some even argued that the air campaign saved Japan from a long period of suffering by ending the war more quickly than conventional methods such as invasion.

The strain from the firebombings and the submarine blockade worsened Japan's already insufficient production of war and consumer goods. Output of warships fell from 250 vessels in 1944 to just 50 in 1945. Over the same period, factories manufactured only 140 tanks (down from 400) and 1,600 fieldpieces, when 3,600 had been made in 1944. Petroleum products plummeted to a handful of barrels. Despite the availability of Korean rice, food was so scarce that the people were compelled to eat tofu, which was considered to be lowbrow. Both military personnel and civilians starved by the Summer 1945 as their caloric intake fell below life-sustaining levels. Japan could not possibly go on, but doggedly persist it did.

STRUGGLE IN THE CHINA-BURMA-INDIA THEATER

The Allies also closed up the pincers on land as well as from the air and sea. Actually, in China, the Imperial Army made headway with its impressive IchiGo campaign. Joseph Stilwell continued to spar with Chiang Kai-shek over supplies, military performance, and corruption, and he disdained air commander Claire Chennault's plan to interdict sea-lanes by air attacks from southeastern China. Chiang liked this idea because it allowed his forces to avoid combat and let him avoid domestic reforms. By mid-1944, the Japanese proved Stilwell right. Ichi-Go captured airfields, and Chiang's armies melted away. Japan called off the operation in May 1945, but the damage done undercut the Nationalists Chinese appeal. Resistance broke down and with it confidence that Chiang could do nothing more than tie down troops and possibly help develop a staging area for the invasion of Japan itself. The victory also kept open Japanese lines of communications from China into Indochina, undermined efforts to harass shipping from air bases, and threatened Chiang's capital of Chungking. All the while Chiang took aim on his communist foe. Roosevelt certainly saw the effort against Mao as a diversion of resources from the war and in late 1944, his personal emissary Patrick Hurley demanded that Chiang undertake political and military reforms and make peace with Mao. Yet as usual, Chiang stonewalled until Ichi-Go petered out. In any case, and regardless of the politics, China became a tertiary concern in the war. In October 1944, the Allies divided the China-Burma-India theater into a distinct China partition and a Burma-India area. The diplomatic Albert Wedemeyer, who had drafted the U.S. Victory Plan of 1941 and had served in China as a deputy to Marshall and Lord Mountbatten, replaced Vinegar Joe Stilwell. Wedemeyer tactfully persuaded Chiang to prevent enemy troops from leaving China by abandoning his dream of a viable air force and modernizing the Nationalist Army through Lend-Lease aid. He also managed to open the Ledo Road from India through northern Burma to the Burma Road that ended in Kunming in January 1945. An oil pipeline ran alongside this 478-mile supply road. By this time, China diminished in strategic value as internal intrigue intensified. America would not send troops there because it focused on the race to Berlin and securing Luzon in the Philippines. Hurley also allowed a virtual civil war between the despised Communists and Chiang's forces, and suspected his own headquarters of sympathizing with Mao. Chiang's Nationalist generals hunted the Communists rather than the Japanese. At Yalta in February 1945, FDR and Churchill played the Soviet card, asking Stalin to pressure Mao to cooperate with Chiang and then got Moscow's assent to enter the war on the Asian mainland. Breaking the USSR-Japan neutrality treaty would hinder the transfer of enemy troops to central China and the home islands. In return, the Allies granted Stalin aid and territorial concessions, including parts of Manchuria and land lost to Japan in 1905. Chiang was obliged to accept these conditions, which then permitted him to fight Mao while the Americans (and soon the Red Army) fought the Japanese.

As China receded in importance, the campaign in Burma and India accelerated. After attempts to invade India through Kohima and Imphal ended in disaster in mid-1944, the Imperial Army was sent reeling through Burma by the British. The Japanese lost thousands of casualties, many from starvation. William Slim drove to the Chindwin River in northern Burma and linked with the Americans under Daniel Sultan who had assumed command of U.S. and Chinese units in central Burma. Slim fixated on pushing the enemy out of Rangoon and back to Thailand by counting on new Indian divisions. Since performing badly in 1942, fresh recruits and an expanded officer corps had professionalized the Indian Army, and better coordination converted it into a more effective force. Divided into three corps with only two European divisions, Slim's Fourteenth Army drove into the Arakan. Coming upon bodies of enemy soldiers executed because they were too hurt to evacuate, Slim knew he had the initiative, and he also enjoyed a huge edge in manpower. British Fourteenth Army numbered 260,000 soldiers to Fifteenth Japanese Army's 21,000 troops, and furthermore, the Allies more than quadrupled the Japanese in combat and transport aircraft. Slim directed two corps east toward Mandalay and a third to the south along the Arakan coast. Two West African divisions of VX Corp occupied the communications hub of Myohaung on January 25, 1945 after seizing Buthidaung. The 25th Indian Division also landed on Akyab. Because the Japanese had withdrawn most of their troops, Commonwealth forces advanced southward to take the islands of Ramree and Cheduba and to cut off an escape route.

With the coast secured, Slim intended to approach Rangoon from central Burma. The initial step required defeating Shihachi Katamura's Fifteenth Army, which had been retreating since the Imphal offensive. Slim's XXX Corps under Montagu Stopford, a hero of the Kohima siege, crossed the Irrawaddy River for Mandalay, as a British and two Indian divisions made the longest river crossings (1,000 to 4,500 yards) of the war at points west of Sagaing in February. One of the Indian divisions turned south toward Rangoon and severed rail and road links while British troops came from the east and south toward Mandalay. Japanese Burma Area Army and collaborators determined to hold Mandalay as long as possible, but it fell in March after engagements in the colonial fortifications of Mandalay Hill and Fort Dufferin. The loss was more a blow to Japanese prestige than a military setback. Because Katamura enjoyed substantial strength in the town, the key clash occurred to the south at Meiktila.

The battle for Meiktila occurred from February to March 1945. To trap Katamura, Slim tricked the Japanese with radio signals into believing that he would assault Mandalay. Feinting toward the town, he secretly moved elements of the IV Corps—namely, the 17th Indian Division and the 255th Tank Brigade—through the Myittha valley and across the Irawaddy. From this position, Allied armor charged Meiktila and overran enemy communications and supplies. After the British swept aside the Indian National Army, 300 Japanese infantrymen fought for and lost Meiktila. Slim was ecstatic as his men buried over 2,000 Japanese. Hyotaro determined to retake Meiktila with Masaki Honda's 49th Division and other troops but the 17th Indian Division held on and resupplied by air drops. Honda could not break through, and he withdrew on March 28 to cover Katamura's retreat from Mandalay. After a brief stand at Pyawbwe, Imperial troops vacated the area. The route to Rangoon lay open to the Allies in a major strategic victory for Slim. Both sides suffered similar numbers of casualties, but the Japanese had four times as many killed.

Rangoon came under attack from the Arakan forces. Stopford's XXX Corps descended the Irrawaddy valley, and two Indian divisions of the IV Corps under the command of the dashing Africa and Burma campaign veteran Frank Messervy jumped from Meiktila to Pyinmana to Toungoo—250 miles—in 19 days. Burma Independence Army led by former Japanese ally turned Allied friend Aung San protected his flank. This allowed one of Messervy's divisions to reach Pegu on April 29, just 50 miles from Rangoon. Rainstorms delayed the trucks and tanks and hampered air cover, but Slim wanted the capital before the monsoon season began in earnest and thus turned to an amphibious landing by the other Indian unit. Burma Area Army had already escaped the city to Moulmein with a loss of 7,000 soldiers. Stopford met Messervy coming down from Mandalay. Although the Burma campaign was not over, Rangoon was finally back in British hands after three years and Burma was no longer a jewel in the crown of the Co-Prosperity Sphere.

SECURING THE PHILIPPINES

The Pacific was now clearly the decisive theater in the war against Japan. MacArthur had the job of liberating Luzon and Manila and then cleaning out the rest of the Philippines. Taking Luzon would fulfill his obligation to liberate the Filipinos. He had at his disposal 16 divisions, or more U.S. soldiers than had served in operations in North Africa, Italy, and southern France combined. MacArthur's invasion was not without worries, however. The U.S. Seventh Fleet's Thomas Kinkaid as well as air fleet commanders thought that Japanese suicide bombers might prevent landings in northern Luzon. The Americans also needed air bases but since October 1944, kamikazes had damaged several carriers to the point that Bull Halsey had called off raids on airfields. Subordinates thus persuaded MacArthur to take Mindoro to the south of Luzon and build airstrips from which they could cover a landing. The effort, MacArthur hoped, might divert Yamashita's attention to the south of Luzon while the Americans circled around to the north of the island for their main invasion. This exercise delayed the Luzon invasion, but it was a prudent course and reminiscent of his successful New Guinea campaign. Amphibious units of Robert Eichelberger's Eighth Army came ashore on Mindoro on December 15, 1944, with minimal resistance. They captured the airfields and put two into operatio, but a kamikaze killed 133 and injured over 200 naval and army personnel on the light cruiser *Nashville*. Flying from bases in the northern Philippines, other planes penetrated the antiaircraft screen and sunk three LSTs and five Liberty ships. U.S. engineers built an airfield by Christmas Eve, however.

MacArthur's impatience grew. He wanted Manila by his sixty-fifth birthday on January 26, 1945, and he also hoped to rescue thousands of prisoners. His haste caused the U.S. Army to underestimate Yamashita's forces on Luzon even though the cautious Walter Krueger put the numbers nearer to their actual mark of 267,000. On January 9, U.S. Sixth Army landed in Lingayen Gulf. Kamikazes damaged the invasion fleet and just missed MacArthur's flagship as it moved up the coast, yet Yamashita lacked equipment, transport, aircraft, and the best troops to counter the enemy's mobility. The Americans came ashore elsewhere in small amphibious and airborne forces in an attempt to keep the defenders off balance. They had their lodgment, and now the real battle began. Rather than seek a decisive battle in the central Luzon plain, Yamashita fought a war of attrition from the mountains. He predicted correctly that MacArthur would follow the Japanese course of three years before down the central valley to the prize of Manila. As a result, Yamashita kept an armored division of 150 tanks in reserve to hit the Americans' flanks. He divided his defense into three groups and placed another under Sanji Iwabachi, ordering the men to fight to the last and punish the enemy. The 152,000-man Shobu Group in the Carabello Mountains sought to attack U.S. Sixth Army's left flank at Lingayen Gulf while Shimbu Group's 80,000 troops in the Sierra Madres defended south of Manila. The 30,000 men of Kembu Group set up in the western mountains to block Clark Field and stop an advance on Manila from Bataan. Iwabachi's task was to gut the capital city as a military site. Drawn from a naval base and remnants of warship crews, his forces set out to destroy facilities and ammunition that could not be carted into the mountains. After eviscerating Manila, Iwabachi would then link with Shimbu Group.

To MacArthur's dismay, Yamashita's strategy slowed down the U.S. advance in one of the most brilliant defensive maneuvers of World War II. Logistical snafus plagued the 175,000 American troops, but mainly the Japanese hindered progress. MacArthur ordered Eighth Army to land on Bataan and south of Manila to divert Yamashita's attention. Krueger and Eichelberger fought on the central plain, holding its eastern edge while countering Shobu Group. Three divisions took Clark airfield, but resistance from Kembu Group required two corps of Sixth Army to help out. Meanwhile, Shobu Group fell back to Yamashita's headquarters at Baguio. MacArthur was livid. He issued direct orders to Krueger as his birthday deadline passed without his presence in Manila, and he personally sent three divisions racing toward the capital on January 30. They entered the city's outskirts within five days and a column of the 1st Cavalry Division liberated 500 prisoners at Santo Tomas University. Yet about a million people sheltered in the old thick walls and buildings of Manila. Unlike the Americans in 1942, Yamashita fought ferociously for the capital.

Lasting almost a month, the battle for Manila witnessed some of the worst destruction of any urban area during the Second World War and it also represented one of America's most costly engagements in the Pacific. To save the city from ruin in 1942, MacArthur had declared the city open. Iwabachi and Shimbu commander Yokoyama Shizuo had no such qualms. Their 16,000 sailors and 3 army battalions refused to withdraw, and instead, they blew up bridges, military installations, and supplies as their perimeter shrunk. Demolition teams burned wood and thatch structures. Tens of thousands became refugees; and thousands more were raped, tortured, and killed. Neither children nor the elderly were immune from the rampage of annihilation by soldiers drunk from looting liquor stores. MacArthur wanted to save Manila, so he refused to use air strikes, but even his own artillery barrages wiped out whatever the fires had left standing. A historian has noted that this was "the Pacific War's most severe slide into savagery," and this was true. Iwabachi turned the modern buildings of the University of the Philippines and the aged walls of the Intramuros section into a bunker where sailors armed with naval artillery, antiaircraft cannon, and machine guns held their own. For his part, Krueger was methodical. The Eleventh Airborne Division advanced from the south toward the new part of the city while the 37th Infantry and 1st Cavalry Division crossed the Pasig River to the Intramuros. Over ten days, he expended thousands of rounds from artillery, tanks, and tank destroyers at point-blank range, and then U.S. infantry then cleared out each enemy soldier. As in Stalingrad and Warsaw, the two sides fought building by building, street by street.

On March 3, the Japanese lost this battle of annihilation. Iwabachi's sailors fought, died, or fled, only to be hunted down in the sewers by gasoline and grenades. All 16,000 perished as Shimbu Group's rescue attempt failed. The Americans had a thousand men killed and 5,600 wounded while nearly 100,000 Filipinos died. Entire families were eliminated, bayoneted or shot after the women were raped. Some were disemboweled, babies included. Civilians were killed at a rate six times that of military combatants. In one incident, the Japanese escorted 3,000 people into a building and killed a third of them before releasing the rest. Several hundred Filipino men were beheaded. Women, men, and children were wired together, drenched in gasoline, and set afire either by grenades or lighters. Second only to Warsaw in its destruction, Manila emerged as a carcass of a city. When MacArthur reestablished Osmena's government on February 27, 1945, he was so overcome with grief by the carnage that he could not finish his speech. Gazing out over a city now among the dead, he closed the ceremonies with the Lord's Prayer.

The liberation of Manila opened the door to the rest of the Philippines, but its fine harbor could not be used until the enemy threat was removed from the western side of the bay on Bataan and at the fortress of Corregidor. Misjudging the strength of the 4,000-troop Kembu Group on Bataan, U.S. officers were responsible for heavy casualties during a tough victory at the end of February. A regiment of paratroopers and two battalions of infantry recaptured Corregidor around this time, to the surprise of the Japanese, yet Yamashita recovered to ignite stockpiles of munitions in the tunnels of the fortress. He killed hundreds, including many Americans. This was another operation to assuage MacArthur's ego and serve political purposes. Tiny Corregidor was neither crucial to the Japan's defensive arrangement nor to U.S. strategy, and without adequate preparation or reserves, soldiers died to take a high-profile target with dubious military value.

The battle for northern Luzon continued as Yamashita pledged to endure. MacArthur and Krueger knew he had to be eliminated to secure Manila as a logistical base. The smallest army unit, comprised of aviation and service personnel, Kembu Group fell back into the Zambales Mountains after defending the roads from Bataan to

Filipinos murdered during Japanese withdrawal from Manila.   Credit: Center for the Study of War Experience at Regis University, Denver, Colorado.

Manila. Eichelberger kept up the pressure but found Shimbu Group to be his biggest headache. Comprised of regular army divisions, it was well supplied and mobile east of Manila. Shimbu also controlled the water supply to Manila by occupying reservoirs, dams, and aqueducts. The Americans assaulted the Wawa Dam until the 6th Infantry Division ground to a halt, and it took three additional divisions to take the Ipo Dam and nullify Shimbu Group. The Japanese effectively traded time and terrain for American lives, as the Wawa Dam did not fall into U.S. hands until May 28. Preoccupation with Shimbu and Kembu Group weakened the battle against Yamashita's Shobu Group in the mountains off Lingayen Gulf. Innis Swift's three divisions of I Corps had been drained by the operations in Manila and he was left with just one division until late February when Krueger gave him three more. To the aid of I Corps came nearly 60,000 Filipino guerrillas including the Hukbalahaps, the military arm of the communist partisans. Many were decorated in the northern Luzon campaign before they assumed positions of power in the postwar years. The Americans and Filipinos labored mightily into the mountains toward Yamashita's redoubt at Baguio where the defenders cleverly conducted a passive battle of attrition that, along with disease and exhaustion, slowed the Allied advance. By the time Baguio fell on April 27, 1945, Yamashita had escaped with over half of his army to Bambang.

The Americans also engaged the Japanese in the vast southern Philippines with its hundreds of islands. MacArthur deemed this campaign necessary to support an Australian seizure of Borneo from which to attack shipping in the Dutch East Indies and to rescue victims of enemy aggression. It was a thankless task involving over 50 landing operations that lasted until the end of the war. The only reason MacArthur escaped censure for the slowness of this effort was that the central Pacific campaign and events in Europe obscured the southern Philippines theater. Eighth Army replaced Sixth Army, which departed to train for the invasion of Japan. MacArthur sent units to clear out forces on Palawan, Zamboanga City, Negros, Bohol, Panay, Mindanao, and Cebu, and they engaged in 14 major and 24 minor landings. About 100,000 badly equipped defenders caused trouble, mostly on Mindanao around Davao City. On the other islands, pockets of Japanese hid until U.S. and Filipino guerrillas rooted them out. On Mindanao, the Americans took Davao City in early May 1945; but the Imperial Army held the eastern part of the island until Tokyo surrendered in September. At the end of the campaign in the southern islands, 18,000 Japanese lay dead while 22,000 were starved into submission. Americans saved many European prisoners, found the bodies of thousands of others, and even rescued Imperial soldiers and citizens from the vengeful Filipinos.

By the war's end, about 50,000 Japanese troops were still on Luzon tying down Sixth Army, including Yamashita, who held out in the rain-soaked Sierra Madres until capitulating with 50,500 men on August 15. Over 400,000 Japanese died, yet 115,000 troops remained at large on Luzon and in the southern Philippines. The last soldier of World War II gave up in March 1974, ordered to do so by a commander dead for thirty years. Yamashita had so effectively resisted and even humiliated MacArthur that the latter had him executed after the war. For his part, MacArthur took criticism for the high number of casualties incurred by his troops in the Philippines. The theater witnessed 10,380 deaths, 36,550 wounded, and over 93,400 noncombat casualties in U.S. Sixth and Eighth Armies. The latter figure ranked the Philippines campaign second only to the Africa-Middle East theater in the number of hospitalized inpatients. The Americans had indisputable control of the Philippines, but the archipelago had become a true killing field.

By 1945, the two Axis powers teetered like boxers on their last legs. Both Japan and Germany had tried surprise attacks on their enemies, and both desperate attempts to save themselves had failed. Japan risked all in a complicated naval attack around the Philippines but met superior firepower and lost its navy as a result. Tokyo faced a tornado of American offensives—on Pacific islands, at sea, and by bombers in the skies overhead. In Germany, Hitler frantically glanced two ways from Berlin. Anglo-American forces drove from the west, and the Russians barreled onward from the east. The Allies had liberated vast areas of Axis-occupied territory, although some fell under the yoke of the Soviet Union. The next year promised freedom for even more people under the Axis thumb and perhaps for ordinary Germans and Japanese as well.

CHAPTER 24

Fall of the Third Reich

My mother referred so frequently to the "darkest time humanity has ever known."...Mom had called it right. Not merely dark. Black.

SCOTT TUROW
Ordinary Heroes

BERLIN

Three deaths in April 1945 signaled the war's end might be near. Two dictators died as losers. Partisans shot Benito Mussolini and hung him from a meat hook in a gas station, and two days later, Adolf Hitler shot himself in his bunker and his minions burned his remains. They actually had outlasted one of their nemeses by a few weeks, for Franklin Roosevelt passed away on April 12. Fascist Italy had long ceased to exist when Il Duce perished and the thousand-year Third Reich was nearly extinguished when the Fuhrer took his life. As allies mourned FDR, however, the Americans and their Allies were primed to end the most destructive war in history if only they could get to Berlin and Tokyo.

The showplace of Nazism, Berlin was the target of the Allied drive across Europe. Designated at Yalta for Soviet occupation, the city would be nonetheless garrisoned by Britain, America, and France as well. Winston Churchill had second thoughts about leaving Berlin to the Russians, but the speed and strength of the Red Army, combined with SHAEF commander Dwight Eisenhower's worry about casualties, left the Yalta decision intact. Control of Berlin (and Germany) emerged as a sticking point in postwar diplomacy; but in April 1945, the Allies united against the capital. Hitler had transferred his headquarters to the Reich Chancellery in Berlin at the beginning of the year and then moved into an underground bunker as bombing grew intense. When the armies of Generals Zhukov and Konev halted within striking distance in March, he demanded that his broken Third Panzer and Ninth Armies of Army Group Vistula hold the line to the last man and bullet. Surrounding the capital were four concentric circles of defensive lines. The outermost was 20 miles from the city center, then one was half that distance, and another followed the suburban railway perimeter. The closest, named Zitadelle, encircled the government seat and the Fuhrer bunker.

Josef Stalin gave Marshal Georgi Zhukov the honors of entering Berlin along the lower Oder River backed by Konev on his left and Rokossovsky to the right. These three army groups numbered 2.5 million troops, 6,250 armored vehicles, 41,600 guns and mortars, and 7,500 airplanes. Seizing the city with ease was not a given; the Soviets had never captured an urban area the size of Berlin. Its underground structures also offered good defensive points, so Zhukov prepared cautiously. By the time he opened the last offensive on April 16, the Russians had guarded their flanks by taking Vienna and blocking Guderian from the Baltic coast. Now they readied to capture the heart of the "fascist beast" that had caused them so much suffering. The Germans proved tougher than the Russians expected, however. To be sure, the defenders did little more than delay an inevitable defeat by a few days, but the Allies underestimated their foe. Zhukov unleashed his assault before dawn on the sandy ridge of the 200-feet high Seelow Heights across the Oder. He exploited an innovation by using searchlights to blind and locate the enemy, a novel tactic that drew praise for permitting an attack before daybreak, but that wreaked havoc on the soldiers themselves. Waves of troops advanced under an ear-splitting barrage from 1,236,000 rounds of ammunition and 6,550 air sorties only to be halted by the Germans, smoke of the bombardment, and glare from the searchlights. The next day, six armies, including two tank armies, tried and failed again to move on the Oder River. On day three, the Soviets advanced into the German lines but again could not break through. Losses on the Seelow Heights numbered 30,000 while Germany suffered 12,000 casualties.

Stalin stepped in, challenging his generals to see which one could get to Berlin first. Stalin sent Zhukov's First Belorussian *front* to the north and Konev, whose First Ukrainian army group had crossed the Neisse River on April 16, to the south. The Second Belorussian *front* under Rokossovsky aided Zhukov by branching off to the south. Because Hitler ordered German Ninth Army to stand on the Oder, Konev enjoyed less resistance. His tanks reached the Wehrmacht's largest ammunition depot at Juterborg on April 20 and headed for the communications center of Zossen below Berlin. The next day, Zhukov reached the outer defensive ring of Berlin, which he and Konev overran four days later. Fighting took place in the streets and houses, but Soviet barrages of heavy artillery and hammering from bombers overhead obliterated the German positions.

Consistent with the surrealism of holding birthday festivities in the midst of his teetering rule, Hitler believed that he could save Army Group Vistula that defended Berlin. He had exalted at the death of FDR—an event, in his view, that paralleled the passing of Elizabeth of Russia in 1762 just as Frederick the Great had faced ruin. Although the new president, Harry Truman, lacked experience in foreign affairs, Allied military omnipotence offered no chance of history repeating itself. Hitler permitted his entourage to evacuate from the capital if they so chose, yet he counted on rescue by Twelfth Army under Walther Wenck. This officer oversaw resistance movements in occupied Germany by the Werewolves, a guerrilla organization tapped to defend the shadowy National Redoubt. The Werewolves never amounted to more than a bunch of Nazi fanatics, and Twelfth Army's capabilities existed only in Hitler's imagination. Wenck's force could not break through the Soviet front to Berlin especially because a substantial number of troops were green Hitler Youth teenagers. On the Fuhrer's birthday, women in Berlin lined up for food. Hearing Soviet artillery in the distance and having experienced another huge Anglo-American bombing raid—also in celebration of Hitler's birthday—they knew the end was near.

Old men and boys were all that remained of the capital's defensive manpower. On April 30 outside of the Berlin pocket, High Command chief Wilhelm Keitel reported that no relief was coming. By that time, the defenders had exhausted their ammunition and civilians were in pure survival mode. Soldiers fled while others quickly changed into civilian clothes and melted into the population. In an urban area comprised mostly of women, the Red Army perpetrated a miasma of rape and killing. The Soviets took whatever loot they could find in an uncontrollable orgy of revenge and annihilation. In the afternoon, they overran the Reichstag building a quarter mile from Hitler's bunker.

The Fuhrer killed himself at this point. Before dying he designated Karl Donitz, the master of submarine warfare, as his successor and chief of the armed forces. On May 1, 1945, the day after Hitler and his new wife Eva Braun committed suicide, Hans Krebs, chief of the General Staff, left the bunker to ask the Soviets for a conditional surrender. Vasily Chuikov rejected the plea. Krebs returned to the bunker to take his own life, and Goebbels and his wife administered poison pills to their six children before committing suicide. The corpses of brown-shirted Nazi Party stalwarts lay in the streets, crushed under tanks around the Reichschancellery, while Soviet soldiers built huge bonfires in the Reichstag. A wall of tree trunks and sandbags stood before the Brandenburg Gate; perched on it, observers witnessed the burning of Berlin. A bungled Soviet investigation into Hitler's whereabouts provoked an enduring postwar myth that the Fuhrer had escaped abroad. In reality, his body was burnt beyond recognition.

On May 2, Berlin's commandant, Karl Weidling, surrendered. The toll in the battle for the city had been 361,367 Red Army and Polish (many of the Poles were virtual conscripts into the Red Army) casualties. The Germans had almost as many, and civilian casualties of rape and plunder exceeded even Soviet standards. The USSR mourned its sacrifice but as its flag flew over the Riechstag, Moscow took grim satisfaction in the destruction of Berlin as partial justice for the savagery of Nazism over the past four years. In his May Day speech just a day before the city's surrender, Stalin exalted the downfall of the Third Reich. In a rare admission of weakness, his historians acknowledged the massive casualties suffered by the First and Second Belorussian and First Ukrainian army groups.

The European theater shut down. In Italy, Harold Alexander destroyed the army group commanded by Heinrich von Vietinghoff. After British Eighth Army captured Argenta, it joined with U.S. Fifth Army at Finale nell'Emilia to effect the finale in the Italian theater. The Allies cut off escape hatches behind the Alps and a cease-fire in Italy occurred the day that Berlin surrendered. The Wehrmacht's attrition warfare and shaky Anglo-American command had drawn out the Italian campaign to the end of the war, and the twenty German divisions that were tied down were ultimately not critical to Hitler. After all, he had shifted 26 divisions from Italy to the Ardennes. The Allied liberation, however, came at a steep price of 188,746 U.S. casualties and 123,254

British losses. The Germans suffered 434,646 casualties, over half of these missing and presumed dead. Thus, unlike the Western and Eastern fronts, the Italian operation was not a resounding defeat for the Third Reich.

GENOCIDE

Italy also did not expose the full terror of the Nazi regime. That was left to the Soviets and the Western Allies who discovered the death camps as they moved into Germany. They had long known about the Holocaust but had yet to directly observe its horrors. The vast system of prison, labor, and extermination camps revealed the murderous ways of the Third Reich. The Soviets had their gulags—dehumanizing camps in which hundreds of thousands of political criminals were tortured and executed—but the Nazi version was based on a racial ideology that left little chance for survival. Hitler initially built concentration camps to detain rivals and such "undesirables" as socialists, gypsies, criminals, and homosexuals. He then expanded them to house slave labor for danger-ous and debilitating work, even including the underground assembly of jet fighters in the Gusen camp network. On invading Poland and the USSR, they became instru-mental to his Final Solution: the systematic annihilation of European Jewry. The Nazis perfected their death machine by using exhaust fumes in closed trucks to kill their victims and then built special gas chambers where masses of prisoners could be effi-ciently murdered.

The news about this process first was carried by a Polish courier named Jan Kozielewski to Western leaders (including FDR) as far back as November 1942. Yet hor-ror on a huge scale was hard to comprehend, and the Nazis used such euphemisms as "resettlement" to disguise their intentions. Notice of the insidious activity at Auschwitz II (Birkenau), for example, did not reach the West until the summer of 1944. This was two years after it had begun killing 6,000 people a day and had exterminated 250,000 Hungarian Jews in just six weeks. The Final Solution could not be ignored. Western Europeans protested, Italy and Hungary resisted deportations, and uprisings arose against the tyranny. When Anglo-American forces established air superiority over Germany, military officials talked of bombing the death camps. Controversy contin-ues as to why the easily located Auschwitz was not destroyed from the air. Roosevelt's wish to hasten the war's end by focusing only on military targets, anti-Semitism, igno-rance of the scope of killing at the camps, and simple infeasibility are given as reasons. Another answer is that few knew about the camps or if they did, what was happen-ing behind the fences. However fragmentary the evidence, it is certain that neighbors knew about the facilities and what was going on. Residents of Lublin, for instance, shut their windows when the winds blew from the Majdanek camp to keep out the smell of human bodies.

The Holocaust was a moral blot on humanity. A total of 6.2 million Jews perished, or one-third of the world's Jewish population, along with an equal number of other undesirables. Suffice it to say that the human carnage and the guilt of those who stood by epitomized a war of annihilation even before the general strategy of mass killing was adopted by the Allies. One scholar has concluded that the "Holocaust is a singular crime, unparalleled in its combination of malice, industrial efficiency, and sheer scale of consistent ruthlessness; but it also holds up a mirror to all humans" to ask themselves if such an apocalypse could happen again. That remains to be seen, but at least for the survivors, there was hope. At least the roughly 300,000 survivors found new homes abroad; most who lived left Europe.

The Final Solution awakened soldiers to the sheer monstrosity of the Nazi regime. As the Soviets advanced westward in September 1944, the Germans evacuated Jewish slave laborers from Auschwitz-Birkenau by rail or on foot. Because little food or shelter was supplied, about 100,000 died. Other forced marches killed many more. When Soviet troops reached Majdanek in July 1944 and liberated Auschwitz-Birkenau the following January, they found few living souls. In a perverse twist, survivors were oftentimes shipped eastward to Siberian gulags thanks to Stalin's paranoid belief that they might be fascist sympathizers. In April 1945, U.S. and British forces opened the camps of Bergen-Belsen, Dachau, Buchenwald, and Mauthausen in Germany and Austria. They found the barely living in a pitiful state and photographs provided the world for the first time with graphic images of the slaughter. Piles of shoes, gold fillings, and hair tormented the liberators who also toured the gas chambers and laboratories of medical experimenters. The dead were so plentiful that they rested either in mass graves or in piles. The military rushed in supplies and doctors to treat the survivors, but instances of hate still surfaced. Patton stood out for his anti-Semitic notions; he permitted German civilians more attention than their Jewish victims. In any event, neither military nor government leaders were prepared to deal with such evil on this scale. For many in the armed forces, however, their disgust intensified the goal of erasing Nazism from the planet. Perhaps the strategy of annihilation over Hamburg and Dresden could be rationalized after all.

SURRENDER AND PEACE

As the gruesome evidence of the Holocaust circulated among the invaders, the Western Allies awaited the Red Army's conquest of Berlin and its subsequent move to the Elbe River. They were certain to claim their zones of influence in Germany, however. This was especially so for Churchill, who had been thwarted by the Yalta agreement and military circumstances. Amidst the Soviet-American toasts, backslapping, and dancing when West met East at Torgau on April 24, the sober British made shrewd judgments regarding territory. They claimed northern Germany and Denmark not only to obtain a role at the postwar occupation table but to prevent the USSR from taking everything. With the support of the U.S. XVIII Corps, Montgomery crossed the Elbe on April 29 and directed Second Army into Lubeck when Berlin capitulated on May 2. The next day, the Americans occupied Wismer on the Baltic and linked with Soviet forces. Admiral Donitz ordered U-boat chief Hans von Friedeburg to surrender the Netherlands, Denmark, and northwestern Germany to the British as part of a plan to ease Germany into the more humane hands of the Western Allies. Donitz tried to buy time by allowing troops to escape westward from the Red Army but the U.S. armies ceased fighting on May 6 after meeting the Soviets at the Elbe and Mulda Rivers. Patton's Third Army made contact with the Soviets in Linz, took Pilsen, and readied for a run to Prague. Patton had taken his forces across seven major rivers to descend on Hitler's hometown of Linz on May 5. At the Brenner Pass on the Austrian border, Seventh and Fifth Armies joined up. Patch's Seventh Army had found nothing more than scattered resistance (and Göring's private cellar of fine liquor at Berchtesgaden) in the alpine National Redoubt where the Nazis were supposedly going to make their last stand. French First Army grew so powerful that it provided the extra muscle of seven divisions to the Allied charge across Europe. De Gaulle thus justified a French hand in the occupation of postwar Germany.

Donitz now had his opportunity to surrender. On May 5, his emissaries arrived at Ike's headquarters in Reims to seek a phased capitulation. Eisenhower flatly refused. He threatened to close the German border when General Alfred Jodl, who was never enamored with Hitler, asked again the next day. SHAEF demanded an unconditional surrender, and the Germans finally obliged at 2:41 a.m. on May 7. Military operations by the Third Reich ceased by 11:01 p.m. on May 8, known afterward as Victory in Europe (V-E) Day. For two parties, this was no day of triumph, however. One was the Germans. Friedeburg signed the surrender papers with the USSR at Karlhorst and at Reims with the Western powers, and committed suicide two weeks later. The other unhappy observer was Stalin, who suspected the West of promising moderate treatment of Germany at the expense of the great Soviet triumph. While Churchill and Truman pronounced V-E Day on May 8, the USSR signed surrender documents on May 9 in a separate ceremony in Berlin. Joy erupted in Moscow. Drunken revelers celebrated by not pondering their immense sacrifices or the future but simply because of elation that the war was over. Irritation over the Third Reich's surrender, combined with arguments over territorial claims, indicated a nascent conflict with Stalin's former allies.

Combat did not end entirely. Konev liberated Czechoslovakia in a drive on Prague in the last large-scale fighting in Europe. Redeployment of his tanks took until May 6. The next day, the First, Second, and Fourth Ukrainian *fronts* marched 1.7 million troops on Army Group Center. Patton approached from the west until stopped by Eisenhower who let the Soviets enter Prague despite pleas of the Czech exile government in London. In Bohemia and Moravia, strikes erupted; and on May 5, the city rose up against Nazism. Donitz added two divisions to the garrison, which lacked tanks and artillery, but Lieutenant-General Andrei Vlasov, a prisoner of the Germans since 1942, blocked the Wehrmacht. Vlasov helped free Prague and then gave way to Konev who treated him as an enemy of the state. Konev did quick work. After being pushed into a pocket just east of Prague, the Germans surrendered on May 11. World War II in Europe was over.

Germany's defense in the West and East had been tenaciously driven by the ideals of Nazism and the inspiration of Adolf Hitler. In the end, the Third Reich collapsed under the overbearing weight of Allied resources, superior enemy command and skills, the sacrifice of its foes, and German hubris. Monty lived in the past of set-piece warfare, but U.S. commanders earned the biggest victory by encircling the Ruhr through maneuver. On the Eastern front, however, the Soviets stood above their allies at the operational level. Their assault on Germany was mercilessly masterful in its plans, organization, and sheer brutal execution. The USSR reversed the near defeat of Barbarossa and registered monumental victories of its own. Its strategy of annihilation caused such losses for itself, as well as Germany, that the Soviets never truly recovered from the nightmare of World War II.

The USSR could shape, if not dictate, the postwar peace because of the Red Army's occupation of most of eastern and central Europe. Because the Americans began to send troops home or redeploy them to the Pacific where the war was expected to persist into 1947, the power vacuum gave Stalin an enormous advantage at the diplomatic table. Germany, Austria, and Berlin were divided into four occupation zones under U.S., France, Britain, and the Soviet administration; but the former Nazi capital was also located deep with the Russian sector. The Western Allies hoped to reunify these countries and they also sought democratic elections in liberated central and eastern European nations. Yet military strength translated into political power. The Soviets aimed to close off their zones of occupation to the capitalist nations and create a buffer of friendly states between them and the West. Within four years, eastern Germany, Poland, Czechoslovakia, Hungary, Rumania, Bulgaria, and the three Baltic states were absorbed into the USSR as communist-bloc satellites. Moscow also exacted revenge on Germany in the form of enormous reparations. Millions of Soviet deaths were not in vain; Stalin derived political benefits from them after the war.

In the summer of 1945, the European continent entered a period of convalescence and flux. The war had forcibly removed tens of millions of people from their homelands, and sixteen million of these were classified as "displaced persons" or refugees from Nazi camps. In a deal with Moscow, the Americans and British sent over two million Soviet personnel who had served the Wehrmacht back home to their likely death or certain incarceration in the gulags. Six million Russians were eventually repatriated. Moscow freed an estimated 20% of them and executed or imprisoned the rest. The USSR's tightening grip in Eastern Europe caused tens of thousands of people to flee westward and create more displaced persons. This refugee stream exacerbated Germany's problems. The war had destroyed roughly half of the country's houses and factories, ruined its transportation system, and undercut food output to the extent that starvation was a major concern. With millions dead and unburied on the battlefields, workers were scarce. The Allies also faced a dilemma. They wanted to revive the German economy but prevent the country from becoming too strong to threaten the peace once again. The USSR fixated on this possibility. By taking reparations in the form of factories, raw materials, and land, Stalin determined to gut Germany's military-industrial capacity and render the former enemy barely self-sufficient. Anglo-American leaders favored this course, at least at first. They pursued de-Nazification and deindustrialization under the Morgenthau Plan, named for the U.S. treasury secretary who sought to pastoralize Germany. But as food became more scarce and women bartered their bodies for something to eat (and conditions in France, Holland, and other western European nations similarly deteriorated) the democracies began to chafe at such a harsh approach.

The sudden end of the American Lend-Lease program in May 1945 complicated the relief and refugee effort. The cutoff of supplies hurt Britain and the USSR in particular, but it also undermined recovery in Europe as a whole. The new United Nations Relief and Rehabilitation Administration stepped in to fill the gap. Even before the war ended, however, the U.S. military began relief work in liberated countries, and then provided medicine and food to Germany once the shooting stopped. At first bent on punishment, the West turned to compensating victims with the vast amount of private property that the Nazis had seized during the war. And as the contours of the Cold War inexorably emerged, the capitalist nations worked toward the rehabilitation of Germany to help in European recovery and offset Russian power. The Western Allies created the Federal Republic of Germany out of their three zones in 1949, and the Soviets confirmed the permanent division between the World War II allies when they went their separate way and established the German Democratic Republic in their eastern zone a few months later. All four (former) allies, however, achieved the mission of preventing a resurgence of German militarism.

There is an irony, though, to the defeat of Nazism. The fatalistic Hitler defeated his own efforts to extend the war by bad decisions and, ultimately, on a focus on wiping out the Jews in the Holocaust, slavs, and other people rather than on military campaigns. He thus spared the German people a terrible fate, for the Third Reich might have been the first recipient of the atomic bomb if he had not undermined German military power and the war had continued longer. There is a further irony, however. Because Nazi racism forced the cream of European scientists and mathematicians to flee the continent, the United States benefited by ushering in the nuclear age. In the end, Hitler did Germany a favor. He also doomed the sole remaining Axis power, Japan, to a terrifying end as a witness to the power of atomic weaponry.

CHAPTER 25

The Inner Ring

Everything was new and apocalyptic. Why was the sky red?
How could it be snowing? And why did the snowflakes burn
her arms?

MARKUS ZUSAK
The Book Thief

THE INNER DEFENSE LINE

In Asia, the war was deteriorating into a senseless and brutal killing time, but it still had a ways to run before people there, as in Europe, could find relief. Simultaneous to the assault on Manila in the Philippines, Chester Nimitz launched the invasion of Iwo Jima to prosecute the central Pacific assault on the Japanese home islands. He sent in a classic amphibious landing. With Tarawa and Saipan in mind, it was preceded by 72 days of air strikes and three days of awesome naval bombardment. Waiting on the pear-shaped, 4-by-2-mile island in the Volcano chain, Tadamichi Kuribayashi mimicked the defense of Peleliu and Luzon by not contesting the Americans as they landed. He would fight instead from networks of cave fortifications. The result was a 36-day American siege, three weeks longer than expected. The bloodiest engagement in the U.S. Marines' 169-year history, the battle for Iwo Jima was the only one in the war in which U.S. casualties surpassed Japan's.

Nimitz deemed the island's capture necessary because of its proximity to the home islands. Just 650 miles from Tokyo and 625 miles from the Marianas, Iwo Jima possessed three airstrips (one under construction) to base escort fighters and land crippled B-29s. The defenders had erected a radar station to warn Tokyo of impending air raids, and this frustrated LeMay's plans for surprising his urban victims. Japanese medium bombers also used Iwo Jima to destroy planes on Saipan and Tinian. In response, U.S. Twentieth Air Force flew a dogleg around the island but this longer route used more fuel and therefore lessened bomb payloads. The smelly "Sulphur Island" had to be captured. It could be, predicted the USAAF's Hap Arnold, but with 10,000 casualties.

The V Amphibious Corps—the largest force ever of U.S. Marines in a single battle—went ashore on February 19, 1945. This was the battle-tested 4th Marine

Division's fourth landing in thirteen months. Joining the assault was the new but well-trained 5th Marine Division that included Raiders and paratroopers from the Solomons campaign, while the 3rd Marine Division from Bougainville and Guam floated off-shore in reserve. Commanders took seriously this invasion into the "inner ring" of Japan's national defense, although circumstances compelled them to rush the schedule. MacArthur's delayed capture of Luzon held up the transfer of naval support and land-ing craft to the central Pacific campaign. Nimitz wanted forces ready for the invasion of Okinawa by April 1 before the monsoon season but the Iwo Jima operation got stuck between those in the Philippines and the larger one on Okinawa. Eventually, 110,000 U.S. Marines under Harry Schmidt landed on Iwo Jima after intensive and continuous bombing shook the awaiting Japanese from mid-January 1945 onward.

Terrain of rocky ridges, caves, and ravines, overseen by 556-foot high Mount Suribachi, provided an ideal holdout for the Japanese defenders. The preliminary bombardment convinced Kuribayashi, who had spent time in North America before service in Manchuria, to construct bunkers within Suribachi and in connected caves, covered by interlocking fire that would force the enemy into close combat. Some 23,000 Imperial Army troops fought from nearly impregnable barricades of 1,500 pillboxes, blockhouses, and miles of trenches and tunnels with 361 artillery pieces, 65 mortars, 33 large naval guns, and almost 100 large-caliber antiaircraft guns. Kurabayashi knew no rescue from Japan was coming because the Imperial Navy had no means to save him. This is why he configured his defenses for the most punishing and drawn-out battle possible; acknowledging that his garrison would never survive, Kurabayashi planned a suicidal defensive mission over an eight-month period. He was clever. He hid his heavy guns and put the biggest minefields of the war at the beach exits. Kurabayashi also con-centrated his forces in the central flatlands around the airfield and the northern ridges and caves. Marksman could pick off the enemy while troops infiltrated the invaders at night. The Japanese leader also stirred up the determined will of his troops to honor the Emperor and avenge the American strategic bombing attacks on the homeland.

Under observation from Mount Suribachi, the 8,000 U.S. Marines in the first land-ings crept up the black beaches of Iwo Jima behind a barrage of naval and air bom-bardment from Task Force 54. This was still not enough, for many targets remained intact. From the vantage of Suribachi, the Americans were "as vulnerable as sitting ducks in a shooting gallery" remembered a 3rd Marine. The Japanese quickly pinned the Marine Corps with machine-gun and artillery fire as they sunk in the deep sand and then tried to move inland across the sandy terraces behind the steep beaches with their heavy packs. Sharpshooters reveled in the killing. Kinryu Sugihara wrote that the enemy were "easy pickings anyway. Come one, come all." Gunners lobbed 700-pound shells and lighter mortars on the hapless U.S. Marines and raked them with dismembering explosive shells from antiaircraft weapons. Still, the 5th Marine Division crossed the narrow southeastern neck of Iwo after landing unscathed and the 4th Marine Division on its right advanced to the southernmost airfield. In just ninety minutes of the first day, Schmidt beached 30,000 men and tanks and artillery. He had his lodgment by nightfall at the cost of 501 dead among a staggering casualty list of 2,420 U.S. Marines.

Turning on Mount Suribachi, the Americans inched upward armed with grenades, large satchel charges, and flamethrowers. The 2,000 defenders counterattacked from subterranean installations, one of which was seven stories deep, as well as from 70 camouflaged blockhouses that only tanks could knock out. On the fifth day (February 23), the U.S. Marines reached the summit with a small U.S. flag on a 20-foot piece of pipe that was later replaced by a larger one so all could see the capture of Mount Suribachi. Joe Rosenthal's photo of the second flag being planted became the most famous image of the Pacific conflict—if not American history.

The battle was far from over. The Marine Corps encountered the defensive strongholds in the central and northern parts of the island. On Day 9, they found out that Kurabayashi possessed eight infantry battalions, five artillery battalions, and 5,000 naval infantry in caves, one of which had an 800-foot long tunnel with 14 exits. He picked his battles by calmly instructing troops when to fire and when to move underground. The Japanese also improvised with the weapons they had. For instance, they concocted a missile that looked like a bucket with pipes and fins attached that exploded and sprayed metal fragments when it hit the ground. For their part, the U.S. Marines welcomed support from medical teams, Native American code talkers who confused enemy code breakers, and air strikes. After two weeks, Kurabayashi withdrew to the north on the same day that the central airstrip rescued the damaged B-29 *Dinah Might* returning from a bombing raid over Honshu. Iwo Jima seemed to have proved its worth, yet ensuing fights in the ravines, gorges, and caves turned merciless. Imperial troops held fast, honored with gifts of cigarettes and candy from the Emperor to whom they pledged their lives. On Hill 382, there were so many casualties that the Marine Corps called it the "Meat Grinder." In a single day, they earned five Medals of Honor, which was the nation's highest award for bravery and sacrifice.

Battle accounts revealed Iwo Jima to be a terrifying field of annihilation and mass destruction of human life. One U.S. Marine with a piece of shrapnel lodged in his back kept running ahead until a blast cuffed his head. Reaching up, he "realized it was Joe Haas's brains that had hit my helmet." Twenty-year old Richard Overton, a U.S. Navy hospital corpsman, also recounted the horrors. Sheltered in a crater as shells screamed overhead—his mouth, eyes, and ears full of sand—he crawled to a neighboring hole where he had run across two young U.S. Marines. They were quiet because the last shell had landed between them. Fragments perforated the chest, stomach, arms, and legs of one, Peter, who was placed on a litter. Noticing his leg hung limply, Overton cut through the trousers and muscle and the leg slid back into the hole and on to the lap of the other U.S. Marine. Overton noted that this American was propped up against the crater's side, dead with the leg still resting in his lap. After covering the corpse with a poncho he met a distraught fellow marine back in his foxhole. "Oh, how can God let this all happen?" sobbed the soldier. "God isn't here!" replied Overton.

The Japanese defenders survived on sheer willpower, hubris, and innovation as many lived under the illusion that the battle was going well. The Americans came across enemy dressed in U.S. Marine clothing or frequently heard cries in perfect English for medical assistance from supposedly hurt comrades. Trickery was a survival skill. As naval bombardment lessened as the battle went on, the Japanese took heart. Wrote an antitank officer, "[b]e persistent! Hold out! Whip the enemy till their blood runs. We must definitely build the foundation of victory for this Greater East Asia War." As U.S. tanks appeared in greater numbers to compel the defenders to repair their cave fortifications, Kurabayashi's men maintained their resolve. "We will resist to the end," wrote one. "In the path of righteousness a gleam of victory can be perceived. We must but fight till victory is in our hands." Nearly his entire antitank battalion was soon wiped out.

The grisly battle finally came to a merciful end. As General Schmidt declared victory on March 16, Kurabayashi prepared for the final fight deep within a gorge appropriately named Death Valley. It took nine days of combat and thousands of tons of explosives to destroy his holdout. Kurabayashi refused to surrender, sending his last message to Tokyo after being promoted to full general and then committing suicide on the night of March 25–26. The remaining handful of troops gathered for one last assault, and then infiltrated U.S. lines and killed 100 sleeping pilots, Seabees, and U.S. Marines. Only a few hundred wounded Japanese survived on Iwo Jima; about 22,000 perished along with 6,821 U.S. Marines (one-third of all Marine Corps deaths in World War II) who were among the more than 26,000 casualties. The Americans began the battle with 24 infantry battalion commanders. Seventeen died or were injured at the hands of Kurabayashi's vicious defense.

Iwo Jima's reputation as a living hell more than made up for its military significance. About 2,400 B-29s with 25,000 crewmen used the island as an emergency base and P-51 Mustangs landed there to provide fighter escort over targets and conducted raids of their own. But the island never became a forward base for the Superfortresses, which turned to night raids launched from the Marianas. Japanese raids from the Marianas ceased although the Imperial Navy relied more on suicide planes. For instance, they sank the escort carrier *Bismarck Sea* and 350 of its crew. In addition, *Saratoga* was put out of action until May 1945 by six bomb hits (though by conventional attack rather than kamikazes). On land, the cost of 700 U.S. Marine deaths for every square mile taken was prohibitive. Five times as many U.S. troops died on Iwo Jima than on Guadalcanal or Tarawa. Entire companies ceased to function, and one left the island with just nine survivors.

While 27 Medals of Honor were bestowed on U.S. Marines and Navy medical corpsman—13 posthumously—the outcry at home was considerable. Why was there not more bombardment? How could such sacrifices be justified for such a small island? One interpretation holds that the effort did not really pay off in terms of saved B-29s. The best that can be said is that many pilots of disabled bombers were thankful for Iwo Jima's emergency airstrips, but in the end, the Marine Corps brass exaggerated its importance as a rationale for the losses. So unproductive was the operation—and so threatening to the very existence of the Marine Corps in its interservice rivalries with the U.S. Army and the Navy over resources in the Pacific—that military leaders quickly covered up the carnage by portraying the battle with a reverence that ensured its institutional survival. It is easy to be cynical about the battle for Iwo Jima but it did impress upon all observers that the war would remain vicious and especially as the Americans zeroed in on Japan. Perhaps the Japanese got a clearer understanding that their enemy would not give up, yet the Americans also realized that the fighting would only get tougher the closer they drew to Tokyo. Nobody in the world needed a reminder of the terrible toll of war, but the death rate on Iwo Jima could not help but stress the sacrifice of thousands of young men who fought a war of annihilation to its ruinous end.

JAPAN'S DOORSTEP

Nothing matched the carnage per square mile of Iwo Jima, but the invasion of Okinawa promised similar bloodshed. Okinawa was the last stop before the home islands and an integral part of Japan itself as a distant prefecture since 1879. There was now a big garrison to guard the nearly half million civilians on the narrow 60-mile long island. Okinawa was pivotal for the Americans. Located 340 miles from the mainland halfway between Tokyo and Manila, this main island in the Ryukyu chain would serve as a staging area for the invasion of Kyushu and Honshu. Its capture would block sea lanes and isolate Formosa, airfields would bring Japan within reach of medium bombers, and ships would enjoy good anchorages. Washington elevated Okinawa to the level of the Normandy invasion, which it equaled in size. A fleet of 1,213 warships included 25 vessels of Task Force 57, the most powerful British naval group of the entire war. Some 190,000 personnel in a Joint Expeditionary Force served in the campaign. The Marine Corps deployed 116,000 men in three divisions of Roy Geiger's III Amphibious Corps, part of a field army of 183,000 assault troops under Aleutians theater veteran Simon Bolivar Buckner, Jr. He led XXIV Army Corps, which included four infantry divisions. Operations on Saipan and Iwo Jima took three divisions each, but Okinawa required eight. Offshore waited reserves as well in a huge logistical train that included, for instance, 7 billion units of penicillin. This testified to the sheer imbalance in forces by this time. Nimitz could afford to leave large numbers of troops in the Philippines but strength in numbers also indicated a sober assessment that Okinawa would be contested every step of the way.

Thirty-Second Imperial Army commanded by General Mitsuru Ushijima waited for the Americans on well-fortified Okinawa. After reinforcements arrived, he had about 110,000 troops, including 20,000 from the Okinawan militia. This former head of the national military academy had seen his best troops transferred to Formosa in November 1944, so he had to compensate with a good defensive plan. Ushijima counted on a large number of field artillery and heavy mortars, and also built a ring of fortifications around a command center located in the thick-walled Shuri Castle to guard airfields and anchorages in the island's southern area. This key defense line ran from Naha up to the Castle and then to Yonaburu on the east coast. Two other lines extended along the bottom of the island. Ushijima planned to fight for the port of Naha from Shuri and defend the northern Motobu peninsula, yet he would give away the airfields on the East China Sea coast. In fact, he planned not to contest the landings but leave kamikazes to drive off the amphibious forces and then hoped that a counterattack would chase the invaders back into the sea. Thirty-Second Army used hand tools to construct a network of tunnels, caves, and fortified positions that capitalized on the ridges and caves in the south. These latter housed hospitals, supply rooms, barracks, and depots for heavy

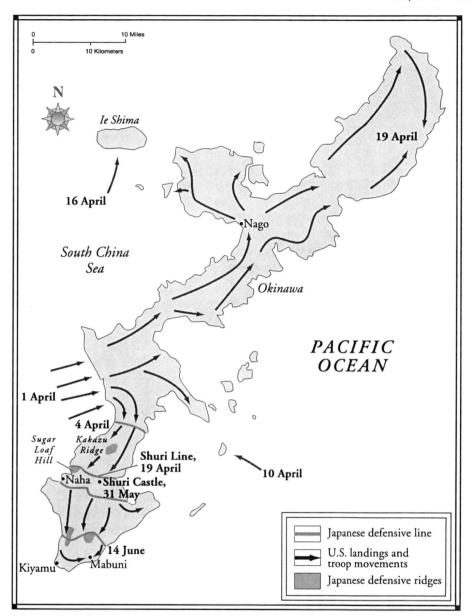

Map 25.1 Okinawa. Credit: Ronald Story, *Concise Historical Atlas of World War II: The Geography of Conflict*, Map 45, p. 95.

weapons. Ushijima dared the Americans to attack at Naha. If they did, the battle would devolve into one of unremitting attrition.

On Easter Sunday, April 1, 1945, U.S. amphibious troops went ashore after a week-long bombardment that was more comforting than effective, yet by the end of the day, 50,000 men rested on the undefended beaches far north of the Shuri Castle complex.

As the armada of ships deposited them on the beaches, they stumbled on a fleet of 300 suicide boats on the outlying island of Kerama Retto and destroyed them. Thanks to a feint by the 2nd Marine Division, Ushijima diverted a group of kamikazes away from the two main landing forces. The suicide missions caused over 100 casualties, but the landings succeeded. The Americans expanded their foothold with just 28 killed and 131 wounded or missing. Geiger's other two Marine Corps divisions landed alongside two Army divisions below the island's midpoint. The U.S. Marines attacked to the north and the U.S. Army headed south. Within a week, the U.S. Marines reached Nago, the largest town in northern Okinawa situated at the base of the Motobu peninsula. Fifty-five miles farther north, the invaders reached the opposite end of the island on April 13. Optimism spread.

But Ushijima showed his true colors. Positioned in caves around Mount Yae above Nago and armed with artillery, 2,000 Imperial troops held off the invaders for five days. Three U.S. commanders were among the casualties. It took bombardment from the battleship *Tennessee* and support from U.S. Marine aviators to secure the Motobu peninsula by April 20 but not until the Americans suffered nearly 1,000 casualties, including 207 killed. Off the western coast, the 77th U.S. Infantry Division took Ie Island after six days and 1,100 casualties, among them popular war correspondent Ernie Pyle, a loss that stunned a nation already reeling from FDR's death a few days before. Troops moved off Ie to help XXIV Corps clear the southern part of Okinawa. The north was under control; but in the south, the landing troops encountered the first sustained resistance. At the Machinato Line north of the Shuri Line, they suffered over 1,500 casualties. On Kakazu Ridge, Ushijima held two hills connected by a saddle from which he stalled the infantry and then counterattacked for three days afterward. A pause preceded another attack on April 14 and ten days of vicious fighting in which the Japanese infiltrated enemy lines at night. Superior firepower eventually convinced the defenders to withdraw from the Ridge. Buckner then opened a three-division attack on the prize of Shuri Castle and got help from the largest concentration of artillery in the Pacific war. Ground batteries, ships, and hundreds of aircraft unleashed a "typhoon of steel" to soften the defenders, but Ushijima withdrew to his underground lair in the Castle to await the ground assault.

Ushijima's defense hinged on the destruction of the American fleet glued to the U.S. ground forces on Okinawa. The naval dimension made his operation different than Kurabayashi on Iwo Jima because he designed to buy time for the First Mobile Fleet of Admiral Toyoda to do its work. Anglo-American forces faced attacks by the aircraft and warships of Operation Ten-Go. The Allies set up a screen of radar pickets to warn of kamikazes, but the fleets could not be sealed off. Between April 6 and June 22, kamikazes flew 2,373 one-way missions. Many never made it to their targets but several did. An initial attack sank three destroyers, a landing craft, and two ammunition ships. Toyoda then let loose the kikusui or "floating chrysanthemums"—ten waves of 350 planes supplemented by smaller night raids—that disrupted Raymond Spruance's operations. Pickets took the brunt of the charge, but no class of Allied vessels was spared. By the battle's end, 36 ships of the Fifth Fleet lay on the bottom while 368 others had been damaged, including carriers and battleships. Five carriers were so beaten up that

Spruance withdrew them. He himself lost a flagship and Marc Mitscher had to switch his flag three times in four days in May due to kamikaze attacks. Furthermore, all of the British carriers in Task Force 57 took hits from kamikazes (although all remained in operation). Ten-Go caused almost 10,000 casualties, nearly half of them dead. This was the largest number ever recorded by the U.S. Navy in a single battle. Over 1,500 Imperial pilots sacrificed their lives.

Operation Ten-Go was heart rending. Kamikazes terrified U.S. sailors, but there was a sad story behind each suicide pilot that spoke to the tragedy behind the Imperial strategy of annihilation. After receiving instructions on the most efficient way to crash their planes into desirable targets, pilots wrote their goodbyes to loved ones. Americans believed the enemy to be either drunk, drugged, or crazy, but many Japanese were reluctant flyers who put a brave face on their doomed missions. An ensign wrote to his family of his hope that his "meager effort" would provide him with the "good fortune to have done something that may be praiseworthy." The Emperor had bestowed a great honor on him, so he wanted no tears shed on his behalf. "Though my body departs, I will return home in spirit and remain with you forever." Many others were not so sanguine. College student Hayashi Ichizu vowed not to look back while he plunged into an enemy vessel. He still hoped Japan could overcome its crisis. "I have dreaded death so much. And yet, it is already decided for us." On learning of her kamikaze husband's death, a new bride was comforted by congratulations. It was good for country, she replied before returning home to cry alone. "I let no one see my tears" because people were told not to cry "but to endure."

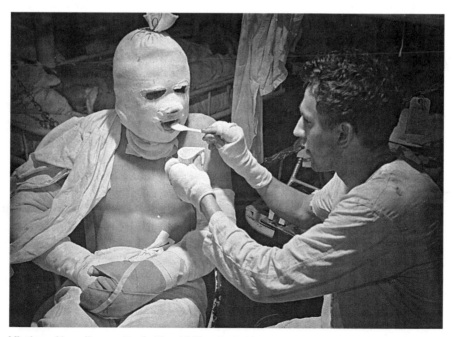

Victim of kamikaze attack, May 1945.   Credit: National Archives.

The last naval battle also occurred as Ten-Go began on April 6. Toyoda dispatched for Okinawa's west coast the biggest battleship in the world, *Yamato*. He provided enough fuel for it to reach the island, beach itself, and bombard the landing force. A cruiser and eight destroyers accompanied the 73,000-ton superbattleship. Subs detected the behemoth exiting the Inland Sea and 300 planes from Task Force 58 attacked 100 miles west of Okinawa. Lacking air cover, most enemy vessels were lost, although *Yamato* required an aerial pounding before sinking. Sailors jumped ship; fatigued, injured, and desolate, many swam in oil-saturated waters after surviving two hours of bombing as well as *Yamato*'s whirlpool suction as the giant went down. Its 3,000 corpses were entombed on the ocean floor. To avoid the same fate, the Mobile Fleet diverted into the East China Sea, and the next morning, Mitscher picked it up and launched 380 aircraft. The battle of the East China Sea destroyed all but four Japanese destroyers. The Imperial Navy had not run out of ships and planes but having lost 3,000 aircraft in the Philippines and another 7,000 by the end of the Okinawa campaign, it had minimal reserves.

The losses and the continued blockade and bombing of the home islands had brought Japan to its knees just as the Allies rolled in Germany in the last half of April 1945. The Empire fought on senselessly, but it was skilled in the field. On Okinawa, Buckner came under pressure to crack the Shuri Line. He logically adopted a World War I-style plan modified by blowtorch and corkscrew tactics to fight from strength, but he also played into the hands of the cool and determined Ushijima, a master of attrition. As American forces got word of the imminent fall of Berlin, Ushijima did make one mistake by changing tactics. Ill advisedly, he decided to heed his impatient chief of staff, Isamu Cho, and counterattack on May 5, yet his attempt to encircle Buckner by an amphibious landing failed. Ushijima lost over 6,000 men and dozens of artillery pieces. He returned to his previous plan of awaiting the Americans under Shuri Castle.

Heavy rains and camouflaged fortifications plagued the U.S. attack. By May 10, mud-slogging troops finally took the Awacha Pocket near the Shuri Line, but at a great loss. The next day, Buckner assaulted the Shuri defenses. The going was rough. The 7th Marine Division moved south on Dakeshi Ridge where these veterans took the crest, withdrew from a withering counterattack, and pushed to the top again. It took three days and 700 casualties to capture Dakeshi. Once at the top, they gazed across a 1,200-yard draw in which the Japanese 62nd Infantry Division engaged in interlocking crossfire for eighteen days. By day, the Americans used tanks to get across the draw to Wana Ridge from which they rolled barrels of napalm into the gorge and cave complexes. By night, the defenders replenished themselves. Clearing the ravine required 200 U.S. Marines for every 100 yards gained. The 96th Infantry Division managed to take the eastern end of the Shuri Line; but at the western tip, the 6th Marine Division had to climb three hills that were reinforced with reverse-slope gun positions that riddled the advance. An eight-day battle for a hill—Sugar Loaf—required a squad leader to hold a shoulder until reinforcements fled from a counterattack. Intense bombardment of Sugar Loaf ensued, but the Japanese remained for three days until tanks and U.S. Marines dislodged them. They left behind craters half full of water and submerged corpses with weapons in hand and flies swarming around them. Bayonets drawn, the Marine Corps beat back another counterattack until the west end of the Shuri Line was theirs for good. After the 6th Marine Division took Naha on May 24 in house-to-house fighting, the outflanked Ushijima abandoned Shuri Castle for an eight-mile long coral escarpment to the southwest corner of Okinawa on the Oroku Peninsula. On May 29, the American flag flew over the Castle.

The fighting was so gruesome that Okinawa epitomized the war of annihilation. "Pieces of bodies were seen everywhere, thrown down in the oozy mud or splashed against boulders flanking the valley," reported a U.S. Marine. "Where flesh could not be identified positively, I assumed it was Japanese. No one walking through or along the area dared to disturb anything. By moving a shoe, we might learn there was a body under it." U.S. Marine E. B. Sledge experienced the mud, maggots, and horror on Dakeshi Ridge. Combat "became the subject of the most tortuous and persistent of all the ghastly war nightmares that have haunted me for many, many years." That both sides demonized the other heightened the ferocity. Nazis viewed undesirables as vermin. But Ernie Pyle had noted in early 1945 "Americans in Europe viewed the enemy as terrible but as people all the same. In the Pacific, however, I gathered that the Japanese were looked upon as something subhuman and repulsive; the way some people feel about cockroaches or mice."

Along an outcropping on the Oroku Peninsula, Ushijima was hurt but not done. Although defense of the Shuri Line cost 64,000 Japanese casualties, the Americans lost 26,000 men, the most in any battle in the Pacific war. The defenders still had several thousand troops and substantial equipment and ammunition. Buckner's Tenth Army began a three-week campaign on the southern escarpment. It pounded away with so many concentrated rounds of artillery, rockets, mortars, and large shells that Ushijima was enveloped in an inescapable hail of fire. Meanwhile, 6th Marine Division took Naha airfield after an amphibious landing on the Peninsula. Over 5,000 Imperial sailors lay dead in their tattered base, but they inflicted over 1,600 U.S. casualties and ruined 30 tanks in a savage ten-day battle until June 14. By then, a week-long day and night battle for Kunishi Ridge gave most of the peninsula to the Americans. Buckner prepared to sweep the rest of the peninsula and obliterate Thirty-Second Army. From an observation post, he watched the advance of the 8th Marine Division across a valley. The Japanese spotted his party, however, and shelled it. Splintered coral pierced his chest. Buckner was one of the highest ranked U.S. officers killed in World War II. Geiger took over Tenth Army for the next five days—the only U.S. Marine and aviator ever to command a field army for the United States—before Joseph Stilwell relieved him. Geiger completed the island's seizure on June 22, 1945 after Cho and Ushijima committed suicide.

The battle's cost was enormous. About 7,400 Imperial troops surrendered—the numbers an oddity during the Pacific War—but nearly 10,000 defenders perished including kamikazes and sailors. Between a tenth and a quarter of the Okinawan civilian population was caught in the battle, even those who fled to caves but were later killed in bombardments. The lowest estimates had 42,000 civilians killed by the strategy of annihilation, but many were murdered by their countrymen to avoid capture by the supposedly demonic Americans. Imperial forces also lost their biggest battleship and dozens of other vessels, as well as over 8,000 planes. At sea and on the beaches, the

U.S. troops among the dead on Okinawa.   Credit: Center for the Study of War Experience at Regis University, Denver, Colorado: U.S. National Archives.

Americans watched 36 warships and landing craft go to the bottom. Kamikazes, mines, and exploding motor boats damaged another 368 vessels. In the air, 763 planes were lost, including British and American aircraft. The results were staggering on land. U.S. Tenth Army suffered nearly 40,000 combat casualties, with 7,613 of these dead. Fatigue and other nonbattle casualties rose and added another 26,000 men. In all, 12,520 Americans died on Okinawa. This was the highest number of any campaign in the Pacific.

Such losses, coupled with the style of Japanese fighting—a ruthlessly efficient defense, terrifying suicide assaults, and courageous counterattacks—made an enormous impression on the Americans. Iwo Jima had been bad; Okinawa was worse in terms of the death count. And now the Japanese home islands awaited their fate. Spruance remarked that Okinawa was "a bloody, hellish prelude to the invasion of Japan," But planners in Manila, Honolulu, Guam, and Washington understood that capturing Honshu and the capital of Tokyo would likely involve an even worse slaughter and cruelty. Beginning in June 1945, they considered the harrowing experience on Okinawa as they devised ways bring about the enemy's final downfall.

TOWARD SURRENDER

How Japan would meet defeat remained the only question mark of the war. The empire had shrunk everywhere. On the Asian mainland, the Imperial Army's Ichi-Go offensive in China had fizzled and the Japanese pulled out of southern China to Manchuria where they defended the border against an invasion by the Red Army. Despite his neutrality treaty with Tokyo, Stalin intended to claim Manchurian territory. Japan vacated a theater that had claimed upward of 5 million lives while they suffered 500,000 casualties of their own since the start of the war in July 1937. That conflict had presaged the war of annihilation in that the number of civilian deaths in China ran as high as 20 million. In Burma, Twenty-Eighth Army moved out of the Arakan after abandoning Rangoon. It linked with the remains of Honda's Thirty-Third Army for a last attack on the Mandalay-Rangoon road. The Allies knew the plan. In the most lopsided engagement of World War II, the Japanese took over 17,000 casualties while the British lost 95 men. A preliminary surrender stopped the fighting on August 28, 1945, two weeks after Emperor Hirohito's capitulation order to his overseas forces. Burma witnessed the demise of two empires. It was free of Japanese rule, but the Imperial Army's steamroller through South Asia hastened the setting sun on the British empire as well.

The dream of the Co-Prosperity Sphere faded elsewhere. In the Netherlands East Indies, the Australians had landed intelligence-gathering forces on Borneo as early as October 1943 but an indigenous rebellion had been crushed by the Imperial Army. But in Spring 1945, training of the locals began in preparation for an invasion. In June, the 9th Australian Division came ashore at Labuan and Brunei Bay. Although 31,000 men of the garrison contested the landings, they were pushed inland by troops and guerrilla bands organized by the Allied intelligence services. On the Dutch side of the island, 13,000 troops in the Australian 26th Brigade Group, along with 5,000 Royal Australian Air Force personnel, took on 2,000 Japanese soldiers and sailors on the island of Tarakan off the coast of Dutch Borneo. The objective was an airfield that the Aussies captured at the end of July with losses of 894 casualties, although it turned out to be useless because the defenders had destroyed it. Of more interest was the oil port of Balikpapan. The 7th Australian Division, backed by Australian, U.S., and Dutch air and naval forces, began the last major operation of the Pacific war on July 1, 1945. A large amphibious assault captured two airfields and the port eight days later. Suffering over 850 casualties, the Australians cleared out the enemy around Balikpapan. Diplomatic wins did not follow military success because even as Europeans recaptured their territories, the United Nations prepared the colonies for independence.

In the Pacific, the Americans turned toward Tokyo. They had unfettered control of the skies, at least during the day. In mid-May 1945, the B-29s diverted to the Okinawa campaign returned to Twenty-first Bomber Command's strategic mission of leveling Tokyo and other cities on Honshu and Kyushu. Nine round-the-clock, month-long, 500-bomber incendiary raids on Tokyo, Nagoya, Osaka, Kobe, Yokohama, and Nagasaki killed over 100,000 civilians, and millions more lost their homes. Daytime runs drew out Japanese fighters who were shot down by the P-51s. Imperial High Command grounded the rest of the planes in June to preserve them for the defense of the home islands. The Japanese turned to night fighting, arming the two-engine Kawasaki Ki-45 Dragon Killer with 20-mm cannon but no radar. The Americans parried with their own two-engine fighter: the large, radar-equipped, and heavily armed P-61 Black Widow. It was no contest as the American bombers got through.

LeMay turned on sixty smaller cities and towns with firebombings, but he also knocked out factories and refineries through precision hits. Sometimes over 800 bombers flew in a single raid. The Americans did not exit unscathed; the USAAF lost nearly 500 bombers and 3,000 aircrew. But LeMay's campaign of annihilation was devastating—so total that by the end of July, Twenty-first Bomber Command had nearly exhausted its targets. Japan's economy and military machine shut down as factories lay in ruins, transport and communications were disrupted, and production was halved. Over 300,000 civilians perished and another half million were hurt, while 8.5 million people no longer possessed homes as the fall approached. LeMay powered on, bent on ending the war by this aerial blitz. There was little room for sympathy toward the Japanese, although some thought about their deeds. "One part of me—a surviving savage voice—says, I'm sorry we left any of them living," wrote a B-29 gunner after a raid. "Of course, as soon as rationality overcomes the first impulse, you say, Now, come on, this is the human race, let's try to be civilized." But few Americans felt merciful.

Faced with an impending humanitarian disaster, some politicians and diplomats quietly intensified their ongoing search for peace. They preferred some sort of

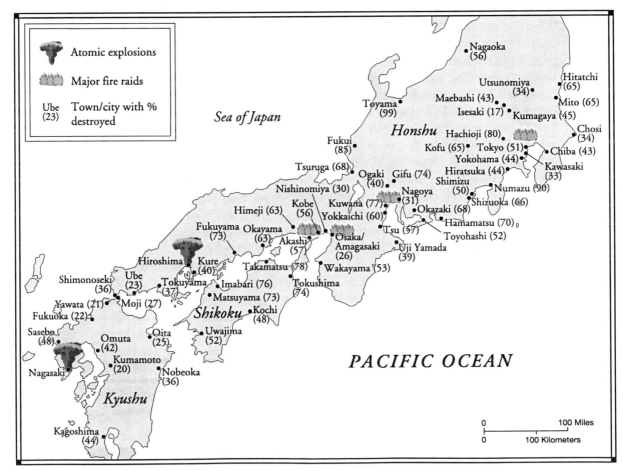

Map 25.2 Air war on Japan.   Credit: Ronald Story, *Concise Historical Atlas of World War II: The Geography of Conflict*, Map 47, p. 99.

conditional surrender to preserve the nation and its institutions. Talking peace was dangerous, however, because it exposed this growing minority of officials and members of the Imperial court to assassination by hard-line, die-hard militarists who believed that if the country survived the Superfortresses, Washington would balk at an invasion of the homeland. The Americans would not wish to repeat the barbarism on Iwo Jima and Okinawa, the fanatics reasoned, a negotiated peace would follow and the empire of Japan would survive. Civilians including the Emperor did not want to bank on U.S. diplomacy saving the day. Therefore, officials made secret approaches through the ostensibly neutral USSR. Stalin, however, planned to make good on his promise at Yalta to enter the war in Asia three months after the conclusion of hostilities in Europe, or around August 8, 1945. He brushed aside the entreaties, declared in April that the USSR would not renew its neutrality treaty with Japan, and then ignored altogether Japanese pleas for negotiation after the fall of Okinawa in late June. The stonewalling led to the demise of the Kuniaki cabinet, some of whom had sought a diplomatic way out. The near-octogenarian Admiral Kantaro Suzuki continued the effort at his peril, but Stalin sought territorial booty, not peace, and had no interest in talking.

Japan had to address the enemy's insistence on total capitulation that had applied to the Axis powers. The Potsdam conference from July 17 to August 2, 1945—the final Big Three summit—reiterated the call for Tokyo's unconditional surrender. While U.S. diplomats, the Joint Chiefs, and Churchill favored the Emperor's retention as a means of providing postwar stability, most U.S. military leaders and the public demanded harsh terms and even sought Hirohito's execution as a war criminal. Truman sided with the voters, Stalin pursued his ambitions, and the British stayed aloof. At Potsdam, Europe joined America in the Pacific war of annihilation, and the result for Japan was a tale of missed signals. The Potsdam Declaration focused on the establishment of a democratic government and did not mention the Emperor. That Hirohito's status seemed negotiable gave Tokyo diplomats hope, but lest there be any ambiguity, the Big Three restated their tough terms. They would punish Japanese officials responsible for the war, strip the armed forces of weapons, ship soldiers home, and occupy the nation. The Proclamation did not mention the Emperor, but the subtlety was lost in the heat of the war. Translations were so tortured that the men in charge in Tokyo believed the pronouncement made no room for compromise. Thus, the government did not respond. Stalin proceeded with war plans and Washington, D.C. took Japanese reticence to mean that it foreswore diplomacy. Truman's goal remained a military victory, whatever the cost.

The Joint Chiefs approved the massive bombing campaigns, but they predicted that the enemy would not abandon the fight without an invasion. Thus, they formulated a strategy that involved bombing, a complete blockade, and landings of 1.3 million men supported by the entire U.S. Pacific Fleet, the British Fleet, and 5,000 aircraft. MacArthur would oversee the Army while Nimitz would command the naval and amphibious forces in the biggest amphibious assaults ever. Operation Olympic would put troops on the southern island of Kyushu starting November 1, 1945. Four months later, Operation Coronet—the invasion of Honshu—would lead to the capture of Tokyo. The fight would not be easy at all. ULTRA showed Imperial headquarter's intention

The Big Three (Stalin, Truman, Churchill) at Potsdam.   Credit: Imperial War Museum.

to bring from Manchuria 60,000 additional troops to bolster the 246,000 garrisoned on Kyushu. By June, the estimate rose to 320,000. The Americans also detected bases hiding suicide aircraft and torpedoes. As Truman sailed home from Potsdam in early August 1945, there were reports that Kyushu's manpower had climbed to 600,000 and that more troops were expected.

In June 1945, the U.S. military presented estimates of manpower losses to Truman should an invasion go forth. The Okinawa campaign had demonstrated that the Japanese would not only fortify every nook of the homeland but that every civilian would take part in some way. That Japan had little air or naval power, severed transport and communication lines, meager economic output, and a dispirited population was beside the point. It was prudent to expect the same, or even more, fanatical resistance in the nation's last stand. The estimates were based on both good and faulty intelligence but also on emotions of hatred, fear, and determination. Of 766,000 men projected to land on Kyushu in Operation Olympic, Admiral William Leahy, head of the Joint Chiefs, initially gave President Truman an estimate of 268,000 killed, wounded, or missing in action. MacArthur put the number lower, while others thought upward of a half million casualties would occur. Officials oftentimes confused deaths with casualties. The Joint Chiefs settled on 60,000 casualties during the first two months of battle based on the 63,360 lost during the first eight weeks of the Normandy campaign and the 133,000 casualties on the Philippines, Iwo Jima, and Okinawa. Scholars have disputed the differing figures ever since but whatever the case, Olympic and Coronet would be deadly affairs and likely mimic the grim battles on the Eastern front. In actuality, they would probably be worse considering that casualties per days of combat in the Pacific were three times more than those in Europe. Tokyo ominously called for "The Glorious Death of One Hundred Million" to prepare for the American onslaught. This attitude so worried some American officials that they considered canceling the invasion plans altogether.

DEATH THE DESTROYER

In this atmosphere of apprehension and revenge, U.S. leaders expressed no qualms about using any weapon in their arsenal to defeat Japan, including blockade and bombing that strangled the enemy over an indefinite period. None of Truman's advisors wanted to extend the war any more than necessary, and the president was a skilled politician who understood that Americans demanded that their boys come home as rapidly and safely as possible. The public knew of the carnage in the Pacific, remembered Pearl Harbor, and had been stirred up into race hatred during this war without mercy. Truman possessed what he believed was the ultimate answer in hand.

On his way to the Potsdam conference, he learned of the successful test of an atomic bomb in New Mexico. Since 1943, the tremendous cost and effort of the Manhattan Project—the atomic bomb research and development program—yielded spectacular results. Scientific ingenuity and U.S. productive acumen brought the Project to fruition in just three years. Researchers delivered an uncontrolled splitting (fission) of the nucleus of an atom in masses of uranium or plutonium large enough to destroy cities. General Leslie Groves oversaw an endeavor that employed over 600,000 people in 37 facilities in 19 states and Canada who were funded by over $2 billion dollars. So massive was the program that it drew on all the uranium of the Congo, the biggest global source of that essential mineral, and it used up so much aluminum that B-29 production suffered. Financing, technology, manufacture, and testing were kept secret from the public. When a plutonium device worked in the New Mexico desert, some scientists worried about the morality of using such a devastating weapon. Groves and the military did not, and neither did Truman at the time. Germany was no longer a target with the European war over but Japan had not surrendered despite the warnings of the Potsdam Proclamation. The atomic bomb might be just the way to conclude a vicious war.

Historians have argued that Truman really had the USSR in mind. He knew Japan was on the brink of collapse, after all, and because of Stalin's obstinance on a host of postwar issues, atomic bombs might prompt Tokyo's immediate surrender. That would make Soviet entry into the war in Asia unnecessary and deny Stalin territory and influence. Diplomatic calculations certainly occupied officials in Washington. Still, the aim of crushing Japan was most prominent. Fresh memories of the horrors of the island-hopping campaign led to the conclusion that the bombs would save lives, and fears of defenses erected to inflict great damage on the invaders validated the use of a weapon designed to stop more carnage. A bomb might even prevent thousands of Japanese deaths that otherwise would be the case from a prolonged ground battle.

The Manhattan Project had to be justified, moreover, and not just financially. Could Truman face a mother whose son died in Operation Coronet's landings on

Honshu when an atomic bomb might have hastened the end of the war and saved his life? Like FDR before him, Truman endorsed a strategy of annihilation. There would be no demonstrations to the Imperial High Command as some scientists urged; the U.S. would not wait for the impact in Tokyo of the Soviet declaration of war. Everything—blockade, strategic bombing, planning for the invasion, and atomic weapons—would be tried. Truman later lamented the killing of so many innocent civilians and he chafed at the moral dilemma of seeking peace while releasing a weapon of mass destruction. The time for guesses, estimates, and future interpretations was over, however. In this war of annihilation, millions had perished in a bloodbath of murder, firebombing, and ground fighting. Evils of medical experiments; massacres of whole towns; and gang rape, torture, and pillage were rampant. The atomic bombs were another weapon—though certainly on a different scale—in a terrible orgy of violence called the Second World War.

If criticism can be leveled at the U.S. plan to end the war against Japan, the doctrine of unconditional surrender deserves the most scrutiny. The atomic bombings were not the only winning weapon in the war of annihilation, and they just might have been avoided because Japan did not surrender until the Soviet Union entered the war. Yet even the insistence on total capitulation must be understood within a context of total war that includes politics as well as military aims. The Americans refused to permit Japan to dictate peace terms, such as limiting trials of war criminals, and they modified their demands in the Potsdam Proclamation rather than negotiate with the Imperial Army. Perhaps by not insisting that the Emperor submit completely to the whims of the Allies, the Proclamation might have convinced more military leaders to surrender. That is a big "if" because fatalistic Imperial Army hard-liners continued to dominate decision making. Still, the Americans might have eased the terms of the Emperor's postwar status a bit more than they did. Speculation remains in the domain of the historians; military plans went forth.

Located in southwestern Honshu, Hiroshima was a commercial and manufacturing center as well as home to Imperial Fifty-Ninth Army and other military units. It had 350,000 inhabitants when the war began, and an influx of Korean and Japanese workers in war plants swelled the population. Because Curtis LeMay left the city untouched by firebombing, it provided a relatively pristine target with a landmark bridge and gave bombardiers a good target. The 509th Composite Group, a special unit of the USAAF, loaded the nine-foot-long, 4 ton *Little Boy*—the world's first atomic bomb—into Colonel Paul Tibbets' Superfortress. A highly regarded combat leader (he had flown in the first USAAF mission over France in 1942), test pilot, and engineer, Tibbets named the plane the *Enola Gay* after his mother. In light of its grisly mission, the name was incongruous. Tibbets took off from Tinian and headed for Hiroshima. At 8:15 a.m. on August 6, 1945 *Little Boy* brought the world into the nuclear age.

The bomb utterly devastated Hiroshima when it exploded 590 yards above the city with a force equivalent to 13,000 tons of TNT. The blast leveled buildings 2 miles from the epicenter and irradiated people in the vicinity. Because the heat reached several thousand degrees, people boiled alive in reservoirs or burned to death as their skin peeled away. Survivors recall the corpses "burning from below and the fat of the bodies

Hiroshima destroyed.   Credit: Center for the Study of War Experience at Regis University, Denver, Colorado:
U.S. National Archives.

was bubbling up and sputtering as it burned." They then "blackened and hardened." A
high school girl remembered being hit by the searing blast and fainting. On regaining
consciousness, she heard constant screaming. Huge blisters covered her face and neck,
and she was unable to control her drooling because her lip had been burned off. About
100,000 people died instantly, and tens of thousands of victims, including twelve U.S.
prisoners of war, perished from wounds or radiation sickness thereafter.

American soldiers who were preparing for the invasion were overjoyed by the
atomic bombing, and most believed that the Hiroshima bombing prompted Japan to
give up. In reality, it was actually one of three events that led to surrender. The shock
did not convince Imperial Army militants to give up, yet it did compel the Emperor to
summon the Imperial court of the nation's governing council of six leaders. The second incident occurred two days later when the USSR declared war on Japan and swept
across the Manchurian border on August 9. In a massive pincer operation that covered an area larger than western Europe, 1.6 million troops commanded by Aleksandr
Vasilevsky overran the Kwantung Army and quickly occupied territory, captured the
Japanese puppet Emperor of Manchukuo, and destroyed resistance before turning
over the region to Mao Tse-tung's Chinese communist forces. The Red Army also
raced into the Korean peninsula and landed on southern Sakhalin Island and the Kuril
Islands. The third event that brought the Japanese surrender came that first day of the
Soviet invasion. A B-29 released a plutonium bomb called *Fat Man* on the port and

steelwork city of Nagasaki in western Kyushu. This fishing, shipbuilding, and mining center suffered 75,000 instant deaths as one-third of the city was ruined. Whether the Nagasaki bombing was necessary remains a valid question. After all, the decision to drop *Fat Man* had not given much time to the Japanese council to meet and decide the country's fate.

It took divine intervention to end the dreams of the Imperial militarists. When the cabinet and the governing council split on whether to negotiate or continue the war, the prime minister called an evening gathering and invited Emperor Hirohito and his advisers to speak. Hirohito had neither welcomed nor tried to prevent the war but now he understood that peace was the only means of saving his country from complete evisceration. On August 10, 1945, he issued a statement signed by the government officials in attendance that accepted the Potsdam Proclamation on the condition that the throne would still represent the people. Because the Emperor would facilitate the surrender of millions of troops overseas, Truman accepted the terms. On August 12, the Allies agreed to permit the Emperor to remain, although they turned his future over to U.S. occupation authorities. At this point, the victors required that he speed the surrender and convert the nation into a democracy.

The war was not over, however. Not all of the Japanese military would lie down, for instance. The same day as the Allied decision, eight U.S. airmen were executed by military extremists and eight more suffered the same fate three days later. The war council continued to debate the proper course until the Emperor simply closed down the government. On August 14, he ordered the cabinet to accept the Allied conditions and then recorded an Imperial Rescript for broadcast to the people. This would ensure that Army and right-wing nationalists would not undo the peace by claiming that the Emperor had not agreed to the terms. That night, however, some junior army officers attempted a coup by seizing the Imperial Guards Division in Tokyo and killing its commander in an attempt to destroy the Emperor's recording before the people heard it. Their search did not turn up the Rescript nor did the coup succeed because senior officers refused to join. The Army chief of staff committed suicide rather than hear the surrender, and the Prime Minister narrowly avoided an assassin's bullet. After hearing the Emperor's broadcast, the chief of the Combined Fleet, Admiral Matomi Ugaki, decided to "follow in the footsteps of those many loyal officers and men who devoted themselves to the country." He climbed into a dive bomber and led kamikaze pilots south toward Okinawa to attack the "arrogant Americans" and display "the real spirit of a Japanese warrior" in defense of an empire that would "last forever." These suicides added to the death toll and showed the fanaticism of many in the Japanese military. The night before Ugaki's fatal flight, over 1,000 American bombers hit Tokyo again, losing not a single plane. As they returned to base, the flyers heard the news of Japan's surrender. Contrary to the expectations of American soldiers, there would be no invasion.

On August 15, the Emperor's recording went out to the crowds who heard the startling news that their country had capitulated. They had never heard the voice of this divine entity, so for people habituated to the notion of sacrifice to the nation, the solemn words could only be believed because the godlike Emperor uttered them. The

Japanese officers surrender their swords.   Credit: Center for the Study of War Experience at Regis University, Denver, Colorado.

enemy had used such a "new and cruel bomb" on the people, he said, that there was no other choice but surrender. Fighting on would only destroy Japan, but civilization as well. In response, many soldiers committed suicide though most lay down their arms. Members of the Imperial family embarked abroad to urge commanders to give up. Less than two weeks later, a Japanese military delegation boarded Admiral Halsey's flagship *Missouri* to provide information on minefields and shipping channels. Elements of the U.S. Third Fleet moved cautiously into Tokyo Bay to watch over Yokosuka air and naval base while other task forces stood on alert and aircraft patrolled overhead. About 19,000 prisoners were freed over the next two weeks.

On August 30, 1945, the 4th Marine Division went ashore as the first Americans to land in the home islands. Nimitz and MacArthur followed them. The Americans discovered positions defended with enormous guns, difficult terrain covered by artillery, and large numbers of troops awaiting U.S. forces at their exact landing spots. The Japanese possibly had acquired plans for the invasion from a spy but luckily, the U.S. Marines would not have to find out. Formal surrender ceremonies took place on *Missouri* on September 2. The new foreign minister, the wooden-legged Mamoru Shigemitsu, morosely signed the documents before Nimitz and MacArthur, and then the conqueror of the Philippines spoke of Japan's return to peace and America's promise to reform its enemy during the impending U.S. occupation. The strategy of annihilation had succeeded in ending the Second World War.

Of the most immediate concern for the Allies was the rescue of their countrymen and civilians from prisoner-of-war camps. The Bataan Death March was still vivid in their minds and they were also well aware of Japan's contempt for fighters who surrendered. Japanese incarcerated at the Cowra camp in Australia, for instance, scoffed at the Geneva Convention for the humane treatment of prisoners of war. In August 1944, they had broken out and 234 of them had either killed themselves or were gunned down by guards. Because many Imperial troops exhibited little concern for dying, the Allies feared the worst for their imprisoned nationals. Liberation of the Philippines and Dutch East Indies yielded 220,000 prisoners, but mistreatment and death typified the experience of 40% of the internees in Japanese camps in Asia.

Some 6.5 million Japanese were stranded in faraway outposts of the former empire. Many possessions remained in Imperial hands, and half of the subjects overseas were civilians who either returned home or were taken prisoner. At U.S. expense and by Japanese ships, all but a half million of those abroad were repatriated in the first ten months of peace. Another half million soldiers, officials, and civilians in Manchuria and Korea were arrested by the Soviets and held in Siberia, from which many never returned. Many more would have fallen victim to acts of revenge by locals had not Anglo-American forces rushed in to ship Imperial citizens home. Repatriation thus proceeded smoothly. In Hong Kong, however, a Chinese mob set on Japanese heading to their waiting ship and killed hundreds. In China, where the world war had started, the fear was not retribution but that the still-powerful Imperial Army might react if threatened. Still wary of Japan's military strength, Chiang Kai-shek did not disarm enemy troops on the coast. He let them either depart on their own, melt into the population to join the fight against communism, or sign up with warlord armies. Japanese civilians went home, secreting out of China as much jewelry or other goods as could be horded in anticipation of the hard times ahead that their country faced.

The end of the fighting in Asia halted the savage eight-year war of annihilation. Battlefield slaughterhouses across several continents revealed millions of corpses while death and destruction were displayed in thousands upon thousands of villages, cities, and farmlands. Civilians no longer needed to fear bombs falling from the skies and commerce could again ply the seas without staying alert for submarines. The vast armies and factories looked forward to converting to peacetime. Substantial housekeeping was in the offing because the victors readied to mete out punishment and organize the recovery effort. The vanquished awaited their fate. Whatever side they were on and wherever they were, people around the world understood that they had peered into the abyss. Many had backed away, but the war had plunged tens of millions more to their demise.

War was a universe unto itself; it didn't make sense that it could be banished in a moment by the say-so of a few men, the scribble of a few signatures. And he had at some point ceased to think it possible that the war would stop with himself alive. Only when he read of the bombs dropped over Hiroshima and Nagasaki did he begin to understand that he was not dead, but he was nevertheless in a new world.

NICK ARVIN
Articles of War: A Novel

The war of annihilation catalyzed change around the globe. Even at the time, World War II seemed like a transformative event and today we acknowledge its influence on the course of history. The war realigned international relations as states and nations adopted new policies, created new institutions, and developed new relationships. An entirely new conflict of the Cold War, which endured roughly six times longer than World War II and consumed millions of more lives—arose from the tensions caused by ideology, interests, fears, destruction, and power caused by the war. Hundreds of millions of lives were altered forever. People viewed the world differently than from the prewar period and they recognized that while such misery must be avoided in the future, they need also remember the lessons of the past.

PUNISHMENT

Of immediate concern to the victors was the pursuit of justice toward the Axis powers. Thousands of Nazi war criminals escaped from or hid out in Europe, although many were caught. Vengeful partisans killed Nazi sympathizers as Allied troops stood by, while courts acted to quash latent fascist movements. For example, collaborator Vidkun Quisling was hanged while 18,000 other Norwegians were jailed. The Dutch and Belgians convicted tens of thousands of collaborators and Austrians tried to purify the body politic by executing 85 of the over 9,000 Nazis brought to trial. The Soviets merely shot most of the fascist suspects they found. In the former Third Reich, the de-Nazification process resulted in trials for over 600,000 Germans and imprisonment for more than 31,000 of them. Many more were banned from government service, even though former Nazis remained as administrators because they were so numerous. Some also lost property or were fined. Even famous Allied figures were not immune from punishment. George Patton spoke out against the de-Nazification process and lost his command of Third Army as a result.

Formal proceedings against the Nazis began in November 1945 in Nuremberg, Germany. An International Military Tribunal brought 22 German leaders before the bar, where Herman Göring was the star defendant. Others heard charges read against them of conspiracy to begin a war, crimes against peace and humanity, and wartime criminal behavior. Ribbentrop, Keitel, Donitz, and other functionaries faced action regarding their collective guilt in perpetrating genocide, and eleven got the hangman's noose. Göring escaped the gallows by poisoning himself while Hitler's private secretary Martin Bormann, who was sentenced in absentia, had committed suicide, unbeknownst to the Allies. Three were acquitted. Speer, Donitz, Raeder, the brutal provincial governor Konstantin von Neurath, Minister of Economic Affairs Walther Funk, and Nazi Party deputy Rudolf Hess received prison sentences ranging from 10 years to life, but only the latter served out his time until his death in 1987.

From 1946 to 1949, the British, French, and Americans followed up with trials of their own. France held them at home, and the other two nations remained at Nuremberg. Included in the British cases was Field Marshal Erich von Manstein who served four years of an eighteen-year sentence (but appeared only as a defense witness at Nuremberg). The U.S. proceedings looked beyond the Nazis, as judges swept up industrial figures and personnel in the Wehrmacht, which resulted in 24 more hangings and 107 prison terms including 20 life sentences. As the tensions of the Cold War worsened by 1949, however, the Americans became less interested in crimes and more in the stability of the new Federal Republic of Germany. Trials came under increasing criticism as the Western democracies questioned Soviet aggression in Poland, Finland, and the Baltic states during World War II. This meant that those who earlier might have been punished for wartime misdeeds were let loose because they were needed to govern West Germany or aid the West in intelligence or military affairs against the Soviet communist threat. Most Nazi criminals, including those involved in the Holocaust, escaped severe punishment, received light sentences from German courts, or were never brought to trial.

The Nuremberg trials were a landmark in international criminal law, and thus World War II had a positive effect on promoting a body of human rights codes. Judges held fair trials that avoided a victor's justice even if there existed no body of international law with which to try the captives. They detailed Nazi bestiality and taught the German public the meaning of Third Reich's war of annihilation. Yet the Nuremberg cases did not focus on the Holocaust and on crimes against humanity. Rather, they dealt with war crimes. It would require the trial and hanging in Israel in 1961 of Adolf Eichmann, the head of the Race and Resettlement Office of the Reich Security Office which administered the Final Solution, to expose the full horror of Nazism to the world.

Vengeance, the treatment of prisoners, and the barbaric conduct of the war in Asia also drove the Allies to punish the Empire of Japan. In the Asian counterpart of the Nuremberg proceedings, the Tokyo war crimes trial took place from 1946 to 1948.

Judges from eleven countries and a U.S. prosecutor convicted 25 officials for "Class A" crimes ranging from waging wars of aggression to condoning atrocities. Treatment of incarcerated Allied personnel during the war received particular attention because the Japanese killed Allied prisoners at a much higher the rate than did the Nazis. The prosecution aimed to inculcate the notion that war was illegal, yet the defendants argued that wars of aggression had not been crimes before 1946. In any case, all were found guilty. The verdicts reflected victor's justice but also the realization that Japan's embrace of a strategy of annihilation (especially in China) demanded harsh punishment. While two men served years in prison, seven, including Tojo, were hanged. Of the sixteen who got life sentences, six died in prison and the rest were released in 1958.

Regional trials of those accused of planning or facilitating crimes convened until 1951. Ten countries including the United States, USSR, France, Canada, and the Philippines held trials for some 5,700 Japanese, convicted over half, and executed 920 men. Among them were Generals Homma and Yamashita. The Allies meted out this justice on behalf of the 27% of Western prisoners who died in camps as well as the even higher percentage of Asians who perished. Medical experiments conducted in Manchuria by Imperial Army Unit 731, which also developed bacteriological agents used against the Chinese and Russians, brought convictions in the USSR. The United States, however, granted Unit 731 members immunity for access to their records. Not one official was tried for the forced prostitution of 200,000 Korean, Chinese, and other Asian women. The government of Japan issued a belated apology to these so-called "comfort women" years later, but they were among the millions of victims of a barbaric war fought decades before.

PEACE AND INFLUENCE

Historians have documented that Germany and its allies lacked the resources for a prolonged war of annihilation. This was true. They occupied areas with raw materials, but their enemies controlled more key resources such as oil, minerals, and foodstuffs. What Britain lost in Asia the United States replaced. What Japan seized it could not ship home due to the Allied blockade. The Nazis harnessed millions of slave laborers in its lebensraum policies and assumed that Europe would feed the Third Reich, but that plan did not work for more than a few years. The Axis powers generally came to rely on quality versus quantity because they could not keep up with either the productive pace or the organizational abilities of their enemies. The Soviets took back their breadbasket, and the Western Allies denied access to ports. German munitions output continued strongly into 1944, but the strategic bombing campaigns and pressure on the ground took their toll. The American arsenal of democracy issued a torrent of mass-produced goods while Hitler ran perilously short of manpower and goods. Germany and Japan became victims of World War II's zero-sum economic game. In the long run, the war's outcome hinged on the productive capacities of the belligerents, but its course was also shaped by the effectiveness of their militaries as well.

Axis losses depended on military decisions and efforts made by leaders. Japan went down to defeat because it fought against a coalition led by an enormously productive foe, the United states. The Empire heralded the "human stuff" of willpower and devotion but Japan lacked flexible military doctrines, strategic imagination, and a systematic decision-making process. Tokyo was "self-hypnotized" by an allegedly invincible bushido mentality. Germany's true believers in the cause also boosted morale and resilience in the Wehrmacht yet Hitler's domination confused the command structure. This led to an inability to master grand strategy, the challenges of industrial warfare, and a response to enemies that united by a coherent strategic vision. In short, Germany's military strategy could not keep pace with the Fuhrer's political ends. When he staked victory on lebensraum through annihilation in the east, the Nazis succumbed. Italy was simply dysfunctional, arrogant, and unable to carry through with its overblown vision of empire. The Axis alliance never had a coherent purpose, like the Allies enjoyed. The dictators fell prey to hubris, bad planning, and militarily improved (and richer) enemies who converted basic Axis deficiencies in command and organization into fatal weaknesses.

On the Allied side, military effectiveness improved as they absorbed the shock of Axis victories into the process of strategic planning. Britain, Holland, Belgium, and France were badly prepared for war because they lacked armor and air forces and suffered for their mistakes. Britain suffered from shaky cohesion and training within army units. But leaders mobilized the population, wisely allocated resources, adopted new techniques (such as ULTRA), and welcomed cooperation with other allied powers. Although at first mistake prone on the battlefield, the United States addressed its operational shortcomings. Defying expectations, America emerged with a potent military propelled to victory by adaptable commanders and overwhelming resources. The USSR entered the war in a panic, but Stalin's ruthless meat-grinder tactic of sacrificing soldiers and materiel over time and distance turned the tide. Determination to defend the homeland from invaders bent on butchery won a vicious ground campaign. In sum, the capacity to survive a strategy of annihilation, and then issue one in return, was a cardinal factor in victory, as were the adaptability, skills, resolve, and strategic vision of the Allies that ultimately halted the Axis threat.

World War II gutted the Axis powers, but its effects were varied. In Europe, Italy joined the ranks of the Western democracies fairly easily. The war ripped Germany in half for forty-five years, but the people prospered largely because of Cold War required that a divided Germany be incorporated into the superpower camps. The USSR plundered its zone of occupation but eventually made East Germany into a showplace of communism whereas the democracies cleaned out Nazi vestiges and rebuilt West Germany. The Germans apologized for their sins—particularly for the Holocaust—and paid reparations by goods, money, aid, and punishment. The vast majority of the population recognized the Nazis as evil. Despite having precipitated the twentieth century's two global armed conflicts, new Germans rose from the ashes of war as pacifists and apologists bent on cooperation with their masters in the ideological struggles of the Cold War.

In Asia, Japan struggled at first. The war of annihilation had destroyed one-third of its wealth and nine million were homeless—a third of Tokyo's residences survived the bombings—and the percentage was worse for the next largest cities of Osaka and Nagoya. Over 2.5 million people died, and double that number were hurt, ill, or

malnourished. From 1945 to 1951, American occupation authorities reformed the political system, instigated economic changes, and altered attitudes. Defeat converted this
military bully into a pacifist with a weak economy reliant on outsiders. The nation's
plight in the postwar period led many to try to forget the cruel behavior and the shame
of defeat. Japan focused instead on material well-being with great success, since it
emerged forty years after the war as the second biggest economy in the world.

Yet not all the Allies benefited from the war. Japanese occupation in Asia sparked
independence movements against colonialism, which had the most far-reaching consequence of the conflict. Like the USSR, Britain and France lost a lot in World War II,
but unlike the Soviets, the war hastened a decline in their global reach. British rule gave
way to nationalism in India, Ceylon, Burma, and Malaya. Only Hong Kong, Gibraltar,
and scattered holdings remained on Britain's colonial ledger. Indonesia emerged from
Dutch control as a state by 1949, and France fought for Indochina only to be ousted
from Vietnam, Laos, and Cambodia within a decade of the war's end. In the Middle
East, neither Arabs nor Britain prevented the loss of Palestine and the creation of the
state of Israel. In Africa, the defeat of Italy and France during World War II loosened
imperial ties that were already under pressure before the conflict. The Second World
War sped up the process of decolonization by severing the links to Europe or, in the
case of French North Africa, putting such stress on them that they unraveled by the
early 1960s. Within thirty years after the end of the war, no colonies remained on the
African continent. Wars of liberation and diplomatic initiatives relegated an imperial
age to the dustbin of history.

The two superpowers were fairly immune to the wave of independence, although
they, too, did not have a free reign. The United States retained influence in Thailand
and in its former colony, the Philippines, but both became independent states after the
war Washington was unable to control the civil war in China that chased Chiang Kai-
shek to Taiwan (Formosa) and brought Mao Tse-tung and the communists to power in
1949. Despite its extensive intelligence contacts during the war, the Americans shunned
a workable alternative to French colonization in Indochina. A different course would
have prevented the disastrous Vietnam War twenty years later. Nonetheless, because
they suffered minimal loss of life and property relative to other combatants, the
Americans swept to influence and prosperity. The Second World War transformed the
United States into the richest and most secure power on earth, propelling it into unparalleled leadership in the West. For their part, the Soviets reabsorbed the Baltic states
of Estonia, Latvia, and Lithuania into their domain. Yet Finland maintained its independence, the Soviets never returned to Manchuria after withdrawing from the region,
and they left northern Norway (the only part of the country devastated by Germany)
after a brief occupation. Of course, Stalin had his prizes in Eastern Europe. Although
imperialism was a dirty word, he retained a virtual empire in the European satellites
that surrounded the USSR.

Because World War II was a transformative event, it also altered world history.
National boundaries actually did not change significantly except in Eastern Europe,
but the war reordered power relationships and activated the rise or demise of entire
structures of governance and socioeconomic arrangements. Some examples were the

dominance of the United States over world economic and Western security institutions, the Soviet grasp on Eastern Europe and influence in the emerging "third World," the supranational integration of Western Europe, new standards for international behavior, the establishment of global nongovernmental organizations that oversaw social and economic policies, and the advent of the nuclear age. Alongside these sweeping developments arose quite traditional national rivalries embedded in the Cold War. As colonization waned, this battle between the capitalist United States and the communist Soviet Union reshaped the world for nearly a half century. Their competition and the emergence of the Cold War was a direct result of the power each gained (and that other nations lost) during the Second World War. The war brought the end of the old regime and ushered in a new, and potentially more dangerous, age of two superpowers, although it was hard to conceive of any development in global affairs more perilous than World War II.

THE WAGES OF WAR

The war's conclusion prompted a search for lost relatives, mourning, and damage assessment. The human element was the top issue. Harm had come to all sides on all fronts and in all theaters of the world during the eight years of war. Few areas escaped death, injury, or destruction caused by total war. In short, nobody was immune to the strategy of annihilation, and as a result, hundreds of millions suffered. Exact tallies of human losses are impossible due to the imprecision of battlefield body counts and the difficulties of tracking civilian casualty figures. Accounting for the missing while distinguishing the real numbers from those distorted by patriotism, insecurity, or secrecy provide only best estimates. One conclusion is evident and bears repeating, however: the Second World War was the most destructive event in recorded human history.

More soldiers fought in World War II than in any other war, so figures on casualty totals are a bit skewed. When taking *military* casualties as a percentage of entire armed forces, the Second World War was actually less of a slaughter than previous wars. For instance, 29% of Union forces in the American Civil War were felled, injured, or hospitalized by disease. By comparison, the U.S. military between 1941 and 1945 suffered 6.7% casualties because soldiers were more dispersed at greater distances to avoid increasingly lethal modern firepower, and medical advances saved many more. Yet in total numbers of people affected, because of the horrific and systematic means of killing, and in the genocidal purposes of Nazism, this war had no parallels. Although the figures on the death toll fluctuated, particularly in regard to the USSR's propensity to hide the toll at first and then switch to high estimates, scholarship has devised a rough total. At the low estimate, over fifty million military personnel and civilians perished in this war without mercy, although the figure is most probably several millions higher (many believe more than sixty million perished) when those that simply vaporized in bombings are included and refugees are accounted for.

World War II was much less discriminatory than other wars when it came to military deaths, a fact that also justifies terming it as a war of annihilation. Eurasian males took the brunt of combat or noncombat losses. In terms of deaths to numbers who served, U.S. forces were the safest place to serve, the Red Army, the Wehrmacht, and

Japanese Army were the most dangerous. Almost 16 million American servicemen and women took part and under 4%, or 405,399, died. About 25 million Soviets served and around half—11–13 million—perished whereas in Germany, a third of the 18 million service personnel died. In direct enemy action, about 2 million Japanese were killed as well as 300,000 Italian servicemen fighting on both sides. The victors actually lost twice as many personnel because Red Army deaths accounted for more than the Axis powers' combined. After the 2.5 million soldiers lost by Nationalist China, the figures drop for the other Allied countries. Britain, America, Yugoslavia, France, and Czechoslovakia each lost in direct action (as opposed to noncombat deaths) between 250,000 and 300,000 personnel. Poland lost 123,000, and the rest of the Allies combined incurred 125,000 killed. No military job was safe, but some were worse than others. Serving in the infantry and tank crews, and as a German submariner and Anglo-American airman, were the most perilous. Of 38,000 German U-boat crewmen, a staggering 32,000, or over 84%, went dead or missing. The RAF's Bomber Command lost nearly half of its 125,000 airmen; and of the 210,000 members of the Eighth USAAF, 25,000 perished. Despite the guesswork, around 21 million people (but likely more) who served in the armed forces worldwide did not make it out of the war alive.

But the slaughter of civilians truly marked this war as one of annihilation and as the most catastrophic event in history. World War II offered a relatively universal source of death. Men, women, and children killed doubled the number of military dead. About 44 million people died, including over 12 million who succumbed in Nazi concentration camps and 2 million who died from strategic bombing in Allied and Axis countries. The Allies saw at least 35 million civilians die—28 million of these were Russian or Chinese, although both nations claimed even more perished. Three million people in the Axis nations were killed, although totals for both sides rise if the numbers for victims of oppression and military operations are fully counted.

While the war exempted no one from its scourge, some suffered disproportionately. Jews died at twice the rate of all Axis civilians. There were 34 million Poles before 1939, but 6 million died in the war, and another 8.5 million left Poland to die in camps

Table C.1 Losses

	Military Dead and Missing	Civilian Dead	Jewish Holocaust Victims	Total Dead and Missing
United States	220,000	—	—	220,000
United Kingdom	370,000	60,000	—	430,000
France	250,000	270,000	90,000	610,000
USSR	13,600,000	6,000,000	1,720,000	21,320,000
China	3,500,000	10,000,000	—	13,500,000
Germany	3,250,000	3,640,000	170,000	7,060,000
Italy	330,000	70,000	15,000	415,000
Japan	1,700,000	360,000	—	2,060,000
All other participants	1,180,000	4,690,000	3,998,000	9,868,000
Total	24,400,000	25,090,000	5,993,000	55,483,000

Source: Hans Dollinger, *The Decline and Fall of Nazi Germany and Imperial Japan: a Pictorial History of the Final Days of World War II* (New York, NY: Bonanza Books, 1965, 1967), 422.

or seek permanent exile. The country eventually was left with just 57% of its prewar population and virtually a nonexistent Jewish population. The Nazis killed most of the Jews, but peasants also had a hand. It is wrong to single out the Poles for such behavior, however, because Lithuanians and Ukrainians massacred Jews well before the Final Solution. Blame for the genocide of this one group can certainly be spread around. Certain countries also bore the burden of dead. The statistics are stunning, especially for eastern and central Europe. For every 1,000 people in their countries, 220 Poles and 116 Soviets died. By contrast, the dead in the Netherlands numbered 22 and in France 15 per 1,000 people while Britain suffered eight, Belgium seven, and America three deaths. Holland, though, suffered strikingly. In a country of nine million people, 16,000 perished from starvation in the winter of 1944–45 during the German occupation and 200,000 more were lost to bombing and incarceration. Again, Poland also can be singled out for losses. It lost 39% of its doctors, a third of its teachers and scientists, and over a quarter of its priests and lawyers. Of the nine million deaths in Asia, the Chinese represented a large share of the killings as did those Asians enslaved in work camps. In addition, hundreds of thousands of Japanese were killed from the U.S. strategic and atomic bombing campaigns.

The efficiency of modern warfare and ideological killing machines wiped out millions of lives as governments perfected ways of systematic mass killing and murder by employing science and industry. Ideas and ideals motivated millions to commit crimes or participate in military operations that swept up civilians as well as armed forces in a miasma of suffering. This was a total war guided by a strategy of annihilation, and no country escaped its horrors. None were completely exonerated for oppression because the major belligerents all perpetuated a strategy of annihilation. Some practices were certainly worse than others, and some regimes were more beastly. Hitler's Third Reich was the worst of all. The Final Solution ranks as the most evil of institutions, and therefore Nazi crimes cannot be placed on the same level as, say, the violation of civil liberties perpetuated by the United States on Japanese-Americans or even the strategic bombing campaign. There is no moral equivalence for the Holocaust. Crimes against humanity were different than killing for military purposes. Still there is ample room for debate moral relativism. The point is not just to assign guilt but to reveal the innocence of many in this so-called good war.

But necessary it was. The Allies' achieved their objectives of defeating fascism and militarism. Berlin collapsed, Europe was liberated, and the Empire of Japan was beaten into submission. Those developments were good. The point is, however, that the means of doing good, through a strategy of annihilation that was as the brutal as any methods ever devised in warfare, were bad. Thus, *how* the war was fought is equally important as why it happened and what its outcome was. Even citizens on the winning side admitted as much. Ordinary people were wiped out by the dozens, hundreds, thousands, and tens of thousands, sometimes in a single fell swoop. All sides, including the Allies, killed prisoners and left their bodies by the roadside. Military personnel who surrendered perished in agonizing ends. They might not have been as innocent as civilians, but they became victims of war all the same.

How do we assess blame in a war of annihilation, or should we? Strategic bombing wrought atrocious results, but were these campaigns worse than Chiang's deliberate drowning of tens of thousands of his own people when he blew up the Yellow River dikes to stem a Japanese advance? Is Stalin's decision to starve civilians including children and the elderly to concentrate resources on the war fronts in 1942 worse than German sieges of Russian towns where tens of thousands perished or famine in Greece perpetuated by vicious occupation and partisan warfare? Unlike Chiang and Stalin, in these cases, the Germans did not kill their own people. Indictments can be spread around. Technology and economic productivity created weapons that when combined with willpower and determination, fear and prejudice, and vengeance and hatred, made World War II the most significant example of mass genocide in history. Discomfort with decisions remained powerful. Nazi and Japanese leaders were tried as war criminals, but the Allies escaped the bar because they were victors. But national consciences forever reproached the air combatants, for instance. Arthur Bomber Harris was denied the peerage granted to all other British commanders after the war and his aircrews did not receive a separate campaign medal. The British, and to some extent the Americans, refused to acknowledge that they had sunk to the level of their enemies' morality, yet they also punished military men for not conducting this barbarous war more nobly.

The human cost should be the focus of any study of war and particularly of this conflict. The theme of annihilation—of destroying noncombatants and economies as well as militaries themselves in a total war—addresses the enormous casualties incurred by the belligerents, bystanders, and victims. Today we worry over such "collateral damage" of military actions as civilian casualties but this was not the case in the Second World War. Allies and Axis alike focused on destruction on the battlefield and of home fronts in the vast war zone. This was no war for the feint of heart or for those seeking a limited engagement. World War II simply spiraled downward into a mass slaughter, an Armageddon of annihilation on a scale never before witnessed.

LEGACY

Yet for all its destructiveness and transformative qualities, the war recedes into the last century, and memory is the battlefront now. The Holocaust receives a large part of the attention. The dwindling number of survivors recall their own struggles and those who did not make it out alive, while nations debate their guilt. Memorialization of the dead occurs beyond the Holocaust, in every affected area in every theater. Thousands of villages and towns mark the war's human toll, as nations honor their casualties and heroes by ceremonies, street names, impressive monuments, and exhibitions. All of these remembrances conjure up questions about the inescapable consequence of industrialized warfare. Survivors were thankful that their lives were spared, but they also wondered whether the war's butchery was necessary. Did people learn from the terror, killings, torture, abuses, and atrocities that attended the relentless campaigns of annihilation in every theater? Would conflict occur again but on an even more monstrous scale in the nuclear age? Memorialization attempts to give succeeding generations answers to these questions by teaching them about a grim past in the hopes that it will not be repeated.

The process of memorialization since 1945 has also dug deeper by exploring the meanings of the war in general and events in particular. This process has stirred controversy about causes, consequences, behavior, and decisions. Even in the victorious United States, which used the war as a springboard to global domination, memory has been contested. A Smithsonian exhibition at the National Air and Space Museum in the nation's capital in 1995 centered on the fiftieth anniversary of the dropping of the atomic bombs, with the *Enola Gay* as the centerpiece. The display so irritated veterans and nonveterans alike by depicting the atomic bombs as shepherding in the Cold War rather than as a catalyst to the end of World War II that it was suspended until the script was reconceived (although in 2003 the full, original exhibition was held). Meanwhile, American deification of the so-called Greatest Generation unrealistically cast the warriors as people without foibles—as some sort of characters in middle-American Norman Rockwell images. Like combatants everywhere, most U.S. soldiers and their leaders were heroes who deserved to be honored but they were also very normal people—good, average, and bad—who reacted in various ways to the horrors of war. Removing them from a pedestal of immortality avoids trivializing the hardships they faced.

Americans are not alone in tending toward amnesia. An exhibition on the crimes of the Wehrmacht toured Germany to popular acclaim from 1995 to 1999; its theme that the military (and not just the Nazi regime) helped plan and implement a war of annihilation was met with amazement. When accusations of inaccuracies led to charges of forgery, the display was suspended, revised, and then reopened in 2001. The image of a Wehrmacht unblemished by Nazism remained strong despite the flood of research showing its complicity in Hitler's crimes. For its part, Italy punished its Axis sympathizers when it switched sides in 1943, yet the public forgot that Il Duce was a perpetrator of aggression. In December 2008, for example, the country's highest court ordered Germany to pay for a 1944 massacre in Tuscany. Germany had long taken moral responsibility for the war, but Italy looked past its trafficking with Hitler to focus on its victim status. Japan not only took its time to apologize for the atrocities it committed in Asia, but for decades, it whitewashed its merciless treatment of enemy civilians and military personnel in school textbooks. The government promised to rectify the distortions after outcries from Koreans, Chinese, and others who had experienced the wrath of the Imperial Army and Navy. Yet Tokyo continued to face censure over its portrayal of the war (even from Japanese citizens who claimed a cover-up regarding army-ordered mass suicides by Okinawa residents). The textbook revision controversy simmered into the new millennium. In sum, memories of World War II remained contested and controversial, as former enemies saw evil in the other but goodness in themselves.

Some buzzwords need to be laid to rest. One wonders if postwar generations appreciate the meaning of the term "good war" when it appears in quotation marks. What was good about a conflict that wrought over fifty million deaths and untold suffering? It is clear that the war was necessary to defeat great evil, but it was not good. Furthermore, there is reason to believe that not everyone learned the lessons of the good war. Anti-Semitism remains in the form of Holocaust deniers, for instance, despite conclusive documentation of the victims and crimes of Nazi genocide.

The notion of a "greatest generation" (mainly an American construct) also should be abandoned. There was no greatest generation any more than any other generation before or since. The World War II generation engaged in the most hideous event in history, but they were one among many who dealt with crises. Did this generation outdo, for instance, those who fought in earlier or subsequent wars or those who toiled to build their countries and provide a livelihood for their families? Are they more deserving of the moniker "greatest" than those who have fought against terrorism, for example? And how should we assess this "greatest generation" when they fought a war against virulent strains of racism but, in the case of the Americans, permitted and even perpetuated race-based segregation at home and abroad? This is not to blame the World War II generation for societal ills nor to discredit their heroic contribution to defeating evil, but it is necessary to caution their memorializers against both warping and cleansing the historical record. The World War II generation should not be cast as supermen saving the world but rather as ordinary people struggling to survive in a violent time. While descendants of the combatants have justifiably honored their relatives who fought in this monumental conflict, they also run the risk of glossing over the real meaning of a terrible war for future generations.

From the 1990s onward, an outpouring of memoirs from combat soldiers and other participants made clear the horrors of the Second World War. Of course, many found in the war a camaraderie, excitement, and commitment to the whole that their countrymen lacked in peacetime, but few soldiers expressed a fondness for combat. They related the fears, tensions, and sadness inherent in fighting for one's life and seeing others killed. Like all events in which humans labor under the most extreme conditions, this one brought out the very essence of human nature. It was oftentimes not a pretty sight to behold. There were petty crimes of robbery and bad behavior induced by alcoholism. Men could panic and exhibit cowardice. At still another level, discrimination of officers against the foot soldier occurred. Even Red Army patriots, arguably the least willing of the war's participants to cast a negative light on their country, confessed that while most Russian soldiers were decent people, a substantial number showed the dark side of the human character. From the debris of carnage arose the uncomfortable fact that World War II had degenerated into a ruinous manmade cataclysm.

Yet global memories have been obscured in the political arguments that compared this good war to later bad ones. Governments, relatives, and museums sought to memorialize this greatest of civilizational conflicts as veterans began rapidly passing from the scene. But they have tended to forget the military details that made the fighters heroes in the first place. We have also overlooked the unintended consequences of the war—military surprises, blunders, successes and losses, and a brutality that accompanied the soldiers every step of the way. Lest we forget, this was the cruelest event in history.

Amidst the story of military campaigns, human suffering is overlooked or downplayed. Accounts by combatants both dead and alive, however, remind us that World War II was just as much about tragedy and loss as it concerned weapons, generals, and grand strategy. A striking (and depressing) element of the war was the number of young who comprised the armed forces in the fields, seas, and air. All armies are young, but it bears reminding all the same, and the youthful dead left millions at home to mourn their loss. Young and old, civilian or soldier, the strategy of annihilation destroyed innumerable lives. These great numbers of deaths, however, were not in vain unless the next generations forget the reality of annihilation experienced by their forbearers. The war put all countries on notice about the dangers of aggression. Although countless millions have perished since, they have heeded that warning by avoiding worldwide war since 1945. This salutary effect of caution is the Second World War's gift to humanity.

In the end, war boils down to not just military machines and masses but to the sacrifice of individuals. Thus, it is appropriate to conclude with the words of a young German soldier who captured the tragedy of this war. "An intoxicating feeling came over me: a burgeoning sense of life, the limitless, exuberant pleasure of being in the world," wrote Willy Peter Reese in his diary entry in the winter of 1943 as he embarked for the Eastern front. "The freedom of an hour in the Russian winterland. I loved life. The war went on. Once more I went out there. I loved life." Like so many millions annihilated in the path of this terrible conflict, he was dead within days.

REFERENCES

INTRODUCTION

Adams, *The Best War Ever*, 7, 9, 157–58.

Ambrose, *The Good Fight: How World War II Was Won*.

Baker, *Human Smoke*.

Bellamy, *Absolute War*, 17–19.

Bourke, "Barbarisation vs Civilisation in Time of War," 19, 30.

Bourke, *An Intimate History of Killing*, xiii, xviii.

Bourke, *The Second World War*, 2–3.

Bradley, *Flyboys*, 15.

Buchanan, *Churchill, Hitler, and "The Unnecessary War"*.

Chickering and Forster, "Are We There Yet?"

Davies, *No Simple Victory: Europe at War, 1939–1945*, 481–90.

Greenfield, *American Strategy in World War II*, 4–5, 10.

Grimsley, *The Hard Hand of War*.

"How Good Was the Good War?," http://www.amconmag.com/article/2008/jul/14/00006/ .

Kashen, *Saints, Sinners, and Soldiers*, 3–4.

Janda, "Shutting the Gates of Mercy," 8.

Manela, *The Wilsonian Moment*, 63–97, 159–75.

Marks, *The Illusion of Peace*, 5–28, 71–80, 130–60.

Mazower, *Hitler's Empire*, 2–7, 43–5.

Megargee, *War of Annihilation*.

Overy, "The Second World War," 39–44.

Strachan, "Total War," 36.

Thompson, *The Lifeblood of War*, 4.

Vonnegut, *A Man Without a Country*, 20.

Weigley, *The American Way of War*.

Weinberg, "World War II Scholarship, Now and in the Future," 340–41, 343–44.

PART I

Beever, *The Battle for Spain*, 152–54, 257–60, 459–64.

Bell, *The Origins of the Second World War in Europe*, 169, 172–82, 185–87, 189–91, 196–98, 250–266.

Bethell, *The War Hitler Won*, 84.

Biddle, *Rhetoric and Reality in Air Warfare*, 94–127.

Bird, *Erich Raeder*, 49–67, 96–133, 145–48, 153–56.

Bird, "The German Navy in World War II," 101–06.

Boatner, *The Biographical Dictionary of World War II*, 188, 206, 435, 570.

Boot, *War Made New*, 221–24.

Bosworth, *Mussolini*, 351–53.

Botman, "The Liberal Age, 1923–1952," 298.

Boyd, "Japanese Military Effectiveness," 164.

Brett, "The Maghrib," 315–328.

Breyer, *Battleships and Battle Cruisers,* 403.

Calvocoressi and Wint, *Total War,* 7–16, 48–49, 49–53.

Carley, *1939,* 35–115.

Carr, *The Twenty Years' Crisis,*.

Chaney, *Zhukov,* 68.

Ch'i, *Nationalist China at War,* 46, 50.

Claasen, *Hitler's Northern War,* 62–140.

Cook and Cook, *Japan at War,* 32.

Cooke, *Billy Mitchell,* 169–84.

Coox, *Nomonhon,* 120–41, 779–841, 952–1010.

Craven and Cate, eds., *The Army Air Forces in World War II,* vol. I.

Dear, ed., *The Oxford Companion to World War II,* 19, 48–49, 110, 140, 184, 228–29, 292–95, 316–18, 370–376, 459–60, 477–79, 493, 499, 519, 526–27, 555, 560, 590, 604, 640–41, 643, 705, 716, 725, 742, 756, 761, 797, 806, 893, 895, 958, 961–63, 1017.

Duroselle, *France and the Nazi Threat,* 192–93.

Edgerton, *Warriors of the Rising Sun,* 222–51.

Ellis, *World War II-A Statistical Survey,* 117, 230.

Evans and Peattie, *Kaigun,* 340–43, 347–91.

Frieser and Greenwood, *The Blitzkrieg Legend,* 18–19.

Gander and Chamberlain, *Weapons of the Third Reich,* 7.

Gat, *British Armour Theory and the Rise of the Panzer Arm,* 1–67.

Gellately, "The Third Reich, the Holocaust, and Visions of Serial Genocide," 246–53.

Gooch, *Mussolini and His Generals,* 385–483.

Green, *Warplanes of the Second World War, Fighters, Vol. II.*

Grossjohann, *Five Years, Four Fronts,* 8.

Gruhl, *Imperial Japan's World War Two, 1931–1945,* 31–36.

Guderian, *Panzer Leader,* 41–2.

Gunston, *World Encyclopedia of Aircraft Manufacturers,* 47–8, 202.

Habeck, *Storm of Steel.*

Hallion, *Strike from the Sky,* 81–8, 111–15.

Harries, *Soldiers of the Sun,* 155–98, 209, 224–25, 235, 240–46.

Hastings, *Bomber Command.*

Herwig, "Innovation Ignored," 228, 231–41.

Huan, "The French Navy in World War II," 79–80.

Ienaga, *The Pacific War,* 97–128.

Iriye, "Japanese Aggression and China's International Position," 525.

Jarrett, ed., *Putnam's History of Aircraft.*

Jeans and Lyle, eds., *Good-Bye to Old Peking,* 62, 71.

Kersaudy, *Norway, 1940,* 175–95.

Kiernan, *Blood and Soil,* 417–39, 445–54, 470–82.

Knox, *Hitler's Italian Allies.*

Knox, *Mussolini Unleashed,* 59–69, 352, 356.

Levy, *The Royal Navy's Home Fleet in World War II,* 19–49.

Li, "The Nanking Holocaust," 732–33.

Lianhong, "The Nanjing Massacre," 122.

Lumans, *Latvia in World War II*, 75–111

Lyons, *World War II*, 15, 19, 22, 71.

MacIntyre, *The Naval War Against Hitler*, 13, 22, 26.

McCormack, "Reflections on Modern Japanese History in the Context of the Concept of Genocide," 266, 268, 271–73.

Mallett, *Mussolini and the Origins of the Second World War*, 48–105.

Masaaki, "One Army Surgeon's Account of Vivisection on Human Subjects in China," 145–52.

Megargee, *Inside Hitler's High Command*, xiii-xiv, 27–28, 230–35.

Millett, "Assault from the Sea," 51, 68–69, 71, 78–84.

Murray, "Armored Warfare," 6–7, 9–15, 48.

Murray and Millett, *A War To Be Won*, 23–28, 31, 33–39, 46–52, 64–66, 151, 156–58.

Overy, *Göring*, 22–75, 109–37.

Parillo, "The Imperial Japanese Navy in World War II," 61–2, 70–2.

Pope, *The Battle of the River Plate*, 200–06.

Record, *The Specter of Munich*.

Richards, *The Hardest Victory*, 340.

Richardson, *Your Loyal and Loving Son*.

Roehrs and Renzi, *World War II in the Pacific*, 30.

Rossino, *Hitler Strikes Poland*, 29, 58, 90, 154–59, 173, 227–35.

Rothwell, *Origins of the Second World War*, 9–20, 45–65, 81–109.

Rutherford, *Prelude to the Final Solution*), 5–6, 36–109.

Sadkovich, "The Italian Navy in World War II," 129–36.

Salerno, *Vital Crossroads*, 1–2, 10–39.

Shachtman, *The Phony War*, 52, 58, 104–20.

Smelser and Davies, *The Myth of the Eastern Front*, 131–49.

Stokesbury, *A Short History of World War II*, 64–66, 69, 71, 75–76, 79, 81–82, 84–88.

Sullivan, "The Path Marked Out by History," 116–26.

Tohmatsu and Willmott, *A Gathering Darkness*, 53–66, 76–82.

Toshihiko, "Essay," 174–202.

Supplying War, 143–46.

Van Dyke, *The Soviet Invasion of Finland* 105–13.

Vehvilainen, *Finland in the Second World War*, 31–45, 55–59, 74–89.

Voss, *Black Edelweiss*, 32–34.

Wasserstein, *Secret War in Shanghai*, 49–115.

Watson, *United States Army in World War II*, 95.

Wegner, *The Waffen-SS*, 14–57;

Weinberg, *A World At Arms*, 15–16, 18–24, 37, 49–55, 61–64, 69, 78, 80–83.

Wilson, *When Tigers Fight*, 30–48, 135–46, 151.

Westwood, *Anatomy of the Ship*, 8–9.

Yamamoto, *Nanking*, 81–150.

Zaloga and Madej, *The Polish Campaign*, 133.

Zhukov, *G. Zhukov*, 183, 187, 193–94, 204.

PART II

Adelman, "German-Japanese Relations," 43–76.

Alexander, *The Republic in Danger*.

Andrew, "British-Polish Intelligence Collaboration During the Second World War in Historical Perspective," 55–56.

Banham, *Not the Slightest Chance*, 93–5, 165–68.

Barnett, *Engage the Enemy More Closely*, 378–426.

Bartsch, *December 8, 1941*, 311–407.

Beevor, ed., *A Writer at War*, 14, 20.

Beevor, *Crete*, 156–62, 240.

Bekker, *The Luftwaffe War Diaries*, 197–257.

Bell, *The Origins of the Second World War in Europe*, 269–70.

Bellamy, *Absolute War*, 28, 99–206, 478–81, 485–91.

Berkhoff, *Harvest of Despair*, 35–88, 114–86.

Bidermann, *In Deadly Combat*, 34.

Boatner, *The Biographical Dictionary of World War II*, 167.

Borch and Martinez, *Kimmel, Short, and Pearl Harbor*, ix, 108–09.

Bosworth, *Mussolini*, 365–72.

Braithwaite, *Moscow 1941*, 211–59.

Broekmeyer, *Stalin, the Russians, and Their War, 1941–1945*, 45–59.

Brown, *Warship Losses of World War Two*, 27.

Callahan, *Churchill and His Generals*, 56–59, 61–134.

Cardozier, *The Mobilization of the United States in World War II*, 74, 82.

Carley, *1939*, 181–212.

Chaney, *Zhukov*, 129, 161–202.

Cherepenina, "Assessing the Scale of Famine and Death in the Besieged City," 13–26.

Chesneau, ed., *Conway's All the World's Fighting Ships*, 240.

Churchill, *The Second World War*, vol. III, 607.

Ciechanowski and Tebinka, "Cryptographic Cooperation-Enigma," 443–55.

Citino, *Death of the Wehrmacht*, 19–84.

Claasen, *Hitler's Northern War*, 141–86.

Cook and Cook, *Japan at War*, 77, 82.

Cressman, *The Official Chronology of the U.S. Navy in World War II*, 45, 59.

Dear, *The Oxford Companion to World War II*, 11, 35, 38, 42–43, 49–50, 52, 54, 60, 79–81, 83, 86, 88–89, 92, 102, 104, 107, 124–27, 130, 132, 135–36, 148–50, 171–73, 180–82, 210, 213, 213, 215, 231–32, 240–41, 243, 245, 247–48, 249, 251, 265, 270, 281, 287, 307–08, 322–24, 326, 332, 334–36, 341–43, 354, 386, 389, 395, 402–03, 412, 427–28, 508, 510–12, 515, 530–33, 535–36, 542, 550, 552–53, 556–57, 558, 560, 572–73, 578, 593, 595, 597, 600, 603, 610–13, 616, 667–69, 674, 677–80, 684–85, 691–92, 713–14, 739, 748, 754, 768, 779, 781, 785, 787, 809, 820, 828–29, 843, 854, 862, 910–11, 919, 922–23, 929, 932, 936–37, 939–40, 963–64, 981, 992, 994–96, 1010–11.

DiNardo, *Germany and the Axis Powers*, 72–83, 192–97.

Divine, *The Reluctant Belligerent*, 147–53.

Doughty, *The Breaking Point*, 1, 131–65.

Ferguson, *The War of the World*, 446–51.

FitzGibbon, *The Winter of the Bombs*, 41–133.

Ford, *Britain's Secret War Against Japan*, 20–75.

Fraser, *Knight's Cross*, 232, 241, 246–47.

Frei, *Guns of February*, 89. 222.

Frei, "The Island Battle," 223.

Frieser and Greenwood, *The Blitzkrieg Legend*, 1–3.

Gatu, *Village China at War*, 357–62.

Gellately, *The Third Reich, the Holocaust, and Visions of Serial Genocide*, 260.

Glantz, *Colossus Reborn*, 60.

Glantz, *Stumbling Colossus*, 83–97, 254–56.

Glantz et al., *Slaughterhouse*, 5–6, 67, 87–88, 100–01, 103, 113–14, 125, 134.

Glover, *An Improvised War*, 37–105.

Gorodetsky, *Grand Delusion*, ix–xi, 294–300, 316–23.

Green, *Famous Bombers of the Second World War*, vol. 1 (Garden City: Hanover House, 1959), 36, 96.

Grossjohann, *Five Years*, 22.

Gruhl, *Imperial Japan's World War Two*, 67–86.

Guderian, *Panzer Leader*, 199–200, 263.

Gunsburg, "The Battle of the Belgian Plain, 12–14 May 1940," 207–44.

Gunsburg, *Divided and Conquered*, 106, 169–72.

Hague, *The Allied Convoy System*, 77.

Heer, "Killing Fields," 55–74.

Hill, *The War Behind the Eastern Front*, 69–87.

Hinsley, *British Intelligence in the Second World War*.

Hionidou, *Famine and Death in Occupied Greece, 1941–1944*, 1, 33–9.

Hondros, *Occupation and Resistance*, 70–2.

Hotta, *Pan-Asianism and Japan's War*, 177–223.

Hough, *The Longest Battle*, 109–13.

Imlay, *Facing the Second World War*, 355–63.

Jackson, *Dunkirk*, 132.

Jackson, *The Fall of France*, 47, 49–52, 55, 190–96.

Jung, *But Not for the Fuehrer*, 119.

Keegan, *The Second World War*, 501–2.

Kemp, *Underwater Warriors*, 66–77.

Kimball, *Forged in War*, 31.

Kirkpatrick, *An Unknown Future and a Doubtful Present*.

Koistinen, *Arsenal of World War II*, 13–32.

Komatsu, *Origins of the Pacific War and the Importance of 'MAGIC'*, 247–84.

LaFeber, *The Clash*, 192–97, 202–07.

Lane, *Ships for Victory*, 4, 174–75, 808–09.

Lasterle, "Could Admiral Gensoul Have Averted the Tragedy of Mers el-Kebir?," 835–44.

Lenton and Colledge, *British and Dominion Warships of World War II*, 51.

Lewis, *The Mammoth Book of Eyewitness World War II*, 155–56.

Lukacs, *Five Days in London*, 39–42, 189–90.

Lyons, *World War II*, 75, 94, 107, 109–12, 115–16, 121, 123, 125, 127, 146, 161.

MacDonell, *One Soldier's Story*, 81–5.

MacKay, *Half the Battle*, 68–87.

Mann, "Combined Operations, the Commandos, and Norway, 1941–1944," 471–95.

Mansoor, *The GI Offensive in Europe*, 11–13.

Manstein, *Lost Victories*, 103–26.

Marix Evans, *The Fall of France*, 103, 147–49.

May, *Strange Victory*, 362–70.

Mazower, *Inside Hitler's Greece*.

Megargee, *Inside Hitler's High Command,* 41, 52.

Megargee, *War of Annihilation,* 65–6, 91–92, 95–97.

Merridale, *Ivan's War,* 106–08, 113.

Messenger, *The Second World War In Europe,* 82–83.

Miller, *The Great Book of Tanks,* 206, 291–312.

Miller, *Bankrupting the Enemy,* 58–74, 84–97, 116–67, 220–43.

Miller, *Nothing Less Than Full Victory,* 270.

Miller, *War Plan Orange,* 213–32.

Miller, *War At Sea,* 111–18, 120–22, 169–200, 230–31.

Milner, "The Royal Canadian Navy in World War II," 41–2.

Moss, *19 Weeks,* 50, 100, 123–26, 174, 213, 289.

Mrazek, *The Fall of Eben Emael,* 13–14, 22–38.

Muir, "The United States Navy in World War II," 1–5.

Mullenheim-Rechberg, *Battleship Bismark,* 116, 176–81.

Mulligan, *Neither Sharks Nor Wolves,* 71–80, 136–37.

Murphy, *What Stalin Knew,* xx, 108–16.

Murray and Millett, *A War to be Won,* 28–30, 32–33, 39–42, 58–62, 68–100, 102–08, 110–15, 118, 120–22, 124–27, 129–35, 137–38, 141, 162, 164–65, 167, 172–75, 178–79, 235–36, 238–40, 242–49, 266–68.

Naumann, "The 'Unblemished' Wehrmacht," 417–27.

Neillands, *The Bomber War,* 44–45.

Nolte, "Partisan War in Belorussia," 1941–1944," 267–73.

Ohl, *Supplying the Troops,* 47–52.

Paterson, *Hitler's Grey Wolves,* 19–80.

Philpott and Alexander, "The French and the British Field Force: Moral Support or Material Contribution?," 743–73.

Pinkus, *The War Aims and Strategies of Adolf Hitler,* 14–18, 167–70.

Place, *Military Training in the British Army,* 168–75.

Ponting, *1940,* 92–3, 163–69.

Potter and Nimitz, *Sea Power,* 528.

Powaski, *Lightning War,* 33–54, 101, 107–202.

Reese, "Lessons of the Winter War," 825–30, 851–52.

Reese, *A Stranger to Myself,* 35.

Reynolds, *Thailand and Japan's Southern Advance,* 25.

Reynolds, *Thailand's Secret War,* 7–10.

Rhodes, *Masters of Death,* 105–79.

Roberts, *Stalin's Wars,* 63–80, 104.

Roehrs and Renzi, *World War II in the Pacific,* 44.

Rommel, *Rommel and His Art of War,* 60, 62, 65–66, 73, 75–76.

Roshwald, *Estranged Bedfellows.*

Sajer, *The Forgotten Soldier,* 20, 37.

Salisbury, *The 900 Days,* 210, 258, 293.

Sawyer and Mitchell, *The Liberty Ships,* 8–9, 20.

Scheck, *Hitler's African Victims,* 28–41, 121–26.

Schaller, *The United States and China in the Twentieth Century,* 58–65.

Schrijvers, *The GI War Against Japan,* 207.

Sebag-Montefiore, *Dunkirk,* 301, 312, 387, 422, 447, 458, 480.

Shepherd, *War in the Wild East*, 58–107.

Spector, *Eagle Against the Sun*, 33–50, 54–69, 78–82.

Stansky, *The First Day of the Blitz*, 32, 131–55.

Stokesbury, *A Short History of World War II*, 89–104, 106–07, 109–14, 116–18, 123, 125–29, 137, 139, 141–48, 150, 152–59, 165–71, 200–03, 207.

Story, *Concise Historical Atlas of World War Two*, 34, 36, 59, 80.

Sullivan, "The Path," 126–39.

Terraine, *The Right of the Line*, 208, 210–11.

Thompson, *The Lifeblood of War,* 53–54.

Titmuss, *Problems of Social Policy*, 97–109, 355–69, 424–30.

Tohmatsu and Willmott, *A Gathering Darkness*, 83–94, 106–09.

The United States Strategic Bombing Surveys, European War and Pacific War, 10, 77–86, 108.

Van Creveld, *Supplying War,* 146–49, 151, 157, 182–90, 192–200.

Van Dyke, *The Soviet Invasion of Finland*, 88.

Vatter, *The U.S. Economy in World War II*, 11–50.

Von Hardesty, *Red Phoenix*, 17, 35.

Von Der Porten, *The German Navy in World War II*, 248.

Wait, *Under Fire at Sidi Rezegh,* http://riv.co.nz/rnza/tales/wait5.htm.

Weinberg, *A World at Arms*, 77–79, 127, 146–48, 208–09, 211–14, 219–20, 223–25, 230–31, 252, 262, 265, 267, 271, 281, 302.

Wette, *The Wehrmacht*, 103–04, 134–35.

Whiting, *Britain Under Fire*, 9, 24.

Williamson, *U-Boat Bases and Bunkers,* 38–40, 49.

Wilson, *When Tigers Fight,* 163–78.

Zhukov, *G. Zhukov*, 264.

PART III

Agarossi, *A Nation Collapses*, 91–138.

Atkinson, *An Army at Dawn*, 241–49, 252–55, 359–86, 389, 513, 537.

Atkinson, *The Day of Battle*, 7, 179–238.

Australian Broadcasting Corporation, *The Men Who Saved Australia*, http://www.abc.net.au/4corners/stories/s12899.htm.

Barr, *Pendulum of War*, 23–41.

Beevor, *A Writer at War,* 125–26, 134–35, 154, 157, 406.

Beevor, *Stalingrad*, 148, 276.

Bess, *Choices Under Fire*, 88–110.

Biderman, *In Deadly Combat*, 57, 136.

Bierman and Smith, *The Battle of Alamein*, 253–335.

Bosworth, *Mussolini*, 391–99.

Breyer, *Battleships and Battlecruisers*, 240, 243, 333, 335.

Buell, *Master of Sea Power*, 197, 216–17.

Callahan, *Churchill and His Generals*, 135–63.

Campbell, *Naval Weapons of World War Two*, 207.

Cannon, *United States Army in World War II*, 25.

Chaney, *Zhukov*, 203–37.

Chesneau, *Conway's All the World's Fighting Ships*, 23–6.

Citino, *Death of the Wehrmacht*, 85–302.

Clemens, *Alone on Guadalcanal*, 126–41.

Cline, *United States Army in World War II*, 235, 379.

Coates, *Bravery Above Blunder*, 96–121, 207–57.

Cook and Cook, *Japan at War*, 268, 271.

Coombe, *Derailing the Tokyo Express*.

Corti, *Few Returned*, 134.

Crane, *Bombs, Cities, and Civilians*, 1, 93–119.

Cressman, *The Official Chronology*, 125–26, 192.

Day, *Reluctant Nation*, 1–43.

Dear, *The Oxford Companion to World War II*, 7, 18, 20, 22, 24, 38, 40, 52–54, 90–91, 98, 102–04, 107, 115, 120–21, 131–32, 134–38, 139, 141, 148, 176–77, 182–83, 189–90, 196–98, 210, 213, 219, 229–30, 232–33, 240, 244, 248, 253–56, 259, 265–66, 274, 296, 328, 339–40, 343–45, 347, 388–89, 404, 406, 410, 412–13, 425, 451, 502, 505–06, 511, 513–14, 516–17, 536, 551–52, 560, 566, 578, 585–87, 591–92, 595, 601, 613,616–17, 620, 625–27, 634–39, 669, 672–73, 677, 685, 710, 714, 716–17, 732, 744, 748, 755, 759, 760–61, 765–66, 775–76, 778–79, 786–87, 800, 804, 808, 823–25, 831–33, 837–38, 847, 855, 857, 862, 865, 867–69, 876, 880, 913, 917–18, 973, 976–77, 990, 992, 994–96.

D'Este, *Patton*, 433, 534.

Donahue, *Guadalcanal Journal*, Http://www.guadalcanaljournal.com/guadalcana12.html

Ehlers, *Targeting the Third Reich*, 112–40.

Farrell, "Introduction," v.

Fay, *The Forgotten Army India's Armed Struggle for Independence*, 87–135.

Frank, *Guadalcanal*, 83, 614.

Fraser, *Knight's Cross*, 401.

Freeman, *The Mighty Eighth War Diary*, 46–47, 154.

Frei, *Guns of February*, 115.

Friedman, *U.S. Aircraft Carriers*, 4, 412–14.

Gailey, *MacArthur Strikes Back*, 117–53, 155–211.

Gander and Chamberlain, *Weapons of the Third Reich*, 154–55.

Gannon, *Operation Drumbeat*, 266.

Glantz, *Slaughterhouse*, 111.

Glantz, *Zhukov's Greatest Defeat*, 2.

Grayling, *Among the Dead Cities*, 83–89, 209–47.

Green, *Famous Bombers*, 360.

Griffith, *MacArthur's Airman*, 101–12, 122–23.

Gruhl, *Imperial Japan's World War Two*, 92.

Hamilton, *Monty*, 153–54, 170.

Hansen, *Fire and Fury*, 53–67; 279–97.

Harrison, *Accounting for War*, 12–13, 128–64, 170–72.

Haskew, *The World War II Desk Reference* , 162, 169, 547, 637.

Hastings, *Bomber Command*, 308.

Hays, *Alaska's Hidden Wars*, xii.

Hayward, "Too Little, Too Late," 769–94.

Hayward, *Stopped at Stalingrad*, 192.

Hickham, *Torpedo Junction*.

Hogg, *German Artillery of World War II*, 138.

Horne, *Race War*, 187–219.

Hough, *The Longest Battle*, 125.

Ienaga, *The Pacific War*, 144.

Isom, *Midway Inquest*, 104–53.

Jackson and Kitson, "The Paradoxes of Vichy Foreign Policy," 79–115.

Jenner, "Turning the Hinge of Fate," 165–72.

Jong, *The Collapse of a Colonial Society*, 47–144.

Keegan, *The Second World War*, 236, 427.

Kennedy, "Symbol of Imperial Defence," 50–62.

Kimball, *The Juggler*, 73, 76.

Knell, *To Destroy a City*, 52–3.

Latimer, *Alamein*, 58–63, 92, 103, 111–17, 119, 134–38, 177, 228.

Leighton and Coakley, *United States Army in World War II*, 535.

Levine, *The War Against Rommel's Supply Lines*, 75–181.

Lewis, *The Mammoth Book of Eyewitness World War II*, 305, 341–42, 499.

Louis, *Imperialism at Bay*, 283.

Lowe, *Inferno*, 183–276.

Lundstrom, *Black Shoe Carrier Admiral*, 85–203, 237–301.

Lundstrom, *The First Team and the Guadalcanal Campaign*, 34–70, 80–82, 129–57, 305–21, 325–459.

Lyons, *World War II*, 163, 166, 168, 171, 178–79, 183, 190–91, 196–97, 201, 225, 235–36.

MacIntyre, *The Naval War Against Hitler*, 420–22.

Matloff and Snell, *United States Army in World War II*, 166

Maung, *Burmese Nationalist Movements*, 32–5.

Meilinger, "Trenchard and 'Morale Bombing'," 243–70.

Melton, *Darlan*, 147–79.

Merridale, *Ivan's War*, 147–50, 157, 164, 173.

Middlebrook, *The Schweinfurt-Regensburg Mission*, 16–21, 258.

Miller, *United States Army in World War II*, 218–19.

Miller, *War at Sea*, 327–52, 357–63.

Monahan and Neidel-Greenlee, *All This Hell*, 98–153.

Mulligan, *Neither Sharks Nor Wolves*, 161–71.

Murfett, "Reflections on an Enduring Theme," 12–22.

Murray and Millett, *A War to be Won*, 181, 187–88, 210–17, 227–30, 250–52, 254, 257, 259–60, 268–73, 275–80, 282–92, 299–303, 307, 310–12, 315–17, 320, 333, 337, 377–78, 380–81.

Neillands, *The Bomber War*, 66–78, 104, 119–20, 154, 204, 218–26, 234–41, 249–56, 292.

Neillands, *The Dieppe Raid*, 66–83, 245–79.

O'Reilly, *Forgotten Battles*, 79–135.

Parshall and Tully, *Shattered Sword*, 19–38.

Partridge, *The Alexandra Massacre*, http://www.nesa.org.uk/html/alexandra_massacre.htm.

Payne, *Franco and Hitler*, 114–205.

Perras, *Stepping Stones to Nowhere*, 136–78.

Porch, *The Path to Victory*, 370.

Potter and Nimitz, *Sea Power*, 595, 726–27.

Powell, *The Third Force*, 25–54.

Prange, *Miracle at Midway*, 370–90.

Roberts, *Stalin's Wars*, 119, 128, 131, 134, 144, 147, 155.

Rommel, *Rommel and His Art of War*, 99, 132–33, 139, 162, 178.

Rottman, *U.S. Marine Corps World War II Order of Battle*, 276, 294.

Roy, "Military Loyalty in the Colonial Context," 497–529.

Sajer, *The Forgotten Soldier,* 133.

Sarantakes, *Allies Against the Rising Sun,* 86–114.

Schrijvers, *The Crash of Ruin,* 33–4.

Schrijvers, *The GI War Against Japan,* 208–09.

Schultz, *The Doolittle Raids,* 150, 276.

Smith, *Carrier Battles,* 83–150.

Smith, *American Diplomacy During the Second World War,* 27, 42–48.

Smith, *Bloody Ridge,* 171–95.

Spector, *Eagle Against the Sun,* 195, 208, 211, 221–22, 229, 234–39, 242–43.

Stewart, *Empire Lost,* 87–114.

Stokesbury, *A Short History of World War II,* 135–36, 204–08, 210–11, 213–15, 218–28, 230–31, 233–41, 249–55, 276–80, 279, 281, 283–86, 291–93, 296–302.

Stoler, *Allies in War),* 66–9, 89–90, 123–26, 140–42, 269–70.

Stone, *War Summits,* 71, 87–88.

Story, *Concise Historical Atlas of World War Two,* 26, 30, 32, 40, 50, 52, 82, 86, 88.

Symonds, *The Naval Institute Historical Atlas of the U.S. Navy,* 154.

Thorne, *Allies of a Kind,* 401–16.

Tohmatsu and Willmott, *A Gathering Darkness,* 118, 124, 126, 128, 130–31, 133–36, 138, 142–48, 149–50, 152.

Van Creveld, *Supplying War,* 162–79.

Vassiltchikov, *Berlin Diaries,* 118, 124–25.

Warren, "The Indian Army and the Fall of Singapore," 253–95.

Weigley, *Eisenhower's Lieutenants,* 36–7, 57, 180.

Weinberg, *A World at Arms,* 326, 344, 380–81, 432–33, 440–50, 580, 595–99, 633.

Willmott, *The War with Japan,* 25–30, 35, 38–50, 56–86, 96, 108–09, 111–14, 118, 120, 127–29, 131–33, 137–38, 140, 151, 158, 161, 163–66, 168.

Y'Blood, *Air Commandos Against Japan,* 3–23.

Y'Blood, *Hunter-Killer,* 12–28.

Zeiler, *Unconditional Defeat,* 10–12, 14–16, 25–26.

PART IV

Alexander, *Utmost Savagery,* 122, 159.

Allan, *In the Trade of War,* 83.

Allen, *Burma,* 170–88.

Ambrose, *D-Day, June 6, 1944,* 418–50.

Atkinson, *The Day of Battle,* 409, 455, 564–67.

Badsey, "Culture, Controversy, Caen and Cherbourg," 48–55.

Barbier, "Deception and the Planning of D-Day," 176–82.

Beavan, *Operation Jedburgh,* 152–58.

Beevor, *A Writer at War,* 218, 233, 236.

Bennett, *Destination Normandy,* 85–96.

Berger, *Breaching Fortress Europe,* 54, 79.

"The Bloody Battle of Tarawa," http://www.eyewitnesstohistory.com/tarawa.htm.

Bookspan, *Slaughterhouse,* 65.

Boyd Yoshida, *The Japanese Submarine Force and World War II,* 134–57.

Bradley, *A Soldier's Story,* 296, 314, 335–36, 355, 366, 371, 377.

Burma Star Association, "The Kohima Epitaph," http://www.burmastar.org.uk/epitaph.htm.

Cardozier, *The Mobilization of the United States,* 25.

Clark, *Anzio,* 70, 91–6, 133, 150, 199, 295–320.

Condon-Rall and Cowdrey, *United States Army in World War II,* 138–40, 441–43.

Cook and Cook, *Japan at War,* 287–90.

Copp, *Fields of Fire,* 133–57.

Cressman, *The Official Chronology,* 229.

Crow, ed., *Armoured Fighting Vehicles in Profile,* 155–57.

Cruikshank, *Deception in World War II,* 170–89.

Dear, *The Oxford Companion to World War II,* 3–4, 8, 24–27, 34–35, 42, 54, 101, 107, 137–38, 149, 182, 189, 209–10, 213, 221, 256, 260, 265, 269, 328–30, 332, 334, 338, 347, 349–50, 406–07, 411, 426, 430, 438, 451–56, 502, 504, 511, 513–15, 517, 527, 530, 561–62, 564, 566–68, 589–91, 597, 601–02, 620–21, 627, 631–34, 653, 656, 667, 673, 681, 690–91, 725–26, 737,-38, 744, 758–59, 764–65, 776–77, 792–96, 813, 840, 852, 855, 862–63, 866, 873, 876–77, 913, 972.

D'Este, *Decision in Normandy,* 116.

D'Este, *Patton,* 593–94, 625, 634, 641.

English, *The Canadian Army and the Normandy Campaign,* xiii, 181–95, 203–30, 263–300.

Erickson, *The Road to Berlin,* 87–135.

Friedman, *U.S. Amphibious Ships and Craft,* 216–17, 223–59.

Friedman, *U.S. Naval Weapons,* 117–18.

Funk, *Hidden Ally.*

Gailey, *MacArthur's Victory,* 262.

Glantz, *Slaughterhouse,* 136–37.

Goldberg, *D-Day in the Pacific,* 29–38, 131–94, 200–02, 215–28.

Grossjohann, *Five Years,* 77, 82, 122.

Gruhl, *Imperial Japan's World War Two,* 96.

Hall, ed., *Case Studies in Strategic Bombardment,* 293.

Hall, ed., *D-Day,* 18.

Hardesty, *Red Phoenix,* 121–47.

Hastings, *Das Reich.*

Haunschmied, Mills, and Witzany-Durda, *St. Georgen GusenMauthausen,* 2008.

Hebras, *Oradour-sur-Glane,* 20–1.

Hesketh, *Fortitude,* 71–9, 168–212.

Holzimmer, *General Walter Krueger,* 101–29.

Hopkins, *Spearhead,* 603–87.

Howard, *Strategic Deception in the Second World War,* 103–32.

Keegan, *Six Armies in Normandy,* 57, 241, 335–37.

Keegan, *The Second World War,* 466.

Kobylyanskiy, *From Stalingrad to Pillau,* 89.

Kramish, *The Griffin.*

Kurzman, *Fatal Voyage,* 1.

Lamb, *War in Italy,* 56–79.

Leventhal, *The American Arsenal,* 105.

Lewis, *Omaha Beach,* 4–5, 210–56, 293–94.

Lewis, *The Mammoth Book of Eyewitness World War II,* 419, 518.

Litvin, *800 Days on the Eastern Front,* 22.

Lyons, *World War II,* 213, 311.

Megargee, *Inside Hitler's High Command*, 81.

Merridale, *Ivan's War*, 217, 219.

Murray and Millett, *A War to be Won*, 293–98, 340–41, 344–50, 354–65, 374, 381–86, 388, 390–405, 407–08, 412–13, 416–26, 428–34, 436–38.

Nash, *Hell's Gate*, 318.

Neiman and Estes, *Tanks on the Beaches*, 81.

Newton, *Kursk*, 10–11, 407–16.

O'Brien, *Battling for Saipan*, 222–23, 314.

Ottis, *Silent Heroes*, 44–75.

Parillo, *We Were in the Big One*, 87.

Pennington, *Wings, Women, and War*, 1–3.

Potter and Nimitz, *Sea Power*, 712, 769.

Prefer, *Vinegar Joe's War*, 1–49.

Reardon, *Victory at Mortain*, 230–86.

Rommel, *Rommel and His Art of War*, 197–206.

Roscoe, *United States Submarine Operations in World War II*, 169.

Rottman, *U.S. Marine Corps*, 301–02, 311–13.

Ryan, *The Longest Day*, 181, 198–203, 225.

Salisbury, *The 900 Days*, 551–60.

Schrijvers, *The GI War*, 218–25, 234–43.

Semelin, *Unarmed Against Hitler*, 168–75.

Sheehan, *Anzio*, 125.

Sledge, *With the Old Breed*, 71, 80, 120–25, 142, 144, 156.

Sloan, *Brotherhood of Heroes*, 153.

Spector, *Eagle Against the Sun*, 60, 262, 265, 280, 283–84, 287, 289–94, 357–60, 368–69.

Stokesbury, *A Short History of World War II*, 241–44, 258–59, 261–64, 302–07, 311–25, 328–41.

Stoler, *Allies in War*, 147–50.

Story, *Concise Historical Atlas of World War Two*, 3, 42, 46, 50, 52, 54, 58, 88.

Thompson, *The Lifeblood of War*, 87, 94–99.

Tooze, *The Wages of Destruction*, 590–624.

Van Creveld, *Supplying War*, 202.

Venzon, *From Whaleboats to Amphibious Warfare*, 101–09.

Weigley, *Eisenhower's Lieutenants*, 81–2, 84–5, 236.

Weinberg, *A World at Arms*, 457, 603–06, 641–42, 657, 677, 687, 691.

Wheeler, *The Big Red One*, 269–83.

Whitlock, *The Fighting First*, 129–234.

Wieviorka, "France," 125–48.

Wieviorka, *Normandy*, 96–121, 255–70.

Wilt, *The Atlantic Wall*.

Y'Blood, *The Little Giants*, 2–9, 11, 17.

Zeiler, *Unconditional Defeat*, 16–17, 18–21, 30, 32–38, 40–43, 45–49, 58–61, 67, 70–76, 80, 82–93, 95–98, 101–06.

PART V

Abrams, "The Second World War and the East European Revolution," 624–25.

Alexander, *The Final Campaign*, 173.

Alperovitz, *The Decision to Use the Atomic Bomb*, 223–75, 377–80, 400–09.

Ambrose, *The Wild Blue*, 212–23.

Astor, *The Bloody Forest*, 148–272.

Astor, *Operation Iceberg*, 15–25, 150, 197–245, 258–73.

Bartholomew-Feis, *The OSS and Ho Chi Minh*.

Baruma, *The Wages of Guilt*, 69–91.

Bayly and Harper, *Forgotten Armies*, 457–62.

Baynes, *Urquhart of Arnhem*, 81–134.

BBC News, "Japan Textbook Angers Chinese, Korean Press," April 6, 2005, http://news.bbc. co.uk/2/hi/asia-pacific/4416593.stm.

Beevor, *A Writer at War*, 273, 276, 279, 281, 326–27, 338–40.

Beevor, *Berlin*, 31, 172–89, 216–56, 295–301, 310–27, 370–405.

Bellamy, *Absolute War*, 616–26, 634–69, 676–82.

Bess, *Choices Under Fire*, 112, 257, 192–253, 263–86.

Biddle, "Dresden 1945," 414–15, 420–25, 430–31, 444–46.

Bidermann, *In Deadly Combat*, 247–53.

Bix, *Hirohito and the Making of Modern Japan*, 503–30.

Boot, *War Made New*, 299–303.

Bradley, *Flags of Our Fathers*, 201–12.

Bradley, *A Soldier's Story*, 416–18, 444, 450, 453–55, 459–62, 467, 506–22, 537–45.

Brokaw, *The Greatest Generation* , 235–36.

Burrell, *The Ghosts of Iwo Jima*.

Cameron, *American Samurai*, 1.

Caruso, *Nightmare on Iwo*, 19–20, 26, 42, 74, 158.

Chaney, *Zhukov*, 278–87, 295–301, 311, 313–16, 322–26.

Ciechanowski, "Reports on the Holocaust," 534–535.

Clark, *Crossing the Rhine*, 299–330.

Connelly, *Reaching for the Stars*, 3, 137–63.

Cook and Cook, *Japan at War*, 325, 345–46, 348, 385–86, 393.

Coox, "Needless Fear," 411–38.

Coox, "The Effectiveness of the Japanese Military Establishment in the Second World War," 39.

Copps, *Cinderella Army*, 87–117, 149–73.

Crane, *Bombs, Cities, and Civilians*, 120.

Cressman, *The Official Chronology*, 59–60, 126–27, 265.

Davies, *No Simple Victory*, 63–72.

De Bruhl, *Firestorm*, 127–67, 255–85.

Dear, *The Oxford Companion to World War II*, 39–40, 42, 58, 60–61, 79, 90, 98–99, 123, 128, 132, 134, 139–40, 177, 182, 201–07, 211, 213, 222, 233, 242–43, 247–48, 252, 262, 266, 271–74, 285, 291, 295–96, 332, 350, 352, 355, 381–82, 390, 401–03, 429, 434, 449, 456, 475, 501, 516, 527, 530–31, 539–40, 542, 549, 558, 561–62, 576, 578, 606, 635, 643–46, 653, 655, 674, 689–90, 714, 732, 737, 739, 747–48, 759, 761, 763–64, 785, 831–33, 840–42, 846, 852, 862, 864, 874, 974, 976, 978, 983–87, 991–92, 995, 1011.

D'Este, *Patton*, 666–69, 676–78, 681, 683–89, 710–12, 727–29.

Dower, *War Without Mercy: Race and Power in the Pacific War*, 77–146.

DuPuy, *A Genius for War*, 1–3.

D.W. World. DE Deutsche Welle, "Germany Sues Italy to Block World War II Compensation Claims," December 24, 2008, http://www.dw-world.de/dw/article/0,3899824,00.html.

Ferguson, *The War of the World*, 546.

Forster, "The Dynamics of Volksgemeinschaft: The Effectiveness of the German Military Establishment in the Second World War," 212–14.

Frank, *Downfall*, 77–79, 117–30, 139–48.

Freeman, *A Mighty Eighth War Diary*, 347, 349.

Friedlander, *The Years of Extermination*, 234–36, 252–55; 458–61.

Fritz, *Endkampf*, 61–124.

Fussell, *Wartime*, 268.

Garbatov, "The Camp at Majdanek," 287.

Garlinsky, *Poland in the Second World War*, 246–99.

Giangreco, "Casualty Projections for the U.S. Invasions of Japan," 1945–1946, 521–82.

Gilmore, ed., *U.S. Army Atlas of the European Theater in World War II*, 122–23, 139.

Giurescu, *Romania in the Second World*, 273–94, 315–36.

Glantz, *Red Storm Over the Balkans*, 23–45.

Glantz, *Slaughterhouse*, 124, 118.

Goldstein and Dillon, eds., *Fading Victory*, 664–66.

Goolrick and Tanner, *World War II*, 14–15.

Gruhl, *Imperial Japan's World War Two*, 142–45.

Grunden, *Secret Weapons and World War II*, 183–91.

Hagan and Bickerton, *Unintended Consequences*, 188.

Hall, *Case Studies in Strategic Bombing*, 274, 306–11, 326.

Hamburg Institute for Social Research, *Crimes of the German Wehrmacht*, 3, 34, http://www.verbrechen-der-wehrmacht.de/pdf/vdw_en.pdf .

Hamilton, *Monty*, 417–25, 460, 466.

Hasegawa, *Racing the Enemy*, 92–102, 130–251.

Holzimmer, *General Walter Krueger*, 184–207.

Jessup, "The Soviet Armed Forces in the Great Patriotic War, 1941–5," 273.

Jung, *Not for the Fuehrer*, 315

Karski, *The Story of a Secret State*, 380–89.

Keegan, *Churchill's Generals*, 236.

Keegan, *The Second World War*, 433.

Knell, *To Destroy a City*, 262–66.

Knox, "The Italian Armed Forces, 1940–3," 170.

Kobylyanskiy, *From Stalingrad*, 139, 179–87.

Koistinen, *Arsenal of World War II*, 499.

Tissier, *Slaughter at Halbe*, 178.

Lewis, *The Mammoth Book of Eyewitness World War II*, 543.

Lilly, *Taken by Force*, 146–63.

Linderman, *The World Within War*, 176.

Litvin, *800 Days on the Eastern Front*, 66–72, 114, 121.

"Diary of First Lieutenant Sugihara Kinryu," 121, 123, 130–31, 133.

Louis, *Imperialism at Bay*, 532–47.

Lyons, *World War II*, 275–76, 279–80, 329, 333–36.

Mann, "Japanese Defense of Bataan, Luzon, Philippine Islands," 1149–76.

Marston, *Phoenix from the Ashes*, 79–110, 217–39.

McManus, *Deadly Sky*, 263.

Meadows, *The Comanche Code Talkers of World War II*, 35–72.

Merridale, *Ivan's War*, 277–79, 287, 305–20, 336–37, 381–82.

Middlebrook, *Arnhem, 1944*, 402–17, 456.

Millett, "The United States Armed Forces in the Second World War," 84.

Ministry of Foreign Affairs of Japan, "Statement by Chief Cabinet Secretary Kiichi Miyazawa on History Textbooks," August 26, 1982, http://www.mofa.go.jp/policy/postwar/state8208.html

Mitcham, *Hitler's Legions*, 440.

Mitcham, *Panzers in Winter*, 95–111.

Mitsuru, *Requiem for Battleship Yamato*, 100, 108, 117, 140–41, 152.

Morison, *History of U.S. Naval Operations, Vol. XIV*, 389–92.

Muang, *Burmese Nationalist Movements*, 110–29.

Murray, "British Military Effectiveness in the Second World War," 129.

Murray and Millett, *A War to be Won*, 335, 365–66, 368–73, 437–44, 446–47, 450–56, 457–63, 469–77, 479–83, 487–89, 491, 493–503, 506–07, 511–15, 519–20, 522, 525–39, 557–61, 565–69.

Neillands, *The Bomber War*, 351–66.

Neufeld and Berenbaum, eds., *The Bombing of Auschwitz*.

Ohnuki-Tierney, *Kamikaze Diaries*, 170.

Overton, *God Isn't Here*, 238.

Perret, *Winged Victory*), 451.

Polonsky and Michlic, eds., *The Neighbors Respond*.

Potter and Nimitz, *Sea Power*, 788–89.

Reese, *A Stranger to Myself*, 165, 564.

Rhodes, *Masters of Death*, 198, 697.

Roberts, *Stalin's Wars*, 180–95, 217–25, 228–53, 260–61, 263, 265, 280–94.

Ryan, *A Bridge Too Far*, 347–49.

Sarantakes, *Allies Against the Rising Sun*, 148–216.

Schrijvers, *The GI War*, 236, 249–60.

Schrijvers, *The Unknown Dead*, 370.

Searle, "'It Made a Lot of Sense to Kill Skilled Workers'," 103–34.

Segesser, "On the Road to Total Retribution? The International Debate on the Punishment of War Crimes, 1872–1945," 362–74.

Sheftall, *Blossoms in the Wind*, 338–51.

Skates, *The Invasion of Japan*, 134–45, 179–216.

Skulski, *Anatomy of the Ship*, 10–11.

Sledge, *With the Old Breed*, 224–25, 235, 270, 292–300.

Smith, *American Diplomacy During the Second World War*, 122–26.

Spector, *Eagle Against the Sun*, 418–20, 429–30, 437–39, 441–42, 493–95, 499–503, 512–16, 523–24, 527–30, 532–34, 538, 540–46.

Stanton, *Order of Battle U.S. Army*, 105–6.

Stokesbury, *A Short History of World War II*, 243–44, 324–26, 280, 287, 332, 342–48, 353–62, 367–73.

Stoler, *Allies in War*, 192–201.

Stone, *War Summits*, 221–24.

Story, *Concise Historical Atlas of World War Two*, 48, 56, 60, 62, 64, 66, 68, 70, 90, 92, 94, 98, 100, 102, 104.

Sturma, *The USS Flier*, 65–72, 85–104.

Suleiman, *Crises of Memory and the Second World War*, 132–59.

Taylor, *Dresden*, xiii, 148–65, 360–72.

Terkel, *"The Good War,"* 196.

Thorne, *Allies of a Kind,* 586–651, 675–88.

Tomasevich, *War and Revolution in Yugoslavia,* 751–85.

Tooze, *The Wages of Destruction,* 461–85, 513–51.

Ungvary, *The Siege of Budapest,* 188, 348–57, 374.

Vego, *The Battle for Leyte,* 335.

Weigley, *Eisenhower's Lieutenants,* 65, 204.

Weinberg, *A World at Arms,* 527, 659–60, 703–08, 713–120, 731–34, 758–60, 769, 776–79, 810–11, 813–14, 816–18, 826–27, 856, 860–66, 881, 894–96, 899–900, 902–13.

White, "Losses in the Second World War," *Historical Atlas of the Twentieth Century,* http://users.erols.com/mwhite28/ww2-loss.htm.

Whiting, *The Battle of Hurtgen Forest,* 53, 98, 224–25.

Wood, *Worshipping the Myths of World War II,* 71–127.

Wood and Jankowski, *Karski.*

Wukovits, *Devotion to Duty,* 141–58.

Yelton, "'Ein Volk Steht Auf,'" 10, 61–83.

Yelton, *Hitler's Volkssturm,* 7–35.

Yoneyama, "For Transformative Knowledge and Postnationalist Public Spheres," 449–64.

Zeiler, *Unconditional Defeat,* 106–112, 114–15, 117–120, 124–26, 128–30, 132–44, 150–54, 157–58, 160–64, 166–70, 177–83, 185–92.

Zumbro, *Battle for the Ruhr,* 227.

BIBLIOGRAPHY

Abrams, Bradley F. "The Second World War and the East European Revolution," *East European Politics and Societies* 16, Fall 2002, 623–664.

Adair, Paul. *Hitler's Greatest Defeat: The Collapse of Army Group Centre, June 1944.* London: Cassell and Co., 2001.

Adams, Michael C.C. *The Best War Ever: America and World War II.* Baltimore: The Johns Hopkins University Press, 1994.

Adelman, Jonathan R. "German-Japanese Relations, 1941–1945" in *Hitler and His Allies in World War II.* Edited by Jonathan R. Adelman. London: Routledge, 2007.

Addison, Paul and Jeremy A. Crang, eds. *The Burning Blue: A New History of the Battle of Britain.* London: Pimlico, 2000.

Agarossi, Elena. *A Nation Collapses: The Italian Surrender of September 1943.* Cambridge: Cambridge University Press, 2000.

Allan, James R. *In the Trade of War.* Tunbridge Wells, UK: Parapress, Ltd., 1994.

Alexander, Joseph H. *The Final Campaign: Marines in the Victory of Okinawa.* Washington, DC: Marine Corps Historical Center, 1996.

Alexander, Joseph H. *Utmost Savagery: The Three Days of Tarawa.* Annapolis: Naval Institute Press, 1995.

Alexander, Martin S. *The Republic in Danger: General Maurice Gamelin and the Politics of French Defence, 1933–1940.* Cambridge: Cambridge University Press, 1992.

Alexander, Martin S., and William J. Philpott. *Anglo-French Defence Relations between the Wars.* Houndsmill, England: Palgrave Macmillan, 2002.

Allen, Louis. *Burma: The Longest War, 1941–45.* New York: St. Martin's Press, 1984.

Alperovitz, Gar. *The Decision to Use the Atomic Bomb.* New York: Vintage Books, 1996.

Ambrose, Stephen E. *D-Day, June 6, 1944: The Climactic Battle of World War II.* New York: Simon & Schuster, 1994.

Ambrose, Stephen E. *The Good Fight: How World War II Was Won* (New York: Atheneum, 2001).

Ambrose, Stephen E. *The Wild Blue: The Men and Boys Who Flew the B-24s Over Germany.* New York: Simon and Schuster, 2001.

Andrew, Christopher. "British-Polish Intelligence Collaboration During the Second World War in Historical Perspective." In *Intelligence Cooperation Between Poland and Great Britain During World War II,* edited by Tessa Stirling, Daria Nalecz, and Tadeusz Dubicki. Edgware, Middlesex, Great Britain: Vallentine Mitchell, 2005.

Arvin, Nick. *Articles of War: A Novel.* New York: Anchor Books, 2006.

Astor, Gerald. *The Bloody Forest: Battle for the Huertgen: September 1944-January 1945.* Novato, CA: Presidio, 2000.

Astor, Gerald. *Operation Iceberg: The Invasion and Conquest of Okinawa in World War II.* New York: Dell Publishing, 1995.

Atkinson, Rick. *An Army at Dawn: The War in North Africa, 1942–1943.* New York: Owl Books, 2002.

Atkinson, Rick. *The Day of Battle: The War in Sicily and Italy, 1943–1944.* New York: Henry Holt and Company, 2007.

Australian Broadcasting Corporation. *The Men Who Saved Australia.* 1995, http://www.abc.net.au/4corners/stories/s12899.htm (accessed November 23, 2009).

Badsey, Stephen. "Culture, Controversy, Caen and Cherbourg." In *The Normandy Campaign, 1944: Sixty Years On,* edited by John Buckley. London: Routledge, 2007.

Buchanan, Patrick. *Churchill, Hitler, and "The Unnecessary War": How Britain Lost Its Empire and the West Lost the World.* New York: Crown, 2008.

Baker, Nicholson. *Human Smoke: The Beginnings of World War II, the End of Civilization.* New York: Simon & Schuster, 2008.

Banham, Tony. *Not the Slightest Chance: The Defence of Hong Kong, 1941.* Vancouver: UBC Press, 2003.

Barbier, Mary Kathryn. "Deception and the Planning of D-Day." In *The Normandy Campaign, 1944: Sixty Years On,* edited by John Buckley. London: Routledge, 2007.

Barnett, Correlli. *Engage the Enemy More Closely: The Royal Navy in the Second World War.* New York: W.W. Norton and Company, 1991.

Barr, Niall. *Pendulum of War: The Three Battles of El Alamein.* Woodstock, NY: The Overlook Press, 2004.

Barrett, David P and Larry N. Shyu. *China in the Anti-Japanese War, 1937–1945.* New York: Peter Lang, 2001.

Bartholomew-Feis, Dixie R. *The OSS and Ho Chi Minh: Unexpected Allies in the War Against Japan.* Lawrence: University Press of Kansas, 2006.

Bartov, Omer. *Hitler's Army: Soldiers, Nazis, and War in the Third Reich.* New York: Oxford University Press, 1991.

Bartov, Omer. *Mirrors of Destruction: War, Genocide, and Modern Identity.* New York: Oxford University Press, 2000.

Bartsch, William H. *December 8, 1941: MacArthur's Pearl Harbor.* College Station: Texas A&M University Press, 2003.

Baynes, John. *Urquhart of Arnhem: The Life of Major General RE Urquhart, CB, DSO.* London: Brassey's, 1993.

Bayly, Christopher and Tim Harper. *Forgotten Armies: The Fall of British Asia, 1941–1945.* Cambridge: Belknap Press, 2004.

BBC News, "Japan Textbook Angers Chinese, Korean Press," April 6, 2005. http://news.bbc.co.uk/2/hi/asia-pacific/4416593.stm (accessed November 23, 2009).

Beavan, Colin. *Operation Jedburgh: D-Day and America's First Shadow War.* New York: Viking, 2006.

Beevor, Antony, ed. *A Writer at War: Vasily Grossman with the Red Army, 1941–1945.* New York: Pantheon Books, 2005.

Beevor, Antony. *The Battle for Spain: The Spanish Civil War, 1936–1939. London: Phoenix, 2007.*

Beevor, Antony. *Berlin: The Downfall, 1945.* London: Penguin Books, 2004.

Beevor, Antony. *Crete: The Battle and the Resistance.* Boulder: Westview Press, 1994.

Beevor, Antony. *Stalingrad.* London: Penguin Books, 1998.

Bekker, Cajus. *The Luftwaffe War Diaries.* New York: Ballantine Books, 1964.

Bell, P. M. H. *The Origins of the Second World War in Europe.* London: Longman Group, 1989.

Bellamy, Chris. *Absolute War: Soviet Russia in the Second World War.* New York: Alfred A. Knopf, 2007.

Bennett, G. H. *Destination Normandy: Three American Regiments on D-Day.* Westport: Praeger Security International, 2007.

Benioff, David. *City of Thieves: A Novel.* New York: Viking, 2008.

Bercuson, David J. and Holger H. Herwig. *The Destruction of the Bismarck.* Woodstock, NY: The Overlook Press, 2001.

Berger, Sid. *Breaching Fortress Europe: The Story of U.S. Engineers in Normandy on D-Day.* Dubuque, IA: Kendall Hunt Publishing, 1994.

Berkhoff, Karel C. *Harvest of Despair: Life and Death in Ukraine Under Nazi Rule.* Cambridge: Belknap Press, 2004.

Bess, Michael. *Choices Under Fire: Moral Dimensions of World War II.* New York: Alfred A. Knopf, 2006.

Best, Antony. *Britain, Japan and Pearl Harbor: Avoiding War in East Asia, 1936–41.* London: LSE/ Routledge, 1995.

Bethell, Nicholas. *The War Hitler Won: The Fall of Poland, September 1939.* New York: Holt, Rinehart and Winston, 1972.

Bethell, Nicholas. *World War II: Russia Besieged.* Alexandria, VA: Time-Life Books, 1977.

Biddle, Tami Davis. "Dresden 1945: Reality, History, and Memory." *Journal of Military History* 72 (April 2008): 413–449.

Biddle, Tami Davis. *Rhetoric and Reality in Air Warfare: The Evolution of British and American Ideas about Strategic Bombing, 1914–1945.* Princeton: Princeton University Press, 2002.

Biderman, Gottlob Herbert. *In Deadly Combat: A German Soldier's Memoir of the Eastern Front.* Lawrence: University Press of Kansas, 2000.

Bird, Keith W. *Erich Raeder: Admiral of the Third Reich.* Annapolis: Naval Institute Press, 2006.

Bird, Keith W. "The German Navy in World War II." In *Reevaluating Major Naval Combatants of World War II,* edited By James J. Sadkovich. New York: Greenwood Press, 1990.

Bierman, John, and Colin Smith. *The Battle of Alamein: Turning Point, World War II.* New York: Penguin, 2002.

Bishop, Chris, ed. *The Encyclopedia of Weapons of World War II.* New York: MetroBooks, 2002.

Bix, Herbert P. *Hirohito and the Making of Modern Japan.* New York: Perennial, 2001.

Blair, Clay. *Hitler's U-Boat War.* Vol. 1, *The Hunters, 1939–1942.* New York: Random House, 1996.

Blair, Clay. *Hitler's U-Boat War.* Vol. 2, *The Hunted, 1942–1945.* New York: Random House, 1996.

Blatt, Joel, ed. *The French Defeat of 1940: Reassessments.* Providence: Berghahn Books, 1998.

"The Bloody Battle of Tarawa." http://www.eyewitnesstohistory.com/tarawa.htm (accessed November 23, 2009).

Blumenson, Martin. *World War II: Liberation.* Alexandria, VA: Time-Life Books, 1978.

Boatner, Mark M., III. *The Biographical Dictionary of World War II.* Novato, CA: Presidio Press, 1996.

Bookspan. *Slaughterhouse: the Encyclopedia of the Eastern Front.* Garden City, The Military Book Club, 2002.

Boot, Max. *War Made New: Weapons, Warriors, and the Making of the Modern World.* New York: Gotham Books, 2007.

Borch, Fred, and Daniel Martinez. *Kimmel, Short, and Pearl Harbor: The Final Report Revealed.* Annapolis: Naval Institute Press, 2005.

Bosworth, R. J. B. *Mussolini.* London: Arnold, 2002.

Botjer, George F. *Sideshow War: The Italian Campaign, 1943–1945.* College Station: Texas A&M University Press, 1996.

Botman, Selma. "The Liberal Age, 1923–1952." In *The Cambridge History of Egypt*, Vol. 2, *Modern Egypt, from 1517 to the End of the Twentieth Century*, edited by M.W. Daly. Cambridge: Cambridge University Press, 1998.

Bourke, Joanna. "Barbarisation vs Civilisation in Time of War." In *The Barbarization of Warfare*, edited by George Kassimeris. New York: New York University Press, 2006.

Bourke, Joanna. *An Intimate History of Killing: Face-to-Face Killing in Twentieth-Century Warfare*. London: Basic Books, 1999.

Bourke, Joanna. *The Second World War: A People's History*. Oxford: Oxford University Press, 2001.

Bowen, Wayne H. *Spain During World War II*. Columbia: University of Missouri Press, 2006.

Boyd, Carl. "Japanese Military Effectiveness: The Interwar Period." In *Military Effectiveness*, Vol. 2, *The Interwar Period*, edited by Allan R. Millett and Williamson Murray. Boston: Allen and Unwin, 1988.

Boyd, Carl and Akihiko Yoshida. *The Japanese Submarine Force and World War II*. Annapolis: Naval Institute Press, 1995.

Bradley, James. *Flags of Our Fathers*. New York: Bantam Books, 2000.

Bradley, James. *Flyboys: A True Story of Courage*. Boston: Little, Brown, and Company, 2003.

Bradley, Omar N. *A Soldier's Story*. New York: The Modern Library, 1999.

Braithwaite, Rodric. *Moscow 1941: A City and Its People at War*. London: Profile Books Ltd., 2006.

Brett, Michael. "The Maghrib." In *The Cambridge History of Africa*, Vol. 7, *From 1905 to 1940*, edited by A. D. Roberts. Cambridge: Cambridge University Press, 1986.

Breyer, Siegfried. *Battleships and Battle Cruisers, 1905–1970*. Garden City: Doubleday and Co., Inc., 1973.

Brion, Irene. *Lady GI: A Woman's War in the South Pacific*. Novato, CA: Presidio, 1997.

Broekmeyer, Marius. *Stalin, the Russians, and Their War, 1941–1945*. Madison: University of Wisconsin Press, 2004.

Brokaw, Tom. *The Greatest Generation*. New York: Random House, 1998.

Brown, David. *Warship Losses of World War Two*. London: Arms and Armour, 1990.

Buell, Thomas. *Master of Sea Power: A Biography of Fleet Admiral Ernest J. King*. Annapolis: Naval Institute Press, 1980.

Burma Star Association. "The Kohima Epitaph." http://www.burmastar.org.uk/epitaph.htm (accessed November 23, 2009).

Burrell, Robert S. *Ghosts of Iwo Jima*. College Station: Texas A&M University, 2006.

Buruma, Ian. *The Wages of Guilt: Memories of War in Germany and Japan*. London: Phoenix, 1994.

Callahan, Raymond. *Churchill and His General*. Lawrence: University Press of Kansas, 2007.

Calvocoressi, Peter, and Guy Wint. *Total War: The Story of World War II*. New York: Pantheon Books, 1972.

Cameron, Craig M. *American Samurai: Myth, Imagination, and the Conduct of Battle in the First Marine Division, 1941–1951*. New York: Cambridge University Press, 1994.

Campbell, D'Ann. "Women in Combat: The World War II Experience in the United States, Great Britain, Germany, and the Soviet Union." *Journal of Military History* 57 (April 1993): 301–23.

Campbell, John. *Naval Weapons of World War Two*. London: Conway Maritime Press, 1985.

Cannon, M. Hamlin. *United States Army in World War II: The War in the Pacific; Leyte, The Return to the Philippines.* Washington, DC: Office of the Chief of the Chief of Military History, 1954.

Cardozier, V. R. *The Mobilization of the United States in World War II: How the Government, Military, and Industry Prepared for War.* Jefferson, NC: McFarland and Company, Inc., 1995.

Carley, Michael Jabara. *1939: The Alliance That Never Was and the Coming of World War II.* Chicago: Ivan R. Dee, 1999.

Carr, Edward Hallett. *The Twenty Years' Crisis, 1919–1939: An Introduction to the Study of International Relations.* New York: Harper and Row, Publishers, 1964.

Carter, Carolle J. *Mission to Yenan: American Liaison with the Chinese Communists, 1944–1947.* Lexington: The University Press of Kentucky, 1997.

Caruso, Patrick F. *Nightmare on Iwo.* Annapolis: Naval Institute Press, 2001.

Chaney, Otto Preston. *Zhukov.* Rev. ed. Norman: University of Oklahoma Press, 1996.

Chang, Iris. *The Rape of Nanking: The Forgotten Holocaust of World War II.* New York: Penguin Books, 1998.

Cherepenina, Nadezhda. "Assessing the Scale of Famine and Death in the Besieged City." In *Life and Death in Besieged Leningrad, 1941–44,* edited by John Barber and Andrei Dzeniskevich. Houndsmill, England: Palgrave Macmillan, 2005.

Chesneau, Roger, ed. *Conway's All the World's Fighting Ships: 1922–1946.* New York: Mayflower Books, 1980.

Chickering, Roger, and Stig Forster. "Are We There Yet?: World War II and the Theory of Total War." In *A World at Total War: Global Conflict and the Politics of Destruction, 1937–1945,* edited by Roger Chickering, Stig Forster, and Bernd Greiner. Cambridge: Cambridge University Press, 2005.

Ch'i, Hsi-Sheng. *Nationalist China at War: Military Defeats and Political Collapse, 1937–45.* Ann Arbor: University of Michigan Press, 1982.

Christ, James F. *Mission Raise Hell: The U.S. Marines on Choiseul, October–November 1943.* Annapolis: Naval Institute Press, 2006.

Churchill, Winston S. *The Second World War.* Vol. 3. Boston: Houghton Mifflin Company, 1948–1953.

Chwialkowski, Paul. *In Caesar's Shadow: The Life of General Robert Eichelberger.* Westport: Greenwood Press, 1993.

Ciechanowski, Jan Stanislaw, and Jacek Tebinka. "Cryptographic Cooperation-Enigma." In *Intelligence Co-Operation Between Poland and Great Britain During World War II,* edited by Tessa Stirling, Daria Nalecz, and Tadeusz Dubicki. Edgware, Middlesex, Great Britain: Vallentine Mitchell, 2005.

Ciechanowski, Jan. "Reports on the Holocaust." In *Intelligence Co-Operation Between Poland and Great Britain During World War II,* edited by Tessa Stirling, Daria Nalecz, and Tadeusz Dubicki. Edgware, Middlesex, Great Britain: Vallentine Mitchell, 2005.

Citino, Robert M. *Death of the Wehrmacht: The German Campaigns of 1942.* Lawrence: University of Kansas Press, 2007.

Citino, Robert M. *The Path to Blitzkrieg: Doctrine and Training in the German Army, 1920–1939.* Boulder: Lynne Rienner Publishers, 1999.

Claasen, Adam R. A. *Hitler's Northern War: The Luftwaffe's Ill-Fated Campaign, 1940–1945.* Lawrence: University of Kansas Press, 2001.

Clark, Lloyd. *Anzio: Italy and the Battle for Rome—1944.* New York: Atlantic Monthly Press, 2007.

Clark, Lloyd. *Crossing the Rhine: Breaking Into Nazi Germany, 1944–1945—The Greatest Airborne Battles in History.* New York: Atlantic Monthly Press, 2008.

Clemens, Martin. *Alone on Guadalcanal: A Coastwatcher's Story.* Annapolis: Naval Institute Press, 1998.

Cline, Ray S. *United States Army in World War II: The War Department; Washington Command Post; The Operations Division.* Washington, DC: Office of the Chief of Military History, 1951.

Coates, John. *Bravery Above Blunder: The 9th Australian Division at Finschhafen, Sattelberg, and Sio.* South Melbourne: Oxford University Press, 1999.

Condon-Rall, Mary Ellen, and Albert E. Cowdrey. *United States Army in World War II: The Technical Services: The Medical Department: Medical Service in the War Against Japan.* Washington, DC: Center of Military History of the United States Army, 1998.

Connelly, Mark. *Reaching for the Stars: A New History of Bomber Command in World War II.* London: I.B. Tauris, Publishers, 2001.

Cook, Haruko Taya, and Theodore F. Cook. *Japan at War: An Oral History.* New York: The New Press, 1992.

Cooke, James J. *Billy Mitchell.* Boulder: Lynne Rienner, Publishers, 2002.

Coombe, Jack D. *Derailing the Tokyo Express: The Naval Battles for the Solomon Islands that Sealed Japan's Fate.* Harrisburg, PA: Stackpole Books, 1991.

Cooper, Matthew. *The German Army, 1933–1945: Its Political and Military Failure.* New York: Stein and Day, Publishers, 1978.

Coox, Alvin D. "Needless Fear: The Compromise of U.S. Plans to Invade Japan in 1945." *Journal of Military History* 64 (April 2000): 411–38.

Coox, Alvin D. *Nomonhon: Japan Against Russia, 1939.* Stanford: Stanford University Press, 1985.

Coox, Alvin D. "The Effectiveness of the Japanese Military Establishment in the Second World War." In *Military Effectiveness.* Vol. 3, *The Second World War,* edited by Allan R. Millett and Williamson Murray. Boston: Allen and Unwin, 1988.

Copp, Terry. *Cinderella Army: The Canadians in Northwest Europe, 1944–1945.* Toronto: University of Toronto Press, 2006.

Copp, Terry. *Fields of Fire: The Canadians in Normandy.* Toronto: University of Toronto Press, 2003.

Copp, Terry, and Bill McAndrew. *Battle Exhaustion: Soldiers and Psychiatrists in the Canadian Army, 1939–1945.* Montreal: McGill-Queen's University Press, 1990.

Corti, Eugenio. *Few Returned: Twenty-eight Days on the Russian Front, Winter 1942–1943.* Columbia: University of Missouri Press, 1997.

Corum, James S., and Richard R. Muller. *The Luftwaffe's Way of War: German Air Force Doctrine, 1911–1945.* Baltimore: The Nautical and Aviation Publishing Company of America, Inc., 1998.

Crane, Conrad C. *Bombs, Cities, and Civilians: American Airpower Strategy in World War II.* Lawrence: University of Kansas Press, 1993.

Craven, Frank W., and James L. Cate, eds. *The Army Air Forces in World War II.* Vol. 1, *Plans and Early Operations-January 1939-August 1942.* Chicago: University of Chicago Press, 1948.

Crawford, John, ed. *Kia Kaha: New Zealand in the Second World War.* Oxford: Oxford University Press, 2000.

Cressman, Robert J. *The Official Chronology of the U.S. Navy in World War II.* Annapolis: Naval Institute Press, 2000.

Crow, Duncan, ed. *Armoured Fighting Vehicles in Profile.* Vol. 4, *American AFVs of World War II.* Garden City: Doubleday and Company, 1972.

Cruikshank, Charles. *Deception in World War II.* Oxford: Oxford University Press, 1979.

Davies, Norman. *No Simple Victory: World War II in Europe, 1939-1945.* New York: Penguin, 2006.

Davis, Richard G. *Carl A. Spaatz and the Air War in Europe.* Washington, DC: Smithsonian Institution Press, 1992.

Day, David. *Reluctant Nation: Australia and the Allied Defeat of Japan, 1942-45.* Oxford: Oxford University Press, 1992.

Dear, I. C. B., ed. *The Oxford Companion to World War II.* Oxford: Oxford University Press, 2005.

De Bruhl, Marshall. *Firestorm: Allied Airpower and the Destruction of Dresden.* New York: Random House, 2006.

De Jong, L. *The Collapse of a Colonial Society: The Dutch in Indonesia during the Second World War.* Leiden, the Netherlands: KITLV Press, 2002.

Denfield, D. Colt. *Hold the Marianas: The Japanese Defense of the Mariana Islands.* Shippensburg, PA: White Mane Publishing Company, Inc., 1997.

D'Este, Carlo. *Decision in Normandy.* New York: Harper Collins, 1983.

D'Este, Carlo. *Fatal Decision: Anzio and the Battle for Rome.* New York: HarperCollins Publishers, 1990.

D'Este, Carlo. *Patton: A Genius for War.* New York: HarperCollins Perennial, 1995.

D'Este, Carlo. *Warlord: The Life of Winston Churchill at War, 1874-1945.* New York: HarperCollins Publishers, 2008.

D.W. World. DE Deutsche Welle, "Germany Sues Italy to Block World War II Compensation Claims." December 24, 2008. http://www.dw-world.de/dw/article/0,,3899824,00.html (accessed November 23, 2009).

Dickson, Paul D. "The Politics of Army Expansion: General H.D.G. Crerar and the Creation of First Canadian Army, 1940-41." *Journal of Military History* 60 (April 1996): 271-98.

DiNardo, Richard L. *Germany and the Axis Powers: From Coalition to Collapse.* Lawrence: University of Kansas Press, 2005.

Divine, Robert. *The Reluctant Belligerent: American Entry into World War II.* New York: McGraw-Hill, Inc., 1979.

Doig, Ivan. *The Eleventh Man: A Novel.* Orlando: Harcourt, Inc., 2008.

Dollinger, Hans. *The Decline and Fall of Nazi Germany and Imperial Japan: A Pictorial History of the Final Days of World War II.* New York: Bonanza Books, 1965, 1967.

Donahue, James A. *Guadalcanal Journal.* http://www.guadalcanaljournal.com/guadalcana12.html (accessed November 23, 2009).

Doolittle, James H. *I Could Never Be So Lucky Again: An Autobiography.* New York: Bantam Books, 1991.

Doughty, Robert Allan. *The Breaking Point: Sedan and the Fall of France.* Hamden: Archon Books, 1990.

Dower, John. *War Without Mercy: Race and Power in the Pacific War.* New York: Pantheon Books, 1986.

Drea, Edward J. *In the Service of the Emperor: Essays on the Imperial Japanese Army* Lincoln: University of Nebraska Press, 1998.

Dulffer, Jost. *Nazi Germany, 1933–1945: Faith and Annihilation.* London: Hodder Headline Group, 1996.

Dull, Paul S. *A Battle History of the Imperial Japanese Navy (1941–1945).* Annapolis: Naval Institute Press, 1978.

Dunn, Walter S., Jr. *Kursk: Hitler's Gamble, 1943.* Westport: Praeger, 1997.

Dunn, Walter S., Jr. *The Soviet Economy and the Red Army, 1930–1945.* Westport: Praeger, 1995.

Dunn, Walter S., Jr. *Stalin's Keys to Victory: The Rebirth of the Red Army.* Westport: Praeger Publishers, 2006.

DuPuy, Trevor. *A Genius for War: The German Army and General Staff, 1807–1945.* Englewood Cliffs, NJ: Prentice-Hall, Inc., 1977.

Duroselle, Jean-Baptiste. *France and the Nazi Threat: The Collapse of French Diplomacy, 1932–1939.* New York: Enigma Books, 2004.

Early, Charity Adams. *One Woman's Army: A Black Officer Remembers the WAC.* College Station: Texas A&M University Press, 1989.

Edgerton, Robert. B. *Warriors of the Rising Sun: A History of the Japanese Military.* New York: W.W. Norton and Company, 1997.

Ehlers, Robert S., Jr. *Targeting the Third Reich: Air Intelligence and the Allied Bombing Campaigns.* Lawrence: University Press of Kansas, 2009.

Ellis, John. *World War II-A Statistical Survey.* New York: Facts on File, 1993.

English, Allan D. *The Cream of the Crop: Canadian Aircrew, 1939–1945.* Montreal: McGill-Queen's University Press, 1996.

English, John A. *The Canadian Army and the Normandy Campaign: A Study of Failure in High Command.* Westport: Praeger, 1991.

Erickson, John. "New Thinking about the Eastern Front in World War II." *Journal of Military History* 56 (April 1992): 283–92.

Erickson, John. *The Road to Berlin: Continuing the History of Stalin's War with Germany.* Boulder: Westview Press, 1983.

Evans, David C., and Mark R. Peattie. *Kaigun: Strategy, Tactics, and Technology in the Imperial Japanese Navy, 1887–1941.* Annapolis: Naval Institute Press, 1997.

Fanning, William J., Jr. "The Origin of the Term 'Blitzkrieg': Another View." *Journal of Military History* 61 (April 1997): 283–302.

Farrell, Brian and Sandy Hunter, eds. *Sixty Years On: The Fall of Singapore Revisited.* Singapore: Eastern Universities Press, 2002.

Fay, Peter Ward. *The Forgotten Army: India's Armed Struggle for Independence, 1942–1945.* Ann Arbor: University of Michigan Press, 1993.

Ferguson, Niall. *The War of the World: Twentieth-Century Conflict and the Descent of the West.* New York: Penguin Books, 2006.

Fieldhouse, D. K. *Colonialism, 1870–1945: An Introduction.* New York: St. Martin's Press, 1981.

Finney, Patrick, ed. *The Origins of the Second World War.* London: Arnold, 1997.

FitzGibbon, Constantine. *The Winter of the Bombs: The Story of the Blitz of London.* New York: W.W. Norton & Company, Inc., 1957.

Ford, Douglas. *Britain's Secret War Against Japan, 1937–1945.* London: Routledge, 2006.

Forster, Jurgen E. "The Dynamics of Volksgemeinschaft: The Effectiveness of the German Military Establishment in the Second World War." In *Military Effectiveness,* Vol. 3, *The Second World War,* edited by Allan R. Millett and Williamson Murray. Boston: Allen and Unwin, 1988.

Frank, Richard B. *Downfall: The End of the Imperial Japanese Empire.* New York: Random House, 1999.

Frank, Richard B. *Guadalcanal: The Definitive Account of the Landmark Battle.* New York: Penguin Books, 1990.

Fraser, David. *Knight's Cross: The Life of Field Marshal Erwin Rommel.* New York: HarperPerennial, 1995.

Freeman, Roger A. *Mighty Eighth War Diary.* London: Jane's Publishing Company Ltd., 1981.

Frei, Henry. *Guns of February: Ordinary Japanese Soldiers' Views of the Malayan Campaign and the Fall of Singapore, 1941-42.* Singapore: National University of Singapore, 2004.

Frei, Henry P. "The Island Battle: Japanese Soldiers Remember the Conquest of Singapore." In *Sixty Years On: The Fall of Singapore Revisited,* edited by Brian Farrell and Sandy Hunter. Singapore: Eastern Universities Press, 2002.

Friedlander, Saul. *The Years of Extermination: Nazi Germany and the Jews, 1939-1945.* New York: HarperCollins Publishers, 2007.

Friedman, Norman. *U.S. Aircraft Carriers: An Illustrated Design History.* Annapolis: Naval Institute Press, 1983.

Friedman, Norman. *U.S. Amphibious Ships and Craft: An Illustrated Design History.* Annapolis: Naval Institute Press, 2002.

Friedman, Norman. *U.S. Naval Weapons: Every Gun, Missile, Mine and Torpedo Used by the U.S. Navy from 1883 to Present Day.* Annapolis: Naval Institute Press, 1985.

Frieser, Karl-Heinz, and John T. Greenwood. *The Blitzkrieg Legend: The 1940 Campaign in the West.* Annapolis: Naval Institute Press, 2005.

Fritz, Stephen G. *Endkampf: Soldiers, Civilians, and the Death of the Third Reich.* Lexington: University Press of Kentucky, 2004.

Fritz, Stephen G. *Frontsoldaten: The German Soldier in World War II.* Lexington: University of Kentucky Press, 1995.

Fugate, Bryan I., and Lev Dvoretsky. *Thunder on the Dnepr: Zhukov-Stalin and the Defeat of Hitler's Blitzkrieg.* Novato, CA: Presidio Press, 1997.

Funk, Arthur Layton. *Hidden Ally: The French Resistance, Special Operations, and the Landings in Southern France, 1944.* New York: Greenwood Press, 1992.

Fussell, Paul. *Wartime: Understanding and Behavior in the Second World War.* New York: Oxford University Press, 1989.

Gailey, Harry A. *MacArthur Strikes Back: Decision at Buna, New Guinea, 1942-1943.* Navato, CA: Presidio, 2000.

Gailey, Harry A. *MacArthur's Victory: The War in New Guinea, 1943-1944.* New York: Ballantine Books, 2004.

Gander, Terry, and Peter Chamberlain. *Weapons of the Third Reich.* Garden City: Doubleday and Co., Inc., 1979.

Gannon, Michael. *Operation Drumbeat: The Dramatic True Story of Germany's First U-Boat Attacks along the American Coast in World War II.* New York: Harper and Row, Publishers, 1990.

Garbatov, Boris. "The Camp at Majdanek." In *World War II: Dispatches from the Soviet Front,* edited by S. Krasilshchik. New York: Sphinx Press, Inc., 1985.

Garlinski, Jozef. *Poland in the Second World War.* New York: Hippocrene Books, 1985.

Gat, Azar. *British Armour Theory and the Rise of the Panzer Arm: Revising the Revisionists.* Houndsmill, England: Macmillan Press, 2000.

Gatu, Dagfinn. *Village China at War: The Impact of Resistance to Japan, 1937-1945.* Vancouver: UBC Press, 2008).

Gebhardt, James F., ed. *Fighting for the Soviet Motherland: Recollections from the Eastern Front Hero of the Soviet Union, Dmitriy Loza.* Lincoln: University of Nebraska Press, 1998.

Gellately, Robert. "The Third Reich, the Holocaust, and Visions of Serial Genocide." In *The Specter of Genocide: Mass Murder in Historical Perspective,* edited by Robert Gellately and Ben Kiernan. Cambridge: Cambridge University Press, 2003.

Gentile, Gian P. *How Effective is Strategic Bombing: Lessons Learned from World War II to Kosovo.* New York: New York University Press, 2001.

Giangreco, D. M. "Casualty Projections for the U.S. Invasions of Japan, 1945–1946: Planning and Policy Implications." *Journal of Military History* 61 (July 1997): 521–82.

Gilbert, Martin. *The Second World War: A Complete History.* Rev. ed. New York: Henry Holt, 1989.

Gilmore, Donald L., ed. *U.S. Army Atlas of the European Theater in World War II.* New York: Barnes and Noble, 2004.

Giurescu, Dinu C. *Romania in the Second World War (1939–1945).* New York: Columbia University Press, 2000.

Glantz, David M. *Colossus Reborn: The Red Army at War, 1941–1943.* Lawrence: University of Kansas Press, 2005.

Glantz, David M. *Kharkov, 1942: Anatomy of a Military Disaster Through Soviet Eyes.* Shepperton, Surrey: Ian Allan Publishing, 1998.

Glantz, David M. *Red Storm Over the Balkans: The Failed Soviet Invasion of Romania, Spring 1944.* Lawrence: University of Kansas Press, 2007.

Glantz, David M., et al. *Slaughterhouse: The Handbook of the Eastern Front.* Bedford, PA: The Aberjona Press, 2005.

Glantz, David M. *Stumbling Colossus: The Red Army on the Eve of World War* Lawrence: University of Kansas Press, 1998.

Glantz, David M. *Zhukov's Greatest Defeat: The Red Army's Epic Disaster in Operation Mars, 1942.* Lawrence: University of Kansas Press, 1999.

Glover, Michael. *An Improvised War: The Ethiopian Campaign, 1940–1941.* London: Leo Cooper, 1987.

Goldberg, Harold J. *D-Day in the Pacific: The Battle of Saipan.* Bloomington: Indiana University Press, 2007.

Goldstein, Donald M., and Katherin V. Dillon, eds. *Fading Victory: The Diary of Admiral Matome Ugaki, 1941–1945.* Pittsburgh: University of Pittsburgh Press, 1991.

Gole, Henry G. *The Road to Rainbow: Army Planning for Global War, 1934–1940.* Annapolis: Naval Institute Press, 2003.

Gooch, John. *Mussolini and His Generals: The Armed Forces and Fascist Foreign Policy, 1922–1940.* Cambridge: Cambridge University Press, 2007.

Goolrick, William K., and Ogden Tanner. *World War II: The Battle of the Bulge* Alexandria, VA: Time-Life Books, 1979.

Gordon, David M. "The China-Japan War, 1931–1945." *The Journal of Military History* 70 (January 2006): 137–182.

Gorodetsky, Gabriel. *Grand Delusion: Stalin and the German Invasion of Russia.* New Haven: Yale University Press, 1999.

Graham, Michael B. *Mantle of Heroism: Tarawa and the Struggle for the Gilberts, November 1943.* Novato, CA: Presidio, 1993.

Grayling, A. C. *Among the Dead Cities: The History and Moral Legacy of the WWII Bombing of Civilians in Germany and Japan.* New York: Walker and Company, 2006.

Green, William. *Famous Bombers of the Second World War,* Vol. 1. Garden City: Hanover House, 1959.

Green, William. *Warplanes of the Second World War, Fighters, Vol. II.* Garden City: Doubleday & Co., 1961.

Greenfield, Kent Roberts. *American Strategy in World War II: A Reconsideration.* Baltimore: The John Hopkins University Press, 1963.

Grenkovich, Leonid D. *The Soviet Partisan Movement, 1941–1944: A Critical Historiographical Analysis.* London: Frank Cass, 1999.

Griffith, Thomas E., Jr. *MacArthur's Airman: General George C. Kenney and the War in the Southwest Pacific.* Lawrence: University Press of Kansas, 1998.

Grimsley, Mark. *The Hard Hand of War: Union Military Policy Toward Southern Civilians, 1861–1865.* Cambridge: Cambridge University Press, 1995.

Gross, Jan T. "Sovietisation of Poland's Eastern Territories." In *From Peace to War: Germany, Soviet Russia and the World, 1939–1941,* edited by Bernd Wegner. Providence: Berghahn Books, 1997.

Grossjohann, Georg. *Five Years, Four Fronts: The War Years of Georg Grossjohann, Major, German Army (Retired).* Bedford, PA: The Aberjona Press, 1999.

Gruhl, Werner. *Imperial Japan's World War Two, 1931–1945.* New Brunswick: Transaction Publishers, 2007.

Grunden, Walter E. *Secret Weapons and World War II: Japan in the Shadow of Big Science.* Lawrence: University of Kansas Press, 2005.

Guderian, Heinz. *Panzer Leader.* Cambridge: Da Capo Press, 1996.

Gunsburg, Jeffrey A. "The Battle of the Belgian Plain, 12–14 May 1940: The First Great Tank Battle." *Journal of Military History* 56 (April 1992): 207–44.

Gunsburg, Jeffery A. *Divided and Conquered: The French High Command and the Defeat of the West, 1940.* Westport: Greenwood Press, 1979.

Gunston, Bill. *World Encyclopedia of Aircraft Manufacturers.* Annapolis: Naval Institute Press, 1993.

Habeck, Mary R. *Storm of Steel: The Development of Armor Doctrine in Germany and the Soviet Union, 1919–1939.* Ithaca: Cornell University Press, 2003.

Hagan, Kenneth J., and Ian J. Bickerton. *Unintended Consequences: The United States at War.* London: Reaktion Books Ltd., 2007.

Hague, Arnold. *The Allied Convoy System, 1939–1945: Its Organization, Defense, and Operation.* Annapolis: Naval Institute Press, 2000.

Hall, R. Cargill, ed. *Case Studies in Strategic Bombardment.* Washington, DC: Air Force History and Museums Program, 1998.

Hall, Tony, ed. *D-Day: Operation Overlord: From Its Planning to the Liberation of Paris.* London: Salamander Books, Ltd., 1993.

Hallas, James H. *Killing Ground on Okinawa: The Battle for Sugar Loaf Hill.* Westport, CT: Praeger, 1996.

Hallion, Richard P. *Strike from the Sky: The History of Battlefield Air Attack, 1911–1945.* Washington, DC: Smithsonian Institution Press, 1989.

Hamburg Institute for Social Research. *Crimes of the German Wehrmacht: Dimensions of a War of Annihilation, 1941–1944: An Outline of the Exhibition.* Hamburg: Hamburger Edition, 2004, 3, 34. http://www.verbrechen-der-wehrmacht.de/pdf/vdw_en.pdf (accessed November 23, 2009).

Hamilton, Nigel. *Monty: the Battles of Field Marshal Bernard Montgomery.* New York: Random House, 1994.

Hansen, Randall. *Fire and Fury: The Allied Bombing of Germany.* New York: NAL Caliber, 2008.

Hardesty, Von. *Red Phoenix: The Rise of Soviet Air Power, 1941–1945.* Washington, DC: Smithsonian Institution Press, 1982.

Harries, Meirion and Susie. *Soldiers of the Sun: The Rise and Fall of the Imperial Japanese Army.* New York: Random House, 1991.

Harrison, Mark. *Accounting for War: Soviet Production, Employment, and the Defence Burden, 1940–1945.* Cambridge: Cambridge University Press, 1996.

Hasegawa, Tsuyoshi. *Racing the Enemy: Stalin, Truman, and the Surrender of Japan.* Cambridge: Belknap Press, 2005.

Haskew, Michael E. *The World War II Desk Reference.* New York: Grand Central Press, 2004.

Hastings, Max. *Bomber Command.* New York: Simon and Schuster, 1989.

Hastings, Max. *Das Reich: The March of the 2nd SS Panzer Division Through France.* New York: Holt, Rinehart & Winston, 1981.

Haunschmeid, Rudolf A., Jan-Ruth Mills, and Siegi Witzany-Durda. *St. Georgen Gusen Mauthausen: Concentration Camp Mauthausen Reconsidered.* St. Georgen an der Gusen, Germany: Books on Demand, 2008.

Hays, Otis, Jr. *Alaska's Hidden Wars: Secret Campaigns on the North Pacific Rim.* Fairbanks: University of Alaska Press, 2004.

Hayward, Joel S. A. *Stopped at Stalingrad: The Luftwaffe and Hitler's Defeat in the East, 1942–1943.* Lawrence: University of Kansas Press, 1998.

Hayward, Joel S. A. "Too Little, Too Late: An Analysis of Hitler's Failure in August 1942 to Damage Soviet Oil Production." *Journal of Military History* 64 (July 2000): 769–94.

Hebras, Robert. *Oradour-sur-Glane: The Tragedy Hour by Hour.* Monteuil-Bellay, France: Editions CMD, 1994.

Hedges, Chris. *War Is a Force That Gives US Meaning.* New York: Anchor, 2003.

Heer, Hannes. "Killing Fields: The Wehrmacht and the Holocaust in Belorussia, 1941–42." In *War of Extermination: The German Military in World War II,* edited by Hannes Heer and Klaus Naumann. New York: Berghahn Books, 2000.

Herwig, Holger. "Innovation Ignored: The Submarine Problem: Germany, Britain, and the United States, 1919–1939." In *Military Innovation in the Interwar Period,* edited by Williamson, Murray and Allan R. Millett. Cambridge: Cambridge University Press, 1996.

Hesketh, Roger. *Fortitude: The D-Day Deception Campaign.* Woodstock, NY: The Overlook Press, 2000.

Hicks, George. "The 'Comfort Women.'" In *The Japanese Wartime Empire, 1931–1945,* edited by Peter Duus, Ramon H. Myers, and Mark R. Peattie. Princeton: Princeton University Press, 1996.

Hinsley, F. H. *British Intelligence in the Second World War.* Abridged version. Cambridge: Cambridge University Press, 1993.

Hickham, Homer H., Jr. *Torpedo Junction: U-Boat War Off America's East Coast, 1942.* Annapolis: Naval Institute Press, 1989.

Hill, Alexander. *The War Behind the Eastern Front: The Soviet Partisan Movement in North-West Russia, 1941–1944.* London: Frank Cass, 2005.

Hionidou, Violetta. *Famine and Death in Occupied Greece, 1941–1944.* Cambridge: Cambridge University Press, 2006.

Hogg, Ian. *German Artillery of World War II.* London: Greenhill Books, 1997.

Holzimmer, Kevin C. *General Walter Krueger: Unsung Hero of the Pacific War*. Lawrence: University Press of Kansas, 2007.

Hondros, John Louis. *Occupation and Resistance: The Greek Agony, 1941–44*. New York: Pella, 1983.

Hopkins, James E. T. *Spearhead: A Complete History of Merrill's Marauder Rangers*. Baltimore: Galahad Press, 1999.

Horne, Gerald. *Race War! White Supremacy and the Japanese Attack on the British Empire*. New York: New York University Press, 2004.

Hotta, Eri. *Pan-Asianism and Japan's War, 1931–1945*. New York: Palgrave Macmillan, 2007.

Hough, Richard. *The Longest Battle: The War at Sea, 1939–45*. New York: William Morrow and Company, Inc., 1986.

Howard, Michael. *Strategic Deception in the Second World War*. New York: W.W. Norton and Company, 1995.

"How Good Was the Good War?" *The American Conservative*, July 14, 2008. http://www.amconmag.com/article/2008/jul/14/00006/ (accessed November 23, 2009).

Huan, Claude. "The French Navy in World War II." In *Reevaluating Major Naval Combatants of World War II* edited by James J. Sadkovich. New York: Greenwood Press, 1990.

Hughes, Terry, and John Costello. *The Battle of the Atlantic*. New York: Dial Press, 1977.

Ienaga, Saburo. *The Pacific War, 1931–1945*. New York: Pantheon Books, 1978.

Imlay, Talbot C. *Facing the Second World War: Strategy, Politics, and Economics in Britain and France, 1938–1940*. Oxford: Oxford University Press, 2003.

Iriye, Akira. "Japanese Aggression and China's International Position, 1931–1949." In *The Cambridge History of China: Volume 13: Republican China, 1912–1949, Part 2*, edited by John K. Fairbanks and Albert Feuerwerker. Cambridge: Cambridge University Press, 1986.

Iriye, Akira. *Power and Culture: The Japanese-American War, 1941–1945*. Cambridge: Harvard University Press, 1981.

Isom, Dallas Woodbury. *Midway Inquest: Why the Japanese Lost the Battle of Midway*. Bloomington: Indiana University Press, 2007.

Jackson, Julian. *The Fall of France: The Nazi Invasion of 1940*. Oxford: Oxford University Press, 2003.

Jackson, Peter, and Simon Kitson. "The Paradoxes of Vichy Foreign Policy, 1940–1942." In *Hitler and His Allies in World War II* edited by Jonathan R. Adelman. London: Routledge, 2007.

Jackson, Robert. *Dunkirk: The British Evacuation, 1940*. London: Cassel, 2002.

Janda, Lance. "Shutting the Gates of Mercy: The American Origins of Total War, 1860–1880." *The Journal of Military History* 59 (January 1995): 7–26.

BBC News. "Japan Textbook Angers Chinese, Korean Press." April 6, 2005, http://news.bbc.co.uk/2/hi/asia-pacific/4416593.stm (accessed November 23, 2009).

Jarrett, Philip, ed. *Putnam's History of Aircraft: Aircraft of the Second World War-The Development of the Warplane, 1939–45*. London: Putnam Aeronautical Books, 1997.

Jeans, Roger B., and Katie Letcher Lyle, eds. *Good-Bye to Old Peking: The Wartime Letters of U.S. Marine Captain John Seymour Letcher, 1937–1939*. Athens: Ohio University Press, 1998.

Jenner, C. J. "Turning the Hinge of Fate: Good Source and the UK-U.S. Intelligence Alliance, 1940–1942." *Diplomatic History* 32 (April 2008): 165–205.

Jessup, John E. "The Soviet Armed Forces in the Great Patriotic War, 1941–5." In *Military Effectiveness*. Vol. 3, *The Second World War*, edited by Allan R. Millett and Williamson Murray. Boston: Allen and Unwin, 1988.

Jones, Matthew. *Britain, the United States and the Mediterranean War, 1942–44.* Houndsmill, England: Macmillan Press, Ltd., 1996.

Jordan, Hillary. *Mudbound: A Novel.* Chapel Hill: Algonquin Books, 2008.

Jung, Helmut. *But Not for the Fuehrer.* Bloomington: Helmut Jung, 2003.

Kaplan, Philip, and Jack Currie. *Convoy: Merchant Sailors at War 1939–1945.* Annapolis, MD: Naval Institute Press, 1998.

Karski, Jan. *The Story of a Secret State.* Boston: Houghton Mifflin, 1944.

Kashen, Jeffrey A. *Saints, Sinners, and Soldiers: Canada's Second World War.* Vancouver: UBC Press, 2004.

Kaufmann, J. E., and H. W. Kaufmann. *The Maginot Line: None Shall Pass.* Westport: Praeger, 1997.

Keegan, John, ed. *Churchill's Generals.* London: Cassell, 2005.

Keegan, John. *The Second World War.* London: Penguin Books, 1989.

Keegan, John. *Six Armies in Normandy: D-Day to the Liberation of Paris, June 6-August 25, 1944.* New York: Viking Press, 1982.

Keegan, John, ed. *Who Was Who in World War II.* New York: Crowell, 1978.

Kemp, Paul. *Underwater Warriors.* Annapolis: Naval Institute Press, 1996.

Kennedy, Greg. *Anglo-American Strategic Relations and the Far East, 1933–1939.* London: Frank Cass, 2002.

Kersaudy, Francois. *Norway, 1940.* New York: St. Martin's Press, 1991.

Kershaw, Ian. *Fateful Choices: Ten Decisions that Changed the World, 1940–1941.* London: Penguin, 2007.

Kiernan, Ben. *Blood and Soil: A World History of Genocide and Extermination from Sparta to Darfur.* New Haven: Yale University Press, 2007.

Kiesling, Eugenia C. *Arming Against Hitler: France and the Limits of Military Planning* Lawrence: University of Kansas Press, 1996.

Kimball, Warren F. *Forged in War: Roosevelt, Churchill, and the Second World War.* Chicago: Ivan R. Dee, 1997.

Kimball, Warren F. *The Juggler: Franklin Roosevelt as Wartime Statesman.* Princeton: Princeton University Press, 1991.

Kirkpatrick, Charles E. *An Unknown Future and a Doubtful Present: Writing the Victory Plan of 1941.* Washington, DC: Center of Military History, 1990.

Kitchens, James H., III. "The Bombing of Auschwitz Re-examined." *Journal of Military History* 58 (April 1994): 233–66.

Knell, Hermann. *To Destroy a City: Strategic Bombing and its Human Consequences in World War II.* Cambridge: Da Capo Press, 2003.

Knox, MacGregor. *Hitler's Italian Allies: Royal Armed Forces, Fascist Regime, and the War of 1940–1943.* Cambridge: Cambridge University Press, 2000.

Knox, MacGregor. "The Italian Armed Forces, 1940–3." In *Military Effectiveness.* Vol. 3, *The Second World War,* edited by Allan R. Millett and Williamson Murray. Boston: Allen and Unwin, 1988.

Knox, MacGregor. *Mussolini Unleashed: Politics and Strategy in Fascist Italy's Last War.* Cambridge: Cambridge University Press, 1982.

Kobylyanskiy, Isaak. *From Stalingrad to Pillau: A Red Army Artillery Officer Remembers the Great Patriotic War.* Lawrence: University Press of Kansas, 2008.

Kochavi, Arieh J. *Prelude to Nuremburg: Allied War Crimes Policy and the Question of Punishment.* Chapel Hill: University of North Carolina Press, 1998.

Kohn, Richard H. "The Scholarship on World War II: Its Present Condition and Future Possibilities." *The Journal of Military History* 55 (July 1991): 365–394.

Koistinen, Paul A. C. *Arsenal of World War II: The Political Economy of American Warfare, 1940–1945.* Lawrence: University of Kansas Press, 2004.

Komatsu, Keiichiro. *Origins of the Pacific War and the Importance of 'MAGIC.'* New York: St. Martin's Press, 1999.

Kramish, Arnold. *The Griffin.* Boston: Houghton Mifflin Company, 1986.

Kurzman, Dan. *Fatal Voyage: The Sinking of the USS Indianapolis.* New York: Atheneum, 1990.

LaFeber, Walter. *The Clash: U.S.-Japanese Relations throughout History.* New York: W.W. Norton and Company, 1997.

Lamb, Richard. *War in Italy, 1943–1945: A Brutal Story.* New York: St. Martin's Press, 1993.

Lane, Frederic C. *Ships for Victory: A History of Shipbuilding Under the US Maritime Commission in World War II.* Baltimore: The Johns Hopkins University Press, 2001.

Lasterle, Philippe. "Could Admiral Gensoul Have Averted the Tragedy of Mers el-Kebir?" *Journal of Military History* 67 (July 2003): 835–44.

Latimer, Jon. *Alamein.* Cambridge: Harvard University Press, 2002.

Leighton, Richard M., and Robert W. Coakley. *United States Army in World War II: The War Department, Global Logistics Strategy, 1940–1943.* Washington, DC: Office of the Chief of Military History, 1955.

Lenton, H. T., and J. J. Colledge. *British and Dominion Warships of World War II.* Garden City, NJ: Doubleday and Company, 1967.

Le Tissier, Tony. *Slaughter at Halbe: The Destruction of Hitler's 9th Army, April 1945.* Phoenix Mill, England: Sutton Publishing, 2005.

Leventhal, Lionel. *The American Arsenal: The World War II Official Standard Ordnance Catalog of Small Arms, Tanks, Armored Cares, Artillery, Antiaircraft Guns, Ammunition, Grenades, Mines, Etcetera.* London: Greenhill Books, 1996.

Levi, Primo. *Survival in Auschwitz and the Reawakening: Two Memoirs.* New York: Summit Books, 1985.

Levine, Alan J. *The Pacific War: Japan Versus the Allies.* Westport: Praeger, 1995.

Levine, Alan J. *The War Against Rommel's Supply Lines, 1942–1943.* Westport: Praeger, 1999.

Levy, James P. *The Royal Navy's Home Fleet in World War II.* Houndsmill, England: Palgrave Macmillan, 2003.

Lewis, Adrian R. *Omaha Beach: A Flawed Victory.* Chapel Hill: University of North Carolina Press, 2001.

Lewis, Jon E. *The Mammoth Book of Eyewitness World War II.* New York: Carol and Graf Publishers, 2004.

Li, Peter. "The Nanking Holocaust: Memory, Trauma and Reconciliation." In *Japanese War Crimes: The Search for Justice,* edited by Peter Li. New Brunswick, NJ: Transaction Publishers, 2003.

Lianhong, Zhang. "The Nanjing Massacre: The Socio-Psychological Effect." In *Japanese War Crimes: The Search for Justice,* edited by Peter Li. New Brunswick, NJ: Transaction Publishers, 2003.

Lilly, J. Robert. *Taken by Force: Rape and American GIs in Europe during World War II.* Houndsmill England: Palgrave Macmillan, 2007.

Linderman, Gerald F. *The World Within War: America's Combat Experience in World War II.* New York: Free Press, 1997.

Litvin, Nikolai. *800 Days on the Eastern Front: A Russian Soldiers Remembers World War II.* Lawrence: University of Kansas Press, 2007.

Lofgren, Stephen J. "Diary of First Lieutenant Sugihara Kinryu: Iwo Jima, January-February 1945." *Journal of Military History* 59 (January 1995): 97–134.

Louis, William Roger. *Imperialism at Bay: The United States and the Decolonization of the British Empire, 1941–1945.* New York: Oxford University Press, 1978.

Lowe, Keith. *Inferno: The Fiery Destruction of Hamburg, 1943.* New York: Scribner, 2007.

Luck, Hans von. *Panzer Commander: The Memoirs of Colonel Hans von Luck.* Westport: Praeger, 1989.

Lukacs, John. *Five Days in London: May 1940.* New Haven: Yale University Press, 1999.

Lumans, Valdis O. *Latvia in World War II.* New York: Fordham University Press, 2006.

Lundstrom, John B. *Black Shoe Carrier Admiral: Frank Jack Fletcher at Coral Sea, Midway, and Guadalcanal.* Annapolis: Naval Institute Press, 2006.

Lundstrom, John B. *The First Team and the Guadalcanal Campaign: Naval Fighter Combat from August to November 1942.* Annapolis: Naval Institute Press, 1994.

Lyons, Michael J. *World War II: A Short History.* 4th ed. Upper Saddle River, NJ: Pearson Prentice Hall, 2004.

MacDonald, Callum. *The Lost Battle: Crete, 1941.* New York: The Free Press, 1993.

MacDonell, George S. *One Soldier's Story, 1939–1945: From the Fall of Hong Kong to the Defeat of Japan.* Toronto: The Dundurn Group, 2002.

MacGregor, Wayne C., Jr. *Through These Portals: A Pacific War Saga.* Pullman: Washington State University Press, 2002.

MacIntyre, Donald. *The Naval War Against Hitler.* New York: Charles Scribner's Sons, 1971.

MacKay, Robert. *Half the Battle: Civilian Morale in Britain During the Second World War.* Manchester: Manchester University Press, 2002.

MacKenzie, S. P. *The Home Guard: A Military and Political History.* Oxford: Oxford University Press, 1995.

Major, James Russell. *The Memoirs of an Artillery Forward Observer, 1944–1945.* Manhattan, KS: Sunflower University Press, 1999.

Mallett, Robert. *Mussolini and the Origins of the Second World War, 1933–1940.* Houndsmill, England: Palgrave Macmillan, 2003.

Manela, Manela. *The Wilsonian Moment: Self-Determination and the International Origins of Anticolonial Nationalism.* Oxford: Oxford University Press, 2007.

Mann, Christopher. "Combined Operations, the Commandos, and Norway, 1941–1944." *The Journal of Military History* 73 (April 2009): 471–95.

Mann, B. David. "Japanese Defense of Bataan, Luzon, Philippine Islands, 16 December 1944–4 September 1945." *Journal of Military History* 67 (October 2003): 1149–76.

Manstein, Erich von. *Lost Victories.* St. Paul: Zenith Press, 2004.

Mansoor, Peter R. *The GI Offensive in Europe: The Triumph of American Infantry Divisions, 1941–1945.* Lawrence: University of Kansas Press, 1999.

Margolian, Howard. *Conduct Unbecoming: The Story of the Murder of Canadian Prisoners of War in Normandy.* Toronto: University of Toronto Press, 1998.

Marix Evans, Mark F. *The Fall of France-Act with Daring.* Oxford: Osprey Publishing, 2000.

Marks, Leo. *Between Silk and Cyanide: A Codemaker's War, 1941–1945.* New York: The Free Press, 1998.

Marks, Sally. *The Illusion of Peace: International Relations in Europe, 1918–1933.* 2nd Ed. Houndsmill, England: Palgrave Macmillan, 2003.

Marston, Daniel P. *Phoenix from the Ashes: The Indian Army in the Burma Campaign.* Westport: Praeger, 2003.

Masaki, Noda. "One Army Surgeon's Account of Vivisection on Human Subjects." In *Japanese War Crimes: The Search for Justice,* edited by Peter Li. New Brunswick, NJ: Transaction Publishers, 2003.

Matloff, Maurice, and Edwin M. Snell. *United States Army in World War II: The War Department, Strategic Planning for Coalition Warfare, 1941–1942.* Washington, DC: Office of the Chief of Military History, 1953.

Maung, U Maung. *Burmese Nationalist Movements, 1940–1948.* Honolulu: University of Hawaii Press, 1990.

May, Ernest R. *Strange Victory: Hitler's Conquest of France.* New York: Hill and Wang, 2000.

Mazower, Mark. *Hitler's Empire: How the Nazis Ruled Europe.* New York: The Penguin Press, 2008.

Mazower, Mark. *Inside Hitler's Greece: The Experience of Occupation, 1941–44.* New Haven: Yale University Press, 1993.

McCormack, Gavan. "Reflections on Modern Japanese History in the Context of the Concept of Genocide." In *The Specter of Genocide: Mass Murder in Historical Perspective,* edited by Robert Gellately and Ben Kiernan. Cambridge: Cambridge University Press, 2003.

McKenzie, John D. *On Time, On Target: The World War II Memoir of a Paratrooper in the 82nd Airborne.* Novato, CA: Presidio, 2000.

McKercher, B. J. C., and Roch Legault. *Military Planning and the Origins of the Second World War in Europe.* Westport: Praeger, 2001.

McManus, John C. *Deadly Sky: The American Combat Airman in World War II.* Novato, CA: Presidio, 2002.

Meadows, William C. *The Comanche Code Talkers of World War II.* Austin: University of Texas Press, 2002.

Megargee, Geoffrey P. *Inside Hitler's High Command.* Lawrence: University of Kansas Press, 2000.

Megargee, Geoffrey P. *War of Annihilation: Combat and Genocide on the Eastern Front, 1941.* Lanham: Rowman and Littlefield, Publishers, Inc., 2006.

Meilinger, Phillip S. "Trenchard and 'Morale Bombing': The Evolution of Royal Air Force Doctrine Before World War II." *Journal of Military History* 60 (April 1996): 243–70.

Melton, George E. *Darlan: Admiral and Statesman of France, 1881–1942.* Westport: Praeger, 1998.

Merridale, Catherine. *Ivan's War: Life and Death in the Red Army, 1939–1945.* New York: Metropolitan Books, 2006.

Mershon, Sherie, and Steven Schlossman. *Foxholes and Color Lines: Segregating the U.S. Armed Forces.* Baltimore: The Johns Hopkins University Press, 1998.

Messenger, Charles. *The Second World War In Europe.* Washington, DC: Smithsonian Books, 1999.

Middlebrook, Martin. *Arnhem, 1944: The Airborne Battle.* Boulder: Westview Press, 1994.

Middlebrook, Martin. *The Schweinfurt-Regensburg Mission.* New York: Charles Scribner's Sons, 1983.

Miller, David. *The Great Book of Tanks: The World's Most Important Tanks from World War I to the Present Day.* London: Salamander Books, 2003.

Miller, Edward G. *Bankrupting the Enemy: The U.S. Financial Siege on Japan before Pearl Harbor.* Annapolis: Naval Institute Press, 2007.

Miller, Edward G. *Nothing Less Than Full Victory: Americans at War in Europe, 1944–1945.* Annapolis: Naval Institute Press, 2007.

Miller, Edward S. *War Plan Orange: The U.S. Strategy to Defeat Japan, 1897–1945.* Annapolis: Naval Institute Press, 1991.

Miller, Jr., John. *United States Army in World War II: The War in the Pacific, Guadalcanal, The First Offensive.* Washington, DC: Historical Division, 1969.

Miller, Nathan. *War At Sea: A Naval History of World War II.* New York: Oxford University Press, 1995.

Millett, Allan R. "Assault from the Sea: The Development of Amphibious Warfare Between the Wars—the American, British, and Japanese Experiences." In *Military Innovation in the Interwar Period,* edited by Williamson Murray and Allan R. Millett. Cambridge: Cambridge University Press, 1996.

Millett, Allan R. "The United States Armed Forces in the Second World War." In *Military Effectiveness.* Vol. 3, *The Second World War,* edited by Allan R. Millett and Williamson Murray. Boston: Allen and Unwin, 1988.

Milner, Marc. "The Royal Canadian Navy in World War II." In *Reevaluating Major Naval Combatants in World War II,* edited by James J. Sadkovich. New York: Greenwood Press, 1990.

Ministry of Foreign Affairs of Japan. "Statement by Chief Cabinet Secretary Kiichi Miyazawa on History Textbooks." August 26, 1982. http://www.mofa.go.jp/policy/postwar/state8208.html (accessed November 23, 2009).

Mitcham, Samuel W., Jr. *Hitler's Legions: The German Order of Battle, World War II.* New York: Dorset Press, 1985.

Mitcham, Samuel W., Jr. *Panzers in Winter: Hitler's Army and the Battle of the Bulge.* Westport: Praeger Security International, 2006.

Mitcham, Samuel, W., Jr. *The Desert Fox in Normandy: Rommel's Defense of Fortress Europe.* Westport: Praeger, 1997.

Monahan, Evelyn M., and Rosemary Neidel-Greenlee. *All This Hell: U.S. Nurses Imprisoned by the Japanese.* Lexington: The University Press of Kentucky, 2000.

Morison, Samuel Eliot. *History of US Naval Operations in World War II.* Vol. 8, *New Guinea and the Marianas.* Boston: Little, Brown and Company, 1947–64.

Moser, Don. *World War II: China-Burma-India.* Alexandria, VA: Time-Life Books, 1978.

Mosley, Leonard. *World War II: The Battle of Britain.* Alexandria, VA: Time-Life Books, 1977.

Moss, Norman. *19 Weeks: America, Britain, and the Fateful Summer of 1940.* Boston: Houghton Mifflin Company, 2003.

Mrazek, James E. *The Fall of Eben Emael: Prelude to Dunkerque.* Washington, DC: Luce, 1971.

Muir, Malcolm, Jr. "The United States Navy in World War II: An Assessment." In *Reevaluating Major Naval Combatants in World War II* edited by James J. Sadkovich. New York: Greenwood Press, 1990.

Mulligan, Timothy P. *Neither Sharks Nor Wolves: The Men of Nazi Germany's U-boat Arm, 1939–1945.* Annapolis: Naval Institute Press, 1999.

Murphy, David E. *What Stalin Knew: The Enigma of Barbarossa.* New Haven: Yale University Press, 2005.

Murray, Williamson. "Armored Warfare: The British, French, and German Experience." In *Military Innovation in the Interwar Period,* edited by Williamson Murray and Allan R. Millett. Cambridge: Cambridge University Press, 1996.

Murray, Williamson. "British Military Effectiveness in the Second World War." In *Military Effectiveness.* Vol. 3, *The Second World War,* edited by Allan R. Millett and Williamson Murray. Boston: Allen and Unwin, 1988.

Murray, Williamson, and Allan R. Millett, *A War To Be Won: Fighting the Second World War.* Cambridge: Belknap Press, 2000.

Nash, Douglas E. *Hell's Gate: The Battle of the Cherkassy Pocket, January-February 1944.* Stamford: RZM Publishing, 2005.

Naumann, Klaus. "The 'Unblemished' Wehrmacht: The Social History of a Myth." In *War of Extermination: The German Military in World War II* edited by Hannes Heer and Klaus Naumann. New York: Berghahn Books, 2000.

Neillands, Robin. *The Bomber War: The Allied Air Offensive Against Nazi Germany.* Woodstock, NY: The Overlook Press, 2001.

Neillands, Robin. *The Dieppe Raid: The Story of the Disastrous 1942 Expedition.* Bloomington: Indiana University Press, 2005.

Neillands, Robin. *Eighth Army.* Woodstock, NY: The Overlook Press, 2004.

Neiman, Robert M., and Kenneth W. Estes. *Tanks on the Beaches: A Marine Tanker in the Pacific War.* College Station: Texas A&M University Press, 2003.

Neufeld, Michael J., and Michael Berenbaum, eds. *The Bombing of Auschwitz: Should the Allies Have Attempted It?* New York: St. Martin's Press, 2000.

Newton, Steven H. *Kursk: The German View.* Cambridge, MA: Da Capo Press, 2002.

Nolte, Hans-Heinrich. "Partisan War in Belorussia, 1941–1944." In *A World at Total War: Global Conflict and the Politics of Destruction, 1937–1945,* edited by Roger Chickering, Stig Forster, and Bernd Greiner. Cambridge: Cambridge University Press, 2005.

Noggle, Anne. *A Dance with Death: Soviet Airwomen in World War II.* College Station: Texas A&M Press, 1994.

Oates, Joyce Carol. *The Gravedigger's Daughter: A Novel.* New York: HarperCollins, 2007.

O'Brien, Francis A. *Battling for Saipan.* New York: Ballantine Books, 2003.

Obryn'ba, Nikolai. *Red Partisan: The Memoir of a Soviet Resistance Fighter on the Eastern Front.* Washington, DC: Potomac Books, Inc., 2007.

O'Hara, Vincent P. *The German Fleet at War, 1939–1945.* Annapolis: Naval Institute Press, 2004.

Ohl, John Kennedy. *Supplying the Troops: General Somervell and American Logistics in WW II.* Dekalb: Northern Illinois University Press, 1994.

Ohnuki-Tierney, Emiko. *Kamikaze Diaries: Reflections of Japanese Student Soldiers.* Chicago: University of Chicago Press, 2006.

O'Reilly, Charles T. *Forgotten Battles: Italy's War of Liberation, 1943–1945.* Lanham: Lexington Books, 2001.

Ottis, Sherri Greene. *Silent Heroes: Downed Airmen and the French Underground.* Lexington: University of Kentucky Press, 2001.

Overton, Richard E. *God Isn't Here: A Young American's Entry into World War II and His Participation in the Battle for Iwo Jima.* 2nd ed. Clearfield, UT: American Legacy Media, 2006.

Overy, Richard. *Göring.* New York: Barnes and Noble Books, 1984.

Overy, Richard. "The Second World War: A Barbarous Conflict?" In *The Barbarization of Warfare,* edited by George Kassimeris. New York: New York University Press, 2006.

Parillo, Mark. "The Imperial Japanese Navy in World War II." In *Reevaluating Major Naval Combatants of World War II*, edited by James J. Sadkovich. New York: Greenwood Press, 1990.

Parillo, Mark, ed. *We Were in the Big One: Experiences of the World War II Generation.* Wilmington: Scholarly Resources, Inc., 2002.

Parshall, Jonathan B., and Anthony P. Tully. *Shattered Sword: The Untold Story of the Battle of Midway.* Washington, DC: Potomac Books, 2005.

Partridge, Jeff. *The Alexandra Massacre.* http://www.nesa.org.uk/html/alexandra_massacre.htm (accessed June 15, 2007).

Paterson, Lawrence. *Hitler's Grey Wolves: U-Boats in the Indian Ocean.* London: Greenhill Books, 2004.

Payne, Stanley G. *Franco and Hitler: Spain, Germany, and World War II.* New Haven: Yale University Press, 2008.

Peattie, Mark R. *Sunburst: The Rise of Japanese Naval Air Power, 1909–1941.* Annapolis: Naval Institute Press, 2001.

Pennington, Reina. *Wings, Women, and War: Soviet Airwomen in World War II Combat.* Lawrence: University Press of Kansas, 2001.

Perras, Galen Roger. *Stepping Stones to Nowhere: The Aleutian Islands, Alaska, and American Military Strategy, 1867–1945.* Vancouver: University of British Columbia Press, 2003.

Perret, Geoffrey. *Winged Victory: The Army Air Forces in World War II.* New York: Random House, 1993.

Peszke, Michael Alfred. *The Polish Underground Army, the Western Allies, and the Failure of Strategic Unity in World War II.* Jefferson, NC: McFarland and Company, Inc., Publishers, 2005.

Phillips, Christopher. *Steichen at War.* New York: Portland House, 1987.

Philpott, William, and Martin S. Alexander. "The French and the British Field Force: Moral Support or Material Contribution?" *Journal of Military History* 71 (July 2007): 743–73.

Pinkus, Oscar. *The War Aims and Strategies of Adolf Hitler.* Jefferson, NC: McFarland and Company, Inc., Publishers, 2005.

Pitt, Barrie. *World War II: The Battle of the Atlantic.* Alexandria, VA: Time-Life Books, 1977.

Place, Timothy Harison. *Military Training in the British Army, 1940–1944: From Dunkirk to D-Day.* London: Frank Cass, 2000.

Polonsky, Antony, and Joanna B. Michlic, eds. *The Neighbors Respond: The Controversy Over the Jedwabne Massacre in Poland.* Princeton: Princeton University Press, 2004.

Ponting, Clive. *1940: Myth and Reality.* Chicago: Ivan R. Dee, Publisher, 1991.

Pope, Dudley. *The Battle of the River Plate: The Hunt for the German Pocket Battleship Graf Spee.* Ithaca: McBooks Press, 2005.

Porch, Douglas. *The Path to Victory: The Mediterranean Theater in World War II.* New York: Farrar, Straus and Giroux, 2004.

Potter, E. B., and Chester W. Nimitz. *Sea Power: A Naval History.* Englewood Cliffs, NJ: Prentice-Hall, Inc., 1960.

Powaski, Ronald E. *Lightning War: Blitzkrieg in the West, 1940.* Hoboken: John Wiley and Sons, Inc., 2003.

Powell, Alan. *The Third Force: ANGAU's New Guinea War, 1942–46.* South Melbourne: Oxford University Press, 2003.

Prange, Gordon W. *Miracle at Midway.* New York: Penguin Books, 1982.

Prazmowska, Anita. *Britain and Poland, 1939–1943: The Betrayed Ally.* Cambridge: Cambridge University Press, 1995.

Prefer, Nathan N. *Vinegar Joe's War: Stilwell's Campaigns in Burma.* Novato, CA: Presidio, 2000.

Prestonn, Anthony. *Jane's Fighting Ships of World War II.* London: Studio, 1989.

Probert, Henry. *Bomber Harris: His Life and Times.* London: Greenhill Books, 2001.

Raus, Edward. *Panzer Operations: The Eastern Front Memoir of General Raus, 1941–1945.* Cambridge, MA: Da Capo Press, 2003.

Reardon, Mark J. *Victory at Mortain: Stopping Hitler's Panzer Counteroffensive.* Lawrence: University Press of Kansas, 2002.

Record, Jeffrey. *The Specter of Munich: Reconsidering the Lessons of Appeasing Hitler.* Dulles, VA: Potomac Books, 2007.

Reese, Roger R. "Lessons of the Winter War: A Study in the Military Effectiveness of the Red Army, 1939–1940." *Journal of Military History* 72 (July 2008): 825–52.

Reese, Roger R. *The Soviet Military Experience: A History of the Soviet Army, 1917–1991.* London: Routledge, 2000.

Reese, Roger R. *Red Commanders: A Social History of the Soviet Army Officer Corps, 1918–1991.* Lawrence: University of Kansas Press, 2005.

Reese, Willy Peter Reese. *A Stranger to Myself: The Inhumanity of War, Russia, 1941–1944.* New York: Farrar, Straus, and Giroux, 2005.

Reynolds, E. Bruce. *Thailand and Japan's Southern Advance, 1940–1945.* New York: St. Martin's Press, 1994.

Reynolds, E. Bruce. *Thailand's Secret War: The Free Thai, OSS, and SOE during World War II.* Cambridge: Cambridge University Press, 2005.

Reynolds, Michael. *The Devil's Adjutant: Jochen Peiper, Panzer Leader.* New York: Sarpedon, 1995.

Reynolds, Michael. *Steel Inferno: I SS Panzer Corps in Normandy.* New York: Sarpedon, 1997.

Rhodes, Richard. *Masters of Death: The SS Einsatzgruppen and the Invention of the Holocaust.* New York: Alfred A. Knopf, 2002.

Richards, Denis. *The Hardest Victory: RAF Bomber Command in the Second World War.* New York: W.W. Norton and Company, 1994.

Richardson, Horst Fuchs. *Your Loyal and Loving Son: The Letters of Tank Gunner Karl Fuchs, 1937–1941.* Washington, DC: Brassey's, Inc., 2003.

Rickard, John Nelson. *Patton at Bay: The Lorraine Campaign, September to December, 1944.* Westport: Praeger, 1999.

Roberts, Geoffrey. *Stalin's Wars: From World War to Cold War, 1939–1953.* New Haven: Yale University Press, 2006.

Roehrs, Mark D., and William A. Renzi. *World War II in the Pacific.* Armonk, NY: M.E. Sharpe, 2004.

Rolf, David. *The Bloody Road to Tunis: Destruction of the Axis Forces in North Africa: November 1942-May 1943.* London: Greenhill Books, 2001.

Rommel, Erwin. *Rommel and His Art of War.* London: Greenhill Books, 2003.

Roshwald, Aviel. *Estranged Bedfellows: Britain and France in the Middle East during the Second World War.* New York: Oxford University Press, 1990.

Roscoe, Theodore. *United States Submarine Operations in World War II.* Annapolis: United States Naval Institute, 1949.

Rossino, Alexander B. *Hitler Strikes Poland: Blitzkrieg, Ideology, and Atrocity.* Lawrence: University of Kansas Press, 2003.

Rothwell, Victor. *Origins of the Second World War.* Manchester: Manchester University Press, 2001.

Rothwell, Victor. *War Aims in the Second World War: The War Aims of the Major Belligerents, 1939–45.* Edinburgh: Edinburgh University Press, 2005.

Rottman, Gordon L. *U.S. Marine Corps World War II Order of Battle; Ground and Air Units in the Pacific War, 1939–1945.* Westport: Greenwood Press, 2002.

Roy, Kaushik. "Military Loyalty in the Colonial Context: A Case Study of the Indian Army during World War II." *The Journal of Military History* 73 (April 2009): 497–529.

Rutherford, Phillip T. *Prelude to the Final Solution: The Nazi Program for Deporting Ethnic Poles, 1939–1941.* Lawrence: University Press of Kansas, 2007.

Ryan, Cornelius. *A Bridge Too Far.* New York: Simon and Schuster, 1974.

Ryan, Cornelius. *The Longest Day: The Classic Epic of D-Day.* New York: Touchstone, 1994.

Sadkovich, James J. "The Italian Navy in World War II: 1940–1943." In *Reevaluating Major Naval Combatants of World War II,* edited by James J. Sadkovich. New York: Greenwood Press, 1990.

Sajer, Guy. *The Forgotten Soldier: The Classic WWII Biography.* Dulles, VA: Brassey Inc., 1990.

Salerno, Reynolds M. *Vital Crossroads: Mediterranean Origins of the Second World War, 1935–1940.* Ithaca: Cornell University Press, 2002.

Salisbury, Harrison E. *The 900 Days: The Siege of Leningrad.* New York: Da Capo Press, Inc., 1985.

Sandler, Stanley. *Segregated Skies: All-Black Combat Squadrons of WWII.* Washington, DC: Smithsonian Institution Press, 1992.

Sarantakes, Nicholas Evan. *Allies Against the Rising Sun: The United States, the British Nations, and the Defeat of Imperial Japan.* Lawrence: University Press of Kansas, 2009.

Sawyer, L. A., and W. H. Mitchell. *The Liberty Ships: The History of the "Emergency" Type Cargo Ships Constructed in the United States During the Second World War.* 2nd ed. London: Lloyd's of London Press, Ltd., 1985.

Schaller, Michael. *The United States and China in the Twentieth Century.* New York: Oxford University Press, 1979.

Scheck, Raffael. *Hitler's African Victims: The German Army Massacres of Black French Soldiers in 1940.* New York: Cambridge University Press, 2006.

Schom, Alan. *The Eagle and the Rising Sun: The Japanese-American War, 1941–1943: Pearl Harbor Through Guadalcanal* New York: W.W. Norton & Company, 2004.

Schrijvers, Peter. *The Crash of Ruin: American Combat Soldiers in Europe during World War II.* New York: New York University Press, 1998.

Schrijvers, Peter. *The GI War Against Japan: American Soldiers in Asia and the Pacific During World War II.* New York: New York University Press, 2002.

Schrijvers, Peter. *The Unknown Dead: Civilians in the Battle of the Bulge.* Lexington: University Press of Kentucky, 2005.

Schultz, Duane. *The Doolittle Raids.* New York: St. Martin's Press, 1988.

Searle, Thomas R. "'It Made a Lot of Sense to Kill Skilled Workers': The Firebombing of Tokyo in March 1945." *Journal of Military History* 66 (January 2002): 103–34.

Sebag-Montefiore, Hugh. *Dunkirk: Fight to the Last Man.* Cambridge: Harvard University Press, 2006.

Segesser, Daniel Marc. "On the Road to Total Retribution? The International Debate on the Punishment of War Crimes, 1872–1945." In *A World at Total War: Global Conflict and the Politics of Destruction, 1937–1945,* edited by Roger Chickering, Stig Forster, and Bernd Greiner . Cambridge: Cambridge University Press, 2005.

Semelin, Jacques. *Unarmed Against Hitler: Civilian Resistance in Europe, 1939–1943.* Westport: Praeger, 1993.

Shachtman, Tom. *The Phony War, 1939–1940.* New York: Harper & Row, Publishers, 1982.

Sheehan, Fred. *Anzio: Epic of Bravery.* Norman: University of Oklahoma Press, 1964.

Sheftall, M.G. *Blossoms in the Win: Human Legacies of the Kamikaze.* New York: NAL Caliber, 2005.

Shepherd, Ben. *War in the Wild East: The German Army and Soviet Partisans.* Cambridge: Harvard University Press, 2004.

Shigeru Sato. *War, Nationalism and Peasants: Java under the Japanese Occupation, 1942–1945.* Armonk, NY: M.E. Sharpe, 1994.

Skates, John Ray. *The Invasion of Japan: Alternative to the Bomb.* Columbia: University of South Carolina Press, 1994.

Skulski, Janusz. *Anatomy of the Ship: The Battleship Yamato.* Annapolis: Naval Institute Press, 1988.

Sledge, E. B. *With the Old Breed: At Peleliu and Okinawa.* New York: Oxford University Press, 1981.

Sloan, Bill. *Brotherhood of Heroes: The Marines at Peleliu, 1944-The Bloodiest Battle of the Pacific War.* New York: Simon & Schuster Paperbacks, 2005.

Smart, Nick. *British Strategy and Politics During the Phony War: Before the Balloon Went Up.* Westport: Praeger Publishers, 2003.

Smelser, Ronald and Edward J. Davies. *The Myth of the Eastern Front: The Nazi-Soviet War in American Popular Culture.* New York: Cambridge University Press, 2008.

Smith, Douglas V. *Carrier Battles: Command Decision in Harm's Way.* Annapolis: Naval Institute Press, 2006.

Smith, Gaddis. *American Diplomacy During the Second World War, 1941–1945.* New York: John Wiley and Sons, 1967.

Smith, Michael S. *Bloody Ridge: The Battle That Saved Guadalcanal.* Navato, CA: Presidio, 2000.

Smith, Kevin. *Conflict over Convoys: Anglo-American Logistics Diplomacy in the Second World War.* Cambridge: University of Cambridge Press, 1996.

Spector, Ronald H. *Eagle Against the Sun: The American War with Japan.* New York: Vintage Books, 1985.

Stansky, Peter. *The First Day of the Blitz, September 7, 1940.* New Haven: Yale University Press, 2007.

Stanton, Shelby. *Order of Battle U.S. Army, World War II.* Novato, CA: Presidio Press, 1984.

Stephan, Robert. W. *Stalin's Secret War: Soviet Counterintelligence Against the Nazis, 1941–1945.* Lawrence: University of Kansas Press, 2004.

Stewart, Andrew. *Empire Lost: Britain, the Dominions, and the Second World War.* London: Continuum, 2008.

Stokesbury, James L. *A Short History of World War II.* New York: William Morrow and Company, Inc., 1980.

Stoler, Mark A. *Allies in War: Britain and America Against the Axis Powers, 1940–1945.* London: Hodder Arnold, 2005.

Stone, David. *War Summits: The Meetings That Shaped World War II and the Postwar World.* Washington, DC: Potomac Books, Inc., 2006.

Story, Ronald. *Concise Historical Atlas of World War Two: The Geography of Conflict.* New York: Oxford University Press, 2006.

Strachan, Hew. "Total War: The Conduct of War, 1939–1945." In *A World at Total War: Global Conflict and the Politics of Destruction, 1937–1945,* edited by Roger Chickering, Stig Forster, and Bernd Greiner. Cambridge: Cambridge University Press, 2005.

Sturma, Michael. *The USS Flier:Death and Survival on a World War II Submarine.* Lexington: University of Kentucky Press, 2008.

Suleiman, Susan Rubin. *Crises of Memory and the Second World War.* Cambridge, MA: Harvard University Press, 2006.

Sullivan, Brian R. "The Path Marked Out by History: The German-Italian Alliance, 1939–1943." In *Hitler and His Allies in World War II* edited by Jonathan R. Adelman. London: Routledge, 2007.

Sulzberger, C. L. *The American Heritage Picture History of World War II.* New York: American Heritage Publishing Co., 1986.

Symonds, Craig L. *The Naval Institute Historical Atlas of the U.S. Navy.* Annapolis: Naval Institute Press, 1995.

Syrett, David. *The Defeat of the German U-Boats: The Battle of the Atlantic.* Columbia: University of South Carolina Press, 1994.

Szarota, Tomasz. "Poland Under German Occupation, 1939–1941: A Comparative Survey." In *From Peace to War: Germany, Soviet Russia and the World, 1939–1941* edited by Bernd Wegner. Providence: Berghahn Books, 1997.

Taaffe, Stephen R. *MacArthur's Jungle War: The 1944 New Guinea Campaign.* Lawrence: University of Kansas Press, 1998.

Taylor, Frederick. *Dresden: Tuesday, February 13, 1945.* New York: HarperCollins Publishers, 2004.

Terkel, Studs. *"The Good War": An Oral History of World War Two.* New York: Ballantine Books, 1984.

Terraine, John. *The Right of the Line: The Royal Air Force in the European War, 1939–1945.* Ware: Woodsworth Editions, 1997.

"The Bloody Battle of Tarawa." 2003. http://www.eyewitnesstohistory.com/tarawa.htm (accessed November 23, 2007).

Thompson, Julian. *The Lifeblood of War: Logistics in Armed Conflict.* London: Brassey's, 1991.

Thorne, Christopher. *Allies of a Kind: The United States, Britain, and the War Against Japan, 1941–1945.* Oxford: Oxford University Press, 1978.

Titmuss, Richard M. *Problems of Social Policy.* London: Longmans, Green and Co., Ltd., 1950.

Tohmatsu, Haruo, and H. P. Willmott. *A Gathering Darkness: The Coming of War to the Far East and the Pacific, 1921–1942.* Lanham: SR Books, 2004.

Tomasevich, Jozo. *War and Revolution in Yugoslavia, 1941–1945.* Stanford: Stanford University Press, 2001.

Tomblin, Barbara Brooks. *With Utmost Spirit: Allied Naval Operations in the Mediterranean, 1942–1945.* Lexington: University Press of Kentucky, 2004.

Tooze, Adam. *The Wages of Destruction: The Making and Breaking of the Nazi Economy.* New York: Viking Penguin, 2007.

Toshihiko, Shimada. "Essay." In *The China Quagmire: Japan's Expansion on the Asian Continent,* edited by James William Morley. New York: Columbia University Press, 1983.

Trew, Simon. *Britain, Mihailovic and the Chetniks, 1941–42.* Houndsmill, England: Macmillan Press, Ltd., 1998.

Turow, Scott. *Ordinary Heroes: A Novel.* New York: Farrar, Straus and Giroux, 2005.

Ueberschar, Gerd R. "The Ideologically Motivated War of Annihilation in the East." In *Hitler's War in the East, 1941–1945: A Critical Assessment,* edited by Rolf-Dieter Muller and Gerd R. Ueberschar. New York: Berghahn Books, 2002.

Ungvary, Krisztian. *The Siege of Budapest: One Hundred Days in World War II.* New Haven: Yale University Press, 2005

United States Army. *U.S. Army in World War II: Pictorial Record: The War Against Germany and Italy: Mediterranean and Adjacent Areas.* Washington, DC: Center of Military History, 2005.

The United States Strategic Bombing Surveys, European War and Pacific War. Maxwell Air Force Base, AL: Air University Press, October 1987.

Urwin, Gregory J. W. *Facing Fearful Odds: The Siege of Wake Island.* Lincoln: University of Nebraska Press, 1997.

Van Creveld, Martin. *Supplying War: Logistics from Wallenstein to Patton.* Cambridge: Cambridge University Press, 1977.

Van Der Zee, Henri A. *The Hunger Winter: Occupied Holland, 1944–1945.* Lincoln: University of Nebraska Press, 1998

Van Dyke, Carl. *The Soviet Invasion of Finland, 1939–40.* London: Frank Cass, 1997.

Vassiltchikov, Marie. *Berlin Diaries, 1940–1945.* New York: Vintage Books, 1988.

Vatter, Harold G. *The U.S. Economy in World War II.* New York: Columbia University Press, 1985.

Vego, Milan. *The Battle for Leyte, 1944: Allied and Japanese Plans, Preparations, and Execution.* Annapolis: Naval Institute Press, 2006.

Vehvilainen, Olli. *Finland in the Second World War.* Houndsmills, England: Palgrave, 2002.

Venzon, Anne Cipriano. *From Whaleboats to Amphibious Warfare: Lt. Gen. "Howling Mad" Smith and the U.S. Marine Corps.* Westport: Praeger, 2003.

Von Der Porten, Edward P. *The German Navy in World War II.* New York: Thomas Y. Crowell Company, 1969.

Von Mullenheim-Rechberg, Baron Burkard. *Battleship Bismark: A Survivor's Story.* Annapolis: Naval Institute Press, 1980.

Voss, Johann. *Black Edelweiss: A Memoir of Combat and Conscience by a Soldier of the Waffen-SS.* Bedford, PA: The Aberjona Press, 2002.

Wait, Robin. *Under Fire at Sidi Rezegh.* http://riv.co.nz/rnza/tales/wait5.htm (accessed November 23, 2007).

Warren, Alan. *Singapore 1942: Britain's Greatest Defeat.* London: Hambledon and London, 2002.

Wasserstein, Bernard. *Secret War in Shanghai.* Boston: Houghton Mifflin Company, 1999.

Waszak, Leon J. *Agreement in Principle: The Wartime Partnership of General Wladyslaw Sikorski and Winston Churchill.* New York: Peter Lang Publishing, Inc., 1996.

Watson, Mark S. *United States Army in World War II-the War Department: Chief of Staff: Prewar Plans and Preparations.* Washington, DC: Department of the Army, 1950.

Wegner, Bernd. *The Waffen-SS: Organization, Ideology and Function.* Oxford: Basil Blackwell, 1990.

Weigley, Russell F. *The American Way of War: A History of United States Military Strategy and Policy.* Bloomington: Indiana University Press, 1973.

Weigley, Russell F. *Eisenhower's Lieutenants: The Campaign of France and Germany, 1944–1945.* Bloomington: Indiana University, 1981.

Weinberg, Gerhard L. *A World At Arms: A Global History of World War II.* Cambridge: Cambridge University Press, 1995.

Weinberg, Gerhard L. "World War II Scholarship, Now and in the Future." *The Journal of Military History* 61 (April 1997): 335–346.

Wells, Mark K. *Courage and Air Warfare: The Allied Aircrew Experience in the Second World War.* London: Frank Cass, 1995.

Westwood, David. *Anatomy of the Ship: The Type VII U-Boat.* Annapolis: Naval Institute Press, 1986.

Wette, Wolfram. *The Wehrmacht: History, Myth, Reality.* Cambridge: Harvard University Press, 2006.

Wheeler, James Scott. *The Big Red One: America's Legendary 1st Infantry Division from World War I to Desert Storm.* Lawrence: University of Kansas Press, 2007.

White, Matthew. *Historical Atlas of the Twentieth Century.* "Losses in the Second World War." http://users.erols.com/mwhite28/ww2-loss.htm (accessed November 23, 2009).

White, Osmar. *Conqueror's Road.* Cambridge: Cambridge University Press, 1996.

Whiting, Charles. *The Battle of Hurtgen Forest: The Untold Story of a Disastrous Campaign.* New York: Orion Books, 1989.

Whiting, Charles. *Britain Under Fire: The Bombing of Britain's Cities, 1940–1945.* London: Century Hutchinson Ltd, 1986.

Whiting, Charles. *The Last Assault: The Battle of the Bulge Reassessed.* New York: Sarpedon, 1994.

Whitlock, Flint. *The Fighting First: The Untold Story of the Big Red One on D-Day.* Boulder: Westview Press, 2004.

Wieviorka, Olivier. "France." In *Resistance in Western Europe,* edited by Bob Moore. Oxford: Oxford University Press, 2000.

Wieviorka, Olivier. *Normandy: The Landings to the Liberation of Paris.* Cambridge, MA: Harvard University Press, 2008.

Williamson, Gordon. *U-Boat Bases and Bunkers, 1941–1945.* Oxford: Osprey Publishing, 2003.

Willmott, H. P. *The Battle of Leyte Gulf: The Last Fleet Action.* Bloomington: Indiana University Press, 2005.

Willmott, H. P. *The War with Japan: The Period of Balance, May 1942-October 1943.* Wilmington: Scholarly Resources, Inc., 2002.

Wilson, Dick. *When Tigers Fight: The Story of the Sino-Japanese War, 1937–1945.* New York: The Viking Press, 1982.

Wilt, Alan F. *The Atlantic Wall, 1941–1944: Hitler's Defenses for D-Day.* New York: Enigma Books, 2004.

Wood, E. Thomas, and Stanislaw M. Jankowski. *Karski: How One Man Tried to Stop the Holocaust.* New York: J. Wiley, 1994.

Wood, Edward W. *Worshipping the Myths of World War II: Reflections on America's Dedication to War* (Washington, D.C.: Potomac Books, Inc., 2006), 19–67.

Wukovits, John F. *Devotion to Duty: A Biography of Admiral Clifton A. F. Sprague.* Annapolis: Naval Institute Press, 1995.

Wylie, Neville, ed. *European Neutrals and Non-Belligerents During the Second World War.* Cambridge: Cambridge University Press, 2002.

Yamamoto, Masahiro. *Nanking: Anatomy of an Atrocity.* Westport: Praeger, 2000.

Y'Blood, William T. *Air Commandos Against Japan: Allied Special Operations in World War II Burma.* Annapolis: Naval Institute Press, 2008.

Y'Blood, William T. *Hunter-Killer: U.S. Escort Carriers in the Battle of the Atlantic.* Annapolis: Naval Institute Press, 1983.

Y'Blood, William T. *The Little Giants: U.S. Escort Carriers Against Japan.* Annapolis: Naval Institute Press, 1987.

Yelton, David K. "'Ein Volk Steht Auf': The German Volkssturm and Nazi Strategy, 1944–45." *Journal of Military History* 64 (October 2000): 1061–83.

Yelton, David K. *Hitler's Volkssturm: The Nazi Militia and the Fall of Germany, 1944–1945.* Lawrence: University Press of Kansas, 2002.

Yoneyama, Lisa. "For Transformative Knowledge and Postnationalist Public Spheres: The Smithsonian *Enola Gay* Controversy." In *The World War Two Reader,* edited by Gordon Martel. New York: Routledge, 2004.

Yoshida, Mitsuru. *Requiem for Battleship Yamato.* Seattle: University of Washington Press, 1985.

Yoshimura, Akira. *Zero Fighter.* Westport: Praeger, 1996.

Zaloga, Steven J., and Leland S. Ness. *The Red Army Handbook, 1939-45.* Thrupp, GB: Sutton Publishing, Ltd., 1998.

Zaloga, Steven, and Victor Madej. *The Polish Campaign, 1939.* New York: Hippocrene Books, 1985.

Zeiler, Thomas W. *Unconditional Defeat: Japan, America, and the End of World War II.* Wilmington: Scholarly Resources, Inc., 2004.

Zhukov, G. K. *G. Zhukov, Marshal of the Soviet Union: Reminiscences and Reflections.* Vol. 1. Moscow: Progress Publishers, 1985.

Zumbro, Derek S. *Battle for the Ruhr: The German Army's Final Defeat in the West.* Lawrence: University Press of Kansas, 2006.

Zusak, Markus. *The Book Thief.* New York: Alfred A. Knopf, 2005.

INDEX

Aachen, 335, 337
ABDA command, 168, 171–74, 179
Abyssinia. *See* Ethiopia
Adachi, Hatazo, 247–48, 264–66
Adams, Michael C. C., 5
Admin Box , 271, 272
Admiral Scheer, 238
Admiralty Islands, 264
Adreatine caves massacre, 280
Afrika Corps, 129, 132, 205, 215
Airborne landings:
    Allied, 217–18, 221, 299, 304, 332–34, 338, 339
    German parachute operations, 75, 80, 82, 127–28,
        299, 333, 338
    U.S., 266, 387
Aircraft carriers: 33, 104–05
    Japan, 319, 322
    U.S., 156, 163, 251–53, 257, 260–61, 319. *See also*
        Japan military; Royal Navy; U.S. Navy
Air gap, 108, 238
Airpower. *See countries*; Luftwaffe; Royal Air Force;
    United States Army Air Force
Akagi, 160, 183
Akyab, 243, 267, 271, 372
Alam Halfa, 207
Albania, 12, 22, 26, 54–55, 123
Aleutian Islands, 182
Alexander, Harold, 175, 176:
    North Africa, 206–07, 215–16
    Sicily and Italy, 217–22, 274, 277–78,
        280–81, 380
Alexander, King, 25
Alexandra Barracks Hospital massacre, 172
Algeria, 28, 119, 210, 278
Altmark, 74
Allied Military Government of Occupied
    Territories, 219
Allied Powers:
    Anglo-American military tensions, 343–44
    Anglo-French declaration of war, 57
    Anglo-French forces in Norway, 77
    Asia/Pacific theater plans, 245–46
    command structure, 211, 214–15, 217, 294–95,
        334, 341

    cooperation, 410
    defeat of Germany, 344, 378–83
    European invasion plans, 211, 216, 220,
        294–96, 299
    invasion of Germany, 329, 349
    Italy, 281
    Mediterranean Allied Tactical Air Force, 276
    Polish exiles, 64
    postwar Germany, 384
    postwar planning, 224–25, 226, 357–58, 372
    production, 226
    war aims and diplomacy, 105, 158, 168, 217, 224–26
    Western Front, 334, 341. *See battles, campaigns,*
        and theaters
Alps, 309
Altenfjord, 238
Ambrose, Stephen, 5
America. *See* United States of America
Amphibious assault, 105, 210, 245:
    Burma, 226, 243
    China, 44, 45
    German, 91
    Gilberts, 253
    Guadalcanal, 185, 190
    Italy, 219, 220, 222, 274, 276
    Iwo Jima, 386–87
    Japan, 399
    Malaya, 152, 166
    Marianas, 316, 319, 322–23
    Marshalls, 257–58, 260, 262–63
    New Guinea, 248–49, 265
    Normandy, 300–01
    Okinawa, 390–91, 394–95
    Pacific, 243, 245, 248, 368, 370, 373, 397
    Philippines, 362, 367
    USSR, 71, 195
Amtracs (LVT), 258–60, 262, 315–16, 318
Anami, Korechika, 264–65
Anderson, Kenneth, 211, 213–14
Anguar Island, 324–25
Anklam raid, 233
Annihilation, 415:
    defined, 1–3
Anschluss, 25, 40, 54

Anti-semitism, 16, 25, 134, 381–82
   in German military, 17. *See also* Hitler
Antonescu, Ion, 292, 352
Antwerp, 80, 312–13:
   German target, 338–39
   liberation, 329–30, 334–35, 337
Anvil. *See* Dragoon
Anzio, 274, 276–78, 280
Aoba, 187
Aosta, Duke of, 120, 122
Apamama islet, 258
Appeasement, 5, 53–54
Arcadia Conference, 168–69
Archangel, 237
Ardennes Forest
   German advance, 79–80, 83
   Western Front, 312–13, 329, 337–38, 340
Argentina, 360
Arizona, 163
Ark Royal, 110
Armored warfare. *See* Mobile warfare
Arnhem, 330, 332–34
Arnim, Jurgen von, 211, 213–16
Arnold, Henry "Hap", 103–04, 179:
   Asia and Pacific, 244, 369, 370, 386
Aryan race. *See* Hitler
Asmara, battle, 122
Astoria, 185
Astrakhan, 195, 198
Atago, 362
Athenia, 64, 106
Atlantic, battle, 106–16, 236–41
Atlantic Charter, 105
Atlantic Wall, 296:
   assault on, 294–304
Atomic bombs, 385, 401–03
Attrition, 2
Attu, invasion of, 182
Atrocities. *See* German military; Imperial Japanese
   Army; Red Army; Strategic bombing
Auchinleck, Claude, 131–33, 204–06
Audacity, 113–14
Auschwitz-Birkenau camp, 353, 381–82
Australia, 164:
   Africa, 120–21, 131, 207, 209, 215
   airforce attacks, 264–65
   Borneo, 376, 397
   Bougainville, 252–53
   Darwin attacked, 173
   Greece, 125
   intelligence services, 298
   Leyte Gulf, 362
   Navy, 120
   New Guinea, 245–50, 266
   Pacific War, 171, 172, 177, 179–81, 184–85, 190, 252
   prisoner camp, 406
   Singapore, 167, 171–72
Austria, 25, 54, 309, 343, 359, 382–83, 384, 407
Awakening of Spring, Operation, 359
Axis Powers:
   diplomacy, 99
   disagreements between, 134, 410
Azores, 110, 238

B-17 Flying Fortress, 105, 110, 158, 162, 165, 227–29
B-24 Liberator, 105, 110, 227–29, 231, 238
B-25 Mitchell, 179–80
B-29 Superfortress, 105, 257, 319, 322–23, 369, 370, 386,
   388–89, 397–99, 401–03
Baatan, 374–75:
   death march, 177, 406
Babi Yar massacre, 143
Badoglio, Pietro Marshal, 23, 118–19, 124, 220
Bagramyan, Ivan, 351
Bagration, Operation, 346–51
Baguio, 374, 376
Bailey bridge, 333
Balikpapan, 173, 397
Baltic states, 20:
   Allied advance, 345
   postwar, 384, 411
   Soviet advance, 346, 351, 354–55, 359
   Winter War, 69 73
Banzai charges, 42, 177, 182, 187, 259, 318, 322–24,
   325, 365
Barbarossa, Operation, 135–46, 192, 195–96, 198, 203
Bardia, battle, 121, 133
Bastogne, 338–40
Battleaxe, Operation, 131
Beaverbrook, Lord, 93
Belgian Gates (Element C), 297
Belgium, 80, 88, 312–13, 329, 407
Belgorod, 283, 285, 288
Bellamy, Chris, 2
Bergen-Belsen camp, 382
Bergonzoli, Annibale, 121
Berlin
   Allied advance on, 329, 332, 341, 343–45, 378–80
   divided, 384
Berlin bombing raids, 230, 234, 235, 341, 380
Berti, Mario, 120
Betio Island, 258–60, 262

Biak, 265
Bialystok, 139–40
Big Three. *See* Allied Powers
"Big Wing" air tactic, 93, 95–96, 294
Bir Hakeim, 204–05
Birmingham, 363
Bismarck, 18, 110–11, 237, 240
Bismarck Sea, 389
Bismarck Sea, battle, 247–48
Blackshirt, 23
Blamey, Thomas, 125, 246, 248
Blaskowitz, Johannes, 310
Blau, Operation, 191, 193, 196–97
Blenheim bomber, 86
Blitzkrieg, 18, 210:
    France
    Poland, 57–59
Blowtorch and corkscrew tactic, 369, 394
Blucher, 77
Blum, Leon, 14
Bobruisk, 347–48
Bock, Fedor von, 79, 137, 142–47, 196
Bogdanov, 355
Boise, 187
Bomber Command. *See* Strategic bombing
Bombing. *See* Combined Bomber Offensive;
    Strategic bombing
Boris, King, 26
Bormann, Martin, 408
Borneo, 158, 166, 168, 174, 319, 376, 397
Bose, Subhas Chandra, 270
Bougainville, 250–52, 264–65, 387
Bradley, Omar:
    Normandy, 295, 300, 302, 304–09, 312
    North Africa, 215
    Sicily, 218
    Western Front, 332, 337–340, 343–45
Brandenberger, Erich, 337–38
Brauchitsch, Walter von, 79, 137, 145, 147
Braun, Eva, 380
Brazil, 66
Bremen raids, 228, 230, 233
Brererton, Lewis, 332
Breskens, 330, 334
Bretagne, 119
Brevity, Operation, 131
Briansk-Vyazma, 145, 191, 193, 196, 283, 285
Britain. *See* Great Britain
Britain, battle, 90–98
Brittany campaign, 295–96, 299, 304, 306–07
Brooke, Alan, 206–07, 220, 344

Brooke-Popham, Robert, 166
Browning, Frederick, 332, 334
Bruce, Andrew, 323
Bucharest, 352
Buchenwald camp, 382
Buckner, Jr., Simon Bolivar, 390, 392, 394–95
Budapest, 353–55, 359
Budyonny, Semyon, 197
Buffer zone. *See* Satellites
Bug River, 291
Bulgaria, 26, 99, 124, 351, 384:
    liberation, 353, 355
Bulge, battle, 338–43, 368
Buna, 247
Bunker Hill, 251
Burma, 158, 226, 411:
    Britain controls, 28, 176, 373
    British advance, 267–73, 371–73
    Burcorps, 176
    Burma Area Army, 243
    Burma Independence (National) Army, 174
    independence, 243
    Japanese advance in, 174–76
    Japanese withdrawal, 397
Burma Road, 152, 176, 244, 371
Busch, Ernst, 347
Bushido. *See* Japan military

Cactus Air Force, 186, 189
Caen, 300, 304–05
Caesar Line, 280
Cairo conference, 225–26
Cairo Declaration, 244
Calabria, battle, 120
California, 163
Callaghan, D.J., 189
Cape Engano, battle, 366
Cape Esperance, battle, 187
Cape Gloucester, 252
Cape Matapan, battle, 125
Canada:
    Air Force, 231, 300
    conscription crisis, 335
    Dieppe, 210, 211
    Italy, 220, 222, 278–80
    Manhattan Project, 401
    Normandy, 300, 303–5, 307–08, 312–13
    Royal Canadian Navy and convoys, 110, 114, 237–38
    Western Front, 329, 330, 332, 334–35, 341–45
Canberra, 185
Cape Hatteras, 236

Caribbean warzone, 66, 114, 236, 240–41
Carlson's Raiders, 258
Carol II, King, 25–26
Caroline Islands, 261, 263–64, 324–25
Carr, E. H., 9
Cartwheel, Operation, 248–49, 250–52
Casablanca conference, 214–15, 217, 225, 229, 245, 294
Casablance Directive, 225
Cash and carry. *See* Neutrality Acts
Caspian Sea, 197
Cassino, battles, 274–80
Casualty totals, 412–15. *See also* Civilians; *various battles, campaigns, theaters*
Caucasus oil fields, 136, 142, 191, 193, 195–98, 202,
Celebes, 168, 174
Central Pacific theater, 182, 190, 245, 250, 252–53, 257–63, 315–26, 386–96, 397, 402–04
    converges with Southwest Pacific theater, 361
Cesare, 120
Ceylon, 174, 176, 180, 411
Chamberlain, Neville, 30, 54, 57, 64, 78
Chamorros, 323
Channel Battle, 94
Channel cross invasion, English. *See* Normandy invasion
Channel ports, 329–30, 334. *See also* Antwerp; Scheldt Estuary
Chans, 243
Chemnitz bombing raid, 341
Chennault, Claire, 153–54, 174, 244, 371
Cherbourg, 295, 300, 305
Cherkassy, 290–91
Chiang Kai-Shek, 39, 242–43:
    confronts Japan, 40
    end of war, 406
    rivalry with Mao Tse-tung, 47, 151–52, 273, 406, 411
    strategy of attrition, 44, 46, 49, 140, 244
    U.S. aid, 112, 153–54, 371–72
    strategic views, 226
Chicago, 185
China, 5, 164, 406:
    Doolittle bombers, 180
    civilian casualties, 172, 180, 409
    forces in Burma, 268–69
    Japanese offensive in, 244, 273, 371–72, 396
    military weakness, 44
    postwar role, 242–43, 372
    resists Japan, 39, 240
    revolution, 411
    theater, 43–50, 151–52, 176, 371
    U.S. air bases, 323

Y-Force, 273
China-Burma-India (CBI) theater. *See* Burma; China; India
Chindits, 243–44, 268–69
Cho, Isamu, 394–95
Choltitz, Dietrich von, 312–13
Christison, Philip, 267–68, 270–71
Chuikov, Vasili, 71, 198–200, 355, 380
Churchill, Winston, 4, 74, 78:
    Africa and Middle East, 119, 131, 205–07, 216
    battle of Britain, 90
    China, 154, 371
    convoys, 238
    Dieppe, 210
    Dragoon, 309, 312
    Dresden, 341
    Eisenhower, 344
    fall of France, 86–88
    Greece, 124–25
    Italy, 217, 220, 274, 277
    Japan, 399
    percentages deal with Stalin, 351–52
    postwar Germany, 378, 382
    postwar planning, 357–58
    second front, 211, 215
    Singapore, 172
    U.S., 99, 100–01, 105, 111, 114, 224–26
    USSR, 199, 224–25, 344, 351
    V-E Day, 383
Citadel, Operation, 285–86, 287–88, 359
Civil Air Transport, 154
Civilians, 2–4, 6, 61, 96, 129, 169, 180, 278, 317, 323, 362, 380, 412–16:
    aerial targets and morale, 95, 97, 104, 224–26, 227, 229, 231–32, 234–35, 316, 341, 369–70, 397–98
    deaths in Asia, 44, 45, 48, 152, 163, 177, 318, 324, 370–71, 374–74, 395, 397–98, 402–03, 404, 406
    deaths in Europe, 63, 82, 85, 192, 198, 203, 229, 232, 235, 239, 280–81, 297, 349–50, 355- 57, 382
    resistance, 297–99, 361
Clark Field, 374
Clark, Mark, 211–12, 220–21,274:
    Cassino, 275–76, 278
    Rome, 280–81
Clausewitz, Carl von, 2
Coast Watchers, 185–86, 319
Cobra, Operation, 305–06
Code talkers, 388
Cold War, 384, 407–08, 410, 412, 416
Collins, J. Lawton, 313
Cologne raid, 227–28

Colorado, 163

Combined Bomber Offensive, 225–26, 229–36, 283, 380:
    France, 297–98, 305

Combined Fleet, 182–84, 190, 251, 258, 263, 267, 273,
    315, 319, 363–67, 392, 404

Communism. *See* Soviet Union; China; Stalin, Josef;
    Mao Tse-tung

Concentration camp system. *See specific camps*

Congo, uranium from, 401

Convoy system, 108:
    Atlantic, 111–14, 116, 236–40
    Arctic, 112–13, 145, 237–38, 240

Cooney teams, 299

Co-Prosperity Sphere. *See* Greater East Asian
    Co-Prosperity Sphere

Coral Sea, 260

Coral Sea, battle, 181–82

Corap, Andre, 86

Cornwall, 176

Coronet, Operation, 399–401

Corregidor, 177, 362, 375

Corregidor, 260

Corsica, 212, 309

Courageous, 106

Courland Peninsula, 347, 351, 355, 359

Countances, 306

Coventry, 93, 98, 232

Cowra camp, 406

Crerar, Henry, 307–08, 313, 329–30, 332, 343

Crete, battle, 122–29

Crimea, 145, 191, 193–95, 283, 291–92

Croatia, 99, 126

Crusader, Operation, 132–33

Cunningham, Alan, 122, 132–33

Cunningham, Andrew, 122, 124–25, 127, 211, 217

Curtin, John, 246

Curtiss P40 fighter, 118

Cyprus, 119

Czechoslovakia, 22, 344:
    independence, 13
    liberation, 359, 383
    Normandy operations, 300
    partisans, 299
    postwar, 384
    Prague occupied, 54
    soldiers in Russia, 20
    Sudentenland, 13, 54

Dachau camp, 382

D'Annunzio, Gabriele, 21

Danube River, 353, 359

Danzig, 12, 56–57, 64, 358

Darlan, Francois, 212–13

Darmstadt raid, 233

Dauntless dive-bomber, 183

Dawley, Ernest, 220

Decolonization. *See* Great Britain; Greater East Asian
    Co-Prosperity Sphere; India; Roosevelt

D-Day. *See* Normandy invasion

Defense Plant Corporation, 101

DeGaulle, Charles, 86, 90, 205, 212, 297–98, 312,
    341, 383

Deladier, Edouard, 54

De Lattre de Tassigny, Jean-Marie, 310, 329, 343, 359

Democracies. *See* France; Great Britain; United States
    of America

Dempsey, Miles, 305, 307–08, 313, 329–30, 332–34

De-Nazification, 384, 407–08

Denmark, 74–75, 344, 382

Destroyers-for-bases agreement, 100–01

Devers, Jacob, 336, 343

Diadem, Operation, 278–80

Dieppe landing, 210–11, 295–96, 313

Dietrich, Josef, 337–40

Dinah Might, 388

Disease. *See* Medical problems

Displaced Persons, 384

Dnieper River, 142, 283, 289–91

Donets Basin, 137, 145, 191, 203, 283, 286

Donitz, Karl, 19, 106–08, 110–11, 114, 236–40:
    surrender, 380, 382–83
    war crimes, 408

Doolittle, James, 179, 211

Doolittle raid, 179–80, 185, 188

Doorman, Karl, 174

Dorman-Smith, Eric, 205–06

Dornier bomber, 94, 96, 227

Dorsetshire, 176

Douhet, Giulio, 24

Dowding, Hugh, 93–94

Dragoon, Operation, 309–12, 334, 336. *See also*
    Riviera landings

Dresden, 2, 341–42, 344–45

Drumbeat, Operation, 236

Duck (DUKW) amphibious truck, 262

Dunkirk, battle and evacuation, 87–89, 277

Dutch Borneo, 397

Dutch East Indies, 155, 158, 165, 168, 171–74, 179, 267,
    376, 397, 406, 411

Dutch Timor, 172, 174

Dyle Line, 80, 84

Dynamo, Operation, 87

88 (Flak) anti-aircraft gun, 131, 205, 207, 227, 230, 305
Eaker, Ira, 229, 233
East African campaign. *See* Egypt; Italy
Eastern European bloc. *See* Satellites
Eastern Front, 26, 112, 116, 133, 135–50, 158, 168,
        191–203, 210–11, 216–17, 220, 224–25,
        235–36, 282–93, 346–51, 354–60. *See also*
        Barbarossa; German military; Red Army;
        selected battles
Eastern Solomons, battle, 186
East Prussia invasion, 290, 336, 349, 351, 354–59
Eben Emael fortress, 80
E-boats, 297, 335
Edelweiss, Operation, 197–98
Eden, Anthony, 125, 352
Egypt, 28, 78, 117, 119–20, 130–31, 204–06, 210
Eichelberger, Robert, 247, 265, 373–74, 376
Eichmann, Adolf, 408
Eindhoven, 332–33
Einsatzgruppen, 61–62, 143, 349
Eisenhower, Dwight D., 211:
    battle of the Bulge, 338
    French Resistance, 299
    German surrender, 383
    liberation of Paris, 312
    Market-Garden, 332, 334
    Normandy invasion, 294–95, 307, 309, 316
    North Africa, 211, 214, 216
    Red Army, 378, 383
    SHAEF decisions, 329, 340
    Sicily and Italy, 216
    Western Front, 335, 341, 343–44
    Zhukov, 354
El Alamein, 204–10
Elba, 310
Elbe River, 341, 345, 354, 359, 382
Emperor Hirohito, 37, 40, 156, 258, 319, 365,
        387–88, 393
    surrender, 397, 399, 402–04
ENIGMA, 91–92, 111, 160, 237
Eniwetok, invasion, 163
Enola Gay, 402:
    exhibition, 416
Enterprise, 160, 182–83, 186, 188
Eremenko, Andrey, 145
Essen raids, 228, 230
Essex (class), 251, 253
Estonia, 290, 347, 351, 354, 411
Ethiopia, 23, 120, 122–23
Exeter, 174
Ezaki, Yoshio, 264

F4F Wildcat fighter, 160
Fairey bomber, 83
Falaise (pocket and gap), 305, 307–09, 312
Falkenhausen, Alexander von, 44
Falkenhorst, Nikolaus von, 74–76, 140
Farouk, King, 130
Fascism. *See* Germany; Italy; Japan
Fatherland Front, 35
Fat Man, 403–04
Federal Republic of Germany, 385, 408
Fellers, Bonner, 204
Fiji, 184
Final Solution, 143, 381–82, 408, 414. *See also*
        Holocaust
Finland, 20:
    Soviet relations, 346–47, 411
    Winter War, 69–73
Finschafen, 248
First World War. *See* World War I
Fiume, 21
Five-Power Treaty, 42
Flamethrower, 103, 252, 317, 367, 369, 388
Flavigny, A. R. L., 86
Fletcher, Jack, 181, 183, 185, 188
Flier, 368
Flintlock, Operation, 261
Flushing, 330, 335
Flying Tigers. *See* Chennault
Formidable, 125
Formosa (Taiwan), 39, 152, 156, 242, 244, 273, 326,
        361–62, 367, 390, 411
Fort Driant, 336
Fourteen Points. *See* Treaty of Versailles
France:
    Air Force, 31
    Armee d'Afrique
    Army strength and strategy, 30–31
    Britain, 27, 119
    fall of, 83–90
    foreign policy, 27, 34, 55
    Free French forces, 205, 276, 278, 280, 310, 312
    Hitler's Germany
    imperialism, 28–29
    Indochina, 152
    insecurities, 14–15, 27, 34
    invasion Riviera and South, 281, 309–12
    and Italy, 34, 276, 278, 280
    Navy, 33–34, 119
    North African invasion, 212–13
    plans for defense of, 79–80
    Poland, 55–57

postwar, 383, 411
Special Air Service, 299
submarine pens, 108
U.S., 27, 212. *See also* de Gaulle; Partisans
Franco, Francisco, 21, 26, 90, 216
Fredenhall, Lloyd, 211–12, 214
Friedeburg, Hans von, 382–83
Freissner, Johannes, 354
French Forces of the Interior (FFI), 298, 310
Freyberg, Bernard, 128, 277–78, 280
Front (Soviet Army Group), 60
Frost, John, 333
Frusci, Luigi, 122
Fubuki, 187
Fuller, Horace, 265
Funk, Walther, 408
Furutaka, 187
Fu Tso-yi, 40

Galahad, 243, 268
Gallivare iron ore, 74–74, 78
Gambier Bay, 365
Gamelin, Maurice Gustave, 79–80, 84, 86
Gandhi, Mohandas, 28
Garand M-1 rifle, 103
Gariboldi, Italo, 129–30
Gazala Line, 204–05, 211
Geiger, Roy, 316, 323, 390, 392, 395
Gelb, Operation, 78, 90, 91
Gemorrah, Operation. *See* Hamburg raid
Gensoul, Marcel, 119
Genzu, Mizukami, 269
George II, King, 352
Georges, Alphonse, 79, 86
German Democratic Republic, 385
German military, 13, 17
    anti-communism, 290
    Army strength, 18
    atrocities, 62, 141–44
    command of, 18
    German-Italian Panzer Army, 207, 210–11, 214,
    France, 83–90
    invasion of Denmark, 74–75
    Italy, 274–80
    losses on Eastern Front, 352
    losses in USSR, 202–03, 282, 287, 348, 355
    Low Countries and France, 78
    Navy, 18–19, 115
    Norway, 74–78
    occupation of Poland, 61–62
    panzers, 17
    plans for USSR, 136–37
    Poland, 55–61
    Sicily, 217–19
    strategic bombing, 227
    views of U.S. military, 305, 337
    war crimes, 408. *See also* Eastern Front;
        Luftwaffe; Market-Garden; Mobile warfare;
        North Africa; Submarines; Western Desert;
        Western Front
Germany:
    division, 384–85
    economy and production, 16–17, 55, 225, 229,
        235–36, 287
    nationalism, 13, 17
    postwar treatment of, 225, 384
    surrender, 380, 382–83
    Treaty of Versailles, 13–15. *See also* Strategic
        bombing
Ghormley, Robert, 185, 188
Ghurka Rifles (Nepal), 243
Gibraltar, 91, 110, 113, 117, 119, 216, 411
Gilbert Islands, 164, 253:
    campaign, 257–61
Glorious, 77
Glowworm, 76
Gneisenau, 18, 76–78, 110–11
Goebbels, Joseph, 138, 341, 380
Gold Beach, 303
Good War, 4, 414, 416, 417
Goodwood, Operation, 305
Gona, 246, 247
Göring, Herman, 16, 19, 87, 127, 201, 383:
    battle of Britain, 92–95
    unit, 218
    war crimes, 408
Gort, Lord, 87
Gothic Line, 222
Govorov, Leonid, 351
Graf Spee, Admiral, 64–65, 74, 106
Graziani, Rodolfo, 120–21, 124
Great Britain:
    decline, 5, 411
    economy, 27–28
    empire, 28, 165–66, 172, 242, 397, 411
    foreign policy, 27–28, 35, 55
    Finland, 74
    France, 27, 30
    intelligence services, 298
    Japan, 399
    military structure, 206
    Norway, 74–78

Great Britain: (continued)
  Poland, 55–57
  postwar, 384
  postwar occupation, 382
  revisionism of war, 4
  U.S., 27, 100–01,
  USSR, 28
Great Britain military:
  Army (British Expeditionary Force) strength and
    strategy, 29–30
  bombing campaign plans, 228–29
  in Burma, 175–76, 243–44, 372–73
  East African campaign, 117–23
  Eighth Army, 132, 204, 205, 207, 209, 215–18,
    220–22, 277–78, 280–81
  Germany, 359
  Malay Barrier, 166–67, 174, 176
  Market-Garden, 332–34
  plans to defend France, 78
  retreats at Dunkirk, 87–88
  views of U.S. military performance, 216. See also
    Airborne landings; Convoy system; Italy;
    Merchant fleet; North Africa; Royal Air Force
    (RAF); Royal Navy; Submarines; Western
    Desert; Western Front
Great Depression, 5, 16, 27, 29–30, 38–39, 98, 102
Greater East Asian Co-Prosperity Sphere, 39,
    47–48, 52, 153–55, 164–65, 169, 174, 244,
    253, 367, 373, 397
Greatest Generation, 416–17
Greece, 12–13, 22, 26, 55, 120, 351, 353:
  Africa and Mediterranean campaigns, 209, 217
  civil war, 352
  communism, 352
  German attack on, 126–29
  Italian attack on, 123–25
  Normandy operations, 300
Greer, 114–15
Grenade, Operation, 343
Grimsley, Mark, 1
Griswold, Oscar, 249, 252
Groves, Leslie, 401
Guadalcanal, 182, 184–90, 248, 304, 310, 319
Guam, 158, 165, 262, 321–23, 387
Guderian, Heinz
  defeat, 379
  Eastern Front, 349, 352, 355, 359
  France, 84–86, 89
  mobile warfare, 18, 57–58
  USSR, 139, 140, 142–43, 146–47, 285
Guernica, 26

Gulags, Soviet, 381–82, 384
Gusen camp, 381
Gustav Line, 222, 274, 276–280
Guzzoni, Alfred, 217–18

Haakon VII, King, 77
Haganah, 298
Ha-Go, Operation, 167–68
Hainan Islands, 49
Halder, Franz, 79, 147
Halifax bomber, Handley Page, 227–28
Halsey, William, 179, 188, 245, 249, 251–52, 257, 315,
    324, 326:
  Leyte Gulf, 362–63, 366
  Philippines, 373
  surrender of Japan, 405
Hamburg, 344, 359:
  bombing raids, 130, 230–31, 342
Hammann, 183
Hampden bomber, 227
Hanover bombing raid, 230
Hansell, Haywood, 369
Harris, Arthur "Bomber," 228–31, 233–36, 341–42, 415
Hart, Thomas, 159
Haruyoshi, Hyakutake, 186, 250
Hausser, Paul, 283
Hawaii, Operation, 159, 164
Hedgerows, 304–06
Hei, 189
Heinkel bomber, 94, 96, 227
Heligoland Bight, battle, 63–64
Hellcat fighter, 321, 363
Hermes, 176
Heron, Operation, 197–98
Herrmann, Hajo, 232
Hess, Rudolf, 408
Heydrich, Reinhard, 62, 299
Higgins boats, 303
Himmler, Heinrich, 16, 350, 355
Hindenburg, Paul von, 16–17
Hipper, 76, 110, 238
Hirohito. See Emperor Hirohito
Hiroshima, 2, 322:
  atomic bombing, 402–03
Hitler, Adolf, 3:
  Aryan and race ideas, 15–16, 135, 195, 298
  assassination attempts, 337
  battle of the Bulge, 337, 339–40
  begins war, 9
  Budapest, 353–54
  counteroffensive in West, 335–40

death, 378, 380
defensive strategy, 309
England, 91
Finland, 346
Franco, 26
halt order at Dunkirk, 87
hatred of communism/USSR, 15, 135
Italian campaign, 277
Japan, 43
lebensraum, 15, 135–36, 287
military decisions in USSR, 142, 193, 195–99,
    201–03, 282, 283, 285–86, 288–92, 347, 351,
    353–55, 359
Mussolini, 123–24, 218
on naval campaigns, 111, 114, 238
Normandy landings, 290, 295, 297, 300, 305, 307,
    309–11, 313
North African campaign, 204
Operation Sealion, 94, 96–97
Paris, 312
planning for war, 53, 55–56
rise to power, 15–17
strategic bombing views, 233
Treaty of Versailles, 15
U.S., 115–16
Vichy France, 211
Wehrmacht, 18
Western Front, 290, 330, 335, 341, 343–44,
Hitler Line, 278, 280
Hitler Youth, 380
Hiyo, 322
Hobart, Percy, 18
Hodges, Courtney, 307–08, 312–13, 329, 335–40,
    343–45
Hoel, 366
Hoepner, Erich, 140, 147
Hollandia, 264–66
Holocaust, 3, 62, 225, 381–82, 408, 410, 414–16
Home Fleet, 33
Home Guard, 91, 131
Homma, Masaharu, 165, 176–77, 409
Honda, Masaki, 267–69, 373
Hong Kong, 158, 165–66, 406, 411
Honshu, 368, 370, 388, 390, 396–97, 399, 402
Hood, 110
Horii, Tomitaro, 245–46
Hornet, 179, 182–83, 188
Horrocks, Brian, 332–34
Horthy, Miklos, 25, 353
Hoth, Hermann, 139–40, 196, 199, 201, 282, 286
Hube, Hans, 218, 221

Hughes, 188
Hukbalahaps, 178, 376
Huon Peninsula, 247, 248
Hull, Cordell, 154, 157, 159, 162
Hump, The, 269
Hungary, 20, 25, 99, 352, 355, 359:
    liberation, 353–54
    Soviet atrocities, 356
    troops in USSR, 195
Hupei raids, 244
Hurley, Patrick, 371
Hurricane fighter, 24, 32, 93–96, 100, 107, 118, 224
Hurtgen Forest, battle, 335–36, 338
Husky, Operation, 217–19
Hutton, Thomas, 174

Iceland, 108–10, 114
Ichi-Go Offensive, 273, 371, 396
Ichiki, Kiyonao, 186
Ida, Shojiro, 174, 176
Illustrious, 124
Imamura, Hitoshi, 168
Imperial Japanese Army:
    advance in Indochina, 48–49
    atrocities, 5, 45–46, 48, 152, 177, 180, 272, 374–75,
        406, 409
    attempted coup, 404
    expansionist aims, 179
    Malaya and Singapore, 171–72
    New Guinea, 245–49
    Pacific battles, 386–92, 394–97
    Philippines, 176–78, 362, 367–68, 373–77
    refusal to surrender, 402
    strength, 40–41
    surrender, 404–05
    victories in China, 44–49, 273
Imperial Japanese Navy:
    Aircraft/pilot losses, 182, 187–88, 190, 252, 316, 319,
        322, 366, 394
    expansionist aims, 155, 158, 164, 179
    Gilbert Islands, 257
    Mariana Islands, 262–63, 316–24
    Marshall Islands, 262
    New Guinea, 180
    Okinawa, 392–94
    Pacific battles, 179–90, 390, 392–94
    petroleum supplies, 156–57
    Philippines defense, 362–67
    Plan A-Go, 319
    ship orders and production, 151
    strength, 42–43, 164, 366

Imperial Japanese Navy: (*continued*)
    Taranto lessons, 124
    Truk, 263
    victories (1941–42), 172–74, 176, 181–82. *See also*
        Combined Fleet; Pearl Harbor;
        selected battles
Imperial Rule Assistance Association, 154
Imphal Offensive, 270–73
Independence (class), 251, 253
India:
    African campaign, 120–21, 209
    Britain, 28–29
    Burma campaign, 167–73, 371–73
    CBI, 176
    Italy, 278
    National Indian Army, 172, 270
    nationalism, 242, 411
    Singapore, 167, 171–72
Indianapolis, 325
Indian Ocean, 211–12, 274
Indochina, 29, 152, 155, 166, 226, 371, 411
Indomitable, 167
Indonesia, 411
Intelligence, 3, 6:
    Asia/Pacific theaters, 298
    Atlantic, 106, 108, 111, 240
    Australian, 397
    British, 55, 76, 78, 91–92, 97, 120, 121, 124, 127,
        208, 333
    Filipino, 361
    French, 79
    German, 94, 197, 204, 210, 297, 302, 408
    Japanese, 42, 182–83, 361–62
    Polish, 209, 212
    Resistance, 298, 309
    strategic bombing, 236–37
    U.S., 155, 160, 162, 167, 181, 214, 261, 165, 168,
        400, 411
    USSR, 136, 138, 139, 285. *See also* ENIGMA;
        MAGIC; ULTRA
Intrepid, 263
Iran, 237
Iraq, 28, 117, 119, 131
Irrawaddy River, 269, 372, 373
Iron Bottom Sound, 185, 188–89
Italian military:
    Air Force, 24, 117–18, 123
    ground forces, 23–24
    Navy, 24–25
    troops in USSR, 195, 217
    weaknesses, 23–25, 123

Italy:
    Albania, 12, 26, 54–55
    Allied invasion of, 220–22, 274–81
    Austria, 54
    cease-fire, 380–81
    East Africa, 29, 53, 117–23
    France, 34, 90
    invades Ethiopia, 29, 35
    North Africa, 204, 207--15
    postwar treatment of, 225
    surrender, 380–81
    rise of fascism, 21
    Greece, 123–25
Iwabachi, Sanji, 374–75
Iwo Jima, 325, 342:
    battle, 386–90, 392, 396, 399–400

Japan
    Anti-Comintern Pact, 40, 52
    Barbarossa, 151
    blockade, 267, 368, 394, 399, 401–02
    diplomacy to end war, 267, 398–99, 402–03,
        405–06
    economic strain, 371, 398
    Emperor, 40
    German defeat, 340
    German-Italian military pact, 40, 43
    imperialism, 29, 270, 397
    interwar, 37–38
    invades China, 9, 43–44
    Manchuria, 39–40
    militarism, 37
    Munich Pact, 49
    neutrality pact with USSR, 52, 154
    postwar, 225, 410–11
    production, 151, 371
    race war, 174, 260–61, 324
    relations with U.S., 39–40, 153–56
    repatriation of citizens, 406
    rivalry with USSR, 40
    rise to international power, 38–39
    surrender, 403–05
    trade, 38, 47, 151
    wartime economy, 43, 47, 157, 361
    wartime expansion, 178–79. *See also* Strategic
        bombing
Japan military:
    air attacks in China, 49
    bomber aircraft, 227
    bushido spirit, 41, 51–52, 365, 409–10
    Kwantung Army, 41–42, 51–52, 152, 403

reprisals for Doolittle raid, 180
Sea Eagles, 42, 162, 166, 183, 248, 321
strategy toward U.S., 43, 155–57, 261. *See also*
Imperial Japanese Army; Imperial Japanese
Navy
Japanese-American intelligence, 268
Java Sea, battle, 173–74
Jedburgh teams, 299
Jeep, 288, 333, 339
Jet aircraft, 227
Jews, 225:
concentration camps, 353
Crete, 128
deaths, 381, 414
Eastern Front, 347
Germany, 15
Greece, 129, 133–34
Hungary, 353, 381
Italy, 134, 280
Poland, 62, 349–50
Yugoslavia, 134
Jodl, Alfred, 383
Johnston, 366
Juneau, 188–89
Junker bomber, 227
Juno Beach, 303–04

Kachins, 243, 268
Kaiser, Henry, 112
Kamikazes, 41, 363, 365, 373–74, 389–90, 392–93,
395–96, 404
Karens, 243
Karlsruhe, 76
Kassel bombing raids, 230, 233
Kasserine Pass, battle, 214
Katamura, Shihachi, 372–73
Kawabe, Masakuze, 243, 267, 270, 272–73
Kawasaki Ki-45 Dragon Killer fighter, 397
Kearny, 116
Keitel, Wilhelm, 142, 144, 380, 408
Kellogg-Briand Pact, 16, 34
Kennedy, Joseph, 98
Kenney, George, 246–48, 264–66, 361
Kenya, 117
Kerch Peninsula, 193–95
Keren, battle, 122
Kesselring, Albert:
Africa, 133, 213, 215
battle of Britain, 92, 95
Sicily and Italy, 219, 221–22, 276–77, 279–80
Western Front, 343

Keynes, John Maynard, 15
Kharkov, 193, 196, 203, 283, 285, 288–89
Kiel bombing raid, 230
Kiev, 142–44, 289–90
Kimmel, Husband, 160, 162, 165
Kincaid, Thomas, 188
King, Edward, 177
King, Ernest, 104–05, 114, 179, 184, 257, 263, 315,
326, 361
Kinkaid, Thomas, 362, 365–66, 373
Kinov, Ivan, 353
Kirishima, 189
Kirponov, M. P., 142–43
Kiska, invasion of, 182
Kleist, Ewald von, 87, 193, 196, 202, 292
Kluge, Gunther von, 58, 142, 147, 191, 286, 305,
307, 309
Knickebien navigational aid, 97
Knox, Frank, 100
Kobayashi, Masashi, 261
Kobe bombings, 370, 397
Kodiak Island, 182
Koga, Meneichi, 248, 251, 263
Koenig, Marie Pierre, 205, 298
Kohima, 271–72, 372
Kohima-Imphal road, 272
Koiso, Kuniaki, 324
Kokoda Trai, 245, 247
Kolombangara Island, 249–50
Komorowski, Tadeusz, 350
Kondo, Nobutake, 166
Konev, Ivan, 145, 285, 288, 291–92, 344, 349,
355, 358–59:
Berlin, 378–79
Czechoslovakia, 383
Konigsberg, 76
Konoe, Fumimaro, 40, 47, 49, 153–54, 157
Korea, 226, 403, 406:
laborers, 260, 262, 318, 409
Koror base, 325
Kozielewski, Jan, 381
Kozlov, D.T., 194
Kozume, Naoyuki, 265
Krebs, Hans, 380
Kretschmer, Otto, 108
Kriiwana, 249
Krueger, Walter, 248, 264, 361, 367, 374–76
Kula Gulf, battle, 249
Kuniaki Cabinet, 399
Kunio, Nakegawa, 325
Kuribayshi, Tadimichi, 386–87

Kuril Islands, 159–60, 182, 264, 403
Kurita, Takeo, 251–52, 362–63, 366
Kursk, 196, 203:
    battle, 283–88
Kutrzeba, Tadeucz, 59
Kutuzov, Operation, 285
Kwajalein, 261–63
Kyushu, 323, 368, 390, 397, 399–400, 404

Lae, 247–48
Lager Nordhausen camp, 357
Lancaster bomber, Avro, 227–29, 232, 341
Langsdorf, Hans, 64
Latin America, 65–66, 360
Latvia, 138, 347, 351, 411
League of Nations, 11, 13, 35, 71, 98, 119
Leahy, William, 400
Leander, 249
Leap, Operation, 202
Lebanon, 212
Lebensraum. *See* Hitler
Leclerc, Philippe, 312
Ledo Road, 243, 267, 269–70, 371
Lee, Willis, 362, 366
Leeb, Wilhelm Ritter von, 83, 89, 137, 140, 143, 145–47
Leese, Oliver, 277–79, 281
Leigh-Mallory, Trafford, 93, 95, 294
LeMay, Curtis, 369–70, 386, 397–98, 402
Lend-Lease, 111–12, 195, 237, 282, 288, 384
Leningrad, 140, 146, 191–93, 196–97, 202, 282, 290, 346, 351
Leopold, King, 80
Le Paradis massacre, 89
Lexington, 160, 181, 182
Leyte, 326, 361–62, 367–68
Leyte Gulf, battle, 361–67
Liberty ships, 112, 114, 373
Libya, 22, 28, 117, 120–22, 130–31, 207, 209–11, 215
Liddell Hart, Sir Basil Henry, 18
Lidice massacre, 299
Lightfoot, Operation, 207–08
Lindbergh, Charles, 324
Liscome Bay, 260
List, Sigmund, 126
Lithuania, 20, 138, 347, 349, 351, 411
Little Boy, 402
Little Saturn, Operation, 201
Locarno Treaty, 14
Logistics, 3:
    Allied, 72, 216, 226, 238, 280, 294–95, 299, 329
    British, 132, 271–72, 334

German, 58, 131, 137, 142, 144, 197, 199, 207, 210, 282, 335, 340
Japanese, 156, 164, 176–77, 243, 267, 367
Latin America, 66
Soviet, 145–46, 195, 288, 349, 355
U.S., 103, 247, 316, 374–75, 390, 409
Western Desert, 131–32, 206
London "Blitz", 95–96, 98
London Naval Treaty, 19
Longcloth, Operation, 243
Long-Range Penetration group, 243
Los Negros Island, 264
Lubeck, 344, 382:
    bombing raid, 228
Lucas, John, 276–77
Luce, Henry, 45, 50
Luftwaffe
    Africa, 130, 213, 216
    battle of Britain, 91–98, 235
    building of, 19–20
    Crete, 128
    Dieppe, 210
    France, 83, 87
    Normandy, 297
    Poland, 57–59
    Sicily and Italy, 217, 276
    Spain, 19
    strategic bombing theory and practice, 226–28, 235
    USSR, 136, 138, 198–201, 282–83, 287
    Western Front, 340. *See also* German military
Lutzow, 76, 238
Luxembourg, 80, 312–13, 329, 338
Luzon, 326, 365, 373–76, 386–87

M2A1 towed howitzer, 103, 216
MacArthur, Douglas, 103, 216, 273:
    invasion of Japan, 399–400
    New Guinea, 245–49, 252, 263–66
    Philippines, 156–59, 165, 176–78, 257, 267, 324, 326
    Philippines invasion, 361–62, 367–68, 373–77, 387
    planning and decision-making, 179, 184, 315, 319
    surrender of Japan, 405
    wades ashore on Leyte, 361–62
Mackensen, Eberhard von, 276–77
McAuliffe, Anthony, 339–40
McCambell, David, 363
McCreery, Richard, 221–22
Madagascar, 212
Mafia, 118, 219
Magdeburg bombing raid, 341
MAGIC, 155, 160

Maginot Line, 31, 34, 57, 63, 79, 83, 89–90, 330, 336
Maikop oil fields, 197, 202
Majdanek camp, 350, 356–57, 381–82
Majuro atoll, 261
Makin Island, 165, 258–60
Malay, 236
Malaya, 152, 158, 166–67, 171–72, 174, 176, 226, 411
Malay Barrier strategy. *See* Great Britain military;
    Royal Navy
Malin, Craig, 103
Malinovsky, Radion, 353–54
Malmedy massacre, 338
Malta, 119
Maltby, Christopher, 165–66
Manchuria, Soviet invasion, 372, 396–97. *See also* China;
    Imperial Japanese Army (Kwantung Army)
Manhattan Project, 401
Manila, 368, 373, 376, 390:
    battle, 374–76, 386
Mannherheim, Carl Gustaf, 70, 346–47:
    Mannherheim Line, 70–73
Manstein, Erich von, 70:
    France, 79
    USSR, 193–95, 197, 201, 273, 283, 286–93
    war crimes, 408
Manteuffel, Hasso-Ecard von, 337–40
Manus Island, 264
Mao Tse-tung, 44, 47, 151–53, 371–72, 403, 411
Maquis, 298
Marco Polo Bridge, 43
Mare Nostrum. *See* Mussolini
Mareth Line, 209, 215
Mariana Islands, 164, 183, 257, 261, 263–65, 386:
    bombing missions, 369, 389
    campaign, 315–24
Marienburg raid, 230, 233
Market-Garden, Operation, 330–34, 336
Marpi Point, 318, 362
Mars, Operation, 201
Marseilles, 309–12
Marshall, George C., 104, 154, 176, 179, 184, 211, 273,
    280, 371
Marshall Islands, 164, 257–58, 273:
    campaign, 261–63
Matsuoko, Yokuke, 154–56
Mauthausen camp, 382
Medenine, 215
Medical problems, 252, 265–66, 377, 390
Megargee, Geoffrey, 1
Meiktila, 372–73
Memory, 416

Merchant fleets, 106–08, 113, 115–16, 118, 123, 133,
    236–37, 239, 267, 368
Merkur, Operation, 127–28
Merrill, Aaron Stanton, 251
Merrill, Frank (Marauders), 268–70
Mersa Brega, battle, 133
Mersa Matruth, 205
Mers el Kebir, 119, 212
Messe, Giovanni, 216, 216
Messerschmitt fighter, 19, 57, 84, 100
Messervey, Frank, 373
Metaxas, John, 26
Metz, 313, 330, 334, 336
Meuse River, 79, 84–86, 312, 330, 332, 338–40
Mexico, 66
Michael, King, 352
Middle East. *See* Egypt; Iraq; North Africa; Palestine
Midway Island, 160, 190:
    battle, 182–84, 362, 366
Mikawa, Gunich, 185, 188
Millervo, 196, 202
Millett, Allan, 125, 272
Mincemeat, Operation, 217
Mindanao, 178, 319, 326, 377
Mindoro, 367–68, 373
Minh, Ho Chi, 29
Minority nationalities, 12–13
Minsk, 140, 347–49
Missouri, 405
Mitchell, Billy, 32, 104
Mitscher, Mark, 261, 263, 316, 319, 321–22, 324, 362, 366:
    Okinawa, 393–94
Mitsubishi "Betty" G4M bomber, 227
Mobile warfare, 17–18, 57, 103
Model, Walther
    Eastern Front, 201, 285–86, 288, 290, 292, 347, 351
    Western Front, 309, 333, 337, 343–44
    death, 344
Molotov Cocktails, 71, 350
Molotovsk, 237
Moluccas, 168, 174
Monte Cassino. *See* Cassino
Montgomery, Alfred, 251
Montgomery, Bernard, 3, 206, 216, 383:
    German defeat, 382
    Italy, 220, 277
    Market-Garden, 330, 332–34
    Normandy, 294, 300, 305, 308–09
    North Africa, 207–09, 215
    Sicily, 219
    Western Front, 330, 335–37, 339–41, 343–345

Morgan, Frederick, 300
Morgenthau, Henry, 153–54
Morgenthau Plan, 384
Morocco, 28–29, 117, 210, 278
Mortain counteroffensive, 307
Moscow, battles for, 140, 145–47, 150, 191, 195–96, 198,
    203, 285
Mosquito bomber, de Havilland, 341
Mountbatten, Louis, 226, 242, 245, 371
Mulberry artificial harbor, 295, 300, 303
Munda Point, 249
Munich crisis, 29, 54
Muraviev, Konstantin, 353
Murmansk, 140, 237–38
Murphy, Robert, 212
Murray, Leonard, 110
Murray, Williamson, 125, 272
Murrow, Edward R., 98
Musashi, 362–63
Mussolini, Benito:
    Albania, 22, 54–55
    Anti-semitism, 134
    bombing target, 230
    death, 378
    Ethiopia, 29
    fall from power, 217–18, 220
    Franco and Spanish Civil War, 22–23
    Hitler, 23, 25, 55, 117
    invasion of Italy, 280
    leadership of, 23, 121–22, 124
    mare nostrum and imperialism, 21–22, 117–18,
        123–24
Mustafa Kemal, 13
Mutaguchi, Renya, 243, 268, 270–73
Myitkyina, 243, 269–70, 273

Nagara, 189
Nagas, 243
Nagasaki, 322, 397:
    atomic bombing, 404
Nagoya bombings, 370, 397
Nagumo, Chuichi, 159–60, 162–63, 165, 183
Naha, 390–91, 395
Nanking, battle, 45–46
Napalm, 370
Narvik, 76–77
Nashville, 373
National Defense Advisory Commission, 101
"National Redoubt", Berchtesgaden, 344, 359, 379, 383
Nationalist (Koumintang) China. *See* Chiang
    Kai-Shek; China

Navy Expansion Act (1938), 104
Nazi, 2
    defined, 15
    propaganda, 12, 195
    punishment, 407–08
Nazi-Soviet Pact, 52, 56, 135
Neame, Philip, 129–30
Neisse Line, 358–59
Neptune, Operation, 294, 296, 299, 304
Netherlands (Holland):
    East Indies, 159
    invasion by Germany, 80–82
    imperialism, 29
    liberation, 344
    Normandy operations, 300
    punishment of collaborators, 407
    surrender of Royal Netherlands East Indies
        Army, 174
    Western Front, 330, 332–33, 335
Neurath, Konstantin von, 408
Neutrality Acts, 98, 111, 123
Nevada, 163
Newall, Cyril, 32
New Britain Island, 165, 264–66
New Caledonia, 188
New Georgia campaign, 249–50
New Georgia Island, 249
New Guinea:
    American-Australian advance, 245–49
    Dutch New Guinea, 174, 265–66
    Japanese advance, 179–81, 184–85, 190
New Zealand, 120, 164:
    Africa, 132–33, 205, 209
    Italy, 277–79
    Greece, 125–28
    Pacific War, 179, 249, 251
Nimitz, Chester, 179:
    battle of Coral Sea, 181–82
    Central Pacific decisions, 190, 252, 257, 386–87
    Gilbert Islands, 253, 260
    Guadalcanal, 185, 188, 190
    invasion of Japan, 399
    Iwo Jima, 386–87
    MacArthur cooperation, 264–65, 273, 315
    Marianas, 315–16, 323
    Marshalls, 262
    message to Halsey, 366
    Midway, 183–84
    Okinawa, 390
    Peleliu, 324
    Philippines, 326, 362

strategy, 179, 245
    surrender of Japan, 405
    Tarawa, 260, 315
Nine-Power Treaty, 39
Nishimura, Shojo, 362–63
Noemfoor Island, 266
Nogues, Auguste, 212–13
Nomonhon, battle, 51–52
Nomura, Kichisaburo, 155, 157, 159, 162
Norden bombsight, 229
Normandy invasion, 390, 400:
    advance inland, 304–09, 312–13
    D-Day, 300–04
    planning, 220, 226, 235, 274, 278, 281
North Africa (1941–42), 117, 129
    Allied landings (Torch), 210–13
    Campaign in, 204–16. See also Western Desert
        campaign
North Carolina, 187
Norway:
    German campaign, 74–78
    neutrality and Winter War, 72
    Normandy, 300
    postwar, 411
    resistance, 298–99
    submarine pens, 108
Nuremberg Trials, 408

O'Connor, Richard, 121, 130
Oder River, 351, 354–55, 358, 379
Office of Strategic Services (OSS), 298
Okinawa, 316, 325, 387, 404:
    invasion, 390–96, 397
    surrender calculations, 399–400
Oklahoma, 163
Oktyabrsky, F.S., 193, 195
Oldendorf, Jesse, 363, 366
Olympic, Operation, 399–400
Omaha Beach, 300–03
Onishi, Takijiro, 363
Oradour-sur-Glane massacre, 299, 304
Orel, 283, 285, 287–88
Organization, military, 7
Ormoc, 367
Osaka bombings, 370, 397
Osmena, Sergio, 361, 363, 375
Overlord, Operation, 220, 277, 280, 292, 294–304.
        See also Normandy invasion
Owen Stanley Mountains, 245
Ozawa, Jizaburo, 166, 319, 321–22, 362–63, 366

P-38 fighter, 265
P-40 fighter, 165, 244
P-47 Thunderbolt fighter, 105, 233
P-51 Mustang fighter, 233, 341, 389, 397
P-61 Black Widow fighter, 397
Pacific war. *See* Central Pacific theater; Imperial
        Japanese Navy, Southwest Pacific theater; U.S.
        military; *selected battles*
Pact of Steel, 22–23, 56
Pahlavi, Reza Shah, 28
Palau Islands, 32, 263, 265, 319, 324–26
Palestine, 13, 117, 119, 298, 411
Papagos, Alexandro, 124–25
Papandreou, Andreas, 35
Papua New Guinea, 245–46
Paris, 80, 85–86, 89–90, 306–08, 312–13, 329
Park, Keith, 93, 95–96
Partisans:
    Albania, 55
    China, 47
    French Resistance, 298–99, 304, 313
    Italy, 221, 280
    Netherlands, 332
    Norway, 298
    Palestine, 298
    Philippines, 178, 361, 376
    Poland, 61, 298–99
    USSR, 143–44
    Yugoslavia, 126, 298
Pas de Calais, 295, 297, 300, 304–05
Patch, Alexander, 189, 309–10, 329, 336, 343, 359
Patton, George, 216:
    anti-semitism, 382
    Czechoslovakia, 383
    Germany, 359, 382
    Nazis, 408
    Normandy, 295–96, 300, 307–09, 311–13
    North Africa, 211–12, 214–15
    Sicily and Italy, 217–19
    Western Front, 329, 334, 336–40, 343, 345
Paulus, Friedrich, 129, 131, 193, 196–99, 201–02, 209
Panay (USS), 46, 98
Pavlov, D. G., 139–40
Pearl Harbor, 42, 151, 158–59, 183–84:
    attack on, 147, 159–64
    cargo explosion (1944), 316
Peenemunde rocket station, 233
Peleliu, 324–26, 386
Pentagon, 103
Percival, Arthur, 167, 171–72

Persian Gulf, 237
Pétain, Philippe, 89–90, 212
Petrov, I.Y., 193, 195
Philippines:
    Japan, 49, 165
    Japanese invasion of, 176–78
    southern islands campaign, 376
    U.S., 29, 156–58, 242, 245, 166, 386–87, 390, 394, 400, 411
    U.S. invasion, 325–26, 361–68, 373–77, 406
Philippine Sea, battle, 188, 319–22, 323
Phony War, 63–66
Pilsudski, Josef, 25
Pingsingkuan, 44
Piva Forks, battle of, 252
Plan Orange, 43, 158, 245
Platt, William, 120, 122
Pointblank, Operation, 229–30
Pointe de Hoc, 301
Poland, 12, 25–26
    airborne forces, 333–34
    attack on, 19, 32, 55–62
    Berlin, 380
    dismembered, 62–63
    exiles, 64, 296
    Home Army, 349–50, 358
    Italy, 279
    Normandy, 300, 307
    postwar, 384
    relations with West, 33
    relations with USSR, 20, 56
    Soviet advance through, 290, 349–51
    uprisings, 349–50
    Western Front, 330
Polish Corridor, 12, 57–58, 358
Popov, A. F., 283
Portal, Charles, 32, 229
Porter, 188
Portland, 188
Port Moresby, 245, 247–48
Potsdam, 400:
    Declaration, 399–402, 404
Pound, Dudley, 238
Prague, battle, 382–83
Prasca, Visconti, 124
Prince Eugen, 110–11
Prince of Wales, 110, 158, 167
Princeton, 251, 363
Pripet Marshes, 137, 292
Prisoners, 2:
    Africa/Mediterranean theaters, 121, 123, 128, 132–33, 218–19

Asia/Pacific, 42, 45, 48, 265, 325, 377, 403, 405–06, 409
Europe, 60–61, 74, 89–91, 304, 334, 338, 341, 343, 345, 352, 354, 381, 384
USSR, 139, 142, 144–45, 150, 194–95, 197, 202–03, 292, 349
Production. See selected countries
Propaganda, 138, 141, 144–45, 216, 341
Prostitution, 409
PT (Patrol Torpedo) boat, 247, 363
Punishment, Operation, 125–26
Purges. See Stalin
PURPLE, 160
Pyle, Ernie, 392, 395

Quebec conference, 225–26, 233–34, 243, 245, 329
Quincy, 185
Quisling, Vidkun, 77, 407

Rabaul, 165, 179, 180, 184–86, 245, 247–52, 257, 264, 266
Race war, 260–61, 324, 401
Radar, 97, 108, 227, 231, 237, 321, 363, 368, 386, 392, 397
Raeder, Erich, 18, 74, 106, 111, 114–15, 238, 408
Ramsay, Bertram, 294–95
Rangoon, 174–76, 270–71:
    liberated, 372–73, 397
Rapallo Treaty, 14
Rape. See Imperial Japanese Army; Red Army atrocities; U.S. military.
Red Army:
    advance in Germany
    air forces, 60, 123, 138, 282
    atrocities, 355–57, 380
    Berlin, 378–80
    Barbarossa, 136
    death camps, 355, 382
    Eastern/Southeastern Europe, 351–55
    East Prussia, 290
    Finland, 69–73
    invades Japanese possessions, 403, 406
    losses, 138, 144, 191, 193–95, 197, 200–01, 286–87, 290, 348
    Poland, 60–61, 290, 337
    purges of, 21, 60–61
    scorched earth policy of, 141
    strength and development, 60
    U.S. meeting, 359–60. See also Soviet military
Refugees. See Displaced Persons
Regensburg-Schweinfurt raids, 230, 233–34
Reichenau, Walther, 59–60, 143, 147
Reinhardt, Georg-Hans, 87
Remagen, 343

Rendulic, Lothar, 359
Renown, 77
Reparations:
    Finland, 347
    German, 13–14, 384
Repulse, 158, 167
Resistance (French). *See* Partisans
Reuben James, 116
Reynaud, Paul, 86, 89–90
Rhine River, 344:
    crossing, 343
    diplomatic borders, 13–14
    Western Front, 330, 332–37, 340–42, 344–45
Rhineland, 16, 35, 229
Rhino device, 305–06
Ribbentrop, Joachim von, 56, 408
Richards, Hugh, 271
Riga, 351
Ritchie, Neil, 133, 204–05
River Plate, battle, 64
Riviera landings, 280, 309–10. *See also* Dragoon;
    France
Rockets, 236, 335
Roer River, 336–38
Rohm, Ernst, 17
Roi-Namur, 261–62
Rokossovsky, Valentin, 202–03, 284–86, 349, 354–55,
    358–59
    Berlin, 379
Romania, 25–26, 90, 99, 124, 129, 292, 351, 355:
    liberation 352–53
    Soviet rule, 356, 358, 384
    troops in USSR, 193–95, 199, 201
Rome, 221–22, 274, 276–80
Rommel, Erwin, 84, 199:
    Africa, 129–34, 204–15, 217
    "asparagus", 297
    death, 305
    Desert Fox nickname, 129
    invasion of France, 84–85, 87
    Normandy, 296–97, 300, 302, 304–05
Roosevelt, Franklin D. (FDR):
    China, 99, 112, 242–43, 371
    Churchill, 100, 105, 111, 114, 220, 224–26
    concentration camps, 381
    convoys, 238
    criticizes Mussolini, 89
    death, 378, 392
    declaration of war, 164
    decolonization, 242
    Doolittle raid, 180

export sanctions on Japan, 154, 158
Europe-first strategy, 105, 158, 165, 211
Guadalcanal, 188
neutrality, 114–16
plea to Axis Powers, 98
Poland, 57
postwar plans, 357–58
pre-war diplomacy of, 35, 40, 99
public pressure, 179
re-election, 368
Stalin, 357–58
Suez Canal, 123
threat of Japan, 153–56
United Nations, 358
Wake Island meeting, 326
Rosenthal, Joe, 388
Rostock raid, 228
Rostov, 196, 202
Rotterdam, 82, 228, 330
Rouen raid, 229
Royal Air Force (RAF): 31–32, 55:
    attacks Wilhelmhaven, 63
    battle of Britain, 93–96
    Bomber Command, 228–29, 233, 235
    competition with Luftwaffe, 19
    defense of France, 79, 83, 86
    against Italy, 24, 117, 123
    Normandy, 300, 305, 307, 309
    Western Front, 330, 337, 341–42. See *also* Combined
        Bomber Offensive; Harris, Arthur; Strategic
        bombing
Royal Marines, 78
Royal Navy:
    African campaign, 121, 207, 209
    Crete, 128
    Dieppe, 210
    French fleet, 119, 212
    Italian fleet, 120
    Malay Barrier strategy, 158–59, 167
    Mediterranean dominance by, 216
    Normandy, 300
    Norway campaign, 74–78
    Okinawa, 390, 396–97, 399
    strength of, 32–33
    submarines, 33, 108, 111. *See also* Convoys; Great
        Britain military
Royal Oak, 64, 106
Ruge, Otto, 77
Ruhr bombing raids, 82, 229–30
Ruhr valley, 330, 332, 334, 341, 343–44
Rumyantsev, Operation, 285, 288

Rundstedt, Gerd von, 58:
   France, 83, 87, 89
   Normandy, 296–97, 299–300, 304–05, 313
   Poland, 58
   USSR, 137, 142, 145–46
   West Wall, 329–30, 337, 340, 343
Rupertus, William, 325
Russo-Japanese War, 39
Ryder, Charles, 211
Ryujo, 186
Rzhev, 191, 201, 282, 285

Saar bombing raids, 229
Sadamichi, Kajioka, 165
Saidor, 264–65
Saipan, 43, 262, 316, 386:
   battle, 316–18, 390
Saito, Yoshitsugu, 316–17
Sakhalin Island, 403
Salazar, Antonio, 25
Samoa, 184
Samuel B. Roberts, 366
San Bernardino Strait, 363, 366, 368
Santa Cruz Island, battle, 188
Saratoga, 187, 251, 389
Sarmi Island, 266
Sasaki, Noboru, 249–50
Satellites (states), Soviet, 351–55, 384, 410–11
Sato, Kotuku, 271–72
Savo Island, battle, 185
Scapa Flow (Scotland), 106, 112
Scharnhorst, 19, 76–78, 110–11, 240
Scheldt Estuary, battle, 329–32, 334–35
Schleswig-Holstein, 57
Schmidt, Harry, 322, 387, 389
Schorner, Ferdinand, 292, 351, 355, 359
Schouten Islands, 265
Scoones, Geoffrey, 267–68
Scott, Norman, 189
Sealion, Operation, 91–92
Second front, 210–11, 224–25
Seine River, 296–97, 299, 304, 306–07, 309, 312
Selassie, Haile, 120, 122–23
Senegalese troops, 278
Sevastopol, 193–97, 292
SHAEF (Supreme Headquarters Allied Expeditionary
   Forces), 294, 296, 298, 302, 304, 309, 329, 337,
   340, 344, 378, 383
Shanghai, battle, 44–45
Shigeyoshi, Inoue, 180
Sherman, Forrest, 251, 261

Sherman, General William T., 1, 3
Sherrod, Robert, 259–60
Shetland Islands, 66
Shibasaki, Keiji, 258–59
Shigemitsu, Mamoru, 405
Shima, Kiyohide, 362–63
Shingle, Operation. *See* Anzio
Shins, 243
Sho Go, Operation, 326
Shoho, 180, 181
Sho Ichi Go, Operation, 362
Shokaku, 180, 182, 188, 321
Shoot Luke bomber, 231
Short, Walter, 160, 162, 164, 166
Shuri Castle, 390–92, 394–95
Sicily, invasion of, 215, 217–19, 287
Sidi Barrani, battle, 120–21
Sidi Rezigh, battle, 132
Siegfried Line, 330, 343. *See also* West Wall
Simonds, Guy, 332, 334
Simpson, W. H., 336, 343–45
Singapore, 166–68, 171–72. *See also* Malaya
Singh, Pritam Giani, 172
Sino-Japanese War (1895), 39
Skip bombing, 247
Skorzeny, Otto, 338
Slavs, 12, 15
Sledge, E. B., 395
Slim, William, 120, 176, 243, 267–68, 270–73, 372–73
Slot, the, 185–86, 189
Slovakia, 25, 57–58, 99, 353:
   troops in USSR, 195
Slovik, Eddie, 336
Smigly-Ridz, Edward, 60
Smith, 188
Smith, Holland, 258, 260, 316, 318, 322–23
Smith, Ralph, 318
Smith, Walter Bedell, 294–95
Smolensk, 140, 142, 147, 191, 203, 285, 290
Smyth, John, 174
Soddu, Ubaldo, 124
Sollum, battle, 131
Solomon Islands, 165, 245, 249–52. *See also*
   Guadalcanal
Sonar, 108
Songkhram, Phibum, 166
Sonngram, Pibul, 155
Soong, T.V., 50, 153
Sosabowski, Stanislow, 334
South African troops, 209, 215
South Beveland Island, 330, 332, 334

South Dakota, 189, 321
Southeast Asian Command (SEAC), 226, 242, 245
Southwest Pacific theater, 179, 182–83, 244–53, 264–67
Soviet military:
    confronts Japan, 51–52
    deficiencies, 137
    doctrine, 61
    manpower, 137, 144, 195, 202, 282, 288, 290,
        347, 355
    production, 60, 138, 195, 198
    Red Banner Fleet, 192
    terrorizes populations, 347, 355–57. *See also* Eastern
        Front; Red Army
Soviet Union
    China, 371–72
    communism, 20, 346, 347, 353–54, 358
    economic distress, 20
    Japan, 51–52, 145, 372
    League of Nations, 71
    mutual aid pacts, 21
    mythology of war, 4–5
    postwar dominance, 384, 410–11
    production, 20–21, 138, 195, 198, 202, 282, 285, 349
    Spanish Civil War, 21, 26
    U.S. aid, 112
    V-E Day, 383. *See also* Eastern Front
Spaatz, Carl "Tooey", 341
Spain:
    Axis powers, 90, 120, 212, 216
    militarists, 14
    partisans, 298
    Spanish Civil War, 19, 21, 26, 35, 71
    troops in USSR, 195, 216
Special Operations Executive (SOE), British, 298–99
Spearfish, 76
Spector, Ronald, 188
Speer, Albert, 195, 233, 309, 408
Sperrle, Hugo, 92, 95
Spitfire fighter, 24, 32, 93–96, 100, 224, 233
Sprague, Clifton, 363, 365–66
Spratcly Islands, 49
Spruance, Raymond, 184, 184, 257, 258, 315, 318–19,
        321–22, 324
    Okinawa, 392–93, 396
SS (Schutz-staffel), 16, 63, 142–43, 198, 280, 299, 338,
        353–55:
    panzers, 283, 285, 287–88, 290, 292, 304, 307,
        333–34, 337–39, 359
Stalin, Josef
    advance in Eastern Europe, 293
    Allied diplomacy, 224–26, 238, 290, 349, 357–58

Berlin, 344, 359
    buffer zone and territory, 346, 349, 351–52,
        357–58, 384
    faces German aggression, 135, 141, 147
    Hitler, 21–22
    ideology, 21
    Japan, 357, 399, 401
    military leadership, 139–40, 144, 191, 193–99,
        202–03, 288, 291, 354, 410
    Order, 227 197
    Polish uprising, 349
    punishes Germans, 349
    purges of, 21, 138
    suspicion toward Allies, 344
    rise to power, 20
    Tripartite Pact, 99
    United Nations, 358
    Yalta, 357–58
Stalingrad, 193, 195–03
Stark, Harold, 104, 114
Stark, Robert, 214
Stavka, 144, 196, 285
Stilwell, Joseph, 175, 242–44, 267–69, 273, 371
    replaces Geiger, 395
Stimson, Henry, 100, 277
Stirling bomber, Short, 227
Stopford, Montagu, 372–73
Strachan, Hugh, 4
Strasbourg, 336, 340
Strategic bombing:
    American losses in Pacific, 398
    Anglo-American losses, 228, 230, 233, 235–36
    Anglo-American planning, 226–28
    annihilation, 1, 2, 6
    Bomber Command, 330, 341
    concentration camps, 381
    German defense against, 227, 236
    Japanese losses, 323
    Pacific and Asian theater, 315–16, 323, 367–71,
        397–98
    technology, 227–29
    theory of, 32, 104
    Western Front (1944–45), 340–42. *See also*
        Combined Bomber Offensive; *various cities*
Student, Kurt, 80, 333
Stuka dive-bomber, 94, 140
Stumme, Georg, 209
Stump, Felix, 365–66
Stumpff, Hans-Jurgen, 92
St. Lo, 365
St. Vith, 337–38

Submarines
    Anglo-American operations, 105–14, 236–41
    dangers, 108
    German bases, 230–31
    German fleet, 19, 78, 105–08, 238, 297, 335
    Italy, 25
    Japanese, 162, 187, 319, 322
    losses, 239, 319, 368
    Norway, 237
    Soviet, 237, 292
    U.S., 267
    U.S. operations against Japan, 317, 321, 323, 362, 368, 370–71
    wolfpack concept, 106. *See also* Convoy system
Suez Canal, 28, 106, 119, 130, 133, 204–05, 210
Sugar Loaf Hill, 394
Suiyan, battle, 40
Sultan, Daniel, 372
Sumatra, 174, 226
Sun Yat-Sen, 39
Suribachi, Mount, 387–88
Suzuki, Kantaro, 399
Suzuki, Sosaki, 367–68
Sussex teams, 299
Sweden, 90:
    Finland and neutrality, 71–72
    iron ore, 72–74, 111
Swift, Innis, 376
Switzerland, 120, 298, 312, 329
Sword Beach, 303
Swordfish biplane, 124
Syria, 28, 131, 212

Tadashi, Hanaya, 271
Taierhchwang, battle, 47
Taiho, 319
Takagi, Takeo, 173–74, 180, 182
Tanaka, Raizo, 186, 189, 249
Tanks, 30, 57, 86–87, 196–97:
    Africa, 131
    British Grant, 269
    British Matilda, 120–21
    German Panther, 286–87, 291
    German Tiger, 222, 286–87, 291
    Soviet T-34 146, 196, 285–86, 291
    U.S. M-3 (British Grant), 204–05
    U.S. M-4 Sherman, 259, 305, 337
    U.S. M-26 Pershing, 337. *See also* Mobile warfare; *selected battles*
Tannenberg, Operation, 62
Taranto, battle, 124

Tarawa, battle, 252, 257–61:
    lessons and memory, 262–63, 276, 303, 315–16, 386, 389
Tassafaronga Point, battle, 189–90
Tawitawi, 319
Technology, 106:
    aircraft, 19, 24, 32, 80, 104–05, 365, 227–30
    ground-based, 30, 71, 102, 297, 316
    naval, 33, 42–43, 108, 240
    nuclear, 385, 401
Tedder, Arthur, 215, 217, 222, 294, 304
Teheran conference, 225–26, 290
Tenaru River, battle, 186
Ten-Go, Operation, 392–94
Tennessee, 392
Terkel, Studs, 5
Thach Weave aerial maneuver, 182
Thailand, 155, 158, 166, 226, 272, 372, 411
Theobald, Robert, 182
Thunderclap, Operation, 341–42
Thunder God Corps, 365
Tibbetts, Paul, 402
Timoshenko, Semyon, 72–73, 138, 140, 144, 193
Tinian, 43, 262, 322:
    B-29 base, 323, 386, 402
Tippelskirch, Kurt von, 347–48
Tirpitz, 18, 111, 237–38, 240
Tito, Josef Brodz, 354
Tobruk, 130–32, 204–05, 209
Tokyo, 315, 323, 386, 390, 396, 399, 404–05:
    bombing, 342, 369–70, 377, 397, 404
Tokyo Express, 186, 189–90, 249
Tokyo War Crimes trials, 408–09
Tojo, Hideki, 40, 119, 153, 157, 266–67, 323–24, 367, 409
Tolbukhin, Fedor, 353
Torch, Operation, 210–13
Torpedo, 111, 119, 124, 160
    electric, 368
    Human (German), 276
    Long Lance, 173–74
    PT boat, 247
Totalize, Operation, 307
Total war, 2–4
Toyoda, Soemu, 319, 326:
    Letye Gulf, 362–63, 366, 368
    Okinawa, 392, 394
Treasury Islands, 251
Treaty of Brest-Litovsk, 20
Treaty of Versailles, 9, 11–15, 19, 34–35, 37, 54
Treblinka camp, 350, 356

Trenchard, Hugh, 32
Tripartite Pact, 99, 152
Truant, 76
Truck, "deuce and a half", 290–91
Truk, 43, 180, 248, 252, 315
Truman, Harry S, 379:
    atomic bomb, 401–02
    Japan, 399–400, 404
    V-E Day, 383
Truscott, Lucian, 277, 280, 310, 313
Tulagi Island, 181–82, 184–85, 248
Tulle massacre, 304
Tunisia, 28–29, 117, 209–15, 218
Turkey, 13, 28, 90, 125
Turner, Richmond Kelly, 185, 189, 316, 319
Tuskegee airmen, 341
Two Ocean Navy Act (1940), 104
Typhoon, Operation, 145–478

U-110 capture, 111
U-boats. *See* Submarines
Ugaki, Matomi, 404
U-Go, Operation, 268
Ukraine, 20, 56, 137, 142–43, 196, 201, 288, 290, 292–93,
    346–47, 349, 353
Ulithi atoll, 324–25
ULTRA, 92, 410:
    Atlantic, 108, 111, 113, 237–39
    battle of Britain, 93, 97
    Italy, 277
    Japan, 399–400
    Mediterranean and North Africa, 123–25, 127–28,
      131, 204–05, 207, 209, 214–15, 219
    Normandy, 304, 307, 310,
    Pacific , 181, 183, 247–49, 264–65, 267
    Western Front, 330, 337
Unconditional surrender, 225, 399, 401
Unit, 731 409
United Front (China), 151
United Nations, 345, 358, 397:
    Declaration, 150, 169, 171, 224–25, 242
United Nations Relief and Rehabilitation
    Administration (UNRRA), 384
United States of America:
    aid to Allies, 195–96, 224, 237–38, 288, 349
    Anglo-French security, 15, 27, 34, 100
    annihilation 6
    ascendance 4
    China, 34, 99, 153–54
    Congress, 40, 98–99, 100–01, 115–16, 153

    draft mobilization, 100–101
    economy, 35
    good war, 4
    hemispheric defense, 66, 98, 114, 155
    imperialism, 29
    isolationism, 35, 40, 53, 90, 98, 100, 115
    Japan, 34–45, 99, 153–59, 396–97, 399
    Japanese invasion of China, 43, 49–50
    London blitz, 98–100
    Manhattan Project, 401
    naval disarmament treaties, 34–35
    occupation of Japan, 411
    postwar dominance, 411
    production of, 100–02, 112, 196, 236–37, 251–53
    surrender terms, 399–400, 405
United States Army Air Force (USAAF), 103–04:
    509th Composite Group, 40
    Asia, 153–54, 156, 160, 244, 246–47, 251, 323, 367–71,
      386, 398, 402
    Europe, 229–30, 231, 233–35, 337, 341–42, 349. *See*
      also Arnold, Henry; Chennault;
    Strategic bombing
United States military:
    African Americans, 341
    Americal Division, 187, 189
    Army, 102–03, 248
    Asiatic Fleet, 104, 156, 159, 176
    atrocities 325
    buildup for Normandy invasion, 294
    defense strategy, 112
    Frogmen, 261, 316
    improvement, 214, 216, 410
    interservice relations, 318, 368, 389
    Joint Chiefs of Staff, 211, 326, 399–400
    Marine Corps, 105, 160, 165, 185–90, 259, 260, 316,
      318, 322–23, 325, 340, 386, 388, 390
    National Guard, 258, 260, 265
    naval blockade of Japan, 267, 368, 394, 399,
      401–02
    naval strategy, 105, 158
    Navy, 104–05, 115–16, 179–90, 261, 267, 300
    Navy air arm, 104–5
    Old Breed, 324–25
    Pacific theater organization, 179, 184, 315, 326
    race war, 260–61, 324, 365
    rape, 356
    Rangers, 301
    Red Army meeting, 359–60
    Seabees, 186, 389
    Special Service Force, 310

United States military: (*continued*)
  surrender of Japan, 405. *See also* Central Pacific
    theater; Convoys; Eisenhower; Kasserine Pass;
    Normandy invasion; North Africa; Overlord;
    Phillipines; Southwest Pacific theater; Strategic
    bombing; Western Front
Uranus, Operation, 201
Urquhart, Roy, 333
U.S. *See* United States of America
Ushijima, Mitsuru, 390–92, 394–95
U.S.S.R. *See* Soviet Union
Utah Beach, 300, 302

V-2 ballistic missile, 236, 335
V-1 cruise missile, 236, 335
Vandegrift, Alexander, 185
Vasilevsky, Aleksandr, 351, 354, 358, 403
Vatutin, Nikolai, 282–83, 285–86, 288, 291
V-E Day, 383
Vegesack raids, 231, 233
Veritable, Operation, 342–43
Vienna, 281
Vistula River, 56, 349, 351–52, 354–55, 359
Volkssturm, 340
Vella Lavella, battle, 249–50
Venezuela, 66
Vasilevsky, Aleksandr, 198, 201, 203
Vichy France, 90, 117, 119, 122, 131, 211–12, 217,
    298, 310
Victor Emmanuel III, King, 23, 54, 118, 218, 222
Vienna, 281, 359, 379
Vietinghoff, Heinrich von, 221–22, 380
Vincennes, 185
Vlasov, Andrei, 193, 383
Volga River, 195–200, 203,
Vogelkop Peninsula, 266
Vonnegut, Kurt, 1, 341
Voronezh, 195–96, 198, 202–03, 283, 285
Voroshilov, Kliment, 192

Waffen-SS, 16, 89, 150, 299, 304, 337
Wainwright, Jonathan, 156, 176–78
Wakde Island, 266
Wake Island, 160, 165, 181
Walcheren Island, 330, 332, 335
Walker, Johnny, 113–14
Wang Ching-wei, 47
Warburton-Lee, Bernard, 77
War crimes, 235:
  trials, 407–09
Warnemunde bomber raid, 230

Warsaw uprisings, 312, 349–50
Warspite, 77, 221
Washington, 189
Wasp, 187
Wavell, Archibald, 117, 120–22, 129, 131, 167–68,
    173–75
Wedemeyer, Albert, 371
Wehrmacht. *See* German military
Weichs, Maximilian von, 196, 199, 353
Weidling, Karl, 380
Weigley, Russell, 1
Weinberg, Gerhard, 6
Wellington bomber, 227
Welsh, William, 211–12
Wenck, Walther, 379
Weser raid, 233
Weserubung, Operation. *See* Norway
Western Desert Air Force, 215
Western Desert campaign (1941), 121, 129–34.
    See also North Africa
West Virginia, 163
Western Front, 294–313, 329–45, 355. *See also* Allied
    Powers; Normandy; Market-Garden; Hurtgen
    Forest; Bulge; *selected countries*
West Wall, 330:
  Allied attack, 329–41
  shift of troops from East, 346, 355. *See also*
    Western Front
Wewak, 248, 264–66
Weygand, Maxime, 31, 86–87, 89
Whitley bomber, 227
Wild Boar night fighter, 232–33
Willow Run plant, 101
Wilson, Maitland, 125–27
Wilson, Woodrow, 11, 13
Window ("snow") anti-radar defense, 227, 231,
Wingate, Orde, 123, 243, 268–69
Winter Line, 222, 278
Winter War, 69–73. *See also* Finland
Wolfpacks. *See* Submarines
Women Accepted for Volunteer Emergency Service
    (WAVES), 104
Women's Air Force Service Pilots (WASP), 104
Women's Army Corps (WAC), 104
Woodlark Island, 249
World War I, 11
Wormhout massacre, 89
Wright, Carleton, 189
Wurzburg raid, 233

X-Gerat navigational aid, 97

Yalta, 195:
 conference, 341, 357–58, 378, 382
 Declaration on Liberated Europe, 358
 Pacific war, 399
Yamamoto, Isoroku, 158:
 death, 248
 Guadalcanal, 189–90
 Midway, 180, 182–84, 186
 Pearl Harbor attack, 159–60, 162, 164
Yamashita, Tomoyuki:
 executed, 409
 Malay, 166–67, 171–72, 177
 Philippines, 367–68, 373–77
Yamato, 362, 394
Yangtze River, 43, 46–47
Yap, 326

Yorktown, 181–84
Yugoslavia, 12, 21, 25, 90, 99, 120:
 end of war, 351, 353–54, 359
 German attack, 125–26

Zangen, Gustav-Adolph von, 330, 332
Zero fighter, 173, 182, 188, 321–22
Zhdanov, Andrew, 192
Zhukov, Georgi, 21:
 Berlin, 344, 354, 378–79
 defense of USSR, 138, 145–47, 191, 198
 Eastern Front, 201–02, 285, 288, 291–92, 347, 355,
  358–59
 Nomonhon, 51
Zuikaku, 180, 182
Zyklon B, 143

Annihilation

A Global Military History of World War II

THOMAS W. ZEILER

From 1937 to 1945 the world witnessed a succession of savage military strategies and actions on land, in the seas, and in the skies that resulted in the slaughter of more than 50 million people. Incorporating the most recent scholarship on the military history of the Second World War, this study offers a chronological and geographical examination of the most destructive event in recorded human history.

Annihilation argues that World War II evolved into a war of annihilation—a total war—that engulfed militants and civilians alike. The book challenges the "good war" thesis by showing that the "strategy of annihilation" was employed by all sides in the conflict. Moving from the onset of hostilities to the final days of battle, the narrative provides a global perspective that links all theaters of the war. Ideal for undergraduate courses on World War II, this uniquely organized text is the first to allow instructors to assign chapters according to time periods or by region.

© 2011   464 pp.   978-019-973473-3   paper

The World in Flames

A World War II Sourcebook

FRANS COETZEE and
MARILYN SHEVIN-COETZEE

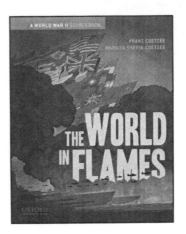

An edited volume of p[...] mary sources from [...] Second World War, [...] *World in Flames: A Wo[...] War II Sourcebook* is [...] first of its kind to prov[...] an ambitious and wi[...] ranging survey of [...] war in a convenient a[...] comprehensive packa[...] Conveying the sheer sc[...] and reach of the confli[...] the book's twelve chapters include sufficient narrat[...] and analysis to enable students to grasp both the wa[...] broad outlines and the context and significance of ea[...] particular source.

Beginning with the growing disenchantment over t[...] World War I peace settlements and the determinati[...] of German, Italian, and Japanese leaders to revise t[...] situation, the book traces the descent into open, arm[...] conflict. It covers the spectacular early successes of t[...] Germans and Japanese, the pivotal campaigns of 194[...] and the Allied effort during the remaining three ye[...] to destroy the Axis' capacity to wage war. Drawi[...] examples from a wide range of documents, the text a[...] includes visual sources: propaganda posters, photos, a[...] cartoons.

© 2011   448 pp.; 15 illus.   978-0-19-517442-7   pape[...]

CPSIA information can be obtained at www.ICGtesting.com
Printed in the USA
BVOW032355180712

295535BV00004B/4/P